Western Balkans

Marika McAdam

Jayne D'Arcy, Chris Deliso, Peter Dragičević,
Mark Elliott, Vesna Marić, Anja Mutić

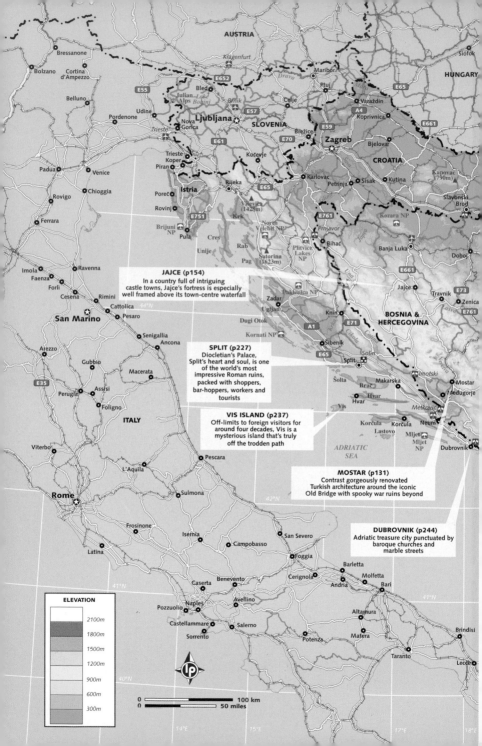

AUSTRIA

HUNGARY

SLOVENIA

Ljubljana

Zagreb

CROATIA

ITALY

JAJCE (p154)
In a country full of intriguing castle towns, Jajce's fortress is especially well framed above its town-centre waterfall

SPLIT (p227)
Diocletian's Palace, Split's heart and soul, is one of the world's most impressive Roman ruins, packed with shoppers, bar-hoppers, workers and tourists

VIS ISLAND (p237)
Off-limits to foreign visitors for around four decades, Vis is a mysterious island that's truly off the trodden path

BOSNIA & HERCEGOVINA

MOSTAR (p131)
Contrast gorgeously renovated Turkish architecture around the iconic Old Bridge with spooky war ruins beyond

DUBROVNIK (p244)
Adriatic treasure city punctuated by baroque churches and marble streets

ADRIATIC SEA

Rome

San Marino

ELEVATION

	2100m
	1800m
	1500m
	1200m
	900m
	600m
	300m

0   100 km
0   50 miles

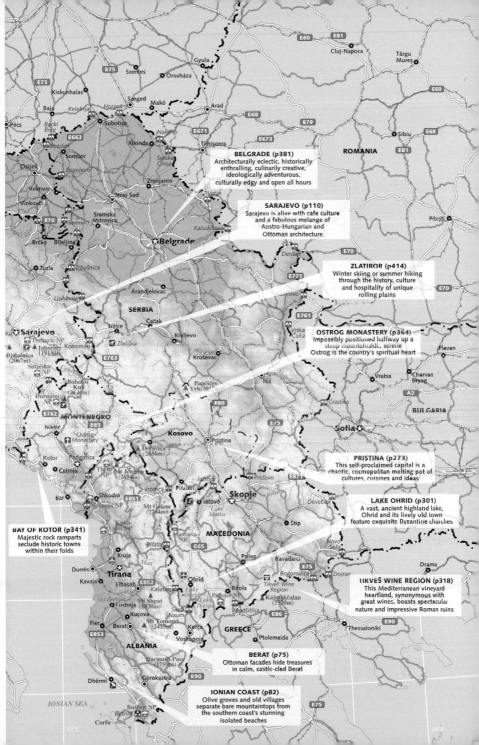

BELGRADE (p381)
Architecturally eclectic, historically enthralling, culinarily creative, ideologically adventurous, culturally edgy and open all hours

SARAJEVO (p110)
Sarajevo is alive with cafe culture and a fabulous melange of Austro-Hungarian and Ottoman architecture

ZLATIBOR (p414)
Winter skiing or summer hiking through the history, culture and hospitality of unique rolling plains

OSTROG MONASTERY (p364)
Impossibly positioned halfway up a steep mountainside, serene Ostrog is the country's spiritual heart

PRISTINA (p273)
This self-proclaimed capital is a chaotic, cosmopolitan melting pot of cultures, cuisines and ideas

LAKE OHRID (p301)
A vast, ancient highland lake, Ohrid and its lively old town feature exquisite Byzantine churches

TIKVEŠ WINE REGION (p318)
This Mediterranean vineyard heartland, synonymous with great wines, boasts spectacular nature and impressive Roman ruins

BAY OF KOTOR (p341)
Majestic rock ramparts seclude historic towns within their folds

BERAT (p75)
Ottoman facades hide treasures in calm, castle-clad Berat

IONIAN COAST (p82)
Olive groves and old villages separate bare mountaintops from the southern coast's stunning isolated beaches

On the Road

MARIKA MCADAM COORDINATING AUTHOR
Chroniclers have written about epic Balkans train travels to the Dalmatian coast, through tunnels to Mostar or overnight to communist capitals. The miniature train (see p408) is rarely considered to be up there among the great train journeys, but I never saw a miniature train I didn't ride. And I'm not ashamed.

MARK ELLIOTT A real Bosnian coffee on Mostar's Kujundžiluk (p137). At last! In 1974 we'd driven right past without seeing even a glimpse of Mostar's delights. That was before the days of guidebooks and we simply didn't happen to look.

VESNA MARIĆ No matter how many times I see Dubrovnik, I can't get enough of it. On this day I was walking around the Ploče area and I stopped to look at the beach and the beautiful old town (p244) above.

ANJA MUTIĆ I'm at over 900m in Učka National Park, just a half-hour ride from fancy Lovran on the Opatija riviera (p214). Surrounded by a multitude of sheep and alpine flowers, right by a half-abandoned shepherd village, I'm floored by this whole other world up here – a world where herbalists make up medicinal potions from local plants, where the sheep cheese is some of the purest and most delicious you'll find in Croatia, and where on a clear day you can see Venice in the distance.

JAYNE D'ARCY There are three ways to get from Corfu to Saranda (p86): on the 45-minute 'flying dolphin' or the slower *Kaliopi* ferry – or, as Albanians have done in the past, swim. I missed the morning's speedy, torpedo-like ferry but scored some wind-in-my-hair moments on the *Kaliopi*'s deck instead.

CHRIS DELISO I could taste the sea salt gusting up from the far-off Aegean on Mt Kozuf (p320), surrounded by wild blueberries, WWI trenches and weird rock formations. This Macedonian communist-era border stone is inscribed SFRJ (Socialist Federal Republic of Yugoslavia). In a few months, these barren slopes will become a skier's paradise…

PETER DRAGIČEVIĆ Nothing compares to driving around the Bay of Kotor (p341) for the first time. At least, that's what I thought, until I took the numerous hairpin turns of the old road behind Kotor and looked down on it from the slopes of the Black Mountain itself. Wow!

For author biographies see p463

Western Balkans Highlights

It wasn't so long ago that you were considered either brave or crazy to travel to the Western Balkans. Well, not any more! Travellers are flocking to discover the gems of the region, and gems there certainly are. Stunning landscapes, gorgeous coastlines, vibrant cities and a warm welcome all await. We asked our readers, staff and authors what they loved most about the region.

© TONY EVELING / ALAMY

1 LAKESIDE IDYLL, MACEDONIA

The lakeside town of Ohrid (p301) has a Mediterranean feel. Walk the old cobblestone streets and visit the monastery on the point. Sip drinks at a lakeside cafe and then jump in for a cool dip. Party at night in one of the many discos. Don't forget to take a boat cruise around the lake.

Carlaanne, traveller

② PARADISE...OR THE MOON, MONTENEGRO

'Am I in paradise or on the moon?' George Bernard Shaw famously quipped from the top of Mt Lovćen (p357). We couldn't help thinking he had a point as we surveyed the same landscape, the spectacular, craggy peaks looking as though they'd been dug up by a giant puppy out of freshly laid concrete. The Adriatic and the Bay of Kotor sparkling away in the southwest aren't particularly lunar, but once you turn your back and gaze at that dramatically fractured landscape...yes, he definitely had a point.

Peter Dragičević, Lonely Planet author

③ MARVELS OF MOSTAR, BOSNIA & HERCEGOVINA

Picture a city of limestone and timber, cobblestones and cafes, chapels and mosques. Now imagine that this city (p131) is nestled into a valley of green and graces the banks of a turquoise river. Stalls offering handcrafted jewellery, local art and copper coffee sets overflow onto streets of friendly faces, eclectic architecture and rich history.

Talia100, traveller

ALL THAT IS DUBROVNIK, CROATIA

Walking around the city walls of Dubrovnik (p244) offers beautiful views of rocky islands, grassy mountains and shimmering seas along with real-life views of people pegging out their washing and winding it along on lines between buildings.

Lisa Vitaris, traveller, Australia

SHANNON NACE

4

EXIT FESTIVAL, SERBIA

It was easy to see what all the hype around Exit (see the boxed text, p401) was about. Its setting is pretty hard to beat: from one music stage in a unique part of the hilltop fortress by the Danube to another, the wildly eclectic sounds and amazing views exhilarate and enchant. And the infectious enthusiasm and friendliness of the region's youth add a deeper meaning to it all. Labelled as the place where 'hedonism meets activism', it really is a State of Exit.

Branislava Vladisavljevic, Lonely Planet staff, Melbourne

© IVAN ZUPIC / ALAM

5

WHITE-MARBLE ZADAR, CROATIA

Zadar (p220) is a bite-sized piece of everything you want from Croatia. Slippery-white cobblestones coat the town like dense marble icing. During the day you race through the labyrinth of twisting laneways until you pop out onto a promenade in time for sunset. Everyone gathers at the sea organ, a series of holes and pipes punched into the stairs descending into the water that are 'played' by the lapping tide. They've been singing all day, but somehow you can only truly hear them when the sun is setting.

Marika McAdam, Lonely Planet author

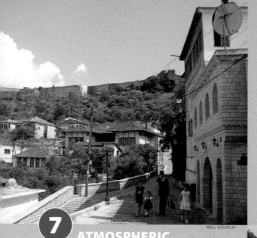

WILL GOURLAY

7

ATMOSPHERIC GJIROKASTRA, ALBANIA

With its steep streets, imposing mansions, lofty views and castle garlanded with circling ravens, Gjirokastra (p88) could have been created especially for a gothic tale or an epic poem told by mountain balladeers.

Will Gourlay, Lonely Planet staff, Melbourne

6

© SUZY BENNETT / ALAM

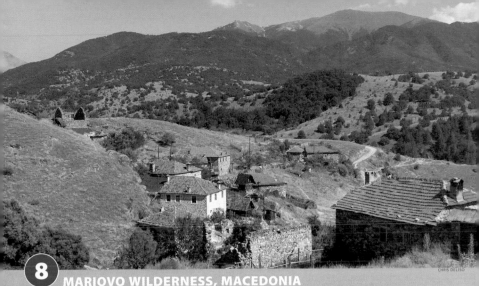

CHRIS DELISO

8 MARIOVO WILDERNESS, MACEDONIA

I had the birthday of my life researching this guide in Mariovo (see the boxed text, p314), a wilderness of mountains and plains between Bitola and the Greece border. Now largely depopulated, the region is the subject of innumerable legends. High in the mountains, an old shepherd spoke rapturously of sipping hidden WWI-era French Cognac. After bursting through dense jungle in a mud-caked Lada Niva, we reached the Bela Reka (White River), where a swim in the icy waters built up my appetite for a hearty lunch. Then we continued to the villages, where the old-timers plied us with wine and regaled us with more eccentric legends from Mariovo's haunted hills.

Chris Deliso, Lonely Planet author

© ROD BRIMSON / ALAMY

9 TRAVNIK'S SPOOKY CASTLE, BOSNIA & HERCEGOVINA

Travnik (p152) is lovely. The castle is all spooky-weird gothic – you typically have to ask at the museum to have it unlocked, and then you get it to yourself to explore.

Iain Shearer, traveller, Australia

CITY OF CHANGE: PRISTINA, KOSOVO

In the 1990s foreign correspondent Robert D Kaplan said 'Defeat...has a name: Pristina.' I wished Kaplan were here with me as my taxi drove through this newly self-proclaimed capital (p273); the streets were pretty much the mess he described, but already, a few months after independence had been declared, blood-red Albanian flags were flapping a new name: change.

Marika McAdam, Lonely Planet author

10

CITY OF FUN: BELGRADE, SERBIA

Belgrade (p381) is a crazy town, where people think only about how to have fun! Even on Monday evening, all cafes and popular river boats are full of people! Fantastic castle in the centre of the city, beautiful view of the rivers...

Anaperunicic, traveller

11

THE MANY FLAVOURS OF ZAGREB, CROATIA

Croatia's capital is a gateway from central Europe to the Adriatic coast and the rest of the Balkans. With an upper and lower town, Croatia's largest metropolis has many flavours. Zagreb (p180) has great architecture and museums, beautiful parks and magnificent views from the hillside.

Michael Sabelli, traveller, Canada

12

WITOLD SKRYPCZAK

GZUREI (CHEERS!), ALBANIA

This post-communist nation (p48), still searching for its identity, has a spirit unlike that of any other place in Europe. With its amazing nature and beaches (and low cost), it's really a diamond in the rough. Hardships have made the people strong, and guests are treated as family.

Ellie Dinnetz, traveller, USA

13

DOUG McKINLAY

CHRIS DELISO

14

POPPIES, MACEDONIA

One thing I'll never forget about Macedonia is the poppies. Everywhere we went outside Skopje (p289), we encountered fields of poppies lining the roads and train tracks.

Carlaanne, traveller

15 CHARMING SVETI STEFAN, MONTENEGRO

SHANNON NACE

Once a fishermen's village and now a luxury island hotel, Sveti Stefan (p353) is one big vehicle-free zone – perfect for a leisurely stroll taking in all its charms: rustic stone buildings, narrow streets, small churches and shops…

Diana Todorovic, traveller, Australia

DOUG McKINLAY

16 EAST MEETS WEST – SARAJEVO, BOSNIA & HERCEGOVINA

If you think Istanbul is where East meets West, check out Sarajevo (p110). This place is an inexpensive and fun amalgam of Austrian and Ottoman.

Stephen George, traveller, USA

Contents

14 CONTENTS

Regional Map Contents

Croatia p01/2-9

Bosnia & Hercegovina p103

Serbia p375

Montenegro p335

Kosovo p271

Macedonia p283

Albania p50

Destination
Western Balkans

The first question many people ask about the Western Balkans is 'where's that?'. Lying in southeast Europe, the region stretches from Croatia's sublimely jagged Dalmatian coast, past Bosnia and Hercegovina's iconic Old Bridge of Mostar to the cultural crossroads of Sarajevo. Further east is Serbia, with its hedonistic music festivals and the pulsing nightlife of Belgrade. Plunge south to newly independent Montenegro, where ancient towns flanked by limestone cliffs are suspended above the azure waters of the Bay of Kotor. East again is controversial Kosovo, abuzz in its bid to have its self-declared independence recognised globally. Drop south into Albania, busy casting off the shadow of communism and welcoming visitors to its quirky capital and dramatic coastline. East of Albania is Macedonia, where other-worldly Lake Ohrid sets the scene for the historical treasures surrounding it.

European dreams that elsewhere on the continent turn out to be too expensive, too crowded or too commercialised are authentic and accessible in the Western Balkans. Sidewalk cafes line cobblestone alleyways, medieval castles preside over historic town centres, and Catholic churches, Orthodox monasteries and Ottoman mosques that vied to stake space throughout history share the terrain today. National parks are untamed patches of wilderness straddling national borders, while translucent turquoise waters lap at the edges of manicured resorts and undeveloped islands. Added to this are riverside restaurants serving world-class cuisine, wine regions ripe for the tasting and nightclubs floating on rivers or thumping underground.

Yet for all this the Western Balkans is still largely known for the wrong reasons. It's true that ethnic complexities led to unspeakable consequences during the troubled 1990s, but as that period seems further and further in the past, differences that once led to conflict now manifest themselves as wondrous diversity.

The 2008 Eurovision Song Contest highlighted that a spirit of regional discourse has overtaken that of discord. International and inter-ethnic conversations spread across social and cultural spheres; musicians cross borders to delight neighbouring fans; artists from one country are revered in another; and tragedies occurring in one part of the region are mourned elsewhere.

We don't want to sound too starry-eyed; some of what you may picture is true. Grim communist architecture still poops the party, some ex-Yugo buildings linger with all the charm of an apocalypse and some fashions are more retro than they know, but in context, on the precipice of Europe, all of this lends distinctive character to an energetically evolving region in which new buildings are being raised, old ones renewed, new ideas exchanged and old ones challenged. The powers that be and the people who elected them are licking their lips at the prospect of EU membership, knowing that getting there means leaving the past in the past and treating neighbours as neighbours.

For all its colour and contradiction, the region is ultimately defined by the similarities between its countries. The Western Balkans is an area of enormous heart and hospitality, and while it aspires to European integration, it stands well and truly on its own as one of the world's great travel destinations.

Getting Started

Some still see the Western Balkans as shrouded in mystery, but for the most part the region is easily accessible for the capable traveller. Visiting Croatia is no more difficult than going to Germany or Italy. Bosnia and Hercegovina (BiH), Serbia, Montenegro and Macedonia are less expensive; they feature lots of signs in Cyrillic, but English is widely spoken. Albania is more challenging; many roads are in dreadful shape, but some main arteries have been rebuilt. Recent years have seen old hotels renovated and new ones built. ATMs and internet cafes are ubiquitous. You need to keep your eye on Kosovo, but when things are calm travelling there is surprisingly smooth.

WHEN TO GO

The Western Balkans has a consistent weather pattern for a region of its size. High tourist season runs from May until September. The volume of visitors (and increased prices) in Croatia, Montenegro, Macedonia and coastal resorts in Albania can be a hassle in peak season (July and August). At these times some places will only take bookings for a week or two, not one night. Migrant locals flocking back to visit family can add to crowds. During major festivals accommodation is scarce and significantly more expensive; it pays to book ahead. The best time to visit is either side of the summer peak: May, June and September stand out, when it's not too hot, crowded or overbooked.

Winter is cold everywhere (particularly mountainous regions) except the Adriatic coast. Ski season runs from late November until March, but sometimes the snow stays longer than skiers do; if there's still snow in late March or early April you may have it to yourself.

See p429 for climate charts.

Travelling off season can reap some bargains, although places where tourism is the main industry all but close down and some hostels are only open in summer. Travelling as early as April will be economical, but you personally may comprise the extent of the social scene.

COSTS & MONEY

There's wide variation in travel expenses across the region. The further north and west you go, the more expensive it is. Prices are steadily rising in popular resorts and cities; the Croatian coast isn't a budget destination in high season, and budget options in Macedonia's Skopje are scarce. Serbia, Montenegro and BiH are moderately priced, especially outside Belgrade and Sarajevo, while Kosovo and Albania are quite budget friendly – certainly comparable to Turkey. But don't expect to live royally on a few euro a day.

DON'T LEAVE HOME WITHOUT...

- Some good travel literature (p22); the Balkans is the place for reading on the road
- An open mind; there's a new shade of grey around every corner
- An international driving licence if you're planning road trips (p446)
- A Swiss army knife (just don't put it in your hand luggage before flying) to slice local cheeses and pop corks on local wines
- An iPod or earplugs to drown out often-overwhelming turbo-folk music
- Appropriate shoes for tramping city streets and nature trails

CONDUCT IN THE WESTERN BALKANS

There's nothing really unusual about the region's customs that might cause you to stumble into a major faux pas, but here are some tips for making (and keeping) friends.

Talking the Talk

Cafes are not places for a quick caffeine refill but somewhere to laze for an hour or three. Conversations about every aspect of your family and marital status are a sign of friendly interest, not nosiness. On entering a shop, a cheerful hello in the local lingo is appreciated before making a beeline to display racks.

Spouting forth your theories on the fall of communism and the wars of the 1990s probably won't win you friends; your views may be met with strained silence or sharpish retorts along the lines of 'You weren't here; you can't possibly know'. Asking people about their experiences during the conflicts may bring up some interesting anecdotes but also maybe some horrendous memories.

If you can speak local languages, be careful when and where you do; speaking Serbian to Albanian Kosovars, for instance, won't endear you to your hosts.

Walking the Walk

The Balkans idea of time is something superefficient global professionals might chafe against. If you're here for work, expect to mix business with pleasure.

When visiting mosques and *tekkes* (shrines or monasteries), wear conservative clothes covering arms and legs, and remove shoes and socks before entering. Women should cover their hair. Don't walk in front of people praying. When visiting Orthodox churches and monasteries, it's customary to buy a few candles and light them; it's an ancient tradition and generates a bit of income for custodians.

Drinking the Drink

Alcohol flows fairly freely in Christian parts of the region, less so in Muslim areas, where coffee is drunk in alcoholic proportions. Being high-spirited is fine, being totally blotto isn't, especially for women. As anywhere in the world, when you are drunk you are more vulnerable (and not just to making a fool of yourself in a foreign country). If people start spouting nationalist rhetoric after a few shots of firewater, it's your turn to be diplomatically quiet.

The major expense is accommodation. Backpackers staying in hostels, eating cheaply and seeing sights can expect to spend around €40 per day, but more in cities such as Zagreb and Belgrade. Those wanting more comfort (midrange accommodation and restaurants) will probably spend between €70 and €100. Staying in private accommodation outside cities will get you by on far less.

If you have an ATM card, you needn't worry about money in decent-sized towns. Major credit and debit cards (including Cirrus and Maestro) are accepted by ATMs. Travellers cheques are much like chastity belts: safe but a pain in the arse. Many banks are unfamiliar with them and commissions can be high. Having €100 in cash safely tucked away is the best insurance – enough for a cheapish room, a meal and a ride to an ATM or phone. Many currencies are difficult or impossible to exchange outside their home country; change them into euros or dollars before leaving.

In Montenegro and Kosovo, where the euro is the official currency, carry small denominations – break notes at the bank if you have to. Even where the euro isn't the official currency, it's sometimes accepted (notes more so than coins), but the bad exchange assumed can make it more expensive than paying in local currency. Conversely, negotiations may be conducted in euro but payment will be expected in the local currency. Hotel prices are often quoted in both currencies.

TRAVELLING RESPONSIBLY

Since our inception in 1973, Lonely Planet has encouraged readers to tread lightly, travel responsibly and enjoy the magic independent travel affords. International travel is growing at a jaw dropping rate, and we still firmly believe in the benefits it can bring – but, as always, we encourage you to consider the impact your visit can have on the global environment and local economics, cultures and ecosystems.

Getting There & Away

If ever there was an easy region in which to travel responsibly, it's the Western Balkans. Taking flights around the region not only increases carbon emissions but also decreases your experiences; overland journeys are often travel highlights. Once in Europe you can enter the region by bus or train (or ferry from Italy or Greece into Croatia or Albania). See p439 for suggestions.

Buses are efficient and a good way of discovering towns you won't find a word about in this book. Old-world adventures can still be found on railway lines; why fly when you can have an epic train journey from Paris or Vienna through to Zagreb or Belgrade and onwards to Moscow? Train enthusiasts should take the scenic route from built-up Belgrade to coastal Bar (Montenegro), then train it between Montenegro's national parks. Or travel overland from Belgrade to Skopje and on to Thessaloniki (Greece). While saving the environment, save on costs; travel by day to see the sights or overnight to save a night's accommodation.

'Old-world adventures can still be found on railway lines; why fly when you can have an epic train journey?'

Slow Travel

What's the rush? The more slowly you move the more time you have to absorb what's around you. Take time to immerse yourself in wherever you are with leisurely day trips and burn nothing but calories by exploring on foot.

When diving, protect the environment by not taking souvenirs and not standing on or touching corals or wrecks. Ask tour companies about their environmental policies.

For more on ecologically ethical ways to enjoy the environment, see the boxed text, p428.

Accommodation & Food

When it comes to accommodation, doing the right thing can be delightfully self-serving. Rather than staying in built-up (and often overpriced) hotels, stay in private homes, which make cosy quarters for passing travellers. They'll often find you or you can find them through local travel agencies.

Large resorts have their place, but when you're choosing them consider how they dispose of waste and do your bit by asking that towels and sheets not be changed daily.

With food that's 'rare' or a 'speciality' consider why it's a rare speciality; Ohrid trout in Macedonia, for instance, has been fished to near-extinction and should be avoided. See the boxed text, p288, for more.

To find real local food, eat where real locals eat and shop where real locals shop. Buying local produce and eating in locally run eateries keeps small businesses and the people behind them afloat. It also keeps your costs low and your interactions genuine.

Responsible Travel Organisations

Supply responds to demand: if more travellers raise environmental issues with operators they're more likely to go green. Useful links:

Black Mountain (www.montenegroholiday.com) Travel agent passionate about Montenegro's environment.

Blue World (www.blue-world.org) Protects bottlenose dolphins and promotes environmental awareness in Croatia's Lošinj-Cres archipelago.
Centre for Sustainable Tourism Initiatives (www.cstimontenegro.org) Organisation committed to sustainable tourism in Montenegro.
Eco-Centre Caput Insulae (www.caput-insulae.com) Part nature park, part sanctuary for the endangered Eurasian griffon.
Green Visions (www.greenvisions.ba) Environmental protection and Bosnian eco-tours.
Responsible Tourism Partnership (www.responsibletourismpartnership.org)
Responsible Travel (www.responsibletravel.com) Database of global green tour operators.
Tourist Bureau Biljana (www.beyondohrid.com) Environmentally friendly agency for the Ohrid region.
Travelling Balkans (www.travellingthebalcans.net) Bosnian-based sustainability projects.

READING UP

The Western Balkans is a region meant to be written about. Before you go, get your head into the discourse (and discord) of the region – you'll appreciate what you see and who you meet if you understand their context. Follow in the footsteps of those who've gone before by taking some literary companionship on the road. See individual chapters and p38 for more.

History & Politics

Misha Glenny's *The Balkans: Nationalism, War & the Great Powers* assumes some prior knowledge but is one of the most comprehensive books on the region from 1804 to 1999. Glenny's *The Fall of Yugoslavia* is an easier-to-read tome on the ex-Yugoslav wars. Though not without critics, Glenny spells out details with verve and clarity.

The Balkans: A Short History by Mark Mazower distils history and culture into an accessible account. John Allcock's *Explaining Yugoslavia* pulls together historical, cultural and political analysis to reach some surprising conclusions.

Historian Noel Malcolm takes on the near-impossible task of clearly presenting disputed histories in *Bosnia: A Short History* and *Kosovo: A Short History* – neither is light but both are authoritative.

Travel Literature

Travel literature in these parts was defined by Rebecca West's gargantuan *Black Lamb & Grey Falcon*. Written in the 1940s, Dame West's journey through the Balkans is heavily dated and has evident bias, but her lyrical observations may become an indispensable travel companion, if you don't mind lugging 1200 pages.

One of many to have stalked West, Tony White's unapologetic *Another Fool in the Balkans: In the Footsteps of Rebecca West* is littered with a cast of interesting characters White encounters on the road.

Robert Kaplan's portable *Balkan Ghosts* takes an engaging look at the region in the mid-1990s and is rumoured to have influenced Bill Clinton's policies in the area.

Through the Embers of Chaos: Balkan Journeys by Dervla Murphy is terrific. At the age of 70, this courageous Irishwoman cycled through Yugoslavia; *Through the Embers* offers political analysis and insight alongside anecdotes of her adventures.

Chris Deliso's *Hidden Macedonia* is an engrossing travelogue that documents a recent journey around the great lakes of Ohrid and Prespa, shared by Greece, Albania and Macedonia.

'Travel literature in these parts was defined by Rebecca West's gargantuan *Black Lamb & Grey Falcon*'

TOP PICKS

MONTENEGRO
KOSOVO   Bulgaria
MACEDONIA
Italy

FESTIVALS

Festivals in the Western Balkans are as diverse as the region itself. Some symbolise triumphant resistance, others are cultural rites of passage, others are revered as timeless rituals, and others are just a good old-fashioned excuse for a party. Here are some – but not all – you should try to be a part of.

- Rijeka Carnival, Rijeka (Croatia), January or February (p211)
- Strumica Carnival, Strumica (Macedonia), beginning of Lent (p326)
- Budva Festival of Mediterranean Song, Budva (Montenegro), June (p352)
- Baščaršijske Noći, Sarajevo (BiH), July (p120)
- Exit Festival, Novi Sad (Serbia), July (see the boxed text, p401)
- Ohrid Summer Festival, Ohrid (Macedonia), July and August (p305
- Summer festivals in Dubrovnik, Split, Pula and Zagreb (Croatia), July and August (p255)
- Sarajevo Film Festival, Sarajevo (BiH), August (p120)
- Dragačevo Trumpet Festival, Kopaonik (Serbia), August (see the boxed text, p414)
- Tirana Film Festival, Tirana (Albania), November or December (p66)

NIGHTSPOTS

A trip(out) through the Western Balkans is rewarding for the nocturnal traveller. Beach boozing on the Dalmatian coast and explorations of the emerging scene in Macedonia are training for the grand finale in the clubbing capital, Belgrade.

- Mumja (p69), Tirana (Albania)
- OKC Abrašević (p137), Mostar (BiH)
- The Garden (p224) and Barbarella's (p224), Zadar (Croatia)
- Jazz Inn (p306), Ohrid (Macedonia)
- Maximus (p349), Kotor (Montenegro)
- Andergraund (p395), Belgrade (Serbia)

Fitzroy Maclean offers the thrill of a spy novel alongside endearing British humour as he parachutes into Yugoslavia for adventures with Tito in *Eastern Approaches*.

Nicholas Bouvier's *The Way of the World* pays literary homage to pre-hippie trail travel. Bouvier's journey kicks off in 1950s Serbia and Macedonia and is written with living, breathing, dizzying vividness.

Wild Europe: The Balkans in the Gaze of Western Travellers by Božidar Jezernik is a collage of 500 years of travellers' impressions of the Balkans.

Magazines

Those wanting to keep their finger on the beating pulse of the Balkans will enjoy the following.

Cafe Babel (www.cafebabel.com) A smart, edgy, multilingual online magazine showing how cosmopolitan young Europe is.

Hidden Europe (www.hiddeneurope.co.uk) A monthly magazine exploring far-flung corners of the continent including the Western Balkans. A free weekly e-newsletter is available.

The Bridge (www.bridge-mag.com/magazine) Online and print editions focusing on European integration.

Websites

Balkan Travellers (www.balkantravellers.com) An upbeat site that'll give you itchier feet than a bad case of tinea.

Balkanology (www.balkanology.com) Impressive home-grown travel site maintained by a Balkans enthusiast.

In Your Pocket (www.inyourpocket.com) Snappy downloadable pocket guides to cities and countries including several in this region.

Southeast European Times (www.setimes.com) Economic and political site for keeping track of serious stuff.

Thorn Tree (http://thorntree.lonelyplanet.com) The Eastern Europe and the Caucasus branch of Lonely Planet's travellers' bulletin covers the Western Balkans.

Virtual Tourist (www.virtualtourist.com) Reviews, forums, photos and tips from travellers and amateur experts.

FESTIVALS & EVENTS

You may need to book accommodation ahead during festivals, but it's well worth the effort. See country chapters for details on local festivals and take a look at the boxed text, p23.

Itineraries
CLASSIC ROUTES

THE ESSENTIAL TOUR
Three Weeks

Start in **Zagreb** (p180) for plazas and parks. Head south for sea breezes on Croatia's dramatic **Dalmatian coast** (p220). Ferry to the island oasis of **Hvar** (p238), before heading to architecturally awesome **Dubrovnik** (p244). Detour into Bosnia and Hercegovina (BiH) for the iconic Old Bridge of **Mostar** (p131) and the captivating city of **Sarajevo** (p110). Hopping south to Montenegro's **Bay of Kotor** (p341) brings you to the walled port towns of **Herceg Novi** (p341) and **Kotor** (p345). Next, make for the Albanian capital **Tirana** (p62) via the mountain town of **Kruja** (p73). Moving to Macedonia, visit churches and lounge by the lake in **Ohrid** (p301) before exploring the old town of **Skopje** (p289). From here, it's a skip to Kosovo's monasteries, which are all accessible from **Pristina** (p273). If all's well at the border, cross into Serbia and pick up the pace in **Belgrade** (p381), party capital of the Balkans. Wind down in **Fruška Gora** (p402) for a taste of Serbia's Orthodox Christian heritage (and its local wines), before coming full circle with your return to Zagreb.

This do-before-you-die trip in the Western Balkans covers every country of the region. It journeys along Croatia's Dalmatian coast and detours into Bosnia before reaching Montenegro, then plunges south into Albania and loops through Macedonia and Kosovo before taking in Serbia on the way back to Zagreb.

ROADS LESS TRAVELLED

THE WILD SIDE   One Month

Pula on Croatia's Istrian coast is the stepping-off point to **Brijuni Islands National Park** (p207). Further south, **Plitvice Lakes National Park** (p224), near Zadar, is a must for its turquoise lakes. From here you could cross over into BiH to explore the **Una Valley** (p161), near Bihać, for its gorges, castles and rapids, then head down to the wet wilds of the **Kornati Islands** (p222). **Makarska** (p235), on the Adriatic, is a great base for hiking up Mt Biokovo. Further south, check out the national park on **Mljet Island** (p242). In BiH, explorations of the shepherd villages behind **Mt Bjelašnica** (p129) are real and rewarding. Then, paying heed to landmine warnings, spend time conquering the canyons, waterfalls and valleys of **Sutjeska National Park** (p146). Over the border is Montenegro's best nature reserve, **Durmitor National Park** (p365), dotted with lakes and home to a ski resort. Here you can also raft through the immense **Tara Canyon** (p365). Head down to the **Bay of Kotor** (p341) and **Lake Skadar National Park** (p360). For something very new and very wild, head into the **Balkans Peace Park** (see the boxed text, p61), where Montenegro, Albania and Kosovo meet. Depending on the safety situation, consider exploring Kosovo's **Šara National Park** (see p273) on your way to Macedonia's **Mavrovo National Park** (p298) in the west. Slice up to Serbia's rugged **Kopaonik** (p413) near the southern city of Novi Pazar. There's also **Đerdap National Park** (p381) on the Romania border, with its striking 'Iron Gate' gorge. The monasteries of **Fruška Gora** (p402) are ensconced by nature and connected by walking trails in Serbia's Vojvodina region.

This trip hikes, walks, rafts and skis through natural wonders to the far edges of the region. Kick off in Croatia and take on the region's crevices and canyons, enjoying as many thrills and spills as you can handle (don't forget your travel insurance).

WORLD HERITAGE SIGHTS

Two to Three Weeks

From Corfu, catch a ferry to Albania's Saranda for the ruins of **Butrint** (p87), and on to the Ottoman-era town of **Gjirokastra** (p88). History buffs will drool in Albania's finest Ottoman town, **Berat** (p75). Bus into Macedonia for the churches of **Ohrid** (p301) and on to **Treskavec Monastery** (p318), near Prilep. From Prilep, head north into Kosovo via **Skopje** (p289) for **Gračanica monastery** (p276) near Pristina, and consider a day trip to Peja for **Dečani Monastery** (p277) and the **Patriarchate of Peć** (p277). It's now a short trip into Serbia's **Novi Pazar** (p410) – if there's no trouble at the border – from where you can see **Sopoćani monastery** (p411) and nearby **Studenica** (p412). Travel through Serbia's stunning Zlatibor region to **Višegrad** (p146), across the border in BiH, for literature's *Bridge on the Drina* (Mehmed Paša Sokolović). Next, travel to Montenegro's spectacular **Durmitor National Park** (p365), from where it's a short hop to Montenegro's old capital at **Cetinje** (p358), and idyllic **Kotor** (p345) on the gulf of the same name. Heading up the Adriatic coast into Croatia, visit **Dubrovnik's old town** (p244), one of the most famous World Heritage sites in the region and a jumping-off point for Croatian islands. From here, detour into BiH, for the iconic Old Bridge of **Mostar** (p131), before moving up the Dalmatian coast to incredible **Hvar island** (p238). Continuing along the coast, make your way to the historical centre of **Split** (p227) and the nearby town of **Trogir** (p235). Further north and a little inland there's the rugged heritage site (and respite from tourist crowds) **Plitvice Lakes National Park** (p224). Finally, head to the Istria region and the enormous Euphrasian basilica at **Poreč** (p199).

This trip weaves indulgently through the cultural and historical treasures of the Western Balkans, offering a taste of the region's ancient and evolving traditions – and its spectacular scenery. Unassuming villages along the way offer insight into the Austro-Hungarian, Orthodox and Ottoman influences that underpin the region's psyche.

TAILORED TRIPS

LAKES & BEACHES

If you like lying by lakes or want to be beside the seaside…from northern Greece, hop over to **Ohrid** (p301) – the jewel of Macedonia – for leisurely days on Lake Ohrid (the deepest lake in the Balkans). Moving south to the tip of Albania, visit the small resort of **Ksamil** (p87), with beach views over to Corfu.

From Saranda (slightly north of Ksamil), catch a ferry for a side trip to Corfu. Head north along the Ionian coast for the blissful beach at **Dhërmi** (p84). The enormous natural repository of **Lake Skadar** (p360) straddles Albania and Montenegro; stop here on your way to **Sveti Stefan** (p353) and **Petrovac** (p353) in Montenegro. Croatia's seaside resorts are booming, but there are still some lesser-known spots to lay your towel. **Cavtat** (see the boxed text, p250) is a good alternative to Dubrovnik, while **Mljet Island** (p242) and **Korčula Island** (p240) are more laid-back than Hvar. **Brela** (p236), near Makarska, has 6km of pebbly beach. Further north, heavenly **Zadar** (p220) is a base for the **Kornati Islands** (p222). **Rab Island** (p217) has dozens of tiny coves and beaches. For a touch of class there's **Opatija** (p214) or, by casual contrast, the many camping grounds around **Pula** (p204) are laid-back bases for beach basking along the Istrian Peninsula.

BALKANS BY RAIL

All aboard for epic old-world train travel! Take a train from Eastern Europe into the Croatian capital **Zagreb** (p180), where Rebecca West's train first pulled in all those years ago. From there, train to the port town **Rijeka** (p210) and chug down the length of Croatia until you spill out at **Split** (p227) on the Dalmatian coast. Leaving aside trains for a while, sunbathe your way south, before crossing into BiH to visit the Virgin of **Međugorje** (p139) and see the Old Bridge of **Mostar** (p131), from where you can pick up a Doboj-bound train, with a stop-off in **Sarajevo** (p110). Crossing back into Croatia, catch a train in Osijek to Serbia's **Novi Sad** (p399) for day trips in the Vojvodina region. Train on to **Belgrade** (p381) for a day trip on the old-world **Romantika train** (p390). From the transport hub of Užice, get to **Mokra Gora** (p416) for

the restored Šargan 8 railway, which once upon a time linked Belgrade with Sarajevo. To end your journey at the beach, continue on the stunning route from Užice via **Podgorica** (p362) to **Bar** (p354) on the Montenegrin coast. Alternatively, go completely off the regular rails by heading to **Skopje** (p289) via **Niš** (p408) and onwards to **Pristina** (p273) – if the train is running.

Snapshots

CURRENT EVENTS

Though the Western Balkans still feels the weight of its past, nowadays it's actively confronting it in a bid to move towards the future. And that future is with Europe.

EU membership is conditional on bringing war criminals to justice. Croatia – the first country of the region to apply for membership, in 2003 – saw the arrest of fugitive General Ante Gotovina in December 2005. Macedonia saw the April 2007 commencement of the Hague trial of former interior minister Ljube Boskovski for alleged war crimes during the 2001 ethnic Albanian rebellion. The July 2008 arrest of Radovan Karadžić – wanted for his alleged involvement in several crimes against humanity, including the 1995 Srebrenica genocide – in Belgrade caused jubilation in the streets of Sarajevo.

Some countries are dealing with heavy issues on their way West. Macedonia's relations with Greece were tested when its long-held dream of NATO membership was vetoed by Greece in April 2008, raising speculation on what will happen when it makes a bid for the EU. Since it became an EU candidate in December 2005, Macedonia has been working to afford its ethnic Albanian minority greater autonomy. In June 2006, Albania increased its EU membership efforts by stamping out crime and corruption and ensuring minority freedoms. The death of media magnate and champion of independent reportage Dritan Hoxha was a blow to Albania. Croatia is making progress in the inclusion of minorities; the deputy prime minister of the new Croatian government as of January 2008 is the first Serb in a key position. Serbia's newly elected government has been moving towards Europe, signalled by its surrender of several war criminals to the Hague. This and the fact that issues of organised crime and state corruption are now openly challenged rather than hopelessly accepted give weight to the EU enlargement commissioner's recent comment that 'there is a new dawn for the Western Balkans, and it is a European dawn'.

But, while most states are busy preening themselves for EU scrutiny, independence issues are not entirely resolved. Kosovo's declaration of independence in February 2008 didn't quite go down in the same smooth way that Montenegro broke from Serbia. While Albanian flags hang defiantly in the streets of Pristina, Serbia remains adamant that 'Kosovo is the heart of Serbia'.

But even with complicated issues like this, the region can generally be said to be on a forward trajectory. Some controversial debates are going on, but the fact that they are is a step towards a more open future. And this won't be achieved purely through political channels.

Take the Eurovision Song Contest. Western and central Europeans may see the event as a bit of kitsch fun, but this blinged-up bonanza is a deeply serious affair in the Western Balkans. The political undertones of past song contests showed how lyrics could replace bullets as performers made controversial pro-independence gestures. Since independence has been largely achieved, the competition now shows how music can transcend ethnic and national divisions, as pop stars earn respect across the whole region. This was never more evident than in 2007, when the tragic death of former Macedonian Eurovision contestant Toše Proeski unified the region in deep mourning. That same year, Serbia's triumph at the song contest was a victory for a 'new Serbia'; the fact that every voting country of the former

The European Stability Initiative (ESI) releases in-depth reports on various countries in the Western Balkans on its website www.esiweb.org.

Richard Burton portrayed Josef Broz Tito in the 1973 big-budget film *Sutjeska*.

Yugoslavia awarded it that victory prompted new reconciliation hopes and gave Serbia the opportunity to lay to rest its pariah past when it hosted the event in 2008.

Beyond Eurovision, every cultural and social sphere is enjoying the fact that insulation is no longer the template for creative expression. Clubs and restaurants, artists and authors, fashionistas and baristas are all pushing and crossing boundaries in the Balkans. Old traditions and new trends are enjoyed free of their former political baggage; artistic movements are moving in creative rather than party-line directions; underground scenes are underground because they want to be, not because they have to be; and turbo-folk music isn't played in the way of propaganda but simply because there's no accounting for taste. New states such as Montenegro are just as excited about Madonna's upcoming concert as American fans would be, and internationally renowned DJs are spinning even in small cities such as Skopje. 'Scenes' ebb and flow, but almost everywhere in the Western Balkans is pumping to some kind of beat.

All in all, while the past doesn't feel so long ago, the future feels even closer.

In 2007, the Bosnian town of Tuzla claimed the world record for simultaneous kissing – almost 7000 couples participated.

HISTORY

Winston Churchill once commented that 'the Balkans produce more history than they consume'. Indeed, the movement of invaders, settlers and traders back and forth across the region over the years has created an intricate – and complicated – patchwork of cultures, societies, religions, ethnicities and conflicts.

Tribes, Colonies & Empires

The region hasn't been controlled by one government since the Roman Empire. Farming came to the area around 6000 BC, and was well established by 4000 BC. By 700 BC the local population grew as increasing amounts of iron tools, horses and chariots helped spread trade routes. By the time Celtic tribes drove south and mixed with native Illyrian and Thracian tribes, there were Greek colonies along the coast of Albania and Croatia. Evidence of Illyrians (ancestors of modern-day Albanians) in the Western Balkans dates to 1200 BC; some areas of Albania have been occupied by their descendants ever since.

The Bosnian town of Visoko may (or may not) be home to a 250m-high, 12,000-year-old pyramid built by an extinct super-culture (see p150).

The Greeks were also early occupants of the Balkans; whether family groups joined extant populations or whether armies of conquerors invaded is not known, but it is clear that Greek influences infiltrated the region early on. From the 2nd century BC, the influence of the Roman Empire began encroaching, particularly into the western part of the region, while Greek influences remained dominant in the east. The first division of the region can be dated to AD 395, when Emperor Theodosius split the unwieldy Roman Empire into an eastern, Greek-influenced half ruled from Byzantium (later Constantinople) and a western, Latin-influenced half ruled from Rome. This division laid the first fault line between the eastern and western churches, even before the original Serbs and Croats had settled in. The Roman Empire was weakened by economic crises and plagues around the time it was divided, and Slavic invaders plundering the region, giving rise to the 'barbarian' dark age in the Balkans. The western part of the empire was significantly weakened, but Greek civilisation survived in sections of the eastern part, and many Slavs were Hellenised. Both Roman and Greek influences remain today; the Romans introduced roads and vineyards and constructed towns and fortresses, while the existence of Greek communities in parts of southern Albania today testifies to the endurance of Greek civilisation.

The Coming of the Slavs

The Avar, Goth and Hun invasions weakened Roman defences along the Danube so much that Slav tribes (farmers and herders originally from eastern Ukraine) were able to move south of the river during the 5th and 6th centuries. Two distinct southern Slavic groups were discernable; one would eventually become Croatians and fall under Charlemagne in the 8th century, leading to the Catholicisation of Croatia and the eventual recognition of the Croatian state by the pope in 879. Meanwhile, the Eastern Orthodox influences of Constantinople prevailed over Slavic Serbs.

In the 9th century Christian monks such as Methodius and Cyril (the early namesake of the Cyrillic alphabet based on Byzantine Greek letters, which eventually became the alphabet of Serbian and Macedonian languages) began to evangelise the Slavs.

Another divide occurred in the same era that Cyril and Methodius were sharpening their quills. The Franks took over the northwest of the region and the Croats and Slovenes came under Western European cultural influence. The first independent Croatian kingdom appeared under Ban Tomislav in 924 and remained a distinct crown right through to the end of the Austro Hungarian Empire, to which it became attached.

In the rest of the region the Byzantine Empire was weakening militarily but still held a great deal of cultural influence. The first Serb principality was established under the Byzantine umbrella around 850, but it wasn't until the 12th century that Stefan I Nemanja established the first fully independent Serbian kingdom. One of his sons, Stefan II, built Serbia into a stable nation, recognised as independent by the pope but still with religious ties to the Orthodox Church in Constantinople. Another son, Rastko, would go on to become St Sava. Many of Serbia's great religious artworks date from this time, as artists combined Byzantine iconography with local styles. It is also this era that gave rise to a strong Serbian national identity. The most powerful of all Nemanjić kings, Stefan Dušan, was crowned in 1331 (after doing away with his father); he established the Serbian Orthodox Patriarchate at Peć in western Kosovo, introduced a legal code and expanded the Serbian empire.

Turkish Overlords: The Ottoman Era

The Seljuk Turks swept out of central Asia into the Byzantine heartland of Anatolia in the 11th century. Their successors, the Ottomans, established a base in Europe in 1354 and steadily increased their European territories over the next century. The Ottoman 'victory' (more of a draw, in fact) over the Serbs at Kosovo Polje in 1389 completed the separation of the southern Slavs; the Catholic Croats remained beyond Turkish rule, while Orthodox Serbs and Macedonians were now under it. The Turks had conquered almost the entire region by 1500. The core of Montenegro remained independent under a dynasty of prince-bishops from their mountain stronghold at Cetinje. Suleyman the Magnificent lead the Ottoman charge, taking Belgrade in 1521 and pushing on as far as Vienna, besieged in 1529.

Over time, some communities (particularly in Bosnia, Albania and Kosovo) adopted Islam. The reasons for the conversion are complex. For Albanians, conversion to Islam occurred gradually in a piecemeal fashion; a famous Albanian poet once said that the true religion of Albania is simply being Albanian. As late as 1900 there were families in central Albania who had Muslim names in public but used Christian names at home. In the mountainous north, some Albanian tribes remained Catholic, while their traditional rivals embraced Islam. Many Roma communities also converted to Islam.

Serbs kept the dream of independence alive through romanticising the *hajduks* (bandits) who had taken to the hills to raid Turkish caravans, and

Don't put your bag on the floor in Serbia – it brings bad luck (and makes the bag easier to pinch).

through epic poems retelling the betrayals that led to the end of their empire at the 1389 battle of Kosovo Polje. Some Serbs moved to the shifting frontier region between the Catholic Austrians and the Turks, which more or less coincides with the modern border between BiH and Croatia. This stark mountain region became known as Krajina, meaning 'borderland'. The Serbs of Krajina were under constant pressure to convert to Catholicism, another theme in Serbian identity.

Beyond the existence of Muslim communities throughout the region, almost five centuries of Ottoman control left marks. Some towns are distinctly Turkish, with strong Ottoman architectural influences. Turkish tastes infiltrated regional cuisines, with *burek* and Turkish coffee becoming Balkans staples, and various words were adopted into the local languages. A less tangible mark is that left on the national psyche, manifesting as both affinity to Turkey and conversely in pride at having resisted it over 500 years and numerous generations.

Ottoman Decline

By 1700 the Ottoman Empire was lagging behind the other great European powers. The Austrians pushed south and reconquered Croatia, and began eyeing territory further south. Over succeeding centuries, the once all-conquering Ottoman Empire failed to adjust to changes in the global economy. As Europe industrialised, the Balkans domains instead descended into corrupt agricultural fiefdoms, over which the empire had little direct control but from which it still demanded financial tribute. By the 1860s, the Ottoman sultans in Istanbul needed ever greater loans to fund their opulent courts and lavish harems; British and French bankers were all too happy to oblige, with juicy interest rates. But, with spiralling debt repayments to make, the empire's peasants were taxed ever more harshly. Unrest spread. In 1873, the empire's debts led to a widespread banking collapse. More than ever the authorities were tax hungry, yet the following year saw disastrous harvests. The result in 1875 and 1877 was a wave of Christian revolts, led initially by Bosnian peasants such as Mrkonjić, who would later become Serbian King Peter I. The Turkish backlash designed to stop the revolt was so brutal that sympathetic 'brother' Slav Tchaikovsky composed his famous *Slavonic March* as a sort of 19th-century Band Aid equivalent. International tempers rose. Serbia declared war on Turkey and suddenly the Bosnian revolts had snowballed into a Balkans-wide tangle of war that was widely known as the Great Eastern Crisis.

The crisis saw Turkey's European forces crushingly defeated, notably through a resurgent Russia and an expanded, newly independent Bulgaria. But the egos of Europe's other big powers had to be stroked. This meant that the eventual carve-up of Turkey's European lands was achieved not on the battlefield but with the 1878 Treaty of Berlin, drawn up with staggering disregard for ethno-linguistic realities. The chairman, German Chancellor Bismarck, quaffed prodigious volumes of port wine to calm the pain of his shingles and hurried the proceedings along, anxious to start his summer holidays. As a counterweight to Russian power in Bulgaria, the Austro-Hungarian Empire was persuaded to take military control of Bosnia in 1878, a decision that would alter Bosnia forever and ultimately lead to Austro-Hungary's downfall.

The Rise of Pan-Slavism

The bloody decline of Turkish power and the emergence of competing nationalisms gave rise to pan-Slavism – the idea of uniting Croatians, Serbians and Slovenians under one flag. Croatian bishop Josip Strossmayer was a

The London-based Bosnian Institute has a good website for Bosnian history (one of the founders was historian Noel Malcolm). Follow the links from www.bosnia.org.uk.

strong proponent of pan-Slavism, and founded the Yugoslav Academy of Arts & Sciences in 1867. An independent Serbian kingdom gradually emerged over the 19th century, expanding from its early base around Belgrade. The Austro-Hungarian claim of Bosnia and competition between Serbia, Greece and Bulgaria for the remaining Ottoman territories in Albania, Macedonia and northern Greece intensified. Ethnic nationalism grew as competing powers manipulated identities and allegiances, particularly in Macedonia, where Greek, Bulgarian and Serbian struggles for expansion resulted in 40 years of rebellion, invasions and reprisals, culminating in the landmark Ilinden uprising of August 1903 and its brutal suppression two weeks later.

The First Balkan War in 1912 pushed the Turks back to Constantinople and forced them to concede Macedonia and Kosovo to Serbia. But the Greeks, Serbs and Bulgarians soon began fighting each other. The conflict spilled into the Second Balkan War of 1913, which drew in Romania and ended unsatisfactorily for all, though it did expand Serbian territory once more. Slavic movements were agitating for the union of Bosnia (controlled by Austria) with Serbia. In this climate, Austrian Archduke Franz Ferdinand was assassinated in Sarajevo on 28 June 1914. Though the assassin was not connected to the Serbian government, this act triggered a domino effect of retaliation throughout Europe, beginning with the Austrian invasion of Serbia. WWI led to unimaginable loss of lives, and the weakened Serbia became an entity of the greater southern Slav Kingdom of Serbs, Croats and Slovenes – a pan-Slavic dream named 'Yugoslavia' in 1929. Albania also emerged as an independent state, ruled by the self-proclaimed king, Zog. Both countries were largely rural, Ruritanian dictatorships with very little industry. Neither regime would be able to resist the Italian and German invasions during WWII.

Homeland Calling: Exile Patriotism and the Balkan Wars by Paul Hockenos explores the fascinating stories of émigrés who involved themselves in the wars back 'home'.

WWII

The Balkans stood between Hitler and Russia, presenting states in the region with two very unattractive choices: join or resist Nazism.

The fascist Croatian Ustaše fought communists and Serbs, the Germans fought communists and royalist Chetniks, and Albanian factions fought the Germans, the Italians and each other. The Germans had installed the far-right Croatian Ustaše party as leaders of the Independent State of Croatia, which included modern Croatia, BIH and parts of Serbia and Slovenia. The Ustaše's brutality towards Serbs in particular was shocking even by Nazi standards; Ustaše attempts to convert Orthodox Serbs to Catholicism on pain of death and its systematic murder of Serbs, Jews, Roma and communists is said to have given rise to the term 'ethnic cleansing'.

Determined Serbian resistance was met with brutal reprisals delivered on civilian populations; at one point the Nazi policy was to murder 100 Serbian civilians for every German killed. Two crucial resistance movements emerged; one was the Chetniks, led by Draža Mihailović, and the other was the pro-communist Partisans, led by Josip Broz Tito. Conflict between the two groups and their common enemy, the Ustaše, resulted in civil war. Ultimately the latter galvanised the most support throughout the region, eventually winning British and Soviet support. Tito and Albanian communist party leader Enver Hoxha took the reins of the region and dispatched their rivals with bullets or sent them to prison camps. Around 10% of the region's population perished during WWII.

After WWII Stalin wanted Yugoslavia, Bulgaria and Albania to be united into one communist federation. The Bulgarian leadership scuppered the idea.

Communism & Collectivisation

Yugoslavia and Albania were the only countries in Europe where communists took power without the assistance of the USSR's Red Army. This gave communist-party leaders an unusual amount of freedom compared with other communist regimes in Eastern Europe. The Yugoslav communist party was quick to collectivise agriculture, but by the late 1940s it faced stagnant growth and dwindling popularity. Fed up with interference from Moscow, Tito broke with Stalin in 1948. The collectivisation of land was reversed in 1953, and within a year most peasants had returned to farming independently. Reforms were successful and the economy was booming in the late 1950s. Albania's leader, Hoxha, looked on Yugoslavia's reforms with utter distaste and kept true to hard-line Stalinism. The Albanian communist party controlled every aspect of society – religion was banned during a Chinese-style cultural revolution in the late 1960s and the country became a communist hermit kingdom.

Tito's brand of socialism was different. Almost uniquely, Yugoslavs were able to travel freely to Western countries as well as within the Eastern Bloc. In the 1960s Yugoslavia's self-management principles contributed to a struggle between the republics within it. Richer republics such as Croatia wanted more power devolved to the republics, while Serbia's communist leaders wanted more centralised control. The Albanian majority in Kosovo started to protest against Serbian control in the 1960s, which began the long cycle of riots, violence and repression that lasted until the UN took control of the territory in 1999. Ripples of tension continue today. There was a saying that the Yugoslav dream began in Kosovo and would end in Kosovo; it seems that this has turned out to be true.

Things Fall Apart

After Tito's death in 1980 the federal presidency rotated annually among the eight members of the State Presidency. The economy stalled as foreign debt mounted, and rivalries between the constituent republics grew. Serbian communist-party boss Slobodan Milošević exploited tensions by playing up disturbances between Serbs and Kosovar Albanians in Kosovo, allowing him to consolidate his power base.

As the democracy movement swept Eastern Europe, tensions grew between central powers in Belgrade, dominated by Milošević, and pro-democracy, pro-independence forces in the republics. Slovenia declared independence in 1991 and after a short war became the first republic to break free of Yugoslavia. Croatia soon followed, but the Serbs of the mountainous Krajina region set up their own state. Macedonia became independent without much trouble, but when Bosnia followed suit the country fell into a brutal civil war between the three main communities: Bosniaks, Serbs and Croats. The war continued until 1995 and cost 200,000 lives.

The Dayton Peace Accords divided the country into a federation, awarding 49% to the Serbs and 51% to a Croat-Muslim federation. In the same year the newly strengthened Croatian army conquered the breakaway Serbs' regions. Meanwhile, in rump Yugoslavia (Serbia and Montenegro) the worst hyperinflation in history occurred between 1993 and 1995, when prices grew by five quadrillion per cent; think of the number five with 15 zeroes after it. Albania's communist regime was toppled in 1992, and the country descended into a free-market vacuum of anarchy; peasants stole animals and equipment from the old collective farms, people pillaged factories for building materials, and gangsters ruled major port towns.

It all came to a head in 1997, when the collapse of pyramid banking schemes set off a violent uprising. In Kosovo, rebel Albanians began a guerrilla campaign against Serb forces in 1996. NATO eventually intervened with a bombing campaign that forced Serbian forces to withdraw from the region. The territory has been under UN control ever since, with the UN recently setting out on a path to extract itself. Serbian strongman Slobodan

---

Thousands of ex-Yugoslavs pay 'homage' to Tito at www.tito ville.com. The site includes songs, speeches, portraits, medals and honours, biographies of his many mistresses, and Tito jokes.

Unhappy with the conflicts during the break-up of Yugoslavia, the villagers of Vevčani in Macedonia voted to declare their home an independent republic in 1991.

The film No Man's Land sees a Serb and a Bosnian soldier trapped in a trench. More complications occur when the media and UN bumble in.

Milošević was finally knocked from power in 2001. The war in Kosovo spilled over into Macedonia, where around a quarter of the population is ethnic Albanian. An accord promising more self-government for Albanian areas helped to restore peace.

By 2002 the region was finally mostly peaceful but for lingering fears over the stability of Kosovo and Macedonia. Montenegro declared independence in June 2006, to which Serbia responded by declaring itself the independent successor state of the former union of Serbia and Montenegro. Kosovo's declaration of independence in February 2008 didn't go down the same way; Serbia held the declaration to be illegal.

Peace Breaks Out

Despite lingering concerns about Kosovo and Macedonia, a historical recap of the region shows just how much progress has been made in the last decade. People who fled the area in search of asylum and livelihood are now drifting back. Where hyperinflation was such that it was cheaper to plaster walls with banknotes than wallpaper, economies are now stable and black markets a thing of the past. Since the international community stepped in to lend a hand to Albania, it has made a successful recovery, going from failed state to EU candidate. Croatia – the first state in the Western Balkans to apply for EU membership – is rising above past persecution and now has a Serb deputy prime minister. After years of communist isolation and the wars of the 1990s, the region has opened up and democratic processes have been established. Former enemies are talking again and almost every ethnic, religious, cultural and national mixture is possible. Obstacles to stability such as organised crime and corruption still linger, but now they are viewed as challenges rather than inevitable by-products of failed statehood.

As countries of the region strive for EU integration, more and more war criminals are being surrendered to the Hague. Where once such criminals hid in government skirts, democratically elected leaders are now stepping forward to acknowledge past wrongs and collaborate in attempts to bring war criminals to justice. Where such trials were once considered to point fingers at particular states, now the region is uniting to acknowledge that the crimes of the past were crimes against the whole of humanity.

PEOPLE

As with anywhere in the world, generalising about people in a region as diverse as this one is near-on impossible. The Western Balkans is inhabited by Slavs, Albanians, descendants of Ottoman Turks, Vlachs, Jews and Roma. A given person can have a fascinating combination of nationality, ethnicity, language and religion. Think for instance about the Muslim Roma in Macedonia whose neighbour is a Catholic Albanian or the nonbelieving Croatian Serb living in BiH. Physically this cast of characters may be indistinguishable, but divisions between them have run deep throughout the region's history.

When it comes to talking about the past, the people you meet will show you many sides of different stories and help you understand that there are few blacks and whites in the Western Balkans. Many will express frustration at how simplistically issues were chalked up by the outside world, and still are. Serbians especially feel that they were demonised by the media, despite the fact that many Serbs were just as victimised by Milošević as people in neighbouring countries were. Indeed, many Serbs lost their lives opposing Milošević. Elsewhere you will encounter still more shades of grey. You will meet people in BiH and elsewhere who will tell you how local criminals were often as heinous during the war as neighbouring aggressors

Brenda Brkusic's *Freedom from Despair* is a riveting film that mixes documentary footage with re-enactments to tell the story of Croatia's struggle against ex-Yugoslavia.

The Culture of Lies by Croatian dissident Dubravka Ugrešić mercilessly examines the little dictators and macho blather of the 1990s.

Nikola Tesla, the brilliant Serbian inventor, was working on a 'death beam' when he died, the plans for which mysteriously disappeared. For more on Tesla, see the boxed text, p389.

In the Albanian *kanun* tradition, 'sworn virgins' are women who assume the role (dress, habits, privileges…) of men. From the day they take their oath, they are respected by the family and community as the male patriarch of the family. See the boxed text, p56.

and blame current problems as much on corruption in their own countries as on foreign policies. On the other hand, you might encounter Albanians who are vocally proud of independence but deafeningly quiet about the 40 years under Hoxha's rule.

In countries of the former Yugoslavia, some of the older generation will recall the extensive opportunities they enjoyed under communism and lament the lack of opportunities for their children today, but nostalgia for the economic certainty of life under Tito is not the same as supporting him.

After many turbulent years, the revolutionary habit of raging against the machine dies hard. Many people are actively engaged in or at least highly opinionated about politics and vocal in support of or in opposition to policies relating to their future. Young people in particular are excited about a European future, with some already joking, 'Where is the Western Balkans? You are in Europe!' On the other hand, you'll also come across people in quiet and prosperous places who have reached opinion-fatigue and just want to get on with their lives without discussing everything along the way.

The movement of people around the region and beyond it has left indelible marks on modern life. Millions of ex-Yugoslavs and Albanians left to work in Western Europe, and just about everyone in the region has an uncle or cousin or hairdresser who left for Canada or Germany or Australia. The wars of the 1990s sparked another wave of departures.

Those who permanently settled in their adopted countries gave rise to new diasporas around the region and beyond. Others returned with new skills, languages, ideas and trends. The increasing cosmopolitanism borne of this movement of people is particularly evident in larger cities; stop someone in the street and they may understand you in a few languages, or step into an innovative new restaurant and chances are it was created by a returnee trying their hand at importing foreign culinary concepts. There is little resentment towards those who left; indeed, the support emigrants provided to friends and family back home was one of the reasons many people survived. And the truth is you will still meet people who want nothing better than to leave.

There is a darker side of movement of people; illegal migrants have used the region as a final staging post for the journey into the wealthier parts of Europe, and many victims of human trafficking originate in the Western Balkans or transit through it en route to destinations in the EU or beyond. Efforts to tackle these problems have increased in recent years.

Most people live in cities and, though fashions are as up to date, bars as sleek and latest releases just as recent as anywhere in Western Europe, strong rural affiliation remains. Many urbanites have country connections and enjoy visits home to revel in the pastoral pace and enjoy homebrewed spirits and homemade condiments. Macho undertones, which still prevail in some areas, are particularly evident in the countryside; women spend Saturday morning grocery shopping while their menfolk idle in cafes. But even in the more conservative Muslim areas you find working women huffily challenging their male counterparts in defiance of traditional gender roles.

The more people you meet in the Western Balkans the more you will be struck by their similarities rather than their differences. You'll have the privilege of meeting opinionated, creative, passionate and slightly eccentric folk in every country of the region, and the one generalisation that can absolutely be made about the lot of them is their shared tradition of warmth and hospitality. Invitations aren't embarrassingly persistent; they are sincere offers that make you feel genuinely welcome wherever you are. A related trait that also transcends ethnic divides is the laid-back approach to time as something to be passed leisurely rather than spent in a hurry.

RELIGION

Religion is an active part of cultural life and identity in the Western Balkans, as it always has been. The Orthodox churches being raised throughout the region and the numbers of pilgrims making their way to monasteries hint at a religious resurgence. On the other hand, many who espouse a religion practise it very loosely.

The role that religion played in conflicts of the past is complex and often misunderstood. As is true the world over, people of different faiths have been pitted against each other in this region, but they also stood side by side and gave their lives in defence of each other. The relationship between religion and ethnicity is often clear; religion generally says more about a person's ethnicity than it does about their nationality or spirituality – even nonbelievers may strongly align themselves with their ancestral faith.

To break it down to bite size: the three key religions in the Western Balkans are Orthodox Christianity, Catholicism and Islam. Precise numbers are impossible to pin down, but of the 24.9 million people living in the region, around 49% are Orthodox, 22% are Muslim, another 22% Catholic and the remaining 7% belong to other faiths or profess no religion.

The biggest Orthodox Church in the Western Balkans is the Serbian Orthodox Church, with adherents in Serbia, Montenegro, Kosovo, BiH and Croatia. Around 85% of Serbians are Orthodox. The Macedonian Orthodox Church split from the Serbian church in 1967, and has the allegiance of about 65% of the Macedonian population. The Albanian Orthodox Church, also a 20th-century creation, is followed by about 20% of Albanians, mostly in the southern half of the country. The Montenegrin Orthodox Church proclaimed itself distinct from the Serbian Orthodox Church as recently as 1993 and tensions still remain between the two.

Around 88% of Croatians are Catholic. The Hungarians of Serbia's Vojvodina region are also predominantly Catholic. Around 10% of Albanians are Catholic too – Mother Teresa of Calcutta was born into an ethnic Albanian family in Skopje, Macedonia. There is also a smallish number of Protestants in the region, mostly ethnic Hungarians in Serbia's Vojvodina region.

The Muslim population is divided into a number of groups, the largest two being the Sunni Muslims of BiH and southern Serbia, who speak Slavic dialects, and the Albanians of Kosovo, Albania and Macedonia. There is also a small Turkish Muslim community, mostly in old Ottoman towns such as Novi Pazar in Serbia, Prizren in Kosovo and Bitola in Macedonia. Ottoman Islam, which many converted to, evolved into a far more moderate and tolerant variety of Islam than is found in many other parts of the world; drinking alcohol is acceptable and a minority of women choose to wear the veil (though more do in Islamic pockets of Macedonia than in Kosovo or Albania). There are also smaller Muslim groups in the region, including the Sufi Bektashi, named for Haji Bektash Veli (though more popularly known as the Turkish Dervishes). Originating in the 12th century, Bektashism incorporates elements of both Sunni and Shia Islam. In Sufi-inspired Bektashism, unveiled women are allowed to take part in rituals and alcohol is not prohibited. The Bektashi moved their headquarters to Tirana after Sufi orders were banned in secular Turkey. For more, see the boxed text, p57.

Despite the moderate Islam that rules in the Western Balkans, there has been increased concern in recent years about the disconcerting rise of fundamentalism. Extremist elements extant in the Balkans have been attributed to complex factors such as the influence of Wahabbis during the conflicts when they fought as mercenaries alongside Bosnian Muslims and Kosovar Albanians in the mid-1990s; foreign-funded missionary activities after the conflicts; and the influence of locals who have returned from Arab states

The Orthodox Christian tradition of Slava celebrates family patron saints. During these celebrations, families come together and the family home is open to anyone who wants to visit.

with devout religious educations. The ability of these factors to infiltrate mainstream ideology is heightened by the susceptibility of local populations that have been economically, socially and culturally displaced.

The majority of the Jewish population was murdered by the Third Reich in the 1940s, though one inspiring exception was Albania, where the Jewish population actually grew during WWII as Jewish people sought refuge there and the government and local population actively protected them throughout the war. Today there are few Jews left throughout the Balkans; there are only around 2500 in Serbia, 1700 in Croatia, 500 in Montenegro, another 500 in Macedonia and, ironically, as few as 10 in Albania. Though commemorative museums and monuments are scattered throughout the region, many synagogues have been left to fall into disrepair.

ARTS

Creative expression has always been integral to expressing identity in the Western Balkans. Invading and prevailing cultures played tug-of-war over buildings that even today show the layers of who was here. Similarly, music not only expresses traditions and cultures but also has been used to garner support for political ideology or to rally resistance against it. Visual arts reflect and record history, and live and breathe triumphantly today after having survived past oppression.

Literature

The region has a penchant for quirky statues; look for Rocky and Bob Marley in Serbia and Bruce Lee in BiH!

Literature in the Western Balkans all began with epic poetry, a tradition which survives in the Dinaric Range from Croatia to Albania and predates Homer. In Serbia, BiH and Croatia, vast epic poems were memorised and recited to the accompaniment of the violin-like *gusle*, played with a bow. They were passed down through generations like this, recording key historical events, dramatising heroic tales and giving rise to myths.

The 1389 battle of Kosovo features prominently in Serbian epic poetry. The slaying of the Turkish sultan by legendary knight Miloš Obilić was portrayed thus:

… Miloš killed the Turkish Sultan, Murad,
And slaughtered many Turkish soldiers with him.
May God Almighty bless the one who bore him!
He leaves immortal fame to all the Serbs
To be forever told in song and story
As long as Kosovo and human kind endure.

An excellent resource for Albanian literary enthusiasts is www.albanian literature.com/en

Serbian epic poetry was first written down by the 19th-century writer and linguist Vuk Karadžić, whose works were brought to a wider audience through translations by the likes of Goethe and Walter Scott.

Contemporary literature in the region has achieved global acclaim. Bosnian-born (but revered throughout the region) Ivo Andrić won the Nobel Prize for Literature in 1961 'for the epic force with which he has traced themes and depicted human destinies drawn from the history of the country'. Andrić's classic *The Bridge on the Drina* offers extraordinarily humanising insight into ethnic conflicts in the region. See p108.

Montenegrin literature is dominated by poet-prince-bishop Petar II Petrović Njegoš; his acclaimed work *The Mountain Wreath* is still a source of pride. Montenegrin writer Milovan Đilas also led a fascinating life beyond his literary pursuits. Partisan leader and one-time vice president to Tito, Đilas was on the verge of becoming president in 1954 but fell from communist grace when works critical of communism landed him in jail.

Contemporary writers include Ismail Kadare, Albania's most beloved novelist and a perennial candidate for a Nobel Prize, who was awarded the Man Booker International Prize in 2005. One of Kadare's most renowned works is *The File on H*, a short, humorous book about the epic-poetry tradition in which two Irish-American academics stumble into local politics.

Another widely acclaimed contemporary writer is Serbia's Milorad Pavić, whose books are not so much read as embarked upon as one would a surreal interactive journey (see p378).

Sarajevo Rose: A Balkan Jewish Notebook by Stephen Schwartz traces the remnants of a lost Jewish world, which intermingled with the other faiths of the region.

Architecture

The region's architecture is a three-dimensional record of previous societies. Buildings have been erected, redesigned, demolished and resurrected throughout history, making for a rich collage of stylistic contrasts.

The Roman amphitheatre at Pula in Croatia is one of the best preserved in the world, while the Euphrasian Basilica at Poreč earned a World Heritage listing for its preservation of Byzantine and classical elements dating back to the 4th century. The Croatian and Montenegrin coasts are strongly Venetian influenced. Serbia's Vojvodina region has Hungarian-influenced elements, particularly in the art nouveau buildings in Novi Sad and Subotica. The Turkish influence in mosques, madrassas (colleges for learning the Koran), hamams (public baths) and domestic architecture spreads from Macedonia to Albania, Serbia and BiH. Berat in Albania has a particularly fine set of Ottoman-era neighbourhoods, and Sarajevo and Mostar in BiH have a delightful mix of Ottoman-style structures, Orthodox churches and Habsburg-era public buildings. Baroque and Gothic architecture mostly appears in Croatia, which also has a strong legacy of Romanesque architecture, continuing long after this style had been supplanted by Gothic design in other parts of Europe.

Communist architecture is easy to spot; it fills you with dread or makes you laugh. While the unmistakable communist influence in the Western Balkans is not particularly celebrated, some of it is certainly distinct. The wackiest in the region has to be Tirana's Pyramid, built in honour of dictator Enver Hoxha. Some surviving Yugo-hotels in Serbia and Montenegro are also thrilling for their grey but groovy character. It's easy to be cynical about these, but some of them truly capture an era and are original enough to be worth hanging on to.

Builders were brought from Turkey to erect authentic structures, so what remains of the Ottoman era is fascinating for the contrast it lends to other styles. Much character has been lost in rebellious assertions of independence from the Ottomans, but interestingly, many Turkish styles left an imprint in post-Ottoman design. The Turkish *konak* is a distinct style of residence throughout the region, generally white with timber framings. The 2nd floor, often balanced on beams, protrudes over the ground floor. These *doksat* (overhanging windowed rooms) would jut over the street so as not to appropriate too much space on it but still afford the people inside a view of its goings-on. Interiors of such residences were adapted to the lifestyles that played out in them; most of the living rooms were on the 1st floor, often adorned with *peškum* (carved hexagonal coffee tables) and *sećija* (benches along the wall), often draped with *ćilim* (hand-woven carpets). Windows were shuttered so sequestered women inside could enjoy the views without being seen. Many such houses now serve as museums. The classical Ottoman mosque features a large cubed prayer area with a dome on top. Minarets on Ottoman mosques in this region are often taller and slimmer than their Arab counterparts. Inside, the *mihrab* (prayer niche) faces Mecca, and the pulpits are often carved from wood.

Tragically, the region's architectural heritage has been caught in the crossfire of its conflicts over the years; hundreds of mosques, churches and monasteries have been vandalised or destroyed. The most recent such spate occurred in Kosovo and Serbia as a result of Kosovo's independence declaration in February 2008; Serbian Orthodox sites in Kosovo and Islamic mosques in Serbia continue to be guarded.

On the brighter side, there has been increased effort to restore key buildings destroyed or damaged during the wars. In Dubrovnik, for instance, dozens of buildings that were attacked from land and sea have been rebuilt. Several brave locals risked their lives during the bombardment to replace roof tiles, and similar courage was shown elsewhere in the region; the people of Sarajevo went to untold effort to protect sacred artefacts. The most iconic structure in the Western Balkans to have been resurrected after its destruction during the war is BiH's Old Bridge (see p133), which was painstakingly rebuilt in 2004 using 16th-century engineering techniques.

Music

'Popular throughout the region, turbo-folk is the crass lovechild of a dirty affair between folk and pop music'

Candidates for the oldest living musical traditions in the Western Balkans are the old Slavonic hymns of the Serbian Orthodox Church and southern Albania's polyphonic singing. Croatia's four-voice *klapa* music is another unusual a cappella tradition. The various Islamic dervish orders have traditions of religious chants on mystical themes. One regional curiosity is *blehmuzika*, Serbian brass music influenced by Turkish and Austrian military music. It's often played by Roma bands at weddings and funerals and at the raucous Guča Trumpet Festival (see the boxed text, p414). Other folk traditions include Macedonian *gajda* (bagpipe) tunes, accompanied by drums, and Serbian peasant dances led by bagpipes, flutes and fiddles. Kosovar folk music bears the influence of Ottoman military marching songs, with careening flutes over the thudding beat of goatskin drums. The beloved traditional music of BiH is *sevdah*, derived from the Turkish word *sevda*, meaning love. The melancholy sound of *sevdah* is sometimes described as the Bosnian blues.

Enormously popular throughout the region, turbo-folk is the crass lovechild of a dirty affair between folk and pop music. During the Milošević era, turbo-folk was appropriated by the regime and heavily impregnated with nationalist messages. The intermingling of pop culture and the political scene was never more epitomised than by the marriage of turbo-folk queen 'Ceca' and Milošević henchman Arkan, described by Matthew Collin in *Guerrilla Radio* as having 'spotlighted the umbilical link between war and pop culture in the most dramatic fashion'. Though its nationalist connotations have diminished, turbo-folk is the loudest thing left over from the former Yugoslavia; video clips are gloriously reminiscent of the 1980s: female leads with gravity-defying bosom and height-defying hair are flanked by groups of choreographed dancing women.

Modern pop artists from BiH, Croatia, Montenegro and Serbia have a bigger audience than imports from other European countries throughout the former federation – 'from Triglav to the Vardar', to quote an old Yugoslav anthem. Indeed, much Balkans talent has been well received in foreign lands; Macedonia's baritone Boris Trajanov has sung all over the world and became an Unesco Artist for Peace in 2005, and classical pianist Simeon Trpčeski is world renowned.

Another influential character on the music scene in the Western Balkans is Goran Bregović. Born in Bosnia to a Serbian mother and a Croat father, the former rock star is now famed for his collaborations with famed filmmaker Emir Kusturica (including composition for the soundtracks of *Time of the Gypsies* and *Arizona Dream*, starring Johnny Depp). Bregović is a strong ambassador for Balkans music and an advocate for Roma music's role in the region's cultural history. Another advocate of Roma traditions is Macedonia's Esma Rexhepova, widely acclaimed for her mastery of the music of her culture.

The music scene in the Western Balkans seems to be in a perpetual state of crescendo, with new artists and sounds emerging all the time. Even hip-hop is building a strong following throughout the region (even for horrifically named outfits like Montenegro's Monteniggers). Some do it tongue in cheek, but others are genuinely dissed. Tuzla in BiH is famed throughout the region as a centre of rap and hip-hop. More challenging types of music also have a strong base among the substantial urban bohemian community. The Skopje Jazz Festival (p293) and Serbia's Exit Festival (p401) draw larger crowds and bigger names each year. Also see the boxed text, p23.

On 16 October 2007, the Western Balkans was shaken by the loss of Tošc Proeski, one of its most successful and beloved pop stars, who died in a car accident at the age of 26. Tošc represented Macedonia in the 2004 Eurovision Song Contest and was a regional Unicef ambassador. He was loved for his powerful voice, compassion and charisma, and his death was met with anguish. October 17 was declared a national day of mourning in Macedonia, and fans throughout the Western Balkans deeply mourned the loss of the young star. For more, see the boxed text, p316.

> In 1934, 12-year-old Jan Yoors ran away from home, joining a Roma clan. His books *The Gypsies*, *Crossing* and *The Heroic Present* offer insight into Roma life.

Visual Arts

Serbian and Macedonian medieval architecture is mostly on a provincial scale compared with Orthodox Christian centres such as Kyiv and Moscow, but in fresco painting local artists rivalled anything produced in the Orthodox world. Many classic frescos painted in churches and monasteries from the 10th to the 14th centuries were hidden by whitewash applied by Turkish rulers (which inadvertently helped to preserve them) and obscured by dense layers of smoke and candle residue. The frescos in the churches of Sveti Pantelejmon near Skopje and Sveti Kliment in Ohrid display a skill for expression that predates the Italian Renaissance by 150 years. Albania has a largely unknown tradition of fine Orthodox art, exemplified by the icon painter Onufri, whose colourful, expressive work is contained in a museum in Berat (p77).

An important 20th-century Yugoslav art movement was Zenitism, from the word zenith, which fused French and Russian intellectualism with Balkans passion. Belgrade's Museum of Contemporary Art (p390) has a fine collection of Zenitist works (returned after works of non-Serbian artists were purged under Milošević).

Socialist realist art dedicated to glorifying the worker and the achievements of communism had only a brief heyday in Yugoslavia – artists were allowed to return to their own styles in the early 1950s – but it lasted right up until the early 1990s in Albania. Tirana's National Art Gallery (p66) has a salon devoted to socialist realist works.

The best-known sculptor of the region is Ivan Meštrović, born into a poor farming family in Croatia in 1883. He taught himself to read from the Bible, and went on to create some of the finest examples of religious sculpture since the Renaissance. Though he emigrated to the USA, around 60 of his works are scattered around the former Yugoslavia, including the *Monument to the Unknown Hero* outside Belgrade (p390).

Conflicts of the 1990s hampered the arts and almost every other sphere of endeavour, but artists of the region survived to re-emerge with much to explore and express. A powerful message was offered by young Bosnian artist Sejla Kamerić, who was growing up in Sarajevo during the time of the siege. In her most recognised and confronting work, *Bosnian Girl,* she has laid graffiti left in Srebrenica by a Dutch soldier ('No teeth…? A mustache…? Smel like shit…? BOSNIAN GIRL!') over her photographic portrait.

Another interesting work to come out of this era was produced by Serbian Ivan Grubanov, who had the opportunity to sit in the press gallery at the Hague during Milošević's trial. The 200-odd portraits that emerged were fused with recordings of the trial as an evocative depiction of the broken dictator.

Cinema

Some exceptional films offer a fascinating window into the Western Balkans. *Lamerica* (1995) depicts the postcommunist culture of Albania. Bosnian Danis Tanović won an Oscar for *No Man's Land* (2002), about the relationship between a Serbian and a Muslim trapped in a trench together during the Sarajevo siege. In *Grbavica* (2006) – written and directed by another Bosnian, Jasmila Zbanic – the protagonist learns that her father was not a war hero but that her mother was a victim of rape during the war. Macedonian director Milčo Mančevski explores ethnic tensions in his Oscar-nominated, cinematically sublime *After the Rain* (1994) and the more recent (and controversial) films *Dust* (2002) and *Shadows* (2007). Montenegro's Veljko Bulajić's films have achieved several international award nominations; his most recent work is *Libertas* (2006). Bojan Bazeli (of *Mr & Mrs Smith* fame) has crossed over to Hollywood. Enigmatic filmmaker Emir Kusturica playfully and energetically dissects the Balkans with vivid portraits in his outlandish films, including his famed black comedy *Underground* (1995).

Emir Kusturica's film *When Father Was Away on Business* addresses Tito's brutal rule. Malik believes his father is away on business. The truth is much darker…

FOOD & DRINK

The cuisines of the Western Balkans mix and match Mediterranean, central European and Turkish influences. Though heavy food may make you feel as though you're packing an artery with every meal, the produce is generally free of fertilisers and pesticides. In most meals, superb use is made of produce from this agriculturally rich region. There's a legion of local cheeses barely known outside the immediate area, and an excellent range of fresh fruits in season: grapes, cherries, apples, peaches, pears, plums, melons, figs and quinces. In colder regions cabbages, walnuts and root vegetables such as turnips are used. Local dishes tend to be fairly simple, relying on abundant quality produce to create tasty meals.

Eating hours across the region are much the same as in the rest of Europe. There are many local terms for restaurants and eateries, from Croatian *gostionica* (restaurant) to Albanian *byrektorë* (bakeries selling *burek,* stuffed filo pastry), and *pekara* (bakeries selling almost everything), which provide a range of sweet and savoury snacks; see the country chapters for details.

Tito's Cookbook by Anja Drulović lets you recreate the meals Tito shared with the likes of Elizabeth Taylor, Saddam Hussein, Winston Churchill and Stalin.

Staples & Specialities

Burek or *byrek,* with a range of fillings including cheese, meat, potato, spinach and mushrooms, is the classic Western Balkans snack. It's often enjoyed with yoghurt for breakfast.

Meals usually begin with spongy Turkish bread slathered with *kajmak* – a salty curd. Appetisers include locally smoked hams, pickled vegetables and feta-style cheeses. For lunch and dinner, the most common restaurant dishes are grilled meats such as *ćevapčići* (grilled spicy kebab fingers), *ražnjići* (shish kebab, called *qebap* in Albanian areas) and *pljeskavica* (spiced mixed meat patties). Kebabs are often served with Turkish-style bread and sliced onions. Stews are popular, often cooked slowly over an open fire, with favourites such as *bosanski lonac* (Bosnian stew of cabbage and meat)

FLAVOURS TO SAVOUR

Had any *ajvar* with a glass of *salep* lately? A few regional rarities to watch out for:

Ajvar Macedonia's national relish, made from red peppers, aubergine (eggplant), paprika, olive oil, onion and garlic.

Hurmastica A Bosnian dessert made from filo pastry with cream and lemon.

Jukvi A breakfast pancake made from semolina, which is cooked and dried, then recooked with water and milk.

Kajmak A dairy dish made from clotted cream, ranging from buttery when fresh to like a soft cheese when matured. Very popular in Serbia – incredibly rich and strangely addictive.

Kukurec A rather fearsome dish made from sheep intestines stuffed with chopped liver.

Raca Pig's head or knuckles, fried in herbs and served cold in slices. A real man's food.

Riblji paprikaš A spicy Slavonian fish stew flavoured with paprika.

Salep A drink made from powdered wild orchid root and hot milk, quite hard to find.

Sheqerpare Balls of sweet dough baked in butter, popular in Kosovo and Albania.

Tartufe Truffles from the hinterland of Croatia's Istrian Peninsula, sold sliced or prepared into oils and pasta sauces.

Tufahija Apples filled with walnuts and almonds, doused in syrup, dusted with cinnamon and topped with *kajmak*.

---

or *kapama* (lamb stew). Where it's available peppery *riblja čorba* fish stew is not to be missed. Goulash made with paprika is a hearty dish found in regions bordering Hungary.

Coastal Croatia, Albania and Montenegro are a dream for fish-fans; grilled fish, shellfish, scampi, calamari, sea bass, bream and hake are drowned with garlic and olive oil. Fried mussels in Albania's Saranda are a treat. *Pastrmka* (trout) is widely available, and usually arrives grilled with a zesty sauce on the side. Macedonian *skara* (barbecue) includes fresh fruit and vegetables.

Salads with diced cucumber and tomato drizzled in olive oil and sprinkled with herbs accompany many main meals. Meals often end with seasonal fruit, or far less healthily with *baklava* (nut-filled pastry heavy with sticky syrup), stuffed *palačinke* (pancakes, which if you're not careful can also constitute a main) and *hurmastica* (syrup-soaked sponge fingers, *urmašice* in Serbia). Cakes and ice creams are also common.

In addition to local fare, ubiquitous Italian food (pizza and pasta) is much loved by locals and international cuisine can be found in larger cities throughout the region.

Drinks

Every country has its favourite locally made beer (*pivo* or *piva* in Slavic languages, *birra* or *birrë* in Albanian), challenged on the shelves by major international brews such as Heineken and Fosters. Local beers worth looking out for are Karlovačko *pivo* from Karlovac in Croatia, Nikšićko *pivo* from Montenegro, and Korca from Korca in Albania. Most beers are lagers, though there are some dark stouts and ales available.

There is also an incredible array of spirits distilled from a variety of fruits; these are called *rakija* in Slavic tongues and *raki* in Albanian. The alcohol content is generally between 40% and 70%, so not surprisingly it's drunk as a shot from special little glasses after meals and for toasts. Macedonia's local variant is *žolta* (yellow) *rakija* with wheat added during a secondary fermentation – even more than most *rakija*, it kicks like a mad mule. The most common fruit *rakija* is made from plums, and is variously called *šljivovica* (Croatia, BiH, Serbia and Montenegro). This is the national drink in Serbia, where something like 70% of the plum harvest goes into its production. The drink appears at any excuse for a celebration, from Christmas to birthdays to anniversaries. Albania's liquor of note is Skënderbeu *konjak*, a surprisingly smooth and subtle brandy. The region also has a range of herbal

Serbs sometimes call a dose of potent *rakija* 'a glass of chat', and back it up with the old saying 'Without *rakija* there is no conversation'.

liqueurs, from Albania's very curious Fernet to Serbia and Croatia's rather medicinal-tasting *pelinkovac*.

More and more, the region is a great one for wine lovers. Wine routes are increasingly being pushed to travellers in the region and yield some splendid surprises both in terms of the wine and the scenery it hails from. Wine connoisseurs should particularly seize the opportunity of being in the Western Balkans to sample offerings from monastery wineries.

Croatia's wine producers are divided into the inland Slavonia region (mostly white wine) and coastal Dalmatia (mostly red wine). Graševina, a gentle golden-hued white similar to riesling, is the most widely grown variety in Slavonia. The Dalmatian coast wineries are increasingly growing merlot and cabernet sauvignon, and some other unusual varieties. The wine routes of Croatia's Istria region are becoming increasingly popular for wine lovers and foodies, who are also starting to flock here for prized truffles and olive oil.

Serbia's workhorse red grape is prokupac, a dense, robust red with high sugar levels, often blended with French varieties such as gamay, merlot and pinot noir. In Serbia, the Fruška Gora region is a major wine producer – and an extremely pretty one. *Bermet* is a traditional Vojvodinian dessert wine worth trying in these parts.

Some fine wines are also coming out of Macedonia, which is putting its endemic grape varieties to good use with vranec, stanošina and temjanika. Boutique wine producers such as Bovin have taken root in Macedonia's vineyard heartland in the Kavadarci-Negotino region. The Tikveš wine region of Macedonia is worth a visit for its scenery as much as its top-notch wines. See the boxed text, p319.

Hercegovina's wine route offers fine žilavka (white) and blatina (red). *Domaći* (house) wines served in restaurants in BiH can be a nice alternative to imported wines on the menu. Many blatina reds are rich and well-balanced, and Stankela white (a prize-winning žilavka), from Međugorje, is crisp and fresh. For more on Hercegovinan wine, see the boxed text, p131.

Albania's wine industry is fairly small, but offers some curiosities like red kallmet from the northern Shkodra region. The Cobo winery near Berat in central Albania is also well worth visiting.

Besides alcohol, coffee is the main social catalyst. The Ottoman aristocracy introduced caffeine in the 16th century, and coffee houses have been pillars of local communities ever since. Turkish-style coffee is the traditional staple, though younger urban clientele opt for Italian- and Austrian-style brews. Turkish coffee (which is not always acknowledged to be Turkish) is prepared by heating finely ground coffee beans and water for 15 to 20 minutes and served in a small cup with a glass of water and a biscuit or Turkish delight on the side. In Serbia, Kosovo and Albania the custom is to mix sugar with the coffee powder and water as well.

Vegetarians & Vegans

There are some delicious Turkish-style vegetable dishes to be had, such as roast peppers and aubergines (eggplants), cauliflower moussaka and vegetarian *burek,* which can be filled with cheese, potato or spinach.

Many entrées are vegetarian as well, such as *ajvar,* but 'vegetarian' soups are sometimes flavoured with smoked ham. Top-end restaurants and those in international hubs are getting more veggie-savvy, but if all else fails you can always fill up on salads: generally a fresh mix of chopped tomato, onion and cucumber, sometimes with grated white cheese and peppers as well. Or enjoy starters tapas style; fried peppers and aubergines, goat cheese and olives can be a happy substitute for a main.

California's popular wine grape zinfandel descends from the ancient Croatian varietal crljenak, which now exists in such small numbers that no pure crljenak is made.

The Best of Croatian Cooking by Liliana Pavicic and Gordana Perker Mosher is just what it says it is.

EAT YOUR WORDS

For a pronunciation guide, see p454.

English	Bosnian/Croatian/Macedonian/Serbian	Albanian
salt	sol or so	kripë
pepper	papar or biber	spec
sugar	šećer	sheqer
bread	kruh or hleb/hljeb	bukë
rice	riža or pirinač	oriz
apple	jabuka	mollë
beans	grah or pasulj	fasulje
grapes	grožđe	rrush
orange	naranča or pomorandža	portokall
pepper (vegetable)	paprika	speca
potato	krumpir or krompir	patate
salad	salata	sallatë
tomato	rajčica or paradajz	domate
meat	meso	mish
beef	govedina	mish lope
chicken	piletina	pülu
fish	riba	peshk
lamb	janjetina or jagnjetina	mish qingji
pork	svinjetina	mish derri
cheese	sir	djathë
milk	mlijeko, mleko or mljeko	qumësht
ice cream	sladoled	akullore
egg	jaje	vezë
tea	čaj	çaj
coffee	kava or kafa	kafe
water	voda	ujë
beer	pivo	birrë
wine	vino	verë

Vegans, good luck. On the upside the region is agriculturally rich and doing your own shopping in produce markets will be a joy.

ENVIRONMENT

The Western Balkans is a rich repository of biological diversity. More than a third of Europe's flowering plants, half of its fish species and two-thirds of its birds and mammals can be found in the former Yugoslavia alone. The area around the borders of Albania, Montenegro and Kosovo is one of the least-touched alpine regions on the continent. Its environmental assets benefit from varied climates, geology and topography and to an extent the continuation of traditional low-intensity agricultural practices. However, the shift towards industry-scale logging and merchandise farming is straining the natural environment, and increasing urbanisation is making metropolitan environments more fragile than before.

The Land

A wide belt of mountains parallel to the Adriatic coast covers about 60% of the region; this strip is usually made of limestone and has long valleys, dramatic gorges, vast cave systems and oddities such as disappearing rivers. The Dinaric Range along Croatia's coast has partly sunk into the sea, creating an incredibly convoluted network of islands, peninsulas and bays. A knot of fault lines in the southern part of the region sometimes causes shattering earthquakes, such as that in 1963, which demolished Macedonia's capital, Skopje. The region's highest mountain is Korab (2764m), on the border of Albania and Macedonia. The Pannonian plain along the Sava and Danube rivers in Croatia and northern Serbia was the floor of an ancient sea around 2.5 million years ago.

An interesting venture is the Balkans Peace Park project (see the boxed text, p61), which aims to create a protected park area cutting across Montenegro, Kosovo and Albania. For more on national parks in the region, see individual country chapters.

The International Commission for the Protection of the Danube River (www.icpdr.org) offers detailed information about cooperative protection and shared use of the water that flows through the region.

Wildlife

The Western Balkans is a refuge for many of the larger mammals that were almost eliminated from Western Europe 150 years ago. Rugged forests of the Dinaric Range from Croatia to Albania shelter wolves, red deer, roe deer, lynx, chamois, wild boar and brown bears. Forests are roughly divided into a conifer zone, beginning between 1500m and 2000m, and including silver fir, spruce and black pine; broad-leafed beech forests, which occur lower down; and a huge variety of oak species below this again. Birds of prey found in the region include griffon falcons, kestrels and peregrine falcons. The great lakes of Ohrid and Prespa in the far south are havens for Dalmatian pelicans, herons and spoonbills.

The more populated shores of the Adriatic coast have endangered populations of golden jackals, red foxes and badgers, while bigger predators such as wolves and brown bears have largely been eradicated. Classic Mediterranean species such as junipers, heaths and olive trees grow well in the high summer temperatures of this area. The Adriatic shore also used to be home to the endangered Mediterranean monk seal, but now all the seals are gone (though colonies are believed to survive in Greece). On a happier note, the number of bottlenose dolphins seems to be growing in Croatia's Kvarner Gulf.

Environmental Issues

The Western Balkans was almost entirely agricultural until after WWII, when communist central planners decreed rapid industrialisation on a massive scale. Between the 1950s and the 1970s, the rate of industrialisation and urbanisation was amongst the highest in the world. Use of energy and raw materials put pressure on natural resources, decreasing forested areas, deteriorating water quality and increasing air pollution. Economic stagnation and UN sanctions imposed during the 1990s contributed to a dramatic slowdown in economic activity; a positive side effect of this was the reduction in air and water pollution, but negative consequences included increased use of low-quality fuels, deprioritisation of environmental policy in industry, and the suspension of international cooperation on environmental management of shared assets. The need for cohesive environmental cooperation has taken on new complexity since the emergence of new Balkans states following the break-up of Yugoslavia, with more states now required to cooperate.

The Dalmatian coast faces a host of environmental challenges, but Sunce, a Split-based environmental organisation, has risen to the occasion. Track its efforts at www.sunce-st.org.

Air pollution is a concern in large cities such as Belgrade and struggling cities such as Pristina. Providing reliable power to Kosovars has often been at the cost of fresh air; time will tell how future decisions fare. Similarly, the flurry of construction taking place in cities throughout the region is not necessarily planned or controlled with respect to its environmental impact.

Sewerage outflows in coastal resorts can be a problem when tourist crowds descend in summer. Dumping of sewage is a problem in Durrës (Albania), and a controversial rock-wool factory has been built in Croatia (see p180).

Litter on land and water throughout the region can be severe, especially in the south. Some steps have been taken to remedy this, but on the whole the locals who contribute to the problem haven't had the benefit of strong ecological education to help them understand the long-term environmental and economic impact of their actions. While you're in the region, take your litter with you (and don't do it subtly – why not try to start a trend?).

For tips on lessening your impact while in the Western Balkans, see p21.

IMPACT OF COMMUNISM

Towns and cities all over the Western Balkans have problems with air, soil and water poisoned by messy industrial plants introduced during the communist era. Pollution from lignite (brown coal) power plants and other industries remains the biggest environmental concern today. Albania's communist party had a particular proclivity for seriously big industrial plants; the humongous Steel of the Party metallurgical plant in Elbasan emitted so much filth that it made agriculture impossible in the surrounding valley. Authorities also terraced thousands of hectares of hillside in a bid to mould hills into fields, an endeavour which had predictable results for soil erosion. As in other communist-controlled regions, damage caused by industrial waste wasn't recognised until much later.

In some instances, communists did go green; the Yugoslav authorities could be surprisingly sensitive to environmental issues. Nomadic sheep and goat herding was banned in 1951 in a bid to prevent soil erosion. Tito's regime also created a network of national parks and protected areas.

The fall of communism introduced new environmental problems. In Albania, uncontrolled logging – previously prevented by the threat of a life sentence in a chrome mine – is now a concern. After the ban on fishing in Lake Ohrid was lifted, the Ohrid trout's numbers dropped perilously (see the boxed text, p288), though the Macedonian government has now declared a fishing moratorium.

IMPACT OF THE WARS OF THE 1990s

Though it's churlish to compare the environmental damage caused by the wars of the 1990s to the human cost, some lingering issues should be flagged. Landmines have meant that areas of BiH, Croatia and Kosovo have become de facto wilderness areas, albeit unexplorable ones.

The NATO air strikes of 1999 heavily targeted industrial areas, causing the release of hazardous substances into the atmosphere and the high-impact movement of people as refugees from rural areas sought safety in cities. Unplanned growth in cities such as Sarajevo, Tuzla, Belgrade, Pristina and Tirana increased demand on already stretched sewerage, waste-disposal and water-supply systems. In addition to the movement of people, the conflicts caused some unusual movement of fauna; wolves wandered into Croatia's Dalmatia region, where they hadn't been seen in decades, after unprotected herds of livestock abandoned by farmers in the Serb-populated Krajina region presented them with an unusual feeding opportunity.

To end this section on a positive note, look to Macedonia's tree-planting day (see the boxed text, p289). On 12 March 2008 more than 200,000 Macedonians planted two million trees (one for every citizen) to heal patches of forest devastated by fires. This initiative of Unesco Artist for Peace Boris Trajanov is expected to plant 30 million trees in the next 10 years.

'the conflicts caused some unusual movement of fauna; wolves wandered into Croatia's Dalmatia region, where they hadn't been seen in decades'

Albania

Albania is a meat-and-three-veg kind of country. The meat – kidney shaped – spreads along the west-coast beaches of the Adriatic and Ionian Seas, while the veg consists of the alpine mountains and brilliant green Lake Koman in the north and the thriving wetlands near Vlora in the south. Tirana, almost smack bang in Albania's heart, makes a tasty and surprisingly colourful and trendy side dish, and there's no doubt that the Unesco-listed and easily accessible Ottoman towns of Berat and Gjirokastra are dessert. Coffee is the extraordinary site of Butrint, bereft of tourists but rich in archaeological finds.

There are millions of ethnic Albanians in neighbouring countries, and as many as a million Albanians make a living in the UK, Italy, Greece, USA and Australia. In summer, hundreds of thousands return, bumping up the local tourism industries and turning quiet seaside spots into loud discos where every day is a thumping weekend. In contrast, northern men and women still wear traditional dress and shepherds guide flocks along grassy ledges in the otherwise inhospitable mountains.

International travellers with no links to Albania are still a relatively new phenomenon, and benefit from practically unrestricted access to castles and century-old houses as well as incredibly generous hospitality and friendliness. Mind the potholes, packs of mangy dogs and undecipherable addresses, and take in the unique sights of Albania: donkeys tethered to bunkers, houses crawling up each other to reach the tops of hills, and pockets of isolated beaches.

Like a good meat-and-three-veg dish, Albania is affordable, filling and ready to eat.

FAST FACTS

- **Area** 28,748 sq km
- **Capital** Tirana
- **Currency** lekë; US$1= 95.25 lekë; UK£1 = 138.74 lekë; €1 = 126.12 lekë; A$1 = 64.20 lekë
- **Famous for** being 'mysterious', concrete bunkers, unique language
- **Key phrases** *tungjatjeta* (hello), *mirupafshim* (goodbye), *ju lutem* (please), *faleminderit* (thank you), *me falni* (excuse me), *më vjen keq* (I'm sorry)
- **Official language** Albanian
- **Population** 3.62 million
- **Telephone codes** country code ☎ 355; international access code ☎ 00
- **Visas** not needed for citizens of the EU, Australia, New Zealand, the US and Canada; see p97 for details

HOW MUCH?

- **Shot of mulberry raki (a local spirit)** 100 lekë
- **Bottle of Albanian wine** 600 lekë
- **Short taxi ride** 300 lekë
- **English translation of an Ismail Kadare novel** 1800 lekë
- **Pizza** 300 lekë

LONELY PLANET INDEX

- **Litre of petrol** 160 lekë
- **Litre of bottled water** 50 lekë
- **Tirana beer** 150 lekë
- **Souvenir T-shirt** 800 lekë
- **Street snack (burek)** 30 lekë

HIGHLIGHTS

- **Tirana** (p62) Wild colour schemes and hip Blloku cafe culture.
- **Lake Koman** (p91) Seemingly mile-high cliffs enclosing bottle-green water.
- **Berat** (p75) and **Gjirokastra** (p88) Unesco-listed museum cities.
- **Dhërmi** (p84) to **Butrint** (p87) The south's dramatic Ionian coast, ranging from beaches to jungly ruins.
- **Theth** (p92) A hard-to-reach village deep in the northern alps.

ITINERARIES

- **One week** Two days in Tirana (p62) will give you time to check out the museums, eat at some of the great restaurants, dance in the pyramid and get some mountain time on the Dajti Express (p74). Then hop on a bus or *furgon* (minibus) to Berat (p75), Albania's loveliest Ottoman-era town, for two days of traipsing around the town's old quarters. Next, make your way to Saranda (p86) by the sea (stopping en route at Dhërmi, p84, for some beach time) and take a day trip to the wonderful jungly ruins of Butrint (p87). On the way to the airport take a detour to Kruja (p73) to check out one of the country's best ethnographic museums and buy your souvenirs in its authentic little bazaar.
- **Two weeks** Spend two days in Tirana, then head to Durrës (p71) for its centrally located ruins and archaeological museum, before catching the rickety early-afternoon train to Shkodra (p90). The next morning head up the terrifying road to the mountain village of Theth (p92) and spend a night with a local family, before heading back to Shkodra and checking out the Marubi photo exhibitions and valley-guarding Rozafa fortress. Take a return trip on the Lake Koman ferry (p91) and find your way to Kruja. Make your way to beautiful Berat for two days of rest, then take a trip to the ruins of Apollonia (p75), near Fier. Catch a bus down through Vlora (p82) and pass through the scenic Llogaraja Pass (p84). Next stop is at the Ionian coast's beaches: choose between busy Dhërmi and quieter Jal (p85) or Himara (p85). Then check out Saranda and the nearby attractions of Butrint, the Monastery of St Nicholas at Mesopotamia and the Blue Eye Spring (p88). Cruise up to Gjirokastra (p88) to explore another Ottoman-era town. Next comes adventure on the stunning road to Korça (p79) – not an easy ride but an unforgettable one. Check out Korça's museums and beer factory before finding your way to lakeside Pogradec (p79) for some R and R.

CLIMATE & WHEN TO GO

Coastal Albania has a pleasant Mediterranean climate. In Tirana and other inland towns on the plains there's plenty of rainfall during winter, but temperatures below freezing are rare. The high mountains often experience heavy snow between November and March, and towns such as Korça become icy. Roads and tracks to mountain villages can be blocked by snow for months, and Theth can be inaccessible as late as June.

In summer Tirana swelters, especially in August, when temperatures reach the high 30s, and even in the mountain towns the mercury frequently rises to 40°C. Temperatures on the coast are milder. See p429 for a Tirana climate chart.

The best time to visit Albania is spring or autumn, particularly May and September, when you can sightsee in the mild sunshine. In August the temperature is high, accommodation is very tight in coastal regions, and most hotels will only take bookings for stays of a week or more.

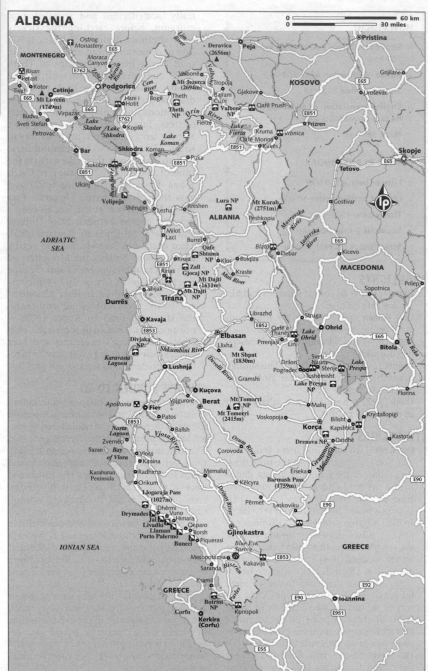

HISTORY

Albanians refer to their country as Shqipëria (pronounced something like *schip*-ree-ya), and trace their roots back to the ancient tribal Illyrians. The Albanian language is descended from Illyrian, making it a rare survivor of the Slavic and Roman influx and a European linguistic oddity on a par with Basque.

Illyrians, Greeks & Romans

The Illyrians occupied the Western Balkans during the 2nd millennium BC. They built substantial fortified cities, mastered silver and copper mining and became adept at sailing the Mediterranean. The Greeks arrived in the 7th century BC to establish self-governing colonies at Epidamnos (now Durrës), Apollonia and Butrint. They traded peacefully with the Illyrians, who formed tribal states in the 4th century BC.

In the second half of the 3rd century BC, an expanding Illyrian kingdom based at Shkodra came into conflict with Rome, which sent a fleet of 200 vessels against Queen Teuta (who ruled over the Illyrian Ardiaean kingdom) in 228 BC. A long war resulted in the extension of Roman control over modern-day Albania by 167 BC, after the capture of the last stronghold of the Ardiaean king Genti – the Rozafa fortress in Shkodra.

Under the Romans, Illyria enjoyed peace and prosperity, though the large agricultural estates were worked by slave labour. Like the Greeks, the Illyrians preserved their own language and traditions despite centuries of Roman rule. The main trade route between Rome and Constantinople, the Via Egnatia, ran from Durrës to Thessaloniki.

Byzantium & Christianity

When the Roman Empire was divided in AD 395, Illyria fell within the Eastern Roman Empire, later known as the Byzantine Empire. Invasions by migrating peoples – Visigoths, Huns, Ostrogoths and Slavs – continued through the 5th and 6th centuries. The Illyrian language survived in the mountains of northern Albania and the adjacent areas of Kosovo and Montenegro. The populace slowly replaced the old gods with the new Christian faith championed by Constantine. Three early Byzantine emperors – Anastasius I, Justin I and Justinian I – were of Illyrian origin.

A SHORT LESSON ON ALBANIAN GRAMMAR

One of the very complicated things about Albania is that there are two common ways of spelling place names. The 'proper' name of Albania's most beautiful Ottoman town is Berati, but road signs and many maps show 'Berat', and so do we. In Albanian grammar, the definite form is 'Berati', meaning 'the Berati', while the indefinite form 'to Berati' changes the spelling to 'Berat'. So when a road sign reads 'Berat – 25km', it means 'to Berati – 25km'. Most locals drop the 'i', so, to make communication a little easier, so do we.

Ottoman Rule

In 1344 Albania was annexed by Serbia, but after the defeat of Serbia by the Turks in 1389 the whole region was open to Ottoman attack. In 1417 Ottoman forces took over Vlora and Gjirokastra. The Venetians held on to some coastal towns, including Durrës (until 1501) and Butrint, which they had bought from Italian kings in 1386. Enter the hero Albanians still admire: Skanderbeg. From 1443 to 1468 Skanderbeg (Gjergj Kastrioti) led Albanian resistance to the Turks from his castle at Kruja. Skanderbeg won all 25 battles he fought against the Turks, and even Sultan Mehmet-Fatih, the conqueror of Constantinople, could not take Kruja. The Ottomans finally overwhelmed Albanian resistance in 1479, 26 years after they had captured Constantinople and 11 years after Skanderbeg's death (from malaria). Albanians proudly assert that Skanderbeg's resistance saved Europe from Ottoman conquest, because their courageous ancestors engaged the attentions of the Ottoman army during one of its strongest periods. After the conquest many Catholic Albanians moved to southern Italy, particularly to the Catanzaro mountains of Calabria and the region around Palermo in Sicily, where they were given their own villages and protection. Their descendents are called the Arbëresh. Today there is a community of something like 280,000 people who speak the Tosk-derived dialect in southern Italy.

The Ottomans settled into a long, largely economically stagnant rule over Albania, which lasted until 1912. The Albanian clan chieftains of the mountains mostly ran their own affairs, except for paying taxes to the imperial treasury. To avoid paying extra taxes and relinquishing their eldest sons to the Janissary system, many Christian Albanians converted to Islam. Later in the Ottoman era some administrators actively pushed for conversions to Islam, especially in the more easily controlled coastal plains. Some northern tribes such as the Shoshi and Mirdite remained Catholic, while in the south the religious mix eventually stabilised at around 50% Orthodox Christian and 50% Muslim.

One of the best-known Ottoman rulers was Ali Pasha of Tepelena. Remains of his castles, aqueducts, bridges and mosques are still dotted around Albania, including the brilliantly preserved Ali Pasha castle at Porto Palermo. Born in Tepelena, he was appointed Ioannina's leader in 1788. Over four decades he skilfully played off French, English, Russian, Venetian and Ottoman interests until his realm encompassed Albania, Thessaly and Epirus. His area of rule became one of the largest in the Ottoman Empire. Lord Byron met him in 1809 and wrote of his wealth, education and refinement, whilst acknowledging he was a 'remorseless tyrant'. The tales of his paedophilia, harems and revenge killings are spine-chilling. He converted to Bektashism (see the boxed text, p57) around 1810 and, after causing the ire of practically everyone and refusing to stand down, was assassinated by Ottoman agents in 1822. His head was sent to Istanbul.

Albania's two Unesco towns, Gjirokastra and Berat, are listed as well-preserved examples of Ottoman settlements. Mosques built during the Ottoman Empire still stand in places such as Tirana and Berat, and there are fine inscriptions from that time.

The Albanian League & National Renaissance

In 1878 the Albanian League at Prizren, in present-day Kosovo (Kosova to Albanians), began a struggle for autonomy that was put down by the Turkish army in 1881. Not initially successful on the battlefield, the new Albanian nationalists were more successful in the cultural field, sparking the National Renaissance (Rilindja Kombétare) movement of great poets and writers. The movement's leaders quickly realised that one of the keys to

building unity among Albanians would be a common script for their language. Previously, Albanian had been written in Arabic, Greek and Latin scripts, depending on the faith of the writer. A couple of unique Albanian scripts briefly appeared in the 19th century – the Elbasani script and Beitha Kukju – but weren't widely adopted. In 1909 a conference of writers and intellectuals agreed on adopting a common Latin alphabet, which is used today.

Further uprisings between 1910 and 1912 culminated in a proclamation of independence and the formation of a provisional government led by Ismail Qemali at Vlora in 1912. These achievements were severely compromised when Kosovo, roughly one-third of Albania, was ceded to Serbia in 1913. The great powers tried to install a young German prince, Wilhelm zu Wied, as ruler of the rump Albania, but he was never accepted and returned home after six months. With the outbreak of WWI, Albania was occupied in succession by the armies of Greece, Serbia, France, Italy and Austria-Hungary. The country suffered appalling damage and essentially broke into warring statelets.

King Zog & Italian Control

In 1920 the capital city was moved from Durrës to less-vulnerable Tirana. A government under the Orthodox priest Fan Noli helped to stabilise the country, but in 1924 Noli was overthrown by Interior Minister Ahmed Bey Zogu. A warlord of the northern Mati tribe, Zogu declared himself King Zog I in 1928, and cooperated extensively with Italy in developing the country. This soon became something of a mixed blessing: the Italians helped develop Tirana from a smallish country town into something like a capital city, but as Albania's debts to Italy stacked up the country increasingly became a de facto Italian colony. Settlers from Italy began moving to the more fertile southern parts of Albania, and Italian advisers increasingly took over the day-to-day running of the country.

During Zog's rule, serfdom was gradually abolished, schools were established and the country's rudimentary infrastructure was vastly improved. Zog himself became a rather eccentric character who played poker relentlessly, hoarded gold and jewels and smoked as many as 150 cigarettes a day. After an assassination attempt in 1931 he became fearful of being poisoned (not by nicotine, evidently) and installed his mother as head of the royal kitchens. In some assassination attempts he actually managed to shoot back. The Great Depression pushed Albania's shaky finances into complete submission to the Italian government. King Zog occasionally managed to get back at the Italians by selling them inaccessible forests and sending them the bill for his lavish wardrobe.

In April 1939, when Mussolini ordered an invasion of Albania, King Zog fled to Britain, along with his young wife, Queen Geraldine, and their newborn son Lekë. He used gold looted from the Albanian treasury to rent a floor at London's Ritz Hotel. In light of the communist regime that followed, elderly Albanians look back on King Zog's reign with some fondness. The first uprising against fascism in Europe occurred in Albania in November 1939, and sparked a long-running fight against the occupiers. King Zog died in Paris in 1961, and Queen Geraldine, who had returned to Albania, died in a Tirana hospital in 2002.

The Rise of Communism

On 8 November 1941 the Albanian communist party was founded with Enver Hoxha as first secretary, a position he held until his natural death in April 1985 (see the boxed text, p54). The communists led the resistance against the Italians and, after 1943, against the Germans, ultimately tying down 15 combined German-Italian divisions.

After the fighting had died down, the communists consolidated power. In January 1946 the People's Republic of Albania was proclaimed, with Hoxha as president and 'Supreme Comrade'.

In September 1948 Albania broke off relations with Yugoslavia, which had hoped to incorporate the country into the Yugoslav Federation. Instead, Albania allied itself with Stalin's USSR and put into effect a series of Soviet-style economic plans. The US and Britain tried to overthrow the regime by sending in Albanians trained in guerrilla warfare, but they were betrayed by the British spy Kim Philby, captured and killed.

Albania collaborated closely with the USSR until 1960, when Nikita Khrushchev demanded that a submarine base be set up at Vlora. A year later Albania broke off diplomatic relations with the USSR and reoriented itself towards the People's Republic of China. The shift also allowed Hoxha to purge some of his rivals in the party on the grounds of being spies for the Soviet Union, just as he had after the split with Yugoslavia.

From 1966 to 1967 Albania experienced a brutal Chinese-style cultural revolution. Administrative workers were suddenly transferred to remote areas, younger cadres were placed in leading positions, churches and mosques were sacked and destroyed, and the collectivisation of agriculture was completed.

Following the Soviet invasion of Czechoslovakia in 1968, Albania left the Warsaw Pact and followed a self-reliant defence policy. Tens of thousands of igloo-shaped concrete bunkers (see the boxed text, p55), conceived of by Hoxha, serve as a reminder of this. The communist-party authorities drained the malarial swamps of the central coastal plains, built some major hydroelectric schemes, raised the literacy level and laid down the country's railway lines.

With the death of Mao Tse-tung in 1976 and the changes that followed in China after 1978, Albania's unique relationship with China also came to an end, and the country was left isolated and without allies. The break with China stunted the economy, and food shortages became more common.

Post-Hoxha

After Hoxha died in April 1985 his long-time associate Ramiz Alia took over the leadership. Restrictions loosened half a notch, but the whole system was increasingly falling apart. In the interests of stability, the regime perfected the art of doing nothing, and doing it slowly. Meanwhile, people were no longer bothering to work on the collective farms, which led to food shortages in the cities, and industries began to fail as spare parts ran out. The party leadership promised reform but remained paralysed.

In June 1990, inspired by the changes that were occurring elsewhere in Eastern Europe, some 4500 Albanians took refuge in Western embassies in Tirana. After a brief confrontation with the police and the Sigurimi (secret police) these people were allowed to board

COMRADE ENVER

Enver Hoxha (*hoe*-dja) ruled Albania for 40 years until his death in 1985. The cliché about ruling with an iron first would be an understatement about his time in power.

Enver Hoxha was born into a middle-class family in Gjirokastra in 1908. He attended a French school in Korça and later the American school in Tirana. In 1930 he won a scholarship to study in France, where he picked up a taste for natty French fashion and hard-line communism, writing articles for communist newspapers under the pseudonym Loulou. He returned to Albania in 1936 and in 1941 founded the Albanian communist party with six others. In WWII Hoxha managed to put himself in control of an increasingly capable guerrilla army, which had 70,000 members by 1944.

After the war he began to purge every possible rival through show trials, executions and forced labour camps. Partly because of the country's poor communications system, the Party of Labour of Albania (Partia e Punës së Shqipërisë, or PPSH) developed a massive secret police force called the Sigurimi to control the populace. They would intrude into every corner of life. The regime denied Albanians freedom of expression, religion and movement. People could be sentenced to 10 years working in chrome mines for listening to foreign radio broadcasts. A strong admirer of Stalin, Hoxha rejected the USSR's relative relaxation after the dictator's death and became a hard-line defender of Stalinism. Hoxha broke with the USSR in 1961, and took the opportunity to purge rivals he accused of being 'revisionists'. Albania then developed close ties with Mao Tse-tung's China.

After Mao's death in 1976, Hoxha felt that China, too, was following a revisionist path, and relations withered by 1978. By then, Hoxha had assessed Eurocommunism, Yugoslav communism, Chinese communism and Soviet communism and found them all to be revisionist errors. Meanwhile his personality cult grew – by 1979 his official title had become 'Comrade–Chairman–Prime Minister–Foreign Minister–Minister of War–Commander in Chief of the People's Army'. In 1980 he engineered the downfall of his long-time deputy Mehmet Shehu, who was driven to suicide (or was murdered; the versions differ). The regime accused Shehu of being a spy for the USA, the UK and Yugoslavia – simultaneously.

Hoxha then crept into a kind of retirement in his villa in the Blloku district of central Tirana, an area that no ordinary Albanian was allowed to see. He died in 1985 and was briefly honoured by an entire museum dedicated to his life and works: the Pyramid building in Tirana (designed by his daughter Pranvera Hoxha and her husband, Klement Kolaneci), which is now a conference centre and disco. For a taste of his writings imagine that this is just the headline of one of his works: 'Reject the Revisionist Thesis of the XX Congress of the Communist Party of the Soviet Union and the Anti-Marxist Stand of Khrushchev's Group! Uphold Marxism-Leninism!' For more information, check the curiously un-ironic www.pksh.org for speeches, photos and more.

ships for Brindisi in Italy, where they were granted political asylum.

After student demonstrations were held in December 1990, the government agreed to allow opposition parties. The Democratic Party, led by heart surgeon Sali Berisha, was formed. Further demonstrations produced new concessions, including the promise of free elections and independent trade unions. The government announced a reform program and party hardliners were purged.

In early March 1991, as the election date approached, some 20,000 Albanians fled the country's crumbling economy. They set out from Vlora to Brindisi by ships they'd commandeered, creating a crisis for the Italian government, which had begun to view them as economic refugees. Most were eventually allowed to stay.

The March 1992 elections ended 47 years of communist rule. After the resignation of Alia, parliament elected Sali Berisha president in April. In September 1992 former president Alia was placed under house arrest after he wrote articles critical of the Democratic government. In August 1993 the leader of the Socialist Party, Fatos Nano, was also arrested on corruption charges.

During this time Albania switched from a tightly controlled communist regime to a rambunctious free-market free-for-all. A huge smuggling racket sprang up, bringing stolen Mercedes-Benzes into the country, and some former collective farms were converted into marijuana plantations. The port of Vlora became a major crossing point for illegal immigrants from Asia and the Middle East into Italy. A huge population shift took place as collective farms were broken up and reclaimed by former landowners. People who had been forced to move to these collectives by the communist party were forced to leave again. Tirana's population tripled as people who were now able to freely move to the city joined internal exiles driven off the old collective farms.

A severe crisis developed in late 1996, when private pyramid investment schemes – which were actually legal at the time, and supported by the Berisha government – inevitably collapsed. Around 70% of Albanians lost their savings, in total over US$1 billion, resulting in nationwide disturbances and riots. People were literally raiding the arms depots and running riot with their quarry. Hoxha's former home in Gjirokastra was blown up (again, and even though he was long gone) and buildings were looted and burnt. Elections were called, and the victorious Socialist Party under Nano –

who had been freed from prison by the rampaging mob – was able to restore some degree of security and investor confidence. But the new wave of violence had destroyed many of the remaining industries from the communist era. Towns where the whole working population had been employed by one mine or factory were left destitute as the economy collapsed again.

In spring 1999 Albania faced a crisis of a different sort. This time it was the influx of 465,000 refugees from neighbouring Kosovo during the NATO bombing and the Serbian ethnic-cleansing campaign. While this put a tremendous strain on resources, the net effect was, in fact, positive. Substantial amounts of international aid money poured in, the service sector grew and inflation declined to single digits. The security situation stabilised and many of the more colourful business activities were shut down.

Stabilisation & Revival

Since 2002 the country has at last found itself in an economic revival, with large amounts of money being poured into construction projects and infrastructure renewal. Over the years, wages have risen, but it's not uncommon for people to have to work two or three

THE BUNKERS

From the hillsides, beaches and, well, most surfaces in Albania, small concrete domes look down on you through their rectangular slits. Meet the bunkers: Enver Hoxha's concrete legacy, built from 1950 to 1985. Made out of concrete and iron and weighing 5 tonnes, these hard little mushroom-like creations are almost impossible to destroy, since they were built to repel the threat of foreign invasion and can resist full tank assault. The Supreme Comrade hired a chief engineer to design a super-resistant bunker. The engineer then had to vouch for his creation's strength by standing inside it while it was bombarded by a tank. The shell-shocked man emerged unscathed and the bunkers were built; the estimated number of these concrete gun posts was 700,000 – one for every four Albanians at the time, although it's more likely 60,000.

Their sheer ubiquity says a lot about the mindset of the previous regime. There are so many bunkers around Albania and they're located in the most unreachable places. They're just a part of a huge legacy of military and security hardware, which includes mysterious tunnels, underground armaments factories, nuclear bunkers under every apartment building (the nuclear bunkers under Tirana built for the leadership are rumoured to be enormous) and nasty surprises like the 16 tonnes of chemical weapons rediscovered at a military base close to Tirana in 2005.

Today the bunkers are the bane of farmers and builders across the country. They are expensive to remove and very hard to destroy. It took one man three months of weekend and after-hours work to demolish one by hand in order to make room for a garage. In places people have tried to decorate them with paint, and some of the few larger command bunkers have been converted into barns. They do have two modern uses. Quite a few Albanians will admit to losing their virginity in the security of a bunker, and, judging by the smell of some of them, they are also used as toilets.

jobs to make ends meet. It is estimated that around one million out of a population of 3.6 million are working abroad. Remittances from these workers (annually estimated at US$600 million to US$800 million) have become crucial to the economy.

The construction boom hasn't been without its problems, however, and the array of ugly concrete apartments and hotels has despoiled many coastal regions. Corruption also remains a real issue. There's still a lingering desire in the electorate for 'strong' leaders, perhaps an echo of the old personality cult of Enver Hoxha.

Albania is expected to join NATO in 2009 and, while the EU's flag flies high throughout the country, Albania is not a member, though it is taking steps to get there and may do so within the next decade.

There's a large American presence in Albania, and you're likely to stumble across Peace Corps volunteers in your travels. Former US president George W Bush received a rapturous reception when he toured the country in 2007, and streets were named after him.

Kosovo's independence in 2008 was enthusiastically greeted by Albanians, to the extent that songs by Albanians celebrating the change became hits. However, at the same time, Albanian independence has its own issues. Berisha returned to power in 2005 after his democrats successfully challenged Nano's socialists and, after a promising start (cracking down on organised crime), there was growing dissatisfaction. Despite promises, Albania's politicians seem incapable of finding ways to provide Albanians with regular water and electricity supply. There is also a change in the dynamics between the traditionally competing factions of socialists and democrats when it comes to land-distribution

deals. Also, while new roads are being built and snazzy apartment blocks are springing up, there are still some seriously poor regions. It is estimated that around 25% of the population lives in poverty.

PEOPLE

In July 2008 the population was estimated to be 3,619,778, of which approximately 95% is Albanian, 3% Greek and 2% 'other' – comprising Vlachs, Roma, Serbs, Macedonians and Bulgarians. The Vlach are an old ethnic group in the Balkans, whose name is supposed to originate from the Greek word *vlach* (shepherd). The Vlach language is related to Romanian; Vlachs are historically a trading community but are now well integrated into all of the Balkan societies.

One of the best things about Albania is its people, who, despite the recent history, are kind, helpful and unquestioningly generous. Most speak more than one foreign language: Italian is almost a second language in the north and centre, as well as the north coast of the country, and Greek is widespread in the southern regions, where the Greek minority is concentrated along the Drinos River. You can rely on the majority of young people to speak English, but learning a few words of the unique Albanian language will delight your hosts. Note that Albanians shake their heads sideways to say yes *(po)* and usually nod and 'tsk' to say no *(jo)*. That's most confusing when you come across an Albanian who is used to dealing with tourists and you can't work out if they're nodding 'your way' or not. The Shkumbini River forms a boundary between the Gheg cultural region of the north and the Tosk region in the south. The people in these regions still vary in dialect, musical

---

SWORN VIRGINS

Albanian women don't have a particularly easy time in male-dominated Albania, so it's not surprising that you can still find sworn virgins in the country's north. It's referred to as a practical decision made by the woman or her family because there's a shortage of males in the community, to escape an unwanted arranged marriage or to keep a male heir in the family. Once the decision is made, she, for all intents and purposes, is a man. She is no longer expected to marry, works and travels as a man, and will take on the appearance and customs of a traditional Albanian man: wearing baggy clothes, keeping her hair short and smoking and drinking. She is treated as a man by other men. Of course, it's worth pointing out that just because an Albanian woman takes on some masculine traits it doesn't mean she's necessarily a 'sworn virgin'; there's a gay and lesbian community in Albania, too.

THE BEKTASHI ORDER

Bektashi Islam is quite different from mainstream Sunni Islam. It allows the consumption of alcohol, for example, and women are less segregated. It takes a more mystical approach, with emphasis on a spiritual relationship with Allah built through prayer and the contemplation of mystical poetry.

The order's founder, Haji Bektash Veli, was born in Iran in the 13th century. He wrote the cornerstone of the order's beliefs, the Makalaat, which lays out a four-stage path to enlightenment. In the first stage, dervishes learn the difference between right and wrong; in the second, they pray constantly; in the third, they come to understand God's love; and in the fourth, they arrive at an understanding of reality through self-effacement and the constant awareness of God. Haji Bektash died in central Turkey, where he is buried at the great *teqe* (shrine) in the little town named after him, Hacîbektaş.

The order grew quite powerful in the 18th century. The Janissaries, the Christian boys taken into the Turkish army and made to convert to Islam, were followers and patrons of the Bektashi order. The order was suppressed in many countries during the 20th century. In its main base, in Turkey, the republican government under Ataturk harshly suppressed the order in the 1920s. In 1925 the headquarters shifted to Albania, where, in turn, the movement was crushed by the communists after WWII. It has undergone something of a revival in Albania since the early 1990s.

---

culture and traditional dress, though the differences are often overstated by outsiders.

RELIGION

Albanians are nominally 70% Muslim, 20% Christian Orthodox and 10% Catholic, but more realistic statistics estimate that up to 75% of Albanians are nonreligious. Religion was ruthlessly stamped out during the 1967 cultural revolution, when all mosques and churches were taken over by the state. By 1990 only about 5% of Albania's religious buildings were left intact. The rest of them had been turned into cinemas and army stores or were destroyed. The 1976 constitution banned 'fascist, religious, warmongerish, antisocialist propaganda and activity'. Despite the fact that the people are now free to practise their faith, Albania remains a very secular society and it's difficult to assess how many followers each faith has. Intermarriage between people of different faiths is quite common.

The Muslim faith has a branch called 'Bektashism' (see the boxed text, above), similar to Sufism, and its world headquarters were in Albania from 1925 to 1945. Rather than mosques, the Bektashi followers go to *teqe* (templelike buildings without a minaret, sometimes housed in former churches). *Teqe* are usually found in mountain towns or on town hilltops, so that followers could escape persecution, and you will no doubt come across at least one of them. Most Bektashis live in the southern half of the country.

ARTS

From Korça's serenades to hand-loomed rugs and wood carvings, Albania has a fairly lively artistic community. Photographers follow in the steps of Shkodra's Marubi and Korça's Sotiri, and filmmakers are given the opportunity to enter Tirana's annual Short Film Festival. Traditional dancing competitions are popular and restaurant proprietors have been known to gather friends and get into a bit of polyphonic singing.

Visual Arts

The art scene in Albania is on the rise. One of the first signs of art that strikes you are the multicoloured buildings of Tirana, a project organised by the capital's mayor Edi Rama, himself an artist. It's worth noting that Tirana's residents may not be so pleased to wake up in a purple building; they get no say in the matter.

There are still some remnants of socialist realism, with paintings and sculptures adorning the walls and gardens of galleries and museums, although many were destroyed after the fall of the communist government as a reflex against the old regime.

One of the most delicious Albanian art treats is to be found in Berat's Onufri Museum (p77). Onufri was the most outstanding

Albanian icon painter of the 16th and 17th centuries and his work is noted for its unique intensity of colour, using natural dyes that are as fresh now as the day he painted with them. Churches around the country feature amazing and original frescos.

Music & Dance

Polyphony, the blending of several independent vocal or instrumental parts, is a southern Albanian tradition dating from ancient Illyrian times. Choirs perform in a variety of styles, and the songs, usually with an epic-lyrical or historical theme, may be dramatic to the point of yodelling, or slow and sober, with alternate male and female voices combining in harmony. Instrumental polyphonic *kabas* (a sedate style, led by a clarinet or violin alongside accordions and lutes) are played by small Roma ensembles. Musical improvisation is accompanied by dancing at colourful village weddings. One well-known group, which often tours outside Albania, is the Lela Family of Përmet (www.kabarecords.com).

There's plenty of Albanian pop, too, and artists like Sinan Hoxha manage to merge the traditional with the new. Other Albanian musicians to check out are the band the Dream as well as Erion Korini.

Literature

There is no substantial body of Albanian literature before the 19th century besides some Catholic religious works (the 6th-century Purple Codex was found hidden in Berat). The Ottomans banned the teaching of Albanian in schools, fearing the spread of anti-Turkish propaganda. They were right. The adoption of a standardised orthography in 1908, when the literary wing of the National Renaissance movement rose together with the Albanian national movement, led to Albanian independence in 1912. A group of romantic patriotic writers at Shkodra, including Migjeni (1911–38) and Martin Çamaj (1925–92), wrote epics and historical novels. Poetry that drew on the great tradition of oral epic poetry was the most popular literary form during this period.

Perhaps the most interesting writer of the interwar period was Fan Noli (1880–1965). Educated as a priest in the USA, Noli became premier of Albania's democratic government until it was overthrown in 1924, when he returned to head the Albanian Orthodox Church in America. Although many of his books have religious themes, the introductions he wrote to his own translations of Cervantes, Ibsen, Omar Khayyám and Shakespeare established him as Albania's foremost literary critic.

The only Albanian writer who is widely read outside Albania is the contemporary Ismail Kadare (b 1936). In 2005 he won the inaugural Booker International Prize for his body of work. These enriching literary works are a great source of information on Albanian traditions, history and social events. His books exquisitely capture the atmosphere of the country's towns, as in the lyrical descriptions of Kadare's birthplace, Gjirokastra, in *Chronicle in Stone* (1971), where wartime experiences are seen through the eyes of a boy. *Broken April* (1990), set in the northern highlands before the 1939 Italian invasion, describes the life of a village boy who is next in line in the desperate cycle of blood vendettas (see the boxed text, opposite). One of Kadare's lighter works is *The File on H*, the tale of two Irish academics who go searching for traditional epic poets in northern Albania in the 1930s, and stumble into local politics.

Cinema

During Albania's isolationist years the only Western actor of whom Hoxha approved was UK actor Sir Norman Wisdom (he became quite a cult hero). However, with so few international movies to choose from, the local film industry had a captive audience that was hungry for anything that would break the cultural tedium. While much of its output was propagandist, by the 1980s this little country was turning out an extraordinary 14 films a year. Despite a general lack of funds, two movies have gone on to win awards at international film festivals. Gjergj Xhuvani's comedy *Slogans* (2001) is a warm and touching account of life during communist times. This was followed in 2002 by *Tirana Year Zero*, Fatmir Koci's bleak look at the pressures on the young to emigrate.

Another film worth seeing is *Lamerica* (1995), a brilliant and stark look at Albania c 1991. Woven loosely around a plot about a couple of Italian scam artists, and Albanians seeking to escape to Italy, the essence of the film is the unshakeable dignity of the ordinary Albanian in the face of adversity.

THE KANUN

The Kanun (Code) was formalised in the 15th century by powerful northern chieftain Lek Dukagjin. It consists of 1262 articles covering every aspect of daily life: work, marriage, family, property, hospitality, economy and so on. Although the Kanun was suppressed by the communists, there has been a revival of its strict precepts in northern Albania. How much so is uncertain, as dramatic incidents may have been overplayed by the media. You can see for yourself its effects in Tirana: walk west along Tirana's Lana River, which was cleared of illegal buildings by Mayor Edi Rama in a clean-up in 2000, bar one imposing grey-and-pink building. It wasn't demolished, as there's a blood feud going on. Whilst the women can leave the house, the men will be killed if they do.

According to the Kanun, the most important things in life are honour and hospitality. If a member of a family is murdered, it becomes the duty of the male members of that clan to claim their blood debt by murdering a male member of the murderer's clan. This sparks an endless cycle of killing that doesn't end until either all the male members of one of the families are dead, or reconciliation is brokered through respected village elders.

Hospitality is so important in these parts of Albania that the guest takes on a godlike status. There are 38 articles giving instructions on how to treat a guest – an abundance of food, drink and comfort is at his or her disposal, and it's also the host's duty to avenge the murder of his guest, should this happen during their visit.

Vdekja e Kalit (1995) covers the harrowing 1980s and the change of regime in 1992, and is the only film that includes Albania's Roma community.

Renowned Brazilian director Walter Salles (*Central Station*) adapted Ismail Kadare's novel *Broken April* and, having kept the novel's main theme, moved the action to Brazil in *Behind the Sun* (2001).

FOOD & DRINK
Staples & Specialities

Food-wise, the only thing you're likely to be lacking in Albania is *mëngjes* (breakfast). In Albania's north, breakfast seems to consist of a shot of the spirit *raki*, and the rest of the country survives on a morning espresso. If you're desperate, most shops sell packet croissants, or try asking your hotel or at a restaurant for some *bukë* and *mjaltë* (bread and honey) to go with your espresso. Albanians make excellent coffee and the local honey (usually sold by the side of the road) is delicious.

Patate të skuqura (potato chips) are served at practically every restaurant, and all meals will come with bread. Korça is famous for its *qofte* (a little like an inside-out sausage), and in coastal areas the calamari, mussels and fish will knock your socks off. Mountain areas such as Llogaraja have roast lamb worth climbing a mountain for.

There's a big trade in offal, and *fërgesë Tiranë* is a traditional Tirana dish of offal,

eggs and tomatoes cooked in an earthenware pot. If the *biftek* (beef) you ordered looks suspiciously like veal, take heart that it's likely to have been reared more humanely than it is in Western countries.

Albanians sometimes drink a shot of *raki* as an aperitif before they tuck into their food. *Raki* is very popular and there are two main types in Albania: grape *raki* (the most common), and *mani raki* (mulberry). Ask for homemade if possible (*raki ë bërë në shtëpi*). If *raki* is not your cup of tea, try *Rilindja* wine, either a sweet white (tokai) or a medium-bodied red (merlot). Wine aficionados should seek out the native red varietal kallmet. The Çobo winery near Berat is certainly worth a visit. Skënderbeu *konjak* (cognac) is the national aperitif, and it's very good indeed.

Where to Eat & Drink

Before you tuck in, you're going to have to work out Albania's bar and restaurant rules. It's complicated, but here are some examples: a cafe with a restaurant downstairs is unlikely to let you eat in the cafe, even if it's nicer and busier. A beachfront bar-restaurant may reserve the tables with the best views for frappé drinkers, not pizza eaters, so if that's what you're after, you'll be sent indoors to the restaurant. It gets more confusing: in some bars an espresso is an inside experience only; outside is reserved for frappé drinkers or ice-cream sundae eaters. To make things more complicated, Albanians rarely eat out, so often you don't have people to 'follow'. It's best to expect to be moved around a little in your Albanian eating adventures.

Long bus trips are usually punctuated by short lunch breaks, and there's nothing better than a quick 60-lekë bowl of rice with a light meat sauce to get you ready for another battering-by-bus. Next up the list is the fast-food *burek* joint, followed by the modest 'room without a view' eateries serving up Albanian food. These are usually an excellent, cheap option. Restaurants that look good and have good views usually offer a mix of Italian and Albanian food at higher prices. Woodfired pizzas are great in Albania, and usually cost 300 lekë. Korça, Himara and some other towns also have some excellent Greek restaurants. A whole meal (grilled meat, potato chips, salad and cheese) at a modest no-name restaurant will cost as little as 300 lekë, while you'll pay more than double that in a large restaurant.

The incidence of brucellosis is increasing and in 2005 there were 16 cases of tuberculosis for every 100,000 people, so avoid unpasteurised milk and stick to imported UHT milk.

Vegetarians & Vegans

Meat rules the menu in Albania, although thankfully the Italian influence means there are plenty of vegetarian pasta and pizza options. If you can't live on pasta alone you can go wild on Turkish-style vegetable dishes, including roast or grilled peppers and aubergines (eggplants), and cauliflower moussaka. 'Vegetable' *bureks* can have sneaky pieces of mince in them, so check. If you're vegan and heading to the alps you'll have a hard time stomaching most meals, as *kos* (yoghurt), cheese and milk are staples.

For a list of Albanian eating and drinking words, see the boxed text, p45.

ENVIRONMENT
The Land

More than three-quarters of Albania is made up of mountains and hills. There are three zones: a coastal plain, a mountainous region and an interior plain in the south. The coastal plain extends approximately 200km from north to south and up to 50km inland. The 2000m-high forested mountain spine, which stretches the entire length of Albania, culminates at Mt Jezerca (2694m) in the north, near the Montenegro border. The country's highest peak is Mt Korab (2751m), on the border with Macedonia. The interior plain is alluvial, with seasonal precipitation. It's poorly drained and therefore alternately arid or flooded and is often as inhospitable as the mountains.

Albania has suffered some devastating earthquakes, including one that struck in 1979, leaving at least 100,000 people homeless.

The longest river in Albania is the Drin (285km), which starts at Lake Ohrid. In the north the Drin flows into the Buna River, which connects Lake Shkodra to the sea. The train line follows the Drin River closely, almost all the way to the coast. The Ionian littoral, especially the 'Riviera of Flowers' stretching from Vlora to Saranda, offers magnificent scenery from the highest peak in this region, the Llogaraja Pass (1027m). Forests cover 40% of the land, and the many olive trees, citrus plantations and vineyards give Albania a Mediterranean air. One of Enver Hoxha's bolder schemes was to turn the hills into fields, and all over the country you can see the result of backbreaking labour where entire ranges of hills have been terraced. In some places this seems to have successfully established new orchards and olive groves, but in other places the terracing has unleashed appalling soil erosion.

Wildlife

Albania's territory is rich in flora, with beech trees and oak, and patches of rare Macedonian pine *(Pinus peuce)* in the lower regions. Birch, pine and fir cover the mountainsides until they reach 2000m, above which all is barren. Forests cover an estimated 36% of the country, much of it in the isolated northern highlands and close to the Greece border. Bears, deer and wild boar inhabit these isolated forests, but they have been pushed out of regions closer to settlements by widespread summer grazing and by the Albanian penchant for hunting.

The endangered loggerhead turtle nests on isolated beaches on the Ionian coast and on the Karaburun Peninsula, where critically endangered Mediterranean monk seals have also been sighted.

There are several wetland sites at the mouths of the Buna, Drin and Mati rivers in the north and at the Karavasta Lagoon south of Durrës, with many interesting and rare birds (white pelicans and white-headed

---

BALKANS PEACE PARK

The Balkans Peace Park project aims to create a relationship between the three countries that share borders in one beautiful alpine area: Kosovo (Rugova), Montenegro (Prokletije) and Albania (Theth). At the moment, there are no official border crossings in this particular region, so, for example, hikers wishing to begin in Albania and finish the hike in Kosovo or Montenegro are not 'officially' entering and leaving the countries involved. While changes like introducing a special visa scheme, or pass, may take some time for the UK-based charity, it's certainly preparing the Albanian town of Theth for tourists. Homes are being transformed into B&Bs, village children are being taught English, the community is being taught about regional environmental issues, maps are being drawn up and tour options are being discussed. In 2005 the **Balkans Peace Park Office** (☎ 225 1704; www.balkanspeacepark.org; rr Marin Barleti 1) opened in Shkodra, and it provides maps and information about the region. Author and seasoned Albanian traveller Antonia Young is heavily involved in the project, and it's worth hunting her down if you find you're in Shkodra when she is. Petrit Imeraj (see p92) runs tours from Shkodra's Hotel Rozafa (p90).

---

ducks, among others) to spot for those with a pair of binoculars. The Albanian portion of Lake Prespa is another important haven for bird life.

National Parks

Albania's national parks have risen from six in 1966 to 15 today, including Mt Dajti, Butrint, Mt Tomorri, Valbonë and Theth. Most of them aren't really protected by anything but their remoteness, and tree felling and hunting still take place. Some hiking maps of the national parks are available, though they can be hard to find, and more guesthouses and camping grounds are popping up. Llogaraja Pass (p84) has an established accommodation scene, and you can go for shorter hikes. Mt Tomorri near Berat is another national park becoming popular with hikers, local organisations in Berat operate guided tours, and plenty of experienced hikers are taking on the Valbonë–Theth route with the assistance of local guides. The Karaburun Peninsula near Vlora is a nature reserve protected largely by its isolation.

Independent camping is not advisable, as the mountains are almost completely uninhabited and have no mobile-phone coverage; in case of an injury, help would be impossible to find.

Environmental Issues

Since the collapse of communism, during which time there were around 2000 cars in the country, the number of roaring automobiles has risen to first-world numbers, many of which are old diesel Mercedes-Benzes stolen from Western Europe. As a consequence of

the explosion, air pollution levels in Tirana are five to 10 times higher than in Western European counties.

Illegal logging and fishing was beginning to reach epidemic proportions during the 1990s and there are signs of it today: fishing for the endangered *koran* trout in Lake Ohrid continues, as does fishing with dynamite along the coast.

Badly maintained oil fields around Fier continue to leak sludge into the surrounding environment and plans for an oil pipeline through Vlora are tinged with environmental concerns.

Several coastal regions discharge raw sewage into seas and rivers. The rapid development of beach areas has compounded the issue, though projects are in place to improve waste disposal in sensitive environmental areas, including Lake Ohrid.

There's a large amount of rubbish on roadsides, beaches and picnic spots everywhere. Albania was practically litter free until the late '90s; everything was recycled. The change seems to be a result both of novelties such as nondegradable plastic bags and of a reaction against the harsh communist-era rules on littering. Even household garbage is an issue: walk around the outside of a picturesque hotel and you're likely to come across its very unpicturesque dumping ground. The ferry trip on gorgeous Lake Koman is punctuated by empty plastic bottles flying over your head and into the lake. Some Albanians are doing their bit to improve these conditions and there's considerable Western investment in aiding this process.

ALBANIA

ALBANIAN ADDRESSES

Albania hasn't developed much of a need for things like postcodes, street signs or street numbers. People usually direct you to places by saying things like 'Turn left at the green building near the old bus depot and it's the third house past Sali's cafe on the right'. This works fine for locals, but visitors won't know that the old bus depot is now a furniture store, and have no idea which of the cafes is owned by Sali. It can take a long time to find a house or even a shop.

The country has a distinctive address system. An example might read, rr Elbasanit, Pall 18, Shk 3, Ap 6. Decoded, rr means *rruga* or street, Pall or sometimes just 'P' means *pallati* or building, Shk means *shkallë* or entrance (there may be several) and Ap means apartment. You may also see the word *përballë* on an address – this means 'in front of', usually referring to some (hopefully) obvious landmark.

In this chapter we've used the abbreviations 'rr' for *rruga* and 'blvd' for *bulevardi*.

TIRANA

☎ 04 / pop 600,000

Lively, colourful Tirana has changed beyond belief in the last decade from the dull, grey city it once was (see the old Albanian movies for evidence). It's amazing what a lick of paint can do – covering one ugly tower block with horizontal orange and red stripes, another with concentric pink and purple circles and planting perspective-fooling cubes on its neighbour.

The trendy Blloku district buzzes with the well-dressed nouvelle bourgeoisie hanging out in bars or zipping between boutiques. Quite where their money comes from is the subject of much speculation in this economically deprived nation, but thankfully you don't need much of it to have a fun night out in the city's many bars and clubs.

The city's grand central boulevards are lined with fascinating relics of its Ottoman, Italian and communist past – from delicate minarets to socialist murals – guarded by bored-looking soldiers with serious automatic weaponry. The traffic does daily battle with both itself and pedestrians in a constant scene of unmitigated chaos.

Loud, crazy, colourful, dusty – Tirana is simply fascinating.

HISTORY

Founded by a Turkish pasha (military governor) in 1614, Tirana developed into a craft centre with a lively bazaar. It became the capital in 1920 when those in power decided it was better to rule the country from its centre rather than from the vulnerable coastal town of Durrës. Diplomats bemoaned the move to what was then a country town, but the Italians built handsome ministry buildings and laid

out the main boulevards that remain today. The city was severely damaged in the liberation battle in 1944, and the new communist regime knocked down a lot of the remains of the old country town to make space for vast plazas. There's been another building boom in the last decade, with many new apartment buildings going up, and new roads and highways being built on the outskirts.

ORIENTATION

Running through Tirana is blvd Zogu I, which changes its name to blvd Dëshmorët e Kombit as it crosses the orientation point of Sheshi Skënderbej (Skanderbeg Sq). The south section ends at Tirana's main university, Mother Teresa University. The main sites of interest are on or very close to this large boulevard. Most of the eating and drinking action is at Blloku, which is roughly a square of 10 blocks of shops, restaurants, cafes and hotels situated one block west of blvd Dëshmorët e Kombit and along the Lana River in south Tirana.

Incoming buses will probably drop you off at the bus and train station at the north end of blvd Zogu I, a five-minute walk from Sheshi Skënderbej (note that not all bus services leave from this station; see p69). *Furgons* (minibuses) drop you at various points around the city, but there are usually taxis waiting and it's an easy and cheap option to catch a taxi to your destination.

INFORMATION
Bookshops

Adrion International Bookshop (☎ 2235 242; Palace of Culture, Sheshi Skënderbej; ⏰ 9am-9pm Mon-Sat) This central bookshop has Penguin literary classics, maps of Tirana and Albania, foreign magazines and newspapers, and an excellent selection of books on Albania and the Balkans.

Internet Access

More and more of Tirana's Blloku cafes offer free wi-fi to go with your frappé, but if you didn't bring your own laptop there are plenty of internet cafes around. The going hourly rate is 100 lekë.

Top Net (☎ 0682085861; cnr rr Vasco Pasha & Ismail Qemali; ⊗ 8.30am-11pm; ✗) Relaxed basement place in the thick of Blloku with comfy chairs, cafe and bar.

Internet Café (rr Presidenti George W Bush; ⊗ 9am-11pm) Small noncafe internet cafe, handy for quick email checks.

Laundry

Drycleaner & Laundry (☎ 0682168268; rr Hoxha Tahsim; per kg 200 lekë; ⊗ 8am-8pm Mon-Sat, 9am-1pm Sun) Near the Stephen Centre.

Media

Shekulli is the largest daily paper. The *Albanian Daily News*, available from major hotels, is a fairly dry English-language publication that has useful information on happenings around Albania. Buy the weekly *Tirana Times* from street kiosks. Foreign newspapers and magazines, including the *Times*, the *International Herald Tribune* and the *Economist*, are sold at most major hotels and some kiosks, though they tend to be a few days old.

The BBC World Service is on 103.9FM; the Voice of America's mainly music program is on 107.4FM.

Medical Services

ABC Clinic (☎ 2234 105; rr Qemal Stafa 260; ⊗ 9am-1pm Mon-Fri) Opposite the New School and with English-speaking Christian doctors; offers a range of services including regular (€50) and emergency (€80) consultations.

All-night pharmacy (☎ 2222 241; blvd Zogu I) Just off Sheshi Skënderbej.

Money

Tirana has plenty of ATMs linked to international networks. The main ATM chains are Alpha Bank, Tirana Bank, Pro Credit Bank, Raiffeisen Bank and the American Bank of Albania.

Independent money exchangers operate directly in front of the main post office and on Sheshi Skënderbej and offer the same rates as the banks. Changing money here is not illegal or dangerous, but do count the money you receive before handing yours over. Travellers cheques are near impossible to exchange outside Tirana, so if you're relying on them (our advice is: don't) try one of the following.

American Bank of Albania (rr Ismail Qemali 27; ⊗ 9.30am-3.30pm Mon-Fri) A reliable, secure place to cash your travellers cheques (2% commission). Also an Amex representative.

National Savings Bank (☎ 2235 035; blvd Dëshmorët e Kombit; ⊗ 10.30am-5pm Mon-Fri) Located in the Rogner Hotel Europapark Tirana; offers MasterCard advances, cashes US dollar, euro and sterling travellers cheques for 1% commission, and exchanges cash.

Post

DHL (☎ 2227 667; fax 2233 934; rr Ded Gjo Luli 6)

Main post office (☎ 2228 262; rr Çameria; ⊗ 8am-8pm) On a street jutting west from Sheshi Skënderbej. There are branch post offices on blvd Zogu I and rr Elbasanit.

Telephone

There's an Albtelecom office next to the main post office.

Tourist Information

Tirana doesn't have an official tourist office, but travel agencies can help. **Tirana in Your Pocket** (www.inyourpocket.com) knows what's going on and can be downloaded free, or bought

---

TIRANA IN TWO DAYS

Start your day with croissants in **Pasticeri Française** (p67) and stroll up to **Sheshi Skënderbej** (p65) to explore the **National Museum of History** (p65). Look around **Et'hem Bey Mosque** (p65) and march down to the **National Art Gallery** (p66). Admire the stunning views of Tirana at sunset as you have a beer, wine or sundae at the **Sky Club Bar** (p68). Drink and party in the trendy **Blloku** (p66) area.

On day two visit **Kruja** (p73), where the castle walls hide the Skanderbeg Museum, a fascinating Ethnographic Museum and the Dollma *teqe* (Bektashi temple), full of history. Don't forget to do some shopping at the lovely bazaar and have a traditional Albanian lunch in one of its small restaurants. Back in Tirana, dinner at **Villa Ambassador** (p68) is obligatory for a diverse, mouth-watering menu.

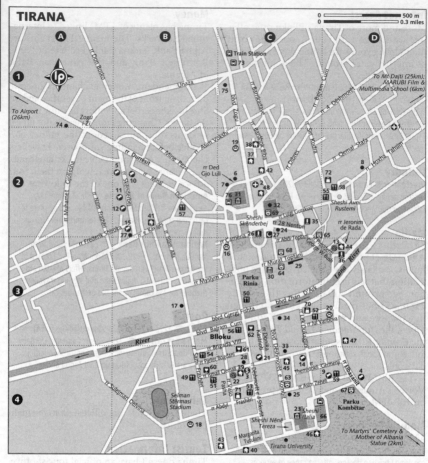

at bookshops, hotels and some of the larger kiosks for 400 lekë.

Another useful reference is *Tirana: The Practical Guide and Map of Tirana* (200 lekë), with telephone numbers and addresses for everything from hospitals to embassies, though some of the entries are only in Albanian. This is also available at the main hotels and bookshops.

Travel Agencies

Travel agencies and airlines of all descriptions and destinations abound on rr Mine Peza, northeast of Sheshi Skënderbej. Nearly all sell tickets to leave Albania, but there are only a few internal tour agencies.

Albanian Experience (☎ 2266 389; Sheraton Hotel, Sheshi Italia) Organises tours and has knowledgable guides.

Outdoor Albania (☎ 0692188845, 2227 121; www .outdooralbania.com; rr Sami Frasheri, Metropol bldg; ☺ 9am-12pm & 2pm-5pm Mon-Fri) Excellent trailblazing adventure-tour agency offering trekking, rafting, ski touring, sea and white-water kayaking and, in summer, hikes through 'hidden valleys' in the alps.

DANGERS & ANNOYANCES

Tirana is a very safe city with little petty crime. The streets are badly lit and there are a few massive potholes, so mind your step and arm yourself with a pocket torch (flashlight) at night to light your way. There are occasional power cuts in the city, so the torch idea stretches further.

Crossing the street is not for the faint-hearted – don't assume the traffic automatically stops at a red light.

SIGHTS
North of the River

Sheshi Skënderbej is the best place to start witnessing the daily goings-on. Until it was pulled down by an angry mob in 1991, a 10m-high bronze statue of Enver Hoxha stood here, watching over a mainly carless square. Now only the **equestrian statue of Skanderbeg** remains, deaf to the cacophony of screeching horns, as cars four lanes deep try to shove their way through the battlefield below.

If you stop to examine Skanderbeg's emblematic goat's-head helmet, the minaret of the 1789–1823 **Et'hem Bey Mosque** will catch your eye. The small and elegant mosque is one of the oldest buildings left in the city, spared from destruction during the atheism campaign of the late '60s because of its status as a cultural monument. Take your shoes off

and go inside to take a look at the beautifully painted dome.

Behind the mosque is the tall **clock tower** (Kulla e Sahatit; ☎ 2243 292, 11 28 Nëntori; admission 50 lekë; ☼ 9am 1pm Mon, 9am 1pm & 4-6pm Thu), which you can climb to watch the square. A little further on, the socialist-realist **Statue of the Unknown Partisan** attracts day-labourers waiting for work, some with their own jackhammers – a fitting image of the precarious position of the postcommunist Albanian worker.

To the east of Sheshi Skënderbej is the white-stone **Palace of Culture** (Pallate Kulturës; Sheshi Skënderbej), which has a theatre, shops and art galleries. Construction of the palace began as a gift from the Soviet people in 1960 and was completed in 1966, years after the 1961 Soviet-Albanian split. The entrance to the National Library is on the south side of the building.

On the northwestern side of the square is the **National Museum of History** (Muzeu Historik Kombëtar; Sheshi Skënderbej; admission 300 lekë; ☼ 9am-1pm & 4-7pm Tue-Sat, 9am-noon Sun), the largest museum in Albania, which holds most of the country's archaeological treasures and a replica of Skanderbeg's massive sword. The hours are strict, and you won't be let in if you arrive half an hour before closing time. The fantastic mosaic mural entitled *Albania* adorning the museum's facade shows Albanians victorious and proud from Illyrian times through to WWII. In case you thought everyone had erased the Hoxha era from their minds, a sombre gallery devoted to its miseries is on the top floor. Its walls are covered with the names of those killed from 1941 to 1985, and there are many, many photos from the time. Even the guides seem to find the exhibit confronting. The museum's better with a guide, and they speak English, French and Italian. There's a good souvenir shop as you exit the museum.

Stroll down the broad, tree-lined blvd Dëshmorët e Kombit to Tirana's **National Art Gallery** (Galeria Kombëtare e Arteve; admission 100 lekë; ☾ 9am-1pm & 5-8pm Tue-Sun), where the garden is adorned with statues of proud partisans. See the astonishing exhibition of icons inside by Onufri, the renowned 16th-century master of colour. If you're lucky you'll catch some modern work by Albanian-born artists in the ground-floor temporary-exhibition area.

If you turn up rr Murat Toptani you pass the 6m-high walls of the **Fortress of Justinian**, the last remnants of a Byzantine-era castle. Strangely, half a cinema spills over the top. East from here, on the corner of rr Presidenti George W Bush and the Lana River, is **Tanners' Bridge**, a small 19th-century slippery-when-wet stone bridge.

South of the River

It's hard not to notice the sloping white-marble and glass walls of the 1988 **Pyramid** (blvd Dëshmorët e Kombit), designed by Hoxha's daughter and son-in-law. Formerly the Enver Hoxha Museum and now used as a disco and conference centre, the building never really took off as a museum but does very well as a slide for children. Nearby is the **Prime Minister's Residence** (blvd Dëshmorët e Kombit), from where Enver Hoxha and cronies would stand and view military parades from the 2nd-floor balcony.

Another creation of the dictator's daughter and son-in-law is the square **Congress Building** (blvd Dëshmorët e Kombit), just a little down the boulevard. Follow rr Ismail Qemali, two streets north of the Congress Building, and enter the once totally forbidden but now totally trendy **Blloku** area. This was once the communist-party elite's hang-out, and when it was first opened to the general public in 1991, Albanians flocked to see the style in which their 'proletarian' leaders lived. If we are to judge by the **former residence of Enver Hoxha** (cnr rr Dëshmorët e 4 Shkurtit & rr Ismail Qemali), a three-storey pastel-coloured house, they lived like the Western suburban bourgeoisie.

If you are an archaeological glutton, they might turn the lights on for you at the **Archaeological Museum** (Muzeu Arkeologik; Sheshi Nënë Tereza; admission 200 lekë; ☾ 10.30am-2.30pm Mon-Fri), which houses an extensive collection close to the main **Tirana University**. The foyer has maps and information about current archaeological digs in Albania.

At the top of rr Elbasanit is the **Martyrs' Cemetery**, where some 900 partisans who died in WWII are buried. The views over the city and surrounding mountains (including Mt Dajti to the east) are excellent. Many people still come here clutching laurel sprigs to pay their respects under the shadow of the immense, beautiful and strangely androgynous **Mother Albania statue** (1972). Hoxha was buried here in 1985 but was exhumed in 1992 and interred in an ordinary graveyard on the other side of town. Catch any municipal bus heading up rr Elbasanit; the grand driveway is on your left.

FESTIVALS & EVENTS

The **Tirana Film Festival** (TIFF; www.tiranafilmfest.com) has been brightening up the city in November or December since 2003. In 2008, 1000 films from 80 countries were vying for the €1200 prizes. An annual event since 2000, the **Tirana Jazz Festival** (www.movingculture.org) is usually held in June or July.

SLEEPING
Budget

Tirana Backpacker Hostel (☎ 0682167357; www.tirana hostel.com; rr Elbasanit 85; dm €12) Albania's first hostel opened in 2005 in a 70-year-old villa close to the city centre. With 25 beds in four rooms, and shared bathrooms, it has big balconies, a great garden with a cosy outdoor kitchen, a summer cinema in the basement and friendly, helpful young managers. Head east along rr Ismail Qemali until it meets rr Elbasanit; it's over the road on your left.

Pension Andrea (☎ 0692904915; rr Jeronim de Rada 103; s/d €20/30) Gina runs this lovely, homely pension; all its rooms have TVs, some have air-con, and there's safe storage for bicycles. On rr Jeronim de Rada take the first right down the court; it's on your right.

Freddy's Hostel (☎ 0682035261; www.freddyshostel .com; rr Bardhok Biba 75; dm €12, r €30) A bunch of clean, basic rooms in different configurations are in two buildings in the same area. To find the main apartment block, walk north of Tirana International Hotel and look for the suburban street parallel to blvd Zogu I. The hostel is past Hestia restaurant (a great place for a snack and a beer), on the left.

Hotel Endri (☎ 2244 168, 2229 334; rr Vaso Pasha 27; r €30; 🔀) The good value Endri is located south of Blloku, where all the action is. The 'hotel' is basically a couple of clean rooms in a building next to owner Petrit Alikaj's apartment. It's on the left at the end of rr Vaso Pasha, but call Petrit if you get lost.

Midrange

Luna Hotel (☎ 2272 950; www.hotels-tirana.com; rr Sami Frasheri 4; s/d €50/60; 🔀) Located just south of Blloku, off rr Sami Frasheri, this modern hotel has had the power of Zen whisk through its rooms and bathrooms. Gigantic stencilled flowers decorate the hall's lime green walls, and everything's been thought of, including hairdryers in the bathroom.

Hotel Nobel (☎ 2256 444; www.hotelnobeltirana.com; blvd Zogu I; s/d €40/50; 🔀) Wi-fi. Albania's two Nobel Peace Prize winners are Mother Teresa and Professor Ferid Murad, the inventor of Viagra. It's good to see a hotel getting into the spirit of things, and charismatic owner Edmond has done a great job giving his hotel some Nobel personality (although the stick of dynamite in his drawer is curious). The six rooms are clean and bright, there's an Italian restaurant downstairs, and it's central (next to VEVE Business Centre).

Firenze Hotel (☎ 2249 099; firenzehotel@albania online.net; blvd Zogu I 72; s/d €50/70; 🅿 🔀) This cheerful and colourful little hotel between the train station and Sheshi Skënderbej has seven cosy, clean rooms with TV and minibar and a great 'magazine corner' in the breakfast room.

Hotel Nirvana (☎ 2235 270; rr e Kavajës 96/2; s/d €60/80; 🔀) With its ostentatious marble staircase and walls dripping in art (apparently this is nothing compared with the owner's house), this hotel may have delusions of grandeur, but

thankfully the price remains reasonably humble and the staff are friendly and helpful.

Top End

Rogner Hotel Europapark Tirana (☎ 2235 035; www .hotel-europapark.com; blvd Dëshmorët e Kombit; s €210-240, d €250-290, ste €320-350; 🔀) Free wi-fi in the lobby. With an unbeatable location in the heart of the city, the Rogner is a peaceful oasis with a huge garden (verging on a park), banks, Avis rent-a-car and travel agencies. The rooms are spacious and very comfortable (with flat-screen TVs), and the restaurant has tasty international cuisine. You can play a game or two of tennis here, too. Accepts all credit cards.

Sheraton Tirana Hotel & Towers (☎ 2274 707; www .starwoodhotels.com; Sheshi Italia; r €220, ste €236-384; 🔀) This is an impressive upper-end business hotel, whose blank mirrored glass and monumental frame might be a nod to the country's totalitarian past. Services and facilities match the prices.

Grand Hotel (☎ 2253 220; grandhotel@icc-al.org; rr Ismail Qemali 11; s/d €120/160, ste €220; 🔀) This small and friendly upmarket hotel is in the heart of trendy Blloku. The rooms are a teensy bit dated but perfectly comfortable and very clean. The hotel's pool and sauna (and massage service) can be privately booked.

Tirana International Hotel (☎ 2234 185; Sheshi Skënderbej; s/d €120/140, ste €300) Originally the Soviet-built Hotel Tirana, the modern incarnation is just as imposing, not exactly friendly and not as good as you'd expect for the price. On the positive side, great artworks are a lobby feature, and some rooms have fantastic views over the busy square.

EATING

If you thought that cuisine in Tirana's restaurants might be monotonous or that eating out would be a downmarket experience, you were wrong. For self-caterers there's a Conan supermarket downstairs at the European Trade Centre.

Era (☎ 2266 662; rr Ismail Qemali; mains 400 lekë; ☒ 11am-midnight; 🅥) In the heart of Blloku, Era serves traditional Albanian and Italian fare. There are some vegetarian choices on the menu, but check first – there may well be mince lurking in your stuffed vegetables.

Pasticeri Française (☎ 2251 336; rr Dëshmorët e 4 Shkurtit 1; breakfast 300 lekë; ☒ 8am-10pm) One of the few breakfast spots in Tirana, this French-owned place has red walls and high ceilings, and small lamps light individual tables, giving it an ooh-la-la feeling!

Villa Ambassador/Chocolate (☎ 0692066257; rr Asim Zeneli 2; meals 1000 lekë; ◔ 8am-midnight; Ⓥ) Now in a new location (in the former Romanian ambassador's residence), this well-regarded restaurant has the same team creating and serving up tasty Albanian dishes for carnivores and vegetarians alike. Crepes and pastries make it a good spot for breakfast, too.

Serenata (☎ 2273 088; rr Mihal Duri 7; mains 600 lekë; ◔ 9am-midnight; Ⓥ) If you're not going to Korça, you can try the region's food here. Serenata specialises in Korçan food, which consists of meat dishes such as oven-baked liver, veal and wild boar, and vegetarian delicacies. It also serves some interesting local wines and *raki* from Korça. This place is decorated in a traditional style and has gentle Korçan music *(serenata)* tinkling from the speakers.

Oda (☎ 2249 541; rr Luigj Gurakuqi; meals around 500 lekë; ◔ noon-late) A cute little traditional Albanian restaurant run by artist Paskal Prifti, with tasty home cooking, an array of powerful *raki* and fragrant homemade wines. Mr Prifti is a fan of traditional Albanian polyphonic singing and sometimes has friends drop by to sing the old melodies. If you're heading towards Sheshi Skënderbej from the northeast, the restaurant is on an alley to your right just past Sheshi Avni Rustemi.

Casa de Pasta (☎ 2251 157; Parku Rinia; meals 700 lekë; ◔ 8am-midnight) The delightfully weird Disneyesque structure called the Taiwan Complex (Taivan Komplekësi) in Parku Rinia houses this excellent Italian restaurant. The food's fine and, if you feel like doing something different, head downstairs for some tenpin bowling (350 lekë per person after 6pm).

Anais (☎ 2246 624; rr Sami Frashëri 20; meals around 2500 lekë; ◔ 11am-11pm) Quite expensive by local standards, the Ottoman cuisine served here by a chef who worked in Turkey is utterly superb. The selection of mezes is tremendous: puréed eggplant, spicy beans and mushrooms, and rich kebabs. Main courses cost around 1000 lekë to 1200 lekë, starters around 400 lekë. If you've been here before you might realise that Anais was once called Efendy.

Green House (☎ 2222 632; rr Jul Varibova 6; meals 1000 lekë; ◔ 9am-11pm) This plush, friendly, modern restaurant is an expat hang-out, and has a varied menu (including un-Albanian fare such

as gnocchi gorgonzola) and a huge wine list. On the road that runs east from the Pyramid, it offers boutique-style accommodation (singles/doubles €100/110) upstairs, too.

La Cantinella (☎ 0692070082; rr Brigada VIII; mains 400 lekë; ◔ noon-midnight) At this delightful courtyard restaurant you can indulge in dishes such as Ali Pasha risotto, oblivious to the traffic chaos of Tirana. There's a good selection of wines, delicious salads and attentive staff.

Stephen Center Café (☎ 2235 924; www.stephen center.com; rr Hoxha Tahsim 1; mains 400 lekë; ◔ 8am-8pm) This American-owned Christian cafe near Sheshi Avni Rustemi is usually full of expats and has free wi-fi. Whilst the coffee may not be as good as you expect, the Western breakfasts will give you a taste of home (pancakes!) if you're tired of cheese.

King House (☎ 2255 559; rr Dëshmorët e 4 Shkurtit; mains 350 lekë; ◔ 7am-midnight) King House, with its usual range of Albanian and Italian food choices in a cosy environment, is also the place to head at 7.30pm on Friday night if you feel like some expat/fellow visitor company. To help you out, the bill is in lekë, euro and US dollars.

DRINKING

Sky Club Bar (☎ 2221 666; Sky Tower, rr Dëshmorët e 4 Shkurtit; ◔ 8am-midnight) Start your night here for spectacular city views from the revolving bar on top of one of the highest buildings in town. If you're just going up for a look, it's cheaper to buy a beer up there than pay the 250-lekë charge reception has been known to request.

Charl's (☎ 2253 754; rr Pjetër Bogdani 5; ◔ 8am-late) Charl's is a consistently popular bar with Tirana's students because of its ever-varying music: jazz, blues, orchestral and rock on different nights of the week. There's a very pleasant, relaxed vibe – fashionable but not pretentious.

Buda Bar (☎ 0682058825; rr Ismail Qemali; ◔ 4.30pm-late) It's all about a relaxed atmosphere here, with subdued lighting, burning incense, chaise longues and armchairs where cushions abound.

ENTERTAINMENT

There's a good choice of entertainment options in Tirana, in the form of bars, clubs, cinemas/performances, exhibitions and even tenpin bowling. For the low-down on events and exhibitions, check out the free fortnightly *Planet Albania* (www.planet-albania.com)

guide as well as the monthly leaflet *ARTirana* (a free supplement to *Gazeta Shqiptare*) and the weekly *Tirana Times*. Free postcards in bars and restaurants also advertise what's coming up.

Cinemas

Kinema Millennium 2 (☎ 2253 654; www.ida-millennium.com; rr Murat Toptani; admission 200-500 lekë) All the current-release movies; the earlier in the day you go, the cheaper it is.

MARUBI Film & Multimedia School (www.afmm.edu.al; rr Aleksander Moisiu 76; admission free; ✆ 7pm Thu) Free art-house movies are shown here during semester. It's located near the last Kino Studio bus stop in the city's northeast.

Imperial Cinema (www.empire-al.com; Sheraton Mall, Sheshi Italia; admission 300-600 lekë) This cinema has three screens and it's easy to get to, especially if you're staying at the neighbouring Sheraton hotel.

Live Music

Qemal Stafa Stadium (Sheshi Italia) Next to the university, this stadium often hosts concerts and other musical events. Look out for street banners and free postcards bearing details of upcoming shows. Football matches are held here every Saturday and Sunday afternoon.

Take 5 (☎ 0684069306; rr Themistokli Gjërmenjl; ✆ 7pm-late) This ain't no candy, it's Tirana's only jazz club and has live performances most evenings and a great theme: 'in jazz we trust'.

Theatre of Opera & Ballet (☎ 2224 753; Sheshi Skënderbej; admission from 300 lekë; ✆ performances from 7pm, from 6pm winter) Check the listings and posters outside this theatre for performances. You can usually buy tickets half an hour before the show for 200 lekë.

Academy of Arts (☎ 2257 237; Sheshi Nënë Tereza) Classical music and other performances take place throughout the year in either the large indoor theatre or the small open-air faux-classical amphitheatre; both are part of the university. Prices vary according to the program.

Nightclubs

Folie (rr Murat Toptani; ✆ 7pm-late) Folks are welcoming here and it's a good place to spend part of your evening, even if it's just to find out which club to go to next, as new places seem to open up weekly. It's at Kinema Millennium 2.

Living Room (☎ 2274 837; rr Presidenti George W Bush 16; ✆ 7.30pm-late) This is the hippest place

to drink and dance in Tirana – with eclectic DJs, a good crowd, cool lampshades and '70s sofas for you to lounge on when you're danced (or drunk) off your feet. The terrace is airy and fun.

Theatre

Teatri Kombëtar (National Theatre; rr Sermedin Said Topani) This theatre may have something of interest on; plays range from the story of Nënë Tereza (Mother Teresa) to Albanian comedies. Posters outside advertise what's on.

SHOPPING

There are a few good souvenir shops on rr Durrësit, blvd Zogu I and around Sheshi Skënderbej. Most of them sell the same things: Albanian flags, carved wooden plates, T-shirts, bunker ashtrays and traditional textiles.

Natyral & Organik (☎ 2250 575; rr Vaso Pasha) This wonderful store in Blloku not only supports small village producers by stocking organic olive oil, honey, herbs, tea, eggs, spices, *raki* and cognac (they make great gifts, but be aware of customs regulations in the countries you're travelling through) but also is a centre for environmental activism.

Public market (Pazari i Ri; Sheshi Avni Rustemi; ✆ 7am-8pm) Tirana's eclectic market, north of the Sheshi Avni Rustemi roundabout several blocks east of the clock tower, is largest on Thursday and Sunday. The fruit market is right on the square, then there's a collection of butchers and cheese shops, and further on there are stalls selling carved wooden trays, small boxes, wall hangings and bone necklaces, though many just sell cheap house supplies for the locals.

European Trade Centre (ETC; cnr blvd Bajram Curri & Lek Dukagjini) The centre has four levels of snazzy European shops.

GETTING THERE & AWAY
Air

Nënë Tereza (Mother Teresa) Airport, also known as Rinas Airport, is at Rinas, 26km northwest of Tirana. Its new passenger terminal opened in 2006. There's a €10 fee to enter Albania by air.

For airlines flying from Albania to other parts of the Western Balkans, see p98.

Bus

Since there are few bus stations in Tirana, it's impossible to pin down where the buses

ALBANIA

BUS SERVICES FROM TIRANA

Destination	Price (lekë)	Duration (hr)	Distance (km)
Berat	400	2½	122
Durrës	100	1	38
Elbasan	300	1½	54
Fier	300	2	113
Gjirokastra	1000	7	232
Korça	800	4	181
Kruja	200	½	32
Pogradec	700	3½	150
Saranda	1200	8	284
Shkodra	400	2	116
Vlora	500	3	147

and *furgons* actually leave from. The easiest is just to jump in a taxi and say '*Dua të shkoj në* (Berat, Vlora, wherever)', meaning 'I want to go to (Berat, Vlora, wherever)'. Taxi drivers always know the latest departure points and, given Albania's unique attitude to assisting travellers, will often secure your ride for you, as well.

See the table, above, for an idea of distances and average costs for departures from Tirana. *Furgons* are usually 20% to 30% more expensive than buses.

Furgons normally leave when full, and buses are usually full by departure time, especially in the afternoon. Pay the driver or conductor on the bus. Only municipal buses tend to give out tickets.

For information on buses arriving in Tirana from other countries in the Western Balkans, see p443.

Car & Motorcycle

Driving around Albania is not as hard as it used to be, although there are bound to be hair-raising moments. The major car-hire companies in Tirana:

Avis (☎ 2235 011; Rogner Hotel Europapark Tirana, blvd Dëshmorët e Kombit)

Europcar (☎ 2227 888; rr Durrësit 61)

Hertz (☎ 2255 028; Tirana International Hotel, Sheshi Skënderbej)

Sixt (☎ 2259 020; rr e Kavajës 116)

Train

The run-down train station is at the northern end of blvd Zogu I. Albania's trains range from sort-of-OK to very decrepit. Albanians travel by train if they can't afford to travel

by bus. Six trains daily go to Durrës (70 lekë, one hour). Trains also depart for Elbasan (190 lekë, four hours, two daily), Pogradec (295 lekë, seven hours, 5.55am), Shkodra (150 lekë, 3½ hours, 1.15pm) and Vlora (250 lekë, 5½ hours, 2.50pm). Check timetables at the station the day before travelling.

GETTING AROUND
To/From the Airport

The brand-spanking-new airport **Nënë Tereza** (Mother Teresa, Rinas, TIA; www.tirana-airport.com) is 26km from Tirana. The Rinas airport bus makes the trip hourly (6am to 6pm) from the western side of the National Museum of History at Sheshi Skënderbej for 250 lekë. If you choose to go by taxi, settle the fee before you hop in – the going rate is €20. You can avoid haggling the minute you arrive in Albania by arranging for a hotel to send someone to collect you, or by going by licensed taxi (which are supposed to park right at the front). It usually takes 20 to 25 minutes to get to the airport, but plan for traffic delays.

Car & Motorcycle

Some of the major hotels offer guarded parking; others have parking available out the front.

Taxi

Taxi stands dot the city and taxis charge 400 lekë for a ride inside Tirana, and 600 lekë at night and to destinations outside the first 'ring'. Make sure you reach an agreement with the driver before setting off. **Radio Taxi** (☎ 377 777), with 24-hour service, is particularly reliable.

CENTRAL ALBANIA

If there's one region of Albania that manages to cram it all in, it's central Albania. Just an hour or two from Tirana and you can be Ottoman house-hopping in brilliantly alive Berat, or musing over ancient ruins in deserted Apollonia or bubbly, beachside Durrës. Don't forget to bargain for antiques under the gaze of Skanderbeg in Kruja or take time out on the cable car to Mt Dajti National Park. To the east, a beer factory and hot spring can add some diversity to your itinerary.

DURRËS

☎ 052 / pop 114,000

Durrës is an ancient city and was, until 1920, Albania's capital. Its 10km-long beach begins a few kilometres southeast of the city (past the port and tangle of overpasses and roundabouts). Here families take up position under rented umbrellas and sun lounges, and the brave cool down in its shallow, and frequently red-flagged, section of the Adriatic Sea. The beaches are something of a lesson in unplanned development; hundreds of hotels side by side, barely giving breathing space to the beach and contributing to the urban-waste problem that has caused outbreaks of skin infections in swimmers.

Away from the seaside, Durrës is a relaxed, amiable city with some gracious early-20th-century buildings, centrally located ancient ruins, a unique museum and an abundance of fun waterfront eating options. Good bus services and its role as the centre of Albania's train network make Durrës a great base for accessing the rest of Albania as well as exploring Kruja to the north and the archaeological site of Apollonia, around 90km to the south.

Orientation

The town centre is easily covered on foot. In the centre, the **great mosque** (Xhamia e Madhe Durrës; Sheshi i Lirisë) serves as a point of orientation: the archaeological attractions are immediately around it, and the train and bus stations are 1km to the northeast. Durrës' main *xhiro* (evening stroll) goes from Sheshi i Lirisë down rr Tregtare to Sheshi Mujo Ulqinaku and along rr Taulantia. East of Sheshi Mujo Ulqinaku is the port. The

large Flagship shopping centre has sprung up on the portside intersection of rr Prokop Meksi and rr Skënderbeg, providing free wi-fi in the middle of Western-style shops. The former palace of King Zog and the lighthouse are to the west, on the ridge.

Information

There are plenty of ATMs near the station and on rr Tregtare.

American Bank of Albania (Sheshi Mujo Ulqinaku)

Century 91 (rr Tregtare; per hr 60 lekë; ☉ 1pm-midnight) Internet access.

Dea Lines (☎ 30 386; dealines@dealines.com; rr Tregtare 102; ☉ 8.30am-8pm) Trustworthy travel agency with branches in the town centre and at Tirana's Rinas airport. It'll also help you find up-to-date information on ferries and flights.

Post office (blvd Kryesor)

Sights

The **Archaeological Museum** (Muzeu Arkeologjik; rr Taulantia; admission 200 lekë; ☉ 9am-3pm Tue-Sun) on the waterfront is well laid out and has an impressive collection of artefacts from the Greek, Hellenistic and Roman periods. Highlights include engraved Roman funeral stelae (memorial stones) and some big carved stone sarcophagi. Back in the day when the city was called Epidamnos, Durrës was a centre for the worship of Venus, and the museum has a cabinet bursting with little busts of the love goddess.

North of the museum, beginning at Bar Torra and following rr Anastas Durrsaku, are the 6th-century **Byzantine city walls**, built after the Visigoth invasion of AD 481 and supplemented by round Venetian towers in the 14th century.

The impressive **Amphitheatre of Durrës** (rr e Kalase; admission 500 lekë; ☉ 8am-7pm) was built on the hillside just inside the city walls in the first decade of the 2nd century AD. In its prime it had the capacity to seat 15,000 spectators, but these days a few inhabited houses occupy the stage, a reminder of its recent rediscovery and excavation. The Byzantine chapel in the amphitheatre is home to mosaics.

Ruins of **Roman baths** are just off the main square at the back of the Alexsandër Moisiu Theatre. Across the road a large circular **basilica** still has some columns standing. Also intriguing are the Roman columns located in

ALBANIA

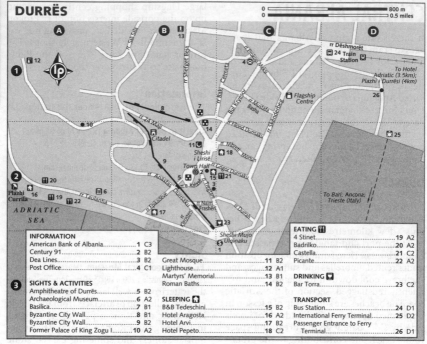

DURRËS

INFORMATION
American Bank of Albania	1 C3
Century 91	2 B2
Dea Lines	3 B2
Post Office	4 C1

SIGHTS & ACTIVITIES
Amphitheatre of Durrës	5 B2
Archaeological Museum	6 A2
Basilica	7 B1
Byzantine City Wall	8 B1
Byzantine City Wall	9 B2
Former Palace of King Zogu I	10 A2
Great Mosque	11 B2
Lighthouse	12 A1
Martyrs' Memorial	13 B1
Roman Baths	14 B2

SLEEPING
B&B Tedeschini	15 B2
Hotel Aragosta	16 A2
Hotel Arvi	17 B2
Hotel Pepeto	18 C2

EATING
4 Stinet	19 A2
Badriko	20 A2
Castella	21 C2
Picante	22 A2

DRINKING
Bar Torra	23 C2

TRANSPORT
Bus Station	24 D1
International Ferry Terminal	25 D2
Passenger Entrance to Ferry Terminal	26 D1

front of the shopfronts, palm trees and road lights on rr Tregtare.

Durrës' attractions are not all ancient. There are some fine socialist-realist monuments, including the **Martyrs' Memorial** (rr Shefget Beja) by the waterfront.

On the hilltop west of the amphitheatre stands the decaying **former palace of King Zogu I** (rr Anastas Durrsaku); it's a 15-minute climb up from the town centre to what was a grand palace (marble staircases, carved wooden ceilings and the like), but it's closed to the public. There are better views from the nearby **lighthouse**.

Festivals & Events

The three main annual festivals to grace Durrës' shores are the **International Festival of Modern & Contemporary Dance** (www.dancealbfest.com) in April; the new **Festival of the Sea**, celebrating the age-old summer solstice in June; and September's **Durrës Jazz Festival**.

Sleeping

Durrës has a variety of accommodation options in the city itself, and there are a few more along the quieter beach Plazhi Currila, west of

the centre, but most line the beach to the east. This is where Albanian holidaymakers and their ethnic kin from Kosovo and Macedonia come to play in summer.

IN TOWN

B&B Tedeschini (☎ 24 343, 0682246303; ipmcrsp@icc .al.eu.org; rr Dom Nikoll Kaçorri 5; s/d €15/30) This gracious 19th-century former Italian consulate has been turned into a homely B&B with airy rooms, antique furniture and portraits of former consuls. Owner (and doctor) Alma prepares great breakfasts in the country-style kitchen. From the square fronting the great mosque, walk past the town hall and down the alley to its left then make a right, then a quick left. Use the doorbell next to the green gates.

Hotel Pepeto (☎ 24 190; rr Mbreti Monun 3; s/d/ ste €20/30/50; ⬛) This well-run (and well-signposted) guesthouse is at the end of a court just off the square fronting the great mosque. The rooms are decent and quiet, some have baths and balconies, and the suite is an attic-dweller's dream. There's a spacious lounge and bar area downstairs. Laundry is €5 and breakfast is included.

Hotel Arvi (☎ 30 403; www.hotelarvi.com; rr Taulantia; d/ste €60/80; 🗶 💻) A polished hotel with friendly staff, neat, modern rooms (all with some kind of sea view), and breakfast, in the perfect location for watching or participating in the Durrës *xhiro*.

Hotel Aragosta (☎ 26 477; www.aragosta.al; rr Taulantia; s/d €60/100; 🗶 💻 🗶) With carpet so cushy you can't walk straight, this new beachfront hotel is close to good restaurants and has one of its own. Staff boast that its private beach is the cleanest in town. Its name means lobster and you can guess the colour scheme of the modern rooms (some with wonderful spa baths).

THE COAST
Hotel Adriatik (☎ 60 850; www.adriatikhotel.com; Plazhi Illiria; s/d €95/125; 🄿 🗶 🗶) Still the grandest hotel on Durrës' beaches, this hotel, located 5km from Durrës' centre, has several restaurants, a tennis court, a sauna and comfortable rooms with all the mod cons.

Eating & Drinking

Castella (rr Grigor Durrsaku; mains 200 lekë; 🕑 10am–4pm Mon-Sat) Popular with locals who prefer a good feed rather than being seen, this casual restaurant provides bargain-priced home-style lunches.

Badrilko (rr Taulantia; mains 500 lekë) This restaurant, on the landward side of rr Taulantia, may lack sea views, but it has the best pizzas in Durrës, a wide range of fish (on display, take your pick), a busy saloon-style interior and a lively terrace bar.

4 Stinet (rr Taulantia; meals 600 lekë) The last of eight pizzerias on the end of the promenade serves tasty light meals, including pasta and pizza, right on the water's edge.

Picante (rr Taulantia; mains 700-4000 lekë) Upping the trendy ante is this stark white restaurant on the promenade. The red-chilli motif may indicate how hot this place is; it's certainly where the young locals are spending their disposable income. The music's good, the furniture's white and minimalistic and the meals are priced to stretch the budget.

Bar Torra (Sheshi Mujo Ulqinaku; beers 150 lekë) Housed inside a fortified Venetian tower at the beginning of the city walls, this was one of the first private cafes in Albania, opened by a team of local artists. After you've had a peek at the tourist information section inside, and at the view from the top, you can drink a local brew in the cosy barred nooks of the old

tower. The ceiling is strangely reminiscent of Hoxha's bunkers.

Getting There & Away

Albania's 720km railway network centres on Durrës. There are six trains a day to Tirana (70 lekë, one hour, 6.10am to 6.40pm), one to Shkodra (160 lekë, 3¾ hours, 1pm) via Lezha, one to Pogradec (300 lekë, 5½ hours, 7.07am) via Elbasan (2½ hours), and one to Vlora (260 lekë, four hours, 4.05pm) via Fier. Times and services change, so check the station's noticeboard beforehand to confirm the train is running. They sometimes depart slightly ahead of schedule. If your train plans fall through there are plenty of buses at the adjacent bus station.

Furgons (150 lekë, one hour) and buses (100 lekë, one hour) to Tirana leave from beside the train station whenever they're full. Buses leave for Shkodra at 7.30am and 1.30pm (300 lekë). In summer, long-distance buses and *furgons* going to and from Saranda, Gjirokastra, Fier and Berat tend to bypass this station, picking up and dropping off passengers at the end of Plazhi i Durrësi, to the far east of the harbour. A taxi there costs 500 lekë, or catch the orange municipal bus to 'Plepa' for 20 lekë.

Numerous travel agencies handle ferry bookings. All offer much the same service (see p444). International ferries leave from the terminal south of the train station.

KRUJA
☎ 0511 / pop 20,000
Your journey to Kruja begins in the slightly grimy town of Fushë Kruja, where George W Bush greeted the crowds in 2007. From here you can see Kruja's houses seated in the lap of the mountain, and the ancient castle jutting out to one side, with the massive Skanderbeg Museum poking out of the castle itself. Fushë Kruja's plaster industry is going full steam ahead, so expect lots of dump-truck activity in the freshly carved-up hills, as well as visibility-reducing plumes of dark-grey smoke.

Kruja is Skanderbeg's town. Yes, Albania's hero was born here, and although it was over 500 years ago, there's still a great deal of pride in the fact that he and his forces defended Kruja until his death. As soon as you get off the bus you're face to knee with a statue of Skanderbeg (Gjergj Kastrioti, 1405-68) wielding his mighty sword with one hand, and it just gets more Skanderdelic after that.

ALBANIA

As for the history, at a young age Kastrioti, the son of an Albanian prince, was handed over as a hostage to the Turks, who converted him to Islam and gave him a military education at Edirne in Turkey. There he became known as Iskander (after Alexander the Great), and Sultan Murat II promoted him to the rank of *bey* (governor), thus the name Skanderbeg.

In 1443 the Turks suffered a defeat at the hands of the Hungarians at Niš in present-day Serbia, and nationally minded Skanderbeg took the opportunity to abandon the Ottoman army and Islam and rally his fellow Albanians against the Turks. Skanderbeg made Kruja his seat of government between 1443 and 1468. Among the 13 Turkish invasions he subsequently repulsed was that led by his former commander Murat II in 1450. Pope Calixtus III named Skanderbeg the 'captain general of the Holy See' and Venice formed an alliance with him. The Turks besieged Kruja four times. Though beaten back in 1450, 1466 and 1467, they took control of Kruja in 1478 (after Skanderbeg's death) and Albanian resistance was suppressed.

Sights

Kruja's sights can be covered in a few hours, making this an ideal town to visit before heading to Rinas airport, which is only 16km away. The main sight in Kruja is the **castle** (admission 100 lekë) and its peculiar **Skanderbeg Museum** (admission 200 lekë; ☺ 9am-1pm & 4-7pm Tue-Sun). Designed by Enver Hoxha's daughter and son-in-law, it opened in 1982, and its spacious seven-level interior displays replicas of armour and paintings depicting Skanderbeg's struggle against the Ottomans. The museum is something of a secular shrine, and takes itself very seriously indeed with giant statues and dramatic battle murals.

The **Ethnographic Museum** (admission 100 lekë; ☺ 9am-7pm) in the castle complex below the Skanderbeg Museum is one of the best in the country. Set in an original 19th-century Ottoman house that belonged to the affluent Toptani family, this museum shows the level of luxury and self-sufficiency the household maintained by producing its own food, drink, leather and weapons. The family even had its very own mini hamam and water mill. The walls are lined with original 1764 frescos. The English-speaking guide's detailed

explanations are excellent; tip him 200 lekë if you can.

A short scramble down the cobblestone lane are the remains of a small hamam as well as a functioning Dollma *teqe* (see the boxed text, p57). This beautifully decorated *teqe* has been maintained by successive generations of the Dollma family since 1789. The knotted and ancient olive tree in front was reputedly planted by Skanderbeg himself.

The bazaar is the best place for souvenir shopping in the country and hides WWII medical kits, antique gems and quality traditional wares, including beautifully embroidered tablecloths, copper coffee pots and plates. You can watch women using looms to make *qilims* (rugs) and purchase the results.

Sleeping & Eating

Hotel Panorama (☎ 30 92; bazaar; s/d €20/25; ✘ ▯) The Panorama has eight wood-panelled rooms with great views of the castle, as well as a bar and a small restaurant with low prices. It's just opposite the entrance to the bazaar, and at the time of research was set to double in size.

Grand Hotel (☎ 45 57; r 3600 lekë) Near the bus stop, the Grand has rooms with balconies, but they don't have much atmosphere and are quite bare. The restaurant has a pleasant terrace.

For more eating options try the upper ridge of the castle.

Getting There & Away

Kruja is 32km from Tirana. A cab from Kruja to Tirana and back with two hours' waiting time costs around 4000 lekë, while a *furgon* one way costs 200 lekë. It's very easy to reach the airport by *furgon* or taxi from here, and there are direct links by bus and *furgon* to Durrës.

MT DAJTI NATIONAL PARK

Just 25km east of Tirana is **Mt Dajti** (1611m) and its surrounding national park. It's the most accessible mountain in the country and many Tiranans go there on the weekend to escape the city rush and have a spit-roast lamb lunch. A cable car, the **Dajti Express** (www.dajti ekspres.com; return 500 lekë), has been plying the route since 2005, cutting the time it takes to chug up the hill down to 15 minutes. Ask around first to see if it's operating.

If you're driving, there's a checkpoint where you pay a park admission fee of 200 lekë per car. Put your sturdy shoes on for a gentle hike in the lovely, shady beech and pine forests, then have a coffee and enjoy the spectacular views from the wide terrace of the **Panorama Restaurant** (☎ 361 124; meals 800 lekë; ☾ 9am-11pm). There are several other restaurants along the road to the Panorama; the **Ballkoni Dajtit** (☎ 0684011021; ☾ 9am-10pm) is right where the Dajti Express stops. The very top of the mountain is a restricted zone with military communication aerials.

To get to the Dajti Express departure point, catch the public bus from outside Tirana's clock tower to 'Porcelain' for 20 lekë, walk uphill for 10 minutes and follow the sign. Taxis seem to charge what they want to the Express, but the 6km trip should only cost 600 lekë. A taxi from the city to the top takes about 45 minutes, and you can arrange to phone the driver to pick you up when you want to go back. The road to Mt Dajti National Park starts on rr Qemal Stafa in Tirana.

APOLLONIA

The ruined city of ancient **Apollonia** (admission 700 lekë; ☾ 9am-5pm) is 12km west of Fier, which is 90km south of Durrës. Apollonia is set on rolling hills among olive groves, and the views of the plains below stretch for miles. Apollonia (named after Apollo) was founded by Greeks from Corinth and Corfu in 588 BC and quickly grew into an important city state, which minted its own currency and benefited from a robust slave trade. Under the Romans (229 BC) the city became a great cultural centre with a famous school of philosophy.

Julius Caesar rewarded Apollonia with the title 'free city' for supporting him against Pompey the Great during the civil war in the 1st century BC, and sent his nephew Octavius, the future Emperor Augustus, to complete his studies here.

After a series of military and natural disasters (including an earthquake in the 3rd century that turned the river into a malarial swamp), the population moved southward to present-day Vlora, and by the 5th century only a small village with its own bishop remained at Apollonia. These days the site is only inhabited by archaeologists and tourists.

Sights

There's far less to see here than at Butrint, but there are some picturesque ruins within the 4km of city walls, including a small original **theatre** and the elegant pillars on the **restored facade** of the city's 2nd-century administrative centre.

The 3rd-century BC House of Mosaics is closed off to the public, and the mosaics have been covered in sand to protect them from the elements.

Inside the **Museum of Apollonia** complex is the **Byzantine monastery** and **Church of St Mary**, which has fascinating gargoyles on the outside pillars. Many of the museum's displays are not ready yet, but interesting and ancient statues are displayed in the church garden and cloisters and labelled in Albanian.

Much of the site remains to be excavated and more recent discoveries include a **necropolis** outside the castle walls, with graves from the Bronze and Iron Ages.

There are a couple of restaurants on the ancient site.

Getting There & Away

Apollonia is best visited on a day trip from Tirana, Durrës, Vlora or Berat, as there's nothing of interest in nearby Fier. The lack of public transport to the site means that you will have to get a bus, *furgon* or train to Fier first. The bus from Durrës costs 200 lekë (1½ hours), and it's 300 lekë from Tirana (two hours). A *furgon* will take about an hour from Berat (500 lekë, 50km) or Vlora (200 lekë, 39km). The train from Tirana (175 lekë, 4½ hours) comes via Durrës. Once in Fier, find a taxi. You should expect to be charged around 2500 lekë for a return journey (15 minutes each way) and an hour's waiting time.

BERAT

☎ 032 / pop 45,500

A highlight of any trip to Albania, Berat is one of the country's most beautiful towns, having been preserved as a museum city by the former communist government. Its most striking feature is the collection of white Ottoman houses climbing up the hill to the castle, earning it the title 'town of a thousand windows'. It joined Gjirokastra in the Unesco ranks in 2008. Its rugged mountain setting is particularly evocative when the clouds swirl

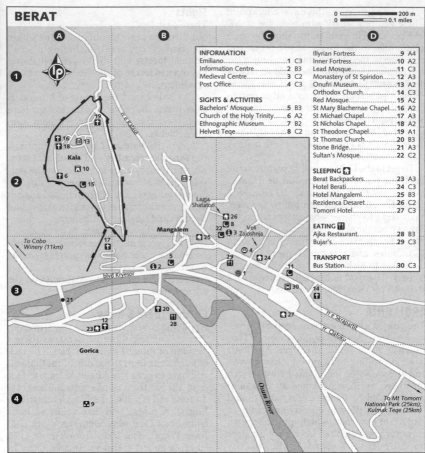

BERAT

around the tops of the minarets, or break up to show the icy top of Mt Tomorri.

The old quarters are lovely ensembles of whitewashed walls, tiled roofs and old stone walls guarding courtyards shaded by grapevines. Surrounding the town, olive and cherry trees decorate the gentler slopes, while pine woods stand on the steeper inclines. In the usual 'religious harmony' style of Albania, an elegant mosque with a pencil minaret is partnered on the main square by a large new Orthodox church. The centre of town and the newer outlying areas along the river flats are less attractive, as they feature housing blocks of rectilinear concrete.

In the 3rd century BC an Illyrian fortress called Antipatrea was built here on the site of an earlier settlement. The Byzantines strengthened the hilltop fortifications in the 5th and 6th centuries, as did the Bulgarians 400 years later. The Serbs, who occupied the citadel in 1345, renamed it Beligrad, or 'White City'. In 1450 the Ottoman Turks took the town. After a period of decline, in the 18th and 19th centuries the town began to thrive as a crafts centre specialising in woodcarving.

For a brief time in 1944 Berat was the capital of liberated Albania.

Information

Berat is in the midst of a tourism transformation. Audio guides to the sights are available for hire from the Medieval Centre, behind the

Sultan's Mosque. There are plenty of ATMs and banks lining the main boulevard.
Albanien Reisen (☎ 0693604259; info@berati-tours .com) This German-Albanian husband-and-wife team organises return trips through southern Albania and can arrange tours to Mt Tomorrt National Park. They're usually only in town in summer.
Emiliano (per hr 100 lekë; ☽ 9am-midnight) Decent internet cafe next to Pro Credit Bank on the main *xhiro* strip.
Information centre (☎ 38 500; blvd Krysor) In the Mangalem quarter; organises tours in and around town.
Post office (rr e Kalasë)

Sights
KALA
There's plenty to see in Berat and you can start by taking a 15-minute walk up to the impressive 14th-century **Citadel** (Kalasa; admission 100 lekë; ☽ 24hr). The neighbourhood inside the walls, Kala, still lives and breathes; you'll see old Mercedes-Benz cars struggling to get up the cobblestone roads to return locals home. If you walk around this busy, ancient neighbourhood for long enough you'll invariably stumble into someone's courtyard thinking it's a church or ruin (no one seems to mind, though). In spring and summer the fragrance of chamomile is in the air (and underfoot), and other wildflowers seem to burst from every gap between the stones.

Kala was traditionally a Christian neighbourhood, but less than a dozen of the 20 churches remain. The quarter's biggest church, **Church of the Dormition of St Mary** (Kisha Fjetja e Shën Mërisë) only holds one service a year, and is now the site of the **Onufri Museum** (Muzeu Onufri; ☎ 32 248; admission 200 lekë; ☽ 9am-4pm winter, 9am-1pm & 4pm-7pm summer, closed Mon). The church itself dates from 1797 but was built on the foundations of a 10th-century church. The building makes a lovely museum, and Onufri's spectacular 16th-century artworks are displayed on the ground level along with a beautifully gilded iconostasis.

It's tough to actually see inside the other churches in Kala, unless you're lucky enough to find the various keyholders. Ask at the Onufri Museum to see the other churches and tiny chapels in Kala, including **St Theodore** (Shën Todher), close to the citadel gates; the substantial and picturesque **Church of the Holy Trinity** (Kisha Shën Triades), below the upper fortress; and the little chapels of **St Mary Blachernae** (Shën Mëri Vllaherna) and **St Nicholas** (Shënkolli). Some of the churches date

back to the 13th century. Also keep an eye out for the **Red Mosque**, which was the first in Berat and dates back to the 15th century.

The rest of Berat and the Osum valley look quite spectacular from Kala. The highest point of the citadel is occupied by the **Inner Fortress**, where ruined stairs lead to a Tolkienesque water reservoir (take a torch/flashlight). Perched on a cliff ledge below the citadel is the artfully positioned little chapel of **St Michael** (Shën Mihell), which is best viewed from the Gorica quarter.

Down from the castle is Berat's **Ethnographic Museum** (Muzeu Etnografik; ☎ 32 224; admission 200 lekë; ☽ 9am-4pm Tue-Sat, to 2pm Sun winter, 9am-1pm & 4-7pm Tue-Sat, 9am-2pm Sun summer). It's based in an 18th-century Ottoman house, which is as interesting as the exhibits. The ground floor has displays of traditional clothes and the tools used by silversmiths and weavers, while the upper storey has kitchens, bedrooms and guest rooms decked out in traditional style. Check out the *mafil*, a kind of mezzanine looking into the lounge where the women of the house could keep an eye on male guests being entertained (and see when their cups needed to be filled). Brochures are available, but to get the most out of it, ask for a guided tour.

MANGALEM
Down in the traditionally Muslim Mangalem quarter there are three grand mosques. The 16th-century **Sultan's Mosque** (Xhamia e Mbretit) is one of the oldest in Albania. The **Helveti teqe** behind the mosque has a beautiful carved ceiling and was especially designed with acoustic holes to improve the sound for meetings held there. The Helveti, like the Bektashi (p57), are a dervish order or brotherhood of Muslim mystics. Staff at the neighbouring Medieval Centre should have the keys.

The big mosque on the town square is the 16th-century **Lead Mosque** (Xhamia e Plumbit), so named because of the lead coating its sphere-shaped domes. The 19th-century **Bachelors' Mosque** (Xhamia e Beqarëvet) is down by the Osum River; you only really notice it because of the enchanting paintings on its external walls. This mosque was built for unmarried shop assistants and junior craftsmen. There are some fine Ottoman-era shopfronts alongside, as well as the information centre.

GORICA

While the seven-arched **stone bridge** (1780) was once the only way to get to Gorica, there are now two more bridges: a new footbridge (leading to Berat's centre) and a modern car bridge. Gorica is another Christian quarter, and is home to the old, but large and still used **Monastery of St Spiridon** with its half-whitewashed frescos, as well as the little church of **St Thomas** (Shën Tomi), next to the new footbridge, which has sadly lost its frescos altogether. When you're here, great views of Kala and the Mangalem quarter's houses stretch before you.

Gorica is tucked under a steep hillside and never sees the sun in winter (it's also one of the coolest places to be in summer). It's a tough, unmarked walk up to the negligible remains of an old **Illyrian fortress** in the woods above Gorica.

Sleeping & Eating

our pick **Hotel Mangalemi** (Hotel Tomi; ☎ 32 093, 0682429803; rr e Kalasë; s/d €17/25) This sprawling Ottoman house is home to the best budget B&B in Albania. Tomi Mio (it's also called Hotel Tomi locally) and his family run a great hotel with a restaurant on the ground floor and a clutch of warm, cosy rooms upstairs, plus a terrace with great views across Berat over to Mt Tomorri. Kind hospitality, tasty food (order by the organ), decent plumbing – does it get any better? It's on the street up to Kala from the main square.

Berat Backpackers (☎ 0693064429; www.beratbackpackers; Gorica; dm €12; ☺ summer) This brand-new backpackers with dorm rooms and camping spots (€6) is located next to the Monastery of St Spiridon and has wonderful views over the castle.

Rezidenca Desaret (☎ 37 593; Lagja Shatatori 13; s/d €20/25) The Desaret has five modern rooms, all individually designed, with great views of the Mangalem quarter. Take the road up to the castle, then follow the signs at the first right past the Sultan's Mosque. The building was designed to resemble an Ottoman-style house.

Tomorri Hotel (☎ 34 462; fax 34 602; s/d €30/50) This tower-block hotel was built in 1975 and has clean rooms that overlook either the citadel or the mountains. It's on the main square by the bus station.

Hotel Berati (☎ 36 953; rr Veli Zaloshnja; dm 1000 lekë, s/d 1800/2000 lekë) This traditional-style building just off rr e Kalasë is hemmed in by modern buildings, and although the restaurant boasts traditional wood-carved ceilings, the rooms are more reminiscent of a fascination with concrete. It's made brighter by old photos of Berat on the walls.

Ajka Restaurant (☎ 34 034; Gorica; meals 800 lekë; ☺ 9am-late) This substantial restaurant is run by an Armenian family whose ancestors settled in Albania early in the 20th century. The restaurant has a lovely setting above the Osum River, looking over the houses of the Mangalem quarter. Pizzas cost around 400 lekë, and a substantial mixed meze platter costs 500 lekë. It also serves grilled dishes and ice cream.

Bujar's (meals 200 lekë; ☺ 9am-9pm) In the *markati* (market) area between the two main roads in the lower town you might be able to find this simple cafe with wonderful home-style meals. The restaurant doesn't have a menu, just a selection of daily offerings. There's a small sign on the single-storey light-blue building in the lane behind the Shpëtimi Bar.

Getting There & Away

Buses and *furgons* run between Tirana and Berat (400 lekë, 2½ hours). From Tirana, buses leave from the Kombinati station (catch the municipal bus from Sheshi Skënderbej to Kombinati for 30 lekë). In Berat, all bus services depart and arrive at the bus station next to the Lead Mosque. *Furgons* leave when full (roughly one an hour) for Tirana until about 4pm. From Berat there are nine buses a day running to Vlora (300 lekë, 2½ hours), three buses a day to Saranda via Gjirokastra (1000 lekë, six hours, 8am, 9.30am and 1.30pm) and one to Gjirokastra (700 lekë, five hours).

One of the most bizarre sights in Albania is on the road from Fier to Berat. Look out for a resplendent concrete replica of a ship on the left-hand side of the road.

AROUND BERAT

Sample the 'white of Berat' (*e bardha e Beratit*) at **Çobo Winery** (☎ 0682070562; www.cobowinery.com; Vajgurore; bottles 400-900 lekë) and celebrate that, after 45 years of silence, Çobo's vines have come to life again. The family will show you around the impressive winery and offer tastings. Of course there's the Çobo version of the 'special natural digestive drink' (*raki*) for sale, too.

Mt Tomorri National Park is Albania's biggest nature reserve. The mountain is some 20km long and 6km wide, and its highest peak of 2415m is visible from Berat and almost always covered in snow. Tomorri has been a holy mountain since pagan times, and is the Albanian equivalent of Mt Olympus. On its southern peak is an important Bektashi shrine, the **Kulmak teqe**, with the grave of the Bektashi saint Abaz Aliu. People head here in droves in August for a huge festival. The roads up to the mountain are pretty hairy and require a 4WD and an experienced guide. Contact Albanien Reisen (p77) for information on getting to the park. If they're not available, try asking at the Medieval Centre in Berat.

ELBASAN
☎ 054 / pop 100,700

Apart from visiting the local **Ethnographic Museum** (Muzeu Etnografik; ☎ 59 626; ☼ 9am-3pm Mon-Fri) and checking out the walls of Elbasan castle along blvd Qemal Stafa, there's little to do in this flat university town. However, travel 15 minutes out of town and you'll find the perfect chill-out spot. Hotel Iliria's **Qender Termale Kurative** (☎ 058-38 0640; www .termaliliria.com; cabins 2200 lekë), just before the town of Llixha, is a green oasis for dust-covered souls. Make yourself at home in a wood cabin perched by the milk-coloured, egg-smelling stream, and breathe deeply. The bargain rates include a horizontal 10-minute stint in a bath full of 'curative' thermal water. The restaurant serves up generous grilled-meat dishes (800 lekë) and will rustle up a breakfast if you ask nicely. The public bus to Llixha (50 lekë) runs regularly; it departs from the south side of Elbasan and stops right outside Hotel Iliria.

In Elbasan, *furgons* to Korça and Pogradec leave from Stadium Ruzhdi, while buses and *furgons* to Tirana or Durrës (300 lekë, one hour 10 minutes) leave from the clock tower.

POGRADEC
☎ 083 / pop 40,000

This 'border town' is much more cosmopolitan than those words give rise to, with plenty of hotels, lake-swimming spots and fresh fish galore (but stay away from Ohrid's endangered trout; see the boxed text, p288). There are tonnes of ATMs and a handy,

central **internet cafe/tourism office** (☎ 22 608; www .explorepogradec.com; rr Reshit Collaku; per hr 100 lekë; ☼ 9am-11pm). If you arrive from the Macedonia border you'll pass through Drilon; look out for 'Vila Art', Enver Hoxha's former summer residence and nature reserve. It's now a hotel and restaurant and a nice spot to hang out for a while. A good place to stay close to Pogradec is **Perla Hotel** (☎ 24 862; rr Per ne Drilon; s/d €20/35). It has clean, bright rooms with massive bed-heads and oversized couches. The showers are sparkling and have shower curtains, and the indoor trees and ferns look great. There's also a good cafe and restaurant in front.

If you get the chance to get up close and personal with Lin (the picturesque lakeside town you first spot when heading down the hill from Tirana), you'll be on Lake Ohrid's only peninsula. Look out for some frescos here as well.

Getting There & Away
Outside summer it's a €5 taxi ride along the 4km to the border (or an easy walk along the lake), but during summer you can catch a *furgon* for 100 lekë. Buses to Durrës leave Pogradec's bus station at 11.45am and 2.45pm and *furgons* ply the road to and from Tirana and Korça half-hourly. The train station is a fair hike from the centre of town, so hail a passing *furgon* to get you the rest of the way, or enjoy the walk along Lake Ohrid.

KORÇA
☎ 082 / pop 58,000

Korça boasts five museums, a beer factory and plenty of snow in winter (made the most of by the ski resort in Dardha, 20km away). Its crown of 'little Paris' fell off after its cultural peak in the 1930s, but it still claims a cinema (in the good old days it had two), a famous pie and a history of serenades. Some cafes and restaurants display New York–trained local photographer Sotiri's images of the town's grander days. There's a busy traditional-style bazaar next to the bus station where goats are sold and carried off like handbags. There are several banks and internet cafes along the main street (blvd Republika), and the town's library has free internet access. Korça is the starting point for the dramatic route along the Greece border down to Gjirokastra and is a good base to explore the city-turned-village of Voskopoja.

Orieta Glozheni operates an **information centre** (Gulliver OK; ☎ 0684023780; zrt_korca@yahoo.com; blvd Gjergi Kastrioti), organises cultural tours (including walking tours), and has loads of information, brochures and maps on the region.

Sights

The **Museum of Albanian Medieval Art** (Muzeu i Artit Mesjetar; ☎ 43 022; rr Stefan Luarasi; admission 200 lekë; ☺ 8.30am-2.30pm & 5-7.30pm Mon-Fri, 9am-noon & 5-7pm Sat & Sun) is a treasury of religious art collected from churches sacked during Albania's cultural revolution. There are no plans to return the works to their old locations; instead they remain preserved here. The gallery has an astonishing array of icons from the 13th to the 19th centuries alongside silver bible covers, grails, crucifixes and two complete carved iconostases. The museum opened in 1980 on the site of an Orthodox cathedral that was dynamited in 1968 during the cultural revolution. To find it, face the new Orthodox cathedral, head left for two blocks along blvd Republika, then turn right and head 150m uphill into the old town, and look for the imposing white Episcopal Residence on a little square; the museum is in the light-brown three-storey building next to the bishop's house.

The **National Archaeological Museum** (Muzeu Arkeologjik; Mihal Grameno; admission 100 lekë; ☺ 8am-2pm Mon-Thu, to noon Fri) houses 1200 objects dating from the Hellenic period. The new **Orthodox cathedral** (blvd Republika) is a striking confection in pink, blue and brown. From Hotel Grand head past the first school in Albania (Educational Museum) and you can't miss it. The oriental facade of the **Bratko Museum** (rr Fan Noli) is hard to miss; inside is mostly Asian art collected on the journeys of Korça-born and once American-based expat Bratko.

One of Korça's newest finds is 3km out of town: the **Tomb of Kamenica**. This prehistoric cemetery contains a rare skeleton of a pregnant woman and her unborn child c 3000 BC. Unless there's a small group of you that can hire a *furgon*, a return taxi to the site costs 2000 lekë.

Sleeping

Hotel Gold (☎ 46 894; rr Kiço Golniku 5; r 3000-3500 lekë) This is the best option in town, with clean rooms, TVs and heating, and en suite bathrooms. The more expensive rooms have balconies. From the post office walk along blvd Gjergj Kastrioti towards Stadiumi Skënderbeu and look out for the sign. It's on the cobblestone road to the left.

Hotel George (☎ 43 794; rr Korça-Mborrje; s/d €20/40) Up past the Korça beer factory is cylindrical Hotel George, one of the friendliest choices in town, with good food, an outdoor bar and a range of good-value rooms (although the cheaper single rooms can be a bit cell-like).

Hotel Grand (☎ 43 168; grandhotelko@hotmail.com; s/d/ste €21/34/50) It's conveniently located on the central square around the corner from the bus station, but the Grand's grand foyer leads to disappointing rooms. It's an extra €10 per room for a non–concrete wall view.

Eating

Taverna Vasili (rr Konstandin Gaçe; meals 1100 lekë) Located on the opposite side of blvd Gjergj Kastiroti to Hotel Gold, this formal restaurant has tasty Korçan meals prepared in front of you in the massive grill, or head downstairs for a cosy basement setting. The soup's great and the mixed grill will totally confuse your tastebuds. Its walls feature wonderful images of an icy, wintry Korça.

Taverna Qilari (rr Bardhyl Pajani 8; mains 500-600 lekë; ☺ 1pm-midnight) This converted basement does a great job of resembling an ethnographic museum, and its owners serve up great local dishes including the local spicy, meaty delight *kernace*.

Birra Korça (rr Fan Noli; mains 600 lekë; ☺ 10am-11pm) Popular because its beer is the cheapest in town, this restaurant–beer garden (attached to Birra Korça's fully automated brewery) does a roaring trade, watering the (male) masses with jug after jug of local beer and feeding them up with local sausage specialities as well as chips, bread and roast chicken. Security will give you a tour of the beer factory if you ask at the factory's gate.

Getting There & Away

Buses to Tirana (700 lekë, six hours) and Saranda/Gjirokastra (1000 lekë, eight hours) leave from the bus station behind the post office. Check departure times the day before as buses to Saranda leave daily at 6am, 7am or 8am depending on the season. *Furgons* start darting around the city at 5am, heading in all directions, but by day *furgons* heading to Tirana (800 lekë, four hours) via Pogradec

THE LONG & WINDING KORÇA–GJIROKASTRA ROAD

The road to Gjirokastra is awe inspiring. The trip certainly has its moments, and one of the first ones is when you notice the conductor handing out sick bags. This epic journey (1000 lekë, six to seven hours) takes you from Korça to Gjirokastra via alpine plains, pine forests, bunker-pocked mountainsides and to the source of Albania's Tepelenë bottled water before hitting the main road to Tirana and curving to Gjirokastra. The bottled water, available throughout the country, is advertised as the 'Water of the Albanian National Football Team', and, according to the English translation on the packaging, it is 'Suffled how it gush from the source of the woods of Tepelena'. This journey takes you right past the very woods where it's 'suffled'.

The journey begins with a slow climb along the Greece border to the highland town of Erseka, about one hour south of Korça. Soon you're in the midst of wild pine forests and cutting along the edge of the Grammoz mountains, before crossing the Barmash Pass (1759m). After the village of Leskoviku the road turns west into raw inner-Albania and descends into the spectacular narrow valley of the Vjosa River to Përmet. Following the gorge of the Vjosa, the road then turns up the Drinos valley to Gjirokastra. There are a few accommodation options en route, including a small hotel called the **Jorgos** (☎ 0821-2700; r €20) about 45 minutes south of Erseka, with a restaurant. Daily buses leave Saranda and Korça in the morning (between 6am and 8am), and pass Gjirokastra's new town en route.

(200 lekë, one hour) congregate on rr e Tiranë. *Furgons* head to Voskopoja at 10am and 1pm each day (100 lekë, 40 minutes) from behind the bazaar near the bus station.

For Greece there are daily buses to Thessaloniki (€20, seven hours); buses to Athens (€35, 16 hours) leave at noon on Sunday, Monday, Thursday and Friday. Buy your tickets from any of the ticket offices around town.

You can take a *furgon* to the border at Kapshtica for 300 lekë to 400 lekë, but a Greek taxi from the Albania–Greece border to Florina or Kastoria alone will cost you between €15 and €30. There are only two or three (inconveniently timed) local buses daily linking the Greek border village of Krystallopigi with Florina, and none to Kastoria. The direct international bus from Korça is by far the best option; the trip to either Florina or Kastoria takes less than two hours.

VOSKOPOJA

It's impossible to believe that in 1764 Voskopoja was the biggest city in the Balkans, with a population of 30,000 and 24 churches. Today this village, 40 minutes' drive from Korça, has a population of a couple of hundred (roughly half Muslim Albanian and half Orthodox Vlach) after repeated sackings and lootings as recently as WWII. Some piles of grey rubble around the village only hint at the scale of the town when it was at its peak, before Ali Pasha of Tepelena (see p52) sacked it in 1788.

Still, it's a nice town, and certainly worth visiting for its churches, of which eight remain. Some have church murals painted by the Zografi brothers Konstantin and Athanas and they're still in superb condition. **St Michael** (Shën Mihali), **St Nicholas** (Shënkolli) and **St Athanasius** (Shën Athanasi) are scattered between old stone houses and around neighbouring fields. About 3km out of town, up a dirt track across the river, the **Monastery of St Prodhomi** nestles in the woods. At the time of research it was being renovated, but the walk to it is pleasant and the views from the monastery are superb.

St Thanasit's incredible apocalyptic frescos are being restored after some depressing years during which the building was used as a magazine; it's the church on the small hill on your right as you return to the town from the monastery. Even if it's not open, the outside frescos are quite brilliant (if a little disturbing).

There's quite a little industry of homestay-like accommodation in Voskopoja, and for 1000 lekë per person they are a good deal. Ask at the cafes and restaurants in town for information. Small hotels are bursting out of the pine forests, but if you prefer your hotel mammoth size, try **Hotel Akademia Voskopoja** (☎ 0692258646; r & cabins €30), which is about 2km out of Voskopoja on the way to the Monastery of St Prodhomi. It's an uphill walk/drive along a rough road. This former communist student camp is a mix of hunting lodge and private school; three large buildings surround a large grassed courtyard with a nonschool-like bar and chairs and tables. It's a bit of a surprise to find such a nice place in this isolated spot. Try to set up home in one of the timber cabins with open fires if you can. The restaurant upstairs in the main building is quite impressive, too, although a little reminiscent of a mess hall.

From Voskopoja town *furgon*s head down (and around some precarious corners) to Korça (100 lekë, 40 minutes) at 1pm and 4pm. Otherwise, it's easy to hire a taxi for a day trip from Korça.

THE SOUTH & THE IONIAN COAST

Is Albania's Ionian coast Europe's next hot spot? It's hard to say, but it's easy to see that the area between Llogaraja Pass National Park and Saranda, where rough mountains fall headfirst into bright blue seas, is ready for a lot more exploration. Some of the south's beaches are jam-packed in August, but outside the peak season you'll probably get entire beaches to yourself. With careful planning by local governments, these areas could shine. Accommodation and restaurant options have boomed, thanks mostly to the growth in both Italian and home-grown tourists. Saranda is home to day trippers from Greece's Corfu, and may soon attract a different clientele if the planned Club Med opens nearby. In the meantime, if the rubbish lying next to you on the beach gets you down, you only have to bend your neck a bit to see the snowcapped mountain peaks and wide green valleys zigzagged by rivers around you. There are still secret, untouched beaches here.

Getting There & Around
If you're planning on spending more than a few days on the Ionian beaches and you're travelling by bus, you'll quickly get used to the local bus timetables. There are usually three or four buses a day travelling the entire Vlora–Saranda route (1000 lekë, six hours), via Llogaraja Pass and Himara. At Llogaraja, the best place to be dropped off is at the Tourist Village, 1km from the summit. Neither buses nor *furgon*s stop at the actual beaches in Dhërmi, Jal (Vuno's beach),

Qeparo or Borsh; all require a walk (usually though beautiful olive groves) or taxi ride.

There are quite a few *furgon*s in the busy summer months, but out of season there are only a few each day, most starting at the crack of dawn. Since services are all but over in the afternoon, many travellers take the risk of hitchhiking or throw away any notion of a schedule and take as much time as it takes.

From Saranda you can pick up a timetable from the information centre and from that estimate what time the bus will pass through the town you're in.

VLORA
☎ 033 / pop 124,000

It's here in sunny Vlora (the ancient Aulon) that the Adriatic Sea meets the Ionian. The beaches are muddy and grubby, but it's a bustling little port city. A long (1.5km) palm-lined avenue stretches from the port and its independence museum through the centre of town to the mosque, bus station and grand independence monument. The outstanding independence and ethnographic museums deserve a few hours' exploration, and a quick hike up the hill to Kuzum Baba behind the bus station is rewarded with good views. The city's 'wild town' label comes from its drug- and people-trafficking days (speedboats used to boldly wait in the harbour for their cargo) and the revolution after the 1997 collapse of the pyramid schemes began here.

Information
Everything you'll need in Vlora is on rr Sadik Zotaj, including ATMs, the post office and the telephone centre.

Colombo Travel Agency (☎ 27 659; www.colombo alb.com; Hotel Sazani, Sheshi i Flamurit; ☷ 8am-7pm) On the hotel's ground floor, near Muradi mosque, this helpful agency sells ferry tickets to Italy. Check to see if it's offering yacht tours; whether they run depends on the rules and regulations of the time.

Internet Café Studenti (rr Kullat Skele 2; per hr 100 lekë; ☷ 7am-midnight) Just off rr Sadik Zotaj, this is the best place to get online. The cafe next door does great crepes, too.

Sights
Start at **Sheshi i Flamurit** (Flag Sq), near the top of rr Sadik Zotaj. The magnificently socialist-realist **independence monument** stands proud against the sky with the flag-bearer hoisting the double-headed eagle into the blue. Near the base of

NARTA LAGOON & MONASTERY OF ST MARY

About 6km north of Vlora is the **Narta Lagoon**, with salt pans on the landward side separated by a dyke from a calm expanse of water closer to the sea. The lagoon attracts water birds in their thousands. Another 4km on, the **Monastery of St Mary** (Shën Mëri; Zvernëcl) occupies a wooded island reached by a wooden boardwalk from the mainland. The church is a modest little country construction with some battered frescos but, combined with the other monastery buildings, it's a very peaceful spot. A return taxi trip from Vlora (10km each way) will cost you 2000 lekë. There's a pilgrimage here every August with feasting and dancing. The road out to Zvernëci passes through neighbourhoods that harboured illegal immigrants during the 1990s – speedboats laden with Kurds, Chinese and marijuana used to zip across the 75km Straits of Otranto to Italy almost nightly.

the monument lies the grave of local Ismail Qemali, the country's first prime minister.

On the other side of the avenue is the **History Museum** (Muzeu Historik; Sheshi i Flamurit; admission 100 lekë; 8am-2pm & 5-8pm), displaying a collection of items dating from the 4th century BC up to WWII. Opposite, behind an inconspicuous metal fence, is the amazing home that houses the excellent **Ethnographic Museum** (Sheshi i Flamurit; admission 100 lekë; 9am-2pm Mon-Sat).

Walk down towards the 16th-century **Muradi mosque**, a small, elegant structure made of red and white stone and with a modest minaret; its exquisite design is attributed to one of the greatest Ottoman architects, Albanian-born Sinan Pasha. The hill overlooking the town is topped by the Bektashi **shrine of Kuzum Baba**. The well-kept gardens, bars and restaurants up here have great views over the Bay of Vlora and you can just spot Narta Lagoon in the distance.

Down by the harbour the **National Museum of Independence** (admission 200 lekë; 9am-1pm & 5-8pm Mon-Sat, 9am-noon & 5-8pm Sun) is housed in the villa that became the headquarters of Albania's first government in 1912. If you're lucky you'll get a passionate pro-independence guided tour; otherwise, the preserved offices, historic photographs and famous balcony still make it an interesting place to learn about Albania's short-lived, but long-remembered, 1912 independence.

Vlora's main beaches stretch south from the harbour, and the further you go, the better they get. Turn left before the harbour to reach Plazhi i Ri, a long public beach that can get quite crowded. Apparently new sand is trucked in each year. A good 2km walk away, **Uji i Ftohtë** (meaning 'cold water') is a better beach choice. It has open-air bars and discos during summer, and plenty of private beaches (where someone actually picks up

the rubbish). You'll need to hire a sun bed and umbrella for 200 lekë per person. Orange municipal buses run from rr Sadik Zotaj to the Uji i Ftohtë post office (20 lekë, 10 minutes, every 15 minutes from 7am to 9pm).

Sleeping & Eating

Hotel Alpin (0692241198; r 2500 leke) This new hotel next to the bus station is named after its owner's passion: climbing Albania's alps. The rooms are spotless and modern, with large bathrooms and excellent beds.

Hotel Vlora International (24 408; www.vlora international.com; rr Sadik Zotaj; s/d €50/60;) Perched by the port, this luxury hotel has modern, comfortable rooms with flat-screen TVs, a fitness centre, an indoor pool and a restaurant.

Hotel Konomi (29 320; rr e Uji i Ftohtë; r 2000 lekë) On the top of a hill with views of the party end of town, this stark former workers' camp has the whiff of socialist idealism in its tatty sheets and dirty bathrooms. It's a short hike up from the last bus stop along the beach road.

Xhokla (Plazhi i Ri; mains 200-1000 lekë) Attentive staff, great Italian food and a good variety of wines make this the best restaurant in town. Being on Vlora's beachfront *xhiro* route makes for great people watching, too.

Belvedere (rr e Uji i Ftohtë; mains 400 lekë; 24hr) One of a few woodfired pizza options near Hotel New York and Vlora's road tunnel, the Belvedere is popular with families. Being a '24 ore' restaurant, it's popular with late-night summer crowds, too.

Getting There & Away

It's easy getting to Vlora from Tirana (bus/*furgon* 500/600 lekë, three/two hours) and Durrës (bus/*furgon* 500 lekë, three hours), with buses and *furgons* whizzing back and forth in the morning hours. Buses from Vlora to Saranda (1000 lekë, six hours) and on to Gjirokastra (1300 lekë, seven hours) leave at 5am, 7am, 1pm and 2pm. There are nine buses a day to Berat (300 lekë, two hours). In Vlora buses leave from rr Rakip Malilaj, although departures to Athens and Italy depart from the Muradi mosque.

There's one train a day from Tirana to Vlora (2.50pm) and from Vlora to Tirana at 5.40am (250 lekë, five hours) via Durrës (210 lekë, four hours). Ferries from Vlora to Brindisi, Italy, take around six hours. There's a departure from Brindisi at 11pm and Vlora at noon Monday to Saturday (deck €35 to €70). You can book tickets through Colombo Travel Agency (p82).

Getting Around

The orange municipal buses to Uji i Ftohtë make getting around town easy; they travel from Muradi mosque to Uji i Ftohtë every 15 minutes (20 lekë, 10 minutes) from 7am to 9pm. Taxis at the terminus can take you to a beach or hotel further along.

LLOGARAJA PASS NATIONAL PARK

Reaching the pine tree–clad Llogaraja Pass National Park (1027m) is one of the special moments of Albanian travel. If you've been soaking up the sun on the Ionian coast it seems impossible that after a steep hairpin-bend climb you're up in the mountains tucking into spit-roasted lamb and homemade wine, miles from rocky beaches. There's great scenery up here, including the Pisha Flamur (flag tree) – a tree in the shape of the Albanian flag, which is registered as a natural monument. Watch clouds descending onto the mountain, shepherds on the plains guiding their herds, and thick forests where deer, wild boar and wolves roam. If you find the **Tourist Village** (Fshati Turistik; ☎ 0693344400; chalets 8000 lekë; ☻) a little too Disneyesque, check out the resident deer before heading across the road to the cute cabins run by the family at **Hotel Andoni** (☎ 0682400929; cabins 4000 lekë). They do a wonderful lamb roast, too (800 lekë).

DHËRMI

As you zigzag down the mountain from Llogaraja Pass National Park, white crescent beaches and azure waters lure you from below. The first beach along the coast is around the alluvial fan at the foot of the pass. There are no hotels here yet, but if you have your own transport it's a wonderfully isolated spot to visit.

Next is Drymades (below), followed closely by Dhërmi (Dhërmiu). Dhërmi is under the tourist trance, as ferry-loads of Italians arrive almost daily, and Tirana-based Albanians and expats pack the beaches, bars and restaurants on the weekend. The beach is about 2km below the Vlora–Saranda road, so ask the conductor to stop at the turnoff on the Llogaraja side of the village. From here, make your own way down to the beach, which is an easy 10-minute walk downhill (not so easy on the way back though). The hillside town itself is quiet, although there are a few sights to see, including the whitewashed church of St Mary (Shën Mëri), which stands on the hill above the village.

Sleeping & Eating

Hotel Luçiano (☎ 0692091431; Dhërmi beach; per person 1000 lekë; ☻) The best place to stay and eat. The water is metres away, the views are sublime, rooms are simple but comfortable, and the staff are busy but helpful. There's a popular restaurant here too, with plenty of pasta choices and good woodfired pizzas (300 lekë). They'll arrange a simple breakfast for you, too. Turn left at the bottom of the hill.

Mena's House (☎ 0684055221; Dhërmi beach; r 3500-5000 lekë; ☼ May-Sep; ☻) On the Himara end of Dhërmi beach (look out for the garishly painted bunkers out front), Mena's has a lively summer atmosphere, with speakers in the trees and a restaurant that serves Albanian meals.

Hotel Riviera (☎ 0682633333; Dhërmi beach; d €40-60; ☻) The Riviera's had a leopard-skin-curtain makeover and is now truly focused on too-cool-for-school orange, lime-green and brown walls. The new futon-style beds and flat-screen TVs make it all acceptable. An ubercool bar is perched on the water's edge.

Toneda (☎ 0692682451; Dhërmi beach; cabins €30; ☻) Further along towards Vlora, the Toneda has clean and comfortable wooden cabins with compact bathrooms and balconies.

Getting There & Away

Buses heading for Vlora can be hailed from the main road at around 6.30am, 7am, 9am and 11am. Ask locally for times for Saranda-bound buses.

DRYMADES & AROUND

Just after the beginning of the walk down to Dhërmi beach is the dirt road to Drymades beach. Turn right and a 45-minute walk through olive groves brings you to this much quieter option where a white virgin beach (albeit with bunkers) stretches before you. You can stay in a cabin, camp, or simply sleep under the stars on the beach. **Drymades Hotel** (☎ 0682285637; cabins 4000 lekë, campsites 500 lekë) is a constellation of cabins and rooms under the shade of pine trees just a step away from the blue sea. There's a bar, a restaurant and a shaded playground, plus a cool beach bar with a straw roof.

Jal beach is an isolated spot 9km down from the charming roadside village of **Vuno**, 8km south of Dhërmi. During summer Tirana Backpackers turns Vuno's school into **South Hostel** (Shkolla; www.tiranahostel.com; dm 800 lekë). It's a long walk down to the beach at Jal or a 400-lekë taxi ride. Jal is bearing the scars of 'development police' who bulldozed 'illegal' constructions and left the mess behind. A military hotel occupies a prominent spot on the cove. If it seems a bit visually polluted, try the small section of beach to the right, where the only view is of the clear water and ice-white pebbles.

HIMARA
☎ 0393 / pop 4500
This sleepy town has fine beaches, a couple of great Greek tavernas, some high-tech, good-looking hotels and an interesting old town. Most of the ethnic Greek population left in the '90s, but many have returned. The lower town comprises three easily accessible rocky beaches, the town's hotels and restaurants. The main Vlora–Saranda route passes the entrance to the castle and, as in Berat, many residents still call it home. A taxi to the castle from Himara costs 300 lekë. From the top you can take in the superb views of Livadhi beach and check out some frescos in the old churches. You can't miss spotting one of Albania's best top-end resorts, **Rapos Resort** (☎ 22 856; www.raposresorthotel.com; d €65-90; 🏊), on the right as you head out of town. The interior decorators have been hard at work: the rooms are full of distinct patterns, defined edges and mood lighting. Outside is no different; there's plenty of marble, stone and glass and a huge pool/bar area. It is a few kilometres from the heart of things, but its upmarket restaurant won't leave you hungry.

Right in the thick of it, **Manolo** (☎ 22 375; d €50) has spacious, glamorous studio apartment–style rooms above a cruisy bar-cafe down-

stairs. Expect floorboards, flat-screen TVs, candles and mosaic-decorated bathrooms. It's located near the port and opposite a nice stretch of beach.

Seafood feasts dominate the bright blue, Greek **Dimitri restaurant** (mains 600 lekë) on the second road back from the main street, near the main post office. Dishes include prawns, calamari and fish.

SOUTH FROM HIMARA
One good beach near Himara is Llaman, 2km away, which has the **Llaman Beach Bar-Restaurant** (☎ 0692412172; pizzas around 400 lekë; 🕐 Jun-Sep). It serves pizza, cold beer and grilled fish on a shaded terrace right on the beach.

Heading towards Saranda the next sight is **Porto Palermo**, an isolated, eye-catching bay with no development on its grassy hills bar a good fish restaurant and a 19th-century castle. The **castle** (admission 100 lekë) was built under Ali Pasha's rule on the foundations of an older fortress. There's some peculiar graffiti in this area and the small, rocky beach is a picturesque spot to cool down – just watch out for sea urchins. If you look carefully you can spot the submarine base in the peninsula, but, not surprisingly, it's off limits. The road then passes **Qeparo**. Half of this picturesque village is perched on cliffs below the main road, with step access down to the icy spring-fed sand, and olive trees meet the beach in the other half. For beachfront accommodation, walk through the olive groves to the vine-clad hotel and restaurant **Riviera** (☎ 0692313475; d 2000 lekë).

Fifteen minutes down the road is **Borsh**, where a rushing mountain stream passes under the main roadside cafe. Below the village there's a fertile plain with a 3km-long bunker-laden beach – the warmest spot in Albania, apparently. The owners of Borsh's cafe can help people find accommodation in village houses, or there are more options on the beach, including, right at the end, **Hotel Elizabeth** (☎ 0692382660; d 2000 lekë; 🍴). If you're planning on heading to the beach, hop off the bus at the petrol station in the valley. There's pleasant accommodation above the shop-bar nearby if you've got an early start.

Next along is the village of Piquerasi, and after 4km there's a turn-off to **Buneci beach**, which has a couple of restaurants. The road then climbs over a pass and loops around behind the mountains before reaching Saranda.

SARANDA

☎ 0852 / pop 32,000

Skeletal high-rises crowd around the horse-shoe-shaped mini city of Saranda, a result of the past few years' astounding level of development. Bar blackouts, a night view of the town shows just how few of the buildings are actually occupied. Despite this development, Saranda is still a pleasant town that is increasingly drawing mostly Albanian tourists into its sea. To make things interesting, a daily stream of Corfu holidaymakers takes the ferry trip to Albania, fills up on Butrint and the Blue Eye Spring and adds the Albanian stamp to their passports before heading back.

The town's name comes from an early monastery dedicated to 40 saints (Ayii Saranda); its bombed remains (including frescos) are still high on the hill above the town. The town was called Porto Edda for a period in the 1940s, after Mussolini's daughter. Saranda's stony beaches are quite decent for a town of this size, and the section near the port even has starting blocks and lanes.

Apart from the beach, Saranda has other attractions: a well-preserved mosaic bizarrely housed in an office complex, as well as a central 5th-century synagogue. The other sights are a bus or taxi trip out of the town itself: the mesmerising ancient archaeological site of Butrint (opposite), the hypnotic Blue Eye Spring (p88), and the Monastery of St Nicholas (p88). Between Saranda and Butrint the lovely beaches and islands of Ksamil (opposite) are perfect for a dip after a day of exploring.

Orientation & Information

Four main streets arc around Saranda's bay, including the waterfront promenade that becomes prime *xhiro* territory in the evening. There are six banks with ATMs along the sea road (rr 1 Maji) and the next street inland (rr Skënderbeu). Card phones abound; mobile-phone users can pick up Greek transmitters as well as Albanian ones. The main bus station is just uphill from the synagogue on rr Vangjel Pando.

Information centre (ZIT; rr Skënderbeu; ⏱ 8am-4pm Mon-Fri) This incredibly helpful centre provides bus timetables and maps.

Internet cafe (rr Milat Hoxha) Near the ferry port, opposite the old flour mill.

Meno's Internet Cafe (rr Skënderbeu; per hr 200 lekë; ⏱ 9am-midnight) Down some concrete steps near the municipal office.

Post office (☎ 23 45; rr Skënderbeu; ⏱ 8am-8pm Mon-Sat) Next to the stone steps that originate at the fishing port.

Sights

The most obvious sight in town is the 5th-century **synagogue** (rr Skënderbeu; ⏱ 24hr), evidence of one of the earliest Balkan-Jewish communities. In the 6th century it was converted to a Christian basilica. The on-site information cabin's hours vary – if it's unoccupied try the information centre across the road.

Hidden in an office building (complete with Venetian blinds) on rr Flamurit is the **Museum of Archaeology** (Muzeu Arkeologjik; ⏱ 9am-noon & 3-10pm). It is well worth visiting for the mosaic floor, which once would have graced the floor of a grand villa.

Sleeping & Eating

Accommodation prices in Saranda vary a lot according to the season: prices rise by about 30% on those given here in the busiest periods of July and August, and drop by 30% during the winter season. The rates are always negotiable, no matter what the time of year. Most of the 60-odd hotels in and around Saranda are in the one-star category and charge similar prices to the Hotel Republica. There are many more bars, cafes and restaurants around the centre of town than we've listed here, as well as several *burek* joints. With the building boom continuing, there are certain to be more still when you visit.

Hotel Grand (☎ 25 574; rr Sarande-Butrint 1; d €40; 🖳) Free wi-fi. This hotel takes up a fair whack of Saranda's eastern foreshore with its swimming pool, children's playground, bar and restaurant. Rooms are spacious, and rates include breakfast.

Hairy Lemon (☎ 0693559317; dm €13) A 10-minute walk from the port (turn left as you exit), this new backpackers is in an orange-and-yellow apartment block.

Hotel Republica (☎ 22 240; rr 1 Maji; s/d €25/30) This is a central hotel with character, and the restaurant on the top floor (there's a lift-with-a-view) comes to life for summer. The bar underneath will bemuse history lovers; you drink coffee at tables wedged between the ruins of the town's ancient walls.

Hotel Palma (☎ 29 29; rr Mithat Hoxha; s/d €20/30, apt €120; 🖳) Free wi-fi. Right next to the port, this hotel has carpets that don't fit, but some rooms have great views with large balconies and the location is great. If you're up for it, guests get free entry into the on-site disco. Breakfast is free.

Zhupa Restaurant (rr 1 Maji; meals 400-800 lekë; ☯ 9am-last customer) This friendly eatery just past Hotel Ari serves Greek, Albanian and Italian dishes. Pastas cost around 200 lekë and steaks around 500 lekë, while fish dishes depend on weight – 800 lekë is a medium-sized meal.

Pupi (rr Saranda-Butrint; seafood dishes 650 lekë; ☯ 9am-midnight) Pupi has an unfortunate name but serves good seafood dishes in a pine-treed terrace setting, about 50m from Hotel Grand towards Butrint. Check out the great wall mosaic inside. In summer you can swim at its private beach.

Castle of Lekursi (Kalaja e Lëkurësit; ☎ 55 55; mains 250-1200 lekë; ☯ 11am-midnight) This restaurant inside the reconstructed castle above Saranda serves traditional Albanian cuisine (grills and fish) plus Italian dishes. You can sit back on the wrought-iron thrones and check out the tremendous views of Saranda and Butrint lagoon. A taxi up to the castle costs about 1000 lekë return; arrange a time for the driver to pick you up. The cheaper Piceri Lekursi (pizza restaurant) operates from the castle's lower tier between May and September.

Getting There & Away

BOAT

Finikas (☎ 60 57; finikaslines@yahoo.com; rr Mithat Hoxha) has two boats a day to Corfu departing at 10.30am and 4pm. A one-way ticket is €17.50 (including the €2.50 port tax). From Corfu it's €15 for the 90-minute trip departing at 9am, or €17.50 for Ionian Cruises' Dolphin boat that departs at the same time. There's a one-hour time difference between Greece and Albania.

BUS

Pick up an up-to-date bus timetable from the information centre (opposite). There are nine regular municipal buses to Butrint via Ksamil (100 lekë, about 40 minutes), leaving from outside the information centre and opposite Hotel Butrinti. Buses to Tirana (1200 lekë, eight hours) leave at 5am, 6.30am, 8.30am, 9.30am and 10.30am. Those to Gjirokastra (300 lekë, 1½ hours) go at 6am, 8am, 11am and 1pm. There's one bus to Durrës (900 lekë, seven hours) at 7.30am. Buses to Himara leave at 5.30am, 6am and 2pm. Daily services to Korça leave at 5.30am (1200 lekë, eight hours). There are also *furgons* to Gjirokastra (one hour, 300 lekë) and Vlora (six hours, 600 lekë)

via Himara, usually leaving between 5.30am and 10am. *Furgons* to Borsh leave at 11am and noon.

TAXI

Taxis wait for customers outside the bus station and opposite Central Park on rr Skënderbeu. A taxi to the Greece border at Kakavija will cost 4000 lekë, while a cab to the border near Konispoli will cost around 5000 lekë.

KSAMIL

Ksamil, 17km south of Saranda, has three small, dreamy islands within swimming distance and dozens of beachside bars and restaurants that open in the summer. The beaches here are getting bigger every year – literally, as presummer bulldozers dig into the rocks and trucks cart in sand. To get to the beach, head past the church and take the second right then the first left. You'll pass **Hotel Jon** (☎ 0692091554; s/d 1000/1500 lekë) near the roundabout, which is the bar and hotel of choice. Rooms cost €20 in summer.

BUTRINT

The ancient ruins of **Butrint** (www.butrint.org; admission 700 lekë; ☯ 8am-dusk), 18km south of Saranda, are renowned for their size, beauty and tranquillity. They're in a fantastic natural setting and are part of a 29-sq km national park. Set aside at least three hours to lose yourself and thoroughly explore this fascinating place.

Although the site had been inhabited long before, Greeks from Corfu settled on the hill in Butrint (Buthrotum) in the 6th century BC. Within a century Butrint had become a fortified trading city with an acropolis. The lower town began to develop in the 3rd century BC, and many large stone buildings had already been built by the time the Romans took over in 167 BC. Butrint's prosperity continued throughout the Roman period and the Byzantines made it an ecclesiastical centre. The city subsequently went into decline, and it was abandoned until 1927, when Italian archaeologists arrived. These days, thanks to Lord Rothschild's Butrint Foundation, the site is well maintained.

As you enter the site the path leads to the right, to Butrint's 3rd-century-BC **Greek theatre**, secluded in the forest below the acropolis. Also in use during the Roman period, the theatre could seat about 2500 people. Close by are the small **public baths**, whose geometric mosaics are buried under a layer of mesh and sand to protect them from the elements.

Deeper in the forest is a wall covered with crisp Greek inscriptions, and a 6th-century palaeo-Christian **baptistery** decorated with colourful mosaics of animals and birds, again under the sand. Beyond are the impressive arches of the 6th-century **basilica**, built over many years. A massive **Cyclopean wall** dating back to the 4th century BC is further on. Over one gate is a relief of a lion killing a bull, symbolic of a protective force vanquishing assailants.

The top of the hill is where the **acropolis** once was. There's now a castle here, housing an informative **museum** (🕓 8am-4pm). The views from the courtyard give you a good idea of the city's layout and you can see the Vivari Channel, which connects Lake Butrint to the Straits of Corfu. There's a community-run shop inside the gates where you can buy locally produced souvenirs.

A taxi to Butrint from Saranda will cost around 2000 lekë; you can usually negotiate to get there and back and see the Blue Eye Spring for 4000 lekë. Saranda-based **Sipa Tours** (☎ 66 75; rr 1 Maji; www.sipatours.com) arranges local tours for around €30 and can include a translator, which is useful to get the whole gist of Butrint. Make sure you pick up a guide to the site from the ticket booth. **Hotel Restaurant Livia** (☎ 0692051263; r €20), next to Butrint's entrance, does good local seafood dishes (mussels and eels) and has rooms available, but they're often taken up by up international archaeological students.

BLUE EYE SPRING & MONASTERY OF ST NICHOLAS

The **Blue Eye Spring** (Syri i Kaltër; admission 50 lekë), about 25km east of Saranda, is a hypnotic pool of deep-blue water surrounded by electric-blue edges like the iris of an eye. It feeds the Bistrica River and its depth is still unknown. It's a pleasant spot; blue dragonflies dash around the water and the surrounding shady oak trees make a good picnic site. There are rustic four-bed cabins for rent a few minutes' walk from the spring, near the on-site **restaurant** (☎ 0694038201; cabins €30). If you don't mind a 3km walk, any bus heading towards Gjirokastra can drop you off at the Blue Eye Spring's turn-off on the main road. Otherwise it's only accessible by taxi or on a private tour.

The Saranda–Gjirokastra road is temptingly close to **St Nicholas' Church** (Mesopotami; admission 100 lekë), where you can check out the extraordinary but decrepit blue interior of the 12th-century monastery that's perched on a little hill. Wonderful carvings of lions, eagles and flying dragons feature on some of the limestone blocks that make up its exterior.

GJIROKASTRA
☎ 0842 / pop 34,000

Austere old Gjirokastra watches over the Drinos valley from its rocky perch. It's sometimes called the city of a thousand steps (Berat is the city of a thousand windows), and you'll see why when you tackle the steep cobbled streets that wind between solid grey stone houses and mansions roofed in slate. Spend a day absorbing the life of the labyrinthine streets of the old town and, for an architectural feast, check out the unique houses and the dark castle splitting the old town in two.

Gjirokastra's Greek name, Argyrokastro, means Silver Castle. The town was well established and prosperous by the 13th century but declined after the arrival of the Turks in 1417. The 17th century brought about improvement and the town became a major trading centre with a flourishing bazaar where embroidery, felt, silk and its white cheese (which is still famous today) were traded. One of the Ottoman Empire's most prominent individuals, Ali Pasha of Tepelena, seized the town in the early 19th century and strengthened the citadel.

Gjirokastra was the birthplace of former dictator Enver Hoxha, who awarded it the status of 'museum city'. Thanks to this, special care was taken to retain its traditional architecture during the communist era; the modern city in the basin below the old town was built during that time. Gjirokastra's other famous son is writer Ismail Kadare, who set the novel *Chronicle in Stone* in his home town. Today, Hoxha's rebuilt birthplace is the Ethnographic Museum, Kadare's home is being reconstructed, and the locals are learning English to help deal with the growing number of tourists to this Unesco World Heritage site.

Information

There are three ATMS in town, including one near the courthouse. Beyond the information centre, the Artisan Centre sells handmade souvenirs and keeps the local arts industry alive.

Information centre (☎ 67 077; www.gjirokastra.org; rr e Kalase; 9am-5pm) On the road to the castle, just past the five-street junction; provides free information and stocks a good range of Kadare's novels.
Internet cafe (per hr 100 lekë) Opposite the mosque.
Old Bazar Travel and Tour Agency (tours €20-25) Near the information centre.

Sights

Gjirokastra's incredible 19th-century houses were mostly built between 1800 and 1830. Most have three storeys: the lower floors are used for storage and the upper floors for living quarters, some with lavishly decorated rooms, especially those for receiving guests. The neighbourhoods with these classic Ottoman houses encircle the castle. The houses are fiercely expensive to maintain, and some are falling into disrepair. About 10 of the 400-odd legally protected houses have collapsed in the last five years. The local **Ethnographic Museum** (old town; admission 200 lekë; 9am-7pm) is a good example of a traditional house, but twin-towered **Zekate House** (admission 100 lekë), on the road past Hotel Kalemi, is much more interesting, especially with its 'conception room', where new couples were given some privacy. You walk down the owners' driveway to get to the foot of the looming 200-year-old house.

The splendidly gloomy **castle** (old town; admission 200 lekë; 9am-7pm) is the city's dominant feature. Built from the 6th century onwards, this brooding giant was used as a prison by King Zog I, then the Nazis, and then the communists until 1971, when it became the **Albanian National Armaments Museum** (admission 200 lekë). The main entrance is in the middle of the castle's flank; to the left as you enter, eerie silhouettes of cannons and tanks fill the main, dim gallery of the fortress. Outside, the shell of a 1957 US military jet is a bizarre addition to the ramparts of the castle. The communist party used to explain that it was a spy plane that had been forced down and captured. In fact it was a training jet from an Italian NATO base that had run into mechanical trouble and made an emergency landing in Albania.

If the mountains around town look inviting, jump on a local bus to Këlcyra and the 'city of flowers' Përmet. The route up the Vjosa valley is nothing short of breathtaking. There are regular *furgons* between Gjirokastra and Përmet (300 lekë, 1½ hours) until about 5pm.

Festivals & Events

The **National Albanian Folk Festival** began in 1968 and packs the castle with over 1000 local and international performers every four years in September, although there's a five year gap between the 2004 and 2009 festivals.

Sleeping & Eating

our pick Hotel Kalemi (☎ 63 724; draguak@yahoo.com; Lagja Palorto; r 4000 lekë;) Somewhere between a hotel and a museum, this is a great authentic experience of old Albania, with carved wood ceilings and stone fireplaces in the 1st-floor rooms. The 2nd floor's balcony has fantastic rooftop and castle views. The included breakfast in the basement is delicious.

Kotoni B&B (☎ 35 26; Lagja Palorto 8, rr Bashkim Kokona; s/d 1500/2000 lekë) Expect cosy and clean double/twin rooms with TV and heating. A cooked breakfast is included and served downstairs, where it's hard to keep your eyes off the carved wooden decor.

Hotel Relax (Sheshi Çerçiz Topulli; d 3000 lekë;) It may be in a modern building, but after climbing six floors, the four bright and airy double and twin rooms are a pleasant surprise. Some rooms have great views of the castle.

our pick Kujtimi (Pazar i Vjetër; meals 600 lekë; 11am-midnight) From fried Saranda mussels (only on the menu if they're fresh) to delicious vegetable *qofte*: it's Albanian food with flair. The Dumi family are doing everything right, including keeping prices incredibly low. Kujtimi is the small, tree-shaded restaurant en route to the hard-to-miss Fantazia restaurant.

Kurveleshi (rr e Kalase; mains 200 lekë; 11am-midnight) Opposite the information centre, Kurveleshi offers beer on tap and simple Albanian food at low prices (meat 200 lekë, rice 60 lekë).

Getting There & Around

Buses to and from Gjirokastra stop on the main highway, 1.5km from the old town. Taxis from the new to the old town cost 400 lekë. There's a taxi rank on the old town's main square, Sheshi Çerçiz Topulli. Buses to Tirana (1000 lekë, eight hours) are fairly frequent. There are three buses a day to Saranda (250 lekë, one hour), leaving at 8am, 9am and 10am, and Berat (700 lekë, five hours). The 7am bus to Korça (1000 lekë, six hours) takes the spectacular route through Përmet and Erseka. You'll need to take a taxi to get to the Greece border at Kakavija (1500 lekë, 30 minutes), or catch the bus to Ioannina that passes through in the morning.

NORTHERN ALBANIA

The northern Albanian landscape has rich wildlife, swamps and lagoons around Shkodra and Lezha, and high, unforgiving mountains around Theth in the northeast (named the Accursed Mountains, Bjeshkët e Namuna, in Albanian). Reports indicate that instability in the neighbouring areas is no longer an issue. The main road corridor from Tirana to the border with Montenegro (the area where Shkodra and Lezha are located) is fine.

LEZHA
☎ 0215 / pop 14,000
This small town was home to one of Albania's most significant historic moments: it's the place where Gjergj Kastrioti, Skanderbeg (see p51), brought the Albanian clan heads to unite against their common enemy, the Ottomans. He was buried here in 1468, in Lezha's cathedral. The Ottomans ravaged his tomb some years later, turning his bones into talismans and the cathedral into a mosque.

The ruins of St Nicholas' cathedral house Skanderbeg's **memorial tomb** (admission 100 lekë), where a red mosaic of the double-headed eagle flag stretches behind a bronze bust of the man himself. The cathedral is artfully protected from the elements and you can just make out the red fresco featuring St Nicholas (aka Santa) himself.

Outside Lezha is **Hotel i Gjuetisë** (☎ 0692170898; Ishulli i Lezhës; r 2000 lekë), a dilapidated hunting lodge offering meals (mains 500 lekë) as well as accommodation. Built by Mussolini's son-in-law Count Ciano, the lodge is set in a quiet (though rubbish-strewn) wetland park rich with flora and rare birds. To get here take a taxi, which shouldn't cost more than 500 lekë.

SHËNGJIN
Shëngjin, 7km north of Lezha, has moved quickly from being a quiet fishing village to being a major oil port. Its sand is grey and so is its water. **Hotel Ermiri Palace** (☎ 0281-2444; www .ermiripalace.com; s/d €25/40) is the best of a similar bunch of beachfront hotels. A different beach option is to head to Velipoja, near the border with Montenegro, although Shkodra's 'construction police' have been hard at work

here demolishing illegal buildings (including hotels) and leaving behind the mess.

Furgons from Tirana to Shkodra stop at the bus station–taxi rank in Lezha (200 lekë, 1½ hours), and there are plenty of *furgons* from there to Shëngjin. *Furgons* make the 34km Shkodra–Velipoja journey for around 100 lekë.

SHKODRA
☎ 022 / pop 91,300
Shkodra (Shkodër), the traditional centre of the Gheg cultural region, is one of the oldest cities in Europe. Rozafa fortress is beautiful and the Marubi photography exhibition is small but fascinating. A section of town (between the mosque and the cathedral) has benefited from sensitive renovations of most of its older-style houses and shopfronts, and Shkodra's locals are more likely to own a bicycle than a Mercedes-Benz. Out of the centre, tatty grey apartment buildings lend a rather sombre air. Travellers pass through here on their way between Tirana and Ulcinj in Montenegro, but more are beginning to use the town as a base for forays into the alpine area of Theth and the isolated wonder of Lake Koman.

As the Ottoman Empire declined in the late 18th century, Shkodra became the centre of a semi-independent *pashalik* (region governed by a pasha, an Ottoman high official), which led to a blossoming of commerce and crafts. In 1913 Montenegro tried to annex Shkodra (it succeeded in taking Ulcinj), a move not approved of by the international community, and the town changed hands often during WWI. Badly damaged by the 1979 earthquake, Shkodra was subsequently repaired and is Albania's fourth-largest town. The communist-era Hotel Rozafa in the town centre is not the most welcoming hotel, but it makes a good landmark – restaurants, transport to Montenegro and most of the town's sights are close by.

Information
ArtCom (☎ 52 555; rr Çajupi; per hr 100 lekë; 🕑 7.30am-10pm) Buzzing internet cafe downstairs between Hotel Rozafa and Hotel Europa.
Tirana Bank (rr 13 Dhjetori) Next to Hotel Colosseo; has an ATM.

Sights
Near the southern end of Lake Shkodra is **Rozafa fortress** (admission 200 lekë), founded by the

Illyrians in antiquity and rebuilt much later by the Venetians and Turks. The fortress derives its name from a woman named Rozafa, who was allegedly walled into the ramparts as an offering to the gods so that the construction would stand. The story goes that Rozafa asked that two holes be left in the stonework so that she could continue to breastfeed her baby. There's a spectacular wall sculpture of her breastfeeding near the entrance to the castle's **museum** (admission 150 lekë). Some nursing women come to the fortress to smear their breasts with the milky water that appears annually in January and February. The castle is about 3km south of the city centre; a return taxi (with waiting time) is 800 lekë, or, if you're up for a steep walk, municipal buses stop near the turn-off to the castle.

Hidden behind a building that looks like a block of flats, the **Marubi Permanent Photo Exhibition** (rr Muhamet Gjollesha; admission 100 lekë; ☺ 8am-4pm Mon-Fri) boasts fantastic photography by the Marubi 'dynasty', Albania's first and foremost photographers. The first-ever photograph taken in Albania is here, taken by Pjetër Marubi in 1858. The exhibition shows fascinating portraits, places and events. Not only is this a rare insight into what things looked like in old Albania, it's also a small collection of mighty fine photographs. To get there, go northeast of the clock tower into rr Çlirimi; rr Muhamet Gjollesha darts off to the right. The exhibition is on the left in an unmarked building, but locals will help you find it if you ask. Postcards of some of the images are available for 100 lekë.

Sleeping & Eating

Hotel Kaduku (HK; ☎ 42 216; Sheshi 5 Heronjtë; r €30) This popular and clean hotel is set behind Raiffeisen Bank on the roundabout near Hotel Rozafa. The two wings have been renovated, and staff and other guests are great information providers. Breakfast is an extra €4.

Hotel Europa Grand (☎ 41 211; www.europagrand hotel.com; Sheshi 2 Prilli; d €65; 🖳) One of only a few Albanian five-star hotels worth splashing out on, the Europa Grand has the lot: water features, luxuriously large rooms, two ATMs, a shop, free fitness access and two bars. One of the bars, the top-floor 'Red Bar', is worth spending a sunset at, even if you're not staying here, and the lake and mountain views and cool atmosphere are worth paying 250 lekë a beer for.

Hotel Parku (☎ 49 683; rr Vaso Kadia; s/d €5/10) It ain't beautiful (it's very, very bare), but it's cheap, not so far from the centre and very close to the rr 13 Dhjetori xhiro route.

G&T Tradita (Tradita Gegë dhe Toskë; rr Skenderbeu; meals 1100 lekë) Great food (fresh fish is a speciality) is on offer in what could be an ethnographic museum, and you can watch your grills and pita being cooked on the huge hearth. It's really dim inside, but no doubt that's part of the Gheg and Tosk's atmosphere.

Piazza Park (rr 13 Dhjetori; meals 800 lekë) Here's where the locals return to, night after night, day after day. Once you get past security (?!), people watch (or be watched) next to the fountains.

Getting There & Away

There are frequent *furgons* to and from Tirana (350 lekë, 2½ hours), leaving Tirana from the train station and dropping you off in the centre of Shkodra. From Shkodra, *furgons* depart from Radio Shkodra near Hotel Rozafa. The train station is a fair walk away, but *furgons* meet arriving trains (160 lekë to Durrës).

Furgons to Ulcinj (Ulqini in Albanian) in Montenegro leave at 9am and 3pm (500 lekë) from outside Hotel Rozafa. They fill quickly, so get in early. The length of the trip depends on how busy the border at Muriqan is. Taxis to Hani i Hotit on the way to Podgorica charge about 2500 lekë, or catch a *furgon* to Koplik (the turn-off to Theth) and a taxi from there.

LAKE KOMAN

The breathtaking, two-hour ferry journey from Koman to Fierzë takes you through the Drina valley, which was dammed in the 1970s and still produces hydropower. The ferry glides through deep green water and you almost feel wedged in by the sharp stone cliffs that reach dizzying heights. The snowy mountains in the distance only add to the feeling of isolation. There are caves and grottoes, but even in this wilderness you'll still see people waving from goat tracks high above the lake's edge.

Getting There & Away

Buses go from Bajram Curri all the way to Tirana (1000 lekë including ferry ticket) or, if you're coming from Shkodra, you can do a return ferry trip in one day, although there's not much to Fierzë's pier precinct. A complete Shkodra–Koman–Fierzë–Koman–Tirana

ALBANIA

journey is possible, too. There's a loop from here to Bajram Curri (buses meet the arriving boat) to alpine Valbonë, where you can discover the Balkans Peace Park walking tracks (see the boxed text, p61), but you'll need to be well prepared as it's pretty isolated going.

Furgons for Koman depart Shkodra from the corner of rr Skenderbeg and rr Marin Barleti at 6.30am, 7am and 7.30am (400 lekë, two hours) and meet the passenger ferry and car ferry heading to Fierzë at 10am (400 lekë, two hours). If you're driving, get to the port early as it's first in, best dressed for vehicles, and the queue of cars, trucks and buses quickly fills the tunnel to the pier. For the return journey (and you may need to check that there actually is one) the ferry departs Fierzë at 2pm; however, *furgons* don't usually meet the ferry and you may need to ask the captain to help find a lift with someone going to Shkodra, or the more popular Tirana (but see the hitchhiking warning, p448).

THETH

Heading to Theth is seriously heading into Albania's unknown. From the precariousness of the three-hour *furgon* trip up there, to the breakfast you'll be served by your host family, it truly feels like you're a part of something very new but, at the same time, mind-blowingly old.

Information

The trip there gets exciting as soon as the asphalt road finishes. You're cruising along bumpily for some time before you start ascending the narrow road, and it seems like mere minutes before your *furgon* is precariously perched on the edge of a chasm. There's slight relief when you cross the Buni i Thores pass (this is where the local passengers cross themselves) and begin the descent into the Valley of Theth.

Theth's a tiny town in summer, and even tinier in winter when only eight of the families stay here, although that number is increasing because of tourism. Theth residents have a rich history of making travellers welcome; even Edith Durham, who travelled the country solo in the 1900s, had an incident-free time.

The tourist season lasts from June to September, and even during that time it's possible that snow will have blocked access, so contact the Balkans Peace Park Office (see the boxed text, p61) beforehand. It's not unusual to hear of people snowshoeing their way in (apparently it takes a day).

Sights & Activities

The town itself doesn't really have a centre, but wander around and you'll walk over icy, fast-flowing rivers on rickety wooden bridges and find wooden water mills that are still in use. You may even stumble upon the lock-in tower *(kulla e ngujimit)*, where men waited, protected, during a blood feud (see the boxed text, p59). Various attempts have been made to turn the tower into accommodation or a museum, so check its status when you get there.

The region is home to wild animals including brown bears, mountain goats, otters and wildcats, and plant species including beech, ash, walnut, maple and birch. Locally, each family seems content with a cow (with a noisy bell), chooks and a few sheep. The only way to see the more exotic fauna and flora of the area is on a trek, and it's possible to ask around for a local guide. Expect to pay at least 2000 lekë for a day-long hike. Be prepared with wet-weather gear as Theth holds the title as one of the wettest areas in Albania and sees 130 to 160 days of snow per year.

Petrit Imeraj (☎ 0692065205) is a Shkodra-based mountain man linked to the Balkans Peace Park project who offers plenty of varieties of all-inclusive tours around the region.

Sleeping & Eating

Accommodation in Theth is in local homes, although there is one hotel-style option (Hotel Kampi). A recent push has led to a level of donor-funded development not seen elsewhere in Albania. In true donor style, traditional homes are being renovated to a Western standard rather than being demolished. The standard of accommodation inside the old stone houses dotted in the valley is quite unexpected but certainly desired; hot showers in brand-new bathrooms definitely make alpine living very comfortable (just don't expect central heating).

There are no restaurants in town, and the only 'shop' is just outside town, near Hotel Kampi as you descend. Most guesthouses offer a package deal of 2500 lekë per person per day, which includes three meals. It's back-to-basics stuff: most of what you'll be served for breakfast will come from the cows or sheep that roam the property (and vegans beware: there's a lot of dairy: milk drinks, yoghurt drinks and hard white cheeses abound) or what was baked that day. It's mostly organic.

There are now 10 guesthouses in the region, but the following are convenient if you want to be based in the village.

Harusha Family Home (☎ 0692770294; per person 2500 lekë) This friendly homestay is in Theth's 'centre' (on the left, over the bridge). The Harushas are the biggest family in the village, so look out for a bunch of (English-speaking) children and you won't be far.

Tërthorja (☎ 0692831287; per person 2500 lekë) One of the largest homes here, Tërthorja has incredible views of the valley, centre and surrounding peaks. There's a field for volleyball and football in front of the house.

Getting There & Away

A *furgon* makes a daily trip (500 lekë, three hours), departing at 7am from outside Café Rusi. To find this tiny cafe, head northeast from Sheshi 5 Heronjte to Sheshi i Rusit and keep going until you see a small vegetable market. The cafe is on the left.

The turn-off for Theth is at Koplik, halfway between Shkodra and Hani i Hotit along Lake Shkodra. It's a spine-chilling drive from the tiny village of Bogë to Theth, and roadside memorials attest to its danger. Hiring a 4WD and driver is also an option, but make sure the driver is well acquainted with the road.

The routes vary, but it's possible to hike from Theth to Valbonë (eight hours).

ALBANIA DIRECTORY

ACCOMMODATION

The accommodation reviews in this chapter are listed in order of preference. Albania's budget accommodation is usually decent and clean; breakfast is sometimes included in the price. Midrange hotels are a notch up, with wi-fi, telephones and evidence of attempts to spruce up the rooms. Top-end hotels are mostly on a par with modern European hotels in terms of comfort and facilities, and offer fitness centres, satellite TV, internet access and swimming pools.

Accommodation has undergone a rapid transformation in Albania, and custom-built, private hotels operate alongside dilapidated ex-state-run ones. Beaches are lined with hotels in Saranda, Durrës and Vlora, while homestays

abound in places like Theth. For budget travellers, finding people who've partly converted their homes into private accommodation is a good way to go, although backpacker-style hostels are sprouting up in Tirana, Saranda and Berat. Whatever town you're in there's usually at least a few good hotel or B&B options in most price categories. The local hotel-booking company **Albania-hotel.com** (www .albania-hotel.com) is a reliable resource for finding out about new lodgings; the company does a good job assessing recently opened hotels.

Find unofficial accommodation in private homes by asking around in cafes. Camping is possible in the southern area and sometimes on deserted beaches.

ACTIVITIES

The further south you get, the better the swimming is. South of Vlora the sandy Adriatic gives it up for its rockier and much more picturesque Ionian counterpart. You can go birdwatching around Lezha (p90), Velapoja and the Drina delta and hiking in Mt Dajti National Park (p74). For challenging hiking, find a local guide and try Theth (opposite) and Valbonë in the Balkans Peace Park (see the boxed text, p61). Hiking and adventure sports are in their infancy in Albania, and the national leaders are the enthusiastic young team at Outdoor Albania (p64). A few Berat operatives run tours to Mt Tomorri National Park.

ALBANIA

Cyclists, take comfort: there are more than a few two-wheeled adventurers carving up the Albanian countryside. International operators lead mountain-bike tours through the rocky hills of northern Albania, while lone cyclists have been spotted along the Ionian coast and even tackling the Korça–Gjirokastra route.

Don't forget kayaking, caving and the ski slopes of Dardha (p79).

BOOKS

For a helpful list of Albanian words and phrases check out the *Mediterranean Europe Phrasebook* from Lonely Planet. *Colloquial Albanian* (2007) by Isa Zymberi is a good teach-yourself language course, accompanied by a CD.

The Albanians – A Modern History (1999) by Miranda Vickers is a comprehensive and very readable history of Albania from the time of Ottoman rule to the restoration of democracy after 1990.

James Pettifer's *Albania and Kosovo Blue Guide* (2001) is a thoroughly informed source for answering any questions on Albanian history and a good guide of things to see.

Albania – From Anarchy to a Balkan Identity (1999) by Miranda Vickers and James Pettifer covers the tumultuous 1990s in great detail, while managing to convey a sense of the confusion Albania faced as it shed its communist past.

Biografi (1993) by New Zealander Lloyd Jones is a rather arresting story set in post-1990 Albania, and is a semifactual account of the writer's quest for the alleged double of former communist dictator Enver Hoxha.

Rumpalla – Rummaging Through Albania (2002) by Peter Lucas is a personal account by an American journalist of Albanian descent detailing several visits to Albania before and after the revolution.

The Best of Albanian Cooking (1999) by Klementina Hysa and R John Hysa is one of scant few books on Albanian cuisine and contains a wide range of family recipes.

High Albania (published in 1909 and reprinted in 2000), written by Albania's 'honorary citizen' Edith Durham, recounts the author's travels in northern Albania in the early 20th century.

The Accursed Mountains (1999) is written by a seemingly miserable Robert Carver, who doesn't have many nice things to say about his journey through Albania in 1996.

Black Lambs & Grey Falcons (1991) is a collection of stories by women writers who travelled through the Balkans. It's edited by John B Allcock and Antonia Young.

BUSINESS HOURS

Most offices open at 8am and close around 5pm. Shops usually open at 8am and close around 7pm, though some close for a siesta from noon to 4pm, opening again from 4pm to 8pm. Banking hours are shorter (generally 9am to 3.30pm). Restaurants, cafes and bars are usually open from 8am till midnight or later.

COURSES

The **Lincoln Centre** (Map p64; ☎ 04-2230 880; www .lincoln-intl.org; rr Qemal Stafa 184, Tirana) runs Albanian language courses. Private tutorial is another way of picking up the language, so if you're keen stop by the secretariat office of the University of Europe on the Lana River and ask for students who can teach Albanian.

DANGERS & ANNOYANCES

Even though the country is safe for travel, some folk love to tell stories of bloodcurdling danger if you say you're going to Albania. First of all, the notion that travellers stumble into Albanian blood feuds isn't true. Poverty is a problem, but not this old custom. Locals suggest it's best to travel with a local guide to Bajram Curri and Tropoja in the far north, and even in the area around Theth. There are still land mines near the northern border with Kosovo, but Albania expects to be landmine-free by the end of 2009. Tirana itself was the scene of a massive munitions explosion in March 2008, which claimed the lives of 26 people and injured 302 others.

Otherwise, personal safety in Albania is very good. The number of people walking around central Tirana late on a summer evening shows that the locals are confident about safety. There isn't a hard-core drinking culture here so it's almost unheard of to be bailed up by drunks after dark. Take the usual precautions about avoiding rowdy demonstrations, and beware of pickpockets on crowded city buses. The most serious risk is on the roads – Albania has a high traffic-accident rate. Other dangers are the ripped-up pavements, ditches and missing manhole covers – watch your step!

To avoid being overcharged, travellers who've just entered Albania from Montenegro should know that the real price for a mini-bus trip to Tirana is 400 lekë, or about €4. Sometimes it pays to show taxi drivers how much you will pay, as mysterious things can happen with the number '0', and a taxi ride may cost 3000 lekë instead of the 300 leke you thought you had negotiated (and even, perhaps, written down).

As Albania was closed for so long, black travellers may encounter some curious stares; in fact, most visitors to Albania can expect a certain amount of curiosity.

There are risks in drinking tap water or local milk; plenty of bottled water and imported UHT milk is available. The standard of health care in Albania is variable: local hospitals and clinics are understaffed and underfunded, but pharmacies are good.

EMBASSIES & CONSULATES

There are no Australian, New Zealand or Irish embassies in Albania. The following embassies and consulates are in Tirana (Map p64; area code ☎ 042); note that – except for the American, Dutch and Italian embassies, which are near the university – the missions are on a high-security, blocked street off rr e Kavajës.

France (☎ 2234 054; ambafrance.tr@adanet.com.al; rr Skënderbej 14)

Germany (☎ 2274 505; www.tirana.diplo.de; rr Skënderbej 8)

Greece (☎ 2274 670; gremb.tir@mfa.gr; rr Frederik Shiroka 3)

Italy (☎ 2275 900; www.ambtirana.esteri.it; rr Lek Dukagjini 7)

Macedonia (☎ 2230 909; makambas@albnet.net; rr e Kavajës 116)

Netherlands (☎ 2240 828; www.mfa.nl/tir; rr Asim Zeneli 10)

Serbia (☎ 2232 091; www.tirana.mfa.gov.yu; rr Donika Kastrioti 9/1)

UK (☎ 2234 973; www.uk.al; rr Skënderbej 12)

USA (☎ 2247 285; rr Elbasanit 103)

FESTIVALS & EVENTS

Albania is getting right into festivals, and most towns claim at least one. There are festivals celebrating the sea and dance in Durrës, and folk festivals in Përmet and Gjirokastra. Elbasan has its Day of Spring, which has now extended into Tirana, and way down south Butrint holds its annual Theatre Festival on the ancient site each summer. Tirana's winter film festival is popular, and its June or July jazz festival is bringing in international names each year.

GAY & LESBIAN TRAVELLERS

Gay and lesbian life in Albania is alive and well but is not yet organised into out clubs or NGOs. It's no problem to be foreign and affectionate with your same-sex partner in the street, keeping in mind that no couples are overly demonstrative in public in Albania, so any public sexual behaviour beyond holding hands and kissing will be a spectacle. For gay and lesbian visitors, your gaydar will serve you well, and ask anyone who looks funky on the street where the parties are – the alternative music and party scene is queer friendly.

HOLIDAYS

Albania respects the holy days of four different faiths and sects, which makes for a busy religious and secular holiday schedule. The dates of the Muslim religious holidays of Bajram i Madh (the 'big feast' at the end of the fasting month of Ramadan) and Bajram i Vogël (the 'little feast' commemorating the prophet Ibrahim's willingness to sacrifice his son Ismail to God) fall 11 or 12 days earlier every year. Over the next couple of years Bajram i Vogël falls in November, while Bajram i Madh falls in September. See the boxed text, p433, for precise dates. In addition, the Catholic and Orthodox Easter (Pashkët) dates only rarely fall on the same day (4 April 2010 is one of those rare instances); see the boxed text, p433, for precise Easter dates in upcoming years. The main holidays:

New Year's Day 1 January
Summer Day 14 March
Nevruz 22 March
Catholic Easter March or April
Orthodox Easter March or April
May Day 1 May
Bajram I Madh September
Mother Teresa Day 19 October
Bajram i Vogël November
Independence Day 28 November
Liberation Day 29 November
Christmas Day 25 December

LANGUAGE

Albanian (Shqip) is an Indo-European language, a descendent of ancient Illyrian, with a number of Turkish, Latin, Slavonic and (modern) Greek words, although it constitutes a linguistic branch of its own. It has 36 characters (including nine diagraphs or double letters, eg ll and dh). It shares certain grammatical features with Romance languages such as Romanian, but it's fair to say the Albanian language is a world unto itself. Most of the vocabulary sounds completely unfamiliar at first.

The core words of the main dialects of Albanian – Tosk and Gheg – were the same, but the grammar was slightly different. For example the word 'working' was *punuar* in Tosk but *punue* in Gheg. A unified form of Albanian was established in 1972 and is now taught wherever Albanians live.

Most Albanian place names have two forms, as the definite article is a suffix. An example of this is *bulevardi* (the boulevard), as opposed to *bulevard* (a boulevard). See also the boxed text, p51.

Many Albanians speak Italian, thanks to Italian TV broadcasts which can be picked up along the populated coast. During the communist period people grew skilled at rewiring their TVs to overcome the Albanian government's attempts to block Italian channels.

Quite a few people in the south also speak Greek, and younger people are learning English.

See the Language chapter, p454, for pronunciation guidelines and useful words and phrases.

MONEY

Albanian banknotes come in denominations of 100, 200, 500, 1000 and 5000 lekë. There are 5-, 10-, 20-, 50- and 100-lekë coins. You may come into contact with the larger-than-life 1000-lekë note, with the familiar head of Skanderbeg, which is still being used. Bring out a 5000-lekë note to pay for a quick meal and you'll see a lot of teeth gritting, but that's what ATMs dish out. In 1964 the currency was revalued 10 times; prices on occasion may still be quoted at the old rate (3000 lekë instead of 300). Happily, if you hand over 3000 lekë you will probably be handed 2700 lekë in change.

Everything in Albania can be paid for with lekë, but most of the hotel prices are quoted in euros. Day trippers from Corfu can rely on euros, though they won't get a good exchange rate.

ATMs

A variety of ATMs can be found in most towns and cities, excepts for villages like Theth and Dhërmi. ATMs frequently offer you your currency in euros or lekë. The main

networks are Alpha Bank, Raiffeisen Bank, American Bank of Albania, Pro Credit Bank and Tirana Bank.

Credit Cards
Credit cards are accepted only in the larger hotels and travel agencies, and in only a handful of establishments outside Tirana. Major banks can offer credit-card advances.

Moneychangers
Travellers cheques are about as practical and useful here as a dead albatross, though you can change them at Rogner Hotel Europapark Tirana (p67) and at major banks in Tirana. Some banks will change US-dollar travellers cheques into US cash without commission. Travellers cheques (in euros and US dollars) can be used at a few top-end hotels, but cash (euros and lekë) is preferred everywhere.

Every town has its free currency market, which usually operates on the street in front of the main post office or state bank. Such transactions are not dangerous or illegal and it all takes place quite openly, but do make sure you count the money twice before tendering yours. The advantages are that you get a good rate and avoid the 1% bank commission. There are currency-exchange businesses in major towns, usually open 8am to 6pm and closed on Sunday.

Euros are the favourite foreign currency. You will not be able to change Albanian lekë outside of the country, so exchange them or spend them before you leave.

Tipping
It's usually good to round up the bill, and best to hand the coins or notes to the waiter rather than leave them on the table.

POST
Outside main towns there are few public post boxes, but there is an increasing number of modern post offices springing up around the country where you can hand in your mail directly, though whether they have stamps is another matter. Sending a postcard overseas costs around 60 lekë, while a letter costs 80 lekë to 160 lekë. The postal system is fairly rudimentary – there are no postcodes, for example – and it does not enjoy a reputation for efficiency. Don't rely on sending or receiving parcels through Albapost.

TELEPHONE & FAX

Long-distance telephone calls made from main post offices (Albtelecom) are cheap, costing about 90 lekë a minute to Italy. Calls to the USA cost 230 lekë per minute. Calls from private phone offices are horribly expensive, though – 800 lekë per minute to Australia. Faxing can be done from the main post office in Tirana for the same cost as phone calls, or from major hotels, though they will charge more. Albania's country code is ☎ 355. For domestic directory enquiries call ☎ 124; international directory assistance is ☎ 12.

Mobile Phones

The three established mobile-phone providers are Vodafone, AMC and Eagle, and a fourth licence has been promised. Nearly all populated areas of the country are covered, though the networks can become congested. Prepaid SIM cards cost around 1000 lekë and usually include credit. Mobile tariffs are roughly 45 lekë to 60 lekë a minute nationally, and 200 lekë to 245 lekë a minute to zone 4 areas (including USA, Australia and Japan). International texts are 20 lekë. You can also check to see if a roaming agreement exists with your home service provider. Numbers begin with ☎ 067, ☎ 068 or ☎ 069. To call an Albanian mobile number from abroad, dial ☎ 355, then either ☎ 67, ☎ 68 or ☎ 69 (drop the 0).

Phonecards

Phonecards are available from Albtelecom in versions of 50 impulses (350 lekë), 100 impulses (600 lekë) and 200 impulses (1100 lekë). Long-distance calls use 20 impulses per minute. It's quite common to buy some phonecard time from men waiting around public phones: you use one of their cards, then they check how much credit you've used up and you pay them. Be wary of kids trying to sell you phonecards – sometimes they have no credit left on them.

EMERGENCY NUMBERS

- Ambulance ☎ 127
- Fire service ☎ 128
- Police ☎ 129

TOURIST INFORMATION

Tourist information offices operate in Saranda, Gjirokastra, Berat and Korça, and hotel receptionists or travel agencies will also usually help you with directions. You can buy city maps of Tirana in bookshops, and maps of Vlora, Saranda, Gjirokastra, Durrës and Shkodra from the respective towns' travel agencies or hotels. It's difficult to find street signs and numbers, and your destination will probably still be referred to by what's around it (for example, the cathedral next to the TV station). The Tourism Ministry has started producing a weighty but colourful **Albania Guide** (Guidë Turistike; marketing@albania-guide .com; €11), which is useful and covers all the tourism areas (in English and Albanian). Look for a copy at major hotels. The **In Your Pocket** (www.inyourpocket.com) series covers Tirana and Shkodra and has excellent up-to-date tourist information.

TRAVELLERS WITH DISABILITIES

There are few special facilities for travellers in wheelchairs: to get onto footpaths in Tirana you have to step up from the road, steps are everywhere, and gutters have no ramps. However, there are toilets that cater to people with disabilities in the Tirana International Hotel (p67), the Rogner Hotel Europapark Tirana (p67) and the Sheraton (p67). The roads and castle entrances in Gjirokastra, Berat and Kruja are cobblestone, although taxis can get you reasonably close to the action.

VISAS

No visa is required by citizens of EU countries or nationals of Australia, Canada, New Zealand, Japan, South Korea, Norway, South Africa or the USA. Travellers from other countries should check with an Albanian embassy for appropriate visa requirements or consult www.mfa.gov.al. Citizens of all countries – even those entering visa-free – are required to pay €1 to enter the country; those arriving at Tirana Airport pay €10.

Upon arrival you fill in an arrival and departure card. Keep the departure card, which will be stamped, with your passport and present it when you leave.

WOMEN TRAVELLERS

Albania is quite a safe country for women travellers, but it's important to be aware of

ALBANIA

the fact that outside Tirana it's mainly men who go out and sit in bars and cafes in the evenings. While they are not threatening, it may feel strange to be the only woman in a bar. It's extremely unlikely that you'll be involved, but be aware that Albania is a source country for people-trafficking.

TRANSPORT IN ALBANIA

This section covers transport connections between Albania and the other countries in this book. For information on getting to Albania from further abroad, see p439.

GETTING THERE & AWAY
Air
Albania's international airport is the recently renovated Nënë Tereza Airport (aka MTA, Mother Teresa Airport or Rinas Airport), 26km northwest of Tirana. There are no domestic flights within Albania, and the selection of flights within the region is limited to Belgrade in Serbia and Pristina in Kosovo. Airlines flying to and from Albania within the Western Balkans:

Albanian Airlines (airline code LV; ☎ 04-2235 162; www.albanianairlines.com.al) Hub Tirana.

JAT Airways (airline code JU; ☎ 04-2272 540; www.jat .com; rr Abdi Toptani, Tirana) Hub Belgrade.

Land
For information on travelling to and from Greece, see p443. There are no passenger trains into Albania, so the options are buses, *furgons* or taxis to a border and picking up transport on the other side.

BORDER CROSSINGS
Kosovo
The two main crossings are at Qafë Morina between Kukës and Prizren and Qafë Prush. The popularity of the Lake Koman car ferry means you're unlikely to be alone on the 20-minute drive to Qafë Prush.

Macedonia
The two best crossings are on either side of Lake Ohrid. The southern crossing is at Tushëmisht/Sveti Naum, 29km south of Ohrid; the northern crossing is at Qafë e Thanës, between Struga and Pogradec. If you are taking a bus to/from Macedonia (Tirana–

Struga–Tetovo–Skopje), use the Qafë e Thanës crossing. The Tushëmisht/Sveti Naum crossing is most commonly crossed on foot, as taxis from Pogradec will drop you off just before the Macedonia border. Albania's Pogradec is 4km from the border.

There are two smaller border crossings at Blato, 5km northwest of Debar, and at Stenje on the western shore of Lake Prespa. There is no public transport on these routes.

Montenegro
At the time of writing there were two border crossings, one is at Hani i Hotit (between Shkodra and Podgorica) and another at Muriqan between Ulcinj and Shkodra. There are no regular buses from Tirana to cities in Montenegro, but *furgons* leave Shkodra for Ulcinj at 9am and 3pm (one way €5, around 40 minutes). See p91 for details.

BUS
Kosovo
Buses to Pristina depart daily from beside the Tirana International Hotel on Sheshi Skënderbej at 6pm (€30, 10 hours).

Macedonia
There are buses from Tirana via Struga (€10, five hours) to Tetovo (€15, seven to eight hours) and Skopje (€25, eight hours). The **Pollogu travel agency** (Map p64; ☎ 04-2235 000, 0692094906; Pall 103, blvd Zogu I, Tirana) sells tickets for the Macedonian bus company Polet, which has services at 9am and 9pm daily from the bus stand next to the train station. The Pollogu office is a little hard to find – it's upstairs in a modern apartment building at the top end of blvd Zogu I. **Drita Travel and Tours** (Map p64; ☎ 04-2251 277; www.dritatravel.com) has offices at the Tirana train station and behind the museum, and runs an evening service to Skopje.

In July and August there are additional services to ethnic Albanian towns in Macedonia from Durrës.

CAR & MOTORCYCLE
Macedonia
The busiest route to Macedonia is from Tirana to Struga via Qafë e Thanës, and there are sometimes delays because of trucks. The route around the southern end of Lake Ohrid via Tushëmisht/Sveti Naum is quieter and delays are much less common.

Sea
There are sea links with Italy and Corfu (Greece). Ferries depart Corfu for Saranda at 9am and take either 45 minutes (€17.50) or 90 minutes (€15). The return ferry leaves Saranda at 4pm, and there's a €2.50 departure tax included in the ticket's price. In low season the daily ferry trip from Vlora to Brindisi or from Durrës to Bari costs €35, rising to €50 in peak season.

GETTING AROUND
Bicycle
Cycling in Albania has been given a bad rap over the years – it's tough but certainly doable. Expect lousy road conditions including open drains, some abysmal driving from fellow road-users, and roads that aren't really roads (for example, the road from Boga to Thcth). Shkodra is one of the few places you'll see the locals embracing cycling.

Bus
Most Albanians travel around their country in private *furgons* or larger buses. These run fairly frequently throughout the day between Tirana and Durrës (38km) and other towns north, east and south. Buses to Tirana depart from towns all around Albania at the crack of dawn. Pay the conductor on board; the fares are low (Tirana–Durrës costs 150 lekë). Tickets are rarely issued.

Municipal buses operate in Tirana, Durrës, Shkodra and Vlora and trips usually cost 30 lekë. Watch your possessions on crowded city buses.

Car & Motorcycle
Albania has only acquired an official road-traffic code in recent years and most motorists have been driving for a maximum of 15 years. During the communist era car ownership required a permit from the government, which in 45 years issued precisely two to nonparty members. As a result, the government found it unnecessary to invest in new roads and most Albanians were inexperienced motorists. Nowadays the road infrastructure is improving, especially on the routes from the Macedonia border to Dhërmi; from Durrës to Korça, and on the stretch from Fier to Gjirokastra. If you're keen to drive, spend a few hours in a taxi first so you can see what conditions to expect. Off the main routes a

4WD is a good idea. Driving at night is particularly hazardous, and driving on mountain 'roads' at any time is a whole new field of extreme sport. Cars, *furgons,* trucks and buses DO go off the edge. There is no national automobile association in Albania as yet.

DRIVING LICENCE
Foreign driving licences are permitted, but it's recommended that you have an international driving permit as well. Car-hire agencies usually require that you have held a full licence for one year.

FUEL & SPARE PARTS
There are plenty of petrol stations in the cities and increasing numbers in the country. Unleaded fuel is available along all major highways, but fill up before driving into the mountainous regions. A litre of unleaded petrol costs 170 lekë, while diesel costs 160 lekë. There isn't yet a highly developed network of mechanics and repair shops capable of sourcing parts for all types of vehicles, but no doubt if you're driving an old Mercedes-Benz there will be parts galore.

HIRE
There are four hire-car companies operating out of Tirana: Avis, Europcar, Hertz and Sixt. Hiring a small car costs from €35 per day. Keep your wits about you and you'll find driving here now is like driving in Ireland was 10 years ago.

ROAD RULES
Drinking and driving is forbidden, and there is zero tolerance for blood-alcohol readings. Both motorcyclists and passengers must wear helmets. Speed limits are as low as 30km/h in built-up areas and 35km/h on the edges of built-up areas. Keep your car's papers with you as police are active paper-checkers.

Local Transport
Most Albanians travel around in private *furgons* or larger buses. Bus/*furgon* activity starts at the crack of dawn and usually ceases by 2pm. Fares are low, there are no tickets and they leave when they're full or almost full (or if you pay for the missing customers). They cost more than the bus, but they're still cheap. On intercity *furgon*s people usually pay the driver or assistant en route.

Train

Prior to 1948 Albania had only a few minor military and mining-industry railway lines, but the communist party built up a limited rail network. Today, however, nobody who can afford other types of transport takes the train, even though train fares are seriously cheap. The carriages are almost invariably in poor condition (you may well get wet if it rains) and journeys proceed at a pace best described as leisurely. That said, they are an excellent adventure. The line between Pogradec and Tirana is rather attractive, especially when it crawls along the shores of Lake Ohrid (it actually stops a few kilometres from Pogradec). There is only one class of travel, and there is no reservation system. Ticket offices generally open 10 minutes before a train is due to depart, and trains can leave early.

Daily passenger trains leave Tirana for Shkodra (150 lekë, 3½ hours), Fier (205 lekë, 4¼ hours), Vlora (250 lekë, 5½ hours) and Pogradec (295 lekë, seven hours). Six trains a day also make the trip between Tirana and Durrës (70 lekë, one hour).

Relying on the internet for Albanian train timetables is hopeless; you need to check the boards at the station itself.

Bosnia & Hercegovina

Bosnia and Hercegovina (BiH) describes itself as the 'heart-shaped land', which is surprisingly accurate anatomically. Emotionally, too, the deep yet unimposing human warmth of this craggily beautiful country fits the bill. And despite some lingering scars, the heartbreaking societal haemorrhaging of the 1990s has been completely stemmed (if not forgotten). The BiH of today has regained its once-famed religious tolerance. Rebuilt churches, mosques and synagogues huddle closely, rekindling that intriguing East-meets-West atmosphere born of Bosnia's fascinatingly blended Ottoman and Austro-Hungarian histories.

Socialist urban planning and war damage still combine to give certain post-industrial city-scapes all the charm of a Molvanian nightmare. But such scenes are surprisingly rare blots on a beautiful, largely rural landscape. Meanwhile the reincarnated Austro-Ottoman centres of Sarajevo and especially Mostar are unexpected delights. And the majority of Bosnian towns are lovably small, wrapped around medieval castles and surrounded by mountain ridges, verdant hills or merrily cascading river-canyons. Few places in Europe offer better rafting or such accessible and excellent-value skiing.

Fashionable bars and wi-fi–equipped cafes abound, but unemployment concerns remain as the fledgling state comes to terms with post-communist realities that were masked for years by more pressing war worries. Roads remain slow and winding, but they're extremely scenic, mostly well surfaced and relatively quiet, making for delightful random adventures, especially if you're driving. Indeed, however you travel, BiH offers a great sense of discovery, of real personal interaction and of very fair value for money that's all too rare in the heart of 21st-century Europe.

FAST FACTS

- **Area** 51,129 sq km
- **Capital** Sarajevo
- **Currency** KM (BAM); US$1 = 1.48KM; UK£1 = 2.15KM; €1 = 1.96KM; A$1 = 0.99KM
- **Famous for** the 1984 Sarajevo Winter Olympics, the bridge at Mostar
- **Key phrases** *zdravo* (hello), *hvala* (thanks), *molim* (please)
- **Official languages** Bosnian, Croatian and Serbian
- **Population** four million (estimate)
- **Telephone codes** country code ☎ 387; international access code ☎ 00
- **Visas** not required for most visitors; see p166

HIGHLIGHTS

- **Old Bridge** (Stari Most; p133) Seek ever-new angles from which to photograph young men throwing themselves off this magnificently rebuilt icon, in Mostar's delightful old town.
- **Jajce** (p154) One of BiH's most appealing fortress towns, which hides some compelling historical curiosities and makes an ideal base for visiting the stunning mountain lakes nearby.
- **Sarajevo** (p110) Potter round the timeless Turkish- and Austrian-era pedestrian lanes sampling the city's fashionable cafes and eclectic nightlife or gazing down on the mosque-dotted, red-roofed cityscape from the Park Prinčeva restaurant (p124).
- **Best Activity** (p163) Rafting dramatic canyons down one of BiH's fast-flowing rivers, whether from Foča, Bihać, Banja Luka or Konjic, or even starting with a quad-bike 'safari' through the wild upland villages behind the Bjelašnica ski resort (p129).

ITINERARIES

- **Six days** Arriving from Dubrovnik in coastal Croatia, roam Mostar's old town (p131) and join a day tour visiting Počitelj (p141), Blagaj (p138) and the Kravice waterfalls (p142). After two days in Sarajevo (p110) head for Jajce (p154), then bus it down to Split in Croatia. Or visit Višegrad (p146) en route to Mokra Gora and Belgrade in Serbia.
- **Two weeks** As above, but add quaint Trebinje (p143) and historic Stolac (p142) between Dubrovnik and Mostar, ski or go quad-biking around Bjelašnica (p129) near Sarajevo, visit the controversial Visoko pyramid (p150) and old-town Travnik (p152) en route to Jajce and consider adding in some high-adrenalin rafting (p163) from Banja Luka, Bihać or Foča.

CLIMATE & WHEN TO GO

Bosnia gets cold, snowy winters and baking hot summers. Hercegovina has milder winters and truly scorching summers, though even here the bare mountaintops can stay snow-whitened till mid-April. In spring the days are gently warm (if often wet) and the country-side bursts forth with dazzling blossoms and

---

HOW MUCH?

- **Short taxi ride** 5KM
- **Internet access per hour** 1.50-3KM
- **Espresso coffee** 0.50-2KM
- **Shot of šljia (plum brandy)** 1.50KM
- **Movie ticket** 3-5KM

LONELY PLANET INDEX

- **Litre of petrol** 2.01KM (diesel 2.18KM)
- **Litre of bottled water** 0.90KM (But why not drink from the tap?)
- **Half-litre of beer** 3KM in midrange bar
- **Souvenir Bosnian coffee set** from 25KM
- **Street snack (burek)** 2KM

---

lush meadow greenery. Bring a sweater for the cool April nights. See p429 for a Mostar climate chart.

In spring and autumn tourists are rare, but in summer the availability of accommodation can be stretched in Sarajevo and Mostar as diaspora Bosnians come 'home'. The peak ski season is mid-December to mid-March, but prices fall considerably in later March if you're prepared to gamble on the snow conditions (often excellent but much less predictable at that time).

Rafting in April and May is high-adrenalin, world-quality stuff best left to the most experienced. Rivers calm down in mid-summer, making rafting conditions much less taxing for novices in July.

HISTORY

From the faith of medieval kings to the who-did-what of the 1990s conflict, much of BiH's 'history' remains highly controversial and is seen very differently according to one's ethno-religious viewpoint.

Early History

The region's ancient inhabitants were the Hellenic Illyrian people, whose peaceable existence became steadily tougher around 2500 years ago, leading them to build hefty fortifications like those at Daorson near Stolac (p143). They were nonetheless conquered by the Romans in AD 9. After a period of pacification, the Romans started building fine

BOSNIA & HERCEGOVINA

mosaic-floored villas around the country, most notably around Bileća, Stolac (p142) and Ilidža (p119). Slavs arrived from the late 6th century and were dominant by 1180, when Bosnia first emerged as an independent entity under former Byzantine governor Ban Kulina.

For periods between 1180 and 1463 Bosnia became one of the most powerful states in the Western Balkans, helped by lucrative lead mines at Olovo, salt extraction at Tuzla and silver deposits at Srebrenica. By the late 1370s and under King Tvtko, Bosnia gained Hum (future Hercegovina) and controlled much of Dalmatia. But the Turks were coming. For 80 years Turkish raids whittled away at the country and by the 1460s most of Bosnia was under

Ottoman control. Resistance continued under Herceg (Duke) Stjepan Vukčić in Hum, later renamed Hercegovina in his honour. Despite fratricidal family quarrels, his son held out until 1482 when his dramatic mountaintop castle at Blagaj (p138) finally fell.

Ottoman Rule

Without the strong supra-national religious infrastructures prevalent in neighbouring Serbia (Orthodox) and Croatia (Catholic), BiH assimilated into the Ottoman Empire comparatively swiftly (see p107). Within a few generations, Islam had become dominant amongst townspeople and landowners, though a sizeable proportion of the *rayah* (serfs) remained Christian. Bosnians also became

BOSNIA & HERCEGOVINA

particularly prized soldiers in the Ottoman army, many rising eventually to high rank within the imperial court. Most notable of these was Mehmed-paša Sokolović, who became Grand Vizier (1565–79), effectively running the whole vast empire for three sultans. Such folk often remembered their homeland with a *vakuf* (bequest) to build mosques or public facilities: in Sokolović's case these were the famous stone bridges at Višegrad (p146) and Trebinje (p143).

But after three centuries the Ottoman economy was foundering. All attempts to modernise the archaic feudal system were strenuously resisted by the entrenched Bosnian-Muslim elite, while to the east the Serbs fought for quasi-independence in the 1804 and 1807 rebellions, initially planned from Dobrun (p148) in eastern Bosnia.

In 1874, just a year after Istanbul's banking collapse (p32) had left the empire reeling, Bosnia had a disastrously bad harvest. Starving, mostly-Christian Bosnian peasants with nothing to lose kicked off a wave of revolts that snowballed into a tangle of pan-Balkan wars. Ottoman reprisals were so harsh that peasants started to flee en masse. Flooded by around 200,000 desperate Bosnian-Christian refugees, Austria-Hungary reluctantly agreed to the 1878 Congress of Berlin's invitation…to occupy BiH.

Austro-Hungarian Rule

Austria-Hungary's invasion swiftly stabilised Bosnia such that the refugees could go home. Theoretically it remained under Ottoman sovereignty but, treating it like a colony, the Austro-Hungarians rapidly launched BiH into an unprecedented period of development. Roads, railways and bridges were built and coal mining and forestry became booming industries. Education encouraged a new generation of Bosnians to look increasingly towards Vienna, which at that time was approaching a peak of intellectual and artistic brilliance. But political unrest was simmering. Nationalism had been on the rise amongst Bosnian Catholics, who increasingly identified with neighbouring Croatia (itself within Austria-Hungary). Meanwhile Orthodox Bosnians, identifying with recently independent Serbia, increasingly imagined becoming part of a greater Serbian homeland. In danger of being lost in between lay Bosnia's Muslims who had, since 1878, lost their 400-year 'right' to economic dominance. Although emigration to Turkey considerably reduced their numbers after 1878, they still constituted around 40% of the population and belatedly started to develop a distinct Bosniak (Bosnian Muslim) 'ethnic' consciousness.

While Turkey was distracted by the 1908 Young Turk revolution, Austria-Hungary annexed BiH. On the face of things, this only formalised the de facto situation since 1878. But it was a slap in the face for all those who dreamed of a pan-Slavic or greater Serbian future. The resultant scramble for the last remainders of the Ottoman Empire in Europe kicked off the Balkan Wars of 1912 and 1913. No sooner had these been (unsatisfactorily) resolved than the heir to the Austrian throne was shot dead while visiting Sarajevo (see the boxed text, p114). One month later Austria declared war on Serbia and the whole Western world swiftly followed.

World Wars, Communism & Political Tension

WWI killed an astonishing 15% of the Bosnian population. It also brought down both the Turkish and Austro-Hungarian empires, leaving BiH to be absorbed into proto-Yugoslavia.

During WWII BiH was occupied partly by Italy and partly by Germany, and then absorbed into the newly created fascist state of Croatia. Croatia's Ustaše trumped even Germany's Nazis in the zeal with which they decimated Bosnia's Jewish population. They also persecuted Serbs and Muslims, though, in a very complex situation, there was also a pro-Nazi group of Bosnian Muslims who committed their own atrocities against Bosnian Serbs. Meanwhile Serb Četniks and Tito's Communist Partisans put up some stalwart resistance to the Germans as well as fighting each other. The BiH mountains proved ideal territory for Tito's guerrilla army, who, despite many setbacks, including the loss of the Užice Republic, regrouped to launch campaigns from near Foča (p146) and later from Mrkonjić-Grad (p157). Their major battles at Tjentište (p146) and Mrakovica (p161) are still locally commemorated with vast memorials, and it was at Jajce (p155) in 1943 that Tito's anti-fascist council famously formulated a constitution for a postwar inclusive, socialist Yugoslavia.

Post-WWII, BiH was granted republic status within Tito's initially antireligious Yugoslavia. After Tito fell out with the USSR in 1954 and became prominent in the 'non-aligned movement', Yugoslavia's alliances with Egypt and India meant that having 'token' Muslim Bosnians on the diplomatic staff suddenly became a useful cachet. However, up until 1971 'Muslim' was not considered a nationality, so Bosniaks had had to register as Croat, Serb or 'Other/Yugoslav'.

Despite mining development in the northeast and the boost of the 1984 Sarajevo Winter Olympics, Bosnia remained one of the least developed Yugoslav republics.

The 1990s Conflict

In the post-Tito era, as Yugoslavia imploded, 'ethnic' tensions were ratcheted up by ultranationalist Serb leader Slobodan Milošević and equally radical Croat leader Franjo Tuđman. Although these two leaders were at war by spring 1991, they reputedly came up with a de facto agreement during secret meetings at Karađorđevo and Tikveš in which they planned to divide BiH between breakaway Croatia and rump Yugoslavia.

Under president Alija Izetbegović, BiH declared independence from Yugoslavia on 15 October 1991. Bosnian Serb parliamentarians wanted none of this and withdrew to set up their own government at Pale, 20km east of Sarajevo. BiH was recognised internationally as an independent state on 6 April 1992, but Sarajevo was already under siege both by Serb paramilitaries and by parts of the Yugoslav army (JNA).

Over the next three years a brutal and extraordinarily complex civil war raged. Best known is the campaign of ethnic cleansing in northern and eastern BiH, creating the 300-sq-km 'pure' Serb Republika Srpska (RS). But locals of each religion will readily admit that there were terrible criminals on both sides. In western Hercegovina the Croat population armed itself with the help of neighbouring Croatia, eventually ejecting Serbs from their villages in a less reported but similarly brutal war.

Perhaps unaware of the secret Tuđman-Milošević understanding, Izetbegović had signed a formal military alliance with Croatia in June 1992. But by early 1993 fighting had broken out between Muslims and Croats, creating another war front. Croats attacked Muslims in Stolac and Mostar, bombarding their historic monuments and blasting Mostar's famous bridge into the river. Muslim troops, including a small foreign mujahedin force, attacked Croat villages around Travnik, desecrating churches like that of Guča Gora monastery (p154).

With atrocities on all sides, the West's reaction was confused and erratic. In August 1992, pictures of concentration-camp and rape-camp victims (mostly Muslim) found in northern Bosnia spurred the UN to send a protection force (Unprofor) of 7500 peacekeeping troops. They secured the neutrality of Sarajevo airport well enough to allow the delivery of humanitarian aid but overall proved notoriously impotent.

In the upper Drina Valley, Foča (p146) and Višegrad (p146) had already been ethnically cleansed of Muslims, with uncounted bodies dumped off Višegrad's famous bridge. The UN replied by declaring embattled Muslim enclaves around Srebrenica (p150), Župa and

BOSNIA & HERCEGOVINA

Goražde (p146) 'safe' zones. Rarely has the term 'safe' been more misused. When NATO fighters belatedly authorised air strikes aimed at protecting these areas, the Serbs responded by capturing 300 Unprofor peacekeepers and chaining them to potential targets to keep the planes away.

In July 1995 Dutch peacekeepers could only watch as the starving, supposedly 'safe' area of Srebrenica fell to a Bosnian Serb force led by the infamous Ratko Mladić. An estimated 8000 Muslim men were slaughtered in Europe's worst mass killings since WWII. Somewhat miraculously, Goražde held out, albeit in ruins, thanks to sporadically available UN food supplies.

By this stage, Croatia had renewed its own internal offensive, expelling Serbs from the Krajina region of Croatia in August 1995. At least 150,000 of these dispossessed people then moved to the Serb-held areas of northern Bosnia.

Finally, another murderous Serb mortar attack on Sarajevo's Markale market kickstarted a shift in UN and NATO politics. An ultimatum to end the Serbs' siege of Sarajevo was made more persuasive by two weeks of NATO air strikes in September 1995. US president Bill Clinton's proposal for a peace conference in Dayton, Ohio, was accepted soon afterwards.

Dayton Agreement

While maintaining BiH's prewar external boundaries, Dayton divided the country into today's pair of roughly equal-sized 'entities' (see the boxed text, p104), each with limited autonomy. Finalising the border between the Federation of Bosnia and Hercegovina (the Muslim and Croat portion, including central Sarajevo) and the Republika Srpska (the Serb part) required considerable political and cartographic creativity to ensure that key enclaves remained connected to the 'right' entity, notably Mrkonjić-Grad (p157) to the RS and Goražde to the Federation. In 1999 the last sticking point, Brčko, was belatedly given a special self-governing status all of its own. See p149.

Overseeing BiH as a whole, Dayton created a curious rotating tripartite presidency, kept in check by the EU's High Representative (see www.ohr.int). This powerful position was most famously filled from 2002 to 2006 by the UK's former Liberal Democrat leader Paddy Ashdown.

For refugees (1.2 million abroad, and a million displaced within BiH), the Dayton Agreement emphasised the right to return to (or to sell) their prewar homes. Meanwhile international agencies donated very considerable funding to restore BiH's infrastructure, housing stock and historical monuments.

An embarrassing problem post-Dayton was the failure to find and try as war criminals Ratko Mladić and the Bosnian Serb leader Radovan Karadžić (president of the RS until July 1996). Despite $5 million rewards offered for their arrest, Karadžić was not finally apprehended until July 2008, and some supporters still perceive him as an honest patriot.

THE TWO ENTITIES OF BOSNIA & HERCEGOVINA

BiH Today

Nonnationalist politicians now run the RS while, under EU and American pressure, BiH has centralised considerably in a movement away from the original Dayton 'separate powers' concept. BiH now has a unified army, common passports and indistinguishable car licence plates, and both entities now use the same currency, albeit with banknotes in two somewhat different designs. Many (though by no means all) refugees have returned and rebuilt their prewar homes.

Today it's economics rather than nationalism that is the great concern for most Bosnians. Those few socialist-era factories that weren't destroyed in the 1990s conflicts have downsized to fit tough 21st-century global realities. New business-friendly government initiatives, including a recent wave of privatisations, are eyed with suspicion: the populace fears growing corruption. People assume that one day BiH will join the EU, though for many, nearby Slovenia's experience suggests that EU membership will just push up prices and make life harder. 'Life's tough,' one war-widowed homestay hostess told us, 'but at least there's peace.'

PEOPLE

Bosniaks (Bosnian Muslims), Bosnian Serbs (Orthodox) and Bosnian Croats (Catholics) are all southern Slavs. Physically they are indistinguishable. The prewar population was mixed, with intermarriage common in the cities. Stronger divisions have inevitably appeared since the ethnic cleansing of the 1990s. The war resulted in massive population shifts, changing the size and linguistic balance of many cities. Notably, the population of Banja Luka grew by over 100,000 as it absorbed Serb refugees from Croatia.

Bosniaks now predominate in Sarajevo and central BiH, Bosnian Croats in western and southern Hercegovina, and Bosnian Serbs in the RS, which includes Istochno (East) Sarajevo. Relations between the three groups have virtually normalised on a human level, though in the political sphere contacts remain limited.

RELIGION

Blurring the borderline between Europe's Catholic west and Orthodox east, sparsely populated medieval Bosnia had its own independent church, which remains the source

BOSNIA & HERCEGOVINA

THE BOSNIAN CHURCH

Although theoretically subservient to Rome, medieval Bosnia had a quasi-independent church that adopted certain Orthodox (and unorthodox) teachings. Saints days weren't aligned with Rome's. And monasteries permitted entire families to join the monks, blurring the lines between ordained and lay life. Such details seem fairly petty today, but they led Rome to worry that Bosnians were raving heretics. And heresy was a very serious matter in witch-burning 12th century Europe. For years historians have linked the Bosnian Church with the Bogomils, a ruthlessly persecuted Bulgarian gnostic movement which followed Christ's teachings but rejected Jesus' virginal conception and saw no spiritual merit in venerating his mum. These days, however, scholars believe that the Bosnian Church held masses, read psalms and considered the cross a sacred symbol – all things that Bogomils rejected. After a deal with Ban Kulina in 1203, the Roman Catholic authorities sent in 'approved' priests and later set up a series of Franciscan monasteries (like the one at Guča Gora; see p154) to keep an eye on developments in Bosnia. Even they found few deep heresies to report.

In 1459, King Stjepan Tomaš demanded that the Bosnian clergy convert to mainstream Catholicism. This wasn't a spiritual decision. With the imminent threat of Turkish invasion looming, it was a desperate gamble that he hoped would persuade the pope to send him a defensive force to resist the Muslim onslaught. The ploy failed. Four years later the Turks deposed him and Islamisation began.

Being monastic rather than church based, the philosophical grip that the Bosnian Church held on the general population was probably relatively light. This might explain why, over the century following the arrival of the Ottomans, such a large percentage of Bosnians converted to Islam, albeit mainly as a materialist trade-off to improve civic privileges.

The catacombs in Jajce (see p154) contain what some consider to be one of the last Bosnian Church shrine rooms.

of many historical myths (see the boxed text, p107).

Following their conquest by the Ottoman Turks, many Bosnians converted to the easygoing Ottoman brand of Sufi-inspired Islam as much to gain civil privileges as for spiritual enlightenment. The Ottoman Empire was much more religiously open minded than Western Europe at that time and offered refuge to the Sephardic Jews evicted en masse from Spain in 1492. While conditions varied, Bosnian Jews mostly prospered up until WWII, when most of the 14,000-strong community fled or were murdered by Nazis.

Bosnian Muslims also suffered horribly during WWII, with at least 756 mosques destroyed. Postwar Yugoslavia's Stalinist and initially antireligious line softened when Tito repositioned the country as a 'nonaligned' state, resulting in the growing status of Islam within 1950s Yugoslavia.

Today about 40% of the population is Muslim, 31% is Orthodox (mostly Bosnian Serbs), 15% is Roman Catholic (mostly Bosnian Croats) and 4% is Protestant. There are around 500 Jews. Religion is taken seriously as a badge of ethnicity, but spiritually most people are fairly secular.

ARTS

Sarajevo was once Yugoslavia's unofficial cultural capital. The 1990s conflict abruptly ended that, with artists fleeing back to their home republics or emigrating. But the arts scene is slowly recovering and the conflict itself has spurred much artistic reflection.

Literature

Bosnia's best-known writer, Ivo Andrić (1892–1975), won the 1961 Nobel Prize for Literature. With astonishing psychological agility, his classic epic novel *The Bridge on the Drina* retells 350 years of Bosnian history as seen through the eyes of unsophisticated townsfolk in Višegrad (p146). His *Travnik Chronicles* (aka *Bosnian Chronicle*) is also rich with human insight in its portrayal of Bosnia through the eyes of somewhat jaded 19th-century foreigners (see Travnik, p152). *Death and the Dervish* by Meša Selimović (1910–82) is a melancholy account of life in Bosnia during the Ottoman period, analysing the relationship between man and God.

Stolac-born 20th-century poet Mak Dizdar's most important and linguistically demanding collection, *The Stone Sleeper,* was inspired by the *stećci* (medieval tombstones; see the boxed text, opposite).

Contemporary US-based Bosnian author Aleksandar Hemon is best known for his sharpwitted collection of short stories, *The Question of Bruno*. This eclectic selection includes spiky historical musings, incisive childhood reminiscences and a surreal 'life' story of Alphonse Kauders that's like a literary equivalent of the Rolling Stones's *Sympathy for the Devil*.

Numerous writers have produced thoughtprovoking essays, short stories and poems exploring the prickly subject of the 1990s conflict. Quality varies, but many works fascinatingly contrast the conflict's horrors with the victims' enduring humanity. Recommended collections include Miljenko Jergović's *Sarajevo Marlboro* and Semezdin Mehmedinović's *Sarajevo Blues,* while *Zlata's Diary* (by Zlata Filipović) is a best-selling wartime journal often compared to Anne Frank's WWII diary. Emir Suljagić's *Postcards from the Grave* gives compulsively frightening firsthand insight into the Srebrenica massacre.

Cinema

Danis Tanović's Oscar-winning 2002 film *No Man's Land* portrays the relationship between two soldiers, one Muslim, one Serb, caught in the same trench during the Sarajevo siege.

Go West takes on the deep taboo of homosexuality, as a wartime Serb-Bosniak gay couple become a latter-day Romeo and Juliet.

World-famous director Emir Kusturica (see p378) was born in Sarajevo. His early films, including *When Father Was Away on Business* and *Do You Remember Dolly Bell?*, deal with fraught family life in 1980s Bosnia.

Gori Vatra (aka Fuse) is an irony-packed dark comedy set in Tešanj (p152) just after the Bosnian war, parodying efforts to hide corruption and create a facade of ethnic reintegration for the sake of a proposed visit by US president Bill Clinton.

In Jasmila Zbanic's prize-winning 2006 film *Grbavica* the central figure discovers that her father was not a war martyr as she had believed. In fact her mother had been one of some 20,000 Bosnian women to suffer in a civil-war rape camp.

Craft

Sarajevo's national museum devotes a major section to Bosnian carpet-craft, though most

---

STEĆCI

The most visible reminders of medieval Bosnia's advanced craftsmanship are the carvings on distinctively chunky block gravestones called *stećci* (singular *stećak*). Some designs appear to symbolise the profession or rank of the deceased, while the use of naturalistic forms over more staid Christian iconology has led many to link them to the mysterious Bosnian Church (see the boxed text, p107). These days, in fact, experts insist that they commemorated individuals of all three Bosnian pre-Ottoman Christian faiths. The most famous *stećak* collection is at Radimlja, near Stolac (p142). However, those collected outside Sarajevo's National Museum (p119) are finer, while those near Umoljani (p130) have a much more visually satisfying setting.

---

of the fine-knotted carpets sold in Sarajevo are imported from Iran. The Foča region has a strong tradition of woollen flat-weaves, especially bold, colourful kilims, and Tuzla's BosFam (p148) sponsors carpet weaving as a self-help industry for refugees.

Bosnian copper and brassware, widely sold in Mostar's Kujundžiluk (p137) and Sarajevo's Baščaršija (p126), ranges from traditional coffee-pot sets to curious ornamental items fashioned from ammunition casings and old bullets.

Music

Derived from the Turkish word *sevda* (love), BiH's famous *sevdah* music typically uses heart-wrenching vocals to recount tales of unhappy amours. Safet Isović (died 2007) sang classic *sevdah*, while **Mostar Sevdah Reunion** (www.mostarsevdahreunion.com) offers a more contemporary version. **Ruho** (www.ruho.ba) and **Seljo** (www.seljo.org) have touring Bosnian folkmusic ensembles. *Sevdah* venue Kuća Sevdaha (p126) has recently opened in Sarajevo.

Sarajevo has an annual jazz festival (p121) and there's an occasional 'mini-Woodstock' at Zelenkovac Eco-Village (p157). Listen to Edin Bosnić for a creative fusion of jazz and traditional Bosnian sounds.

BiH's pop-rock scene follows international trends. The post-industrial city of Tuzla has a strong rap scene led by the local Eminem, Brčko-born Edo Maajka, whose group,

Defence, also delves into reggae territory on its excellent *Baga Musin* album. Website www.fmjam.com (in Bosnian) has details of gigs and offers some free song and video downloads.

FOOD & DRINK
Staples & Specialities

As is the case throughout the Balkans, grilled meats are king in BiH. Cylindrical little *ćevapi* (*ćevapčići*) or patty-shaped *pljeskavica* are typically served in spongy *somun* bread and best when a 1KM scoop of *kajmak* (local curd butter) is melted deliciously into the mix. *Ćevabdžinica* are *ćevapi*-specialist eateries, but almost all restaurants serve them along with *šnicla* (steak or schnitzel), *kotleti* (normally veal), *ražnjići* (shish kebab), *pastrmka* (trout) and *ligne* (squid). Pizza and pasta are also ubiquitous.

Aščinica (usually downmarket local canteens) are most likely to serve pre-prepared traditional dishes like *dolme* (cabbage leaves or vegetables stuffed with minced meat) and hearty stews including *bosanski lonač* (cabbage and meat hotpot).

Buregdžinica eateries serve *burek* (meatstuffed filo pastry) or the equivalent, meatfree, *sirnica* (filled with cheese), *krompiruša* (with potato) or *zeljanica* (with spinach). Precooked versions of the same dishes are sold by weight at many a *pekara* (bakery shop). These stay open remarkably long hours and sometimes have tables to sit and snack.

Vegetarians might also consider side dishes of stewed beans or courgettes, though meaty traces can't be discounted. Sarajevo's Karuzo (p124) offers a few chickpea-based veggie options.

Typical desserts include sugar-soaked *baklava*, excellent stuffed *palačinci* (pancakes), *hurmastica* (syrup-soaked sponge fingers) and *tufahije* (baked apple stuffed with walnut paste and topped with whipped cream). Bosnian cakes and ice creams are divine.

Drinks

Tap water is almost always drinkable. Consider carrying an empty bottle to collect fresh mineral water from free roadside springs.

Alcohol is readily available in both Muslim and Christian areas. Hercegovina produces some excellent yet strangely underrated wines (see the boxed text, p131). A *piča* (shot) of *šljiva* (plum brandy) or *loza* (local grappa) makes a good aperitif or digestive.

Good local beers cost as little as 1.50KM per 300mL glass. Try the semi-sweet Nektar from Banja Luka. Sarajevskaya's dark beer is a delight but very hard to find beyond the brewery's own Pivnica HS pub (p125).

Kava (coffee) is the main social lubricant. Traditional *bosanski* coffee is served with the grinds in a *džezva* (small long-handled brass pot) then carefully decanted into thimble-sized cups *(fildžan)*. Add sugar directly or hold the sugar lump between your teeth and sip the coffee through it. A piece of Turkish delight *(lokum)* and a glass of water complete the ritual. Espressos are even more widespread and generally excellent.

For a list of Bosnian eating and drinking words, see p45.

ENVIRONMENT
The Land
BiH is predominantly mountainous. Some 30 peaks rise between 1700m and 2386m, while only 8% of BiH's 51,129 sq km is below 150m. Just a toe of land tickles the Adriatic Sea at Neum. The arid south (Hercegovina) gives way to limestone uplands carved with grey, craggy caves and deep canyons. The mountain core then descends again to the green rolling hills further north, finally flattening out in just the northeasternmost corner.

The country's wild rivers mostly flow north to join the Sava, but the Neretva cuts south towards the Adriatic Sea while the Trebišnjica 'disappears', having cut west through the Popovo Polje Valley.

Wildlife
About half of the country, mostly the north, is covered in forest. The beech woods at lower altitudes shelter rabbits, foxes, weasels, otters, wild sheep, ibex, deer and lynx, while bird life includes eagles, hawks and vultures. Higher up predominantly coniferous forests hide bears and wolves.

National Parks & Protected Areas
BiH's highest mountains are divided by breathtaking canyons, waterfalls and alpine valleys in the magnificent **Sutjeska National Park** (www.npsutjeska.srbinje.net, in Bosnian) – see p146 – which also hides the Unesco-listed remnants of a 20,000-year-old primeval forest *(perućica)*. **Blidinje** (www.tel.net.ba/blidinje), west of Jablanica, protects a sparse, fascinating wilderness

area dotted with curious isolated stone huts. Northwest of Banja Luka is **Kozara National Park** (www.npkozara.com) – see p161 –a gently attractive patchwork of relatively pastoral mountains and forests popular with hunters. The Hutovo Blato wetlands (p142) provide a prime sanctuary for migratory birds.

Environmental Issues
Landmines, wrecked building stock and unexploded ordnance left over from the 1990s war, plus air pollution from metallurgical plants and rubbish-disposal difficulties all remain significant environmental problems for BiH. Small organisations, including **Green Visions** (www.greenvisions.ba), battle to bring environmental issues to the public consciousness.

SARAJEVO

☎ 033 / pop 737,000

In the 1990s Sarajevo was on the edge of annihilation. Today it's a cosy, vibrant capital whose human scale, wonderful cafe scene, attractive contours and East-meets-West ambience are making it a favourite summer destination. Meanwhile in winter it's brilliantly handy for some of Europe's best-value skiing. Don't be surprised if you end up spending longer than you'd planned.

HISTORY
Roman legions, always keen on a bath, developed the settlement of Aquae Sulphurae around the sulphur springs at Ilidža (p119). However, Sarajevo (from *saraj*, meaning palace) was only officially 'founded' once 15th-century Turks incorporated the tiny village of Vrhbosna. Sarajevo rapidly grew wealthy as a silk-importing entrepot and developed considerably during the 1530s when Ottoman governor Gazi-Husrevbey lavished the city with fine buildings, mosques and the covered bazaar that still bears his name.

In 1697 Eugene of Savoy briefly charged south with his Austrian army and burnt most of the city to the ground. The rebuilt city cautiously enclosed its upper flank in a large fortified citadel whose remnants still dominate the Vratnik area.

The Austrians returned more permanently in 1878, connecting Sarajevo to the rest of modernising Europe with railways, erecting

---

SARAJEVO IN TWO DAYS

Plunge into the delightful pedestrianised lanes of **Baščaršija** (p112), the old Turkish quarter. Linger at the street cafes of **Ferhadija** (p125). Stand on the spot where a 1914 assassination kicked off WWI (p114), then cross the cute Latin Bridge for a coffee at **At Mejdan** (p125), a beer at **Pivnica HS** (p125) or dinner overlooking the city rooftops at **Park Prinčeva** (p124).

Next day, tram-hop across town via **Sniper Alley** (p119) and the impressive **National Museum** (p119) to **Ilidža** (p119), from which it's a short bus-hop to the unique **Tunnel Museum** (p120). Hurry back to town for the last 'show' meal at **Mala Kuhinja** (p123). A drink at laid-back **Mash** (p125) or the delightfully Gothic **Zlatna Ribica** (p125) sets you up for a ballet at the **National Theatre** (p126), a feisty gig at **Bock/FIS** (p126) or an old-style party night at **Sloga** (p126).

---

sturdy central-European buildings and even introducing street lighting before doing so in Vienna – there were doubts about the safety of electricity and it was deemed wiser to test it out in the colonies.

Austro-Hungarian rule was put on notice here by the fatal 1914 pistol shot that killed Archduke Franz Ferdinand (see the boxed text, p114).

Seventy years later Sarajevo attracted world attention by hosting the 1984 Winter Olympics. Then from 1992 to 1995 the infamous siege of the city grabbed the headlines and horrified the world. Ratko Mladić, the Bosnian Serb commander, is reported to have said, 'Shoot at slow intervals until I order you to stop. Shell them until they can't sleep; don't stop until they are on the edge of madness.' *Miss Sarajevo*, a heart-rending song by U2 and Pavarotti, belatedly drew public attention to the conflict. The song, with lyrics expressing war-ravaged citizens' desire for the banally ordinary (boy bands, shopping and make-up), was movingly set to a video intercutting Sarajevo's destruction with the besieged city's defiant beauty pageant. The glamorous contestants poignantly hold a sign begging 'Don't Let Them Kill Us'.

Sarajevo's heritage of six centuries was pounded into rubble and its only access to the outside world was via a metre-wide, 800m-long tunnel under the airport (p120). Over 10,500 Sarajevans died and 50,000 were wounded by Bosnian Serb shelling and sniper fire. Endless white-stoned graveyards on Kovači (Map pp116–17) and up near Koševo Stadium (Map p113) are a moving testament to those terrible years.

ORIENTATION

Sarajevo is tightly wedged into the steep, narrow valley of the modest Miljacka River. The city's old Turkish heart beats atmospherically in Baščaršija, a pedestrianised delight full of coffee houses and wooden-shuttered souvenir shops. To its direct west, fine Austro-Hungarian–era buildings line parts of Maršala Tita, Ferhadija and Obala Kulina Bana. North, east and south a pretty fuzz of red-roofed Bosnian houses dotted with uncountable minarets climbs the valley sides towards remarkably rural green-mountain ridges. Further westward, however, Sarajevo sprawls for over 10km through Novo Sarajevo and dreary Dobrinja past contrastingly dismal ranks of bullet-scarred apartment blocks. Park-filled Ilidža, beyond the airport, marks the end of the city's tramway 'spine' with a parkland flourish.

INFORMATION
Bookshops

The following stock maps, guidebooks, magazines and many English-language books on Bosnia and the former Yugoslavia.

BuyBook (Map pp116-17; ☎ 716450; www.buybook.ba; Radićeva 4; ⏱ 9am-10pm Mon-Sat, 10am 6pm Sun)

Šahinpašić (Map pp116-17; ☎ 667 210; www.btcsahin pasic.com; Vladislava Skarića 8; ⏱ 9am-8pm Mon-Sat) Stocks Lonely Planet guides (some pretty dated) and the famous *Sarajevo Survival Guide* (23KM).

Sejtarija (Map pp116-17; ☎ 205233; www.sejtarija .com; Maršala Tita 19; ⏱ 9am-8pm Mon-Sat)

Internet Access

Click (Map pp116-17; Kundurdžiluk 1a; per hr 3KM; ⏱ 9am-11pm; ✗)

Cyber (Map pp116-17; Pehlivanuša 2; per hr 3KM; ⏱ 10am-11pm Mon-Sat, noon-7pm Sun)

Internet Caffe Baščaršija (Map pp116-17; Aščiluk bb; per hr 1.5KM; ⏱ 24hr) Slightly hidden: take the steps marked Sultan Caffe. Connection fast but sometimes temperamental.

BOSNIA & HERCEGOVINA

Laundry

Askos Laundry (Map pp116-17; Halilbašića 2; ✆ 9am-5pm Mon-Fri, to 3pm Sat)

Left Luggage

Main bus station (Map p113; 1st hr 2KM, then per hr 1KM)

Media

Oslobođenje and *Dnevni avaz* are the most popular daily newspapers. *Dani* is a reliable independent weekly.

Medical Services

Baščaršija Pharmacy (Map pp116-17; Obala Kulina Bana 40; ✆ 24hr)
Centar Urgente Medicine (Map p113; ✆ 297 330; Stepana Tomića bb; ✆ 24hr) Emergency assistance section of the vast Koševo Hospital complex. Take bus 14 from Dom Armije to Hotel Belvedere, then walk 300m northwest (signed CUM).

Money

ATMs are sprinkled all over the city centre. Oddly, there's nowhere to change money at the stations, but there is an ATM outside the bus station. There's also an ATM at the airport where a **booth** (✆ 8am-8pm Mon-Fri, 10am-5pm Sat & Sun) cashes travellers cheques but isn't always open on Sunday despite its posted times. **Turkish Ziraat Bank** (Map pp116-17; www.ziraatbosnia.com; Ferhadija 10; ✆ 8.30am-8pm Mon-Fri, 9am-3pm Sat) cashes travellers cheques with the original receipt.

Post & Telephone

The **'central' post office** (Map p113; ✆ 7am-8pm Mon-Sat) for poste restante is beside the bus station. The gorgeous **main post office** (Map pp116-17; Obala Kulina Bana 8; ✆ 7am-8pm Mon-Sat) is actually much much more central. Counters 17 to 19 are for stamps.

Tour Agencies

All the following offer city tours; a minimum group size must sign up.
Green Visions (Map p113; ✆ 717 290; www.green visions.ba; opposite Radnička 66; ✆ 9am-5pm Mon-Fri) Also offers a wide range of set-departure and tailormade hiking trips into the Bosnian mountains and villages.
Ljubičica (Map pp116-17; ✆ 232 109, 061131813; www .hostelljubicica.net; Mula Mustafe Bašeskije 65; ✆ 8am-10pm Oct-Apr, 7am-11pm May-Sep) Helpful and popular.
Sartour (Map pp116-17; ✆ 238 680; Mula Mustafe Bašeskije 63; ✆ 9am-7pm)

Tourist Information

Sonar (www.sonar.ba) Useful new visitor website.
Tourist information centre (Map pp116-17; ✆ 220 724; www.sarajevo-tourism.com; Zelenih Beretki 22a; ✆ 9am-9pm Mon-Fri summer, to 6pm rest of yr, 9am-3pm Sat & Sun all yr) Remarkably helpful, with maps, bus timetables, brochures and ready answers for many an awkward question.

Travel Agencies

Centrotrans-Eurolines (Map pp116-17; ✆ 205 481; www.centrotrans.com; Ferhadija 16; ✆ 8.30am-8.30pm Mon-Fri, 9am-3pm Sat) International bus, train and ferry tickets.
Relax Tours (Map pp116-17; ✆ /fax 263 330; www.relaxtours.com; Zelenih Beretki 22; ✆ 8.30am-8pm Mon-Fri, 9am-5pm Sat) Books airline and ferry tickets.

SIGHTS
Baščaršija & Around

Baščaršija is the bustling old Turkish Quarter, a delightful warren of marble-flagged pedestrian lanes and open courtyards full of cafes, jewellery shops, mosques, copper workshops and charming restaurants.

Nicknamed **Pigeon Square** for all the birds, Baščaršija's central open space centres on the **Sebilj** (Map pp116–17), an ornate 1891 drinking fountain that looks like an enclosed oriental gazebo. It leads past lively if touristcentric coppersmith alley Kazandžiluk to the picturesque, garden-wrapped, 16th-century **Baščaršija mosque** (Map pp116-17; Bravadžiluk) and the six-domed **Bursa Bezistan** (Map pp116-17; ✆ 239 590; www.muzejsarajeva.ba; Abadžiluk 10; admission 2KM; ✆ 10am-6pm Mon-Fri, to 3pm Sat). Originally a silk-trading bazaar, this 1551 stone building is now a museum with bite-sized overviews of the city's history on display boards around a large, compelling model of Sarajevo as it looked back in 1878.

The splendid **Gazi-Husrevbey Vakuf buildings**, built by 1530s Ottoman governor Gazi-Husrevbey, include a **madrassa** (religious school; Map pp116-17; Sarači 33-49) with multiple stone chimneys, a fine **covered bazaar** (see p126) and the imposing **Gazi-Husrevbey mosque** (Map pp116-17; ✆ 534 375; www.vakuf-gazi.ba; Sarači 18; admission 2KM; ✆ 9am-noon, 2.30-4pm & 5.30-7pm May-Sep). Especially at dusk its cylindrical minaret contrasts photogenically with the elegant stone **clock tower** across Mudželeti Veliki alley. The tower would look Italian but for the Arabic numerals on its clock face.

BOSNIA & HERCEGOVINA

GREATER SARAJEVO

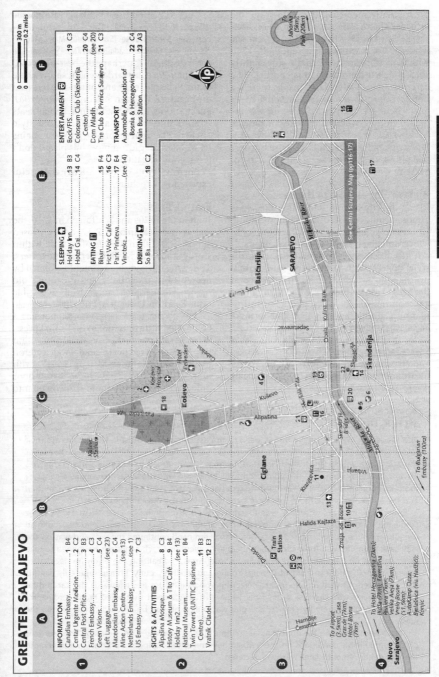

INFORMATION
Canadian Embassy	1 B4
Centar Urgente Medicine	2 C2
Central Post Office	3 B3
French Embassy	4 C3
Green Visions	5 C4
Left Luggage	(see 23)
Macedonian Embassy	6 C4
Mine Action Centre	(see 13)
Netherlands Embassy	(see 1)
US Embassy	7 C3

SIGHTS & ACTIVITIES
Alipašina Mosque	8 C3
History Museum & Tito Café	9 B4
Holiday Inn	(see 13)
National Museum	10 B4
Twin Towers (UNITIC Business Centre)	11 B3
Vratnik Citadel	12 E3

SLEEPING
Holiday Inn	13 B3
Hotel Gaj	14 C4

EATING
Biban	15 F4
Hot Wok Café	16 C3
Park Prinčeva	17 E4
Vinoteka	(see 14)

DRINKING
So Ba	18 C2

ENTERTAINMENT
Bock/FIS	19 C3
Coloseum Club (Skenderija Center)	20 C4
Com Mladih	(see 20)
The Club & Pivnica Sarajevo	21 C3

TRANSPORT
Automobile Association of Bosnia & Hercegovina	22 C4
Main Bus Station	23 A3

See Central Sarajevo Map (pp116-17)

Originally medieval, the little stone **Old Orthodox Church** (Map pp116–17; ☎ 571 065; Mula Mustafe Bašeskije 59; admission 1KM; ☼ 8am-8pm summer, to 4pm winter) was last rebuilt in 1740 with a rectilinear tower that's still slightly shell-shocked from the 1990s conflict. The exterior looks austere, but inside there's a highly impressive iconostasis lavished in gilt. There are even finer icons in the attached cloister, where a three-room **museum** (admission 2KM; ☼ 9am-3pm Tue-Sun) also showcases tapestries, old manuscripts, incense burners and photo-alerts over the recent suffering of Serbs in Kosovo.

Bjelave Slopes & Svrzo House

Rising directly behind Baščaršija, Bjelave is a more genuinely 'lived-in' neighbourhood. Homes range from dreary apartment blocks with crumbling plasterwork and banally modern new brick boxes to traditional Turkish-style houses with courtyards and *doksat* overhanging windows, most impressive at the Svrzo House (right). Dotted throughout are centuries-old mosques, plus a few intimidating Catholic edifices like **Vrhbosnanska Bogoslovija Seminary** (Map pp116–17; Josipa Štadlera bb), Moorish masterpieces like the fabulous **Islamic Science Faculty building** (Map pp116–17; Ćemerlina 54) and striking Austro-Hungarian palaces like the wonderfully indulgent **UK Consulate building** (Map pp116–17; Petrakijina 11).

Tucked behind the 1483 **Jahja Paša mosque** (Map pp116–17; Ćemerlina bb), the wonderful 18th-century **Svrzo House** (Svrzina Kuća; Map pp116–17; ☎ 535 264; Glođina 8; admission 2KM; ☼ 10am-6pm Mon-Fri, to 3pm Sat) is perhaps the best-preserved Ottoman-era courtyard townhouse anywhere in the Balkans. Inner and outer quarters lead off beautiful wooden balconies (*kamarija*), guest rooms sport traditional bench seats (*sećija*) and there's a brilliant old-style kitchen. The upper-storey privy even retains its wooden long-drop pipe, but please don't test its functionality!

Borrow (free) or buy (5KM) the useful explanatory brochure.

Vratnik Area

Built in the 1720s and reinforced in 1816, the **Vratnik citadel** (Map pp116–17) once enclosed almost 500,000 sq metres of hillside within sturdy stone walls and powerful gate towers. Today the most visible remnant is topped by decrepit but potentially grand century-old Austro-Hungarian barracks. More accessible is the **Kula Ploče tower** (Map pp116–17; Ploča bb; admission free; ☼ 10am-6pm Mon-Fri, to 3pm Sat) housing a fascinating little museum to BiH's first president, Alija Izetbegović. Accessed from within the museum, a section of citadel wall leads on to the **Širokac Kula tower** (Map pp116–17), with more exhibits. Ask to have the exit-only door unlocked here if you want to stroll on up into

---

SITTING DUCK

The trigger for WWI is usually traced back to the assassination of Austria-Hungary's royal heir Archduke Franz Ferdinand while on a state visit to Sarajevo in April 1914. During Yugoslav times the assassin, a young Serb called Gavrilo Princip, was considered a hero. The Latin Bridge was renamed in his honour, and the point from which he fired was celebrated by a pair of concrete footprints. Since the 1990s Princip has been redefined as a terrorist. Today the bridge is re-Latinised and the famous concrete footprints have been slung into the museum next door.

Either way, Princip's notoriety was the result of an astonishing chance. On the day, Franz Ferdinand's motorcade had already passed five of Princip's co-conspirators, who had bungled the job when their bomb missed its target. Franz Ferdinand continued the visit and was on the way back from City Hall (now the National Library) when his Czech chauffeur happened to take a wrong turn up Zelenih Beretki (then Franz Josef Strasse). Realizing the error, he decided to reverse, stopping right in front of Princip. Young and relatively puny, Princip reputedly wet his pants with terror but still managed to seize the opportunity. He leapt towards the car and hit Franz Ferdinand with the first shot of his 10mm pistol. A second shot killed Franz Ferdinand's wife too, though entirely by chance: the gun was pulled off-line by a guard trying to stop the massacre.

Serbia was blamed for the double assassination. Pushed by a war-eager Germany, the Austrians placed unfulfillable conditions on the Serbian government in their demands for an enquiry into the foul deed. A month later war was declared.

the charmingly untouristy Vratnik area. It's dotted with red-roofed old houses and traditional mosques, some with central wooden minarets like the **Arapova mosque** (Map pp116-17; Požegina bb), others fronted with timber balconies like the appealing 1560 **Lučevica mosque** (Map pp116-17; Očaktanum 78). Minibus 55 takes you back towards Pigeon Sq, or you can stroll down via the grassy-topped **yellow bastion** (Map pp116-17; Žuta Tabija; Jekovac bb) for stunning views across the city. Directly beneath, in **Kovači martyrs' cemetery** (Map pp116–17), former president Alija Izetbegović's dome-covered grave is guarded by uniformed soldiers.

Riverbank

After a devastating flood, the narrow Miljacka River was canalised with dykes in 1891. This work swept away all the old Ottoman houses except the **Inat Kuća** (Spite House; see p124), so named because of the owner's dogged refusal to accept rehousing and compensation. Instead he insisted that his house be moved stone by stone. History repeated itself a year later when the house was moved a second time, crossing the river to make space for the City Hall, now the **National Library** (Map pp116–17). From a distance that building's intricate Moorish arched balconies make it Sarajevo's most beautiful building. It was here in 1914 that Franz Ferdinand started his little open-top drive that ended up motoring towards world war (see the boxed text, opposite). The building was hit by a Serb incendiary shell on 25 August 1992, deliberately aimed at destroying the unique repository of Bosnian books and irreplaceable manuscripts. Restoration work has stalled and the building remains a stabilised partial ruin.

Built before 1565, the **Emperor's mosque** (Map pp116-17; Konak 2; ☉ prayer times, Muslims only) is one of Sarajevo's biggest and was once the site of the Ulema Majlis palace. A short walk behind, the imposing **St Anthony's Church** (Map pp116-17; Franjevačka bb) has a tall Venetian tower and hosts occasional organ concerts. Nearby, the **Sarajevska Brewery** (Map pp116-17; www.sarajevska-pivara.ba; Franjevačka 15) still operates from its delightfully fanciful 19th-century folly of arches and turrets. Don't miss the associated Pivnica HS bar-restaurant (p125).

Opposite the attractive little Latin Bridge, right beside the spot where Princip shot Franz Ferdinand, the **Sarajevo 1878–1918 Museum** (Map pp116-17; ☎ 533 288; Zelenih Beretki 2; admission 2KM; ☉ 10am-6pm Mon-Fri, to 3pm Sat) is a one-room exhibition on Sarajevo's Austro-Hungarian era that focuses understandably on the assassination. A video loop includes reconstruction footage of Franz Ferdinand's fateful drive.

One block west, **Despića House** (Map pp116-17; ☎ 215 531; Despićeva 2; admission 2KM; ☉ 10am-6pm Mon-Fri, to 3pm Sat) shows off the interior of a rich Bosnian 19th-century merchant's home. Across the river, **Atmejdan Park** is graced by an unusual bandstand-cafe (p125).

Further west, Obala Kulina Bana is patchily flanked with fine Austro-Hungarian-era buildings, best observed across the Mijlacka from behind the **Ashkenazi Synagogue** (Map pp116-17; Hamidije Kreševljakovića 59). With four corner domes, the synagogue itself is potentially attractive but cruelly sandwiched between 20th-century architectural monstrosities.

It's well worth popping into the grand **Main Post Office** (p112) to admire its soaring interior and old-fashioned brass counter dividers. Next door, the **University Rectorate** (Map pp116-17; Obala Kulina Bana 7) is similarly grand. Back across the river, the splendid Gothic revival–style **Academy of Arts** (Map pp116-17; Obala Maka Dizdara) looks like a miniature version of Budapest's magnificent national parliament building.

Ferhadija & Around

In the Austro-Hungarian era the city's centre of gravity shifted westwards from Baščaršija to now-pedestrianised **Ferhadija**. It's still one of Sarajevans' favourite streets for a *passeggiata* (casual stroll) and for *mahalska priča*, a form of friendly neighbourhood gossip that gives Sarajevo a cosy feeling of community beyond anything you'd expect from a cosmopolitan European capital.

The 1889 neo-Gothic **Catholic Cathedral** (Katedrala; Map pp116-17; Trg Fra Grge Martića 2; ☉ 9am-4pm) is where Pope John Paul II served mass during his 1997 visit. The steps in front make a popular meeting point and on the pavement beside the western wing is one of the last remaining **Sarajevo roses** (see the boxed text, p119).

The 1581 **Sephardic Synagogue** (Mula Mustafe Bašeskije 40) has a memorably stark, medieval stone interior soaring three storeys above the dark wooden *bimah* (*tevah*, rabbi's 'pulpit'). It reopened for worship in 2004 but only holds services at Rosh Hashanah (Jewish New Year), otherwise doubling as the interesting **Jewish Museum** (Map pp116-17; ☎ 535 688; admission 2KM;

BOSNIA & HERCEGOVINA

CENTRAL SARAJEVO

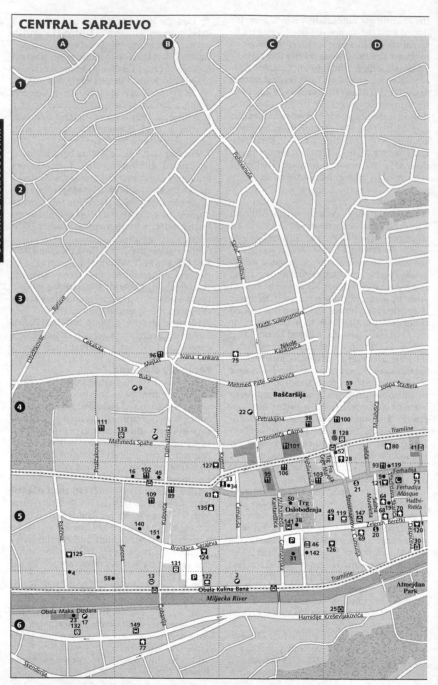

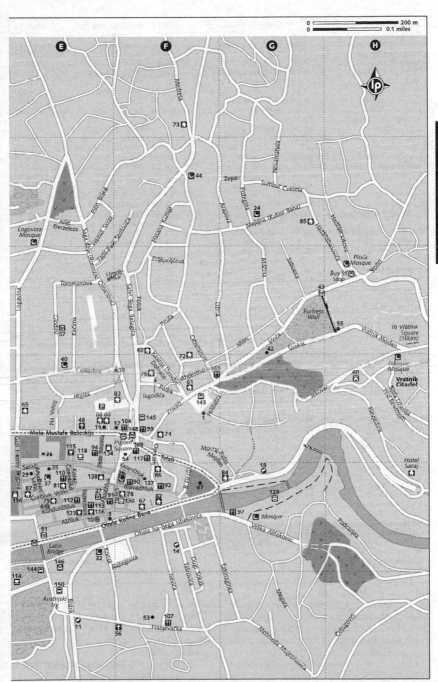

BOSNIA & HERCEGOVINA

🕙 10am-6pm Mon-Fri, to 1pm Sun). Exhibits include thank yous to Sarajevo citizens who saved Jewish lives in WWII, a wince-inducing circumcision knife and a copy of the priceless Sarajevo Haggadah (see the boxed text, p120).

Old men play chess on Trg Oslobođenja (Liberation Sq), with pedestrian paving slabs doubling as squares of a **giant board** (Map pp116–17). Behind, the unfortunate bronze 'Multicultural Man' of a **peace statue** (Map pp116–17) seems to be suffering from genital frostbite.

The large 1872 **Orthodox Cathedral** (Saborna Crkva; Map pp116-17; Trg Oslobođenja), built in

BOSNIA & HERCEGOVINA

WAR WOUNDS

Almost 15 years after the civil war, bombed-out buildings are much rarer here than in Mostar, but Sarajevo still has its scars. A few pavements still sport **Sarajevo roses**, the skeletal, splatter-shaped indentations of mortar-shell impacts, symbolically filled in with hard, once-red paint. Several buildings have rows of little brass plaques for those who died in such shellings. For the ultimate war experience, don't miss a visit to the very thought-provoking Tunnel Museum (p120) near Ilidža or a stroll down 'Sniper Alley' (below) with a wartime survivor.

Byzantine-Serb style, is artfully lit at night. Its soaring interior is atmospheric despite some scaffolding.

Generously endowed with facade mouldings, the **National Gallery** (Umjetnička Galerija; Map pp116–17; ☎ 266 550; Zelenih Beretki 8; admission 2KM; ☑ noon-8pm Tue-Sat) displays a comprehensive range of the country's modern and contemporary art. Across the square is the worn yet potentially attractive **Dom Armije** (Map pp116–17) theatre.

Maršala Tita

An **eternal flame** (Vječna vatra; Map pp116–17; Maršala Tita 62) commemorates the victims of WWII. It's outside the **Finance Ministry Building** (Map pp116–17; Maršala Tita 62), formerly Sarajevo's Grand Hotel, which was used by the Nazis as a makeshift wartime prison. A block further, the **National Bank Building** (Map pp116–17; Maršala Tita 25) is built in a supremacist, post–art deco style and guarded by androgynously muscular lamp-bearer statues. The attractively proportioned **Alipašina mosque** (Map p113; Maršala Tita) dates from 1561.

Novo Sarajevo

During the 1992–95 siege, the wide road in from the airport (Zmaja od Bosne) was dubbed 'sniper alley' because Serbian gunmen in surrounding hills could pick off civilians as they tried to cross it. Built in 1984 for the Olympics, the distinctive, custard-and-pudding-coloured **Holiday Inn** (Map p113; ☎ 288 000; www.holidayinn.com/sarajevo; Zmaja od Bosne 4) by 1992 had become Sarajevo's last functioning hotel and famously housed most of the embattled journalists covering the war. Nearby

are Sarajevo's **Twin Towers** (Map p113). These visor-topped glass skyscrapers spent much of the post–civil war period as burnt-out wrecks, a sad symbol of the city's devastation. Today they're gleamingly reconstructed as the UNITIC Business Centre.

Allow a couple of hours to do full justice to the impressive **National Museum** (Zemaljski Muzej Bosne-i-Hercegovine; Map p113; ☎ 668 026; www.zemaljskimuzej.ba; Zmaja od Bosne 3; adult/concession 5/1KM; ☑ 10am-5pm Tue-Fri, to 2pm Sat & Sun). The complex is a quadrangle of four splendid neoclassical buildings purpose-built in 1913. Especially impressive is the ancient-history section showing fine Illyrian and Roman carvings in a room whose soaring Doric columns create the feel of a Greek temple. Upstairs don't miss peeping through the locked, high-security glass door of room 37 to glimpse the **Sarajevo Haggadah**, possibly the world's most valuable book (see the boxed text, p120).

Across a peaceful botanical garden, the natural-history section has endless stuffed animals and pinned insects, but amid the fine mineral samples is a room full of brilliant Roman mosaics from Bileća and Stolac.

The ethnographic section includes well-presented displays of traditional clothing and Bosnian carpets.

The small but engrossing **History Museum** (Map p113; ☎ 210 418; Zmaja od Bosne 5; admission 2KM; ☑ 9am-4pm Mon-Fri, to 1pm Sat & Sun) 'non-ideologically' charts the course of the 1990s conflict. Affecting personal exhibits include ID cards of 'lost' medics, examples of food aid, stacks of Monopoly-style 1990s dinars and a makeshift siege-time 'home'. The museum is in a dreary, war-battered 1970s building that has been deliberately left partly unrepaired, adding to the thought-provoking effect. To recover from the museum's harrowing impact, wander behind the building to the amusingly tongue-in-cheek **Tito Café** (beers 2KM, coffees 1KM; ☑ 7am-3am), replete with Tito busts, stormtrooper-helmet lampshades and a garden terrace of jeep seats and old artillery pieces.

Ilidža

Tram 3 from Baščaršija terminates in Ilidža, 11km west. The spring waters that once attracted the Romans now fill the multiple pools and summer water slides of **Termalna Rivijera** (☎ 771 000; www.terme-ilidza.ba; Butmirska Cesta 18, Ilidža;

SARAJEVO HAGGADAH

Now estimated to be worth nearly a billion US dollars, the famous **Sarajevo Haggadah** is a small but magnificently illuminated 14th-century holy Jewish codex. It survived WWII thanks to the museum's quick-thinking curator, who managed to get it smuggled out in extremis to a rural village through the fingers of Nazi officers who had turned up to confiscate it. That tale forms a key part of Geraldine Brooks's 2007 historical novel *People of the Book*.

During the 1990s conflict, the book was moved to the vaults of the National Bank Building (p119), where it survived years of bombardment.

There's a Haggadah copy in the Jewish museum (p115) if you want to get a closer look.

adult/child 10/8KM, weekends 14/12KM; 9am-10pm). It's fronted by an Indiana Jones fantasy dome full of cafes and snack bars 600m southeast of the tram terminus.

Across the river directly west of the tram stop, central Ilidža is an unremarkable suburban shopping centre. However, in the parkland behind are several upmarket hotels. One of these, the Casa Grande (p122), marks the start of picturesque pedestrianised avenue **Velika Aleja**, lined with mature plane and chestnut trees whose lantern-lamps twinkle towards a magical infinity. The avenue leads past several 1920s mansions, reaching **Vrelo Bosne** park after 3km. Here the Bosna River gushes out of a rocky cliff then trickles through a patchwork of lush mini-islands linked by half-moon wooden bridges, overlooked by the perfectly positioned **Labud Restaurant** (www.hotelilidza.ba/site/labud; mains 8-25KM, coffees 1.50-2.50KM, beers 3-4KM). Locals jog, but there are horse-and-trap rides (10KM) from the Casa Grande. Alternatively, from Ilidža tram terminus take bus 30 to a grey-and-white Orthodox church (3km), then walk 1.2km south.

Butmir

The tunnel that saved Sarajevo! For much of the war Sarajevo was virtually surrounded by hostile Serb forces, while the airport remained neutral (under tenuous UN control) but uncrossable. Only Butmir village and a narrow corridor of land stretching back to Mt Igman remained in Bosniak hands, thanks to some heroic defence. An 800m-long, metre-wide tunnel running from there beneath the runway was just enough to keep Sarajevo supplied with arms and food during the three-year siege. Most of the tunnel has since collapsed, but the unmissable **Tunnel Museum** (off Map p113; 061213760; Tuneli 1, Butmir; admission 5KM; 9am-4pm), on the south side of the runway, gives visitors just a glimpse of its hopes and horrors. Around the shell-pounded house where the tunnel entrance was secreted is displayed an image-provoking collection of construction equipment and photos, and there's a 20-minute video of the wartime tunnel experience.

To get here from Ilidža tram terminus, take Kotorac bus 68A (formerly 32, 10 minutes, at least twice hourly) to the last stop, walk across the bridge, then turn immediately left down Tuneli for 600m. Several agencies include the museum on their Sarajevo city tours.

TOURS

Each listed tour agency (p112) offers city tours, often fascinatingly accompanied by siege survivors.

The tourist information centre (p112) has a list of private guides and is the starting point for the €10 **Sarajevo Discovery** (061190591; www.sarajevo-discovery.com) walking tour (3pm daily, summer only). Ljubičica's popular €15 tour includes the Tunnel Museum (and transport). Centrotrans-Eurolines (p112) runs simple city bus tours (5KM) without stops.

FESTIVALS & EVENTS

The tourist information centre has a monthly *Programme of Cultural Events*; check www.sarajevoarts.ba as well.

Baščaršijske Noći (Baščaršija Nights; www.bascarsijskenoci.ba) In July a whole range of international events covering dance, music and street theatre are performed at various open-air stages around town.

Sarajevo Film Festival (209 411; www.sff.ba; Zelenih Beretki 12/1; tickets 3-6KM) This globally acclaimed festival brings a special atmosphere to the city every August. New commercial releases and art-house movies are screened, almost always offering English subtitles.

Futura Festival of electronic music every October.

International Jazz Festival (www.jazzfest.ba) Week-long November event showcasing local and international performers.

SLEEPING
Budget
HOSTELS & HOMESTAYS

Tour agencies (p112) and freelance guide-fixers like **Mersad 'Miki' Bronja** (☎ 061836491; www .sarajevo-accommodation.com) can arrange hostel and homestay accommodation (the borderline is rather blurred). A common complaint in many budget hostels is that booked guests might find themselves shifted to a less-central 'overflow' location if the hostel fills up. Ideally, look before you 'buy'.

Hostel City Center (Map pp116-17; ☎ 503 294; www .hcc.ba; 3rd fl, Saliha Muvekita 2; dm/s/d/tr/q €12/18/32/45/54) Head and shoulders above most Bosnian hostels, HCC has smart, brand-new bunk rooms with high ceilings and light wood decor. There's a chill-out space with cushions, TV, kitchen, free internet and help-yourself coffee. Three good bathrooms serve 21 beds. There's no sign ring the bell marked HCC at a doorway beyond archetypal downmarket shot-bar Bife Velež.

Kod Keme (Map pp116-17; ☎ 531 140; www.hostel .co.ba; Mali Ćurčiluk 15; s/d from €20/40) Neat, unfussy rooms here are within a pair of immaculately kept divided apartments fashioned from a once-grand private house: a Corinthian column still pierces two of the rooms! Most share bathrooms. Nera, the charming Bosnian-Aussie owner, will soon open a full hotel at No 11a (see www.hotelnacional.ba).

Hostel Sebilj (Map pp116-17; ☎ 573 500; www.pansion sebilj.com.ba; Bravadžiluk bb; dm/s/d/tr from €15/15/30/45) Around a decent-sized if unsophisticated barnlike sitting area, most rooms share his-or-hers bathrooms, though the €20 four-bed dorms have private facilities.

Pansion Lion (Map pp116-17; ☎ 236 137, 061268150; www.lion.co.ba; Bravadžiluk 30; dm/s/d/tr 30/50/100/120KM; P) Warm antique effects, teddies on some beds, dried flowers, and hair driers in bathrooms all put this 10-room *pansion* a notch above most hostels, though the five- and eight-bed dorms are windowless and less cutesy. There's no real lounge area.

Hostel Posillipo (Map pp116-17; ☎ 061778603; amassko@hotmail.com; Besarina Čikma 5; s/d from €15/30) Tucked away up a tiny lane in central Baščaršija, the three rooms here are small but clean and new and share a decent bathroom. The three-bed apartment (€20 per person) has a bar area, leather sofas and its own bathroom. The overflow sister-building is very close by, and the owners speak good English and are helpful if occasionally a little chaotic.

Zem Zem (Map pp116-17; ☎ 239 649; Mula Mustafe Baseskije 61; s/d €15/30) These four cramped and slightly worn rooms, set above a popular gaming room–cafe, are decent value given the small en suite bathrooms and the super-central location. The place is simply marked 'ROOMS'.

Ljubičica (Map pp116-17; ☎ 232 109; www.hostel ljubicica.com; Mula Mustafe Baseskije 65; dm/homestay/apt from €10/15/20; ☺ 8am-10pm winter, 7am-11pm summer) Ljubičica's mixed bag of simple homestay rooms can be decent value if you score a relatively central one. Its very central bunk bed hostel is contrastingly dingy, tight packed and as jolly as a prison, with battered old shared bathrooms. But it's superbly central, and free transfers from the stations ensure a steady flow of takers.

Other options:

Hostel Marko Polo (Map pp116-17; ☎ 535 000, 061245620, www.hostel-markopolo.com; 1st fl, Logavina 6; dm/d €10/30) Unexceptional but decently located family flat–hostel with tight packed beds and no common area. Emina speaks minimal English

Identico (Map pp116-17; ☎ 233 310; Halači 3; dm/s/d from €15/15/20, s/d with private bathroom €20/40) Unspectacular rooms and minuscule shower booths but perfect old-city location.

Motel Sokak (Map pp116-17; ☎ 570 355; www.sokak -motel.com; Mula Mustafe Baseskije 24; s/d/tr €42/68/93) The 11 fairly plain rooms have limited natural light, but there's a decent communal sitting area. The 'motel' is hopeless for parking but set well enough back from the busy road to avoid noise.

Pansion Baščaršija (Map pp116-17; ☎ 061177952; Ćurčiluk Veliki 41; s/d 60/100KM, breakfast 5KM) With much less atmosphere than the cute exterior suggests, the rooms here are rather pricey given that all four share a single bathroom.

CAMPING

AutoKamp Oaza (off Map p113; ☎ 636 141; www .hoteliilidza.ba/site/oaza; tent/car/camper van 7/8/12KM plus per person 10KM) Tree-shaded camping and cara-van hook-ups (electricity 3KM extra) tucked behind the Hotel Izmit, 1.5km west of Ilidža terminus (12km from Baščaršija). Youthful, international vibe.

Midrange

CENTRAL SARAJEVO

Pansion Vijećnica (Map pp116-17; ☎ 233 433; www .pansionvijecnica.co.ba; Mustaj-Pašin Mejdan 5; s/d €30/50) Four-bedroom mini-hotel with period furni-ture, suave little lobby, attractive lilac interi-ors and excellent private showers. It's slightly more sophisticated than its sister-property, Pansion Stari Grad (Map pp116–17; ☎ 239 898; www.sgpansion.co.ba; Bjelina Čikma 4; singles/doubles from €35/50).

Hotel Hecco (Map pp116-17; ☎ 273 730; www .hotel-hecco.net; Medresa 1; s/tw/d/tr 80/110/130/150KM; P ⬜) Here 29 bright, airy, modern rooms with strong rectilinear lines lead off an artfully designed warren of corridors dotted with arm-chairs, pot plants and even a weight-training machine. Delightful staff, but there's no lift and only the top floor has air-con. Minibus 58 stops outside.

Ada Hotel (Map pp116-17; ☎ 475 870; www.adahotel .ba; Abdesthana 8; s/d/tr/apt 90/140/170/200KM) Popular with embassy guests, this eight-room hide-away has lots of lovable touches. Corridor surprises include a fake fireplace that opens to reveal secret cabinets. Old teapots and a guitar await in the attractive breakfast room. Rooms in peach or pastel green are a little less characterful but pleasant and calm.

Hotel Kovači (Map pp116-17; ☎ 573 700; www.hotel kovaci.com; Kovači 12; s/d €60/80) Barely finished when we visited, this place looks like it will elegantly combine elements of white-on-white minimalism with '70s retro touches and a homely cosiness. But why are the TV stands so low?

Hotel Safir (Map pp116-17; ☎ 475 040; www.hotelsafir .ba; Jagodića 3; s/d 98/140KM) Ultra-white rooms have artistic flashes in sunny colours, stylish coni-cal basins and a kitchenette. Great value.

Guest House Halvat (Map pp116-17; ☎ /fax 237714; www.halvat.com.ba; Kasima Efendije Dobrače (Zije Dizdarevića) 5; s/d/tr 89.80/121/152.30KM; P ⬜) Homely, five-room, family-run guesthouse with friendly, supertalkative hostess still mourning her beloved Dalmatian.

Hotel Gaj (Map pp116-17; ☎ 445 200; www.hotel-gaj .co.ba; Skenderija 14; s/d/apt €60/90/120) The bright, modern-coloured rooms here have polished wooden floors, and some have antique-style bedsteads and gilt-framed pictures. All have great, clean shower booths. Take breakfast in the half-timbered restaurant or on the garden verandah.

AIRPORT AREA

Pansion Suljović (off Map p113; ☎ 627 670; www .suljovic.com; Kurta Šchorka 22; s/d 50/90KM) Functional rooms above a pizzeria beside the EP petrol station, 1.5km from the airport, 10 minutes' (unpleasant) walk from Stup tram stop. Cheaper budget rooms (35KM per person) share bathrooms.

Hotel Octagon (off Map p113; ☎ 471 105; www .hotel-octagon.com; Akifa Šeremeta 48; s/d 120/150KM) Tries overly hard to look upmarket, but staff are friendly and it's just 200m from the airport, albeit well hidden.

ILIDŽA

Hotel Hercegovina (off Map p113; ☎ 772 100; www .hoteliilidza.ba/site/hercegovina; Banjska bb, Ilidža; d 208/226KM; P ⬛ ⬜) The Hercegovina is one of four grandiose boutique hotels occupy-ing pseudo 19th-century mansions that lie in parkland behind the less glamorous Hotel Terme, whose swimming pools they share. The black-and-gilt colour scheme is lavish if overpoweringly showy.

Casa Grande (off Map p113; ☎ 639 280; www .casagrande-bih.com; Velika Aleja 2, Ilidža; s/d/tr from 90/140/210KM; P) If you're staying in Ilidža, this old-style hotel designed like a 1920s villa is perfectly situated at the start of the tree-lined Velika Aleja. The old masters on the corridors are laughable imitations, but rooms are spacious, well equipped and excellent value.

Hotel Bosna (off Map p113; ☎ 771 340; www.hotel bosna.ba; Butmirska Česta 8, Ilidža; s/d 68/106KM; P ⬛) Attractive use of rose-brown woods and cof-fee-cream colours, excellent prices, and a loca-tion slap bang beside the Ilidža tram terminus make this a genuine bargain. Excellent double glazing combats heavy road noise.

Top End

By the time you read this several options in addition to those below should be complete, including the restored classic **Hotel Europa** (Map pp116-17; Vladislava Skarića 3), the Austro-Hungarian-era **Hotel Central** (Map pp116-17; http://hotelcentral.ba/; Zelenih Beretki) and the new Hotel Hayat (Map pp116-17; not in the Hyatt chain).

our pick **Hotel Michele** (Map pp116-17; ☎ 560 310; www.hotelmichele.ba; Ivana Cankara 27; d/apt €100/150) Looking at the unrefined contemporary building doesn't prepare you for the eccentric, lavish luxury of this marvellously offbeat boutique hotel. Most rooms are vast, exotically furnished apartments; guests have included Bono and Richard Gere.

Villa Wien (Map pp116-17; ☎ 232 855; www.europa-garni.ba; Ćurčiluk Veliki 3; s/d 143/186KM) This secret address above the Vienna Café (p124) hides six comfortable rooms with high ceilings, hexagonal Turkish coffee tables and stylish metalwork bedheads. Check in at the Hotel Europa Garni (below).

Hotel Astra (Map pp116-17; ☎ 252 100; www.hotel-astra.com.ba; Zelenih Beretki 9; s/d 153/206KM) Behind a striking Austro-Hungarian-era facade, the hotel has a minimalist reception booth hidden within a '40s-retro cafe. Rooms are impressively spacious and elegantly trendy, sporting over-bed 'flying' drapes. Three rooms have jacuzzi showers.

Hecco Deluxe (Map pp116-17; www.hotel-hecco.net/deluxe.html; 9th-12th fl, Ferhadija 2; s/d/tr 195/254/279KM) Plonked atop a misleadingly scraggy apartment block, the 12 oddly shaped but stylishly appointed modern rooms have unsurpassed views of the city centre. The 11th-floor rooms even have views from the toilet!

Hotel Europa Garni (Map pp116-17; ☎ 232 855; www.europa-garni.ba; Ferhadija 30a; s/d/apt 183/236/306KM; P) Behind a discordantly uninteresting facade this invitingly modern, supercentral hotel has warm, peach-toned rooms with polished pine floors draped in Persian rugs. Some have computers. Check out the gorgeous three-level Moroccan-styled restaurant-cafe. The hotel plans to rename itself 'Art Hotel'.

Hotel Unica (Map pp116-17; ☎ 555 225; www.hotel-unica.ba; Hamdije Kreševljakovića 42; s/d 156/195KM) Tan and brown tones of boutiquey modernism are reflected even in the receptionists' suits. The stylish breakfast room has reverse ceiling beams, 1940s-style square seats and walls partly decorated with old newspapers.

Villa Orient (Map pp116-17; ☎ 232 702; http://hotel-villa-orient.com; Oprkanj 6; s/d 153/206KM;) Great location, neo-Ottoman exterior and soothing modern water features in the stylish lobby set expectations high, so the very ordinary rooms and worn carpets prove sadly disappointing.

However, when occupancy is low, significant discounts are possible.

Holiday Inn (Map p113; ☎ 288 000; www.holiday-inn.com/sarajevo; Zmaja od Bosne 4; s/d 208/226KM;) This famous 10-storey atrium hotel is looking rather dated, with dark-coloured furnishings and the swimming pool out of action.

EATING

There's plenty of choice, but some of Sarajevo's real gems are so small that you might need to book ahead.

Restaurants

our pick **Mala Kuhinja** (Map pp116-17; ☎ 061144741; Josipa Štadlera 6; meals 15-18KM; 9am-6pm Mon-Fri, to 5pm Sat) There's no menu at this tiny, unique, fusion-food gem where TV celebrity chef Muamer Kurtagic simply asks you what you fancy, hands you a shot of homemade *loza* (local grappa) and sets about creating culinary magic. Sit at the three-stool 'bar' to watch the 'show' in all its exquisite glory. Reservations advisable.

Pivnica HS (Map pp116-17; ☎ 239 740; Franjevačka 15; mains 12-22KM; 10am-1am) Tucked in the wings of this magnificent, soaring brewery–beer hall (p125) are dining areas that Condé Nast rated amongst the world's greatest foodie 'discoveries' in 2006. Finely cooked, professionally served meals including scrumptious chicken in gorgonzola (13KM) come with a basket of gourmet breads. It's wise to dine midafternoon to avoid the evening crush, especially at weekends.

To Be or Not to Be (Map pp116-17; ☎ 233 205; Čizmedžiluk 5; meals 10-22KM; noon-11pm) Arched metal shutters creak open to reveal a tiny two-table room lovably decorated in traditional Bosnian style. It serves risottos, curries and pasta, but the top pick is steak in chilli chocolate (18KM), a daring, tongue-tickling success. The crossed-out 'or Not' appearing in the venue's signage dates from the war years, when not surviving was inadmissible as an option.

Vinoteka (Map p113; ☎ 214 996; Skenderija 12; mains 18-32KM; 11am-3pm & 7-11pm Mon-Sat, wine bar 7pm-1am) This expat favourite has an appealing rafter room up top, a mini-rainforest effect on the ground floor and a basement wine bar. The weekly-changing menu has included such delights as venison in forest fruits or John Dory with roast veggies.

Dveri (Map pp116-17; ☎ 537 020; www.dveri.co.ba; Prote Bakovića 10; meals 10-16KM; 11am-11pm Mon-Fri,

8am-11pm Sat & Sun; ✗) This charming 'country cottage' is hung with loops of garlic, corn cobs and gingham-curtained windows. Inky risottos, veggie-stuffed eggplant and plum goulash all wash down a treat with 5KM glasses of the house red, a truly excellent Hercegovinian blatina. But beware when offered 'homemade bread': it's good but costs 5KM extra.

Park Prinčeva (Map p113; ☎ 222 708; www.park princeva.ba; Iza Hidra 7; meals 12-23KM, wine per bottle from 30KM; ✇ 9am-late) Like Bono and Bill Clinton before you, gaze down from this picture-perfect ridgetop perch for fabulous views of Sarajevo's rooftops, mosques and twinkling lights. Try the delicious chicken with cherries. Minibus 56 from the Latin Bridge passes outside.

Biban (Map p113; ☎ 232 026; Hošin Brijeg 95a; grills 6-9KM, trout dishes 10KM, squid dishes 12KM) If you want Park Prinčeva's superbly panoramic views but not its scurrying army of waistcoated waiters, walk 600m further up to the comparatively rustic Biban, where a litre of unsophisticated *domaći* wine costs only 20KM. Turn left after Nalina 15a.

Hot Wok Café (Map p113; ☎ 203 322; Maršala Tita 12; meals 10-15KM; ✇ 8am-midnight) Hot Wok's puntastic menu of Southeast Asian fusion meals is full of unexpected flavour combinations that confuse the palate but leave you wanting to lick the plate. Stylish decor recalls a scene from *Kill Bill*. High stool seating puts fashion before comfort.

Inat Kuća (Spite House; Map pp116-17; ☎ 447 867; Velika Alifakovac 1; most mains 7-12KM, steaks 18KM, beers 4-6KM) This Sarajevo institution is a veritable museum piece, an Ottoman house with great views of the National Library from a perfect riverside terrace. The menu tells its odd history, but much of the typical Bosnian food (stews, *dolme*) is pre-prepared and slightly lacklustre. The *sirnica* (cheese pie) is fresh and might suit vegetarians.

Bosanska Kuća (Map pp116-17; Bravadžiluk 3; mains 6-9KM; ✇ 24hr; Ⓥ) Colour-picture menus make choosing easy. Amongst the Bosnian standards are a couple of veggie options.

Karuzo (Map pp116-17; ☎ 444 647; Dženetića Čikma 2; mains 6-18KM; ✇ noon-3pm & 6-11pm Mon-Fri, 6-11pm Sat; Ⓥ) Tiny, friendly, one-man (ie slow-service) restaurant styled like a yacht interior. Some dishes like the Indian-influenced vegetarian chickpea pockets are successful. However, the strange 'sushi' uses 'tuna' that tastes more like watery beef than *maguro*.

Tavola (Map pp116-17; ☎ 222 207; Maršala Tita 50; mains 14-30KM, pastas 9-25KM; ✇ 10am-11pm Mon-Fri, 2-11pm Sat & Sun) Here sumptuous Italian cuisine is served in an exclusive yet convivial dining room with framed scribbles as an odd choice of artwork.

Cakeshop Cafes

Metropolis (Map pp116-17; Maršala Tita 21; cakes 3.50KM; ✇ 8am-11pm Mon-Fri, 9am-11pm Sat, 11am-10pm Sun) Fashionably relaxed cafe for Švarcvald (Black Forest gateau), Sacher Torte or 'Metropolis' Cake, a lemon meringue delight on an apple and muesli base. Also serves pizzas, tortilla wraps and gourmet ice creams.

Michele (Map pp116-17; ☎ 444 484; Ferhadija 15; coffee 2KM, cakes 3KM, pizzas 7-11KM; ✇ 8am-10.30pm) While some cafes offer more choice, Michele's cakes are delightfully balanced, not oversweet, and its terrace is *the* place for people watching. The period drawing room interior is fun, and there's a secret Arabian Nights basement.

Sara (Map pp116-17; Baščaršija 22; cakes from 1.50KM) Supercentral, this place has amazing bombes, banana splits and a good selection of Bosnian traditional confectionery.

Vienna Café (Caffe Wien; Map pp116-17; Ćurčiluk Mali; cakes 3KM) The try-hard interior is a little too *faux fin-de-siecle* for some tastes, but there are English-language magazines to read while you indulge.

Quick Eats

For *ćevapi* in a stylish, contemporary setting try **Ćevabdžinica Petica** (Map pp116-17; Bravadžiluk 29; ćevapi 3-6KM) or **Urban Grill** (Map pp116-17; www.urban grill.ba; Pruščakova 8; ćevapi 3.50-5.50KM).

Željo (Map pp116-17; ☎ 441 200; Kundurdžiluk 17 & 20; ćevapi 3-7KM; ✇ 8am-10pm) These twin eateries are not as sexy as many surrounding restaurants, but they're veritable institutions famous for offering Sarajevo's best *ćevapi*. They deliver too, and at sensible prices. Skimp on neither the onions nor the 1KM dollop of *kajmak* that adds a delightful creaminess.

There are several bakeries to choose from:
Pekara Edin (Map pp116-17; Mula Mustafe Bašeskije 69; ✇ 5am-midnight) Inexpensive, with sit-in tables offering perfect views of the Sebilj.

Pekara Mahira (Map pp116-17; Kovači 59; ✇ 6am-11pm) Takeaway window with bread and pizza (7KM) baked before your eyes.

Pekara Nina (Map pp116-17; Mula Mustafe Bašeskije; ✇ 24hr) Unremarkable but open all night.

Self-Catering

Markale market (Map pp116–17; Mula Mustafe Bašeskije; 🕙 7am–5pm Mon-Sat, to 2pm Sun) Facing off across a busy road, Markale comprises a huddle of vegetable stalls and the covered 1894 Gradska Tržnica market hall selling meat and dairy products. (Marketgoers were massacred several times in the 1990s by Serbs launching mortar attacks, including a 1995 assault that proved the last straw, triggering NATO air strikes against the forces besieging Sarajevo.)

Butik-Badem (Map pp116–17; Abadžiluk 12) Super little health-food shop selling caramelised nuts, luscious Turkish delight and a variety of tempting snack foods by weight. There's an alternative branch at Maršala Tita 34.

Handy central supermarkets:

Amko (Map pp116–17; Maršala Tita; 🕙 7am–10pm Mon-Sat, 8am–6pm Sun)

DM (Map pp116–17; Ferhadija 25; 🕙 9am–9pm Mon-Sat)

Hoše (Map pp116–17; Mejtaš 5; 🕙 7am–10pm Mon-Sat, to 3pm Sun)

Konsum (Map pp116–17; Safvet Bega Bašagiča; 🕙 7am–10pm)

DRINKING

Sarajevo is one great cafe. In winter the best places can take a little seeking out, but as chilly April melts into sunny May street terraces blossom, diaspora Bosnians pour in and the streets come to endless life. The dividing line between cafes and bars is often vanishingly thin.

Bars

our pick **Zlatna Ribica** (Map pp116–17; Kaptol 5; 🕙 9am–late) This marvellously Gothic little cafe bar is reason enough to visit Sarajevo. Mirrors and sewing-machine parts are just the start. Wine is served in delightful little potion-bottle carafes with complimentary nibbles and dried figs. The uniquely stocked toilet will have you laughing out loud. Unmissable.

Pivnica HS (Map pp116–17; Franjevačka 15; beers from 1.50KM; 🕙 10am–1am) Fabulous Willy Wonka–meets–Las Vegas beer hall that's the only place to be sure of finding Sarajevskaya's excellent dark beer: it's brewed next door! Superb food, too (see p123).

Mash (Map pp116–17; 1st fl, Branilaca Sarajeva 20; beers 2KM; 🕙 8am–1am Mon-Thu, 9am–3am Fri & Sat, 10am–midnight Sun) Hidden upstairs within an entirely unpromising 1970s concrete building, Mash astounds your expectations with its brilliantly chaotic stylistic mishmash of colours, old furniture and bric-a-brac. Though calling itself a 'food club', it's primarily a studenty lounge bar with scuffed board floors and choice of sofa or stool seating.

Babylon (Map pp116–17; Đulagina 4; beers 2KM; 🕙 noon–2am Tue-Sat, 7pm–midnight Sun-Mon) Lou Reed, Bob Dylan and local blues-rock tunes sway this unpretentious incense-edged bar that you just wish could be your local back home.

Hacienda (Map pp116–17; www.placetobe.ba; Bazerdzani 3; mains 6–20KM; 🕙 10am–very late) The not-quite-Mexican food could be spicier. Not so the ambience at 2am, by which time this cosy, cane-ceilinged cantina has metamorphosed into one of the old town's most happening nightspots.

Baghdad Café (Map pp116–17; Bazerdzani 2; teas 2.50KM; cocktails 6–10KM; 🕙 10am–midnight) This entrancing feast of mirrors, Middle Eastern lamps, exotic inlaid tables and majolica-patterned tiles offers a wide range of cocktails. Sadly, the imaginative superjuices are only available during Ramadan, when the bar goes alcohol free.

So.Ba (Map p113; ☎ 278 491; www.soba.ba; Patriotske lige 30; 🕙 8am–10pm Mon-Fri, noon–10pm Sat) No-frills, art-student campus bar and gallery with endless innovation, thick smoke and pumping music. Take bus 16B.

City Pub (Map pp116–17; Despićeva bb; meals 6–9KM; 🕙 8am–late) Despite a could-be-anywhere pub interior, this friendly place is a very popular meeting point with occasional live music.

Restaurant Club Jež (Map pp116–17; ☎ 650 312; Zelenih Beretki 14; beers from 3KM; 🕙 6pm–late) Atmospheric, underlit, pseudo-old basement bar that's a packed-full late-night hotspot with a varying program of themed events and parties.

Cafes

The choice is simply phenomenal.

our pick **Caffe Divan** (Map pp116–17; Morića Ilan, Sarači 77; coffee 1.50–3KM; 🕙 8am–10pm) Relax in wicker chairs beneath the wooden beams of a gorgeous caravanserai courtyard whose stables now contain a fine Iranian carpet shop.

At Mejdan (Map pp116–17; Atmejdan Park; beers 3–5KM, coffee 3KM; 🕙 9am–11pm Mon-Sat, 10am–11pm Sun) Like a Middle Eastern pagoda this open-sided wooden pavilion has curls of communal sofa seating upstairs and oodles of upmarket summer terrace space. Fresh fruit juices and wines are served, but no food.

Central Caffe (Map pp116-17; Štrosmayerova 1; beers 3-5KM; ⏰ 7.30am-3am) Pure '70s retro with beam-me-up-Scottie ceiling effects and hip, youthful clientele. The street outside becomes one long cafe in summer.

Pravda (Map pp116-17; www.pravdasarajevo.com; Radićeva 4c; coffee 2-5KM, cocktails 7-14KM; ⏰ 8am-midnight) Chose from marigold-patterned chill-out sofas or angular perch stools, then strike your pose amid Sarajevo's gilded youth. Oh no, don't say they've all gone next door to the Nivea?!

Club Bill Gates (Map pp116-17; Vladislava Skarića 2; coffee 1-2KM, pizza 5-13KM; ⏰ 8am-10pm) Fun for the Buggles-esque photos of Mr Microsoft but also pleasant for terrace views of the Ferhadija mosque and excellent coffee served with a free chockie.

Delikatesna Radnja (Map pp116-17; Obala Kulina Bana 10; ⏰ 8am-1am, food noon-11pm Mon-Sat) Self-consciously hip cafe full of arty wannabe actors from the nearby performing arts college. Everyone seems strangely oblivious to the traffic fumes that blight the popular narrow strip of river-facing terrace.

Bosanska Kavarna (Map pp116-17; Oprkanj 9; coffee 0.50KM; ⏰ 8.30am-6pm Mon-Sat) Copper bra-pad lamps, tick-tocking wall clocks and not-so-saucy Islamic pin-ups adorn this particularly real, cheap, downmarket coffee house that caters to wizened old local men.

ENTERTAINMENT
Nightclubs & Live Music

The Club (Map p113; ☎ 550 550; www.theclub.ba; Maršala Tita 7; beers 4KM; ⏰ 10am-late) Behind gruffly humourless bouncers, this subterranean trio of stone cavern-rooms contains a highly esteemed DJ bar (live concerts too), a plush chill-out space and a surprisingly decent late-night restaurant. If you arrive too early, the Pivnica Sarajevo (coffee 2KM, beers 2.50KM; open 8am to midnight), behind the same building, offers alternative cavern-rooms plus a plushly cushioned garden terrace.

Sloga (Map pp116-17; Mehmeda Spahe 20; beers from 2.50KM) Downstairs the taverna-style bar Club Gandeamus (open 7pm to midnight) has live Bosnian folk music on Thursday night around 10pm. Upstairs, much bigger, blood-red Seljo-Sloga (open 8pm to 4am) is a cavernous 1990s-style concert/disco/music bar drawing an excitable, predominantly student crowd.

Bock/FIS (Map p113; ☎ 063943431; www.bock.ba; Musala bb; ⏰ 6pm-2am) Barely marked, this is a wonderfully intimate, zebra-striped venue for live alternative and 'urban' music. Uncompromisingly real. Dress in black.

Kuća Sevdaha (Map pp116-17; Halači 5) At the time of writing, this new pseudo-Ottoman cloister-house venue for *sevdah* (traditional Bosnian music) was shortly due to open.

Dom Mladih (Map p113; ☎ 201 203; Skenderija Center) Occasional rock gigs.

Club Toplik (Map pp116-17; 062942979) Sporadically open weekend house-techno club in a river-side cave opposite Bentbaša.

Coloseum Club (Map p113; ☎ 250 860; www.coloseum-club.com; Skenderija Center) This somewhat cheesy new casino offers a decent roster of concerts plus free salsa/merengue lessons on Sunday (9pm) to entice potential gamblers. Bring ID.

Cinemas

Oslobođenje, Sarajevo's daily paper, has cinema listings under 'Kina'.

Obala Meeting Point (Map pp116-17; ☎ 668 186; Hamdije Kreševljakovića 15a; admission 3-5KM; ⏰ 5pm & 7pm Mon-Fri, noon & 2pm Sat & Sun) Great cinema hidden in an alley between Galerija Palenta and the Serbian embassy.

Bosniak Institute (Map pp116-17; ☎ 279 800; www.bosnjackiinstitut.org; Mula Mustafe Bašeskije 21) Library and club with occasional film screenings, exhibitions and concerts.

Theatres

National Theatre (Narodno Pozorište; Map pp116-17; ☎ 221 682; www.nps.ba; Obala Kulina Bana 9; tickets from 10KM; ⏰ season mid-Sep–mid-Jun, box office 9am-noon & 4pm-7.30pm) Classically adorned with fiddly gilt mouldings, this proscenium-arched theatre hosts a ballet, opera, play or philharmonic concert (www.sarf.com.ba) virtually every night in season.

SHOPPING

The narrow lanes of Baščaršija are packed with wooden-shuttered souvenir shops flogging oriental slippers, Bosnian kilims, imported carpets, BiH flags, wooden spoons and jewellery (especially on Saraći). Metalwork, most archetypally found at coppersmiths' workshops on Kazandžiluk, is also common here, ranging from coffee-pot sets and rather tacky embossed 'pictures' to 'war souvenirs' including pens and plant pots hammered out of mortar cases and empty bullets. Note that if you're heading to Mostar you might find prices better there.

The attractive, one-street, stone-domed **Gazi-Husrevbey covered bazaar** (Map pp116-17; ☎ 534 375; www.vakuf-gazi.ba; ⏰ 8am-8pm Mon-Fri, 9am-2pm Sat) gives a vague taste of Istanbul, but the stalls within sell relatively inexpensive souvenirs, fake bags and sunglasses (from 5KM).

Buying a pair of knitted mitts or slippers from nonprofit **Bosnian Handicrafts** (Map pp116-17; Ćulhan 1) helps out a cause that works with refugees.

Tim Clancy's photo-book *Bosnia and Hercegovina: People and Places* makes a great gift to show people back home the country's beautiful side. Still in print, the *Sarajevo Survival Guide* (23KM) remains a fascinating, darkly humorous chronicle and life manual to siege-era Sarajevo (1992–93). It bills itself as the 'first guide to death in the modern era' and is often sold with the cartoon-style *Survival Map* (15KM). Bookshops are listed on p111.

CDs of highly suspect legality cost 3KM from stalls (Map pp116–17) filling a hidden yard behind the Hecco Deluxe hotel.

GETTING THERE & AWAY
Air
Sarajevo's international **airport** (off Map p113; ☎ 234 841; www.sarajevo-airport.ba; Kurta Schorka 36) is about 12km southwest of Baščaršija. For flight details see p166.

Bus
Sarajevo's **main bus station** (Map p113; ☎ 213 100; Put Života 8) primarily serves locations in the Federation, Croatia and Western Europe, while most services to the Republika Srpska and Serbia leave from **Lukavica bus station** (off Map p113; ☎ 057-317 377; Nikole Tesle bb), the common if misleading nickname for the Autobus Stanica Istochno Sarajevo. The latter lies way out in the Dobrinja suburb, 400m beyond the western terminus of trolleybus 103 (and not in Lukavika). Buses to some destinations (Banja Luka, Belgrade, Pale, Srebrenica) leave from both stations.

Buses to the mountain villages of Bjelašnica and to Butmir start from behind the Ilidža tram terminus.

For bus-service details, see the table, p128.

The 10pm bus to Novi Pazar (€15, eight hours) 'secretly' continues to Pristina (around 12 hours) and Prizren in Kosovo, for which you'll pay an extra €5 fare once you reach Novi Pazar.

For services to Western Europe, see p167.

Train
The **train station** (Map p113; ☎ 655 330; Put Života 2) is close to the main bus station. Useful trains run to Mostar (9.90KM, three hours, 6.45am and 6.18pm) and Konjic (1½ hours, 7.15am and 3.40pm). For Banja Luka (23.30KM, five hours) take Zagreb-bound trains at 10.27am or 9.20pm. For Belgrade (46KM, nine hours) take the 9.20pm service and change at Doboj (13.60KM) or the 7.14am Budapest train, changing in Strizivojna-Vrpolje (Croatia) with 1½ hours' wait.

GETTING AROUND
To/From the Airport
There's no direct airport to centre bus. Blue bus 36 departs from directly opposite the airport to Nedžarići on the Ilidža–Baščaršija tram line, but it only runs twice an hour. Much more frequent is trolleybus 103, which picks up around 700m away. To find the stop, turn right out of the airport then take the first left. Shimmy right-left-right past Hotel Octagon, then turn right at **Panda car wash** (Braće Mulića 17). Just before the **Mercator Hypermarket** (Mimar Sinana 1), cross the road and take the bus going back the way you've just come.

Metered airport taxis charge around 7KM to Ilidža, 25KM to Baščaršija.

Car
Sarajevo is not driver friendly. One-way systems are awkward, and Baščaršija is largely pedestrianised and has minimal parking. However, renting a car makes it much easier to reach the surrounding mountain areas. Most major car-hire agencies have offices at Sarajevo airport, including **Budget** (☎ 766 670), **Hertz** (☎ 235 050), **Avis** (☎ 469 933), **Sixt** (☎ 622 200) and **National** (☎ 267 590), but booking ahead (online) is advisable.

Public Transport
Tram 3 runs every four to seven minutes from Ilidža, passing the Holiday Inn then looping anticlockwise around Baščaršija. Tram 1 (every eight to 20 minutes) does the same starting from the main bus station, though it's only seven minutes' walk from the No 3 line to the stations.

BOSNIA & HERCEGOVINA

BUS SERVICES FROM SARAJEVO

Destination	Station	Price (KM)	Duration	Departures
Banja Luka	M	29	5hr	5am, 7.45am, 9.15am, 2.30pm, 3.30pm & 4.30pm, all via Jajce
	L	31	5hr	9.30am & 11.30am
Belgrade	M	55	10hr	6am
	L	55	10-11hr	6.15am, 8am, 9.45am, 11am, 12.30pm, 3pm & 10pm, all via Zvornik
Bihać	M	41	6½hr	7.30am, 1.30pm & 10pm
Dubrovnik	M	30-44	5-7hr	7.15am &10am, plus 2.30pm & 10.30pm summer
Foča	L	9	1½hr	11am, 4.35pm & 6.25pm, plus Trebinje & Višegrad services
Goražde	M	11	2¼hr	6 Mon-Fri, 4 Sun
Gradačac	M	31	4¼hr	8.30am, 5pm via Srebrenik
Herceg Novi	M	38	7½hr	11am, 10.30pm summer only
Jahorina	M	10	1hr	9am Fri, Sat, Sun in ski season
Mostar	M	16	2½hr	15 daily
Niš	L	40	11hr	8.40am, 6pm
Novi Pazar	M	30	7-8hr	9am, 3pm, 6pm, 9pm, 10pm
Pale	L	3.50	40min	14 daily Mon-Fri, 3.15pm only Sat & Sun
	M	4	25min	7am, 10am & 2pm
Podgorica	L	31	6hr	8.15am & 2pm
Split	M	41	7½hr	via Čapljina 10am & 9pm
			7¼hr	via Livno 6am & 11pm
			6¾hr	via Imotski 2.30pm
Srebrenica	M	32	3½hr	7.10am
	L	27.50	3¾hr	8.40am & 3.30pm
Tešanj	M	23	3hr	7am, 1.15pm & 5.15pm
Travnik	M	15	2hr	9 daily
Trebinje	L	23	5hr	7.45am, 1pm & 4.05pm via Sutjeska National Park
Tuzla	M	20	3¼hr	hourly 10am-4pm, plus 6.50pm
Višegrad	L	14	3hr	3pm
Visoko	M	5.70	50min	at least hourly by Kakanj bus
Zagreb	M	54	9½hr	6.30am, 9.30am, 12.30pm & 10pm

M: Main bus station
L: Lukavica bus station (Autobus Stanica Istochno Sarajevo)

Handy for Lukovica bus station and the airport, usefully frequent trolleybus 103 runs along the southern side of the city from Austrijski Trg to Dobrinja (30 minutes) with stops near Hotel Unica, the Skenderija Center and Green Visions en route.

From Dom Armije, bus 16B runs past the US embassy and So.Ba to the Koševo area.

Many lines (including tram 3, trolleybus 103 and minibus 56) operate 6am to 11pm daily, but some stop after 7pm and all have reduced services on Sunday. Full timetables are available on www.gras.co.ba (in Bosnian).

Click 'Redove Voznje', then select mode of transport.

Single-ride tickets cost 1.60/1.80KM from kiosks/drivers and must be stamped in a special machine once aboard the bus/tram: inspectors have no mercy on 'ignorant foreigners'. Some major kiosks (with red-on-yellow signs) sell good-value 5.30KM day passes, valid for almost all trams, buses and trolleybuses.

Taxi

Charges usually start at 2KM, plus about 1KM per kilometre. While all of Sarajevo's taxis have meters, **Žuti Taxis** (Yellow Cabs; ☎ 663 555) actually turn them on.

There are handy central taxi ranks near Latin Bridge, Hotel Kovači and outside Zelenih Beretki 5.

AROUND SARAJEVO

JAHORINA ЈАХОРИНА
☎ 057

This purpose-built **ski resort** (per day ski pass 30KM, ski rental around 24-50KM) offers world-class pistes designed for the 1984 Winter Olympics. The majority are short, intensely fast red and black runs, but it's also possible to take longer forest-cut pistes and return via the Skočine lift. In summer there's mountain biking and hiking, and up near the Rajska Vrata **AeroKlub Trebević** (☎ 065350201; per hr €25; ⊙ Jun-Sep) offers paragliding.

Sleeping & Eating

A large selection of accommodation spreads along Jahorina's single main road that wiggles 2.5km up from a little seasonal shopping 'village', past the Termag Hotel (300m), S-bending past the Dva Javora (1.5km) to the post office and the still-ruined Hotel Jahorina, then tunnelling beneath the main piste (under the Rajska Vrata) before dead-ending at the top of the Skočine lift.

Whichever accommodation option you choose, there'll be one of Jahorina's six main ski lifts within about 300m of your door. Note that most smaller *pansions* close outside the ski season. Larger resort hotels stay open all year but in ski season won't take bookings for less than seven-day stays. One night visitors can always risk turning up on spec, hoping for a cancellation. We quote lowest (summer) and highest (New Year) rates, but several shoulder pricings exist within the main December–March ski season.

our pick **Rajska Vrata** (☎ 272 020; www.jahorina-rajskavrata.com; d/tr €50/75) Beside the longest piste, this perfect alpine ski-in cafe-restaurant (beers 2.50KM to 3.50KM, mains 7KM to 14KM) has rustic sheepskin benches around a centrally flued real fire. Fully equipped bedrooms with fabulously oversized antique locks are available to casual tourists in the summer, making this one of Jahorina's most tempting off-season choices. Sadly, in ski season all rooms are precontracted to agencies.

Termag Hotel (☎ 270 422; www.termaghotel.com; r per person Dec-Mar from 132KM, Apr-Nov 96KM; P ⊠ 🖳 ⏟) Within an oversized mansion built in Scooby-Doo Gothic style, the Termag is a beautifully designed fashion statement where traditional ideas and open fireplaces are given a stylish modernist twist. Sumptuous rooms have glowing bedside tables and high headboards. The swimming pool and steam rooms are open to nonguests for 18KM.

Hotel Club Dva Javora (☎ 270 481; www.dvajavora .com; s/d/apt 47.50/65/125KM, peak season 118/150/300KM) The refreshingly modern lobby bar feels like a trendy London coffee house. Rooms are very presentable if less hip, and there's a seasonal shopping centre downstairs.

Hotel Bistrica (☎ 270 020; www.oc-jahorina.com; half board s/d 71.50/123KM, peak season 160/214KM; P ⏟) With 152 rooms, this vast, unsophisticated 1984 resort complex feels somewhat dated (especially the bathrooms), but there are lovely views and many family-style facilities, though these close down off season. It's set back 300m from the Dva Javora. Useful website.

Pansion Sport (☎ 270 333; s/d 80/160; ⊙ 20 Dec–10 Apr) Pleasant Swiss chalet–style guesthouse at the bottom 'village area' of the resort.

Getting There & Away

On Friday, Saturday and Sunday in peak ski season, buses depart from Sarajevo's main bus station at 9am, returning at 3.45pm. On weekdays, start by heading to Pale. Jahorina is 15km above Pale, 30KM by taxi or 3KM (25 minutes) by season-only bus departing 6.15am, 2.15pm and 8pm (returning 7am, 3.15pm and 11pm). In summer all public transport stops, but you might be able to hitch a ride on the Hotel Bistrica's staff bus (free), departing 7am and 2pm from Pale's Bartova Market.

With your own vehicle, consider driving the very pretty 22.5km back road starting up Sarajevo's Derviša Numica street. Cross Mladih Muslimana, turn left at a T-junction 1km beyond, then enjoy fabulous views across Sarajevo and a winding lane through joyous alpine meadow. Turn right at the only other junction 13km further.

Mountain bikes can be rented from Termag Hotel for 10KM per day plus deposit.

BJELAŠNICA
☎ 033

Sarajevo's second Olympic ski field offers five lifts (rides/day pass 5/30KM) and a decent

BOSNIA & HERCEGOVINA

> **WARNING**
>
> Stay on the groomed ski runs and hiking paths around Jahorina and Bjelašnica as there are mines in the vicinity of both resorts.

selection of longer forest-cut pistes at altitudes between 1270m and 2067m. Good snowfalls are not uncommon even in late March (ie out of season when accommodation prices fall). In summer the exploration potential of the nearby mountain villages makes this area an unexpectedly delightful getaway from Sarajevo.

Hidden away near Pizza Piccolo Mondo on the parallel back road behind Bjelašnica's short main strip, **Eko Planet** (☎ 579 035; www.touristbiro.ba) offers information, winter ski hire and summer quad-bike trips. It can also organise year-round apartment rental (100KM to 200KM).

Hotel Maršal (☎ 279 100; www.hotel-marsal.ba; s/d €46/62, winter €59/78; P ☐) offers Bjelašnica's only formal accommodation. Fronted by what looks like a giant Plexiglas pencil, it's very friendly but ageing, haphazardly patched-up and somewhat lacklustre. In season seven-day minimum bookings apply. A second hotel was slated to open in 2009. There's also a basic hostel in Šabići (right)

Of Bjelašnica's four eateries, much the most appealing is the somewhat pricey **Srebrna Lisica** (☎ 579 000; www.srebrnalisica.ba; mains 9-34KM, espresso 2KM), offering a wide range of drinks, pastas and Bosnian favourites.

On weekends in ski season buses leave Sarajevo at 9am and 9.20am from beside the National Museum and also from Ilidža, returning at 4pm and 4.30pm (7.40KM return). Five weekly Ilidža–Sinanovići minibuses pass through year-round. See right for the timetable.

AROUND BJELAŠNICA

Newly asphalted roads now link Bjelašnica to a dozen little **shepherd villages** set in fabulous upland scenery simultaneously reminiscent of the Alps, the Scottish Highlands and northern Scandinavia. Photos from the 1970s show that many of these villages were once graced with a unique and very inspiring local architecture, with houses sporting tall, pointy shingle roofs pulled down close to their floors like a hat drawn across a face for shelter from the wind. Tragically, almost all the traditional homes

were burnt during the 1990s conflict. The main exception is at **Lukomir**, which retains many old houses, albeit now mostly roofed with rusty, beaten-flat oil drums. Access is by an unsurfaced track, passable by car in dry weather from **Umoljani**, 16km from Bjelašnica. The approach to Umoljani is delightful in itself. Turn right off the Sinanovići road just before the Rakitnica River bridge (3km before Umoljani). Hairpin bends lead up a ridge topped near the roadside by a set of partly carved, beautifully set **stećci** (see the boxed text, p109).

Around 1km further look left across the Sedernik Valley to spy an almost vertical array of eight mini **water mills**. Just before entering Umoljani village you'll pass the region's only genuinely old mosque to have survived both the communist era and the 1990s conflict, though its odd metal-wrapped minaret looks more like a missile silo dressed for a KKK meeting. **Gradina**, a hamlet on the Umoljani–Lukomir track, was once an Illyrian settlement and retains a few traditional-style barns.

Tours

With a guide, the area is marvellous for hiking. April to October, given a minimum sign-up of five people, Sarajevo's Eco-tourism outfit **Green Visions** (p112) organises fixed-departure trips from the capital to Umoljani (Monday), Lukomir (Tuesday) and the Rakitnica Canyon (Wednesday) for €40 per person including three or four hours' guided hiking.

From Bjelašnica, **Eko Planet** (p129) runs excursions to Lukomir (four hours, from €50) and ultimate day-trip loops quad-biking to Boračko Lake then rafting down the Neretva to Konjic (opposite). Minimum four, maximum eight people, from €110 per person.

Sleeping

The very rustic **Hojta Hostel** (☎ 437 874; emina2708@ yahoo.com; Šabići; dm 20KM, dinner 6KM) is run by a gruff, Bosnian Basil Fawlty, but the beds are cheap and the front room forms the de facto village pub, attracting a wonderfully genuine cross-section of farming folk for a beer and a chat. No English spoken. There's a little huddle of *stećci* (see the boxed text, p109) almost outside. Šabići is 11km from Bjelašnica, 5km before Umoljani.

Getting There & Away

In this area it's great to have your own wheels. Every lonely side lane offers its scenic attractions, yet the only public transport is minibus 85 from Ilidža to Sinanovići via Bjelašnica, Šabići and the Rakitnica River bridge (for Umoljani). It leaves Ilidža at 7.30am Monday and Saturday, 7am Tuesday, and 4pm Friday and Sunday. Return trips leave Sinanovići around 9.15am Monday and Saturday, and 6.15pm Tuesday, Friday and Sunday.

KONJIC
☎ 036 / pop 32,000

As an armament factory and a key town on the Sarajevo–Mostar road, Konjic suffered substantially in both WWII and the 1990s conflict. Under reconstruction in beautiful golden stone, Konjic's six-span Ottoman Bridge is like a miniature version of the Višegrad classic. Apart from this and some interesting craft shops, central Konjic has no pressing attractions, but it's ringed by dramatic mountains and makes the ideal end point for rafting trips down the upper Neretva canyon, typically starting around 30km up the R435 at Glavatičevo, beyond lovely **Boračko Lake**. Local adventure-sports outfits include **Badžo-Raft** (☎ 726 716; www.badzoraft.com; Huseinbegova 15).

Whether by luck or by design, **Motel Konjic** (☎ 734 150; s/d 35/55KM) has turned its incorrigible 1970s slab-cake design to advantage with mild hints of retro-chic fashion. It's relatively handy for public transport, facing the river some 500m south of the R435 junction at the southern edge of Konjic town.

Mostar–Sarajevo buses pass through.

HERCEGOVINA

Hercegovina is the part of BiH that no one in the West ever mentions, if only because they can't pronounce it. Its arid, Mediterranean landscape has a distinctive beauty punctuated

by barren mountain ridges and photogenic river valleys. Famed for fine wines and sun-packed fruits, Hercegovina is sparsely populated but has several intriguing historic towns, and the Adriatic coast is just a short drive away.

MOSTAR
☎ 036 / pop 94,000

At dusk the lights of numerous mill-house restaurants twinkle delightfully across gushing streamlets. The impossibly quaint Kujundžiluk (Gold Alley) bustles joyously with trinket sellers. And in between, the Balkans' most celebrated bridge forms a truly majestic stone arc between reincarnated medieval towers. It's a magical scene.

Meanwhile, behind the delightful cobbled lanes of the attractively restored Ottoman quarter, a less palatable but equally unforgettable 'attraction' lies in observing the devastating urban scars that still recall the brutal 1990s conflict all too vividly.

Add in a selection of fascinating day trips for which Mostar makes an ideal base and it's not surprising that this fascinating little city is starting to attract a growing throng of summer visitors. Visit off-season and you'll have it much to yourself.

History
Mostar means bridge-keeper and the crossing of the Neretva River here has always been its raison d'être. In the mid-16th century Mostar boomed as a key transport gateway within the powerful, expanding Ottoman Empire. Some 30 craft guilds (esnafi) included tanners (for whom the Tabahana was built) and goldsmiths (hence Kujundžiluk). In 1557, Suleyman the Magnificent ordered a fine stone arch to replace the suspension bridge whose wobbling had previously terrified tradesmen as they

BOSNIA & HERCEGOVINA

WINE DIVINE

Hercegovina produces some splendidly well-balanced wines, typically dry yet densely fruit filled and often every bit as good as more expensive Slovenian and Croatian vintages. Vranac and blatina grapes make wonderfully rich reds. Some žilavka whites such as the very drinkable Kameno brand (from Čitluk) are 'stone wines', the vines growing out of virtually soil-free rocky ground. In Hercegovinian restaurants, play clever and ask your waiter for local domaći (house) wine. It comes by the carafe and, while not always sophisticated, some domaći reds prove every bit as excellent as bottled blatinas for less than half the price (from 12KM per litre). Hercegovina is just waking up to the tourist potential of its numerous wineries (see www.wineroute.ba); while many producers now offer tastings, relatively few speak English. Advance notice is often required.

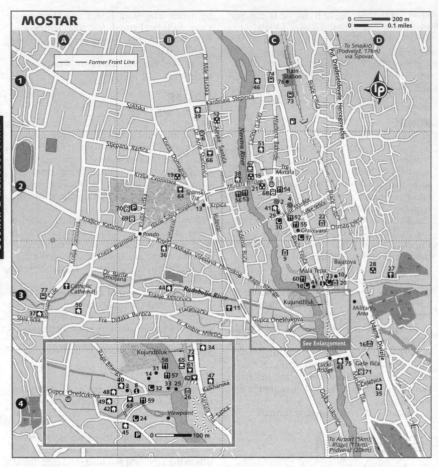

MOSTAR

gingerly crossed the fast-flowing Neretva. The beautiful Old Bridge (Stari Most) that resulted was finished in 1566 and came to be appreciated as one of the world's engineering marvels. It survived the Italian occupation of WWII, but after standing for 427 years the bridge was destroyed in November 1993 by Bosnian Croat artillery. That was one of the most poignant, pointless and depressing moments of the whole Yugoslav civil war.

Ironically, Muslim and Croat citizens had initially fought together against Serb and Montenegrin forces, who had started bombarding Mostar in April 1992. However on 9 May 1993 a bitter conflict erupted between the former allies. Bosnian Croat forces expelled many Bosniaks from their homes; some were taken to detention camps, while others fled to the very relative 'safety' of the Muslim east bank of the Neretva. For two years the two sides swapped artillery fire and the city was pummelled into rubble.

By 1995 Mostar resembled Dresden after WWII, with all its bridges destroyed and all but one of its 27 Ottoman-era mosques ruined. Vast international assistance efforts have since rebuilt almost all of the Unesco-listed old city core. By 2004 the Old Bridge had been painstakingly reconstructed using 16th-century-style building techniques and Tenelija stone from the original quarry. But significant quantities of ghostlike rubble remain, particularly along the old front-line area. And the psychological scars will take at least a generation to heal.

INFORMATION
Almira Travel.............................. **1** C3
Barbados.....................................**2** C2
BuyBook...................................... **3** B4
Europa Club................................**4** C2
Fortuna Travel........................... **5** C3
GPO & Telephone Centre........ **6** B2
Left-Luggage office................(see **73**)
Post Office...................................**7** C2
Tourist Information Centre........**8** B4

SIGHTS & ACTIVITIES
Art Gallery.............................(see **72**)
Bišćevića Ćošak (Turkish
    House).....................................**9** C3
Clock Tower............................. **10** D3
Franciscan Church.....................**11** C3
Gutted Apartments...................**12** B1
Gymnasium................................**13** B2
Hamam.......................................**14** B4
Hotel Neretva.......................... **15** C2
Kajtaz House............................. **16** D3
Karađozbeg Mosque................**17** C2
Koski Mehmed Paša Mosque .. **18** C3
Ljubljanska Banka Tower...........**19** B2
Museum of Hercegovina...........**20** D3
Music School........................... **21** C2
Muslibegović House................ **22** C2
Nesuh-aga Vučijaković
    Mosque...................................**23** D3
Neziraga Mosque......................**24** C3
Old Bridge **25** D4
Old Bridge Museum..................**26** B4
Orthodox Chapel **27** D3
Orthodox Church Ruins............ **28** D3

Roznamedži Ibrahimefendi
    Madrassa................................**29** C2
Roznamedži Ibrahimefendi
    Mosque...................................**30** C2
Tabahana....................................**31** B4
Tabačica Mosque...................... **32** B4
Tara Gunpowder Tower............**33** B4

SLEEPING 🅰
Apartments Konak.....................**34** B3
Hostel Nina............................... **35** D4
Hostel Nina Annex....................**36** B3
Hotel Bevanda.......................... **37** A3
Hotel Bristol..............................**38** C2
Hotel Ero...................................**39** B1
Hotel Old Town.........................**40** B4
Hotel Pellegrino........................ **41** C2
Kriva Ćuprija............................. **42** A4
Kriva Ćuprija 2...........................**43** D4
Majda's Rooms..........................**44** B3
Motel Deny................................**45** B4
Muslibegović House..............(see **22**)
Pansion Aldi...............................**46** C1
Pansion Armin...........................**47** B4
Pansion Emen............................ **48** A4
Pansion Oscar............................**49** A4
Salve Regina.............................. **50** A3
Vila Sara.................................... **51** C2

EATING 🍽
ABC..**52** C2
Dan-i-Noć...................................**53** C2
Grill Centar................................ **54** C2
Mercur Supermarket.................**55** C2
MM Restaurant..........................**56** C2

Restaurant Bella Vista...............**57** B4
Restoran Babilon........................**58** B4
Šadrvan...................................... **59** C3
Tepa Market...............................**60** C3
Urban Grill.............................(see **5**)

DRINKING 🍸 🏳
Ali Baba Bar................................ **61** B4
Bijeli Bar.....................................**62** B4
Caffe Marshall............................ **63** B4
Coco Loco Bar............................**64** B2
Košćela **65** B4
OKC Abrašević........................... **66** B2
Villa Neretva..............................**67** C2

ENTERTAINMENT 🎭
Club Oxygen...............................**68** C2
Dom Kultura Herceg Stjepan
    Kosača.....................................**69** B2
Heineken Inn.............................**70** B2
Pavarotti Music Centre............. **71** D4

SHOPPING 🛍
Ismet Kurt..................................**72** B4

TRANSPORT
BH Airlines.............................(see **52**)
Bus Station.................................**73** C1
Bus Stop for Blagaj...................**74** C1
Helax.......................................(see **39**)
Lucki Bridge Bus Stop for
    Blagaj & Podveležz................**75** D4
MaxLine.....................................**76** C1
Sixt..(see **39**)
Bus Stop for Međugorje **77** A3

Orientation

The little old town is a small web of narrow pedestrian alleys around the Old Bridge. Kujundžiluk becomes Mala Tepa, which becomes Braće Fejića, Mostar's mostly pedestrianised commercial street. This is paralleled by Maršala Tita, which runs one way northbound for its central section. Southbound traffic crosses the river and uses the Bulevar or bypasses town altogether on the considerably higher M17.

Information

Almost any business accepts euros (at favourable 2:1 rates for small purchases) or even Croatian kuna (4:1). There are numerous ATMs down Braće Fejića. Several banks around Trg Musala change money, but rates are better at the post office.

Both travel agencies listed below can arrange guided tours, accommodation and car hire.

Almira Travel (☎ /fax 551873; www.almira-travel.ba; Mala Tepa 9; 🕑 9am-5pm Mon-Sat, later in season) Very human agency with French- and English-speaking guides and a vast range of imaginative options including wine-tasting tours. Sells decent BiH-Croatia maps (€7).

Barbadus (Braće Fejića 26; per hr 2KM; 🕑 9am-11pm) Internet access. Upstairs, entered from side door.
BuyBook (☎ 558 810; Onešćukova 24; 🕑 9am-9pm Mon-Sat, 10am-6pm Sun) A useful array of English-language books, guidebooks and CDs.
Europa Club (Huse Maslića 10; per hr 1KM; 🕑 7am-midnight) Internet access. Beneath a stationery shop.
Fortuna Travel (☎ 552 197; www.fortuna.ba; Rade Bitange 34; 🕑 8am-4.30pm Mon-Fri, 9am-1pm Sat) Major local agency with sub-offices on Mala Tepa and at Hotel Ero.
GPO & Telephone Centre (Dr Ante Starčevića bb; 🕑 7am-7pm Mon-Sat, 8am-noon Sun) Poste restante; bureau de change.
Left-luggage office (per item per day 2KM) In the bus station.
Post office (Braće Fejića bb; 🕑 8am-8pm Mon-Sat) ATM outside.
Tourist Information Centre (☎ 397 350; www.hercegovina.ba; Onešćukova bb; 🕑 9am-9pm) Useful but subject to sporadic closures out of season.

Sights
OLD BRIDGE

The world-famous **Stari Most** is the indisputable visual focus that gives Mostar its unique magic. Nicknamed Petrified Moon for its slender, refined beauty, the bridge's pale stone magnificently throws back the golden glow of sunset or the tasteful night-time floodlighting. Numerous well-positioned cafes and restaurants tempt you to admire the scene from a dozen varying angles. Directly east is a five-storey stone defence tower housing the **Old Bridge Museum** (admission 5KM; ☯ 11am-2pm, 10am-6pm summer) with brief, informative historical information boards. Two slow-moving 15-minute videos on the bridge's destruction/ reconstruction are shown in the 'labyrinth' beneath, where archaeologists have discovered the remnant supports of an older 15th- to 16th-century suspension bridge.

Directly west, the semicircular **Tara Gunpowder Tower** is now the 'club house' for the town's unique breed of divers. Nicknamed the Icaruses of Mostar, they plunge 21m off the bridge's parapet into the icy Neretva River below. Originally this display of masculinity gave townsmen a certain pulling power. Today it's more a (well-deserved) summer money-spinner, a diver only taking the plunge once his energetic hustler has collected enough photo money from impressionable tourists.

The annual bridge-diving competition is still held each July, as it was even when the war-shattered bridge had been replaced by a temporary wooden gantry pre-2004.

OLD TOWN

On the west bank of the Neretva, pretty old shopfronts line Prječka Čaršija from the bridge to the **Tabačica mosque** and tourist office. Set back is a cobbled square with a restored former hamam and a gateway leading through into the **Tabahana**. This Ottoman-era enclosed courtyard originally housed leather workshops but is now full of lively bars and (on the far side) restaurants with fabulous Old Bridge views.

Just across Onešćukova, delightful footpath-stairways link half a dozen superquaint eateries in old houses and stone mills. These are layered down a mini-valley around the quaint little **Crooked Bridge** (Kriva Ćuprija). Originally built in the 16th century, this looks like a miniature Old Bridge, for which it was reputedly the model. And, like its bigger cousin, the Crooked Bridge is also a 21st-century stone replica. The original, weakened by 1990s bombardment, was washed away by floods in 1999.

If there's a happy twist to all the 1990s destruction, it's that it created space for the reconstruction of the attractive 1550 **Neziraga mosque** and its *mekteb* (former school, now Radio Stari Most). The originals had been entirely demolished and replaced by the communists in 1951.

On the east bank, very picturesque **Kujundžiluk** is a cobbled alley of miniature shops selling appealingly colourful tourist tat (see p137). There's a great view back towards the Old Bridge from opposite the tiny **Art Gallery** (Kujundžiluk 1).

Entered from a gated courtyard, the originally 1618 **Koski Mehmed Paša mosque** (Mala Tepa 16; mosque/mosque & minaret 3/5KM; ☯ 9am-6pm) has decor that lacks finesse. But if claustrophobia doesn't overcome you in the climb, its minaret offers commanding panoramas. The 1781 *šadravan* (ablution fountain) is original.

The **Bišćevića Ćošak** (Turkish House; ☎ 550 677; www .biscevicakuca.bravehost.com; Bišćevića 13; admission 2KM; ☯ 9am-3pm Nov-Feb, 8am-8pm Mar-Oct) is a charmingly ramshackle 350-year-old Ottoman-Bosnian home with pebble-paved courtyard, an outhouse filled with butter churns and a colourfully furnished interior sporting a selection of traditional metalwork and carved wooden furniture. Partly supported on extraordinarily long stilts, a three-sided window overhangs the riverbank way below.

For interesting comparisons, also visit the grander 18th- to 19th-century **Muslibegović House** (admission 3KM; ☯ 10am-8pm mid-Apr–mid-Oct), which doubles as a boutique guesthouse (see opposite), and the less central, 16th-century **Kajtaz House** (☎ 550 913; Gaše Ilića 21; admission 2KM; ☯ unpredictable).

BRAĆE FEJIĆA

Mostar's main shopping street leads up to **Trg Musala**, the square that was once the grand heart of Austro-Hungarian Mostar, passing the large, rebuilt 1557 **Karađozbeg mosque** (Braće Fejića; admission/minaret 3/2KM; ☯ 9am-6pm Sat-Thu) with its distinctive wooden verandah and four-domed madrassa annexe (now a clinic).

The early-17th-century **Roznamedži Ibrahim-efendi mosque** (Braće Fejića) was the only mosque to survive the 1993–95 shelling relatively unscathed. Its associated **madrassa** has just been rebuilt, the original having been demolished in 1960.

BAJATOVA

The fine 16th-century **Nesuh-aga Vučijaković mosque** (Maršala Tita bb) spent much of the communist era as a warehouse, then the 1992–95 war overloaded its graveyard with sad, pointy white graves. From here a stairway-lane (Bajatova) leads up past partly shattered houses and a 17th-century **clock tower** (Bajatova 5). Roughly opposite, the little **Museum of Hercegovina** (☎ 551 602; Bajatova 4; admission 1.5KM; ⊗ 9am-2pm Mon-Fri, 10am-noon Sat) is housed in the former home of Džemal Bijedić, ex-head of the Yugoslav government, who died in mysterious circumstances in 1978. The museum's most interesting exhibit is a well-paced 10-minute film featuring pre- and post-1992 bridge-diving plus war footage, including the moment the Old Bridge was blown apart.

At the top of Bajatova an underpass takes you beneath the M17 to the site of the once imposing **Orthodox church**. Only two pillars and a leaning portal arch survived the Croat shelling of 1993, but from amidst the rubble there are superb views across the city to the looming grey crags beyond. A small, older **Orthodox chapel** behind survived the shelling but is only open for occasional services.

WAR DAMAGE
While it might sound in bad taste, visiting the dramatic ruins of the **former front line** is both moving and intensely thought provoking, especially in the company of a wartime 'survivor'. One central wreck that is under slow renovation is the once-stately 1896 **Gymnasium** (High School; Španski Trg), a grand piece of Austro-Hungarian architecture with intricate Moorish flourishes. From here various eerie ruins run down the Bulevar to the rebuilt 1866 **Franciscan church** (Franjevačka Crkva), whose unfeasibly tall postwar tower smacks of campanile-versus-minaret one-upmanship. On Trg Musala the once-beautiful 1898 **Hotel Neretva** (www.cinv .co.ba/en/neretva.htm) and 1920s **Music School** remain tragic shells. Yet somehow the bombed-out nine-storey former **Ljubljanska Banka Tower** (Kralja Zvonimira bb) and the **gutted apartments** on Aleske Šantića seem even more heartrendingly poignant, being so comparatively modern.

Sleeping
There's an ever-growing wealth of accommodation, but if you're stumped for a place the tourist information centre and travel agencies can help you find a bed. Almira Travel (p133) also offers homestays in rural villages in the area. Note that midsummer prices can rise 20% to 50% when demand is high.

BUDGET
All places listed are effectively glorified home-stays. None has a full-time receptionist, so calling ahead is wise, especially off-season when some are virtually dormant (and un-heated). At such times you'll probably get a whole room for the dorm price. All but the Armin have shared bathrooms.

Majda's Rooms (☎ 061382940; 1st fl, Franje Milicevica 39; dm/d €11/24; ⊠) By sheer force of personality, and a very human awareness of traveller needs, sharp-witted Bata and his surreally delightful mother have turned a once-dreary tower-block apartment into Mostar's cult hostel. Most rooms are eight-bed dorms. Bata's regional tours are superb value.

Hostel Nina (☎ 061382743; www.hostelnina.ba; Čelebica 18; dm/s/d €10/15/20; ⌨ P) Good-value homestay-style accommodation with three rooms per neat bathroom run by a very obliging English-speaking lady. Her overflow annexe is out near the Rondo.

Pansion Oscar (☎ 061823649; Oneščukova 33; per person €10-20; ⊠) Six very presentable rooms, some with balconies, share two bathrooms in a truly unbeatable location near the Old Bridge. Washing machines are available (€5 per load) and breakfast is €5; there's no communal sitting area. Seid speaks good English.

Vila Sara (☎ 555 940; www.villasara-mostar.com; Sasarogina 4; dm/s/d/tr 20/30/40/60KM) Crammed-together new beds with fresh duvets share a decent kitchen and cramped but piping-hot showers. Phone ahead off-season. Check-out is a yawny 10am.

Pansion Aldi (☎ 552 185, 061273457; www.pansion -aldi.com, Lačina 69a; dm/d/apt €10/20/42) This no-frills hostel has 13 beds in five spacious if simple rooms (two air-conditioned) sharing a kitchenette and riverside garden terrace but only one shower and two squat toilets. It's unmarked but very handy for the bus station. No heating; limited English.

Pansion Armin (☎ 552 700; Kalkhanska 3; s/d from €15/30) Excellent-value en suite rooms in a bright yellow new house with trellis frontage facing the eerie ruin of a bombed-out school.

MIDRANGE & TOP END
If you want a business-standard hotel, consider staying in Čapljina (p141).

ourpick Muslibegovic House (☎ 551 379; www .muslibegovichouse.com; Osman Đikća 41; s/d €40/70; ⊠) In summer tourists pay to visit this superbly restored 18th-century Ottoman courtyard house. But it's simultaneously an extremely convivial 15-room homestay-hotel. Room sizes and styles vary significantly, mixing excellent modern bathrooms with elements of traditional Bosnian-Turkish design. Room 2 is especially atmospheric.

Pansion Emen (☎ 581 120, 061848734; Oneščukova 32; www.motel-emen.com; s/d/tr from €30/50/60; 🐾 📖) More a fashionable mini-hotel than a *pansion*, the Emen is one of old Mostar's most prized addresses, with understated chic and a remarkably reasonable price tag. It features wonderful sitting areas, two shared internet computers and angular bath fittings straight from a design magazine.

Hotel Old Town (☎ 558 877; www.oldtown.ba; Oneščukova 30; d/tr/ste from €90/120/150) This delightful, supercentral boutique hotel is full of specially designed handmade furniture, uses energy-saving waste-burning furnaces for water heating and has eco-friendly air circulation to save on air-conditioning wastage.

Kriva Ćuprija (☎ 550 953; www.motel-mostar.ba; s/d/apt from €30/55/65; 🐾) Soothe yourself with the sounds of gushing streams in new, impeccably furnished (if not necessarily large) rooms ranged above this charming stone millhouse restaurant overlooking the Crooked Bridge. Don't be fobbed off with Kriva Ćuprija 2, a new annexe on the main road across Lučki Bridge.

Hotel Pellegrino (☎ 061480784; www.hotel-pellegrino.ba; Faladjica 1c; s/d/tr 90/130/150KM; 🐾) Above a surprisingly spacious neo-Tuscan restaurant-lounge, expansive rooms have excellent anti-allergenic bedding and a kitchenette. Each room has its own oddity, be it a giant black-lacquer vase, a bundle-of-twigs lamp or a whole-cow mat.

Motel Deny (☎ 578 317; www.mdmostar.com; Kapetanovina 1; s/d 53/86KM, in summer 63/106KM; P 🐾) This modern mini-hotel overlooks the mill area of the old town and has a charming lobby decked out with flickering candles. Rooms are slightly plain in comparison but well furnished and clean.

Apartments Konak (☎ 551 105, http://apartmani-konak.com/; Maršala Tita 125; d/tr/q €30/45/60; 🐾) Good-value homely apartments, central and fairly well set back from the noisy main road up a little stairway.

Other Mostar options:

Hotel Ero (☎ 386 777; www.ero.ba; Dr Ante Starčevića bb; s/d/apt 99/166/215KM; P 🐾 📖 ♿) The 165 solidly renovated rooms have balconies and peachy-cream

new decor, though rickety doors and abandoned floor-lady areas faintly recall its previous Tito-era incarnation.

Hotel Bevanda (☎ 332 332; www.hotelbevanda.com; Stara Ilića 1; s/d/ste 199/255/425KM; P 🐾) The over-shiny atrium does little to support the Bevanda's delusions of grandeur, though rooms are perfectly comfortable, and very plush suites come with a waiting decanter of brandy.

Hotel Bristol (www.bristol.ba; Mostarskog Bataljona bb; 🐾) Undergoing full-scale renovation at research time.

Eating

Cafes and restaurants with divine views of the river cluster along the western riverbank near the Old Bridge. Remarkably, although these are unabashedly tourist-oriented, prices are only a *maraka* or two more than any ordinary dive (though wine can get comparatively costly).

Restoran Babilon (☎ 061164912; Tabahana; mains 8-15KM) Along with the almost indistinguishable Restaurant Teatr next door, the Babilon has wonderful open terraces with stupendous views across the river to the old town and the Old Bridge. Choose from grills, fish dishes, dolma or a great-value set 'tourist meal' (€7).

Restaurant Bella Vista (☎ 061656421; Tabahana; pizzas 7-10KM, mains 7-17KM) Even nearer to the Old Bridge than the Babilon, the Bella Vista adds several Italianish options to the menu and has a more atmospheric interior should you want *that* view on a colder winter's evening.

Dvije Pecine (Two Caves; ☎ 061175245; Jusovina 66; mains 8-22KM; ⏰ 9am-11pm) Two sections of this novel place are indeed tucked within indentations in the cliff just behind the Crooked Bridge. However, their terrace and little chalet-style main room are more convivial places to sample the somewhat pricey fish dishes (16KM to 22KM). Several other streamside mill-restaurants nearby are every bit as good, so simply pick the atmosphere that suits.

Šadrvan (☎ 579 057; Jusovina 11; dishes 6-17KM) On a quaint corner where the pedestrian lane from the Old Bridge divides, this appealing, gently upmarket restaurant has tables set around a trickling fountain made of old Turkish-style metalwork, shaded by the spreading tentacles of a kiwi-fruit vine. The menu covers all Bosnian bases.

ABC (☎ 194 656; Braće Fejića 45; pizza & pasta 6-9KM, mains 12-15KM; ⏰ 8am-11pm Mon-Sat, noon-11pm Sun) Downstairs is Mostar's most popular cake shop and a narrow see-and-be-seen pavement cafe. Upstairs is a relaxed pastel-toned Italian restaurant. Pizzas are rather bready, but the plate-lickingly creamy Aurora tortellini comes with an extra bucketful of parmesan.

Options for snacks and self-catering:

Dan-i-Noć (Mostarskog Bataljona 8; ☾ 24hr) All-night bakery.

Grill Centar (Braće Fejića 13; grills 5KM; ☾ 8am-11pm) Unsophisticated *ćevadžinica* (shop selling meat grills) attached to an old Bosnian courtyard house.

Mercur Supermarket (Braće Fejića 51; ☾ 7am-10pm) Sizeable, central grocery.

MM Restaurant (Mostarskog Bataljona 11; meals 6-12KM; ☾ 8am-10pm Mon-Sat) Easy-to-use buffet-style feeding station.

Tepa market (Braće Fejića bb; ☾ 6.30am-2pm) Some of the gnarled characters working at this modest fruit-and-veg market look like they've been here for centuries. Great views from the parapet behind.

Urban Grill (www.urbangrill.ba; Mala Tepa; ćevapi 3.50-5.50KM) Can *ćevapi* ever be cool? They think so here.

Drinking

our pick **OKC Abrašević** (☎ 561 107; www.okcabrasevic .org; Alekse Šantića 25; beers 2KM; ☾ variable) This uncompromising yet understatedly intellectual bar offers Mostar's most vibrantly alternative 'scene', with an attached venue for off-beat gigs. You'll need the guts to seek it out, hidden away between the prison and the city's most daunting burnt-out war ruins.

Ali Baba Bar (Kujundžiluk; ☾ summer) Remarkable, seasonal bar-club tucked into the cliff face that looms directly above Kujundžiluk.

Bijeli Bar (Stari Most 2; coffee 2KM, beers 4KM; ☾ 7am-11pm) The ubercool main bar zaps you with a wicked white-on-white *Clockwork Orange* decor. Meanwhile, around the corner the same bar owns an utterly spectacular perch-terrace from which the Old Bridge and towers appear from altogether new angles. The latter is entered from Maršala Tita, through a wrought-iron gate marked 'Atelje Novalić': cross the Japanese-style garden and climb the stone roof-steps.

Košćela (Kujundžiluk; coffee 2KM; ☾ 10am-7pm) Bridge views are almost as perfect as from the Bijeli Bar terrace, and Bosnian coffee (2KM) comes with full traditional copper regalia complete with Turkish delight. Light grill-meals are served, but there's no alcohol.

Caffe Marshall (Oneščukova bb; beers 3KM; ☾ 8am-midnight) Minuscule but appealing box-bar draped with musical instruments.

Villa Neretva (Trg Musala; ☾ 7am-11pm) This spacious, modern cafe attracts a calm, literate crowd, while the attached Monkey Bar has a

livelier music vibe that pumps harder as the evening progresses.

Coco Loco Bar (Kralja Zvonimira bb; ☾ 8am-late) With minimal decor and wafting, question-able vapours, this place is nonetheless packed to the gunnels at weekends for deafening DJ parties.

Entertainment

OKC Abrašević (see left) and the **Pavarotti Music Centre** (☎ 550 750; Maršala Tita 179) host occasional concerts.

Club Oxygen (☎ 512 244; www.biosphere.ba/bios fere-stranice-oxigen en.html; Braće Fejića bb; ☾ variable) Oxygen has movie nights, DJ discos and Mostar's top live gigs. In summer its rooftop SkyBar takes over as the place to party.

Dom Kultura Herceg Stjepan Kosaća (☎ 323 501; Rondo; ☾ variable) This large cultural centre offers diverse shows, concerts and exhibitions. Visiting opera, ballet and theatre companies from Croatia show up occasionally.

Heineken Inn (beers from 2.50KM; ☾ 10.30pm-late Thu-Sat) Enjoy busty live acts and oriental tinged disco at the biggest of four, free-entry weekend discos around the Rondo. No guns please.

Shopping

The stone-roofed shop-houses of Kujundžiluk throw open antique-styled metal shutters to sell agreeably colourful, inexpensive, if some-what trashy Turkish souvenirs, from amulets to glittery long-toed velveteen slippers (€7), pashmina-style wraps (from €5), fezzes (€5), *boncuk* (evil-eye) pendants, and five-deep Russian-style *matryoshka* nested dolls. Many stalls sell pens fashioned from old bullets, while master coppersmith **Ismet Kurt** (☎ 550 017; Kujundžiluk 5) hammers old mortar-shell casings into works of art while you watch.

Getting There & Away
AIR

Mostar airport (☎ 350 992; code OMO) is 6km south of town off the Čapljina road. **BH Airlines** (☎ 551 820; Braće Fejića 45; ☾ 9am-5pm Mon-Fri) flies to Istanbul on Sunday morning for €180.

BUS

From the main **bus station** (☎ 552 025; Trg Ivana Krndelja), tickets for most services are presold through **Autoprevoz-bus** (☎ 551 900). For bus-service details, see the table, p138.

Yellow **Mostar Bus** (☎ 552 250; www.mostarbus.ba /linije.asp) services to Blagaj and Podvelež depart

BUS SERVICES FROM MOSTAR

Destination	Price (KM)	Duration (hr)	Departures
Banja Luka	25	6	1.30pm via Jajce
Belgrade	48	11	7.30pm
Dubrovnik	27	3½	7am, 10.15am & 2.30pm
Sarajevo	16	2½-3	hourly 6am-3pm, plus 6.15pm & 8.30pm
Split	25	4½	9.30am, 10.45am, 12.50pm, 17.30pm & midnight
Stolac	4	1	6.15am, 3.30pm & 8.15pm, or change in Čapljina
Tešanj	34	6	5.30pm
Trebinje	19	3	via Stolac 6.15am, 3.30pm, via Nevesinje 5.30pm
Visoko	20	3¾	6.30pm
Zagreb	43	9½	9am

from opposite the station and also pick up from the Lučki Bridge stop. On weekdays buses for Međugorje (4KM, 45 minutes) pick up from a stop very near the Bevanda Hotel at 6.30am, 11.30am, 1.10pm, 2.30pm, 3.30pm, 6.10pm and 7.30pm. All but those at 1.10pm, 2.30pm and 3.30pm also run on Saturday; only the 7.30pm bus runs on Sunday.

CAR

Vehicle rentals are available from **Helax** (☎ 382 114; Hotel Ero; per week from 490KM; ☺ 8am-5pm Mon-Fri, to noon Sat) and **MaxLine** (☎ 551 525; www.maxline.ba; Station Sq; per day/week from €45/245; ☺ 8am-6pm Mon-Fri, 9am-3pm Sat) or through travel agencies. **Sixt** (☎ 317 166; www.sixt.com; Hotel Ero; per week from €220) offers the possibility to drop off at Sarajevo airport for no extra cost, but its online-booking system doesn't always work.

TRAIN

The **train station** (☎ 552 198) is beside the bus station. Two daily services run to Sarajevo (9.90KM, 2¾ hours) at 7.38am and 6.40pm, connecting or continuing to Doboj (six hours) and Zagreb (12 hours). The little three-carriage trains puff alongside fish farms in the pea-green Neretva River's magnificent dammed gorge before struggling up a series of switchbacks behind Konjic to reach Sarajevo after 65 tunnels.

AROUND MOSTAR

Blagaj

At the far end of pretty Blagaj village the Buna River gushes out of a gaping cave backed by soaring cliffs. Beside it is a very picturesque, half-timbered **Tekija** (Dervish monastery; ☎ 573 221; admission 3KM; ☺ 8am-10pm). The charmingly wobbly interior has carved wooden ceilings and entombs two Tajik 15th-century dervishes.

Pilgrims pay their respects and dervishes still gather regularly, while the quaint courtyard also doubles as souvenir shop and terrace cafe.

From the **tourist information booth** (☺ 10am-7pm in season) in central Blagaj there are two 10-minute walking routes to the Tekija. Following the direct road you'll pass the delightful **Oriental House** (Velagic House; ☎ 572 712; www.velagomed.ba; Velagicevina bb; admission 2KM; ☺ 10am-7pm), signed Velagomed. This unique, artistically appointed 18th-century Ottoman ensemble has fabulous island-meadow gardens, a former mill house and a private riverside cave for sipping coffee. Visits include tasting the owners' famous honey.

Two dainty bridges near the Tekija cross to the splendidly located riverside-view restaurant **Vrelo** (☎ 572 556; mains 7-18KM; ☺ 9am-11pm), from which you can loop back to town along the quieter east bank, crossing the modest, 16th-century Karađozbeg stone bridge and passing the octagonal **Sultan Sulejman mosque**, rebuilt in 1892.

The high crag above Blagaj is topped by the impressively massive ruined **fortress** (admission free) of Herceg Stjepan, whose dynasty ruled Hum (present-day Hercegovina) until his son finally capitulated to the Ottoman Turks here in 1482. The sweaty but relatively obvious climb to the top starts from the hill's western flank, around 600m west of the tourist booth via the road that heads away from the river.

SLEEPING

Kayan Pansion (☎ 572 299; nevresakajan@yahoo.com; tw €20) This new homestay offers four unfussy, very well-kept rooms sharing two toilets and two air-conditioned sitting rooms. The family is delightful and Merima (mobile ☎ 061346969) speaks English. The house has a blue 'Velez Mountain Eco-Tourism' plaque and is approximately opposite the Sultan Sulejman mosque.

Oriental House (Velagic House; ☎ 572 712; www .velagomed.ba; Velagicevina bb; d €30) At the time of writing, two simple but authentic rooms sharing a decent bathroom were being prepared for guest use in this classic Blagaj museum-home. Semir (mobile ☎ 061273459) speaks excellent English.

Hotel Ada (☎ 572 500; www.ada-hotel.com.ba; s/d €35/60) New if unremarkable waterfront hostelry tucked 200m down the second Blagaj–Buna road, around 3km from the Tekija.

Motel-Restoran Kolo (☎ 061106203; www.motel -kolo.com; d/apt €20/40) If you're driving, consider continuing 4km from the Ada towards Buna, where this modest but inexpensive motel is idyllically set overlooking an especially scenic bend on the Buna River, complete with large waterwheel.

GETTING THERE & AWAY

Mostar Bus lines 10, 11 and 12 run patchily to or near Blagaj (1.80KM, 30 minutes), but check www.mostarbus.ba/linije.asp for the frequently changing schedule. There's no public transport from Blagaj to Podvelež or Počitelj.

The tourist booth can organise hikes, mountain biking and canyoning adventures.

Podvelež

Mt Velež is a desolate, strikingly long, tent-shaped ridge almost 2000m high. Widely scattered along its base is Podvelež, a group of 13 isolated shepherd villages. With a car, driving through Podvelež makes a fascinating back-road loop from Mostar. Endless hairpin bends with superb panoramas take you up to some harrowing reminders of the 1990s conflict and into a fascinatingly stark moonscape. Then villages begin to usher in patches of dwarf woodlands before the lane descends again via the Nevesinje road with brilliant views of Blagaj's castle, inaccessibly looming across a dramatically deep-cut valley.

Smajkići is the only Podvelež village with any facilities. A **turbe** (Muslim graveyard) here commemorates the area's vast number of 1990s deaths. Facing it, where the road turns, **Motel Sunce** (☎ 560 082; www.motel-sunce-podvelez.com; per person B&B/half board from 45/52KM) offers rustic homemade meals (mains 5KM to 9KM) and decent rooms (some with shared bathroom). Despite the well-translated website, the motel's kindly owner, Ismet, speaks minimal English.

If you can handle the language barrier, he can organise walking guides (50KM to 100KM) to explore the tracks up towards Velež Ridge. Alternatively, snap a digital photograph of the high-quality topographic map outside and use that to strike off alone, but remember to stick to worn paths as some mine dangers remain.

From Mostar weekday bus 16 runs to appealing Šipovac village via Smajkići (2.50KM, 45 minutes) at 7am, noon, 3.30pm and 8.30pm, returning around an hour later. There's no public transport at all on the hairpin-fraught short-cut between Mostar and Šipovac.

MEĐUGORJE

☎ 036 / pop 4300

Once a nondescript, poor Hercegovinian village, Međugorje rapidly became one of the most visited places in the former Yugoslavia after six teenagers claimed that the Holy Virgin spoke to them on 24 June 1981. Unlike similar apparitions at Lourdes (France, 1858) and Fatima (Portugal, 1917), the Catholic Church has not officially acknowledged the legitimacy of these visions. Indeed the Virgin's decidedly open-minded pronouncement that 'all religions are accepted' by her son has caused consternation among some Christian groups. This hasn't stopped Međugorje from becoming a magnet for Catholic visitors from all over the world. The hope of catching a personal glimpse of the Virgin Mary is very real among believers and three of the original six witnesses still claim to see the vision daily. According to 'scientific' studies, the three do all see the exact same thing at the same moment, whatever that might actually be (www.medjugorje.org/science.htm).

If you don't spot her personally you can console yourself by shopping for Virgin statuettes or by drowning your disappointment in some of BiH's best wine, sampled at a local vineyard or three.

Orientation

From St James's Church, Međugorje's unnamed main drag is a strip of visionabilia, kitschy religio-souvenir shops, restaurants and travel agencies stretching 500m north to the main post office and bus station. Here the road swerves abruptly left (west) passing two large supermarkets (200m), the Čapljina/Dubrovnik turn (600m), and Sport Centar (1.2km) before crossing the R424 Mostar–Čitluk–Ljubuški road by the Circle International petrol station (Tromeđa, 1.5km).

Around 100m southwest of St James's, go straight across the Stari Crkva one-way loop for the Stankela winery (1.2km) and the Mt Križeva path (1.5km). Or turn left (initially northeast) for Apparition Hill (2.1km), with right turns after 400m (Forum shop) and 1.1km (Surmanci junction).

Artist's-eye maps are available from travel agents or by download from the **tourist association** (www.tel.net.ba/tzm-medjugorje/1%20karta100.jpg).

Information

Busy prayer schedules are posted on multilingual boards outside St James's Church. Arrive early, as masses can get packed.

Globtour (☎ 651 393; www.globtour.com; ⏰ 8.30am-4.30pm) Books ferries and flights, and runs its own bus network.

Main post office (⏰ 7am-8pm Mon-Sat, 10am-5pm Sun) Telephone, money changing and internet access (per hr 4KM). There's a smaller post office beside St James's Church.

UniCredit Zagrebačka Bank (⏰ 8am-2.30pm Mon-Fri, to noon Sat) Travellers cheques, ATM.

Ured Informacije (☎ 651 988; www.medjugorje.hr; ⏰ 8am-6pm Mon-Sat, 9am-2pm Sun) Collect church schedules, town maps and the Virgin Mary's monthly message from a yellow-orange building beside St James's.

TOUR AGENCIES

The following, all very central, can arrange accommodation, wine tastings and tours to the Kravice waterfalls. All shut on Sunday.

Global Travel (☎ 651 489; www.global-medjugorje .com)

Medjugorje Travel (☎ 650 389; www.medjugorje travel.ba)

Paddy Travel (☎ /fax 651 482; paddy@tel.net.ba)

Sights & Activities

A large open-air pilgrims' prayer area is tucked behind the 1969 double-towered **St James's Church** (Župna Crkva). From here the tree-lined **Via Domini** (Path of Contemplation) leads 200m past several religious mosaics to Međugorje's most memorable site, the mesmerising **Resurrected Saviour** (Uskrsli Spasitej). A masterpiece of modernist sculpture, this gaunt 5m-tall metallic Christ stands crucified yet crossless, his manhood wrapped in scripture. Erected in 1998, the statue 'miraculously' weeps a colourless liquid from its right knee. Pilgrims queue to dab a drop of this holy fluid onto specially inscribed pads.

It's possible to walk on up Via Domini to Mt Križevac (see right).

On **Apparition Hill** (Brdo Ukazanja), a white statue marks the site at which the Virgin was first seen on 24 June 1981. This supposedly represents Jesus' mother, though her straight, European nose and nunlike clothing hardly seem characteristic of a 1st-century Palestinian Jewess. The site is a 10-minute climb above Podbrdo village, accessed by an unstabilised network of red-earth paths studded with sharp stones. Some pilgrims walk barefoot in deliberately painful acts of penitence.

Around 400m east on the road that eventually curves back to Mt Križevac (2km), **Oaza Mira** (admission free; ⏰ 9am-2pm) is a delightfully peaceful garden of reflection leading to a small chapel backed by fields and drystone walls. Behind, a remarkable castle-palace folly is under construction in surreal MC Escher style.

The delightful ivy-draped **Stankela Winery** (Vinarija Stankela; ☎ 651 042; tastings €5-10; ⏰ by arrangement) makes what is arguably BiH's best žilavka white wine: fresh and dry, yet fruity like a sophisticated muscat sec. By prearranging a day ahead you can visit the atmospheric wooden-beamed tasting room and little subterranean cave where the owner keeps his vast array of international awards.

To work off the alcohol you could climb **Mt Križevac** (Mt Cross) for terrific views towards Velež Ridge. The mountain is topped by a white cross planted in 1934 to commemorate the 1900th anniversary of Christ's death. The stations-of-the-cross path starts between cafebars just 300m west of Stankela.

In summer, cooling off in the three swimming pools of the very extensive **Sport Centar** (☎ 651 402; www.sport-centar.com; Tromeđa bb; day admission €5; ⏰ 10am-7pm May-Sep) might just be the answer to your prayers. Its smart cafe has an internet corner.

Sleeping

Most of Međugorje's *pansion* rooms are fundamentally alike, and as likely as not you'll be sleeping under a cross or an image of the Virgin Mary. Some places only accept group bookings, but unless the Virgin walks down the main street the town's 18,000-plus rooms can generally cope with all accommodation demands. Nonetheless, booking is wise at the following peak times, when prices will rise somewhat:

Catholic Easter Dates vary; see p433.

Late June This is when the apparition's anniversary is celebrated in the Peace Walk parade.

August Especially around the Feast of the Assumption (15 August).

First Sunday after Mary's birthday Mary's birthday is 8 September.

Villa Regina (☎ 651 808; www.hotel-villaregina.com; s/d/tr €41/64/84) Stylish Italian-contemporary design, a superbly central location and the best pizzeria in town make this new 107-room hotel Međugorje's foremost choice.

Pansion Park (☎ 651 155; s/d/tr €25/40/60; **P**) Facing the Gardens restaurant across a manicured lawn, the rooms are typically generic but impeccably clean and great value.

Pansion Mate-i-Zdenka (☎ 651 697; mate.vasilj1@tel.net.ba; per person €10) Three doors away from Globtour towards St James's Church, this family house is a warren of plain, monastic rooms, typical of Međugorje's cheapest options but more central than many.

Eating

Gardens (☎ 650 499; dishes 10-24KM; fish per kg from 36KM) Downstairs the buzzing cafe-bar is Međugorje's top post-prayer party spot, with an atmosphere somewhere between a Louisiana speakeasy and an Irish pub. Upstairs the predominantly Italian restaurant is altogether more refined, with winsome cherubs plucking lyres and fresh fish of the day waiting on ice. It's located near the main post office.

Lukas (☎ 653 830; mains 6-15KM; ☽ 7am-late) Informal and decorated with humorously tacky cloud-burst paintings on the fake-pyramid ceiling, Lukas offers inexpensive squid-and-chips (10KM) washed down with 2KM glasses of slightly effervescent *domaći* red wine.

Dubrovnik (☎ 651 472; mains 11-24KM; ☽ 7am-late) Popular for its very central terrace, Dubrovnik has Guinness on tap and offers 20KM Irish fry-up breakfasts.

Getting There & Around

Buses to Mostar (3KM, 40 minutes) run eight times on weekdays, five times on Saturday. On Sunday there's just the Sarajevo-bound 9am minibus. **Globtour** (☎ /fax 651 393) runs daily services to Zagreb (8am via Jajce), Dubrovnik (25KM, 4½ hours, 6.10am) and Split (20KM, three or four hours, 7.30am, 11am and 5.20pm). Taxis charge €40 to Mostar, €40 return to the Kravice waterfalls or €5 per hop in town.

ČAPLJINA
☎ 036

Although in itself an entirely uninteresting junction town, Čapljina offers some useful transport connections to Stolac and Ljubuški. Beside the Villa Rustica restaurant, 1km south of the bus station, are the chunky Roman ruins of Mogorjelo Vila, now used as a little park. Directly beyond the **Vranac Riding Club** (☎ 063357231; www.villa-rustica.ba) offers horse-riding lessons or canters along pretty riverside trails (€12 per hour). Owner Mato also organises canoeing and kayaking safaris including transfers to a put-in near the Studenci rapids, from which you paddle back to a point just 1km south of Mogorjelo.

On the riverfront 900m east of the bus station, the stylish **Mogorjelo Hotel** (☎ 810 815; www.hotelmogorjelo.ba; Kraljice Katarine bb; s/d from 90/140KM) is far more impressive than any equivalent business hotel in Mostar, and the giant Michelangelo-style murals in its restaurant-cafe area are a sight in themselves.

Hotel J&B (☎ 801 382; Mostarska 15; s/d/tr 50/80/100KM) is hopelessly dated.

Getting There & Away

Buses to Mostar (6KM, 40 minutes) via Počitelj (5km) run twice hourly on weekdays, less often on Saturday and only six times on Sunday. Buses to Stolac (5KM, 45 minutes) depart at 8am and 10am and then hourly till 4pm on weekdays, but only five times on Saturday and not at all on Sunday. To Ljubuški (3.50KM, 40 minutes) they leave at 6.50am, 7.30am, noon, 1.40pm and 6.25pm Monday to Saturday.

AROUND ČAPLJINA
Počitelj
☎ 036

Cupped in a steep, rocky amphitheatre, this stepped Ottoman-era fortress village is one of the most picture-perfect architectural ensembles in BiH. Its strategic Hungarian garrison fell to Hamazbey's Turkish army in 1471, and the fortifications were vastly enlarged in 1698 after Venice grabbed once-important Gabela, leaving Počitelj as Ottoman Hercegovina's frontier post with hostile Dalmatia. During the Yugoslav era Počitelj became an artists' community, but it was systematically despoiled in the 1990s conflicts. Today much has been repaired, while those old stone homes that remain in ruins almost add to the antique if slightly maudlin atmosphere of the place.

Entering beside the vine-trellised Stari Grad Café, climb via the imposing **gate tower** towards the 16th-century **Šišman Ibrahim Madrassa**, with five domes and a lovely stone portico. Further up, the **Gavrakapetanović House** was the centre of the 20th-century artists' colony till 1993. Steps to the right lead up beside the 1563 **Hadži Alijna mosque** and curve round to the 16m, 17th-century **clock tower** (Sahat Kula), whose bell was melted down to make bullets during WWI. Alternatively, turn left to reach the uppermost fort, whose **Gavrakapetan Tower** is the village's landmark feature.

There's no accommodation and not even the apricot-vending urchins offer homestays. Near the madrassa the **Počitelj Pizzeria** (čevapi 7KM; 🕑 8am-10pm) has a pleasant terrace but no pizza.

Počitelj is right beside the main Split–Mostar road, 4km north of the Čapljina bridge. Take Mostar–Čapljina buses (p141). In summer arrive early to avoid the heat and the Croatian tour groups.

Kravice Waterfalls

In spring this stunning arc of **25m cascades** pounds itself to a dramatic, steamy fury that's smaller than Niagara but in some ways more beautiful thanks to the verdant vegetation through which the rivulets and leaps explode. In summer the falls themselves are less impressive, but the pools become shallow enough for swimming and seasonal cafes materialise to serve the merry holidaymakers.

Kravice is 4km down a dead-end road (no public transport) that turns off the Čapljina–Ljubuški road at kilometre 42.5. Taxis cost around 8KM from **Ljubuški** (7km), a sprawling, unexciting town that's backed by a superb **medieval fortress ruin** and is famous for the new-meets-old **Franciscan monastery** in its Humac suburb, 3km south.

Good-value one-day tours from Mostar often visit Kravice along with Počitelj, Blagaj and Međugorje.

Hutovo Blato

☎ 036

This **wetland park** (☎ 814 715; www.hutovo-blato.ba; admission free) is BiH's top reserve for migratory birds. The starting point for exploring Hutovo Blato's marshy terrain is the superfriendly if slightly dated **Motel Karaotok** (☎ 814 990; s/d/tr 62/104/111KM; 🗷 🅿). It's set in a lonely wood-

land that's magically serenaded by millions of croaking frogs at dusk. Right outside is the park's limited 'Educational Walk' with pictures of local wildlife to spot (text in Bosnian), and the starting points for a 5km cycling trail and a waterborne **photo safari** (6/10/20 people from 40/60/100KM). Longer 2½-hour boat trips (from 150KM) chug right through the overgrown waterways to a lake that's seasonally choked in lotus flowers. Alternatively, rent a self-paddle canoe (20KM) or simply look down upon the scene when driving along the new 5.4km access road. That turns east off the Mostar–Split road 1.2km south of the Čapljina-Stolac junction. There's no public transport.

NEUM

BiH's tiny toehold of Adriatic is crammed with concrete apartment-hotels for holidaying locals, but the water isn't as inviting as parts of neighbouring Croatia. For most travellers it's enough to glimpse Neum (www.neum.ba) from a Split–Dubrovnik bus. Most of these make refreshment breaks at unexotic shop-cafes on the Neum bypass. No need to change money!

STOLAC

☎ 036

The attractive yet little-touristed castle town of Stolac guards an impressive craggy canyon dappled with cypress trees. Site of 3rd-century Roman Diluntum, it became a prominent 15th-century citadel that only fell to the Ottomans in 1465. Much more recently Stolac suffered serious conflict in 1993, when Serbs and Bosniaks were carted off to concentration camps by Croat militias. Some awful physical and psychological damage remains, but the displaced population has returned and reconstruction continues apace.

Sights

From the bus station walk past the Auro petrol station, cross two small bridges and pass the almost-rebuilt 1732 **Podgradska mosque**, with its *bezistan* (covered market) arches, to reach the pretty main street, Hrvatske-Brante (aka Ada). This arcs towards the centre (700m) following a gurgling river lined with shady plane trees. The overgrown **Vidoški Grad** castle hill looms above. Access is 100m beyond Krypton Pizzeria, via a lane that winds up past the **Donja Kapija** (lower gate), through which steps climb on past a creeper-covered four-storey stone tower. Further up in the Gornji Grad summit section it's all too easy to see how the town could be bombarded by whoever controlled this perch.

In the town centre, the memorable, mural-fronted **Čaršija mosque** has been rebuilt with stone roof, fountain and cloister to look much like the 1519 original. Facing it, the fine 1735 **Šarić House** had been a celebrated gallery till it was torched in July 1993.

The dainty **Cuprijška mosque**, 1km upstream, overlooks the historic but modest five-arched **Inat Bridge**. For another 800m upstream there are several delightfully picturesque if partly ruined collections of 17th-century stone **mill races**.

Sleeping & Eating

Villa Ragusa (☎ 853 700; s/d/tr 35/70/105KM) Stolac's only hotel offers mostly clean but worn triple rooms with uncurtained showers. It's on the riverside, somewhat hidden across a small bridge just north of the central area.

Restaurant Behar (☎ 854 012; meals 5-16KM; ☷ 7am-11pm) Near the Auro petrol station, Behar looks like a private house but has a simple terrace area with (partially obscured) castle views. Perfectly cooked trout is washed down a treat with powerful if slightly green *domaći* white wine (12KM per litre) made in Stolac.

Getting There & Away

To Čapljina (5KM, 45 minutes) weekday buses run most hours on the hour until 5pm. They leave at 8am, 10am, noon, 3pm and 5pm on Saturday; there's no Sunday service. Weekdays only, buses to Mostar via Rotimlja leave at 6.30am and 12.30pm. Two Mostar–Trebinje buses pass through town but oddly *don't* call at the bus station. There's an overnight bus to Zagreb via Jajce at 7pm.

AROUND STOLAC
Radimlja

Around 3km west of Stolac, **Radimlja Necropolis** was the medieval burial ground of Stolac's preeminent Hraben-Milovadović dynasty. Today its collection of around 110 *stećci* (see the boxed text, p109) is often cited as BiH's most important. However, many carvings are hard to discern, and the unexotic location beside a bombed-out tourist centre at kilometre 21 of the M6 Čapljina road doesn't make an impressive visual impact.

Daorson Archaeological Park

Rediscovered in 1891 on a lonely, windswept ridge is the remarkable if lumpy cyclopean wall of a 4th-century-BC Illyrian citadel. The stone blocks weigh up to 7 tonnes apiece. The very narrow access lane starts at kilometre 24 of the M6, 200m east of Stolac bus station, then winds up for 7km. Fork right after 1.5km, then left 1km beyond, after which there's no asphalt. The lane passes near two attractive villages and there's a great viewpoint at the end; there's no public transport.

Stolac to Trebinje

Only two daily buses use this fascinatingly lonely road that crosses the desolate scrub-land hills of the former Croat-Serb front line to **Ljubinje** with its two modest collections of *stećci* (see the boxed text, p109). The road then winds grandly down between some picturesque, very isolated hamlets (notably pretty **Kotezi**, kilometre 55) into the wide, relatively fertile **Polopov Polje** valley with its mysterious 'disappearing river'. Around kilometre 61 a side road via Ravno (3.5km) allows motorists to follow a parallel lane to **Zavala** with its famous monastery and **Vjetrenica Cave**, known ever since Roman times for its 'windy breath'. The more major road passes many other attractive villages, **Tvrdoš monastery** (p145) and several waterwheels (*dolap*) before reaching Trebinje.

TREBINJE ТРЕБИЊЕ
☎ 059 / pop 36,000

Leafy squares, a charming little old town and a unique Ottoman-era bridge make Trebinje a beguiling quick stop between Dubrovnik (28km) and Mostar or Višegrad. But don't expect snooty Dubrovnik citizens to encourage the trip. Remembering the 1990s conflict, some coastal Croatians imagine Trebinje to be a nest of murderers. In fact Trebinje's greatest charm lies in the residents' disarmingly unpretentious friendliness, making it a great place to hear Serb viewpoints on recent history. Street signs are largely in Cyrillic, but finding English speakers is rarely a problem.

Orientation & Information

Central Trebinje sits on an S-bend where a section of the otherwise east–west Trebišnjica River briefly swings south. Since 2007 the new 'bus station' (Vojvode Stepe Stepanovića) is an unmarked parking area between the mirror-glassed Electrical Utility building and Njegoševa. Njegoševa runs east, passing close to Trg Svobode before swerving south past the old town's main

BOSNIA & HERCEGOVINA

JOVAN DUČIĆ ЈОВАН ДУЧИЋ

Born around 1874 (nobody's sure when) in Trebinje (they're very sure where), Jovan Dučić was a poet whose work embodied Serb consciousness. By 1907 he'd left BiH (then Austrian controlled) to become a diplomat for Serbia. He was initially against the post-WWI union of southern-Slav countries, but by 1937 he'd changed his mind, waxed up his moustache and taken the job as Yugoslavia's ambassador to Romania. Fleeing the Nazis in 1941, he took exile in the USA, where he returned to organising Serbian nationalist work, albeit at a distance and possibly with proto-CIA backing. He died and was buried in Illinois during 1943. However, during the 1990s his Serbian-consciousness ideas belatedly turned him into an iconic figure in the RS. So it was that almost 60 years after his death his remains were returned to his home town for a grand reburial at the specially built Hercegovacka Gracanica (see below).

---

gateway and Dučić Park. After one short block, opposite the large Saborna church, Preobraženska cuts east, passing the **tourist office** (☎ 273 122; www.trebinjeturizam.com; Preobraženska 10; ⏰ 8am-3pm Mon-Fri), hidden in an unlikely apartment building. That's tucked behind the **Balkan Investment Bank** (☎ Preobraženska 6; ⏰ 8am-4pm Mon-Fri), which offers money changing and an ATM. After the large Market 99 supermarket, Preobraženska crosses the river on Andrić Bridge, becomes Vidovdanska for a block, then reaches a T-junction at Dušanova. Turn left to find motels Viv and Etage after one block. A block further is the main **post office** (Srpska 2; ⏰ 7am-8pm Mon-Fri, to 6pm Sat), covering two blocks. Left again here and Kralja Petra Prvog Oslobodioca brings you back past Hotel Leotar then across the river on Kameni Bridge beside the old town's northern flank.

Somewhat dated city maps are downloadable from www.trebinje.info/trebinje/mape.

Sights

Trebinje's small, walled **old town** (Stari Grad) has a human charm that rests more on its inviting, unpretentious cafes than on any grand monuments. The ramparts back onto the riverside near a 19th-century former Austro-Hungarian barracks that now houses the **Hercegovina Museum** (☎ 271 060; Stari Grad 59; admission 1KM; ⏰ 8.30am-2pm). As well as ethnographical exhibits, there's a collection of valuable Roman sculptures bequeathed by Jovan Dučić (see the boxed text, above), whose medals and diplomatic finery are also displayed.

Host to Saturday markets, lovely **Trg Svobode** sports an angel-topped stone monolith paid for by the ubiquitous Jovan Dučić. It celebrates November 1918, when Serbian forces kicked the Austrians out of Trebinje. Doze off on this square and when you awake you might think yourself transported to southern France. Chestnut trees and stone-flagged pavements, old stone buildings with wrought-iron overhangs, all those lovely street cafes, and directly southeast, shaded by mature plane trees, Dučić Trg looks like it's just waiting for a game of pétanque. Pedestrianised Jovana Dučića alongside leads down to Dučić Park, where there's a statue of…guess who?

Potentially even more iconic than the Višegrad equivalent, Trebinje's 1574 **Arslanagić Bridge** (Perovića Most) is a unique double-backed structure that survived explosive damage during WWII but was outrageously submerged by a 1960s hydroelectric scheme. The drowned bridge was belatedly disassembled in 1965 but left like a stone jigsaw. Only in 1972 was it eventually put back together in its present, disappointingly unexotic location. Find it by following the curving river road round for 700m, starting directly north of the Hotel Leotar.

Crowning Crkvina Hill, the compact but eye-catching **Presvete Bogorodice Church** is a feast of arches and domelets built in layers of alternating stone and brick. Financed by a Chicago-Bosnian businessman, it was erected in 2000 to rehouse the bones of local hero Jovan Dučić (did you read that boxed text yet?). The design is based on the 1321 Gračanica monastery (p276) in Kosovo, a building that's symbolically sacred to many Serbs. The site also includes a freestanding bell tower, a small museum, a bookshop, a summer cafe and religious offices. But the main attractions for non-Serbs are the phenomenal views.

Hercegovacka Gracanica is 2km northeast of the hospital (itself diagonally behind Motel Etage). The winding, switchback route is regularly indicated by brown signposts (in Cyrillic: 'ХЕРЦЕГОВАЧКА ГРАЧАНИЦА').

Gloriously set amid vines, beehives and orchards overlooking the river 6km west of Trebinje, the delightful **Tvrdoš monastery** (M3, km97; admission free; ☺ 10.45am-2pm & 4-7pm) welcomes those visitors who have a spiritual interest in Serbian Orthodox monasticism. If you've only come to buy the famous wine, that's available from a little shop-kiosk by the driveway gate. For Bosnian Serbs Tvrdoš is of great religious significance as the place where St Basil of Ostrog took his monastic vows. Based around the site of a 4th-century Roman church, it became the 16th-century seat of the Metropolitan (Orthodox archbishop) of Hercegovina until 1694. The monastery's icon-packed little campanile church is brilliantly painted with interior murals incorporating a few fragmentary remnants of the 1517 originals. It's surrounded across an irregular garden courtyard by a very attractive collection of buildings with stone bases and overhanging uppers held on wooden beams.

Sleeping

Hotel Platani (☎ 225 134; www.hotelplatani.com; Trg Svobode; s/d/tr 79/115/135KM; P 🐾) Perfectly located above the town's top street cafe, this cosy 12-room hotel feels gently upmarket, though the tiny reception can take a bit of finding.

Motel Etage (☎ 261 443; www.hoteletage.com; Dušanova 9; s/d/tr €30/45/55) Bright and colourful but not overlarge rooms, with a decent buffet breakfast included. It's near the hospital: cross the river east of the tourist office, then turn left.

Motel Viv (☎ 273 500; www.hotelviv-trebinje.com; Dušanova 11; s/d/tr 60/90/120KM) Marginally smarter but slightly more prone to road noise than the next-door Motel Etage.

Hotel Leotar (☎ 261 086; www.hotelleotar.com; Obala Luke Vukalovića bb; s/d 51.50/83KM, deluxe 81.50/113KM) This growling four-storey socialist-era remnant faces the old-town ramparts across the river. So far 35 deluxe rooms have been attractively upgraded, but twice that many are sorry old affairs with all the glamour of a 1960s hospital ward.

Eating & Drinking

Pizza Castello (☎ 223 192; Trg Travunije 3; pizzas 6.50-7.50KM; ☺ 7.30am-midnight) Castello's three-table terrace is great for people watching, jovial host Snezhan speaks great English, and the thin-crust pizza is excellent. Several other relatively downmarket eateries share this same old town square with the recently rebuilt Osman-Paša mosque.

Galerija Veritas (Stari Grad 17; beers 2.50KM; ☺ 9am-11pm) Eccentric brick-domed cavern cafe dotted with antique TV sets. Check out the beamed upper level! It's hidden in an old-town alley between the museum and Kameni Bridge.

Azzovo (Stari Grad 114; beers 2KM; ☺ 8am-11pm Mon-Sat, 10am-11pm Sun) Cosy, old-town blues-oriented bar with ceilings of bamboo and vine stems. Nearby, several others have similarly great terraces, while Kafe Serbia and Bajica Caffe are built right into the old-town ramparts.

Underground (off Vldovdanska; beers 1.50KM; ☺ 8am-2am Mon-Sat, 3pm-1am Sun) Spacious stone-walled basement pub beneath a fine old mansion facing Andrić Bridge. Look for the Jim Beam-style logo-sign.

Shopping

Say 'filatelia' at the post office and the kind staff might scuttle off to find a selection of relatively rare Republika Srpska stamps for sale at face value.

Getting There & Away

For bus services, see the table, below.

BUS SERVICES FROM TREBINJE			
Destination	**Price (KM)**	**Duration (hr)**	**Departures**
Belgrade	40	11	8am & 6pm via Foča & Višegrad
Bileća	5	½	11 daily
Dubrovnik	5	¾	10am Mon-Sat, returns 1.30pm
Herceg Novi	13	1¾	6am via Risan, handy for Perast & Kotor
Ljubinje	9	1½	2.10pm Mon-Fri & 7pm daily
Mostar	19	3	6.15am & 2.30pm via Stolac, 10am via Nevesinje
Pale	22	4½	5am via Foča
Podgorica	20	3½	8.30am, 3pm & 4.30pm via Nikšič
Sarajevo	20	4	5am, 7.30.am & 11am via Foča

EASTERN BOSNIA

DRINA VALLEY

Drina is BiH's best-known brand of cigarettes. More relevantly, it's also Eastern Bosnia's most important river, the confluence of the beautiful Sutjeska and Tara rivers and a natural sculptor of some truly awesome rocky canyons. Anyone who's read Ivo Andrić's epic *The Bridge on the Drina* will find it hard to resist a literary 'pilgrimage' to Višegrad. Hard-core rafting fans should make a beeline for Foča. In between, **Goražde** has no sights per se, but the desperate story of its 1992–95 siege is brilliantly retold in Joe Sacco's very humane, darkly humorous comic strip *Safe Area Goražde*.

Sutjeska National Park

Национални Парк Сутјеска

☎ 058

North of the almost comically miserable eyesore town of **Gacko**, the Trebinje–Foča road becomes extremely scenic, winding across a magnificent woodland pass into the glorious **Sutjeska National Park** (www.npsutjeska.srbinje .net). Here the road follows a tight canyon whose soaring, spiky limestone sides are topped with improbably perched conifers as though designed for a Chinese woodcut. The valley opens out at the northern edge of the park, where an impressively vast concrete **Partisans' Memorial** commemorates a classic WWII battle. Around 600m beyond, just a few of the 68 rooms at the rather institutional **Hotel Mladost** (☎ 233 118; s/tw/tr/q 30/60/90/120KM; ☺ May–Oct) have been upgraded, though most have great mountain-view balconies. There's also a campsite. Just a few buildings scattered between here and a petrol pump 1km further north constitute the settlement of **Tjentište**.

Trebinje–Foča buses pass right through. But to get a better idea of the park's treasures, you'll need wheels. Take the tiny, somewhat degraded lane almost opposite the petrol station signed 'Prijevor 20km'. After 5km pay the 3KM per person fee at a gate, or if it's unstaffed just open it (and close it behind you). From a car park around halfway to Prijevor, it's a 10-minute stroll to a viewpoint of the 72m **Skakavac Waterfalls**. From the road's end at Prijevor, it's around two hours' trek to the achingly beautiful **Trnovačko Lake**, popular with locals for summer camping.

Foča Фоча

☎ 058 / pop 24,000

Foča's central street, Kraljapetra-I, stretches 600m east from the Drina Bridge to the bus stand where Jevrejska (right) doubles back past the market to a one-street **old town** (Karađorđeva). Here you'll find a few tile-roofed old shop-houses, a pretty stone **clock tower** and the shattered facade-wall of the 1752 **former Kukavića mosque**, dynamited in May 1992.

However, the only reason you're likely to come is for the world-class **rafting** on the Tara River. That comes cascading out of Europe's deepest canyon across the Montenegro border, then thunders over 21 rapids (grade III–IV in summer, IV–V in April). Very professional extreme-sports outfit **Encijan** (☎ 211 220; www.pkencijan.com; Kraljapetra-I 1; ☺ 9am-5pm), at the westernmost end of town, can organise everything. In July and August you'll pay €27 per person, assuming a minimum group of six people, plus €8 to the put-in (37km away), where Encijan offers a very decent **hut-camp** (☎ 484 099; Brštanovica; dm €6). Prices rise significantly in April and May, when ferocious water conditions necessitate three skippers per raft. Encijan also offers a range of outdoor pursuits in the Sutjeska National Park.

Tucked behind Hypo Bank (ATM available), the sorry **Hotel Zelengora** (☎ 210 013; Njegoševa 2; s/d/tr 45/66/75KM) is Foča's only central accommodation, with droopy curtains, worn carpets and a creaky old lift.

Višegrad Вишеград

☎ 058 / pop 20,000

Višegrad's internationally famous 1571 old bridge is a Unesco World Heritage site. While the town is otherwise architecturally unexotic, it's set between some of Bosnia's most impressive river canyons.

ORIENTATION & INFORMATION

The ultra-helpful **tourist office** (☎ 620 821; tovgd@teol.net; Užičkog 11; ☺ 8am-3pm Mon-Fri) operates a summer information kiosk right by the south end of the old bridge, but the main office is, oddly, unmarked in the town centre, 400m further east opposite a dinky little steam train.

Download town maps from http://vise grad24.info/galery/data/media/17/Karta _Visegrada_AB.jpg.

If you haven't read Ivo Andrić's *The Bridge on the Drina* you can buy copies (30KM) at the bookshop kiosk facing Hotel Višegrad.

SIGHTS
Immortalised in Andrić's classic, the 10-arch **Mehmet Paša Sokolović Bridge** (www.pbase.com/vmarinkovic/the_bridge_on_the_drina) still incorporates a central *kapia* (sitting area) marked by a tall rectangular plinth featuring the Grand Vizier's inscription stone. Here Alihoja was nailed by the ear, the beautiful Fata dived to a marriage-avoiding death and the magnificent Pop Nikola led the terrified town notables to meet the Austrian Commander in one of the novel's most splendidly anticlimactic moments. Readers remembering one-eyed Ćorkan's death-defying rum-soaked traverse of the bridge's icy parapet might be surprised by how wide that parapet is these days. The much narrower original was washed away in the terrible 1896 flood.

The bridge looks especially picturesque at night overlooked by the floodlit **Serbian Orthodox Church**. That sits on the Mejdan hillock above, to which the old Alihodja would struggle home at night.

In early July there's a very popular Mostar-style **bridge-diving competition**.

ACTIVITIES
Drina **boat rides** can take you through some of Europe's deepest and most spectacular canyons. Ask the tourist office about the *Sonja*, which makes round trips north from Višegrad. Alternatively, **Vodeni Ćiro** (☎ 711 155, 0654022111) links Ustiprača (a tiny junction town on the once-murderous 'Blue Rd' from Sarajevo) to Ruda. Bookings are essential, price depends on group size.

SLEEPING
Motel Okuka (☎ 065998761; Vojvode Stepe bb; s/d/tr 50/80/120KM) Shaped like a Pennsylvanian barn, the Okuka has adequate rooms, but they lack style. The similarly unsophisticated restaurant (mains 9KM to 14KM) has good if distant views of the old bridge, 1.2km upstream.

Motel Aura (☎ 631 021; auravgd@teol.net; Kraljapetpui bb; s/d from 45/65KM) Swish new rooms are better than equivalents at Okuka but lack any views. The motel is behind AutoGas LPG station, just across the new bridge from town (1km northeast of the old bridge).

Hotel Višegrad (☎ 620 378) At the time of research this garishly coloured 1970s block, right beside the southeastern end of the old bridge, was under total reconstruction. The smaller cubic building in front, recently refaced in less than tasteful stone cladding, was the site of Lotte's Hotel in *The Bridge on the Drina*.

EATING
Restoran Kruna (☎ 620 352; Kraljapetra-I; mains 7-16KM) Opposite Zoka supermarket in the main street, Kruna looks horrible from the outside, but the interior is charmingly decorated with olde-style windows, sepia photos, gingham tablecloths and strings of paprika. Wide-ranging trilingual menus.

Na Drini Cuprija (☎ 620 534; Nikole Tesle bb; mains 5-16KM) Down a side street just beyond Zoka supermarket, Višegrad's best food is served at a covered but open terrace decked with artisans' implements. English menu; no views.

DRINKING
For perfect bridge views sip a coffee in the wonderful tree-shaded garden terrace outside Hotel Višegrad or a beer on the attractive floating barge bar **ARS** (beers 2KM, ✆ 8am-11pm) on the opposite bank.

GETTING THERE & AWAY
Buses to Belgrade (9.30am and 1.30pm) and Užice (7.30am, 11.30am and 6pm) pass Dobrun and Mokra Gora. Other useful departures include Sarajevo (8am), Mostar (4am), Foča (7am) and Trebinje (10am) via Foča and Sutjeska National Park. Many longer-distance buses pick up at the Motel Okuka, beside which a new bus station is planned.

The Sarajevo–Višegrad–Belgrade railway was scrapped in 1974, but reconstruction of the narrow-gauge line to Mokra Gora (Serbia) is nearly complete. From 2009 tourists should be able to use this to conveniently combine Višegrad, Dobrun and Serbia's popular Šargan 8 tourist train (see p417).

Around Višegrad
VILINA VLAS ВИЛИНА ВЛАС
To build Višegrad's famous bridge, the 16th-century Turks needed lots of appropriate stone. Quarrying for it in pine-covered hills, 6km northeast of Višegrad, they found

thermal springs instead and ended up building a lonely little bathhouse (still extant). In the 1980s, **Vilina Vlas** (☎ 620 311; www.vilinavlas.teol .net; s/d/tr half board with treatment 46/72/102KM, bathing only 3KM; ☯ 10am-3pm & 5-9pm) thermal-waters resort was built nearby. It's almost worth visiting for the perverse curiosity of its time-warp Soviet-sanatorium atmosphere. Using controversial radioactive radon baths, the resort's 'medical centre' specialises in postsurgery recovery and gynaecological problems. That's a spooky irony considering that in 1992 it was infamously used as a 'rape camp' during Višegrad's ethnic cleansing.

DOBRUN ДОБРУН

In a pretty, rural setting 11km east of Višegrad, **Dobrun Monastery** (☎ 612 747; ☯ 11am-5pm Mon-Fri, 11-7pm Sat & Sun) has a strong historical resonance for Serbs as it was here that Karađorđević hid out immediately before launching the 1804 Serb uprising. At the heart of the complex is an originally 14th-century church, used by German troops in WWII. The Germans exploded most of the building on retreat, but miraculously the porch survived, complete with its original interior murals featuring Serbian emperor Dušan. The church is flanked by new monastery buildings that look more like a luxury hotel complex than a hermitage. A **museum** (suggested donation 2KM) here celebrates the 1804 rising, displays religious artefacts and presents an impressive gallery of paintings resulting from the artists' colony that meets here each August.

Steps lead up the crag behind to a hefty bronze Karađorđević statue.

NORTHEASTERN BOSNIA

Dotted amongst the relatively faceless industrial towns of this virtually untouristed region are several small but photogenic medieval castles.

TUZLA
☎ 035 / pop 165,000

A satanic, smoke-belching power station and platoons of 17-storey apartment blocks bode ill as you approach BiH's third-largest city. It's certainly not a prime attraction, but the old-town area has a certain modest charm, with many partly restored Austro-Hungarian-era buildings fanning out in seven pedestrianised directions from a junction called Kapia.

Sights

Tuzla initially grew rich on the salt industry for which it's named. Salt *(tuz)* was retrieved from beneath the town by pumping in water and pumping out brine. However, too much was removed, leaving great cavities and unstable ground. The disastrous results remain obvious in some twisted, collapsing buildings on intriguing Solni Trg, directly southwest of Kapia. A mini **ethnographic museum** here explains traditional salt-making processes. The two display rooms are glassed in, so you don't need to enter (or pay).

North of Kapia, the snappily named Trg Žrtava Genocida u Srebrinici will be transformed if a large 19th-century-style palace building is built as proposed in front of Tuzla's main market. Beyond, the lovably tatty downmarket shopping street, Gradska, continues north to a roundabout known as Skvera, where the 18th-century **Šarena mosque** faces a contemporary neo-Moorish portal.

From Skvera go 50m up VI Bosanske Brigade, then right for 100m to find **BosFam** (☎ 257 534; www.bosfam.ba; Stjepana Matijevića 11; ☯ 9am-5pm Mon-Sat), a self-help organisation for refugee women whose workshop is above its appealing craft and carpet shop (crochet work from 5KM).

South of Kapia, street cafes fill Turalibegova, where Volksbank occupies a grandly spired 19th-century mansion. Two blocks east up Đorđa Mihaijlovića is the large, rather austere 1926 **Orthodox cathedral**, with splendid triple-level iconostasis and cut-glass 1920s chandeliers inside.

Behind, across a major road from the 'Kajmak' city-bus station, **Pannonica** is a sizeable park around a small **salt lake**. There's a mini **zoo** (mainly ostriches), a reconstructed salt-drilling derrick, and an appealing **Arheologiški Park** (☯ 9am-4pm Sat & Sun) of wooden hut-houses showing how Tuzla folk lived centuries ago.

Sleeping & Eating

Pansion Nargalic-Komerc (☎ 256 160; Kazan Mahala 40; d/tr 55/75KM; ☒) Look before you pay as the same *pansion* offers a strange mix of appealing, high-ceilinged rooms and dingy little windowless boxes at similar prices. It's 200m beyond Volksbank.

Pansion Kipovi (Tabašnice bb; s/tw/d/tr 30/40/50/60KM) Simple but central *pansion* west of the market facing the Kipovi Bridge where four metal goliaths bear lamps in potted globes of stained glass.

BOSNIA & HERCEGOVINA

BOSNIA & HERCEGOVINA'S TOP CASTLES

- **Srebrenik** (below) for its dramatic setting
- **Ostrožac** (p162) for its spooky atmosphere
- **Vranduk** (p151) as the most idyllic castle village
- **Tešanj** (p152), rising above a lovable old-town square
- **Počitelj** (p141) for its picture-perfect ensemble
- **Jajce** (p155) for its sheer power and the waterfall frontage
- **Doboj** (p151) for its costumed festivals and cafe-tower
- **Gradačac** (right) because you can sleep in it

Hotel Tuzla (☎ 250 050; www.hoteltuzla.com; Zavno BiH 13; s/d 91/165KM; P ☒ ☒) Supposedly Tuzla's best, this distinctive if far from beautiful 12-storey tower of grey prefab concrete has dated, vaguely musty rooms that are redecorated but not remodelled. There's burlap sacking for wallpaper. Staff are friendly, but the location, 1km east of the old town, isn't very helpful.

Čaršijska Česma (☎ 258 408; Trg Žrtava Genocida u Srebrinici; meals 5–8KM) Here there are well-executed pseudo-antique interiors, a popular terrace frontage and a wide range of Bosnian meals.

Heartland Pizzeria (☎ 255 111; Kazan Mahala 10; pizzas 6–8.50KM, beers 2KM) Amusingly overstretched wrought-iron tables and tasteful dried-flower displays give this place a gently stylish modern vibe.

Getting There & Around

Tuzla's long-distance bus and train **stations** (www.transturist.ba/pretraga.html) are 1.7km west of Skvera. Take bus 7 for Hotel Tuzla. Take buses 5 or 11 for Skvera and the Kajmak Stanica (city-bus terminal), from which buses depart frequently to Srebrenik (3KM) until 8pm.

AROUND TUZLA
Srebrenik
☎ 035 / pop 45,000

The dramatic ruins of Srebrenik's impregnable 1333 **castle** sit on a spike of partly wooded crag, accessed by wooden steps and a footbridge across its deep defensive gully. Inside there's

relatively little to see, but there are several spectacular views of the site along the winding 6km lane that leads here from unremarkable Srebrenik town (about 10KM return by taxi).

At Srebrenik's central crossroads, the great-value **Motel Park** (☎ 645 820; Magistralni Put; s/d/apt 50/80/100KM; P ☒) has impeccably clean rooms that aren't as tacky as one might fear from the overglitzy restaurant. The motel was the scene of a 2004 hostage drama that ended in the arrest of an infamous Albanian criminal.

Directly behind, rooms at **Motel Gradina** (☎ 645 931; s/d 45/70KM) are simpler and less attractive, but less prone to traffic noise.

Srebrenik is served by at least two buses hourly from Tuzla's Kajmak terminal. Many buses continue to Brčko (last at 6.45pm). On weekdays, nine daily buses run to Gradačac (3KM, last at 6pm). The bus station is 300m west of Motel Gradina.

Gradačac
☎ 035

Just before northern Bosnia's pretty rolling hills fade into the flat Brčko plain, Gradačac is a bowl-shaped town wrapped around a remarkable central fortress hill. The **castle complex** sits within double-fortified medieval walls, themselves within a walled former citadel that's now the town park. Uniquely for Bosnia, the castle's central keep-tower has been converted into the comfy, four-room **Gradina Hotel** (☎ 816 625; www .zebed.com.ba; s/d 40/80KM). Room 101, decorated in traditional Bosnian-Ottoman style, is a free 'museum' and not for guest stays. The top-floor **restaurant** (mains 5–9KM, beers 1.50–3KM; ☒ 7am–10.30pm) surveys the town with 360-degree views from overhanging window boxes.

Until 1.45pm on weekdays, buses run every hour to Tuzla via Srebrenik (3KM). Only three run on Sunday. Change in Srebrenik for Brčko and in Modriča for Doboj. To Sarajevo the 5.30am and 1.45pm buses go via Olovo, the 6am via Zenica.

Brčko
☎ 049 / pop 65,000

This vibrantly rejuvenated river port commands the only flat area in all of BiH. Apart from the splendid but sadly decrepit 1895 neo-Moorish **Umjetničke Gallery** (☎ 211 738; Trg Mladih 2; ☒ during exhibitions 7.30am–4pm Mon–Fri) there's precious little to see. But for travellers who find a thrill in seeking out the world's most forgotten enclaves and quasi-states, Brčko offers the cachet of being its own 'entity', neither really Federation nor Republika Srpska, though technically in both! To reach the very limited old-town area, 1.7km from the bus station, walk north up Jusufa Čamare, Tina Ujevića and Bosne Srebrne streets. Then luxuriate with coffee and cakes at the 1891 **Hotel Grand Posavina** (☎ 220 111; www.grand-hotel-posavina.com; Trg Mladih 4; s/d 60/80KM), whose sturdy Austro-Hungarian building has been (over)restored after serious war damage. Its rooms are great value albeit often taller than they're wide.

Buses run hourly to Tuzla, or you could take a train at 4.34am, 11.20am or 5.30pm. From near the Hotel Grand Posavina, a 900m-long bridge crosses to Gunja (Croatia). Gunja's station, a further 3.5km away (north, then east) has trains to Vinkovci (55 minutes) on the Zagreb–Belgrade line departing at 5.18am, 10.35am, 1.20pm, 4.11pm and 9.11pm.

SREBRENICA СРЕБРЕНИЦА
☎ 056 / pop 12,000

Known in antiquity for its silver mines, Srebrenica's peaceful green-hill setting is hard to equate with its terrible modern history: up to 8000 Muslim men were killed in cold blood during July 1995. The massacre is commemorated by a large cemetery and open-air modernist mosque at **Potočari**, some 8km northwest, accessible by regular buses.

During summer a series of 10-day **international youth-exchange camps** (www.youthcamp-vlasenica.ba) attracts 14- to 19-year-olds to Bratunac (north of Srebrenica) and Vlasenica (between Srebrenica and Kladanj).

From Sarajevo three buses run daily (32KM, 3½ hours). There's a 4.30pm bus back to Sarajevo's main station and a 2pm bus to Belgrade (4½ hours). There's no easy route between Višegrad and Srebrenica.

CENTRAL BOSNIA

VISOKO
☎ 032 / pop 17,000

Once a major neolithic settlement, historical Visoko (Visoki) became the capital of King Tvrtko's medieval Bosnian state and the spiritual centre of the controversial Bosnian Church (see the boxed text, p107). By the 20th century minimal signs of antiquity remained and the town was known mainly for its leather industry. Suddenly, however, Visoko has become one of BiH's top tourist draws as the curious arrive to see whether the 250m-high Visočica Hill really looks like the **World's Greatest Pyramid** (Sun Pyramid; www.piramidasunca.ba). That's the theory of Bosnian archaeologist Semir Osmanagic, who claims that it was built around 12,000 years ago by a long-disappeared superculture. Excavations have revealed what seem to be 'paving' and 'tunnel entrances'. And, despite a covering of pine forest, the hill does have a remarkably perfect pyramidal shape. A long ridge at the back, however, rather spoils the idea.

The main **archaeological diggings** (admission free) are up a steep, 200m wood-and-mud stairway above **Bistro Vidikovac** (coffee 1.5KM; ☉ 8am-11pm), whose sugar sachets sport the ubiquitous Sun Pyramid logo. The pyramid/hill's summit, site of the medieval **citadel of Visoki**, can be reached in a further 20 sweaty minutes by scrambling up through steep forest, though it's easier and not much longer to take the paved road starting at the Bistro Vidikovac. The bistro itself is around 15 minutes' walk from Visoko bus station. Start by crossing the river bridge towards the Motel Piramida-Sunca tower. Turn immediately left down Visoko's relatively attractive main street (variously named Jalija, Alije Izetbegovića and Čaršijska), passing the **museum** (Alije Izetbegovića 29), **tourist office** (☎ 733 189; Alije Izetbegovića 29; ☉ 9am-4pm Mon-Fri) and **post office** (Čaršijska 75; ☉ 8am-8pm Mon-Fri, to 3pm Sat). After the bazaar, merge left into Tvrtka, which becomes Mule Hodžić. Opposite Mule Hodžić 25 climb steeply up winding Pertac, then turn left at the top.

Sleeping & Eating

our pick **Hotel Centar** (☎ 730 030; www.hotelcentar.ba; Alaudina 1; d/apt 156/206KM; ☒) This design-book boutique hotel has dark-wood interiors, top-quality linens and an excellent city-centre location above Volksbank (Alije Izetbegovića 37). Apartment 301 has pyramid views, and the remarkable basement restaurant is designed like an old Bosnian village courtyard.

Motel Piramida-Sunca (☎ 731 460; www.motelpiramidasunca.co.ba; 6th fl, Musala 1; s/d/tr/q 50/80/100/120KM; P ☒) Good, unfussy new rooms aren't nearly as wacky as you'd expect from the triangular key-fobs, crazy nozzle lamps and acid-trip colours in the corridors.

Caffe Fashion (Čaršijska 14; coffee 1KM, beers 2.50KM; ☉ 7am-10pm) This curious little multilevel cafe near the bazaar has unexplained stove-doors, token beams and a ribbon-wrapped piano.

Getting There & Away

Buses stop here twice hourly until 8.30pm between Sarajevo (5.50KM, 50 minutes) and Kakanj (4.40KM, 35 minutes). For Travnik (10.50KM) buses leave at 8.10am, 9.50am, 2.10pm, 4.10pm and 10.30pm, or you can change in Zenica (to which there are 14 buses on weekdays).

AROUND VISOKO
Bobovac

Incredible as it seems today, Bobovac was once the medieval capital of Bosnia until the approaching Turkish threat caused a royal retreat to Jajce. The uninhabited site is appealingly situated on a shoulder of some high, partly wooded hills. Only one recently rebuilt house-like structure, King Tvrtko's mausoleum, now occupies the ruinous tiered **citadel** that seems oddly chosen in defensive terms. Easiest access is 12km by looping road (or around two hours' short-cutting hike) from the compact, valley-bottom village of **Kraljeva Sutjeska**. That village is dominated by a huge **Catholic monastery** (Samostan; ☯ mass 7am), and its semiquaint centre sports a celebrated 18th-century Bosnian house. Both can be visited by arrangement with the **tourist office** (Turistički Ured; ☎ 552 160; http://visit-ks.info/indexen.php) or **Katarina Travel** (☎ 779 091, 061443470; www.turist-katarina.vze.com; Kraljice Katarine 6). The latter is in reality just a friendly local family who also offer a village apartment for rent (€10 per person).

Kraljeva Sutjeska is reached by nine daily buses from Kakanj, except on Sunday, when only the 10.30am bus runs. The Bobovac–Vareš road (20km) is unpaved as far as Pogar (13km).

ZENICA & VRANDUK
☎ 032 / pop 125,000

The industrial city of **Zenica**, BiH's fourth biggest, has a little **gallery-museum** (Jevrejska bb; admission 2KM), housed in what was originally a synagogue. There's also a useful regional tourism website (www.turizam-zdk.net). But you're only likely to stop here to change transport for Vranduk, for which local Maglaj-bound trains depart at 7.25am and 3.23pm (13 minutes), returning from Vranduk at 10.42 and 6.12pm. Bus and train stations are together.

Surely Bosnia's most beautiful village, tiny **Vranduk** – an undeveloped but magical huddle of red roofs – wraps itself around a sturdy mini **castle-museum** (☯ 8am-9pm), whose Michael Palin–lookalike caretaker will generally open up on request – phone the number on the door, usually ☎ 032-676 337. Vranduk commands a tight, idyllic woodland bend in the Bosna River, just 600m from an unmarked halt on the Zenica–Maglaj railway line. Alternatively, take any bus using the Zenica–Doboj road and get off just before kilometre 66. From here it's safest to follow signs east (a very beautiful 2km loop). A shorter but potentially dangerous alternative is to cross the busy highway, then, near the tunnel, double back as though coming from the railway.

DOBOJ ДОБОЈ

The site of at least 18 historical battles, Doboj is now a dreary railway-junction town. However, rising above its dull apartment blocks, Doboj's 13th-century hilltop **fortress** (Meshe Selimovića [Beslagića] bb; adult/student 2.50/1KM; ☯ 10am-8pm) remains impressive. One tower is topped by a reconstructed wooden guard box that's now a quaint 'ethno-cafe'. Here your entry ticket entitles you to a free coffee or half-priced beer served by a waiter in medieval garb. More costumed characters materialise during the annual **FestTour** (http://festtour.dobojlive.com/; ☯ late May).

To get there from the central **regional museum** (Vidovdanska 16), under reconstruction, curve north up Kralja Aleksandra (Kapetanovića) past a pretty **Catholic church**, the pink 2004 **Donje mosque** with its unusual clock tower and the recently restored **Bet Shalom synagogue**. Here Meshe Selimovića branches north, leading in 500m to the castle's northwest entry gate.

Sleeping & Eating

Hotel Integra (☎ 224 274; hotintdo@teol.com; Vidovdanska 156; s/d/tr/apt 60/95/120/130KM) Beside the big B&D shopping centre, 800m south of the museum, the Integra's tasteful modern rooms come with monogrammed towels and ultrawhite linen.

Hotel Bosna (☎ 242 012; Kneza Lazara 2; s/d 56/80KM) This unreconstructed Tito-era throwback is very central (a block east of the museum) but entirely uninviting.

Konoba Grazia (☎ 225 248; pizzas 6.50-8.50KM; Vidovdanska 22; ☯ 8am-11pm) Overloaded by intricate wrought ironwork and wooden panelling, this restaurant's interior is as much an attraction as its vast dessert menu.

Getting There & Away

The **bus station** (Svetoga Sobe bb) is 900m southeast of the museum. The train station, BiH's busiest, is across the river 600m beyond. Useful departures include Sarajevo (18KM, three hours) at 3.12pm, Belgrade (23KM, seven hours) at 12.23am (yes, after midnight), Tuzla (1½ hours) at 7.28am and 3.28pm and Zagreb (30KM, six hours) via Banja Luka (two hours) at 3.29pm and 12.32am. Slower local trains to Banja Luka (2½ hours) leave at 7.20am, 10.58am, 3.32pm and 7.30pm.

AROUND DOBOJ
Tešanj
☎ 032 / pop 5700

Old Tešanj enfolds around a **medieval castle** (admission free; ☾ 8am-4pm Sat-Thu) whose sturdy ruins sport two reconstructed towers (empty). In front lies a well-placed 17th-century **bell tower** and a quaint little triangle of old-town square (Trg Gazi-Ferhadbega). The scene here is especially picturesque on market day (Friday morning), when grizzled farmers in berets and Islamic skullcaps sip coffees on the cafe terraces.

Just 30m away, the helpful **tourist office** (☎ 650 651; www.turizam-zdk.net; Titova 18; ☾ 8am-4pm Mon-Fri, 10am-2pm Sat) has maps and lists of regional events.

Tešanj's only hotel, **Motel RM** (☎ 656 600; motel _rm@yahoo.com; Smailbegovića 6; s/d 55/80KM), has a tatty reception area, but rooms are presentable and breakfast (in the pizzeria next door) is included. It's tucked down a dead-end lane, 500m south of the centre, signed from the main road.

At **HD Caffe-Slastičarna** (Trg Gazi-Ferhadbega; pizzas 4.50-6KM, coffee 1KM) excellent thin-crust pizza and brilliantly tart homemade lemonade are served right on the old-town square.

From the **bus station** (☎ 650 445), 300m north, buses leave for Doboj (4KM, six daily) and Sarajevo (23KM, three hours, 7am, noon and 4.30pm).

TRAVNIK
☎ 030 / pop 27,500

Once the seat of Bosnia's Turkish viziers (Ottoman governors), Travnik was the setting for Ivo Andrić's *Travnik Chronicles* (aka *Bosnian Chronicle*), in which Napoleonic-era French and Austrian consuls find the town to be an impossibly harsh, middle-of-nowhere posting. Today it feels much more inviting, its sizeable castle ruin and patchily attractive architecture making it a good half-day stop between Sarajevo and Jajce. You can ski at Vlašić, 22km away.

Orientation & Information
Central Travnik wiggles along the deep Lavša Valley, with traffic rumbling constantly along

Sehida (the M5 highway), which is roughly paralleled by Bosanska, Travnik's main street. The **bus station** (☎ 792 761) is between the two, west of centre: exit through the yellow fencing, walk past the **post office** (☎ 547 102; Prnjavor) and you'll emerge on Bosanska near the Lipa Hotel. There, turn right for the **tourist office** (☎ 511 588; www.tzsbk.com; Bosanska 75; ☾ 8am-4pm Mon-Fri), opposite the 1820 Alibeyova mosque and its Rumelian clock tower. Or turn left and walk 400m east to reach the many-coloured mosque, the heart of old Travnik, passing several ATMs and useful city map boards.

Dernek Internet Club (per hr 2KM; ☾ 9am-10pm Mon-Fri, to 10pm Sat & Sun) is hidden away immediately west of the bus station facing a rusty little steam train.

Sights
Memorable for its lively if faded exterior murals, the **many-coloured mosque** (Bosanska 203) is remarkable for the *bezistan* (mini bazaar) built into the arches beneath the main prayer house.

Readers who enjoyed his *Bosnian Chronicle* should visit the **Ivo Andrić museum** (☎ 518 140; Zenjak 19; admission 2KM; ☾ 10.30am-5pm Thu-Tue), in an old-style house designed to simulate Andrić's birthplace. There's minimal English, but the curator can point out portraits of Pierre David, the real French consul on whom the book's boorish main character, Jean Daville, was based. Note also the myriad documents (shown as photocopies) from which Andrić spent 15 years exhaustively researching the book. The museum is one block off Bosanska (between 171 and 169). If it's locked, the key is available from the somewhat stuffy **regional museum** (Zavičajni Muzej Travnik; ☎ 518 140; opposite Bosanska 145; adult/concession 1.50/1KM; ☾ 9am-3pm Mon-Fri, 10am-2pm Sat & Sun).

Chronicle fans might also be intrigued to see the partly ivy-covered **Hafizadić House** (Bosanska 135). In the book it was from a plum tree in the garden here that Salko the barber's apprentice would spy on the Austrian consul's unapproachable daughter Agatha. Today the garden houses the downmarket but appropriately named **Café Consul** (coffee 0.50KM; ☾ 5am-10pm).

Outside the Hotel Lipa, the **Viziers' turbe** is the best known of several Travnik tombs gathered under open-sided gazebos.

Behind the many-coloured mosque a pedestrian underpass crosses beneath the M5. To reach the **medieval castle ruins** (Stari Grad; admission 2KM; ☾ 9am-6pm Oct-Apr, 8am-8pm May-Sep), walk steeply up Varoš, past the originally 18th-century **Mahala**

bell tower and two pretty mosques, then cross a tall stone causeway-bridge that replaced the castle's drawbridge after a 19th-century fire. Built in the 15th century to hold the Turks at bay, the fortress was never tested: the Bosnian state was already collapsing and its defenders simply surrendered. Enough of the rampart walls have been repaired to allow some enjoyable scrambles, and the central 14-sided keep now features a two-room **historical museum** (extra 1KM), opened on request.

Descending from the castle, turn first left then left again to follow Hendek alley down to Šumeće. Turning left again, you'll come quickly to **Plava Voda** (Blue Water), where a rushing mountain stream is crisscrossed by small stone bridges and overlooked by several delightful restaurants. Just beyond is the 1780 **Muftijino Turbe** (tomb of the vizier's poet) and a **Mekteb-Madrassa complex** (Šumeće 184) designed in colourfully ornate 19th-century neo-Moorish style.

Sleeping

All central accommodation suffers somewhat from road noise. There are six more motels within 10km along the eastbound M5.

Motel Aba (☎ 511 462; www.aba.ba; Šumeća 166a; s/d/tr/q 30/40/50/70KM) Central Travnik's best yet cheapest option offers highly acceptable, unfussy en suite rooms at excellent prices. But it's not really a motel: getting a car to this area near Plava Voda can prove modestly challenging given the one-way system. Breakfast is 10KM.

Motel Consul (☎ 514 195; www.consultravnik.20fr.com; s/d 52/84KM; P) With a private orchard, sepia photos of old Travnik, big double beds and an art-filled dining room, this peaceful new eight-room retreat is more comfortable than the Aba but inconveniently situated 1.5km west of centre overlooking the industrial zone.

Hotel Lipa (☎ 511 604; Lažajeva 116; s/d 52/84KM) Entering from Bosanska, the Lipa's zinc-wrapped retro-trendy cafe creates a misleadingly hip image. In fact its renovated rooms are uninspired and the corridors dingy. But at least the showers are good and the location's handy.

Restoran Oniks (☎ 512 182; Bosanska bb; s/d/tr 35/60/80KM) Simple bedrooms for rent above an unsophisticated, diner-style restaurant in the pedestrianised shopping area just east of the many-coloured mosque.

Eating

Restaurant Divan (☎ 061786471; Zenjak 19; meals 5-17KM; ☼ 8am-11pm) Dine on fish, squid or Bosnian grills around the piano in thick-walled, timber-beamed rooms beneath the Ivo Andrić museum. Or sip coffee in the attractive courtyard behind.

Konoba Plava Voda (☎ 512 171; Šumeće bb; meals 5.50-12KM) Three restaurants called Plava Voda all have lovely summer terraces overlooking the attractive springs area. However, *Konoba Plava Voda* has the nicest interior, with the homely touches of a traditional Bosnian house and great upper window seats.

Čevabdžinica Asko (ćevapi 3.50-6KM; ☼ 7am-10pm) Just 30m south of the many-coloured mosque, Asko's streamside terrace is the best central cheapie for warm sitting-out evenings. But on colder nights Čevabdžinica Hari (*ćevapi* 3.50-6KM; open 8am to 10pm) is more appealing.

SELF-CATERING

Ðino Samir (Bosanska 157; ☼ 8am-5.30pm Mon-Sat) is one of many shops selling Travnik's famous white cheese. There's a big **Konzum supermarket** (Bosanska bb) opposite the regional museum and a sizeable market behind Bosanska 137. All-night bakery **Pekara Aba** (Bosanska 117; ☼ 24hr) sells decent *burek*.

Getting There & Away

For bus services, see the table, below.

BUS SERVICES FROM TRAVNIK

Destination	Price (KM)	Duration (hr)	Departures
Bihać	28-31	6	6.50am, 9.30am, 3.30pm, 4.20pm & 11.50pm
Guča Gora	2.30	½	approx hourly, weekdays only (Maline bus)
Jajce	8-12	1½	9 daily
Sarajevo	15	2	hourly in morning, plus 3.40pm, 6.20pm & 7.10pm
Split	28-36	4½	up to 6 daily via Bugojno
Vranduk	7.50	1¼	8.40am, noon or 3.30pm (Tuzla bus)
Zenica	4.50-7	1	25 daily

AROUND TRAVNIK
Vlašić
☎ 030

With only three main lifts, **Vlašić** (www.babanovac .net; ski passes 26KM; ☼ lifts 9am-4pm in season) is somewhat more limited than Jahorina (p129), but at its base, **Babanovac village** offers a wide selection of accommodation. The swishly inviting **Hotel Paluljica** (☎ 540 022; www.pahuljica.com; s/d 90/108KM, peak season 140/208KM) and less stylish **Hotel Vlašić** (☎ 540 690; www.hotel-vlasic.com; s/d 60/80KM, peak season 90/140KM) are just a stone's throw from the main lift. They usually enforce five-day minimum stays during peak season (mid-December to mid-March), but not so the homely **Hotel Central** (☎ 540 165; www.hotel-central-vlasic.net; s/d 35/70KM, peak season 70/140KM), which is just 300m further back, facing the ski jump.

Buses from Travnik (4KM, 40 minutes) leave at 10am and 3.10pm in summer, or at 7.15am, 11.30am and 6pm in winter, returning around 90 minutes later.

Guća Gora
This large **Catholic monastery** features frequently in Andrić's chronicles. But its double-towered sandstone church, which today so dominates little Guča Gora village, only took its present form in 1897, when it was one of BiH's biggest buildings. Entered through the attractive cloister, the interior is vast if rather plain. The 8km drive from Travnik is appealing and passes through the pretty, mosque-dominated hamlet of **Mosor**.

Prusac
☎ 030 / pop 1800

This hilltop village is the starting point for what is reputedly Europe's biggest Muslim pilgrimage: in late June thousands of people hike around 5km through pine forests to **Ajvatovica holy spring**. According to legend, water started to flow here when a mountain rock was split open through the force of a 40-day prayer stint, thereby ending a terrible drought. Outside the colourful pilgrimage day, Ajvatovica can seem visually disappointing and the prevalence of surrounding minefields is disconcerting. But Prusac itself, along with twin hilltop village **Srt Brdo**, has a considerable if unfocused charm. There are several fine **mosques** and some wonderful **viewpoints**, and Prusac's picturesque **castle ruin** is fronted by the unusual **Sahat Kula** tower. A big open-pit mine directly across the valley is much less attractive.

Access is via **Donji Vakuf** (6km north) where the congenial new **Hotel Vrbas** (☎ 203 100; hotelvrbas@bih.net.ba; Trg Malkoča; s/d/tr 39/70/96KM) is perfectly central. Donji Vakuf's bus station, 500m down the Bugojno–Prusac road from the hotel, has buses to Travnik (7KM, 9.45am daily, plus 7.15am, 1pm and 8.45pm weekdays), Jajce (5KM, six on weekdays, 12.05pm on Saturday), and Prusac (1.50KM, 7.30am and 3.15pm daily, seven on weekdays). Most Prusac buses continue to Bugojno, 10km east on the Travnik–Livno road.

JAJCE
☎ 030 / pop 30,000

Above an impressive arc of waterfall, Jajce's fortified old town climbs a steep rocky knoll to the powerful, ruined castle where Bosnia's medieval kings were crowned. The surrounding array of glorious mountains, lakes and canyons makes Jajce a great exploration base, while curious catacombs and a Mithraic temple will intrigue fans of mysterious 'lost' religions.

Information
Several central, money-changing banks have ATMs.

Eko Kuća (Eko House; ☎ 654 100; www.plivaturism.ba; Pijavice bb; ☼ 8am-3pm Mon-Fri, to 1pm Sat) Regional eco-tourism and rural self-help group selling local organic produce.

Kantonal Tourist Office (1st fl, Sadije Softića 1; ☼ 8am-3pm Mon-Fri, to 1pm Sat) In historic Omirbegović House. Brochures available; minimal English spoken.

Network Internet (Trg Jajačkih Branitelja; per hr 1.50KM; ☼ 9am-midnight)

Tourist information booth (☎ 065323782; ☼ 9am-8pm May-Sep) Alida is very helpful, arranges homestay accommodation and has the key for closed attractions. If the booth is closed she's probably conducting a tour.

Sights
Old-town Jajce's attractions can be seen in a two-hour ramble, assuming you can locate the sites' various key holders: the tourist booth can help.

CATACOMBS
Built as a family mausoleum around 1400 by the powerful Duke Hrvoje, the **catacombs** (Svetog Luke bb; admission 1KM) are unique for their boldly sculpted interior featuring a sun and crescent moon design that is considered one of the best surviving memorials to the in-

dependent Bosnian Church (see the boxed text, p107). Some tour guides still insist that this was 'Bogomil', though the central cross motif suggests otherwise. Either way, the small, half-lit subterranean space is very atmospheric. Tito is said to have hidden here during 1943.

The key is usually available from the little cafe-hairdresser opposite, built onto the side of the sturdy round **Bear Tower** (Medvjed Kula).

Other attractive buildings on Svetog Luke (Ademovića) include an 1880 **schoolhouse** and the fine 15th-century campanile **tower of St Luke**.

FORTRESS
A stairway leads up to a **square castle tower** (Čolića bb) and the small **Dizdar mosque** (women's mosque), beyond which it's a short stroll to the main **fortress** (Tvrđava; admission 1KM). Get the key from Mediha at the second house on the right before the stone **entry portal**, inscribed with the heraldic device of Bosnian king Stjepan Tomaš.

All you'll find within the ramparts are a well house and the intact if unlit two-storey **barutana** (powder tower). However, do walk the partly crenellated battlements for sweeping views of surrounding valleys and crags.

From the **Velika Tabija** (Gornja Mahala) it's possible to descend a further section of citadel wall to the **Midway Tower** (Mala Tabija) behind the attractively renovated **Old Kršlak House**.

WATERFALLS
Jajce's impressive 21m **waterfalls** mark the confluence of the Pliva and Vrbas rivers. You can peer down on the falls from the gardens behind the Travnik gate or admire them from a platform near the petrol station. But for the classic brochure-view photos in which the whole of old-town Jajce rises majestically above the cascades, you'll need to cross the big Vrbas bridge, then turn left on the Banja Luka road (Vrbaska). Walk 500m to the third lay-by on the left, then climb over the low crash-barrier and double back 150m down a footpath through the pine woods to the viewing point.

AVNOJ MUSEUM
In 1943 the second congress of AVNOJ (Antifascist Council of the People's Liberation of Yugoslavia) formulated Yugoslavia's postwar socialist constitution in a building that's now the small **AVNOJ-a Museum** (☎ 657 712; admission 2KM; ◷ 8am-6pm). Peep in to see a large, brooding statue of Partisan Tito in gold-painted polystyrene.

MITHRAS SCULPTURE
Protected by an unassumingly suburban, house-like building – get the key from the tourist booth – are the remarkable remnants of a 1700-year-old **Mithras temple** (Mitrasova 12; admission 1KM). Once worshipped in a now-mysterious, forgotten religion, Mithras is thought by some to have been a pre-Zoroastrian Persian sun god 'rediscovered' by mystical Romans. He's seen here in a comparatively well-preserved 4th-century sculpture fighting a bull (that looks more like a wolf), helped by a crow, a snake, a scorpion and an audience of ladies and centurions.

Sleeping
The tourist booth can arrange old-city **homestays** (s/d 30/50KM), while Eko Kuća can find rooms in rural village homes from 30KM.

Hotel Stari Grad (☎ 651 006; hotel.stari.grad @tel.net.ba; Svetog Luke 3; s/d/apt 55/80/160KM; P ⊠) Although it's not actually old, beams, wood panelling and a heraldic fireplace give this comfortable little hotel a look of suavely modernised antiquity. Unbeatably central, it's the ideal address as long as you can manage the stairs. An added curiosity is the lobby-restaurant's glass floor, beneath which are the excavations of an Ottoman-era hamam.

Hotel Tourist 98 (☎ 658 151; Kraljice Katerine bb; s/d/tr/q/apt 57/84/106/135/120KM; P ⊠ ⅚) This bright-red box beside Jajce's big hypermarket offers new, very straightforward rooms that are clean and mostly spacious. Smaller single rooms 214 to 216 plus jacuzzi-shower apartment 211 offer impressive castle views.

For lakeside alternatives, see p156.

Eating & Drinking
Several potentially intriguing cafe-bars are cut out of the cliff face on HV Hrvatnica. There's also a 24-hour bakery nearby.

Stari Grad Hotel (mains 9-14KM; ◷ 7am-9pm) Decent Bosnian and Italian food is served in the hotel's appealing little lobby-restaurant.

Restoran Una (mains 4-12KM; ◷ 10am-9pm) Of all the HV Hrvatnica cafe-bars, only the lovably incompetent Una serves full meals, and even here most items were 'off' when we tried to dine.

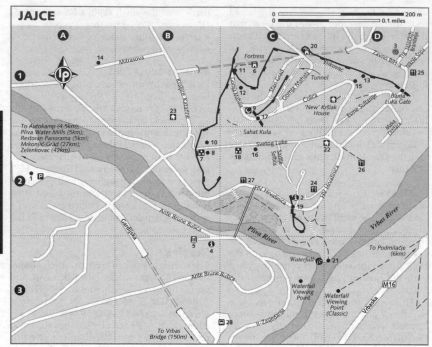

Dea (☎ 657 173; pizzas 6-8KM; ✆ 8am-11pm) Opposite the Hotel Stari Grad, Dea bakes acceptable pizzas.

Ćevabdžinica Tomy (grills from 3KM; ✆ 8am-3pm Mon-Sat) Fast(ish) food is on offer from this cube of ancient stone building.

Omerbegović House Café (coffee 0.50KM, beers 2KM; ✆ 7am-11pm) This unpretentiously local place is intriguingly hidden in the bare-stone former guard house of the medieval Travnik gate. Enter via the stairway of the Kantonal tourist office.

Getting There & Away

For services from the **bus station** (☎ 659 202; II-Zasjedanja AVNOJ-a), see the table, opposite.

Take Zenica or Sarajevo buses for Travnik (8KM to 12KM). Take Bihać buses for Mrkonjić-Grad (4.50KM to 6.20KM).

AROUND JAJCE
Pliva Lakes (Plivsko Jezero)

Wooded mountains idyllically reflected in these two pretty lakes create a scene that seems too perfect to be real. A park between the two contains the superquaint collection of 17 miniature **water mills** that features in so many BiH tourist brochures. To reach the water mills take a Jezero-bound bus to kilometre 92 on the M5 (around 4km from Jajce), then walk 800m, passing the **autokamp** (campsite without/with electricity 8/12KM, plus adult/child 10/5KM; ✆ mid-Apr–Sep) partway. An attractive waterside lane leads on for another kilometre, rejoining the M5 beside the lakefront **Plaža Motel** (☎ 647 200; s/d 40/70KM) and the plusher if slightly set back **Hotel Plivsko Jezero** (☎ 654 090; www.hoteljajce.bet .net.ba; s/d/tr/q/apt 57/84/106/135/120KM).

For a great alternative view down across the lakes, snack or dine at the brilliantly located **Restoran Panorama** (M5, km93; mains 8-15KM, beers 2.50KM; ✆ 8am-11.30pm).

Podmilačje

Just before the superscenic Banja Luka road disappears into a thrilling trio of rocky canyons, Podmilačje village is a minor Catholic pilgrimage site sporting the shingle-roofed 15th-century stone **Church of St Ivo** (M16, km69.3). It was one of the only medieval churches to survive the Ottoman era intact but was virtually destroyed in the 1990s conflict and only rebuilt in 2000. Right beside it, an unusual concrete spiral of a new church is nearing completion.

Mrkonjić-Grad Мркоњић-Град
☎ 050 / pop 12,000
Set in rolling woodland hills, the predominantly Serb town of Mrkonjić-Grad is his-

torically famed for being one of several places from which Tito relaunched his Partisan movement (after Ušice and Foča). The Gene Hackman movie *Behind Enemy Lines* was loosely based on the shooting down of a US air force plane here in June 1995. In October that year 181 Bosnian Serbs were massacred by Croat forces following a three-day NATO bombardment. The Serb population fled but returned in 1996 once the area was allotted to the RS in a controversial 'swap' for lands around Brčko.

Rebuilt Mrkonjić-Grad (see www.mrkonjic-grad.com/magazine.asp?page=6 for a map) is not a great attraction, but you'll probably change buses here to reach Zelenkovac. If stranded, **Hotel Kraijina** (☎ 211338; Karađorđeva 23; s/d 52/74KM) has peeling ceilings but is otherwise much better than you'd guess, with remodelled rooms and good bathrooms. It's marked simply 'ХОТЕЛ', 300m from the bus station.

Note that long-distance buses (notably Bihać–Sarajevo services) don't come into town, picking up instead at the big bypass junction. The **bus station** (☎ 211 093; Karađorđeva bb), 600m east, has five weekday services to Baraći that pass Zelenkovac and 10 more to Podrašnica that get you pretty close.

Zelenkovac Зеленковац
The eccentric eco-village of **Zelenkovac** (☎ 278 649; www.zelenovac.org; John Lennon Sq; dm 20KM) is based around a picturesque old wooden water mill that its amply bearded owner, Boro Yanković, has transformed into a wonderful little **art gallery–bar-cafe** (beers 2KM; ⏰ 7am-11pm). Numerous earth-friendly initiatives emanate from this inspiring place that also holds occasional outdoor jazz festivals, international voluntary camps and a July artists' colony week. Simple accommodation, mostly with shared toilet and shower,

BUS SERVICES FROM JAJCE			
Destination	**Price (KM)**	**Duration (hr)**	**Departures**
Banja Luka	9.50	1½	7.30am, 9.15am, 1pm, 4.40pm & 5.30pm
Bihać	23.50	3½	8.30am, 11.15am, 12.40pm & 5.25pm
Jezero	2.50	¼	9 daily, last return at 5.30pm
Mostar	18.50	3	2.20pm
Sarajevo	23.50	3½	7am, 9.15am, 10.20am & 5.20pm
Split	30.50	4½	6am (returns at 12.30pm)
Zenica	14	2¼	8.15am, 1.45pm & 3.15pm

BOSNIA & HERCEGOVINA

is available in Tolkienesque wooden bungalows in the surrounding woodland. Hiking
possibilities abound or just hang out and
strum guitar with like-minded locals. The
woodland site is just 400m off the Baraći
road, 15km from Mrkonjić-Grad, 1.5km
beyond Podrašnica.

WESTERN BOSNIA

BANJA LUKA БАЊА ЛУКА
☎ 051 / pop 232,000
Welcome to one of Europe's least known
'capital cities' (of the RS since 1998). OK, so
Banja Luka is unlikely to engross you with
its architecture: it was devastated by a 1969
earthquake, then in 1993 local Serbs updated
the damage by exploding all 15 of the city's
mosques. However, it does make a decent
hub for adventure sports in the dramatic river
valleys nearby.

Information
Internet Diana (Kralja Petra 65a; per hr 2KM; ☽ 8am-
11pm Mon-Sat) Upstairs over a gambling bar.

Post office (☎ 211 336; Kralja Petra 93; ☽ 7am-8pm
Mon-Fri, to 6pm Sat) Telephones, RS stamps, ATM and
money exchange.
Tourist office (☎ 232 760; www.banjaluka-tourism
.com; Kralja Petra 87; ☽ 8.30am-5.45pm Mon-Fri, 9am-
2pm Sat) Copious brochures, free maps and useful help in
seeking out adventure-sport contacts.

Sights
Selectively photographed, the fine buildings
within a block of Trg Srpskikh Vladaraz
could make the folks at home believe that
Banja Luka was actually beautiful. The centrepiece is an iconic **Orthodox Church of Christ
Saviour** (Crkva Hrista Spasitelja) with a gilded
dome and brick bell tower that looks like
a Moroccan minaret on Viagara. Flanking
it, the **Banski Dvor** was once the 1920s palace of the Yugoslav royal governor. It now
hosts the RS Assembly and a concert hall.
The essentially identical **City Hall** (Opština) is
better renovated and magically lit at night.
Across Kralja Petra, the **Republika Srpska Art
Gallery** (Trg Srpskikh Junaka 2) occupies an 1891
pile with impressively soaring ceilings but
no permanent collection.

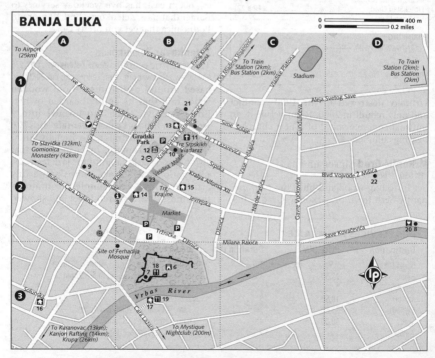

Down by the gently attractive riverbank, the chunky walls of a large, squat 16th-century **castle** (Kaštel) enclose parkland that hosts a summer festival of music, dance and theatre.

The once-famous Unesco-listed **Ferhadija mosque**, originally constructed in 1580 with the ransom money for an Austrian count, has yet to be rebuilt.

Activities

Kanu Klub (☎ 303 368; basement, Save Kovačevića 44; ☺ 8am-2pm Mon-Sat) Visit Banja Luka by paddle: slightly ageing kayaks rent for €10 per hour.

Klub X-treme (www.xtremebl.com; Sokolski Dom, Marije Bursać 18; ☺ 8pm Sun, 9.30pm Mon & Thu) A climbing club with three weekly training evenings.

Kanjon Rafting (☎ 065420000; www.kanjonraft.com) This reliable, well-organised adventure outfit offers rafting at €25 per person (three hours including transport, four person minimum) and guided canyoning (€25, no minimum). Its riverside campsite-cafe is at Ada-Karanovac on the Jajce road.

Sleeping

Prenoćište vl. Marija C (☎ 218 673; Solunska 21; s/d 27/54KM) Four slightly spartan rooms share a

decent bathroom in this inexpensive family homestay. Turn diagonally right at the south end of Kralja Petra; enter from the rear.

Hotel Palace (☎ 218 723; Kralja Petra 60; www.hotelpalasbl.com; s/d/tr/ste from 63.50/117/130.50/147KM; P ⌘) Built in 1933, the Palace retains its original round tower and brass topknot. It looks almost elegant behind its copious street cafe, and the lobby makes hypnotic use of new art deco–inspired design. Most rooms are straightforward, midrange international standard, but cheaper singles are small and built into the sloping roof. The surreal buffet breakfast includes chocolate gateau and fish fingers.

Vila Vrbas (☎ 433 840; Brace Potkonjaka 1; s/d/ste 70/110/120KM) Excellent-value boutique hotel peering through the plane trees at the castle ramparts from above a try-hard riverside restaurant. Some rooms have PC, internet and wraparound shower pod.

Hotel Vidović (☎ 217 217; www.hotelvidovic.com; Jevrejska bb; s/d 105/125KM; P ⌘) Think international business room, then expand by about 50% and you've got the Vidović's new if slightly impersonal formula.

Hotel Bosna (☎ 215 775; www.hotelbosna.com; Kralja Petra 97; s/d C-Standard 77/124KM, A-Lux 162/224KM; P) Perfectly central the Bosna's excellently refurbished A-Lux rooms seem perfectly good business propositions. However, the C-Standard rooms look like unkempt 1970s student digs, leading off sickeningly worn corridors.

Eating & Drinking

Running parallel to Kralja Petra, Veselina Maslaše offers a wide range of tempting street cafes, bars, pastry shops and ice-cream vendors. There are several other appealing cafebars on the riverbank.

Sur Sedra (Braće Potkornjaka 3; meals 4-10KM, beers 1.50KM; ☺ 8am-6pm) For fish or grills, Sur Sedra is cheaper and less pretentious than the Vila Vrbas restaurant next door, yet with a summer riverside terrace that's every bit as tempting.

Kazamat (☎ 224 460; www.kazamat.mapabih.com; Kaštel; mains 12-20KM; ☺ 10am-midnight) With a riverside terrace and stone-dungeon cellar room, the location is fun, though you might be subjected to 'music' that's cheesier than the pricey pastas.

Monet (Save Kovačevića 42; coffee 1.20KM, beers 2KM; ☺ 9am-midnight) This wooden chalet-style barcafe has rattan chairs and a real fire in winter, but it's only really worth the trek if visiting the next door Kanu Klub. Or for the great

BOSNIA & HERCEGOVINA

BUS SERVICES FROM BANJA LUKA

Destination	Price (KM)	Duration (hr)	Departures
Belgrade	35	7	15 daily
Bihać	20	3	5.30am, 7.30am (except Sun), 1pm & 2pm
Doboj	16	2	5am, 6.30am, 9am, 2.30pm, 4pm & 5pm
Jajce	11.50	1½	6.40am, 7.45am (except Sun), 12.25pm, 1pm, 2pm & 4pm
Prijedor	6.50	1	20 daily via Kozarac
Sarajevo	31	5	6.30am, 7.45am, 2.30pm, 4pm, 5pm & midnight
Zagreb	24	7	8.45am, 9.10am, 4.10pm & 5.30pm

*Note that returning *from* Zagreb all buses depart by 10.30am.

Thursday-evening concerts of Serbian folk rock (reserve in person as there's no phone!).

Mystique Nightclub (☎ 065743677; Miloša Obilića 35; beers 3-5KM; ☺ 10pm-4am Tue-Sun) Blood-red music bar within a devilish all-black mirrored interior. Reserve or arrive early at weekends.

Getting There & Away
AIR
The **airport** (☎ 535 210; code BNX) is 25km north, near Laktaši. **JAT** (☎ 535227) flies to Belgrade four times weekly. BH Airlines flies Wednesday and Saturday to Zurich, with tickets (from 140KM) sold by **ARS Travel** (☎ 219 974; Kralja Petra 109).

BUS
For services from the **main bus station** (☎ 315 555; Prote N Kostića 38), see the table, above.

Yellow buses to Bronzani Mejdan and Slavićka use the city-bus terminal 50m behind, in front of the train station.

TRAIN
Useful rail connections include Zagreb (4¼ hours, 3.30pm), Sarajevo (five hours, 1.15pm) and Belgrade (eight hours, 10.30pm). Slow trains to Doboj (2½ hours) depart at 7.30am, 9.55am, 1.03pm, 3.32pm and 7.30pm. To Novi Grad (two hours) via Omarska (3.20KM, one hour) they leave at 7.20am, 1.40pm, 3.40pm and 7.16pm.

Getting Around
From Trg Krajine, take buses 6, 8 or 10 for the bus/train stations. Take loop-line 14 to Borik for the Kanu Klub and Monet.

AROUND BANJA LUKA
Vrbas Canyons
Between Jajce and Banja Luka the Vrbas River descends in a wonderful series of lakes and

gorges that together form one of BiH's foremost adventure-sport playgrounds. Nearest to Banja Luka, the Vrbas Valley is filled with homely villages and overhung with willows. After **Karanovac** (13km), sections of canyon become rugged and wooded. The valley opens again at **Krupa** (26km) where, 600m west of the main road, a pretty set of cascades tumbles down between little wooden mill huts. A map here marks several long-distance hiking and biking routes, and mountaineers scale the canyon sides nearby to reach the ruins of forgotten medieval settlements. Grottoes in the dolomite limestone attract cavers. At the time of research an extreme-sports centre was slated to open here shortly.

The next canyon up offers top-class rafting, and at one sizeable rapid 1km before the first (low) dam, spectator seating allows the curious to watch for waterborne mishaps.

The Jajce road then winds steeply up past a castle ruin and the high dam into the long, beautiful Bočac Reservoir gorge.

Slavićka Славиħка
This tiny village is little more than a half-timbered tavern-shop facing a pair of small churches. But one of those churches is a truly remarkable wooden affair with an extraordinary timber tower. That's probably not enough to justify the 50-minute bus ride from Banja Luka – departing 7am (weekdays only), 3.10pm and 7.45pm, returning 5.15am, 8.45am (weekdays) and 4.35pm. However, if you have a car, it makes part of a very attractive drive that you could begin by heading via Bronzani Majdan to the icon-rich 1541 **Gomionica Monastery** (www.gomionica.org). After doubling back to Slavićka, wind through lovely meadowlands to **Omarska** (a dreary iron-ore warehousing town infamous for its 1990s

concentration camp) before rejoining the main Banja Luka–Prijedor road at **Lamovita**, where there's another fine wooden-towered Orthodox church.

Ljekarice Eko Centar (☎ 065629128; www.eko-centar ljekarIce.com; ✆ May-Oct) offers rural camping accommodation and large, popular bathing pools in a forest-ringed field at lonely Lončari, though it's more family summer camp than 'eco'-centre. The site is 10km from Slavićka or 11km from Omarska, down a 5km dead end off the Omarska–Bronzani Majdan road. Turn at Flamingo Café.

Kozara National Park
Национални Парк Козара
☎ 052

From Kozarac, between Banja Luka and Prijedor, a pretty 12km **toll road** (adult/child 2/1KM) climbs through dainty beech forests then shaggy pines to the heart of this **national park** (☎ 480 898; www.npkozara.com). It's a hilltop forest clearing called **Mrakovica**, crowned by a vast cylindrical concrete monument to the WWII Partisans. Opposite the access stairway, Mrakovica's spanking-new **Hotel Monument** (☎ 483 777; www.monument-kozara .com; s/d/apt 80/140/216KM) rents mountain bikes (5KM per hour) should you wish to explore the national park's lengthy circuit of cycle paths. The scenery is very pleasant but not mind-blowingly dramatic. Taxis want 20KM from Kozarac.

BIHAĆ
☎ 037 / pop 80,000

A closely clumped **church tower, turbe** and 16th-century stone **tower-museum** (☎ 223 214; admission 2KM; ✆ 9am-4pm Mon-Fri, to 2pm Sat) rise very photogenically above the Una River's gushing rapids and green meadow parkland. But, sadly, that's about all there is to see in central Bihać apart from the nearby **Fethija mosque**, converted from a rose-windowed medieval church in 1595. If you're driving, Bihać could make a decent staging post for reaching the marvellous Plitvice Lakes (p224), 30km away in Croatia. Otherwise, grab a map-brochure from the **tourist booth** (Bosanska 1; ✆ 8am-4pm), then head out into the lovely Una Valley (right), preferably on a raft!

Sleeping & Eating
Consider staying at Kostela (p162) instead of Bihać.

Villa Una (☎ /fax 311 393; Bihaćkih Branilaca 20; s/ d/tr 50/70/90KM; P) Behind a jewellery shop, halfway between the bus station and the Una Bridge, Villa Una is a friendly homestay-style *pansion* with decent pine furniture. Some road noise.

Hotel Park (☎ 226 394; www.aduna.ba; ul 5-Korpusa bb; s/d/apt 69/125/160KM; P 🔁) The lobby looks very dated, but rooms have been thoroughly spruced up with good new bathrooms and wheelchair access. Singles are pretty small. Reception can help with information if the nearby tourist-info booth is closed. Very central.

Restaurant River Una (☎ 310 014; Džemala Bijedića 12; mains 7-15KM, beers 2KM; ✆ 7am-11pm) Of several riverside eateries facing central Bihać's pretty rapids, River Una has the most appealing wooden-rustic interior with stone platforms, giant hooks and 'flying' fish. There's a great terrace too, though views from the cheesier Restoran B-Adis, 100m beyond, are even better. The latter offers rooms from single/double €25/40. Buy the whole place for €400,000!

Getting There & Away
Looking more like a downmarket casino, the **bus station** (☎ 311939; Put V-Korpusa bb) is 1km west of the centre, just off Bihaćkih Branilaća. Buses run to Zagreb (25KM, 2½ hours, 4.45am, 10.20am, 2pm and 4.45pm), Banja Luka (20KM, three hours, 5.30am, 7.30am, 1pm and 3pm) via Bosanska Krupa, and Sarajevo (40.50KM, seven hours, 12.45am, 7.30am, 2.30pm and 10pm) via Travnik. Cazin bound buses (5.50KM, 11 daily except Sunday) pass through Kostela and Ostražac. **Super-Matrix** (☎ 061257098; Zagreb Hwy) rents cars.

UNA VALLEY
Locals claim that the Una ('number one') River was so named by Romans who considered it the most beautiful in their whole empire. Its green gorges, scattered castles, pounding cascades and widely fanned rapids range from lovably pretty to powerfully dramatic. Village homes are mostly new but frequently have attractive wooden *kuruzana* (corn-drying stands) in their blossom-filled yards.

Activities
Several adventure-sports companies in and around Bihać offer rafting, kayaking and climbing, run their own campsites and provide transfers from town. Rafting prices vary

BOSNIA & HERCEGOVINA

BOSNIA & HERCEGOVINA

WARNING

The Bihać area was mined during the war, so stick to paths and concreted areas.

---

according to difficulty and distance (€25 to €40 per person); minimum group size is six. The section from Kostela to Bosanska Krupa is good for beginners: mostly grades I to II, but with plenty of gentle rapids to keep things fun. The Una's top rafting section is between the impressive 24m **Štrcački Buk** waterfall and Troslap/Lohovo (grades II to IV in July, IV to V in April). In late July the festive **Una Regatta** (registration fee 55KM) sees hundreds of water lovers rafting or kayaking from Kulen-Vakuf to Bosanska Krupa via Bihać over three days. Useful contacts:

Limit (☎ 061144248; www.limit.co.ba; Džanića Mahala 7, Bihać) Canyoning, caving, guided mountaineering and biking.

Sport Bjeli (☎ 388 555; www.una-rafting.ba) Based at Klokot, about 10km west of Bihać up a side river.

Una Kiro Rafting (☎ /fax 223 760; www.una-kiro-rafting.com) Based at Golubic, 6km southeast of Bihać.

North of Bihać
KOSTELA
At Kostela, 9km north of Bihać, the Una plunges over the thundering **Kostelski Buk**, rapids so high that they're more of a waterfall. Perfectly positioned to admire the scene, **Pansion Kostelski Buk** (☎ 302 340; www.kostelski-buk.co.ba; M14, km9; s/d 60/90KM; P ✖) offers superb-value, lavishly equipped rooms almost overembellished with gold fabrics and white-leather padding. Food at the excellent view-restaurant downstairs is impeccable and is accompanied by walnut bread and artistic garnishes.

OSTROŽAC
By far the most dramatic of several medieval castle sites surveying the valley is up a 3km ladder of hairpin bends from lower Srbljani (M14 kilometre 12). **Ostrožac fortress** (☎ 061236641; www.ostrozac.com; admission IKM; ✆ 8am-6pm by phoning caretaker) was originally built in 1286. Its remarkably complete citadel walls enclose a modernist sculpture garden and sport several towers whose pointy, Gothic spires would make the perfect set for a Dracula movie. Inside, the atmosphere is even spookier, as the once-splendid interiors are now

semiderelict following heartless vandalism during the 1990s conflicts.

Little Ostražac village has a handful of restaurants 300m southwest of the castle. **Motel Estrada** (☎ 531 320; s/d 30/60KM; P) offers homely en suite rooms in the fifth unmarked house on the left up the Prečići road: look for the beer signs.

BOSANSKA KRUPA
Locals overstate the charm of Bosanska Krupa, whose old-town core is little more than a stubby central castle knoll. Nonetheless, that knoll makes a pleasant view when pondered from Pizzeria Palaco or Bistro Dino, two cafe-restaurants on stilts above the Una waters on an island linked by an old plank bridge to the bus station.

An alternative lunch stop if driving to Novi Grad (formerly Bosanski Novi) is **Otoka Bosanska** where Stari Mlin (kilometre 43) and Bistro Kron (kilometre 44) are both delightful little mill-cottage restaurants with functioning waterwheels. Stari Mlin is the more genuine, but Kron's fried trout (6KM) comes deliciously brushed with subtle sorrel-garlic dressing.

South of Bihać
SOKOLAC & ORLIJANI
Rearing above the Golubić road, a green hilltop is crowned by the shattered stone tower and 10m-high gated wall of **Sokolac castle**. Inside there's little to see, but the castle looks dramatic from below and (more distantly) from across the river at Orlijani, 3km south of Bihać. Orlijani has a **campsite** (www.aduna.ba; ✆ May-Sep) and a pair of riverside restaurants, of which **Biffe Mlin** (☎ 333 249; M5, km17; mains 5-12KM) is much the more atmospheric, perched on creaky wooden walkways and with its own waterwheel.

BOSNIA & HERCEGOVINA DIRECTORY

ACCOMMODATION
Prices quoted are for the low season. That's October till May in most areas, though only a few towns (notably Mostar) raise prices significantly in summer (maybe 20% to 50%). For ski resorts the high season is mid-

December to mid-March, during which ski-hotel prices double and bookings are rarely accepted for stays shorter than seven days (though you can try turning up on spec). Sarajevo and Mostar are fairly well set up for budget accommodation, with seasonal touts waiting at the bus stations and a wide selection of home-hostels bookable via international hostel-booking sites. Unlike hostels in Western Europe, these are almost never purpose built, being instead a cheap homestay with multibed rooms, occasionally unlicensed. Higher-class homestays are also fairly common in tourist areas, and organised rural homestays are starting to catch on, as in Blagaj and around Jajce.

Most towns have *pansions* that range from glorified homestays to sophisticated little boutique hotels. Virtually every town in BiH has at least a couple of suburban motels, ideal for those with cars or for anyone finding all in-town accommodation booked up. Note that not all motels provide parking facilities: the term can simply imply a lower midrange hotel.

Medium-sized towns generally have at least one hotel inhabiting the husk of an old Tito-era concrete monster. Some of these have been elegantly remodelled; others remain gloomy and a little forbidding, despite prices that usually exceed better motels'.

Unless otherwise mentioned, breakfast is not included with private or hostel accommodation but is included for *pansions*, motels and hotels. *Pansions* and hotels will usually do laundry if asked, albeit at wildly varying prices. Less than 10KM per load is unusual.

ACTIVITIES

BiH is an outdoor wonderland, with enormous potential for extreme sports, especially rafting and skiing. Trekking and wild camping have been compromised since the 1990s by the presence of landmines, but many upland areas and national parks now have safe, marked trails for hiking and mountain biking. Of numerous outdoors companies that can get you into the wilderness, expat-run ecotourism organisation **Green Visions** (see p112) is especially accustomed to working with foreign guests.

Skiing

Sarajevo hosted the 1984 Winter Olympics, and Bosnia's very accessible main ski resorts

---

PRACTICALITIES

- *Oslobođenje* and *Dnevni avaz* are the most popular daily newspapers in Sarajevo; *Dani* is a reliable independent weekly. *Nezavisne novine* is a Banja Luka daily.

- Most public radio and TV stations are operated by the Bosnian Muslim-Croat and Serb entities; a national public broadcasting service is being developed.

- Electrical supply is 220V to 240V/50Hz to 60Hz. BiH uses the standard European round-pronged plugs.

- BiH uses the metric system.

Jahorina (p129), Bjelašnica (p129) and Vlašić (p154) offer excellent yet remarkably inexpensive pistes. Daily lift passes cost barely €15. Jahorina has the liveliest après-ski scene. The season starts on 20 December, running officially till mid-March, though good snowfalls can continue into early April.

Rafting

Bosnia's fast-flowing river-canyons offer excellent rafting. In April-May when waters are high, sections of the Tara (p146), Una (p161) and Vrbas (p160) rivers can reach grade V (the highest difficulty level that's raftable) and will host the 2009 **International Rafting Federation** (www.intraftfed.com) championships. In midsummer waters are calmer and each river has 'beginner' stretches of lower difficulty. The Neretva above Konjic (p131) also has picturesque, highly raftworthy white water.

BOOKS
Historical Background

Noel Malcolm's very readable *Bosnia: A Short History* is a great introduction to the complexities of Bosnian history and is helpful at deconstructing many commonly-held myths. Ivan Lovrenović's less readable *Bosnia: A Cultural History* throws in more about writers and artists but covers essentially the same ground. For more on regional history read any of ex-BBC correspondent Misha Glenny's excellent books on the Balkans or Yugoslavia. Get a movingly personal insight into the 1990s wartime sufferings with Joe Sacco's deeply humane comic-strip books.

Matija Mažranić's *Glance into Ottoman Bosnia* is a historical curiosity offering snapshots of daily life and highlighting the rigours of travel during a trundle through 1830s Bosnia.

For Bosnian literature see p108.

Guidebooks

Time Out's excellent annual *Sarajevo and Bosnia-Herzegovina for Visitors* magazine-guide (15KM) is available locally. Babić and Bozja's *Mountaineering Tourist Guide* (35KM) is a great resource for hikers, with detailed topographic maps and many photos. Tim Clancy has written several ponderous BiH guidebooks, both for Bradt and for Bosnian bookshop-publisher **BuyBook** (www.buybook.ba). They are very comprehensive but cry out for better editing. BuyBook also produces Matias Gomez's *Forgotten Beauty: A Hiker's Guide to Bosnia and Herzegovina's 2000m Peaks.*

BUSINESS HOURS

Official hours are 8am to 4pm Monday to Friday; banks open Saturday morning as well. Shops are open longer hours (usually from 8am to 6pm), and many open on Sunday. Restaurants often open from 7am to 11pm but until around 11am are likely to act only as a cafe. When custom is sparse any place might simply close, ignoring its posted opening hours, possibly pinning a mobile-phone contact number to the door in the case of museums or tourist offices.

DANGERS & ANNOYANCES

As of 2007 BiH was still estimated to have over a million mines and fragments of unexploded ordnance (bullets and bombs) spread over 1890 sq km. While that's only 3.9% of the country's area, mines were generally laid by individuals who kept poor or no records, so there's a certain level of uncertainty as to their location. BiH averages around 40 mine casualties per year, only a 20th of the number in Cambodia, but caution remains key. The golden rule is to stick to asphalt and concrete surfaces. Don't enter war-damaged buildings and avoid areas that look abandoned or where there's no clearly worn path.

Sarajevo's **Mine Action Centre** (Map p113; ☎ 033-209 762; www.bhmac.org; Zmaja od Bosne 8; ⏰ 8am-4pm Mon-Fri) has more information.

EMBASSIES & CONSULATES

The nearest embassies for Ireland and New Zealand are found in Ljubljana and Rome respectively. Representation in Sarajevo (area code ☎ 033):

Australia (Map pp116-17; ☎ 206 167; Obala Kulina Bana 15\1) Honorary consulate.
Canada (Map p113; ☎ 222 033; Grbavička 4/2)
Croatia (Map pp116-17; ☎ 444 331; Mehmeda Spahe 16)
France (Map p113; ☎ 282 050; Mehmed-bega Kapetanovica Ljubusaka 18)
Germany (Map pp116-17; ☎ 275 000; Buka bb)
Hungary (☎ 208 353; www.hungemb.ba; Splitska 2)
Japan (Map pp116-17; ☎ 209 580; Bistrik 2)
Macedonia (Map p113; ☎ 206 004; Splitska 57)
Montenegro (Map pp116-17; ☎ 239 925; Talirovića 4)
Netherlands (Map p113; ☎ 562 600; www.netherlandsembassy.ba; Grbavička 4/1)
Serbia (Map pp116-17; ☎ 260 080; Obala Maka Dizdara 3a)
Slovenia (Map pp116-17; ☎ 271 251; Bentbaša 7)
UK (Map pp116-17; ☎ 208 229; Petrakijina 11)
USA (Map p113; ☎ 445 700; Alipašina 43)

In Banja Luka there's a **US Consulate** (Map p158; ☎ 051-211 500; Jovana Dučića 5).

GAY & LESBIAN TRAVELLERS

Although homosexuality was decriminalised per se in 1998 (2000 in the RS) attitudes are very conservative and laws remain against 'insulting the moral feelings of citizens'. This leaves judges a free hand to interpret the limits of public morality. Understandably, this, along with occasional assaults on homosexuals, means that there are no open displays of affection between same-sex couples. The gay characters in *Go West* made it a particularly controversial prizewinner at the 2005 Sarajevo Film Festival.

Logos (www.logos.org.ba/cont/) focuses on combating discrimination against sexual minorities, while Association Q attempts to empower the self-reliance of the gay community in BiH. English-language chat website www.gayromeo.com reportedly has around 400 Sarajevo members, and www.queer.ba (in Bosnian) organises occasional local meet-ups.

HOLIDAYS

Major Islamic festivals are observed in parts of the Federation, their dates changing annually according to the Muslim lunar calendar. The feast of sacrifice is known locally as Kurban Bajram, while the end-of-Ramadan celebration is called Ramazanski Bajram. Orthodox Easter (variable) and Christmas (7 January) are observed in the RS. Western Easter (variable) and Christmas (25 December) are celebrated in the Federation. For variable holiday dates, see the boxed texts, p433. Other national holidays:

New Year's Day 1 January
Independence Day 1 March
May Day 1 May
National Statehood Day 25 November

INTERNET RESOURCES

BiH Ministry of Foreign Affairs (www.mvp.gov.ba) Visa and embassy details.
BiH Tourism (www.bhtourism.ba)
Bosnian Institute (www.bosnia.org.uk) Bosnian cultural affairs.
Grad Sarajevo (www.sarajevo.ba) City site.
Herceg-Bosna (www.hercegbosna.org) BiH seen from a Croat angle.
HIdden Bosnia (www.hiddenbosnia.com) Useful tourist information.
InsideBosnia (www.insidebosnia.com) Events and interesting links.
Office of the High Representative (www.ohr.int) Constitutional news and background information from the EU's overseeing office; useful, but at the time of research was imminently due to wind down.

LANGUAGE

Notwithstanding different dialects, the people of BiH basically speak the same language (see p455) but it's referred to as 'Bosnian' (Bosanski) in Muslim parts of the Federation, 'Croatian' (Hrvatski) in Croat-controlled parts and 'Serbian' (Српски) in the RS. The Federation uses the Roman alphabet; the RS uses predominantly Cyrillic (Ћирилица), but Roman (Latinica) is gaining wider parallel usage too. The mixed Brčko area uses both alphabets equally.

MAPS

Freytag & Berndt's very useful 1:250,000 BiH road map costs 12KM in Sarajevo bookshops but is virtually impossible to find anywhere else in the nation. A very decent BiH map is available free from the **Zdrava Voda restaurant** (www.zdravavoda.co.ba) 2km south of Jablanica:

well worth the 1.50KM price of a coffee should you stop here on a Mostar–Sarajevo bus. Most other country maps range from incomplete to downright inaccurate.

City maps are patchily available from bookshops, kiosks or tourist information centres. Many places post town plans on their websites. Otherwise, it can be useful to take digital photos of occasionally displayed map boards in town centres and navigate using your camera image.

MONEY

Bosnia's convertible mark (KM or BAM) is pronounced *kai-em* or *maraka* and divided into 100 fenig. It's tied to the euro (approximately €1=1.96KM). Many establishments (shops, restaurants and especially hotels) unblinkingly accept euros, though this is slightly rarer in the RS. In Mostar even Croatian kuna are also accepted without fuss.

ATMs accepting Visa and MasterCard brands are ubiquitous.

Travellers cheques can be readily changed at Raiffeisen and Zagrebačka banks, though you'll usually need to show the original purchase receipt.

PHOTOGRAPHY & VIDEO

Photographing military installations (including airports, bridges, checkpoints, troops and bases) and embassies is forbidden. If in doubt, ask first.

POST

Post and telephone offices are usually combined. Poste-restante service is available for a small fee but only at main-city central post offices. BiH's complex postal history makes it fascinating for philatelists, and three postal organisations still issue their own stamps. The Cyrillic lettering makes RS **Srpske Poste** (www.filatelija.rs.ba) stamps obviously distinctive. Those from Mostar-based **HP Post** (www.post.ba) and Sarajevo's **BH Post** (www.bhp.ba) have their

---

EMERGENCY NUMBERS

- Fire service ☎ 123
- Medical emergency ☎ 124
- Police ☎ 122
- Roadside emergency ☎ 1282/1288

BOSNIA & HERCEGOVINA

own designs but are both marked Bosnia i Hercegovina in Latin.

TELEPHONE

Phonecards for public telephones can be purchased at post offices or from some street kiosks for 10KM. Different cards are required for the Federation and for the RS.

It's usually somewhat cheaper to use the telephone section of post offices for longer calls. Dial ☎ 1201 for the international operator, ☎ 1188 for local directory information.

Telephone codes 061 to 065 are for mobile phones. BH Mobile (061 and 062) is most widely used in the Federation. Its prepaid 'Ultra' SIM cards cost 15KM including 10KM credit. Alternatives are 063 (HT/EroNet), popular among Croats, and 065 (M-Tel), which is most widespread in the RS, though with marginally cheaper call costs M-Tel's popularity is growing in the Federation too.

TOURIST INFORMATION

All Bosnia's larger cities and many smaller towns have tourist offices. The typically underemployed staff are generally delighted to see travellers, dispensing maps, brochures and advice, and sometimes helping with accommodation. However, don't be surprised by unexplained office closures.

TRAVELLERS WITH DISABILITIES

Most of Bosnia's most appealing town and village cores are based around steep, rough streets and stairways. That's visually charming, but awkward if you have limited mobility. A few places have wheelchair ramps in response to all the war wounded, but smaller hotels won't have lifts, and wheelchair-accessible toilets are still extremely rare.

VISAS

EU nationals don't need visas. Nor do citizens of Andorra, Australia, Brunei, Canada, Croatia, Japan, Kuwait, Liechtenstein, Macedonia, Malaysia, Monaco, Montenegro, New Zealand, Norway, Qatar, Russia, San Marino, Serbia, Switzerland, the Vatican, Turkey and the USA.

For other nationals, single-/multi-entry visas cost from €31/57. Visa applications must be accompanied by one photograph and either a letter of invitation or a tourist-

agency voucher. For full details, see www.mvp.gov.ba.

TRANSPORT IN BOSNIA & HERCEGOVINA

GETTING THERE & AWAY

Air

Even BiH's main airport, **Međunarodni Aerodrom Sarajevo** (off Map p113; ☎ 033-289 100; www.sarajevo-airport.ba; code SJJ) is decidedly modest, served by just the following airlines:

Adria Airways (Map pp116-17; airline code JP; ☎ 033-232 125; www.adria-airways.com; Ferhadija 23, Sarajevo) Hub Ljubljana.

Austrian Airlines (airline code OS; ☎ 033-202 059; www.aua.com) Hub Vienna.

BH Airlines (Map pp116-17; airline code JA; ☎ 033-218 605; www.bhairlines.ba; 15 Branilaca Sarajeva, Sarajevo; ⏰ 9am-5pm Mon-Fri, to 2pm Sat) Hub Sarajevo.

British Airways (airline code BA; www.ba.com) Hub London.

Croatia Airlines (airline code OU; ☎ 033-666 123; www.croatiaairlines.hr) Hub Zagreb.

JAT (Map pp116-17; airline code JU; ☎ 033-259 750; www.jat.com; Zelenih Beretki 6, Sarajevo) Hub Belgrade.

Lufthansa (airline code LH; ☎ 033-278 590; www.lufthansa.com) Hub Frankfurt.

Malév Hungarian Airlines (airline code MA; ☎ 033-473 200; www.malev.hu) Hub Budapest.

Turkish Airlines (Map pp116-17; airline code TK; ☎ 033-666 092; www.thy.com; Branilaca Sarajeva, Sarajevo) Hub Istanbul.

Between them all of BiH's other airports have only seven scheduled flights a week on three routes: Mostar–Istanbul, Banja Luka–Zurich and Banja Luka–Belgrade.

The national carrier, BH (pronounced 'Bay-Ha') Airlines, flies inexpensively to Belgrade, Frankfurt, Cologne/Bonn, Istanbul, Skopje, Stuttgart, Zagreb and Zurich. (The Belgrade and Zagreb flights are codeshares.) Although it's slowly getting more user-friendly, at present BH generally advises customers to phone in reservations then pay at the airport immediately before departure.

If prices to Sarajevo seem high, consider taking budget flights to Dubrovnik, Split or Zagreb in Croatia, then connecting to BiH by bus or train.

BUS SERVICES FROM BOSNIA & HERCEGOVINA

Destination	Price (KM)	Departures
Amsterdam	206	Tue, Thu, Sat & Sun
Berlin	167	Wed, Thu & Sat
Brussels	206	Sun
Dortmund/Köln via Frankfurt	209/235	daily except Fri
Ljubljana	74	Tue, Wed, Thu & Sun
Munich	190	daily
Paris	260	Thu
Stockholm	280	daily
Vienna ('Beč')	92	2 daily

Land

BORDER CROSSINGS

Crossing borders is generally hassle free. By bus or train, just wait on board. Either a border guard boards to check documents or the driver collects passports and takes them to the guard post. Don't panic; this is normal.

When driving, simply queue up and flash your passport and car documents.

BUS

Towns in the Federation usually have buses to Zagreb and/or Split (Croatia) at least daily, while from some RS towns, services to destinations in Serbia and Montenegro are often more frequent than those to the Federation.

Bigger towns generally have weekly services to at least a couple of Western European destinations, typically in Germany. For international bus services from Sarajevo see the table, above.

CAR & MOTORCYCLE

Drivers need to ensure that they have Green Card insurance for their vehicle and an EU or international driving permit. Petrol (95 and 98 octane) and diesel are readily available in any town, though many service stations close between 11pm and 7am.

TRAIN

Two daily services connect Ploče (on the Croatian coast) to Sarajevo via Mostar. Both either connect or continue to Zagreb. The overnight Zagreb–Sarajevo section (56.60KM, 9½ hours, 9.20pm) has one carriage of comfortable six-berth couchettes (19.60KM supplement).

The Banja Luka–Belgrade train (eight hours) runs overnight eastbound (depart-ing 10.30pm), but you'll be woken twice for Croatia and Serbia border crossings. The westbound train returns by day, departing Belgrade at 1.20pm. Sarajevo–Belgrade tickets (46KM) are sold but require a train change (p127).

The Budapest train (96KM, 12 hours) leaves Sarajevo at 7.14am, routed via Doboj, Šamac and Osijek (Croatia). It returns from Budapest-Keleti at 9.25am. From Budapest a return ticket is cheaper than a one-way.

GETTING AROUND

Air

Although BH Airlines flies Sarajevo–Banja Luka en route to Zurich it won't sell tickets for the internal sector.

Bicycle

Roads are very hilly, but for tough cyclists BiH's calm secondary routes offer a delight-ful playground. Several mountain areas now have suggested off-road trails for mountain bikers, but beware of straying off-route into minefields.

Bus

BiH's bus network can be annoyingly in-frequent on many of the routes that would most interest tourists. Long-distance buses maintain the same schedules every day, but local, shorter-hop buses reduce services at weekends, often stopping altogether on Sunday. Bus stations presell tickets, but it's normally easy enough to wave down any bus en route. Buses depart even when virtually empty. Normally, reservations are only nec-essary for overnight routes or during peak holiday times.

Stowing luggage on long-distance buses typ-ically costs 2KM per item extra. Buses usually run on time but are slow due to the winding roads, meal stops and side trips to collect passengers in intermediate town centres.

A return ticket is usually significantly cheaper than two singles but limits you to a specific bus company, which can prove inconvenient. Fares average around 7KM per hour travelled but vary somewhat between different companies.

Car & Motorcycle

Given the minimal transport to BiH's most spectacular backwoods areas, having wheels can really transform your trip. Bosnian roads are winding, lightly trafficked and almost always beautiful, a delight for driving as long as you aren't in a hurry. Flowers and memorials mark crash spots at many sharper bends, suggesting the contrary, yet in our experience most local drivers drive relatively calmly and the main frustration is getting past slow trucks, tractors or occasional horse carts. Some country roads are not asphalted.

AUTOMOBILE ASSOCIATIONS
Automobile Association of Bosnia & Hercegovina (Map p113; ☎ 033-212 771; www.bihamk.ba; Skenderija 23, Sarajevo; annual membership 25KM; ⏲ 8am-4.30pm Mon-Fri, 9am-noon Sat) offers road assistance and towing services for members.

HIRE
Most bigger towns offer car hire starting at around €43/245 per day/week with unlimited mileage and basic insurance. Before signing, check car condition, insurance deductible and whether the 17% tax costs extra. EU or international driving permits are accepted.

ROAD RULES
Driving is on the right, seat belts must be worn and headlights must be kept on day and night. The maximum blood-alcohol level is 0.05% (roughly 0.5g/L). Speed limits are 80km/h for rural roads, dropping to 60km/h or less in town, often without reminder signs for many kilometres. Police spot checks are very common.

Parking is relatively easy in most towns: in the central areas expect to pay 1KM per hour to an attendant. Mostar and Sarajevo are contrastingly awkward, with tow-away trucks ruthless in the capital.

Train
RS Railways (www.zrs-rs.com/red_voznje.php) has full, up-to-date timetables. Trains depart much less frequently than buses, but they're generally 30% cheaper, and there's a comfy Sarajevo–Zagreb sleeper. The whole Mostar–Sarajevo run is delightful, though tunnels obscure many of the views.

Croatia

Touted as the 'new this' and the 'new that' for years upon its re-emergence on the world tourism scene, it is now apparent that Croatia is a unique destination that can hold its own, and then some: this is a country with a 1778km-long coast and a staggering 1185 islands. The Adriatic coast is a knockout: its limpid sapphirine waters pull visitors to remote islands, hidden coves and traditional fishing villages while also offering a glitzy beach and yacht scene. Istria is captivating with its gastronomy and wine, and the bars, clubs and festivals of Zagreb, Zadar and Split remain little-explored delights. Eight national parks protect pristine forests, karst mountains, rivers, lakes and waterfalls in a landscape of primeval beauty. Punctuate all this with Dubrovnik in the south, and a country couldn't wish for a better finale.

Sitting on a see-saw between the Balkans and central Europe, Croatia has suffered from something of a love-hate-love affair with the EU. Statistics show that the support for joining the union – once vast and palpable – is lately hovering around the 50% mark, thanks to the already slightly elusive joining date (is it 2010? or 2011? or even 2012?) snagging on a number of hurdles. Developers and investors are more present by the year, but despite this the country has, with few exceptions, managed to keep the lack of (massive) development at bay and maintain the extraordinary beauty of the coast – the very thing that keeps the punters coming for more.

CROATIA

FAST FACTS

- **Area** 56,538 sq km
- **Capital** Zagreb
- **Currency** kuna (KN); 1KN = 100 lipa; US$1 = 5.55KN; UK£1 = 8.08KN; €1 = 7.35KN; A$1 = 3.74KN
- **Famous for** neckties, Slaven Bilić, Tito
- **Key phrases** *bog* (hello); *doviđenja* (goodbye); *hvala* (thanks); *pardon* (sorry)
- **Official language** Croatian
- **Population** 4.5 million
- **Telephone codes** country code ☎ 385; international access code ☎ 00
- **Visas** not necessary for citizens of Australia, Canada, the EU, New Zealand and the USA (see p256)

HIGHLIGHTS

- **Dubrovnik** (p244) A walled old town with luminous marble streets and finely ornamented buildings.
- **Hvar town** (p238) Venetian architecture and vibrant nightlife.
- **Split** (p228) The incredible, lively and historic delights of Diocletian's Palace.
- **Mljet** (p242) Lakes, coves and an island monastery.
- **Rovinj** (p202) Cobbled streets and an unspoilt fishing port.

ITINERARIES

- **One week** After a day in dynamic Zagreb (p180) head down to Split (p227) for a day and night in Diocletian's Palace (p228). Then take a ferry to Hvar (p238), windsurf in Brač (p237) and end with two days in Dubrovnik (p244), taking a day trip to Mljet (p242) or the Elafiti Islands (p248).
- **Two weeks** After two days in Zagreb (p180), head to Rovinj (p202) for a three-day stay, taking day trips to Pula (p204) and Poreč (p199). Head south to Zadar (p220) for a night and then go on to Split (p227) for a night. Take ferries to Hvar (p238), Brač (p237), and then Vis (p237) or Korčula (p240), spending a day or three on each island before ending with three days in Dubrovnik (p244) and a day trip to Mljet (p242).

CLIMATE & WHEN TO GO

The climate varies from Mediterranean along the Adriatic coast, with hot, dry summers and mild, rainy winters, to continental inland, with cold winters and warm summers. You can swim in the sea from mid-June until late September. Coastal temperatures are slightly warmer south of Split. See p429 for a Zagreb climate chart.

The peak tourist season runs from mid-July to the end of August. Prices are highest and accommodation scarcest during this period. The best time to be in Croatia is June. The weather is beautiful, the boats and excursions are running often, and it's not yet too crowded. May and September are also good, especially if you're interested in hiking.

HISTORY

In 229 BC the Romans began their conquest of the indigenous Illyrians by estab-

---

HOW MUCH?

- **Short taxi ride** 60KN
- **Plate of fish stew** 50KN
- **Loaf of bread** 4KN
- **Bottle of house white wine** 40KN
- **Newspaper** 8KN

LONELY PLANET INDEX

- **Litre of petrol** 9.65KN
- **Litre of bottled water** 10KN
- **33cL of Karlovačko beer** 12KN
- **Souvenir T-shirt** 90KN
- **Street snack (slice of burek)** 10KN

---

lishing a colony at Solin (Salona), close to Split in Dalmatia. Emperor Augustus then extended the empire and created the provinces of Illyricum (Dalmatia and Bosnia) and Pannonia (Croatia). In AD 285 Emperor Diocletian decided to retire to his palace fortress in Split, today the greatest Roman ruin in Eastern Europe. When the empire was divided in 395, what are now known as Slovenia, Croatia and Bosnia and Hercegovina (BiH) stayed with the Western Roman Empire, while present-day Serbia, Kosovo and Macedonia went to the Eastern Roman Empire, later known as the Byzantine Empire.

Around 625, Slavic tribes migrated from the Caucases and the Serbian tribe settled in the region that is now southwestern Serbia. The Croatian tribe moved into what is now Croatia and occupied two former Roman provinces: Dalmatian Croatia along the Adriatic, and Pannonian Croatia to the north.

By the early part of the 9th century both settlements had accepted Christianity, but the northern Croats fell under Frankish domination while Dalmatian Croats came under the nominal control of the Byzantine Empire. The Dalmatian duke Tomislav united the two groups in 925 in a single kingdom that prospered for nearly 200 years.

Late in the 11th century the throne fell vacant and the northern Croats, unable to agree upon a ruler, united with Hungary in 1102 for protection against the Orthodox Byzantine Empire.

In the 14th century the Ottomans began pushing into the Balkans, defeating the Serbs in 1389 and the Hungarians in 1526. Northern Croatia turned to the Hapsburgs of Austria for protection in 1527 and remained part of their empire until 1918.

Some Dalmatian cities changed hands repeatedly until Venice imposed its rule on the Adriatic coast in the early 15th century and occupied it for nearly four centuries. Only the Republic of Ragusa (Dubrovnik) maintained its independence.

After Venice was shattered by Napoleonic France in 1797, the French occupied southern Croatia, abolishing the Republic of Ragusa in 1808. Napoleon merged Dalmatia, Istria and Slovenia into the 'Illyrian Provinces', but following his defeat at Waterloo in 1815, Austria-Hungary occupied the coast.

It wasn't long before Croatia began itching for independence from the Austrian empire and for the unification of Dalmatia and Slavonia. When an uprising in Hungary threatened Austrian rule, Croatia seized the opportunity to intervene in return for greater autonomy. The Croatian commander Josip Jelačić set out to fight the rebels, but his campaign was unsuccessful and Croatian hopes were crushed. Disillusionment spread after 1848, and deepened when the monarchy placed Croatia and Slavonia within the Hungarian administration, while Dalmatia remained within Austria.

The river of discontent running through late-19th-century Croatia forked into two streams that dominated the political landscape for the next century. On the one side was Bishop Josif Juraf Strossmayer, who believed that Jugoslavenstvo (south-Slavic unity), brought together by a common language, was the only way forward for the aspirations of the southern Slavs. His opponent, the militantly anti-Serb Ante Starčević, envisaged an independent Croatia made up of Slavonia, Dalmatia, Krajina, Slovenia, Istria and part of BiH.

South Slavic Unity

The first organised resistance against the Austro-Hungarian Empire formed in Dalmatia. Croat representatives in Rijeka and Serb representatives in Zadar joined together in 1905 to demand the unification of Dalmatia and Slavonia with a formal guarantee of Serbian equality as a nation. The spirit of unity mushroomed, and by 1906 Croat-Serb coalitions had taken over local government in Dalmatia and Slavonia, forming a serious threat to the Hungarian power structure.

Similar resistance was going on in neighbouring BiH, and with the outbreak of WWI the idea that only Slavic unity could check great-power ambitions in the region was cemented. With the collapse of the Austro-Hungarian Empire in 1918, the Kingdom of Serbs, Croats and Slovenes was established. Italy seized Pula, Rijeka and Zadar in November 1918.

Problems with the kingdom began almost immediately, with the abolition of Croatia's Sabor (parliament) and the centralisation of power in Belgrade. The new electoral districts underrepresented the Croats, and the new government gave away Istria, Zadar and a number of islands to Italy.

One of the main opposition leaders was Stjepan Radić, who, together with Svetozar Pribićević, advocated a federal democracy within the kingdom and tried to promote the idea of an egalitarian state. He formed HSS (the Croatian Peasant Party), a political party that remains influential to this day. Following a number of heated parliamentary debates, Radić was assassinated, along with two of his party members. Exploiting fears of civil war, on 6 January 1929 King Aleksandar in Belgrade proclaimed a royal dictatorship, abolished political parties and suspended parliamentary government.

Ustaše, Chetniks & Partisans

One day after the coup d'état, a Bosnian Croat, Ante Pavelić, set up the Ustaše Croatian Liberation Movement in Zagreb, with the stated aim of establishing an independent state by force if necessary. Fearing arrest, he fled to Sofia in Bulgaria and then to Italy. There, he established training camps for his organisation, favoured by Mussolini. Pavelić succeeded in assassinating King Aleksandar in Marseilles in 1934; Italy responded by closing down the training camps and imprisoning Pavelić and many of his followers.

When Germany invaded Yugoslavia on 6 April 1941, the Nazis installed the exiled Ustaše with the support of the Italians. In return, Pavelić agreed to cede a good part of Dalmatia to Italy, which left him with the Lika region southwest of Zagreb and western Hercegovina as his political base.

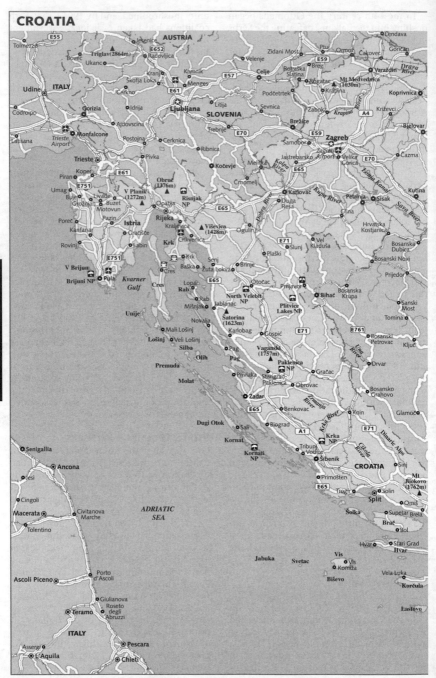

CROATIA

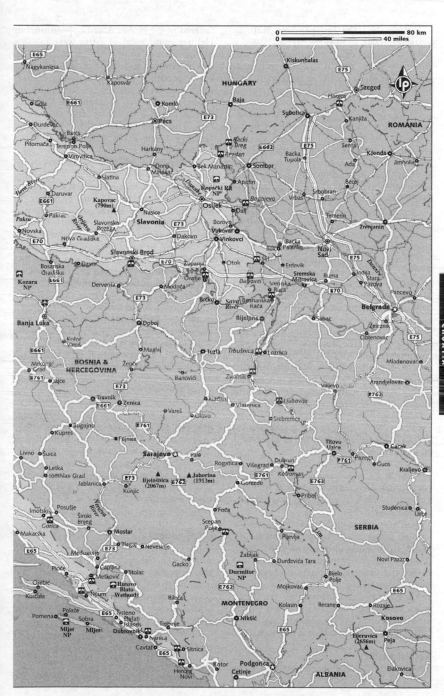

Within days the Independent State of Croatia (NDH), headed by Pavelić, issued a range of decrees designed to persecute and eliminate Serbs, Jews, Roma and antifascist Croats. Villages conducted their own personal pogroms against Serbs, and extermination camps were set up, most notoriously at Jasenovac (south of Zagreb). The extermination program was carried out with appalling brutality. The exact number of Serb victims is uncertain and controversial, with Croatian historians tending to minimise the figures and Serbian historians tending to maximise them. The number of Serb deaths range from 60,000 to 600,000, but the most reliable estimates settle somewhere between 80,000 and 120,000. Whatever the number, it's clear that the NDH and its supporters made a diligent effort to eliminate the entire Serb population.

The Serbs did not quietly accept their fate. Armed resistance to the regime took the form of Serbian 'Chetniks', led by General Draža Mihajlović, which began as an antifascist rebellion but soon degenerated into massacres of Croats in eastern Croatia and Bosnia.

In the meantime, Croat-Slovene Josip Broz, leader of the outlawed Yugoslavian Communist Party, fronted the partisans, who consisted of left-wing Yugoslav intellectuals, Croats disgusted with Chetnik massacres, Serbs disgusted with Ustaše massacres, and antifascists of all kinds.

Although the Allies initially backed the Serbian Chetniks, it became apparent that the partisans were waging a far more focused and determined fight against the Germans. On 20 October 1944 Tito entered Belgrade with the Red Army and was made prime minister. When Germany surrendered in 1945, Pavelić and the Ustaše fled and the partisans entered Zagreb.

The remnants of the NDH army, desperate to avoid falling into the hands of the partisans, attempted to cross into Austria at Bleiburg. A small British contingent met the 50,000 troops and promised to intern them outside Yugoslavia in exchange for their surrender. Tricked, the troops were forced into trains that headed back into Yugoslavia, where the partisans claimed the lives of at least 30,000 men (although the exact number is in doubt).

Recent History

Tito's attempt to retain control of the Italian city of Trieste and parts of southern Austria

faltered in the face of Allied opposition, but Dalmatia and most of Istria were made a permanent part of postwar Yugoslavia. Tito was determined to create a state in which no ethnic group dominated the political landscape. Croatia became one of six republics – Macedonia, Serbia, Montenegro, BiH and Slovenia – in a tightly configured federation. Tito effected this delicate balance by creating a one-party state and stamping out opposition.

During the 1960s, the concentration of power in Belgrade became an increasingly testy issue as it became apparent that money from the more prosperous republics of Slovenia and Croatia was being distributed to the poorer regions, such as BiH, Kosovo, and Montenegro. Serbs in Croatia were over-represented in the government, the armed forces and the police – this was, allegedly, partly because state service offered financial certainty and career opportunities among the poorer Yugoslavs.

The dissatisfaction with Tito's government manifested itself in many student and other demonstrations across Yugoslavia during the late '60s, but Croatia's unrest reached a crescendo in 1971, during the 'Croatian Spring'. Led by reformers within the Communist Party of Croatia, intellectuals and students first called for greater economic autonomy and then constitutional reform to loosen Croatia's ties to Yugoslavia. Tito's crackdown meant that leaders of the movement were either jailed or expelled from the party. Serbs viewed the movement as the Ustaše reborn, and jailed reformers blamed the Serbs for their troubles. The stage was set for the later rise of nationalism and war that followed Tito's death in 1980, even though his 1974 constitution afforded the republics more autonomy.

Independence

After Tito's death, Yugoslavia was left with a large external debt. The country was unable to service the interest on its loans and inflation soared. The authority of the central government sank along with the economy, and mistrust among Yugoslavia's ethnic groups resurfaced.

In 1989 the repression of the Albanian majority in Serbia's Kosovo province sparked renewed fears of Serbian hegemony and heralded the end of the Yugoslav Federation. With political changes sweeping Eastern

Europe, many Croats felt the time had come to separate from Yugoslavia, and the elections of April 1990 saw the victory of Franjo Tuđman's Croatian Democratic Union (HDZ; Hrvatska Demokratska Zajednica). On 22 December 1990 a new Croatian constitution was promulgated, changing the status of Serbs in Croatia from that of a 'constituent nation' to a national minority.

The constitution's failure to guarantee minority rights, and mass dismissals of Serbs from the public service, stimulated the 600,000-strong ethnic Serb community within Croatia to demand autonomy. In early 1991 Serb extremists within Croatia staged provocations designed to force federal military intervention. A May 1991 referendum (boycotted by the Serbs) produced a 93% vote in favour of independence, but when Croatia declared independence on 25 June 1991, the Serbian enclave of Krajina proclaimed its independence from Croatia.

War & Peace

Under pressure from the EC (now EU), Croatia declared a three-month moratorium on its independence, but heavy fighting broke out in Krajina, Baranja (the area north of the Drava River opposite Osijek) and Slavonia. The Serb-dominated Yugoslav People's Army intervened in support of Serbian irregulars, under the pretext of halting ethnic violence.

When the Croatian government ordered a blockade of 32 federal military installations in the republic, the Yugoslav navy blockaded the Adriatic coast and laid siege to the strategic town of Vukovar on the Danube. During the summer of 1991, a quarter of Croatia fell to Serbian militias and the Yugoslav People's Army.

In early October 1991 the federal army and Montenegrin militia moved against Dubrovnik to protest the blockade of their garrisons in Croatia, and on 7 October the presidential palace in Zagreb was hit by rockets fired by Yugoslav air-force jets in an unsuccessful assassination attempt on President Tuđman. When the three-month moratorium on independence ended Croatia declared full independence. On 19 November the city of Vukovar fell after a bloody three-month siege. During six months of fighting in Croatia 10,000 people died, hundreds of thousands fled and tens of thousands of homes were destroyed.

To fulfil a condition for EC recognition, in December the Croatian Sabor (which was re-established under Tito) belatedly amended its constitution to protect minority groups and human rights. A UN-brokered ceasefire from 3 January 1992 generally held. The federal army was allowed to withdraw from its bases inside Croatia and tensions diminished. In January 1992 the EC, succumbing to strong pressure from Germany, recognised Croatia. This was followed three months later by US recognition, and in May 1992 Croatia was admitted to the UN.

In January 1993 the Croatian army launched an offensive in southern Krajina, pushing the Serbs back and recapturing strategic points. In June 1993 the Krajina Serbs voted overwhelmingly to join the Bosnian Serbs (and eventually greater Serbia). Meanwhile, continued 'ethnic cleansing' left only about 900 Croats in Krajina, out of an original population of 44,000.

On 1 May 1995 the Croatian army and police entered occupied western Slavonia, east of Zagreb, and seized control of the region within days. The Krajina Serbs responded by shelling Zagreb in an attack that left seven people dead and 130 wounded. As the Croatian military consolidated its hold in western Slavonia, some 15,000 Serbs fled the region, despite assurances from the Croatian government that they were safe from retribution.

Belgrade's silence throughout this campaign showed that the Krajina Serbs had lost the support of their Serbian allies, encouraging the Croats to forge ahead. On 4 August the military launched a massive assault on the rebel Serb capital of Knin, and vastly outnumbered, the Serb army fled towards northern Bosnia and into Serbia. An estimated 150,000 civilians fled and many were murdered. The military operation ended in days but was followed by months of terror. Widespread looting and burning of Serb villages and attacks upon the remaining Serbs cemented the huge population shift. The Dayton accord signed in Paris in December 1995 recognised Croatia's traditional borders and provided for the return of eastern Slavonia, which was effected in January 1998. The transition proceeded relatively smoothly, but the two populations still regard each other with suspicion.

Although the central government in Zagreb has made the return of Serb refugees a priority in accordance with the demands of the international community, its efforts have been less than successful. Serbs intending to reclaim their property face an array of legal impediments.

Franjo Tuđman's combination of authoritarianism and media control, and tendency to be influenced by the far right, no longer appealed to the postwar Croatian populace. By 1999 opposition parties united to work against Tuđman and the HDZ. Tuđman was hospitalised and died suddenly in late 1999, and planned elections were postponed until January 2000. Still, voters turned out in favour of a centre-left coalition, ousting the HDZ and voting the centrist Stipe Mesić into the presidency.

The country gradually began welcoming tourists again, and the economy opened up to foreign competition. General Mirko Norac turned himself in to the Hague in 2001 and General Ante Gotovina was arrested in 2005 for crimes against Krajina's Serb population. The EU required Gotovina's handover before it would begin discussing Croatia's eventual membership. The arrests of both men were accompanied by some nationalist protest. Discussions with the EU have been slowed down by various hurdles – such as the reforms of the country's judicial system and the fight against corruption – and the proposed joining date is anywhere between 2010 and 2012.

PEOPLE

Croatia has a population of roughly 4.5 million people. Before the war Croatia had a population of nearly five million, of which 78% were Croats and 12% were Serbs. Bosnians and Hercegovinians, Hungarians, Italians, Czechs, Roma and Albanians made up the remaining 10%. Today Croats constitute 89% of the population and slightly less than 5% are Serbs, followed by 0.5% Bosnians and about 0.4% each of Hungarians and Italians. Most Serbs live in eastern Croatia (Slavonia). The largest cities in Croatia are Zagreb (780,000), Split (188,700), Rijeka (144,000), Osijek (114,600) and Zadar (72,700).

Croats are united by a common religion, Catholicism, and a common sense of themselves as European. If you ask a Croat what distinguishes Croatian culture from Bosnian or Serbian culture, the answer is likely to be a variant of 'We are Western and they are Eastern'. The Croats, however, share in the Balkan-wide passion for turbo folk, ćevapčići

(grilled minced lamb or beef) and burek (filled filo-pastry pie).

The shelling of Dubrovnik and the atrocities committed in eastern Slavonia and Krajina have left a bitter taste in those regions. Despite this, many Croatian books and articles examining the country's war conduct have become a staple of the country's intellectual life.

RELIGION

Croats are overwhelmingly Roman Catholic, while the Serbs belong to the Orthodox Church. Catholicism is undergoing a strong resurgence in Croatia. Pope John Paul II visited Croatia several times before his death, though Benedict XVI had not visited at the time of writing. Muslims make up 1.2% of the population and Protestants 0.4%, with a small Jewish population in Zagreb.

ARTS
Architecture

Examples of Roman architecture are abundant in Dalmatia, where the style persisted long after Gothicism had swept the rest of Europe. In the 13th century the earliest examples of Gothic style appeared, usually still mixed with Romanesque forms. The most stunning work from this period is the portal on Trogir's Cathedral of St Lovre, carved by the master artisan Radovan. Depicting human figures performing everyday chores was a definite break with traditional Byzantine reliefs of saints and apostles. The Cathedral of the Assumption of the Blessed Virgin Mary (formerly St Stephen's) in Zagreb was the first venture into the Gothic style in northern Croatia.

In independent Ragusa (Dubrovnik) Renaissance art and sculpture flowered. By the second half of the 15th century, Renaissance influences were appearing on late-Gothic structures. The Sponza Palace, formerly the Customs House, is a fine example of this mixed style. By the mid-16th century, Renaissance features began to supplant the Gothic style in the palaces and summer residences built in and around Ragusa by the wealthy nobility. Unfortunately, much was destroyed in the 1667 earthquake and now Dubrovnik is more notable for the mixed Gothic-Romanesque Franciscan monastery, the 15th-century Orlando column and Onofrio fountain, and the baroque St Blaise's Church and Cathedral of the Assumption of the Virgin.

Northern Croatia is well known for the baroque style introduced by Jesuit monks in the 17th century. The city of Varaždin was a regional capital in the 17th and 18th centuries and, because of its location, enjoyed a steady interchange of artists, artisans and architects with northern Europe. The combination of wealth and a creatively fertile environment led to its becoming Croatia's foremost city of baroque art.

In Zagreb good examples of the baroque style are found in the Upper Town (Gornji Grad), Kaptol and Gradec. Notice St Catherine's Church and the restored baroque mansions that are now the Croatian History Museum and the Croatian Naive Art Museum.

Visual Arts

The painter Vincent of Kastav was producing lovely church frescos in Istria during the 15th century. The small church of St Maria near Beram contains his frescos, most notably the *Dance of Death*. Another notable Istrian painter of the 15th century is Ivan of Kastav, who has left frescos throughout Istria, mostly in the Slovenian part.

Many artists born in Dalmatia were influenced by, and in turn influenced, Italian Renaissance style. The sculptors Lucijano Vranjanin and Frano Laurana, the miniaturist Julije Klović and the painter Andrija Medulić left Dalmatia while the region was under threat from the Ottomans, and worked in Italy.

Vlaho Bukovac (1855–1922) was the most notable painter in the late-19th century. Early-20th-century painters of note include Miroslav Kraljević (1885–1913) and Josip Račić (1885–1908), but the most internationally recognised artist was the sculptor Ivan Meštrović (1883–1962), who created many masterpieces on Croatian themes. Antun Augustinčić (1900–79) was another internationally recognised sculptor – his *Monument to Peace* is outside New York's UN building.

Postwar artists experimented with abstract expressionism, but this period is best remembered for the naïve art movement that began with the 1931 *Zemlja* (Soil) exhibition in Zagreb. Fronted by Ivan Generalić (1914–92) and other peasant painters, the movement was committed to producing art that could be easily understood and appreciated by ordinary people.

Postwar avant-garde art evolved into installation, minimalism, conceptualism and video art. Contemporary Croatian artists worth seeing are Lovro Artuković, whose highly realistic style is contrasted with surreal settings; on the video scene look for Sanja Iveković and Dalibor Martinis. The multimedia works of Andreja Kulunčić and the installations of Sandra Sterle are attracting international notice, while the performances of Slaven Tolj could be called 'extreme art'. Lana Šlezić is a New York–based but Croatian-born photographer whose excellent work is often inspired by Croatia.

Music

Although Croatia has produced many fine classical musicians and composers, its most original musical contribution lies in its rich tradition of folk music. Croatian folk music itself bears many influences, much of them dating back to the Middle Ages, when the Hungarians and the Venetians vied for control of the country.

The instrument most often used in Croatian folk music is the *tamburica*, a three- or five-string mandolin that is plucked or strummed. Introduced by the Turks in the 17th century, the instrument rapidly gained a following in eastern Slavonia and came to be closely identified with Croatian national aspirations. *Tamburica* music predominates at weddings and local festivals.

Vocal music followed the *klapa* tradition. Translated as 'group of people', *klapa* is an outgrowth of church-choir singing. The form is most popular in rural Dalmatia and can involve up to 10 voices singing in harmony about love, tragedy and loss. Traditionally the choirs were all-male, but now women have been getting into the act, although there are very few mixed choirs.

There's a wealth of homegrown talent on Croatia's pop and rock music scene. Some of the most prominent pop, fusion and hip-hop bands are Hladno Pivo (Cold Beer), Pips Chips & Videoclips, TBF, Edo Maajka, Vještice (The Witches), Gustafi, and the deliciously insane Let 3. The fusion of jazz and pop with folk tunes has been a popular musical direction in Croatia, and prominent names on this scene are Tamara Obrovac, a talented singer from Istria, and Mojmir Novaković, formerly the singer of the popular band Legen. The Croatian queen of pop is Severina, famous for her good looks and eventful personal life, which is widely covered by local celebrity and gossip magazines. Gibonni, from Dalmatia, is another massively popular singer; his major influence is Oliver Dragojević, a legendary singer of loveable schmaltz.

Dance

Like the music, Croatian traditional dances are kept alive at local and national festivals. Look for the *drmeš*, a kind of accelerated polka danced by couples in small groups. The *kolo*, a lively Slavic round dance in which men and women alternate in the circle, is accompanied by Roma-style violinists. In Dalmatia, the *poskočica* is also danced by couples creating various patterns.

Literature

Croatia's towering literary figure is 20th-century novelist and playwright Miroslav Krleža (1893–1981). His most popular novels include *The Return of Philip Latinovicz* (1932), which has been translated into English, and *Banners* (1963–65), a multivolume saga about middle-class Croatian life at the turn of the 20th century.

Gold, Frankincense and Myrrh by Slobodan Novak, originally published in Yugoslavia in 1968, has recently been translated into English. It's considered to be one of the pivotal works of 20th-century literature.

A great introduction to contemporary Croatian writers is the collection of short stories *Croatian Nights,* edited by Tony White, Borivoj Radaković and Matt Thorne. The anthology features prominent Croatian writers such as Gordan Nuhanović, Vladimir Arsenijević, Jelena Čarija, Zoran Ferić, Miljenko Jergović and Zorica Radaković. Some contemporary writers have been strongly marked by the implications of Croatian independence. Journalist Alenka Mirković wrote a powerful memoir of the siege of Vukovar. Expat writer Dubravka Ugrešić has been a figure of controversy in Croatia and acclaimed elsewhere. Now living in the Netherlands in self-imposed exile, she is best known for her novels *The Culture of Lies* and *The Ministry of Pain*. Ugrešić (www .dubravkaugresic.com) published *Nobody's Home* in 2007, a book that is part memoir, part travelogue, with stories of travel across Europe and the US. Slavenka Drakulić's *Café Europa – Life After Communism* is an excellent read, detailing the continuing conflict between the pervasive infiltration of Eastern Europe by Western culture, and the reluctance with which the West handles Eastern European culture. Miljenko Jergović, Sarajevo born but living in Croatia, is a witty, poignant writer whose *Sarajevo Marlboro* and *Mama Leone* powerfully conjure up the atmosphere of and life in prewar Yugoslavia.

FOOD & DRINK

If thoughts of Croatian cuisine conjure up images of greasy steaks with a side of boiled potatoes and sauerkraut, think again. While it still holds true to its Eastern European roots and positively pleases meat-happy Balkan palates, Croatian food is a savoury smorgasbord of taste, echoing the varied cultures that have influenced the country over the course of its history. You'll find a sharp divide between the Italian-style cuisine along the coast and the flavours of Hungary, Austria and Turkey in the continental parts.

Most restaurants cluster in the middle of the price spectrum – few are unbelievably cheap and few are exorbitantly expensive. If you're willing to splurge, you can spend hours feasting on slow-food delicacies or savour forward-thinking concoctions created by up-and-coming young chefs.

A restaurant *(restauracija* or *restoran)* is at the top of the food chain, generally presenting a more formal dining experience. A *gostionica* or *konoba* is usually a traditional family-run tavern. A *pivnica* is more like a pub, with a wide choice of beer. A *kavana* is a cafe. Self-service cafeterias are quick, easy and inexpensive, though the quality of the food tends to vary.

The cheapest dishes are pasta and risotto, which can make filling meals. Fish is often priced by weight; an average portion is about 250g. Some restaurants tack on a 10% cover charge, which is *supposed* to be mentioned on the menu.

Breakfast is included in the price of the hotels in this chapter and usually includes a juice drink, bread, cheese, yoghurt, cereal and cold cuts, as well as coffee and tea. Self-caterers can easily get coffee at a cafe and pastries from a bakery.

A load of fruit and vegetables from the local market makes a healthy, cheap picnic lunch. There are plenty of supermarkets in Croatia. If you ask nicely, the person behind the deli counter will usually make a *sir* (cheese) or *pršut* (prosciutto) sandwich, and you only pay the regular price of the ingredients.

Staples & Specialities

Zagreb and northwestern Croatia favour the kind of hearty meat dishes you might find in Vienna. Juicy spit-roasted and baked meat features *janjetina* (lamb), *svinjetina* (pork) and *patka* (duck), often accompanied by *mlinci* (baked noodles) or *pečeni krumpir* (roast potatoes). Meat slow-cooked under *peka* (a domed baking lid) is especially delicious but at many restaurants needs to be ordered in advance. *Purica* (turkey) with *mlinci* is practically an institution on Zagreb and Zagorje menus, along with *zagrebački odrezak* (veal steak stuffed with ham and cheese, then fried in breadcrumbs).

Spicier than in other regions, cuisine in Slavonia uses liberal amounts of paprika and garlic. The Hungarian influence is most prevalent here, as many typical dishes are in fact a version of *gulaš* (goulash). The nearby Drava River provides fresh fish such as carp, pike and perch, which is stewed and served with noodles in a dish known as *fiš paprikaš*. The region's sausages are renowned, especially the paprika-flavoured *kulen*.

Coastal cuisine is typically Mediterranean, using a lot of olive oil, garlic, fresh fish and shellfish, and herbs. Along the coast, look for lightly breaded and fried *lignje* (squid) as a main course. For a special appetiser, try *paški sir*, a pungent hard cheese from the island of Pag. Dalmatian *brodet* (stewed mixed fish served with polenta; also known as *brodetto*) is another regional treat, but it's often only available in two-person portions.

Istrian cuisine has been attracting international foodies for its long gastronomic tradition, fresh foodstuffs and unique specialities. Typical dishes include *maneštra*, a thick vegetable-and-bean soup, *fuži*, hand-rolled pasta often served with truffles or game meat, and *fritaja* (omelette often served with seasonal veggies). Istrian wines and olive oil are highly rated; the tourist board has marked wine and olive routes along which you can visit local growers and taste these nectars from the source. The best seasonal ingredients include the prized white truffles picked in autumn and wild asparagus harvested in spring.

For fast food you can snack on *ćevapčići* (small spicy sausages of minced beef, lamb or pork meat), *ražnjići* (shish kebab), *pljeskavica* (a kind of hamburger) or *burek* (a layered pie filled with meat or cheese).

It's customary to have a small glass of brandy before a meal and to accompany the food with one of Croatia's many wines. Croatians often mix their wine with water, calling it *bevanda*. *Rakija* (brandy) comes in different flavours. The most commonly drunk are *loza* (grape brandy), *šljivovica* (plum brandy) and *travarica* (herbal brandy). Istrian grappa is particularly excellent and ranges in flavour from honey *(medica)* to mistletoe *(biska)*. Other popular drinks include *vinjak* (cognac), *maraschino* (cherry liqueur made in Zadar), *prosecco* (sweet dessert wine) and *pelinkovac* (herbal liqueur). Coffee is served Italian-style, in espresso shots.

Zagreb's Ožujsko *pivo* (beer) is very good, but Karlovačko *pivo* from Karlovac is even better. You'll probably want to practise saying *živjeli!* (cheers!).

Vegetarians & Vegans

Outside major cities like Zagreb, Rijeka, Split and Dubrovnik, vegetarian restaurants are few, but Croatia's vegetables are usually locally grown and quite tasty. *Blitva* (Swiss chard) is a nutritious side dish often served with potatoes. The hearty *štrukli* (baked cheese dumplings) are a good alternative too. Pasta, risotto and pizza are often made from scratch, and lacto-ovo vegetarians will appreciate Croatia's wide variety of cheese. If seafood is part of your diet, you'll be fine.

For a list of Croatian eating and drinking words, see p45.

ENVIRONMENT
The Land

Croatia is just over half the size of Serbia and Montenegro combined in area and population. The republic swings around like a boomerang from the Pannonian plains of Slavonia between the Sava, Drava and Danube rivers, across hilly central Croatia to the Istrian Peninsula, then south through Dalmatia along the rugged Adriatic coast.

The narrow Croatian coastal belt at the foot of the Dinaric Alps is only about 600km long as the crow flies, but it's so indented that the actual length is 1778km. If the 4012km of coastline around the offshore islands is added to the total, the length becomes 5790km. Most of the 'beaches' along this jagged coast consist of slabs of rock sprinkled with naturists. Don't come expecting to find sand, but the waters are sparkling clean, even around large towns.

Croatia's offshore islands are every bit as beautiful as those off the coast of Greece. There are 1185 islands and islets along the tectonically submerged Adriatic coastline, 66 inhabited. The largest are Cres, Krk, Lošinj, Pag and Rab in the north; Dugi Otok in the middle; and Brač, Hvar, Korčula, Mljet and Vis in the south. Most are barren and elongated from northwest to southeast, with high mountains that drop right into the sea.

National Parks

The eight national parks occupy nearly 10% of the country. Brijuni near Pula is the most carefully cultivated park, with well-preserved Mediterranean holm oak forests. The mountainous Risnjak National Park near Delnice, east of Rijeka, is named after one of its inhabitants – the *ris* (lynx).

Dense forests of beech and black pine in the Paklenica National Park near Zadar are home to a number of endemic insects, reptiles and birds. The abundant plant and animal life, including bears, wolves and deer, in the Plitvice Lakes National Park between Zagreb and Zadar has warranted its inclusion on Unesco's list of World Natural Heritage sites. Both Plitvice Lakes and Krka National Parks (near Šibenik) feature a dramatic series of cascades and incredible turquoise lakes.

The 101 stark and rocky islands of the Kornati Archipelago and National Park make it the largest in the Mediterranean. The island of Mljet near Korčula also contains a forested national park, and the North Velebit National Park includes Croatia's longest mountain range.

Environmental Issues

The lack of heavy industry in Croatia has left the country largely free of industrial pollution, but its forests are under threat from acid rain from neighbouring countries. The dry summers and brisk *maestral* (strong, steady westerly winds) pose substantial fire hazards along the coast. Waste disposal is a pressing problem in Croatia, with insufficient and poorly regulated disposal sites.

Istria has recently seen the building of the Danish-owned Rockwool International, the world's leading producer of the mineral fibre rock wool. Some of the region's environmental groups have accused the factory of threatening to pollute one of Istria's most fertile and wildlife-rich valleys, just under Učka National Park. Its construction was halted by protests and inspections several times, but the factory is now in operation.

Croatia came into conflict with the EU in late 2007 and early 2008 over Europe's fishing laws. The country had set up a law in 2003 that protected its fishing zone from foreign fishing fleets, with the exception of EU countries. According to the Croatian government, however, the stocks are being depleted by Italy's large fishing fleet – the government says that Italy's annual catch of 200,000 tonnes of fish is 10 times the size of Croatia's own – and the government banned EU members from fishing in the Adriatic. The EU has responded by stating that refusing access to member states could affect Croatia's plans to join the EU; the debate was still going on at the time of writing.

Wildlife

Deer are plentiful in the dense forests of Risnjak, as are brown bears, wild cats and lynx. Occasionally a wolf or wild boar may appear but only rarely. Plitvice Lakes National Park, however, is an important refuge for wolves. A rare sea otter is also protected in Plitvice as well as in Krka National Park.

The griffon vulture, with a wing span of 2.6m, has a permanent colony on Cres Island, and Paklenica National Park is rich in peregrine falcons, goshawks, sparrow hawks, buzzards and owls. Krka National Park is an important migration route and winter habitat for marsh birds such as herons, wild duck, geese, cranes, rare golden eagles and short-toed eagles. Kopački Rit swamp near Osijek in eastern Croatia is an extremely important bird refuge, but its status as a visit-worthy place is vague – there are still mines there.

Two venomous snakes are endemic in Paklenica – the nose-horned viper and the European adder – and the nonvenomous leopard snake, four-lined snake, grass snake and snake lizard can also be found in Krka National Park.

ZAGREB

☎ 01 / pop 780,000

Everyone knows about Croatia, its coast, beaches and islands, but a mention of the country's capital still draws confused questions of whether 'it's nice' or 'worth going to for a weekend'. Well, here it is, once and for all: yes, Zagreb is a great destination, weekend or week-long. There's lots of culture, arts, music, architecture, nightlife, gastronomy and all the other things that make a quality capital. Admittedly, it doesn't register highly on a nightlife Richter scale, but it does have an ever-developing art and music scene and a growing influx of fun-seeking travellers.

Zagreb is made for strolling the streets, drinking coffee in the almost permanently full cafes, popping into museums and galleries, and enjoying the theatres, concerts, cinema and music. It's a year-round outdoor city; in spring and summer everyone scurries to Lake Jarun in the southwest to swim, boat or dance the night away in a lakeside disco, and in autumn and winter Zagrebians go skiing at Mt Medvednica, only a tram ride away, or hiking in nearby Samobor.

Visually, Zagreb is a mixture of straight-laced Austro-Hungarian architecture and rough-around-the-edges socialist structures. Its character is a sometimes uneasy combination of the same two elements: try as they may, the frequenters of Zagreb's elegant galleries, high-class restaurants and alternative art and music venues cannot quite ignore the vast turbo folk crowds, attesting to the city's – and the country's – lasting struggle between perceived Central European sophistication and Balkan 'savagery'. But perhaps therein lies much of its charm – the mixture of and the schism between these two traits have given Zagreb a personality all of its own.

HISTORY

Medieval Zagreb developed from the 11th to the 13th centuries in the twin villages of Kaptol and Gradec, which make up the city's hilly old town. Kaptol grew around St Stephen's Cathedral (now renamed the Cathedral of the Assumption of the Blessed Virgin Mary) and Gradec centred on St Mark's Church. The two hilltop administrations were bitter and often warring rivals until a common threat in the form of Turkish invaders emerged in the 15th century. The two communities merged and became Zagreb, capital of the small portion of Croatia that hadn't fallen to the Turks in the 16th century. As the Turkish threat receded in the 18th century, the town expanded and the population grew. It was the centre of intellectual and political life under the Austro-Hungarian Empire and became capital of the Independent State of Croatia in 1941 after the German invasion. The 'independent state' was in fact a Nazi puppet regime in the hands of Ante Pavelić and the Ustaša movement, even though most Zagrebians supported Tito's Partisans.

In postwar Yugoslavia Zagreb took second place to Belgrade but continued expanding. The area south of the Sava River developed into a new district, Novi Zagreb, replete with the glum residential blocks that were a hallmark of postwar Eastern European architecture. Zagreb has been capital of Croatia since 1991, when the country became independent.

ORIENTATION

The city is divided into Lower Zagreb, where most shops, restaurants, hotels and businesses are located, and Upper Zagreb, defined by the two hills of Kaptol and Gradec. As you come out of the train station, you'll see a series of parks and pavilions directly in front of you and the twin neo-Gothic towers of the cathedral in Kaptol in the distance. Trg Jelačića, beyond the northern end of the parks, is the main city square of Lower Zagreb. A bus runs from the airport to the bus station (see p192). The bus station is 1km east of the train station. Trams 2 and 6 run from the bus station to the train station, with tram 6 continuing to Trg Jelačića.

INFORMATION
Bookshops

Algoritam (Gajeva 1; ⊗ 8am-7pm Mon-Fri, 9am-5pm Sat) A wide selection of books and magazines to choose from in English, French, German, Italian and Croatian.

Emergency

Police station (☎ 45 63 311; Petrinjska 30) Assists foreigners with visa problems.

Internet Access

Sublink (☎ 48 11 329; Teslina 12; per hr 15KN; ⊗ 9am-10pm Mon-Sat, 3-10pm Sun) Was the city's first cybercafe and remains the best.

Laundry

If you're staying in private accommodation you can usually arrange with the owner to do your laundry, which would be cheaper than the two options listed below (5kg of laundry will cost about 65KN).

CROATIA

CROATIA

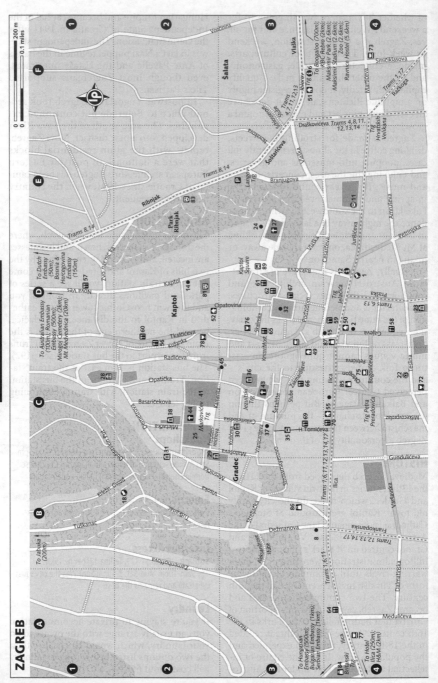

ZAGREB

0 200 m
0 0.1 miles

To Jabuka (200m)

Tuškanac

To Hungarian Embassy (500m); Bulgarian Embassy (1km); Serbian Embassy (1km)

To Hotel Ilica (250m); H&M (2km)

To Australian Embassy (100m); Romanian Embassy (50m); Mirogoj Cemetery (2km); Mt Medvednica (20km)

To Dutch Embassy (500m); Bosnia & Hercegovina Embassy (150m)

Nova Ves

Park Ribnjak

Šalata

Kaptol

Kaptol Square

Opatovina

Gradec

Markovićev Trg

Matoševa

H Tomićeva

Trg Petra Preradovića

Trams 1, 6, 11, 12, 13, 14, 17

Trams 1, 6, 11

Trams 1, 2, 13, 14, 17

Trams 6, 13

Trams 4, 7, 11, 12, 13

Trams 4, 8, 11, 12, 13, 14

Trams 8, 14

To Bogaljevo (700m); KBC Rebro (2km); Maksimir Park (2.6km); Maksimir Stadium (2.6km); Zoo (2.6km); Ravnice Hostel (5.6km)

Draškovićeva.

Britanski Trg

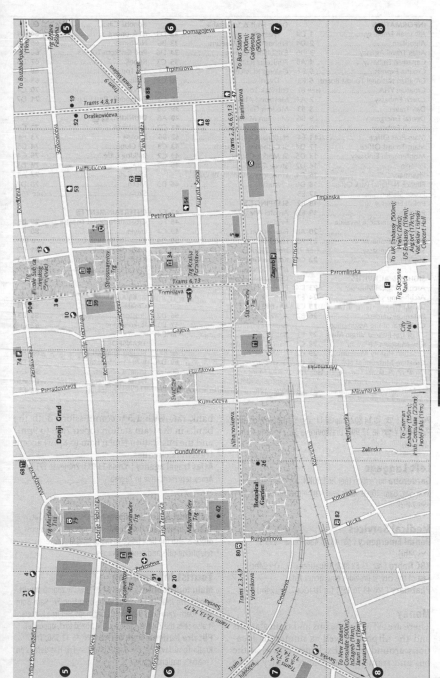

CROATIA

INFORMATION		
Albanian Embassy	**1**	D4
Algoritam	**2**	D4
Atlas Travel Agency	**3**	D5
Canadian Embassy	**4**	A5
Croatia Express	**5**	E7
Croatian National Tourist Board	**6**	F3
Croatian YHA	(see 8)	
Czech Embassy	**7**	A7
Dali Travel	**8**	B3
Dental Emergency	**9**	B6
French Embassy	**10**	D5
Main Post Office	**11**	E4
Main Tourist Office	**12**	D4
Montenegrin Embassy	**13**	D5
Petecin	**14**	D2
Pharmacy	**15**	D4
Plitvice National Park Office	**16**	D6
Police Station	**17**	E5
Polish Embassy	**18**	B2
Predom	**19**	F5
Savez Organizacija Invalida Hrvatske	**20**	A6
Slovakian Embassy	**21**	A5
Slovenian Embassy	(see 7)	
Sublink	**22**	C4

SIGHTS & ACTIVITIES		
Archaeological Museum	**23**	D4
Archbishop's Palace	**24**	E3
Banski Dvori	**25**	C2
Botanical Garden	**26**	B7
Cathedral of the Assumption of the Blessed Virgin Mary	**27**	E3
City Museum	**28**	C1
Croatian History Museum	**29**	C2
Croatian Museum of Naïve Art	**30**	C3
Croatian National Theatre	(see 79)	
Croatian Natural History Museum	**31**	C2

Dolac Fruit & Vegetable Market	**32**	D3
Ethnographic Museum	**33**	B6
Exhibition Pavilion	**34**	D6
Funicular Railway	**35**	C3
Galerija Klovićevi Dvori	**36**	C3
Lotrščak Tower	**37**	C3
Meštrović Atelier	**38**	C2
Modern Gallery	**39**	D5
Museum Mimara	**40**	A6
National Assembly	**41**	C2
National Library	**42**	B6
St Catherine's Church	**43**	C3
St Mark's Church	**44**	C2
Stone Gate	**45**	C3
Strossmayer Gallery of Old Masters	**46**	D5

SLEEPING ☆		
Arcotel Allegra	**47**	F7
Evistas	**48**	F6
Fulir Hostel	**49**	C3
Hotel Dubrovnik	**50**	D4
Hotel Jadran	**51**	F3
Krovovi Grada	**52**	D2
Never Stop	**53**	E5
Omladinski Hostel	**54**	E6
Pansion Jägerhorn	**55**	C4

EATING 🍴		
Agava	**56**	D2
Baltazar	**57**	D1
Boban	**58**	D4
Fruit & Vegetable Market	(see 84)	
Gavrilović	**59**	D4
Ivica i Marica	**60**	D2
Kaptolska Klet	**61**	D3
Kerempuh	**62**	D3

Konoba Čiho	**63**	E6
Makronova	**64**	A4
Nocturno	**65**	D3
Pod Gričkom Topom	**66**	C3
Rubelj	**67**	D3
Tip Top	**68**	B5
Vallis Aurea	**69**	C3
Vincek	**70**	C4
Zinfandel's Restaurant	**71**	D7

DRINKING 🍷 🍸		
Apartman	**72**	C4
Booksa	**73**	F4
BP Club	**74**	C5
Bulldog Café	**75**	C4
Cica	**76**	D3
Eli's Café	**77**	A4
Melin	**78**	D2
Škola	(see 75)	

ENTERTAINMENT 🎭		
Croatian National Theatre	**79**	B5
David	**80**	B7
Kazalište Komedija	(see 85)	
Komedija Theatre	**81**	D2
KSET	**82**	B8
Purgeraj	**83**	E2

SHOPPING 🛍		
Antiques Market	**84**	A4
Croata	**85**	C4
Prostor	**86**	B3
Rukotvorine	**87**	D4

TRANSPORT		
Budget Rent-a-Car	**88**	F6
Buses to Mirogoj	**89**	D3
Croatia Airlines	**90**	D5
Hertz	**91**	A6
Hrvatski Autoklub	**92**	F5

Petecin (☎ 48 14 802; Kaptol 11; ☾ 8am-8pm Mon-Fri)
Predom (☎ 46 12 990; Draškovićeva 31; ☾ 7am-7pm Mon-Fri)

Left Luggage
Garderoba bus station (per hr 1.20KN; ☾ 5am-10pm Mon-Sat, 6am-10pm Sun); train station (per hr 1.20KN; ☾ 24hr)

Medical Services
Dental Emergency (☎ 48 28 488; Perkovčeva 3; ☾ 24hr)
KBC Rebro (☎ 23 88 888; Kišpatićeva 12; ☾ 24hr) East of the city, it provides emergency aid.
Pharmacy (☎ 48 16 159; Trg Jelačića 2; ☾ 24hr)

Money
There are ATMs at the bus and train stations and the airport as well as numerous locations around town. Exchange offices at the bus and train stations change money at the

bank rate with 1.5% commission. Both the banks in the train station (open 7am to 9pm) and the bus station (open 6am to 8pm) accept travellers cheques.
Atlas travel agency (☎ 48 13 933; Zrinjevac 17) The Amex representative in Zagreb.

Post
Main post office (Branimirova 4; ☾ 24hr Mon-Sat, 1pm-midnight Sun) Holds poste-restante mail. This post office is also the best place to make long-distance telephone calls and send packages.

Tourist Information
Main tourist office (☎ 48 14 051; www.zagreb-tourist info.hr; Trg Jelačića 11; ☾ 8.30am-8pm Mon-Fri, 9am-5pm Sat, 10am-2pm Sun) Distributes city maps and free leaflets. It also sells the Zagreb Card (see the boxed text, opposite).
Plitvice National Park Office (☎ 46 13 586; Trg Kralja Tomislava 19; ☾ 9am-5pm Mon-Fri) Has details on Croatia's national parks.

Travel Agencies

Croatia Express (☎ 49 22 237; www.zug.hr; Trg Kralja Tomislava 17; ☯ 9.30am-7pm Mon-Fri, 9am-3pm Sat) At this office opposite the train station you can change money, make train reservations, rent cars, buy air tickets and ferry tickets, and book hotels around the country.
Dali Travel (☎ 48 47 472; travelsection@hfhs.hr; Dežmanova 9; ☯ 9am-5pm Mon-Fri) The travel branch of the Croatian YHA can provide information on HI hostels throughout Croatia and make advance bookings.

SIGHTS

As the oldest part of Zagreb, the Upper Town offers landmark buildings and churches from the earlier centuries of Zagreb's history. The Lower Town has the city's most interesting art museums and fine examples of 19th- and 20th-century architecture.

Upper Town
KAPTOL

Zagreb's colourful **Dolac** (☯ 6am-3pm daily) is just north of Trg Jelačića. It's the buzzing centre of Zagreb's daily activity, with traders coming from all over Croatia to flog their products here. The Dolac has been heaving since the 1930s, when the city authorities set up a market space on the 'border' between the Upper and Lower towns. The main part of the market is on an elevated square; the street level has indoor stalls selling meat and dairy products, and there are flower stands a little further towards the square. The stalls at the northern end of the market are packed with locally produced honey, handmade ornaments and supercheap food stands.

The twin neo-Gothic spires of the 1899 **Cathedral of the Assumption of the Blessed Virgin**

Mary (Katedrala Marijina Uznešenja; formerly known as St Stephen's Cathedral) are nearby. Elements of the medieval cathedral on this site, destroyed by an earthquake in 1880, can be seen inside, including 13th-century frescos, Renaissance pews, marble altars and a baroque pulpit. The baroque **Archbishop's Palace** surrounds the cathedral, as do 16th-century fortifications constructed when Zagreb was threatened by the Turks.

GRADEC

From Radićeva 5, off Trg Jelačića, a pedestrian walkway called stube Ivana Zakmardija leads to the **Lotrščak Tower** (Kula Lotrščak; ☎ 48 51 768; admission 10KN; ☯ 11am-7pm Tue-Sun) and a **funicular railway** (one way 3KN; ☯ 6.30am-9pm) built in 1888, which connects the Lower and Upper Towns. The tower has a sweeping 360-degree view of the city. To the east is the baroque **St Catherine's Church** (Crkva Svete Katarine), with Jezuitski trg beyond. The **Galerija Klovićevi Dvori** (☎ 48 51 926; Jezuitski trg 4; adult/student 40/20KN; ☯ 11am-7pm Tue-Sun) is Zagreb's premier exhibition hall, where superb art shows are staged. Further north and to the east is the 13th-century **Stone Gate**, with a painting of the Virgin, which escaped the devastating fire of 1731.

Gothic **St Mark's Church** (Crkva Svetog Marka; ☎ 48 51 611; Markov trg; ☯ 11am-4pm & 5.30-7pm) marks the centre of Gradec. Inside are works by Ivan Meštrović, Croatia's most famous modern sculptor. On the eastern side of St Mark's is Croatia's 1908 **National Assembly** (Sabor).

West of the church is the 18th-century **Banski Dvori**, the presidential palace, with guards at the door in red ceremonial uniform. Between April and September there is a noon changing of the guard ceremony at the weekend.

Not far from the palace is the former **Meštrović Atelier** (☎ 48 51 123; Mletačka 8; adult/concession 30/15KN; ☯ 10am-6pm Tue-Fri, to 2pm Sat), now housing an excellent collection of some 100 sculptures, drawings, lithographs and furniture created by the artist. There are several other museums nearby. The best is the **City Museum** (Muzej Grada Zagreba; ☎ 48 51 364; Opatička 20; adult/concession 20/10KN; ☯ 10am-6pm Tue-Fri, to 1pm Sat & Sun), with a scale model of old Gradec, atmospheric background music, and interactive exhibits that fascinate kids. Summaries in English and German are in each room of the museum, which is in the former Convent of

---

ZAGREB CARD

If you're in Zagreb for a day or three, getting the Zagreb Card is a pretty good way to save money. It costs 60/90KN for 24/72 hours and with it you get free travel on all public transport, a 50% discount on museum and gallery entries, plus discounts in some bars and restaurants, car rental etc. A booklet lists all the places that offer discounts, or check www.zagrebcard.fivestars .hr for more details. The card is sold at the main tourist office and many hostels, hotels, bars and shops.

CROATIA

ZAGREB IN TWO DAYS

Start your day with a stroll through Strossmayerov Trg, Zagreb's oasis of greenery. While you're there, take a look at the **Strossmayer Gallery of Old Masters** (below) and then walk to Trg Jelačića, the city's centre. Head up to **Kaptol Square** (p185) for a look at the **Cathedral of the Assumption of the Blessed Virgin Mary** (p185), the centre of Zagreb's (and Croatia's) religious life. While you're in the Upper Town, pick up some fruit at the **Dolac fruit and vegetable market** (p185). Then, get to know the work of Croatia's best sculptor at **Meštrović Atelier** (p185) and take in a contemporary-art exhibition at **Galerija Klovićevi Dvori** (p185). See the lie of the city from the top of **Lotrščak Tower** (p185). The evening is best spent having a drink at lounge bar **Škola** (p190) or bar-crawling along **Tkalčićeva** (p190).

On the second day, tour the Lower Town museums, reserving a good two hours for the **Museum Mimara** (below). Lunch at **Tip Top** (p189). Early evening is best at **Trg Petra Preradovića** (p190) before dining at one of the **Lower Town restaurants** (p189) and sampling some of Zagreb's **nightlife** (p190).

St Claire (1650). There's also the lively and colourful **Croatian Museum of Naïve Art** (Hrvatski Muzej Naivne Umjetnosti; ☎ 48 51 911; Ćirilometodska 3; adult/concession 10/5KN; ☼ 10am-6pm Tue-Fri, to 1pm Sat & Sun) and the **Croatian Natural History Museum** (Hrvatski Prirodoslovni Muzej; ☎ 48 51 700; Demetrova 1; adult/concession 15/7KN; ☼ 10am-5pm Tue-Fri, to 1pm Sat & Sun), which has a collection of prehistoric tools and bones plus exhibits on the evolution of plant and animal life in Croatia.

Lower Town

There are four museums in the parks between the train station and Trg Jelačića. The yellow **exhibition pavilion** (1897) across the park from the station presents changing contemporary-art exhibitions. The second building north, also in the park, houses the **Strossmayer Gallery of Old Masters** (Strossmayerova Galerija Starih Majstora; ☎ 48 95 115; www.mdc.hr/strossmayer; Zrinjevac 11; adult/concession 10/5KN; ☼ 10am-1pm & 5-7pm Tue, 10am-1pm Wed-Sun). When it's closed you can still enter the interior courtyard to see the Baška Slab (1102) from the island of Krk, one of the oldest inscriptions in the Croatian language.

The fascinating **Archaeological Museum** (Arheološki Muzej; ☎ 48 73 101; www.amz.hr; Trg Nikole Šubića Zrinjskog 19; adult/concession 20/10KN; ☼ 10am-5pm Tue-Fri, to 1pm Sat & Sun) has a wide-ranging display of artefacts from prehistoric times through to the medieval period. Behind the museum is a garden of Roman sculpture that is turned into a pleasant open-air cafe in the summer.

The **Modern Gallery** (Moderna Galerija; ☎ 49 22 368; Andrije Hebranga 1; adult/concession 20/10KN; ☼ 10am-6pm Tue-Sat, to 1pm Sun) presents temporary exhibitions that offer an excellent chance to catch up with the latest in Croatian painting.

The **Museum Mimara** (Muzej Mimara; ☎ 48 28 100; Rooseveltov trg 5; adult/concession 20/15KN; ☼ 10am-5pm Tue, Wed, Fri & Sat, to 7pm Thu, to 2pm Sun) houses a diverse collection amassed by Ante Topić Mimara and donated to Croatia. Housed in a neo-Renaissance palace, the collection includes icons, glassware, sculpture, oriental art, and works by renowned painters such as Rembrandt, Velázquez, Raphael and Degas.

The neobaroque **Croatian National Theatre** (☎ 48 28 532; Trg Maršala Tita 15; ☼ box office 10am-1pm & 5-7.30pm Mon-Fri, to 1pm Sat, 30 min before performances Sun) dates from 1895 and has Ivan Meštrović's sculpture *Fountain of Life* (1905) in front. The **Ethnographic Museum** (Etnografski Muzej; ☎ 48 26 220; Trg Mažuranićev 14; adult/concession 15/10KN; ☼ 10am-6pm Tue-Thu, to 1pm Fri-Sun) has a large collection of Croatian folk costumes, accompanied by English captions. To the south is the art nouveau **National Library** (1907). Laid out in 1890, the **Botanical Garden** (Mihanovićeva; admission free; ☼ 9am-7pm Tue-Sun) has 10,000 species of plant, including 1800 tropical flora specimens. The landscaping has created restful corners and paths that seem a world away from bustling Zagreb.

Out of Town

A 20-minute ride north of the city centre on bus 106 from the cathedral takes you to **Mirogoj** (Medvednica; ☼ 6am-10pm), one of the most beautiful cemeteries in Europe. The cemetery was designed in 1876 by one of Croatia's finest architects, Herman Bollé, who also created numerous buildings around Zagreb. The sculptured and artfully designed tombs lie beyond a majestic arcade topped by a string of cupolas.

Another suburban delight is **Maksimir Park** (Maksimirska; ☺ 9am-dusk), a peaceful wooded enclave covering 18 hectares; it is easily accessible by trams 4, 7, 11 and 12. Opened to the public in 1794, it was the first public promenade in southeastern Europe. There's also a modest **zoo** (adult/child under 8 20/10KN; ☺ 9am-8pm).

TOURS
The main tourist office sells tickets for two-hour walking tours (95KN) which operate Monday through Thursday leaving from Trg Jelačića, as well as three-hour bus and walking tours (150KN) that operate Friday through Sunday, leaving from the Arcotel Allegra hotel.

FESTIVALS & EVENTS
During odd-numbered years in April there's the **Zagreb Biennale** (www.biennale -zagreb.hr), Croatia's most important classical-music event. Zagreb also hosts the gay **Queer Zagreb FM Festival** (www.queerzagreb.org), a **festival of animated films** (www.animafest.hr) during even-numbered years in June, and a **film festival** (www.zagrebfilmfestival.com) from 19 to 24 October. Croatia's largest international fairs are the Zagreb spring (mid-April) and autumn (mid-September) grand trade fairs. Zagreb's highest profile music event is **Vip INmusic Festival** (www.vipinmusicfestival.com), a two-day extravaganza on 3 and 4 June, taking place on Jarun Lake's island. In July and August the **Zagreb Summer Festival** presents a cycle of concerts and theatre performances on open stages in the Upper Town. For a complete listing of Zagreb events, see www.zagreb-convention.hr.

SLEEPING
Zagreb's accommodation scene has been undergoing a small but noticeable change with the arrival of some of Europe's budget airlines: the budget end of the market (so far rather fledgling) has started to get a pulse. Although the new hostels cater mainly to the backpacker crowd, it's a good beginning. For midrangers and those wanting more privacy and a homely feel, there are private rooms and apartments, arranged through agencies. The city's business and high-end hotels are in full flow, thanks to Zagreb's role as an international conference hotspot.

Prices stay the same in all seasons, but be prepared for a 20% surcharge if you arrive during a festival, especially the autumn fair.

If you intend to stay in a private house or apartment, try not to arrive on Sunday because most of the agencies will be closed. Prices for doubles run from about 300KN and apartments start at 400KN per night for a studio. Try **Evistas** (☎ 48 39 554; evistas@zg.htnet.hr; Augusta Šenoe 28; s from 200KN, d 250KN; ☺ 9am-1.30pm & 3-8pm Mon-Fri, 9.30am-5pm Sat), recommended by the tourist office; **InZagreb** (☎ 65 23 201; www.inzagreb .com; Remetinečka 13; apt per night €65-86), with great, centrally located apartments (minimum two-night stay; price includes bike rental and pick up and drop off from railway and/or bus station); and **Never Stop** (Nemoj Stati; ☎ 48 73 225; www .nest.hr; Boškovićeva 7a; ☺ 9am-5pm Mon-Fri), which has apartments in the centre of town (minimum three-night stay; contact for prices).

Upper & Lower Town
our pick **Arcotel Allegra** (☎ 46 96 000; www.arcotel .at/allegra; Branimirova 29; d €152-162; P ⊠ ⊠ 🖳) The Arcotel Allegra is Zagreb's first designer hotel, with airy, elegant rooms and a plush, marble-and-exotic-fish reception. The bed linen is covetable and soft and the bed throws are printed with the faces of Kafka, Kahlo, Freud, Lorca and numerous other iconic personalities. There's a DVD player in each room and the hotel has movies you can borrow. The top floor has gym, sauna and great views of the city. The on-site Radicchio restaurant is good and Joe's Bar's hot on Latino music.

Hotel Ilica (☎ 37 77 522; www.hotel-ilica.hr; Ilica 102; s/d/tr/apt 399/499/599/849KN; P 🌐) A great central option, with rooms ranging from super kitsch to lushly decorous – there are gilded motifs, plush beds, wall-long paintings and lots of red. The bathrooms are well equipped and the setting is quiet. Trams 6, 11 and 12 stop right outside the entrance, or walk down buzzy Ilica for 15 minutes.

Pansion Jägerhorn (☎ 48 33 877; www.hotel-pansion -jaegerhorn.hr; Ilica 14; s/d/apt 590/690/890KN; 🌐) A great little hotel that sits right underneath Gradec and Lotrščak Tower, the 'Hunter's Horn' (don't snigger!) has spacious, classic rooms with good views (you can gaze over Gradec from the top-floor attic rooms) and friendly service. The downstairs restaurant serves wild game.

Hotel Dubrovnik (☎ 48 73 555; www.hotel-dubrovnik .t-com.hr; Gajeva 1; s/d from 875/1350KN; 🌐) Right in the centre of town, this glass wannabe New York building is a real city landmark. It buzzes with business travellers who love being at the centre of the action. The 260 rooms are elegant and have all you need, and the style is old-school classic. Try to get a view of Jelačića and watch Zagreb pass by under your window.

Buzzbackpackers (☎ 23 20 267; www.buzzbackpackers.com; Babukićeva 1B; dm from 120KN, d from 400KN; 🄳 🖳) Slicker than the Fulir but a bit further out, Buzzbackpackers is another great-value newcomer. It's clean and the rooms are bright, and there's wi-fi access, free internet, a shiny kitchen, a laundry service (at a charge), and a BBQ area for the summer months. Take tram 4 or 9 from the main train station to Heinzelova stop; it's a short walk from there (check the website for detailed directions).

Fulir Hostel (☎ 48 30 882; www.fulir-hostel.com; Radićeva 3a; dm low-high 100-140KN; 🖳) Right in the centre of town and seconds away from the bustle of Jelačića and bars on Tkalčićeva, the Fulir has 16 beds, friendly owners, self-catering (perfect for its proximity to Dolac market), a DVD-packed common room, satellite TV and free internet. Opened in summer 2006, it's a popular spot for shoestring travellers, so book in advance.

Krovovi Grada (☎ 48 14 189; Opatovina 33; s/d/tr 200/300/400KN) Possibly the most charming of Zagreb's central options, this place is right in the Upper Town. The restored old house is set back from the street and has creaky-floor rooms with pieces of vintage furniture and grandma blankets. There are two large apartments with shared bathrooms that can sleep eight.

Hotel Jadran (☎ 45 53 777; www.hup-zagreb.hr; Vlaška 50; s/d 517/717KN; 🄳) This six-storey hotel has a superb location only minutes from Trg Jelačića. The 48 rooms are laid out in a cheery, modern style and the service is good and friendly.

Omladinski Hostel (☎ 48 41 261; www.hfhs.hr; Petrinjska 77; 6-/3-bed dm 103/113KN, s/d 193/256KN) A bit of a sad place that although recently refurbished maintains the old gloomy feel. But the rooms are sparse and clean, and it's relatively central and the cheapest in town.

Out of Town

Hotel Fala (☎/fax 61 94 498; www.hotel-fala-zg.hr; Trnjanska 18; s/d 350/495KN; 🄿 🄳) The rooms are small and frill-free, and it takes a tram ride or a 20-minute walk to get from here to the centre, but it's all neat and clean. Take tram 5 or 13 to Lisinski.

Ravnice Hostel (☎/fax 23 32 325; www.ravnice-youth-hostel.hr; Ravnice 38d; dm 125KN; 🖳) Quite far out of the centre, this place is possibly the weakest link in the hostel choices in Zagreb due to its location – it's a good 45-minute hike from the centre or a 20-minute tram ride (take tram 4, 7, 11 or 12 and get off at the Ravnice stop). Having said that, the quiet, residential area, past Maksimir park, is quite lovely. The rooms are clean but spartan, there's a big kitchen downstairs where tea and coffee are free, and the nice garden has ping-pong tables for your entertainment. The internet is charged at 16KN per hour, laundry 50KN per load and (oddly) you have to pay 7KN for your locker.

EATING

You'll have to love Croatian and (below par) Italian food to enjoy Zagreb's restaurants, but new places are branching out to include Japanese and other world cuisines. The biggest move is towards elegantly presented haute cuisine at haute prices.

You can pick up excellent fresh produce at Dolac market (p185). There's also a **fruit and vegetable market** (🕥 7am-3pm) on Britanski trg.

Kaptol

our pick Kerempuh (☎ 48 19 000; Kaptol 3; mains 50-70KN) Overlooking Dolac market, this is a fabulous place to taste a) Croatian cuisine cooked well and simply and b) the market's ingredients on your plate. The daily set menu changes, well, daily, and the dishes are decided on in the morning, when the chef gets that day's freshest ingredients from Dolac. Get an outside table and enjoy the excellent food and market views.

Baltazar (☎ 46 66 999; www.restoran-baltazar.hr; Nova Ves 4; mains from 120KN; 🕥 Mon-Sat) Meat – duck, lamb, pork, beef and turkey – are grilled and prepared the Zagorje and Slavonia way in this upmarket old timer, and there's a good choice of local wines. The summer terrace is a great place to dine under the stars.

Agava (☎ 48 29 826; Tkalčićeva 39; mains 100-120KN) Right on Tkalčićeva, this is a smart and sophisticated place for smart and sophisticated people. The food ranges from starters such as swordfish *carpaccio* (50KN) to mains of steak and truffle (120KN), while the delectable risottos and pastas feature seafood seared in cognac (60KN). The wine list is good, with plenty of Istrian and Slavonian choices.

Kaptolska Klet (☎ 48 14 838; Kaptol 5; mains from 70KN; **V**) This friendly restaurant is comfortable for everyone from solo diners to groups of noisy backpackers. There's a huge outdoor terrace and a brightly lit beer hall–style interior. Although famous for its Zagreb specialities such as grilled meats and homemade sausages, it also turns out a nice platter of grilled vegetables and a vegetable loaf.

Ivica i Marica (☎ 48 17 321; Tkalčićeva 70; mains from 40KN; **V**) Based on the Brothers Grimm story of Hansel and Gretel, this little restaurant–cake shop is made to look like the 'food house' from the tale, with waiting staff clad in traditional costume. It's not exactly veggie, but it does have a decent range of veggie and fish dishes, plus meatier fare. The ice creams and cakes are good too.

Rubelj (☎ 48 18 777; www.rubelj-grill.hr; Tržnica Mala Terasa; mains from 25KN) One of the many Rubeljs across town, this Dolac branch is a great place for a quick portion of *ćevapi*. And though none are as tasty as those in neighbouring BiH (the spiritual home of the *ćevap*), these are Zagreb's best.

Gradec
Vallis Aurea (☎ 48 31 305; Tomićeva 4; mains from 30KN) This is a true local eatery that has some of the best home cooking you'll find in town, so it's no wonder that it's chock-a-block at lunchtime. Taste the Dalmatian staple *pašticada* (beef stew) or the slightly spicy beans, and accompany either with some house red. Right by the lower end of the funicular.

Pod Gričkom Topom (☎ 48 33 607; Stube Zakmardijeve 5; mains from 90KN) Tucked away by a leafy path below the Upper Town, this restaurant has a somewhat self-conscious charm, but it has an outdoor terrace and good Croatian meat-based specialities. It's a great place to hole up on a snowy winter evening or dine under the stars in the summer months.

Lower Town
our pick **Tip Top** (☎ 48 30 349; Gundulićeva 18; mains from 35KN) Oh, how we love Tip Top and its waiting staff that still sport old socialist uniforms and the scowling faces that eventually turn to smiles. But how we mostly love the excellent Dalmatian food. Every day has its own set menu (in addition to à la carte), but Thursday is particularly delicious with the octopus *brodet* (octopus stewed in red wine, garlic and herbs). Owned and run by Korčulans, you'll find that island's wines on offer – the wines that were no doubt enjoyed by Tin Ujević, Tip Top's once most loyal customer.

Zinfandel's Restaurant (☎ 45 66 666; www.regent hotels.com; Mihanovićeva 1; mains 90–200KN; ☷ Mon-Sat; **V**) The tastiest, most creative dishes in town are served with polish in the dining room of the Regent Esplanade Zagreb. For a simpler but still delicious dining experience, head to Le Bistro, also in the Esplanade. Don't miss the *štrukli* (baked cheese dumplings).

Boban (☎ 48 11 549; Gajeva 9; mains 40–60KN; **V**) Italian is the name of the game in this cellar restaurant that's owned by Croatian World Cup star Zvonimir Boban. Devised by an Italian chef (who hasn't quite instilled the concept of *pasta al dente* into the local chefs), the menu is a robust range of pastas, salads and meats. It's a popular lunch and dinner spot; the upstairs cafe's terrace attracts Zagreb's youngsters.

Konoba Čiho (☎ 48 17 060; Pavla Hatza 15; mains from 55KN; ☷ Mon-Sat) Another old-school Dalmatian *konoba*, where, downstairs, you can get fish and seafood grilled or stewed just the way the regulars like it. Try the wide range of *rakija*.

Makronova (☎ 48 47 115; www.makronova.com; Ilica 72; mains 80–120KN; ☷ Mon-Sat; **V**) This macrobiotic restaurant is elegant and peaceful and more than welcoming for those of the vegan persuasion. It's part of a whole healthy emporium – there's a health-food shop downstairs, shiatsu treatment, yoga classes and feng-shui courses.

Nocturno (☎ 48 13 394; Skalinska 4; mains 20–50KN; **V**) Right on the sloping street underneath the cathedral, this place is very popular for its Italian menu and lively outdoor terrace. There are all the usual pizzas, and some good salads too, which will gladden vegetarian hearts. The risottos are pretty huge, so order one of those if you're starving.

Quick eats:
Gavrilović (Trg Jelačića; ☷ closed Sun) Pick up local cheese, smoked meat and cold cuts.
Vincek (☎ 45 50 834; Ilica 18) This *slastičarna* (pastry shop) serves the best ice cream in town. The long lines as soon as summer starts attest to its popularity.

CROATIA

DRINKING

The architecture may be sober but the nightlife definitely is not, especially as the weather warms up and Zagrebians take to the streets. In the Upper Town, the chic Tkalčićeva is throbbing with bars. In the Lower Town, Trg Petra Preradovića is the most popular spot for street performers and occasional bands in mild weather. One of the nicest ways to see Zagreb is to join in on the *špica* – the Saturday morning and pre-lunch coffee drinking on the many terraces along Preradovićeva and Tkalčićeva.

ourpick Booksa (☎ 46 16 124; www.booksa.hr; Martićeva 14d; ☻ 9am-11pm Tue-Sun) Bookworms and poets, writers and performers, oddballs and artists, and anyone on the creative side of things in Zagreb comes to chat and drink coffee, buy books, and hear readings at this lovely bookshop. There are English-language readings here too, so check the website.

ourpick Škola (☎ 48 28 197; www.skolaloungebar .com; Bogovićeva 7) This has to be the best-designed bar in the whole of Zagreb with its huge, differently themed rooms, lounge sofas, an olive tree in the middle of the main room, and notebook-style menus (it's called School, you see). There are DJ nights, various 'after-school' parties and it's packed with the trendiest of people (and, of course, students).

Eli's Café (☎ 0915277990; www.eliscaffe.com; Ilica 63; ☻ 8am-9pm Mon-Sat, 9am-3pm Sun) You'll see why this tiny place was declared to have the 'Best Coffee in Croatia' in 2008 when you try the excellent espresso or smooth cappuccino. There are also breakfast pastries for dipping.

Bulldog Café (☎ 49 17 393; Bogovićeva 6) It's easy to sit for hours outside, watching the activity on this busy pedestrian street. At night, it's a good place to meet and have a few drinks before clubbing.

Cica (Tkalčićeva 18) It's the size of an east London bedsit, with a similar vibe to go: an underground place with a massive choice of *rakija* in all flavours – herbal, nutty, fruity – you think it, they have it. Lovers of hedonistic pleasures, Cica is your place.

Apartman (☎ 48 72 168; Preradovićeva 7) A 1st-floor space decked out with large cushions and an unpretentious, relaxed crowd, the Apartment gets going with DJ music on weekends. You can also come and lounge around during the day.

Melin (☎ 48 28 966; Tkalčićeva 47) This is rock and roll as it used to be, with grotty seats, oddly painted walls, smoke curtains and music that bursts ear drums. A corner of grungy old Zagreb on a fast-gentrifying street.

BP Club (☎ 48 14 444; Teslina 7; ☻ 10pm-2am) One of a couple of cafes and music shops that share the lively complex at the corner of Teslina and Gajeva streets. In the basement, check it out for jazz, blues and rock bands.

ENTERTAINMENT

Zagreb is definitely a happening city. Its theatres and concert halls present a great variety of programs throughout the year. Many (but not all) are listed in the monthly brochure *Zagreb Events & Performances*, which is available from the main tourist office.

The gay and lesbian scene in Zagreb is finally becoming more open than it had previously been, although 'free-wheeling' it isn't. Many gay people discreetly cruise the south beach around Jarun Lake and are welcome in most discos. **David** (☎ 0915337757; Marulićev Trg 3) is a sauna, bar and video room popular on Zagreb's gay scene.

Nightclubs

The dress code is relaxed in most Zagreb clubs. It doesn't get lively until near midnight.

KSET (☎ 61 29 999; www.kset.org; Unska 3; ☻ 8pm-midnight Mon-Fri, to 3am Sat) Zagreb's best music venue, with everyone who's anyone performing here. Saturday night is dedicated to DJ music, when hundreds of young Zagrebians drink, dance and stay up late. You'll find gigs and events to suit most tastes.

Aquarius (☎ 36 40 231; Jarun Lake) A truly fab place to party, this enormously popular spot has a series of rooms that open onto a huge terrace on the lake. House and techno are the standard fare here.

Boogaloo (☎ 63 13 021; www.boogaloo.hr; OTV Dom, Vukovarska 68) A great venue that hosts DJ nights and live music. It's a 15-minute walk from Jelačića.

Purgeraj (☎ 48 14 734; Park Ribnjak) This is a funky, relaxed space to listen to live rock, blues, rock-blues, blues-rock, country rock and avant-garde jazz. And there's a daily two-drinks-for-one happy hour from 9pm to 11pm.

Jabuka (☎ 48 34 397; Jabukovac 28) This is a bit of an old-time favourite, with 1980s hits played to a 30-something crowd that reminisces about the good old days. It's a fun place, really, and much loved by Zagrebians.

Sport

Basketball is popular in Zagreb, and from October to April games take place in a variety of venues around town, usually at the weekend. The tourist office can provide you with the schedule.

Football (soccer) games are held every Sunday afternoon at **Maksimir Stadium** (Maksimirska 128), on the eastern side of Zagreb; catch tram 4, 7, 11 or 12 to Bukovačka. If you arrive too early for the game, Zagreb's zoo is just across the street.

Theatre

It's worth making the rounds of the theatres in person to check their programs. Tickets are usually available for performances, even for the best shows. A small office marked 'Kazalište Komedija' (look out for the posters) also sells theatre tickets; it's in the Oktogon, a passage connecting Trg Petra Preradovića to Ilica 3.

The neobaroque Croatian National Theatre (p232) was established in 1895. It stages opera and ballet performances.

Komedija Theatre (☎ 48 14 566; Kaptol 9) Near the cathedral, the Komedija Theatre stages operettas and musicals.

Vatroslav Lisinski Concert Hall (☎ ticket office 61 21 166; Trg Stjepana Radića 4; ☒ 9am–8pm Mon–Fri, to 7pm Sat) Just south of the train station, this concert hall is a prestigious venue where symphony concerts are held regularly.

SHOPPING

Ilica is Zagreb's main shopping street.

Croata (☎ 48 12 726; www.croata.hr; Ilica 5, Oktogon) Since the necktie originated in Croatia, noth-

ing could make a more authentic gift, and this is the place to get one. The locally made silk neckties are priced from 175KN to 380KN.

Rukotvorine (☎ 48 31 303; Trg Jelačića 7) Sells traditional Croatian handicrafts such as dolls, pottery and red-and-white embroidered tablecloths.

GETTING THERE & AWAY
Air

The airport is south of the centre. For information about flights to and from Zagreb, see p257 and p258.

Bus

Zagreb's big, modern **bus station** (☎ 61 57 983; www.akz.hr, in Croatian) has a large, enclosed waiting room and a number of shops, including eateries and grocery stores. You can buy most international tickets at windows 17 to 20.

Buses depart from Zagreb for most parts of Croatia and places beyond. For information on domestic services, see the table, p192.

Train

Domestic trains depart from **Zagreb train station** (☎ 060 33 34 44; www.hznet.hr); see the table, p193, for services.

All daily trains to Zadar stop at Knin. Reservations are required on fast InterCity (IC) trains, and there's a supplement of 5KN to 15KN for fast or express trains.

For international train connections see p193.

GETTING AROUND

Zagreb is a fairly easy city to navigate, whether by car or public transport. Traffic isn't bad, there's sufficient parking, and the efficient tram system should be a model for other polluted, traffic-clogged European capitals.

MARKET DAYS

Zagreb doesn't do many markets, but those that it does do, it does well. The Sunday **antiques market** (☒ 9am–2pm) on Britanski Trg is one of central Zagreb's joys, but to see a flea market that's unmatched in the whole of Croatia you have to make it to **Hrelić** (☒ 7am–3pm). It's a huge space that's packed with anything – and we mean anything – from car parts, cars and antique furniture to clothes, records, kitchenware, you name it. Apart from the shopping, though, it's just a great experience and a side of Zagreb you probably won't see anywhere else – expect lots of Roma, music, general liveliness and grilled meat smoking from the food section. If you're going in the summer months, take a hat and put on some sunscreen – there's no shade. Take bus 295 to Sajam Jakuševac from behind the train station.

BUS SERVICES FROM ZAGREB

Destination	Price (KN)	Duration (hr)	Daily departures
Dubrovnik	250	11	7-8
Korčula	224	11	1
Krk	160-190	4-5	4
Makarska	210	8	10
Mali Lošinj	260-280	6½	2
Osijek	125-160	4	8
Plitvice	80	2½	19
Poreč	170/210	5	6
Pula	170/230	4-5	6
Rab	195	5	2
Rijeka	125-150	2½-3	14
Rovinj	170-190	5-8	8
Šibenik	165	6½	15
Split	195	5-9	27
Varaždin	69	2	20
Zadar	120-140	3½-5	20

To/From the Airport

The Croatia Airlines bus to Pleso airport leaves from the bus station every half-hour or hour from about 4am to 8.30pm depending on flights, and returns from the airport on about the same schedule (50KN one way). A taxi would cost about 300KN.

Car

Of the major car-hire companies, you could try **Budget Rent-a-Car** (☎ 45 54 936; Kneza Borne 2) in the Hotel Sheraton and **Hertz** (☎ 48 46 777; Vukotinovićeva 4). Prices start at 300KN per day. Bear in mind that local companies will usually have lower rates. Try **H&M** (☎ 37 04 535; www.hm -rentacar.hr; Grahorova 11), which also has an office at the airport.

Zagreb is relatively easy to navigate by car but remember that the streets around Trg Jelačića and up through Kaptol and Gradec are pedestrian only. Watch out for trams sneaking up on you.

The **Croatian Auto Club (HAK) Information Centre** (☎ 66 11 999; www.hak.hr; Avenija Dubrovnik 44) helps motorists in need. It's just east of the centre.

Public Transport

Public transport is based on an efficient network of trams, though the city centre is compact enough to make them unnecessary. Buy tickets at newspaper kiosks for 8KN. Each ticket must be stamped when you board. You can use your ticket for transfers within 90 minutes, but only in one direction.

A *dnevna karta* (day ticket), valid on all public transport until 4am the next morning, is 25KN at most Vjesnik or Tisak news outlets. (See the boxed text, p185 for details of discounts with the Zagreb Card.) Controls are frequent on the tram system; there are substantial fines for not having the proper ticket.

Taxi

Zagreb's taxis ring up 8KN per kilometre after a flag fall of 25KN. On Sunday and from 10pm to 5am there's a 20% surcharge.

AROUND ZAGREB

SAMOBOR

pop 14,000

Samobor is the Zagrebians' version of the Hamptons for New Yorkers, only it doesn't have a beach and it's much smaller. OK, we may be stretching the comparison, but this is where the stressed-out city dwellers come to wind down and get their fix of hearty food, creamy cakes and pretty scenery. A shallow stream stocked with trout curves through a town centre that is composed of trim pastel houses and several old churches, while the verdant woods of Samoborsko Gorje are perfect for hiking.

In keeping with its mission to preserve a little piece of the past, the main economic activity centres on small family businesses involved in handicrafts, restaurants, and the production of mustard and spirits. The town's literary and musical traditions, which produced

TRAIN SERVICES FROM ZAGREB			
Destination	Price (KN)	Duration (hr)	Daily departures
Osijek	113	4	5
Pula	131	6½	7
Rijeka	96	5	5
Šibenik	149	6½-10	3
Split	160	6-8½	6
Varaždin	59	3	13
Zadar	156	7-9¾	5

the poet Stanko Vraz and the composer Ferdo Livadić, are reflected in a number of annual festivals, most famously the **Fašnik** (Samobor Carnival) on the eve of Lent.

Orientation & Information

The bus station (no left-luggage office) is on Šmidheva, about 100m uphill from the town, which centres around Trg Kralja Tomislava.

In the town centre, the **tourist office** (☎ 33 60 044; www.samobor.hr, in Croatian; Trg Kralja Tomislava 5; ✆ 8am-7pm Mon-Fri, 9am-7pm Sat, 10am-7pm Sun) has limited documentation, but you can get hiking maps.

Sights & Activities

The **Town Museum** (Gradski Muzej; ☎ 33 61 014; Livadićeva 7; adult/student 8/5KN; ✆ 9am-3pm Tue-Sat, to 1pm Sun) has moderately interesting exhibits on regional culture. It's housed in Livadićev Dvor Villa, which once belonged to composer Ferdinand Livadić and was an important centre for the 19th-century nationalist cause.

Stop by the **Museum Marton** (☎ 33 64 160; admission 15KN; ✆ 10am-1pm & 3-6pm Sat & Sun) for a look at a private art collection that centres on paintings from the Biedermeier period as well as porcelain, glass and furniture.

Sleeping & Eating

Most people come to Samobor on a day trip from Zagreb, but you can also stay here and commute into Zagreb.

Hotel Livadić (☎ 33 65 850; www.hotel-livadic.hr; Trg Kralja Tomislava 1; s 360, d low-high season 465-530KN) This atmospheric place is decorated in 19th-century style and provides spacious, comfortable rooms with TV and phone. Since cuisine is a major draw for Samobor, you can count on the quality of the restaurant and cafe.

Samoborska Pivnica (☎ 33 61 623; Šmidhena 3; mains 35-90KN) An excellent array of local specialities is served in this vaulted space, with a variety of sausages, eye-watering horseradish and the delicious, cheesy *štrukli*. It's a beer house (*pivnica*), so accompany your food with a glass of crisp local beer.

Pri Staroj Vuri (☎ 33 60 548; Giznik 2; 2-course meal 90-110KN) About 50m uphill from Trg Kralja Tomislava, this restaurant serves traditional dishes in a cosy cottage, and sometimes hosts poetry readings. The specialities of

TAKE A HIKE

Samobor is a good jumping-off point for hikes into the Samoborsko Gorje, a mountain system (part of the Žumberak Range) that links the high peaks of the Alps with the karstic caves and abysses of the Dinaric Range. Carpeted with meadows and forests, the range is the most popular hiking destination in the region. Most of the hikes are easy and there are several mountain huts that make pleasant rest stops. Many are open weekends only (except in high season).

The range has three groups: the Oštrc group in the centre, the Japetić group to the west and the Plešica group to the east. Both the Oštrc and the Japetić groups are accessible from Šoićeva Kuća, a mountain hut 10km west of Samobor, only reachable on foot. From there, it's an easy 30-minute climb to the hill fort of Lipovac and an hour's climb to the peak of Oštrc (753m). Another popular hike is the 1½-hour climb from Šoićeva Kuća to Japetić (780m). You can also follow a path from Oštrc to Japetić, which will take about two hours. If you want to explore the Plešica group, head east to the hunting cabin Srndać on Poljanice (12km), from which it's a 40-minute climb to the peak of Plešivica (780m). The tourist office in town has maps and information on hikes in the region.

the house are *hrvatska pisanica* (beef steak in a spicy mushroom, onion, tomato and red-wine sauce) and *struklova juha* (soup with *štrukli*).

our pick **U Prolazu** (☎ 83 66 420; Trg Kralja Tomislava 5) This eatery on the main square serves the best *kremšnite* (custard pie) in town.

Getting There & Away

Samobor is easy to reach by public transport. Get a **Samoborček** (www2.samoborcek.hr, in Croatian) bus from the main bus station in Zagreb (one way 12KN, 30 minutes, every half-hour).

HRVATSKO ZAGORJE

Despite its proximity to Zagreb, the bucolic region of Hrvatsko Zagorje in the country's northwest receives few tourists even at the height of the summer season. Undeservedly so – these leafy landscapes with the Austrian-influenced food and architecture present an alternative to the busy Mediterranean south and make a good escape from the summer heat. The Zagorje region begins north of Mt Medvednica just outside of Zagreb, and extends west to the Slovenia border and as far north as Varaždin, the area's largest city.

VARAŽDIN
☎ 042 / pop 49,000

Varaždin, 81km north of Zagreb, is a largely overlooked destination, often used as a mere transit point on the way to or from Hungary. In fact, the town is well worth a visit in its own right, its centre a showcase of scrupulously restored baroque architecture and well-tended gardens and parks. It was once Croatia's capital and most prosperous city, which explains the extraordinary refinement of its buildings. Topping off the symphony is the gleaming white, turreted Old City (Stari Grad), which contains a city museum. Today the pleasant town is an increasingly popular day-trip destination – at the time of writing its historic core was being spruced up, with plans to complete the renovations by 2010.

Orientation

The bus station lies just southwest of the town centre, while the train station is to the east, at the opposite end of town. About 1km apart, the stations are linked by a minibus that serves the town and the nearby villages (5KN). The pedestrian zone of attractive 18th-century buildings

centres on Trg Kralja Tomislava, with the old streets radiating from this square.

Information

Caffe Bar Aquamarin (☎ 311 868; Gajeva 1; per hr 15KN; ☼ 7am-midnight Mon-Thu, to 1am Fri-Sun) Popular student hangout with internet terminals.
Garderoba bus station (per bag 7KN; ☼ 5am-8.30pm); train station (per day 15KN; ☼ 24hr) Left luggage.
Post office (Trg Slobode 9; ☼ 7am-7pm Mon-Fri, to 2pm Sat)
Tourist office (☎ 210 987; www.tourism-varazdin .hr, in Croatian; Ivana Padovca 3; ☼ 8am-6pm Mon-Fri, 9am-1pm Sat Apr-Oct, 8am-4pm Mon-Fri Nov-Mar) Plenty of colourful brochures and a wealth of information.
Varaždin Tours (☎ 320 400; www.varazdintours.com; Alojzija Stepnica 1; ☼ 8am-7.30pm Mon-Fri, to 1pm Sat) Books domestic and international bus tickets.
Zagrebačka Banka (Kapucinski Trg 5) This bank is diagonally opposite the bus station.

Sights

Varaždin offers a fine ensemble of baroque buildings in the town centre, a number of which have been turned into museums. Many of the aristocratic mansions and elegant churches are being restored as part of the town's bid to be included in Unesco's list of World Heritage sites. Conveniently, most buildings have plaques with architectural and historical explanations in English.

The **Town Museum** (Gradski Muzej; ☎ 658 754; www .gmv.hr; Strossmayerovo Šetalište 7; adult/student 20/12KN; ☼ 10am-6pm Tue-Sun May-Sep, 10am-5pm Tue-Fri, 10am-1pm Sat & Sun Oct-Apr) is inside the Old City, a gem of medieval defensive architecture surrounded by a lovingly manicured park. Construction of this whitewashed fortress began in the 14th century, and it was shaped into the present Gothic-Renaissance structure by the 16th century. Today it's a museum that houses furniture, paintings, decorative objects, insignia and weapons amassed over centuries. Far more interesting than the historic collections is the architecture – enter via a drawbridge and wander around archways, courtyards, chapels and towers of this sprawling castle-fortress.

A 10-minute stroll west takes you to the serene **Varaždin Cemetery** (Hallerova Aleja; ☎ 7am-9pm May-Sep, to 5pm Oct-Apr), a horticultural masterpiece designed in 1905 by Viennese architect Hermann Helmer. A meander amidst tombstones, avenues, promenades and over 7000 trees, including magnolia, beech and birch, reveals some superb landscaping.

The fascinating **Entomological Collection** (Entomološka Zbirka; ☎ 658 760; Franjevački Trg 6; adult/student 20/12KN; ✆ 10am-6pm Tue-Sun May-Sep, 10am-5pm Tue-Fri, 10am-1pm Sat & Sun Oct-Apr), housed in the classicist **Hercer Palace**, comprises nearly 4500 exhibits of the bug world, including 1000 insect species. The examples of nests, habitats and reproductive habits are informative and well displayed, with interactive stations and free audio guides.

The town's newest attraction, the **Traditional Crafts Square** (Trg Tradicijskih Obrta; ✆ 10am-6pm Mon-Sat Apr-Oct), recreates olden times. Here the town blacksmith forges 'Varaždin Medallions', and there are demonstrations of pottery, weaving and hat making.

Festivals & Events
Varaždin is famous for its baroque music festival, **Varaždin Baroque Evenings** (www.vbv.hr), which takes place over two to three weeks each September. Local and international orchestras play in the cathedral, churches and theatres around town. Tickets range from 75KN to 150KN, and become available one hour before the concert at travel agencies or the **Varaždin Concert Bureau** (☎/fax 212 907) at the Croatian National Theatre.

In late August, the eclectic **Špancirfest** (www.spancirfest.com) enlivens the town's parks and squares with world music (from Afro-Cuban to tango), acrobats, theatre, traditional crafts and illusionists.

Sleeping
Generally less expensive than in Zagreb, most hotels in Varaždin are clean and well maintained and offer decent value for money. If you're looking for private accommodation, turn to the tourist office, which has listings of single/double rooms from about 150/250KN.

ourpick Hotel Varaždin (☎ 290 720; www.hotel-varazdin.com; Kolodvorska 19; s/d from 388/576KN; P ✖ ◻) Sparkling contemporary rooms at the city's newest hotel, opposite the train station, are jam-packed with amenities such as internet and minibars. On the premises is a restaurant with bar and terrace.

Maltar (☎ 311 100; www.maltar.hr; Prešernova 1; s/d 220/405KN; P ✖) Good value for money can be had at this cheerful little family-run *pansion* (guesthouse) near the centre. Rooms are well kept and complete with satellite TV and air-con. Four suites have kitchenettes.

Hotel Turist (☎ 395 395; www.hotel-turist.hr; Kralja Zvonimira 1; s/d from 353/546KN; P ✖ ◻) The lack of character is balanced out with 35 years of service, solid facilities and functional rooms at this six-floor hotel with freshly painted facade a stroll away from the centre.

Studentski Centar Varaždin (☎ 332 910, 332 911; hostel@scvz.hr; Julija Merlića bb; s low-high 180-225KN, d high only 310KN; ◻) This student hall–hostel has 12 newly renovated single rooms available for rent year-round, each with TV, cable internet and fridge. Doubles can be booked in summer only, when students leave.

Eating
While it doesn't stand out as a gastronomic destination, Varaždin offers plentiful opportunities to try Croatia's continental cuisine. There is a daily **market** (Augusta Šenoe 12), open until 2pm. Many bakeries sell Varaždin's savoury finger-shaped bread, *klipič*.

ourpick Zlatna Guska (☎ 213 393; Jurja Habdelića 4; mains 57-119KN) The medieval theme runs through this basement restaurant that evokes a knights' dining hall with plenty of armour and imaginatively named items, like 'the last meal of the inquisitions victims' (a hearty bread-and-sausage soup). Dishes are well prepared and portions copious.

Grenadir (☎ 211 131; Kranjčevićeva 12; mains from 32KN) No-frills but great-value *gableci* (lunches) are popular with locals at this traditional town-centre eatery.

Angelus (☎ 303 868; Alojzija Stepinca 3; pizzas from 25KN, mains from 45KN) Housed in a vaulted basement, this cosy pizzeria-trattoria churns out excellent pizza, pasta (from gnocchi to tagliatelle), risottos and meat mainstays.

Zlatne Ruke (☎ 320 650; Ivana Kukuljevića 13; mains 49-116KN) The latest outpost by the owners of Zlatna Guska, this subterranean spot is the town's most design-conscious choice, with white-stone walls and creative dishes such as venison tartare and goose liver with peaches.

Getting There & Away
Varaždin is a major transport hub in north Croatia, with bus and train lines running in all directions. Remember that northbound buses originate in Zagreb, stop at Varaždin and cost the same whether you buy the ticket in Zagreb or Varaždin.

There's a daily bus to Vienna (210KN, six hours) and two daily buses to Munich

(345KN, eight hours). A bus goes to Berlin (773KN, 15 hours) and Zurich (509KN, 13 hours) twice weekly. Most buses to the coast go through Zagreb. They run hourly on weekdays (69KN, 1¾ hours), with reduced service on weekends.

There are 11 to 14 daily trains to Zagreb (53KN, 2½ hours); connect in Zagreb for trains to the coast. One direct train runs daily to Budapest (205KN, six hours).

SLAVONIA

Pancake-flat Slavonia is a fertile region bounded by three major rivers, the Sava, Drava and Danube, and bordering Hungary in the north, BiH in the south and Serbia in the east. For a visitor, Slavonia provides a landscape nearly untouched by tourism, with unique natural wonders like the wetlands of Kopački Rit and tasty regional cuisine. Osijek, Slavonia's largest town, is well worth a visit for its riverfront setting, remarkable fortress quarter and Secessionist architecture.

OSIJEK
☎ 031 / pop 90,411
Photographs of Osijek before the 1990s reveal a relaxed river city of wide avenues, leafy parks and grand 19th-century Secessionist mansions. Sadly, the shells that fell during the 1991 civil war scarred the pretty image of this lively university town.

Although many buildings along the avenues have been restored to their former lustre, the pits and pockmarks on other structures are grim reminders of the war that ravaged eastern Slavonia in the early 1990s. However, the economy is kicking back, with people returning to their hometown after years of exile, new hotels and restaurants popping up and tourists slowly trickling in. The pleasant waterfront promenade along the Drava River, the imposing 18th-century fortress and the resilient spirit of this relaxed city are all reasons to visit Osijek.

Orientation
Stretching along the southern bank of the Drava River, Osijek is composed of three boroughs: the Upper Town (Gornji Grad), the Lower Town (Donji Grad) and the 18th-century fortress, Tvrđa. The bus station (at the time of writing a new one was being built just to the west) and train station are adjacent in the southern part of the Upper Town. Most of the sights, hotels, cafes and shops are between the train and bus stations and the river.

The main shopping street is Kapucinska, which becomes the wide Europska Avenija in the east, bordered by a series of parks planted with chestnut and linden trees. A pleasant riverfront promenade stretches all the way to the city's outskirts.

Information
Hospital (☎ 511 511; Josipa Huttlera 4)
OK Tours (☎ 212 815; www.ok-tours.hr; Trg Slobode 7; ☼ 9am-7pm Mon-Fri, to noon Sat) Good source of local information and some private accommodation.
Panturist (☎ 214 388; www.panturist.hr; Kapucinska 19; ☼ 8am-8pm Mon-Fri, to 1pm Sat) Slavonia's largest travel agency, it runs buses to the coast as well as to international destinations.
Post office (Kardinala Alojzija Stepinca 17; ☼ 7.30am-7pm Mon-Sat) You can make phone calls and get MasterCard cash advances.
Press Cafe (☎ 212 313; Lorenza Jägera 24; per hr 15KN; ☼ 7am-11pm Mon-Sat, 8am-11pm Sun) Internet access.
Privredna Banka (Stjepana Radića 19) Bank.
Tourist office (☎ /fax 203 755; www.tzosijek.hr; Županijska 2; ☼ 9am-5pm Mon-Fri, to 4pm Sat) Distributes plentiful brochures, booklets and maps.
Zlatna Greda (☎ 565 180; www.zlatna-greda.org; Opatijska 26f; ☼ 8am-4pm Mon-Fri) An offshoot of the Zeleni Osijek environmental nonprofit organisation (www.zeleni-osijek.hr), which runs an eco-centre in the wetlands of Baranja, this agency organises hiking trips, photo-safaris, boat and canoe rides along the Danube, and bike tours.

Sights
TVRĐA
Built under Habsburg rule as a defence against Turkish attacks, the 18th-century **citadel** was relatively undamaged during the recent war. This baroque complex of cobblestone streets, spacious squares and stately mansions reveals a remarkable architectural unity, lending it the feel of an open-air museum.

The **Museum of Slavonia** (Muzej Slavonije Osijek; ☎ 250 730; Trg Svetog Trojstva 6; adult/student 15/10KN; ☼ 8am-2pm Tue-Fri, 10am-1pm Sat & Sun) on the main square traces Slavonia's long history, beginning with implements from the Bronze Age and displays of coins, pottery and utensils from the Roman colony of Mursa. Diagonally opposite is the city's newest museum, the **Archeological Museum of Osijek** (Arheološki Muzej Osijek; ☎ 232 132; Trg Svetog Trojstva 2; adult/student 15/8KN; ⊙ 10am-3pm Tue-Fri, to 1pm Sat & Sun), in the renovated city guard building with a glass dome over an arcaded patio. It showcases recently unearthed finds – from Roman stones to Celtic helmets.

UPPER TOWN

The towering **Church of St Peter & Paul** (☎ 310 020; ⊙ 8am-7.30pm) looms over Trg Ante Starčevića with its 90m-high tower, surpassed in height only by the cathedral in Zagreb. Built in the 1890s, this red-brick neo-Gothic structure features an interior with 40 elaborate stained-glass windows in Viennese style and vividly coloured frescos by Croatian painter Mirko Rački.

Housed in an elegant neoclassical mansion, the **Gallery of Fine Arts** (Galerija Likovnih Umjetnosti; ☎ 251 280; Europska Avenija 9; adult/student 10/5KN; ⊙ 10am-6pm Tue-Fri, to 1pm Sat & Sun) contains a collection of paintings and sculptures by Slavonian artists from the 18th century onwards.

BEYOND THE CENTRE

As an escape from museums and churches, take the emblematic **kompa** (free; ⊙ 8am-midnight Jul-Sep, 9am-6pm Oct-May), a wooden pedestrian ferry propelled by the water current from the shore of Gornji Grad to **Zoo Osijek** (☎ 285 234; Tvrđavica 1; adult/child 7/3KN; ⊙ 9am-7pm summer & spring, to 5pm winter & autumn) on the other side of the Drava. Croatia's largest zoo spreads over 11 verdant riverside hectares, with 80 animal species and a reptile-filled aquarium.

Worth a trek to the semi-industrial zone of Bosutsko Naselje is Osijek's most offbeat sight, **Gloria Maris Museum** (☎ 273 008; Svetog Josipa Radnika 35; adult/children 20/15KN; ⊙ 10am-1pm & 4-7pm Tue-Sat, 10am-1pm Sun) of sea shells and marine life. This private collection of over 250,000 items – from the giant mammoth tooth found in the Sava River to pearl shells from the Indian Ocean – has been gathered over a lifetime by the avid collector Ivan Filipović, who will share a million fascinating titbits on an educational guided tour (request in advance for English).

Sleeping

Osijek recently got a fresh crop of hotels, and a few more are in the works. There are no hostels and there's limited private accommodation. For private rooms (from 165KN per person), ask at the tourist office or at OK Tours.

our pick Waldinger Pansion (☎ 250 450; www .waldinger.hr; Županijska 8; s/d 290/440KN; P 🐾 🖳) In the quiet backyard of Osijek's boutique Waldinger Hotel, its three-star annexe – with a pond and garden – offers less elaborate

CROATIA

WORTH THE TRIP: KOPAČKI RIT NATURE PARK

Only 12km northeast of Osijek, **Kopački Rit Nature Park** (Park Prirode Kopački Rit; www.kopacki-rit .com; adult/child 10/5KN) is one of the largest wetlands in Europe, home to 141 bird species nesting throughout its 23,000 hectares. Formed by the meeting of the Drava and Danube rivers, this vast flood plain is surrounded by a remarkable variety of vegetation – from aquatic and grassland flora to willow, poplar and oak forests. Look for the rare black storks, white-tailed eagles, great crested grebes, mallard ducks, purple herons, cormorants, falcons and wild geese. Bring a tonne of mosquito repellent, as mosquitoes – 21 kinds of them – are bloodthirsty little devils. The best time to come is during the spring and autumn bird migrations.

The park was heavily mined during the war and closed for many years as a result. Most mines have now been cleared and safe trails have been clearly marked, but it's still not wise to wander off into the woods. The **visitor centre** (☎ 752 320; ⊙ 9am-5pm daily) is located at the main entrance along the Bilje–Kopačevo road. You can walk the two marked educational trails nearby, but the best way to take in the wetlands is on a one-hour **boat tour** (adult/child 60/45KN Apr-Jun & Sep-Nov, 40/25KN Jul & Aug); it's best to book in advance.

There's no public transport to the park, but you can take local bus line 6 (route 24, 25 or 27) with the Darda-Bilje sign and then walk the 3km to the park. Alternatively, rent a bike in Osijek at **CetraTour** (☎ 372 920; Ružina 16; www.cetratour.hr; ⊙ 8.30am-3.30pm Mon-Fri, 9am-1pm Sat) or take a day trip with Zlatna Greda (opposite).

but gracious rooms. The hotel rooms (singles/doubles 650/950KN) in the elegant Secessionist building come with jacuzzis. The elegant tearoom showcases rotating exhibits and fantastic cakes.

Villa Sveti Rok (☎ 310 490; www.villa-sveti-rok.hr; Svetog Roka 13; s/d 585/785KN; P 🎮 🖳) Hole up in one of the plush rooms at this swank little guesthouse on a leafy residential street near the centre. You may not want to leave – there are DVD players, hydro-massage showers, wifi and music piped in the bathrooms.

Hotel Central (☎ 283 399; www.hotel-central-os.hr; Trg Ante Starčevića 6; s/d 335/514KN; P 🖳) While it no longer holds its status as the grandest of Osijek hotels, this old-fashioned property still has a prime location on the main square. The room decor is out of date, but perks include wi-fi and nice panoramas from the square-facing units.

Hotel Drava (☎ 250 500; www.hotel-drava.com; Ivana Gundulića 25a; s/d 380/680KN; P 🎮 🖳) Tucked away from the busy street a hop and a skip from the train and bus stations, this small family-run hotel has colourful rooms, each slightly different but all with modern furnishings.

Eating

Osijek is the place to sample the hearty and spicy Slavonian cuisine, which is strongly influenced by neighbouring Hungary. Paprika is sprinkled on almost every dish, and meat and riverfish have a prominent presence. Note that all restaurants below are closed on Sunday evening.

our pick **Kod Ruže** (☎ 206 066; Kuhačeva 25a; mains from 45KN) Clad in wood and villagey knick-knacks, one of the city's newest restaurants has quickly become a locals' favourite for its excellent regional mainstays. Try the *čobanac* stew with game and don't miss the homemade cakes.

Slavonska Kuća (☎ 369 955; Kamila Firingera 26a, Tvrđa; mains from 40KN) This rustic old house on the edge of Tvrđa serves mean *fiš paprikaš* and venison *perkelt* (goulashlike stew) as well as other regional specialities. Wash your meal down with Graševina, a fruity white wine.

Laguna Croatica (☎ 369 203; Dubrovačka 13; mains 35-75KN) Once you've studied the extensive and varied menu, you can admire the bric-a-brac on the walls of this dark basement restaurant steps from the centre. Try the uniquely Slavonian version of calamari – filled with *kulen* (spicy pork sausage) and cheese!

DOMESTIC BUS SERVICES FROM OSIJEK

Destination	Price (KN)	Duration (hr)	Daily departures
Dubrovnik	300	14	1
Rijeka	235	7	1
Split	283	11	1
Zagreb	128	4	9

Getting There & Away

Osijek is a major transport hub with buses and trains arriving and departing in all directions.

BUS

For some international bus services from Osijek see the table, below. Many more buses leave for destinations in Germany than can be listed here.

For domestic bus services from Osijek see the table, above.

TRAIN

There's one train a day in either direction between Pećs and Osijek (56KN, two hours). The train from Osijek connects to Budapest (207KN, six hours). There is a daily train to Sarajevo (138KN, seven hours).

Seven daily trains run to Zagreb (130KN, four to five hours), two to Rijeka (200KN, nine to 10 hours) and one to Šibenik (242KN, 14 hours, with a change in Perković).

Getting Around

Osijek has a tram line that dates from 1884 and makes transport within the city easy. The fare is 8KN each way from the driver, or 7KN from a *tisak* (newsstand).

For visitors, the most useful tram lines are the 2, which connects the train and bus station with Trg Ante Starčevića in the centre, and the 1, which goes to the Tvrđa.

INTERNATIONAL BUS SERVICES FROM OSIJEK

Destination	Price (KN)	Duration (hr)	Departures
Belgrade	107	3½	5 daily
Tuzla	112	4	1 daily
Vienna	302	10	2 weekly
Zurich	675	7½	1 weekly

ISTRIA

☎ 052

Continental Croatia meets the Adriatic in Istria (Istra to Croatians), the heart-shaped 3600-sq-km peninsula just south of Trieste in Italy. While the bucolic interior of rolling hills and fertile plains has been attracting artists and visitors to its hilltop villages, rural hotels and farmhouse restaurants, the verdant indented coastline is enormously popular with the sun-and-sea set. Vast hotel complexes line much of the coast, and the rocky beaches are not Croatia's best, but the facilities are wide ranging, the sea is clean and there are still secluded spots aplenty.

The northern part of the peninsula belongs to Slovenia. Just across the water is Italy, but the pervasive Italian influence makes it seem much closer. Italian is, in fact, a second language in Istria, many Istrians have Italian passports, and each town name has an Italian counterpart. Perhaps they dream of the days when the string of Istrian resorts belonged to Italy. Italy seized Istria from Austria-Hungary in 1918, kept it until 1920 and then gave it up to Yugoslavia in 1947. Tito wanted Trieste (Trst) as part of Yugoslavia too, but in 1954 the Anglo-American occupiers returned the city to Italy so that it wouldn't fall into the hands of the 'communists'.

Visit Poreč, Rovinj and Pula on the coast and then move on to the interior, known for its hilltop towns and acclaimed gastronomy, starring prime truffles, wild asparagus, top olive oil and award-winning wines.

POREČ

pop 17,000

Poreč (Parenzo in Italian) sits on a low, narrow peninsula halfway down the western coast of Istria. The ancient Roman town is the centrepiece of a vast system of resorts that stretch north and south, entirely devoted to summer tourism. While this is not the place for a quiet getaway (unless you come out of season), there is a World Heritage basilica, well-developed tourist infrastructure, a strip of rocky beaches nearby and the pristine Istrian interior within easy reach.

Orientation

The compact old town, called Parentium by the Romans, is based on a rectangular street plan. The ancient Decumanus with its pol-

ished stones is still the main street running through the peninsula's middle, lined with shops and restaurants. Hotels, travel agencies and excursion boats are on the quay, Obala Maršala Tita, which runs from the small-boat harbour to the tip of the peninsula. The bus station is just outside the old town, behind Rade Končara.

Information

You can change money at any of the many travel agencies or banks. There are ATMs all around town.

Atlas Travel Agency (☎ 434 933; www.atlas-croatia .com; Eufrazijeva 63; ⏱ 9am-2pm & 6-9pm) Books excursions.

CyberM@c (☎ 427 075; Mire Grahalića 1; per hr 42KN; ⏱ 8am-10pm) A full-service computer centre.

Di Tours (☎ 432 100; www.di-tours.hr; Prvomajska 2; ⏱ 9am-10pm Jul & Aug, to 9pm Jun & Sep) Finds private accommodation.

Garderoba (per day 22KN; ⏱ 7am-9pm daily) Left luggage; at the bus station.

Main post office (Trg Slobode 14; ⏱ 8am-noon & 6-8pm Mon-Sat)

Poreč Medical Centre (☎ 451 611; Maura Gioseffija 2)

Sunny Way (☎ 452 021; Alda Negrija 1; sunnyway@pu .t-com.hr; ⏱ 9am-9pm Jul & Aug) Specialises in boat tickets and excursions to Italy and around Croatia.

Tourist office (☎ 451 293; www.to-porec.com; Zagrebačka 9; ⏱ 8am-10pm Mon-Sat, 9am-1pm & 6-10pm Sun Jul & Aug, 8am-4pm Mon-Sat rest of yr)

Sights

The main reason to visit Poreč is the 6th-century **Euphrasian basilica** (☎ 431 635; Eufrazijeva bb; admission free, to climb belfry 10KN; ⏱ 7am-8pm Apr-mid-Oct or by appointment), one of Europe's finest intact examples of Byzantine art. What packs in the crowds are the glittering wall mosaics in the apse, veritable masterpieces featuring biblical scenes, archangels and martyrs. The belfry affords an invigorating view of the old town. Worth a visit is the adjacent **Bishop's Palace** (admission 10KN; ⏱ 9am-7pm Apr-mid-Oct or by appointment), which contains a display of ancient stone sculptures, religious paintings and 4th-century mosaics from the original oratory.

The numerous historic sites in the old town include the ruins of two **Roman temples** between Trg Marafor, once the site of the Roman forum, and the western end of the peninsula. There's also a medley of Gothic and Romanesque buildings to look out for, as well as the baroque Sinčić Palace that houses

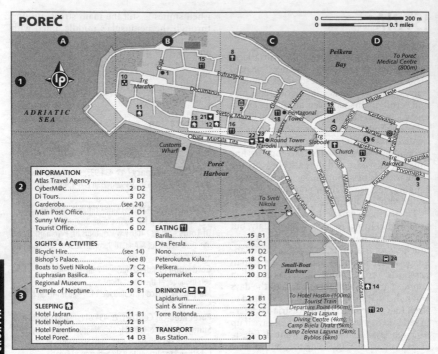

POREČ

the **Regional Museum** (Decumanus 9; www.muzejporec
.hr), under renovation at the time of research.

From May to October there are passenger
boats (15KN) travelling to **Sveti Nikola**, the
small island that lies opposite Poreč harbour.
They depart every 30 minutes to an hour from
the wharf on Obala Maršala Tita.

Activities

Nearly every activity you might want to enjoy
is outside the town in either Plava Laguna
or Zelena Laguna. Most of the sports and
recreational centres are affiliated with hotels.
For details, pick up the yearly *Poreč Info* booklet from the tourist office, which lists all the
recreational facilities in the area.

From March to early October a **tourist train**
operates regularly from Šetalište Antuna
Štifanića by the marina to Plava Laguna
(10KN) and Zelena Laguna (15KN). There's
an hourly passenger boat that makes the same
run from the ferry landing (25KN).

The well-marked paths make **cycling** and
hiking prime ways to explore the region. The
tourist office issues a free map of roads and

trails. You can rent a bike at many places
around town; try the **outlet** (☎ 098335838; per
day 70KN) just below the Hotel Poreč.

There is good diving in and around shoals
and sandbanks in the area, as well as to the
nearby *Coriolanus*, a British Royal Navy
warship that sank in 1945. At **Plava Laguna
Diving Center** (☎ 098367619; www.plava-laguna-diving
.hr) boat dives start at 100KN (more for caves
or wrecks).

Sleeping

Accommodation in Poreč is plentiful but gets
booked ahead of time, so reservations are
essential if you come in July or August.

There's a handful of hotels in the old town,
but most of the camping grounds, hotels,
apartment complexes and resorts spread along
the coast north and south of Poreč. The major
tourist complexes are in Plava Laguna, 4km
south of the old town, and Zelena Laguna,
2km further. Most hotels are managed by
Valamar Hotels & Resorts (☎ 465 100; www.valamar
.com) or **Plava Laguna** (☎ 410 101; www.plavalaguna
.hr). Only a few hotels remain open all year.

For stays of fewer than three nights, expect a 20% surcharge during summer.

If you want to find private accommodation, consult the travel agencies listed on p199. Expect to pay between 200KN and 250KN for a double room in high season (up to 350KN for a two-person apartment), plus a 30% surcharge for stays of fewer than four nights. There are a limited number of rooms in the old town, where there's no parking. Look for the *Domus Bonus* certificate of quality in private accommodation.

our pick **Hotel Hostin** (☎ 408 800; www.hostin .hr; Rade Končara 4; low-high s 300-650KN, d 395-920KN; P ⚙ 🏊 ⚒) Each of the well-equipped rooms here comes with a balcony. The indoor swimming pool, fitness room, Turkish bath and sauna are nice perks, as are the pebble beach 70m away and the parkland setting.

Hotel Neptun (☎ 400 800; www.valamar.hr; Obala Maršala Tita 15; low-high s 370-515KN, d 500 785KN; P) It's the best of the harbourfront hotels, but the rooms are unspectacular (and slated for renovation). If you pay extra for sea vistas, you'll also get noise from the promenade below. There are two cheaper annexes further down the waterfront: Jadran (doubles low season 250KN, high season 670KN) and Parentino (doubles low season 265KN, high season 740KN).

Hotel Poreč (☎ /fax 451 811; www.hotelporec.com; Rade Končara 1; low-high s 285-495KN, d 395-730KN; ⚒) While the rooms inside this concrete box have uninspiring views over the bus station, they're acceptable and an easy walk from the old town. It's open all year.

Camp Zelena Laguna (☎ 410 700; www.plava laguna.hr; per adult/site 55/75KN; ☉ Apr-Sep) Well equipped for sports, and with access to many beaches, this campsite is only 5km from the old town.

Camp Bijela Uvala (☎ 410 551; www.plavalaguna .hr; per adult/site 55/75KN; ☉ Apr-Sep; 🏊) It can be crowded, as it houses up to 6000, but there are two outdoor pools and the facilities of Zelena Laguna are a stone's throw away.

Eating

A large supermarket and department-store complex is situated next to Hotel Poreč, near the bus station.

our pick **Dva Ferala** (☎ 433 416; Obala Maršala Tita 13a; mains from 50KN) Savour well-prepared Istrian specialities, such as Istarski Tris for two (a co-

pious trio of homemade pastas; 110KN) at the terrace of this *konoba* (family-run bistro).

Nono (☎ 435 088; Zagrebačka 4; pizzas 45-80KN) Nono serves the best pizza in town, with puffy crust and toppings such as truffles. Other dishes are tasty too.

Barilla (☎ 452 742; Eufrazijeva 26; mains from 45KN) Comforting Italian concoctions in all shapes and forms – penne, tagliatelle, fusilli, tortellini, gnocchi… There are tables on the square and a quieter patio in the back. Try the spaghetti with seashells (170KN for two).

Peterokutna Kula (☎ 451 378; Decumanus 1; mains from 65KN) Inside the medieval Pentagonal Tower, this upscale restaurant has an alfresco terrace in a stone vault, where a full spectrum of fish and meat can be yours to taste. The oven-baked sea bass is particularly good.

Peškera (☎ 432 890; Nikole Tesle bb; meals 35-60KN; ☉ 10am-9pm) Seemingly stuck in the socialist era, this self-service canteen offers simple, cheap meals like fried chicken and grilled calamari. It has a sea-facing terrace.

Drinking & Entertainment

Byblos (www.byblos.hr; Zelena Laguna bb) Celeb guest DJs such as David Morales and Eric Morillo crank out house tunes at this humongous open-air club, one of Croatia's hottest places to party.

Lapidarium (Svetog Maura 10) This gorgeous bar behind the regional museum has a large courtyard and a series of antique-filled inner rooms. Wednesday is jazz night in summer, with alfresco live music.

Saint & Sinner (☎ 434 390; Obala Maršala Tita 12) A B&W plastic theme runs through this latest opening on the waterfront, where the young ones sip *chococcinos* during the day and strawberry *caipiroskas* at night.

Torre Rotonda (Narodni Trg 3a) Take the steep stairs to the top of the historic Round Tower and grab a table at the open-air cafe to watch the action on the quays.

Getting There & Away

Buses from the **bus station** (☎ 432 153; Rade Končara 1) go to Rovinj (38KN, 40 minutes, seven daily), Zagreb (217KN, five hours, seven daily), Rijeka (81KN, two hours, 11 daily) and Pula (50KN, one to 1½ hours, 11 daily).

The nearest train station is at Pazin, 37km to the east. There are about 10 buses daily from Poreč (34KN, 30 minutes).

CROATIA

For information about boat connections to Italy, see p444.

ROVINJ
pop 14,200

Rovinj (Rovigno in Italian) is coastal Istria's star attraction. While it can get overrun with tourists in summer months and residents are developing a sharp eye for maximising their profits by upgrading the hotels and restaurants to four-star status, it remains one of the last true Mediterranean fishing ports. Fishers haul their catch into the harbour in the early morning, followed by a horde of squawking gulls, and mend their nets before lunch. The massive Cathedral of St Euphemia, with its 60m-high tower, punctuates the peninsula. Wooded hills and low-rise hotels surround the old town, webbed by steep, cobbled streets and piazzas. The 13 green, offshore islands of the Rovinj archipelago make for a pleasant afternoon away, and you can swim from the rocks in the sparkling water below the old town.

Orientation

The old town of Rovinj is contained within an egg-shaped peninsula, with the bus station just to the southeast. There are two harbours – the northern open harbour and the small, protected harbour to the south.

Information

There's an ATM next to the bus station entrance, and banks are all around town. Most travel agencies will change money.

Futura Travel (☎ 817 281; www.futura-travel.hr; Matteo Benussi 2; ☒ 8.30am-9pm Mon-Sat, 8.30am-1pm & 5-9pm Sun May-Sep) Private accommodation, excursions and transfers.

Garderoba (per hr 1.40KN; ☒ 6.30am-8.15pm Mon-Fri, 7.45am-7.30pm Sat & Sun) Left luggage; at the bus station. Note the three half-hour breaks at 9.15am, 1.30pm and 4.30pm.

Globtour (☎ 814 130; www.globtour-turizam.hr; Alda Rismonda 2; ☒ 9am-10pm Jul & Aug, reduced hr rest of yr) Excursions, private accommodation, and bike rental (60KN per day).

Kompas (☎ 813 211; www.kompas-travel.com; Trg Maršala Tita 5; ☒ 9am-10pm Jul & Aug, reduced hr rest of yr) Daily excursions.

Main post office (Matteo Benussi 4; ☒ 7am-8pm Mon-Fri, to 2pm Sat)

Medical Centre (☎ 813 004; Istarska bb)

Planet (☎ 840 494; Svetog Križa 1; per 10min 6KN; ☒ 9am-10pm Mon-Sat, 9am-1pm & 5-9pm Sun) Travel agency with an internet terminal.

Tourist office (☎ 811 566; www.tzgrovinj.hr; Pina Budicina 12; ☒ 8am-10pm Jul & Aug, to 9pm Sep-Jun) Just off Trg Maršala Tita, the office has plenty of brochures, maps and materials.

Sights

The town's showcase is the imposing **Church of St Euphemia** (Sveta Eufemija; ☎ 815 615; Petra Stankovića; ☒ 10am-6m Jul & Aug, 11am-3pm Sep-Jun) that dominates the old town from its hilltop location. Built in 1736, it's the largest baroque building in Istria, reflecting the period during the 18th century when Rovinj was its most populous town, an important fishing centre and the bulwark of the Venetian fleet.

Inside the church behind the right-hand altar, don't miss the marble tomb of St Euphemia, Rovinj's patron saint, martyred in AD 304, whose body mysteriously appeared in Rovinj according to legend. On the anniversary of her martyrdom (16 September) devotees congregate here. The mighty 60m tower is topped by a copper statue of St Euphemia, which shows the direction of the wind by turning on a spindle. You can climb it for 10KN.

The **Heritage Museum** (☎ 816 720; www.muzej-rovinj.hr; Trg Maršala Tita 11; adult/concession 15/10KN; ☒ 9am-3pm & 7-10pm Tue-Fri, 9am-2pm & 7-10pm Sat & Sun mid-Jun–mid-Sep, 9am-3pm Tue-Sat rest of yr), in a baroque palace, contains a collection of contemporary art and old masters from Croatia and Rovinj, as well as archaeological finds and a maritime section.

Nearby is the elaborate **Balbi Arch**, built in 1679 on the location of the former town gate. The cobbled street of **Grisia** leads uphill from behind the arch to St Euphemia, lined with galleries where local artists sell their work. On the second Sunday in August each year, narrow Grisia becomes an open-air **art exhibition** with anyone from children to professional painters displaying their work. The winding narrow backstreets that spread around Grisia are an attraction in themselves. Windows, balconies, portals and squares are a pleasant confusion of styles – Gothic, Renaissance, baroque and neoclassical.

On the harbour, **Batana House** (☎ 812 593; www.batana.org; Pina Budicina 2; admission free, with guide 15KN; ☒ 10am-1pm & 7-10pm Tue-Sun May-Sep, 10am-

1pm Tue-Sun rest of yr) is a multimedia museum dedicated to the *batana*, a flat-bottomed fishing boat that stands as a symbol of Rovinj's seafaring and fishing tradition.

When you've seen enough of the town, follow the waterfront on foot or by bike past Hotel Park to the verdant **Golden Cape Forest Park** (Zlatni Rt, or Punta Corrente) about 1.5km south. Covered in oak and pine groves and boasting 10 species of cypress, the park was established in 1890 by Baron Hütterott, an Austrian admiral who kept a villa on Crveni Otok. Here you can swim off the rocks or just sit and admire the offshore islands.

Activities

Most people hop aboard a boat for swimming, snorkelling and sunbathing. A trip to Crveni Otok or Sveti Katarina is easily arranged. In summer, there are 18 boats daily to Sveta Katarina (15KN, five minutes) and on to Crveni Otok (15KN return, 15 minutes). They leave from just opposite Hotel Adriatic and also from the Delphin ferry dock near Hotel Park.

Diver Sport Center (☎ 816 648; www.diver.hr; Villas Rubin) is the largest operation in Rovinj, offering boat dives from 210KN, with equipment rental. The main dive attraction is the wreck of the *Baron Gautsch*, an Austrian passenger steamer sunk in 1914 by a sea mine.

Biking around Rovinj and the Golden Cape park is a superb way to spend an afternoon. You can rent bicycles at many agencies around town, from 60KN per day. The cheapest bike rental (5KN per hour) is at the town entrance, by the Valdibora parking lot and the market.

Tours

Most travel agencies listed on opposite sell day trips to Venice (450KN to 520KN), Plitvice (580KN) and Brijuni (380KN to 420KN). There are also fish picnics (250KN), panoramic cruises (100KN) and trips to Limska Draga fjord (150KN). These trips can be slightly cheaper if booked through one of the independent operators that line the waterfront; **Delfin** (☎ 813 266) is reliable.

Sleeping

Rovinj has become Istria's destination of choice for hordes of summertime tourists, so reservations are strongly recommended.

If you want to stay in private accommodation, there's little available in the old town,

plus there's no parking and the cost is higher. Double rooms start at 180KN in high season, with a small discount for single occupancy; two-person apartments start at 380KN. You can book directly through www.inforovinj .com or one of the listed agencies.

The surcharge for a stay of fewer than three nights is 50%, and guests who stay only one night are punished with a 100% surcharge. Outside summer months, you should be able to bargain the surcharge away.

Except for a few private options, most hotels and campsites in the area are managed by **Maistra** (www.maistra.com).

our pick **Casa Garzotto** (☎ 811884; www.casa-garzotto .com; Via Garzotto 8; s low-high 510-760KN, d 650-1015KN; P ⊠ ⬚) Each of the four nicely outfitted studio apartments have original detail, a stylish touch and up-to-the-minute amenities. The historic townhouse couldn't be better placed. Bikes are complimentary.

Hotel Villa Angelo d'Oro (☎ 840 502; www.angelo doro.hr; Vladimira Švalbe 38-42; low-high s 619-990KN, d 1005-1762KN; P ⊠) In a renovated Venetian townhouse, the 24 plush rooms and (pricier) suites of this boutique hotel have lots of antiques plus mod perks aplenty. There's sauna, jacuzzi and a lush interior terrace, a great place for a drink amidst ancient stone.

Hotel Adriatic (☎ 815 088; www.maistra.hr; Pina Budicina bb; s low-high 392-589KN, d 522-784KN; ⊠ ⬚) The location right on the harbour is excellent; the rooms are spick and span and well equipped but on the kitschy side. The sea view rooms are more spacious.

Vila Lili (☎ 840 940; www.hotel-vilalili.hr; Mohorovičića 16; low-high s 333-385KN, d 505-730KN; ⊠ ⬚) Bright rooms with all the three-star perks, including air-con and minibar in a small modern house a short walk out of town.

Porton Biondi (☎ 813 557; www.portonbiondi.hr; per person/tent 40/23KN; ☀ Apr-Oct) This camping ground that sleeps 1200 is about 700m from the old town.

Eating

Most of the restaurants that line the harbour offer the standard fish and meat mainstays at similar prices. For a more gourmet experience, you'll need to bypass the water vistas. Note that many restaurants shut their doors between lunch and dinner. For an evening snack of local cheese, cured meats and tasty small bites, head to **Ulika** (Vladimira Švalbe 34; ☀ evenings

CROATIA

only), a tiny tavern a few doors down from Angelo d'Oro. Picnickers can get supplies at the supermarket next to the bus station or at one of the Konzum stores around town.

La Puntuleina (☎ 813 186; Svetog Križa 38; mains 100-160KN) Sample creative Med cuisine on three alfresco terraces – from traditional recipes like *žgvacet* of calamari to revamped ones like truffle-topped fish filet. Pastas are more affordable (from 55KN). At night, grab a cushion and sip a cocktail on the rocks below this converted townhouse. Reservations recommended.

Trattoria Dream (☎ 830 613; Joakima Rakovca 18; mains from 75KN) Tucked away in the maze of narrow streets, and with two earthy-coloured outdoor terraces, this stylish trattoria does flavourful dishes like salt-baked sea bass and some global favourites like chilli con carne and chicken curry.

Cantinon (☎ 816 075; Alda Rismonda 18; mains 29-74KN) A fishing theme runs through this high-ceilinged canteen that specialises in fresh seafood at low prices. The Batana fish plate for two (68KN) is great value.

Veli Jože (☎ 816 337; Svetog Križa 3; mains from 35KN) Graze on good Istrian standards, either in the eclectic interior crammed with knick-knacks or on the outdoor tables with water views.

CROATIA

Drinking

Havana (Aldo Negri bb) Tropical cocktails, Cuban cigars, straw parasols and the shade of tall pine trees make this open-air cocktail bar a popular spot to chill and watch the ships go by.

Monte Carlo (☎ 830 683; Svetog Križa 21) This low-key cafe-bar has great views of the sea and St Katarina across the way.

Zanzibar (☎ 813 206; Pina Budicina bb) Indonesian wood, palms, wicker lounge chairs and subdued lighting on the huge outdoor terrace of this cocktail bar create a tropical and definitely upscale vibe.

Getting There & Away

Eurostar Travel (☎ 813 144; Pina Budicina 1; 🕑 9am-9pm Mon-Sat, 9am-1pm & 5-8pm Sun) has schedules and tickets for boats to Venice and Trieste.

Buses go to Pula (35KN, 40 minutes, 13 daily), Dubrovnik (593KN, 16 hours, one daily), Poreč (37KN, one hour, eight daily), Rijeka (112KN, 3½ hours, four daily), Zagreb (173KN to 255KN, five hours, four daily) and Split (417KN, 11 hours, one daily).

The closest train station is at Kanfanar, 20km away on the Pula–Divača line.

PULA

pop 65,000

The wealth of Roman architecture makes the otherwise workaday Pula (ancient Polensium) a standout among Croatia's larger cities. The star of the Roman show is the remarkably well-preserved Roman amphitheatre, which dominates the streetscape and doubles as a venue for summer concerts and performances. Historical attractions aside, Pula is a busy commercial city on the sea that has managed to retain a friendly small-town appeal. A series of beaches and good nightlife awaits just a short bus ride away in the resorts that occupy the Verudela Peninsula to the south. Further south along the indented shoreline, the Premantura Peninsula hides a spectacular nature area, the protected cape of Kamenjak.

Orientation

The oldest part of the city follows the ancient Roman plan of streets circling the central citadel. Most shops, agencies and businesses are clustered in and around the old town as well as on Giardini, Carrarina, Istarska and Riva, which runs along the harbour. The bus station is 500m northeast of the town centre. The harbour is west of the bus station. The train station is near the sea less than a kilometre north of town.

Information

You can exchange money in travel agencies and banks or at the post offices. There are numerous ATMs around town.

Arenaturist (☎ 529 400; www.arenaturist.hr; Splitska 1a; 🕑 8am-8pm Mon-Fri, to 6pm Sat) In the Hotel Riviera, it books rooms in the network of hotels it manages. It also offers guide services and excursions.

Garderoba (per hr 2.20KN; 🕑 4am-10.30pm Mon-Sat, 5am-10.30pm Sun) Left luggage; at the bus station.

Hospital (☎ 376 548; Zagrebačka 34)

Istra Way (☎ 214 868; www.istraway.hr; Riva 14; 🕑 9am-9pm Jul–mid-Sep) On the harbour, it books private accommodation, offers excursions to Brijuni, Rovinj and Lim, and has bikes for rent (100KN per day).

Main post office (Danteov Trg 4; 🕑 7.30am-7pm Mon-Fri, to 2.30pm Sat) You can make long-distance calls here. Check out the cool staircase inside!

MMC Luka (☎ 224 316; Istarska 30; per hr 20KN; 🕑 8am-midnight Mon-Fri, to 3pm Sat) Internet access.

Tourist information centre (☎ 212 987; www.pulainfo.hr; Forum 3; 🕑 8am-9pm Mon-Fri, 9am-9pm Sat & Sun summer, 8am-7pm Mon-Fri, 9am-7pm Sat, 10am-4pm Sun rest of yr) Knowledgable and friendly, it

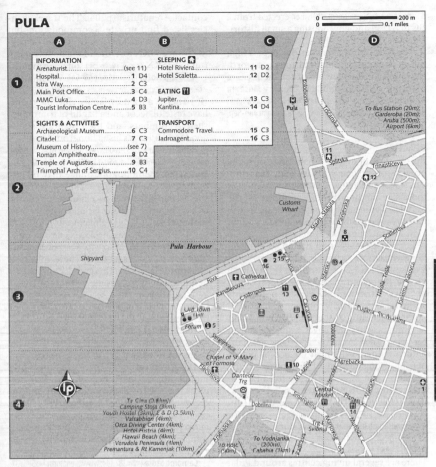

PULA

0 — 200 m
0 — 0.1 miles

INFORMATION
Arenaturist....................................(see 11)
Hospital..1 D4
Istra Way...2 C3
Main Post Office....................................3 C4
MMC Luka..4 D3
Tourist Information Centre..................5 B3

SIGHTS & ACTIVITIES
Archaeological Museum......................6 C3
Citadel..7 C3
Museum of History.........................(see 7)
Roman Amphitheatre..........................8 D2
Temple of Augustus..............................9 B3
Triumphal Arch of Sergius................10 C4

SLEEPING
Hotel Riviera......................................11 D2
Hotel Scaletta....................................12 D2

EATING
Jupiter...13 C3
Kantina..14 D4

TRANSPORT
Commodore Travel..........................15 C3
Jadroagent..16 C3

provides heaps of maps and brochures. Pick up the useful *Domus Bonus* booklet, which lists the best-quality private accommodation in Istria.

Sights

Pula's most imposing sight is the 1st-century **Roman amphitheatre** (☎ 219 028; Flavijevska bb; adult/concession 40/20KN; ⏰ 8am-9pm summer, 9am-8pm spring & autumn, 9am-5pm winter) overlooking the harbour northeast of the old town. Built entirely from local limestone, the amphitheatre with seating for up to 20,000 spectators was designed to host gladiatorial contests. In the chambers downstairs is a small museum with a display of ancient olive-oil equipment. Every summer, Pula Film Festival is held here, as are pop and classical concerts.

The **Archaeological Museum** (Arheološki Muzej; ☎ 218 603; Carrarina 3; adult/concession 20/10KN; ⏰ 9am-8pm Mon-Sat, 10am-3pm Sun May-Sep, 9am-2pm Mon-Fri Oct-Apr) presents archaeological finds from all over Istria. Even if you don't enter the museum, be sure to visit the large sculpture garden around it, and the **Roman theatre** behind. The garden, entered through 2nd-century twin gates, is the site of concerts in summer.

Along Carrarina are **Roman walls**, which mark the eastern boundary of old Pula. Follow these walls south and continue down Giardini to the **Triumphal Arch of Sergius** (27 BC). The street beyond the arch winds right around old Pula, changing names several times. Follow it to the ancient **Temple of Augustus** (☎ 218 603; Forum; adult/concession 10/5KN; ⏰ 9am-8pm Mon-Fri, 10am-3pm Sat

& Sun summer, by appointment otherwise), erected from 2 BC to AD 14 and now housing a small historical museum with captions in English.

The 17th-century Venetian **citadel**, on a high hill in the centre of the old town, is worth the climb for the view if not for the meagre maritime-related exhibits in the tiny **Museum of History** (Povijesni Muzej Istre; ☎ 211 566; Gradinski Uspon 6; adult/concession 15/7KN; ☼ 8am-9pm Jun-Sep, 9am-5pm Oct-May) inside.

BEACHES

Pula is surrounded by a half-circle of rocky beaches, each one with its own fan club. The most tourist-packed are undoubtedly those surrounding the hotel complex on the Verudela Peninsula, although some locals will dare to be seen at the small turquoise-coloured Hawaii Beach near the Hotel Park.

For more seclusion, head out to the wild **Rt Kamenjak** (www.kamenjak.hr, in Croatian; pedestrians & cyclists free, cars 20KN, scooters 10KN; ☼ 7am-10pm) on the Premantura Peninsula 10km south of town. Istria's southernmost point, this gorgeous, entirely uninhabited cape has wild flowers, including 30 species of orchid, 30km of virgin beaches and coves, and a delightful beach bar, **Safari** (snacks 25-50KN; ☼ Easter-Sep), half-hidden in the bushes near the beach. Watch out for strong currents if swimming off the southern cape. Take city bus 26 from Pula to Premantura (15KN); to get inside the park, rent a bike (50KN to 100KN per day) from **Windsurf Bar** (☎ 0915123646; Camping Village Stupice; www.windsurfing.hr) near the bus stop.

Activities

There are several diving centres around Pula. At **Orca Diving Center** (☎ 224 422; www.orcadiving.hr; Hotel Histria) on the Verudela Peninsula you can arrange for boat dives, wreck dives and introductory dives.

In addition to windsurfing courses, the Windsurf Bar in Premantura offers biking (250KN) and kayaking (300KN) excursions.

Sleeping

Pula's peak tourist season runs from the second week of July to the end of August. During this period it's wise to make reservations. The tip of the Verudela Peninsula, 4km southwest of the city centre, has been turned into a vast tourist complex replete with hotels and apartments.

Any travel agency can give you information and book you into one of the hotels, or you can

contact Arenaturist (p204). The travel agencies listed find private accommodation, but there's little in the town centre. Count on paying from 250KN to 490KN for a double room (up to 535KN for a two-person apartment).

our pick **Hotel Scaletta** (☎ 541 599; www.hotel-scaletta.com; Flavijevska 26; low-high s 398-498KN, d 598-718KN; P) There's a friendly family vibe, the rooms have tasteful decor and a bagful of trimmings, such as minibars, and the restaurant serves good food. Plus it's just a hop from town.

Hotel Histria (☎ 590 000; www.arenaturist.hr; Verudela; low-high s 400-666KN, d 650-1190KN; P ✗ ☒ ☒) Its concrete-behemoth appearance may be off-putting, but the extensive facilities, balconied rooms and easy beach access make up for the lack of character. It shares facilities with the new, slightly cheaper Hotel Palma (doubles low season 485KN, high season 935KN) next door.

Hotel Riviera (☎ 211 166; www.arenaturist.hr; Splitska 1; low-high s 283-354KN, d 464-600KN) There's plenty of old-world elegance at this grand 19th-century building, but the rooms need a thorough overhaul and the carpets a serious scrub. On the plus side, it's in the centre and the front rooms have water views.

Youth Hostel (☎ 391 133; www.hfhs.hr; Valsaline 4; low-high dm 85-114KN, mobile 103-134KN; ☐) This hostel overlooks a beach in Valsaline bay, 3km south of central Pula. There are dorms and mobile homes split into two tiny four-bed units, each with bathroom and air-con on request (15KN per day). There's bike rental (80KN per day) and campsites (70/15KN per person/tent). Take bus 2 or 3 to the 'Piramida' stop, walk back to the first street, then turn left and look for the sign.

Camping Stoja (☎ 387 144; www.arenaturist.hr; Stoja 37; per person/tent 52/30KN; ☼ Apr-Oct) The closest camping ground to Pula, 3km southwest of the centre, has lots of space on the shady promontory, with a restaurant, a diving centre and swimming possible off the rocks. Take bus 1 to Stoja.

Eating

There are a number of decent eating places in the city centre, although most locals head out of town for better value and fewer tourists.

our pick **Gina** (☎ 387 943; Stoja 23; mains from 60KN) Istrian mainstays like *manestra* and *fritaja* are prepared with care, pastas are handmade, and veggies picked from the garden. This stylish but low-key eatery near Stoja campsite draws in a local crowd. Try the semifreddo with a hot sauce of figs, pine nuts and lavender.

Vodnjanka (☎ 210 655; Vitezića 4; mains from 30KN; ☽ closed dinner Sat & all day Sun) Locals swear by the home cooking here. It's cheap, casual and cash only, and has a small menu that concentrates on simple Istrian dishes. To get here, walk south on Radićeva to Vitezića.

Valsabbion (☎ 218 033; www.valsabbion.hr; Pješčana Uvala IX/26; mains 95-175KN) The creative Croatian cuisine conjured up at this award-winning restaurant, one of Croatia's best, is an epicurean delight. The decor is showy but stunning; the menu's gimmicky in its descriptions, but the food is tops. Sampling menus range from 395KN to 555KN. It doubles as a plush 10-room hotel (doubles 860KN) with a top-floor spa. It's in upscale Pješčana Uvala, south of the city.

Jupiter (☎ 214 333; Castropola 42; pizzas 21-37KN) The thin-crust pizza here would make any Italian mamma proud; the pasta is yummy too. There's a terrace upstairs and a 20% discount on Wednesday.

Kantina (☎ 214 054; Flanatička 16; mains 55-125KN; ☽ closed Sun) The beamed stone cellar of this Habsburg building has been redone in a modern style. It won't help you fit into your bikini, but you'll appreciate the ravioli Kantina, stuffed with *skuta* (ricotta) and *pršut* (prosciutto) in a cheese sauce.

Drinking & Entertainment

You should definitely try to catch a concert in the spectacular amphitheatre; the tourist office has schedules.

Although most of the nightlife is out of the town centre, in mild weather the cafes on the Forum and along the pedestrian streets, Kandlerova, Flanatička and Sergijevaca, are lively people-watching spots. For the most underground experience, check the program at **Rojc** (Gajeva 3; www.rojcnet.hr), a converted army barracks that now houses a multimedia art centre and art studios with occasional concerts, exhibits and other events.

ourpick **Cabahia** (Širolina 4) An artsy hideaway in Veruda, with cosy wood-beamed interior, eclectic decor of old objects, dim lighting, South American flair and a great garden terrace in the back. It hosts concerts and gets packed on weekends.

Aruba (☎ 300 535; Šijanska 1a) On the road to the airport, this popular cafe-bar-disco is a relaxing hang-out during the day and, come night, turns into a hopping venue for live music and parties. The outdoor terrace gets crowded. Wednesday is salsa night.

E&D (☎ 894 2015; Verudela 22) Lounge just above Umbrella beach on Verudela, on the lush outdoor terrace with several levels of straw-chair seating interspersed with small pools and waterfalls. The sunset views are great and weekend nights spiced with live DJ tunes.

Getting There & Away
BOAT
Jadroagent (☎ 210 431; www.jadroagent.hr; Riva 14; ☽ 7am-3pm Mon-Fri) has schedules and tickets for boats connecting Istria with Italy and the islands. It also represents Jadrolinija.

Commodore Travel (☎ 211 631; www.commodore -travel.hr; Riva 14, ☽ 8am-8pm Jun-Sep) sells tickets for a catamaran between Pula and Zadar that runs five times weekly from July through early September (100KN, five hours) and twice weekly in June and September. There's a weekly boat to Venice between June and September (370KN, 3½ hours).

BUS
From the Pula **bus station** (☎ 500 012; Trg 1 Istarske Brigade bb) there are buses heading to Rijeka almost hourly (86KN to 91KN, two hours). In summer, reserve a seat a day in advance and be sure to sit on the right-hand side of the bus for a stunning view of the Kvarner Gulf.

Other destinations you can reach by bus include Rovinj (35KN, 45 minutes, 15 daily), Poreč (54KN to 65KN, one to 1½ hours, 13 daily), Zagreb (210KN, four to five hours, 18 daily), Zadar (249KN to 257KN, seven hours, three daily), Split (360KN to 396KN, 10 hours, three daily) and Dubrovnik (568KN, 10½ hours, one daily).

TRAIN
There are two daily trains to Ljubljana, with a change in Buzet (133KN, two hours), and four to Zagreb (125KN to 148KN, 6½ hours), but you must board a bus for part of the trip, from Lupoglav to Rijeka.

Getting Around
The city buses of use to visitors are the 1, which runs to the Autocamp Stoja, and the 2 and 3 to Verudela. Tickets are sold at *tisak* for 6KN, or 10KN from the driver.

AROUND PULA
Brijuni Islands National Park
The Brijuni (Brioni in Italian) archipelago consists of two main pine-covered islands and

CROATIA

12 islets off the coast of Istria, just northwest of Pula. Now a highly groomed and scrupulously maintained national park, the islands owe their fame to Tito, the extravagant Yugoslav leader who turned them into his private retreat. He hosted many illustrious guests at his Brijuni hideaway, including Josephine Baker, Sophia Loren, Elizabeth Taylor and Richard Burton. Some 680 species of plants grow here, including many exotic subtropical species which were planted at Tito's request. Tito's former private hunting grounds are now a safari park where elephants, zebras and antelope roam.

You may only visit Brijuni National Park with a group on a three-hour guided tour, or if you stay at one of the hotels on the islands. **Hotel Istra-Neptun** (☎ 525 807; www.brijuni.hr; low-high s 297-716KN, d 463-1215KN) is the ultimate in communist chic. Instead of booking an excursion with one of the travel agencies in Pula, Rovinj or Poreč, you could take public bus 21 from Pula to Fažana (8km), then sign up for a tour (110KN to 190KN) at the **national park office** (☎ 525 883; www.brijuni.hr) near the wharf. It's best to book in advance, especially in summer, and request an English-speaking tour guide.

PAZIN
pop 5200

Most famous for the gaping chasm that so inspired Jules Verne and for its medieval castle, Pazin is a workaday provincial town in central Istria. It deserves a stop mainly for the chasm and the castle, but part of the appeal is the small-town feel and the lack of fashionable foreigners stomping its streets.

Lying at the geographic heart of Istria, Pazin is the county's administrative seat and excellently connected by road and rail to virtually every other destination in Istria. The hotel and restaurant pickings in town itself are skimpy, so you're better off visiting on a day trip, since you're within an hour of most other places in Istria.

Orientation & Information

The town is relatively compact, stretching little more than a kilometre from the train station on the eastern end to the Kaštel on the western end, which is at the edge of Pazin Cave. The bus station is 200m west of the train station, and the old part of town comprises the 200m leading up to the Kaštel.

The best source of information about Pazin and its surrounding area is the **tourist office** (☎ 622 460; www.tzpazin.hr; Franine i Jurine 14; ☺ 8.30am-6pm Jul & Aug, 8am-3pm Mon-Fri Sep-Jun), which also manages all of central Istria. They distribute a map of hiking trails and honey spots (you can visit bee-keepers and taste their delicious acacia honey).

Sights

Pazin's most renowned site is the **Pazin Cave** (☎ 622 220; www.pazinska-jama.com; adult/concession 30/15KN, free & at your own risk May-Oct; ☺ 10am-6pm Tue-Sun mid-Apr–mid-Oct, 10am-3pm Tue-Thu, noon-5pm Fri, 11am-5pm Sat & Sun mid-Oct–mid-Apr), a deep abyss of about 100m through which the Pazinčica River sinks into subterranean passages forming three underground lakes. Its shadowy depths inspired the imagination of Jules Verne, who set his *Mathias Sandorf* (1885) novel here. Visitors can walk the 1200m path inside the abyss. If the trip into the abyss doesn't appeal, there's a viewing point just outside the castle.

Looming over the chasm, Pazin's **Kaštel** (Trg Istarskog Razvoda 1; ☺ 10am-6pm Tue-Sun mid-Apr–mid-Oct, 10am-3pm Tue-Thu, noon-5pm Fri, 11am-5pm Sat & Sun mid-Oct–mid-Apr) is the largest and best-preserved medieval structure in Istria. Within are two museums, both open the same hours as the castle. The **town museum** (☎ 622 220; adult/concession 15/8KN) has a collection of medieval Istrian church bells, an exhibit about slave revolts, and torture instruments in the dungeon. The **Ethnographic Museum** (☎ 622 220; www.emi.hr; adult/concession 15/8KN) has about 4200 artefacts portraying traditional Istrian village life, including garments, tools and pottery.

Festivals & Events

The **Days of Jules Verne** in the last week of June is Pazin's way of honouring the writer that put Pazin on the cultural map. There are races, re-enactments from his novel, and journeys retracing the footsteps of Verne's hero Mathias Sandorf.

Sleeping & Eating

The tourist office helps arrange private accommodation. Count on spending from about 100KN per person for a room.

Poli Luce (☎ 687 081; www.konoba-marino-gracisc .hr; r per person 125KN, breakfast 25KN; ℗) If you don't mind being out of town, try this lovingly restored townhouse with charming rustic rooms. It's in Gračišće, a sleepy medieval town just 7km southeast of Pazin.

Hotel Lovac (☎ /fax 624 324; tisadoo@inet.hr; Šime Kurelića 4; s 240KN, d 420KN; **P**) The late 1960s architecture of Pazin's only hotel, on the western edge of town, could be a hit, if only the rooms were done up right. The hotel restaurant serves acceptable food – especially as there are no notable restaurants in Pazin itself.

Konoba Marino (☎ 687 081; Gračišće; mains from 35KN; ⊗ closed Wed) The owners of Poli Luce also run this cosy tavern next door, dishing out homemade Istrian food.

Getting There & Away

From the **bus station** (☎ 624 364; Šetalište Pazinske Gimnazije) there are services to Motovun (27KN, 40 minutes, two daily Monday to Friday), Poreč (34KN, 45 minutes, seven daily), Pula (41KN, one hour, six daily), Rijeka (53KN, one hour, nine daily) and Rovinj (37KN, one to 1½ hours, five daily). Service is reduced on weekends.

Pazin **train station** (☎ 624 310; Od Stareh Kostanji 3b) has services to Ljubljana (107KN, 3½ to 4½ hours, two daily) with a transfer in Buzet or Divača, Pula (30KN, one hour, nine daily) and Zagreb (111KN to 127KN, five to eight hours, three daily), with a bus portion from Lupoglav to Rijeka.

MOTOVUN
pop 590

Motovun is a captivating little town perched on a 277m hill in Mirna River Valley, about 25km northeast of Poreč. The Venetians fortified the town in the 14th century, building two sets of thick walls. Within these, a cluster of ancient stone buildings now houses a smattering of artists, who have set up studios in this atmospheric tumble of Romanesque and Gothic houses. A popular film festival takes place here every summer.

Orientation & Information

If you come by car, there are three parking spots. The first one is at the foot of the village, from where there's a steep 1km hike up to the city gates. Another parking spot is 300m below the old town. The last one is for residents and guests of Motovun's only hotel. Otherwise, there's a 15KN-per-day charge in season.

The hotel's **tourist agency** (☎ 681 607; Trg Andrea Antico 8; ⊗ 7.30am-3.30pm Mon-Fri) acts as the source of information about Motovun, since there is no official tourist office. There's an ATM just after the town entrance on the right.

Sights

A Venetian lion scowls down from the outer gate, after which sprawls a terrace with a baroque loggia and outside cafe tables, perfect for watching the sun go down below the valley. A cheerier lion adorns the inner gate, which holds a long-running restaurant. Beyond the inner gate is a tree-shaded square with the town's only hotel, an old well and the Renaissance church of St Stephen, under long-term renovation.

Along the inner wall that encloses the old town rises a 16th-century **bell tower** (admission 5KN; ⊗ 10am-5pm), which you can climb for a magnificent view. Make sure to walk on the outer walls of the ramparts for memorable vistas over the vineyards, fields and oak woods below.

There are a number of galleries and crafts shops before you enter the old town and between the town gates, including a wine-tasting shop and another chain of the Zigante food emporium.

Festivals

The **Motovun Film Festival** (www.motovunfilmfestival.com) presents a roster of independent and avant-garde films in late July or early August. It attracts quite a crowd, with nonstop outdoor and indoor screenings, concerts and parties.

Sleeping & Eating

Hotel Kaštel (☎ 681 607; www.hotel-kastel-motovun.hr; Trg Andrea Antico 7; s low-high 308-352KN, d 506-594KN; **P** 🖳) The town's only hotel is in a restored stone building with 28 simply furnished rooms. For 100KN more, get room 202 with a balcony overlooking the square. There's a good restaurant offering truffles and Istrian wines. At research time a wellness centre was being built.

Pod Voltom (☎ 681 923; Trg Josefa Ressela 6; mains from 55KN; ⊗ closed Wed) In a vaulted space within the town gates, just below the hotel, this wood-beamed place serves simple down-home Istrian cuisine and pricier truffle dishes. Try the steak carpaccio with fresh truffles.

Restaurant Zigante (☎ 664 302; www.zigantetartufi.com; Livade 7, Livade; mains from 160KN) Gourmets from afar come to this destination restaurant, repeatedly named one of Croatia's top 10, a few kilometres below Motovun in the village of Livade. Expect five-star fancy dining, with truffles as the showcase – celery and black truffle cappuccino, pigeon with black truffles, even tiramisu with black truffles... Menus start at 440KN.

CROATIA

Getting There & Away

It's not easy to visit Motovun without your own car, but there are bus connections, on weekdays only, from Pazin (27KN, 40 minutes, two daily) and Poreč (29KN, 45 minutes, one daily).

GROŽNJAN

pop 193

Until the mid-1960s, Grožnjan, 27km northeast of Poreč, was slipping towards oblivion. First mentioned in 1102, this hilltop town was a strategically important fortress for the 14th-century Venetians. They created a system of ramparts and gates, and built a loggia, a granary and several fine churches. With the collapse of the Venetian empire in the 18th century, Grožnjan suffered a decline in its importance and its population.

In 1965 sculptor Aleksandar Rukavina and a small group of other artists 'discovered' the crumbling medieval appeal of Grožnjan and began setting up studios in the abandoned buildings. In 1969 a summer school for musicians, Jeunesses Musicales Croatia, was established in Grožnjan and has been going strong ever since. Concerts and musical events are held almost daily in summer, and you can overhear the musicians practising while you browse the many crafts shops and galleries.

Orientation & Information

The tiny town is a jumble of crooked lanes and leafy squares. Near the centre is the **tourist office** (☎ 776 349; www.tz-groznjan.hr; Umberta Gorjana 3; ⌚ 8am-4pm Mon-Fri), which provides a list of private accommodation options in and around town and a small map with a list of galleries.

Sights & Activities

The Renaissance **loggia** is immediately to the right of the town gate by the tourist office. Keep going and on your right you'll see the baroque **Spinotti Morteani Palace**, its patio taken over by the outdoor tables of the **Zigante Tartufi** (☎ 721 998; www.zigantetartufi.com; Umberta Gorjana 5) shop and its adjacent wine bar. Next to the right comes the **Kaštel**, where many concerts are held.

Summer music concerts are organised by the **International Cultural Centre of Jeunesses Musicales Croatia** (☎ 776 223; www.hgm.hr, in Croatian). Held in various locations around town, the concerts are free and no reservations are necessary.

There are over 30 galleries and studios scattered around town; most are open daily from May to September. **City Gallery Fonticus** (Gradska Galerija Fonticus; ☎ 776 349; www.gallery-fonticus-groznjan.net; Trg Lođe 3; ⌚ 10am-1pm & 5-8pm Tue-Sun) promotes recent work of Croatian and some international artists.

Sleeping & Eating

The tourist office can put you in touch with private room owners. Count on spending about 100KN per person.

Bastia (☎ 776 370; 1 Svibnja 1; mains from 45KN) The town's oldest restaurant sits on the verdant main square. The decor is bright and cheerful, the menu extensive and heavy on the truffles.

Getting There & Away

There are no buses directly to Grožnjan unless it's a school day. If you're driving from Motovun, do not take the first marked turnoff for Grožnjan – it's unpaved and takes a lot longer. Continue along the road for another kilometre or so until you get to another sign for Grožnjan – this is a far better approach.

KVARNER REGION

☎ 051

The Kvarner Gulf (Quarnero in Italian) covers 3300 sq km between Rijeka and Pag Island in the south, protected by the Velebit Range in the southeast, the Gorski Kotar in the east and the Učka massif in the northwest. Covered with luxuriant forests, lined with beaches and dotted with islands, the region has a mild, gentle climate and a wealth of vegetation.

The metropolitan focus is the busy commercial port of Rijeka, Croatia's third-largest city, only a few kilometres from the aristocratic Opatija Riviera. The islands of Krk, Rab, Cres and Lošinj offer picture-perfect old towns just a ferry ride away, as well as plenty of beaches for scenic swimming.

RIJEKA

pop 147,700

While Rijeka (Fiume in Italian) doesn't fit the bill as a tourist destination, it does offer an insightful glimpse into the workaday life of Croatia's largest port. Most people rush through en route to the islands or Dalmatia, but for those who pause, a few assets await. Blend in with the coffee-sipping locals on the bustling Korzo pedestrian strip, stroll along the tree-lined promenade that fronts the harbour, and visit the imposing hilltop fortress of Trsat. Rijeka also boasts a burgeoning nightlife and, every year, Croatia's biggest and most colourful carnival celebration.

Much of the centre contains the ornate, imposing public buildings you would expect to find in Vienna or Budapest, evidence of the strong Austro-Hungarian influence. The industrial aspect is evident from the boats, cargo and cranes that line the waterfront, but there's a seedy beauty to it. As one of Croatia's most important transportation hubs, Rijeka has buses, trains and ferries that connect Istria and Dalmatia with Zagreb.

Orientation

Korzo runs through the city centre, roughly parallel to Riva (seafront), towards the Rječina River in the east. The intercity **bus station** (☎ 060 302 010; Trg Žabica 1) is at the western edge of Riva. The train station is a five-minute walk west of the intercity bus station, along Krešimirova.

Information

There are two ATMs at the train station and a number of them along Korzo and around the city centre. The exchange offices adjacent to the train and bus stations keep long hours. There's free wi-fi along Korzo and in parts of Trsat.

Blitz (Krešimirova 3a; small load 51KN; ☒ 7am-8pm Mon-Fri, 7am-2pm Sat) Laundry.

Cont (☎ 371 630; Andrije Kačića Miošića 1; per hr 15KN; ☒ 7am-10pm) This cafe inside Hotel Continental has a full bank of computers.

Garderoba intercity bus station (per day 13KN; ☒ 5.30am-10.30pm); train station (per day in locker 15KN; ☒ 4.30am-10.30pm) The bus station left-luggage office is at the cafe next door to the ticket office.

Hospital (☎ 658 111; Krešimirova 42)

Main post office (Korzo 13; ☒ 7am-8pm Mon-Fri, to 2pm Sat) Has a telephone centre and an exchange office.

Tourist Information Centre (☎ 335 882; www.tz-rijeka.hr; Korzo 33a; ☒ 8am-8pm Mon-Sat, 9am-2pm Sun summer, 8am-8pm Mon-Fri, 8am-2pm Sat rest of yr) This spiffy centre has plentiful free materials and info about private accommodation.

Sights

Rijeka's main orientation point is the distinctive yellow **City Tower** (Korzo), originally a gate from the seafront to the city and one of the few monuments to have survived the devastating earthquake of 1750.

Just up from the Korzo on the 2nd floor of the university library is the **Museum of Modern &**

Contemporary Art (Muzej Moderne i Suvremene Umjetnosti; Dolac 1; ☎ 334 280; www.mmsu.hr; adult/student 10/5KN; ☒ 10am-1pm & 6-9pm Tue-Sun summer, 10am-1pm & 5-8pm rest of yr), in an L-shaped space which puts on rotating shows. The **Maritime & History Museum** (Pomorski i Povijesni Muzej Hrvatskog Primorja; ☎ 553 666; www.ppmhp.hr; Muzejski Trg 1; adult/student 10/5KN; ☒ 9am-8pm Tue-Fri, to 1pm Sat) gives a vivid picture of life among seafarers, with model ships, sea charts, navigation instruments and portraits of captains. A five-minute walk to the east is the **Natural History Museum** (Prirodoslovni Muzej; ☎ 553 669; Lorenzov Prolaz 1; adult/student 10/5KN; ☒ 9am-7pm Mon-Sat, to 3pm Sun), devoted to the geology and botany of the Adriatic, inside a 19th-century villa.

Also worth a visit is the **Trsat Castle** (☎ 217 714; adult/student 15/5KN; ☒ 9am-8pm May Oct, to 5pm Nov-Apr), a 13th-century hill fortress that houses two galleries and has great vistas from its open-air cafe. During summer the fortress features concerts, theatre performances and fashion shows. The other hill highlight is the **Church of Our Lady of Trsat** (Crkva Gospe Trsatske; ☎ 452 900; Frankopanski Trg; ☒ by appointment only), a centuries-old magnet for believers that showcases an apparently miraculous icon of the Virgin Mary.

Festivals & Events

The **Rijeka Carnival** (www.ri-karneval.com.hr) is the largest and most elaborate in Croatia, with two weeks of partying that involves pageants, street dances, concerts, masked balls, exhibitions and an international parade. Check out the *zvončari*, masked men clad in animal skins who dance and ring loud bells to frighten off evil spirits. The festivities take place anywhere between late January and early March, depending on when Easter falls.

Sleeping

Prices in Rijeka hotels generally stay the same year-round except at popular carnival time, when you can expect to pay a surcharge. There are few private rooms in Rijeka itself; the tourist office lists these on its website. Opatija (see p215 for details on getting there) is a much better choice for accommodation.

our pick Hotel Jadran (☎ 216 600; www.jadran-hoteli.hr; Šetalište XIII Divizije 46; s/d 672/793KN; P ☒ ☐) The four-star upgrade of this long-standing hotel produced airy rooms with huge glass windows or balconies offering sea vistas. Perks include a restaurant, a small gym and a private

(see p215 for details on getting there)

CROATIA

lonelyplanet.com

RIJEKA

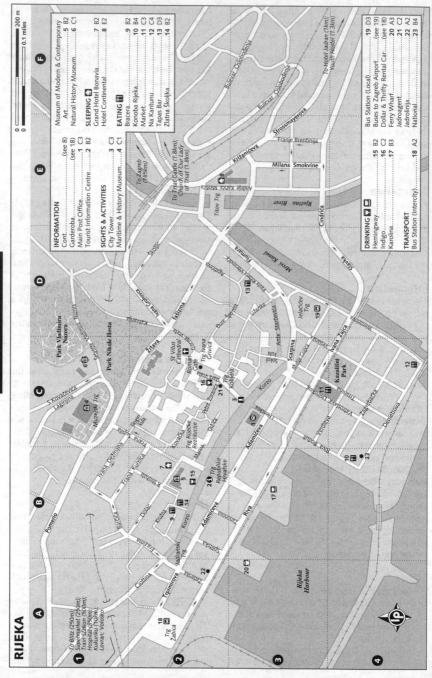

INFORMATION		
Cont.		(see 8)
Garderoba.		(see 18)
Main Post Office.		1 C3
Tourist Information Centre.		2 B2

SIGHTS & ACTIVITIES		
City Tower.		3 C3
Maritime & History Museum.		4 C1

Museum of Modern & Contemporary		
Art.		5 B2
Natural History Museum.		6 C1

SLEEPING		
Grand Hotel Bonavia.		7 B2
Hotel Continental.		8 E2

EATING		
Bracera.		9 B2
Konoba Rijeka.		10 B4
Market.		11 C3
Na Kantunu.		12 C4
Tapas Bar.		13 D3
Zlatna Školjka.		14 B2

DRINKING		
Hemingway.		15 B2
Indigo.		16 C2
Karolina.		17 B3

TRANSPORT		
Bus Station (Intercity).		18 A2
Bus Station (Local).		19 D3
Buses to Zagreb Airport.		(see 19)
Dollar & Thrifty Rental Car.		20 A3
Ferry Wharf.		21 C2
Jadroagent.		22 A2
Jadrolinija.		23 B4
National.		(see 18)

beach below. Worth the 1km trip east of the city centre.

Grand Hotel Bonavia (☎ 357 100; www.bonavia.hr; Dolac 4; s/d from 945/1135KN; P X X Q) Bet on high-brow luxury at this top hotel, one of Croatia's best. Slick rooms are equipped with all top-of-the-line amenities. The restaurant serves outstanding creative cuisine, while the spa offers treats like aromatherapy showers.

Hotel Continental (☎ 372 008; www.jadran-hoteli .hr; Andrije Kačića Miošića 1; s/d 384/449KN; P Q) At the time of writing, more than half of the rooms inside this grand building were being revamped. Once they're primped up, the rating will go up to three stars and the prices by 15%. The location is prime, just northeast of the centre.

Youth Hostel (☎ 406 420; rijeka@hfhs.hr; Šetalište XIII Divizije 23; dm/s/d 130/235/310KN; Q) Five bus stops east of the centre (bus 2) in a leafy residential area of Pečine, this renovated 19th-century villa has clean and snug units and a communal TV room. Breakfast available (15KN); reservations advisable in summer.

Eating

If you want a meal on a Sunday, you'll be limited to fast food, pizza or a hotel restaurant, as nearly every other place in Rijeka is closed.

For self caterers, there're a large supermarket between the bus and train stations and a **market** (btwn Vatroslava Lisinskog & Trninina; ⏱ early-7pm Mon-Sat, to noon Sun).

OUR PICK Na Kantunu (☎ 313 271; Demetrova 2; mains from 35KN) If you're lucky enough to grab a table at this tiny lunchtime spot on an industrial stretch of port, you'll be treated to a superlative daily catch.

Kukuriku (☎ 691 417; Trg Matka Laginje 1a, Kastav; 6-course meals 370-510KN; ⏱ closed Mon winter) Among the pioneers of the slow-food movement in Croatia, this gastronomic destination in the old town of Kastav, Rijeka's hilltop suburb, offers delectable meals amidst lots of rooster-themed decoration. It's worth the splurge and the trek on bus 18.

Tapas Bar (☎ 315 313; Pavla Rittera Vitezovića 5; tapas around 25KN) This small and stylish spot churns out Croatian-inspired tapas. Delicious bruschetta are topped with anchovies, truffles, fresh tuna...at 9KN per piece. Portions are small and the bill adds up.

Konoba Rijeka (☎ 312 084; Riva Boduli 7c; mains from 25KN) Tasty and cheap fish meals can be had at this restaurant right on the harbour,

with high ceilings, stone walls and plenty of fish nets. Try the dried octopus omelette, a house speciality.

Zlatna Školjka (☎ 213 782; Kružna 12; mains 65-95KN) Savour the superbly prepared seafood and choice Croatian wines at this classy maritime-themed restaurant. The mixed fish starter Conco d'Oro is pricey (100KN) but worth it. The adjacent Bracera, by the same owners, serves crusty pizza, even on a Sunday.

Drinking

With several recent openings, Rijeka's nightlife got a boost of energy. Bar-hoppers cruise the bars and cafes along Riva and Korzo for the liveliest of social hubbub. Many of the bars double as clubs on weekends.

Hemingway (☎ 211 696; Korzo 28) This stylish venue for coffee sipping, cocktail drinking and people watching pays homage to the bar's namesake with the hero's large B&W photos and drinks named after him. It's part of a fashionable chain.

Indigo (☎ 315 174; Stara Vrata 3) On weekends the owner likes to lay tracks at this snazzy hang-out next to an archaeological dig. Salsa dancing and after-work parties take place on weeknights. There's a restaurant that, atypically, serves brunch.

Karolina (☎ 211 447; Gat Karoline Riječke bb) Trendy but not self-conscious about it, this waterfront bar-cafe is a relaxed place for a daytime coffee. At night, crowds spill out onto the wharf in a huge outdoor party.

Getting There & Away

BOAT

Jadrolinija (☎ 211 444; www.jadrolinija.hr; Riva 16; ⏱ 8am-8pm Mon-Fri, 9am-5pm Sat & Sun) sells tickets for the large coastal ferries that run all year between Rijeka and Dubrovnik on their way to Bari in Italy, via Split, Hvar and Korčula. Other ferry lines include Rijeka–Cres–Mali Lošinj and Rijeka–Rab–Pag. All ferries depart from Rijeka's **wharf** (Adamićev Gat).

Jadroagent (☎ 211 626; www.jadroagent.hr; Trg Ivana Koblera 2) has information on all boats around Croatia.

BUS

If you fly into Zagreb, there is a Croatia Airlines van directly from Zagreb airport to Rijeka twice daily (at 3.30pm and 9pm; 145KN, two hours) and back from Rijeka (5am and 11am).

BUS SERVICES FROM RIJEKA

Destination	Price (KN)	Duration (hr)	Daily departures
Baška	71	2¼	4-8
Dubrovnik	340-485	12-13	2-3
Krk	50	1-2	14
Poreč	72-114	1-3	7-11
Pula	78-88	2¼	8-10
Rab	125	3	2
Rovinj	81-112	2-3	4-5
Split	241-327	8	6-7
Zadar	153-202	4-5	6-7
Zagreb	95-174	2½-3	13-17

From the intercity bus station there are six daily buses to Trieste (60KN, 2½ hours) and one daily bus to Plitvice, with a change in Otočac (130KN, four hours). For some of the more popular domestic routes, see the table, above.

CAR
Dollar & Thrifty Rental Car (☎ 325 900; www.sub rosa.hr), with a booth inside the intercity bus station, has rental cars from 466KN per day (2500KN per week) with unlimited kilometres. You can also try **National** (☎ 212 452; www .nationalcar.hr; Demetrova 18b).

TRAIN
The **train station** (☎ 213 333; Krešimirova 5) is a five-minute walk from the city centre. Seven trains daily run to Zagreb (96KN, 3½ to five hours). There's a daily train to Split that changes at Ogulin, where you wait for two hours (160KN, 10 hours). Reservations are compulsory on some *poslovni* (executive) trains.

OPATIJA
pop 9073
Just 13km west of Rijeka, Opatija stretches along the coast, its forested hills sloping down to the sparkling sea. It was this breathtaking location and the agreeable all-year climate that made Opatija the most fashionable seaside resort for the Viennese elite during the days of the Austro-Hungarian Empire. The grand residences of the wealthy have since been revamped and turned into upscale hotels, with a particular accent on spa and health holidays. Foodies have been flocking from afar too, for the clutch of fantastic restaurants in the nearby fishing village of Volosko.

Orientation & Information
Opatija sits on a narrow strip of land sandwiched between the sea and the foothills of Mt Učka. Ul Maršala Tita is the main road that runs through town; it's lined with travel agencies, ATMs, restaurants, shops and hotels.
Da Riva (☎ 272 990; www.da-riva.hr; ul Maršala Tita 170; ☼ 8am-8pm Jun–mid-Sep, shorter hr rest of yr) Finds private accommodation and offers excursions around Croatia.
Linea Verde (☎ 701 107; www.lineaverde-croatia.com; Andrije Štangera 42, Volosko; ☼ 8am-10pm Mon-Sat, to 9pm Sun summer, to 4pm Mon-Sat rest of yr) Hiking excursions to Risnjak, gourmet tours to Istria and shepherds' picnics to Učka.
Tourist office (☎ 271 310; www.opatija-tourism.hr; ul Maršala Tita 101; ☼ 8am-10pm Mon-Sat & 5-9pm Sun Jul & Aug, 8am-7pm Mon-Sat Apr-Jun & Sep, 8am-4pm Mon-Sat Mar-Oct) Distributes maps, leaflets and brochures.

Sights & Activities
Visit the exquisite **Villa Angiolina** (Park Angiolina 1), which houses the **Croatian Museum of Tourism** (☼ 9am-1pm & 4.30-9.30pm Tue-Sun summer, reduced hr rest of yr) with its collection of old photographs, postcards, brochures and posters tracing the history of travel. Don't miss a stroll around the park, overgrowing with ginkgo trees, sequoias, holm oaks and Japanese camellia, Opatija's symbol. Note that museum admission was free at the time of writing but was expected to go up to 20KN.

The pretty **Lungomare** is the region's showcase. Lined with plush villas and ample gardens, this shady promenade winds along the sea for 12km, from Volosko to Lovran. Along the way are innumerable rocky outgrowths where you can throw down a towel and jump into the sea – a better option than Opatija's concrete beach.

Opatija and the surrounding region offer some wonderful opportunities for **hiking** and **biking** around the Učka mountain range (the tourist office has maps and information).

Sleeping

There are no real budget hotels in Opatija, but the midrange and top-end places offer surprisingly good value for money considering Opatija's overall air of chic. **Liburnia Hotels** (☎ 710 444; www.liburnia.hr) manages 15 hotels in the area and is a good bet for getting a room. Note that Opatija gets booked up over the Christmas holidays so reserve for this time.

Private rooms are abundant and reasonably priced. The travel agencies, opposite, find private accommodation. In high season, rooms cost between 80KN and 115KN per person, depending on the amenities. A 30% surcharge applies for stays under three nights.

Hotel Kvarner (☎ 271 233; www.liburnia.hr; Pave Tomašića 1-4; low-high s 462-578KN, d 653-1039KN; 🏊) Feel like a jet setter of a bygone time in Opatija's oldest hotel – splash in an indoor-outdoor pool, walk through plush hallways, and recline on period furniture in high-ceilinged rooms that, despite the fame, could use an update.

Hotel Mozart (☎ 718 260; www.hotel-mozart.hr; ul Maršala Tita 138; low-high s 660-920KN, d 1095-1530KN; 🅿) Light-flooded rooms feature old-school style and Secessionist furniture, the stars add up to five, and the spiffy new spa offers saunas and steam baths. Most rooms come with sea-facing balconies.

Hotel Residenz (☎ 271 399; www.liburnia.hr; ul Maršala Tita 133; low-high s 293-524KN, d 354-816KN) While rooms boast no frills – unless you pay extra for a unit with a balcony – the building is a classic right on the seafront, with a private beach below.

Camping Opatija (☎ 704 836; www.rivijera-opatija .hr; Liburnijska 46, Ičići; adult/site 36/27KN; 🕑 Apr-Oct) In a pine forest 5km south of town before you reach Lovran.

Eating

Maršala Tita is lined with serviceable restaurants that offer pizza, grilled meat and fish. The better restaurants are away from the main strip.

Istranka (☎ 271 835; Bože Milanovića 2; mains from 45KN) Graze on flavourful Istrian mainstays like *maneštra* and *fuži* at this rustic-themed tavern in a small street just up from Maršala Tita.

Bevanda (☎ 493 888; Zert 8; mains from 80KN) It recently switched the ownership that built its reputation, but this elegant restaurant on the Lido still delivers terrific fresh fish and shellfish. Get a table at the all-white terrace right on the sea.

Drinking

Viennese-style coffee houses and hotel terraces dominate the scene, but a few stylish bars add extra punch.

The ever-popular **Hemingway** (Zert 2) on the harbour is an enjoyable place for a seaside drink. For a cocktail on the beach, head to **Tantra** (Lido) just around the corner, a lounge bar with chill-out music and unbeatable coastal views. The trendiest place in town is still **Monokini** (☎ 703 888; ul Maršala Tita 96), a watering hole of choice for Opatija's scenesters. **Disco Seven** (www.discoseven.hr; ul Maršala Tita 125) is Opatija's only club, with the typical roster of electronic tunes and a seaside terrace.

Getting There & Away

Bus 32 stops in front of the train station in Rijeka (15KN, 20km) and runs along the Opatija Riviera west of Rijeka to Lovran every 20 minutes until late in the evening.

AROUND OPATIJA
Volosko

Volosko, 2km east of Opatija, is an old fishing village rising up on a gentle hill in a warren of narrow alleyways, stone townhouses and flower-laden balconies. The chief reason to visit is a set of stellar restaurants that has sprouted around the small harbour. Volosko is now a mecca for foodies, with several dining choices, however deep your pockets.

our pick Skalinada (☎ 701 109; Put Uz Dol 17; mains from 25KN) One of Volosko's best-kept secrets, this small, colourful and artsy restaurant hides behind a stone vault entrance just below the second bus stop on the road from Rijeka. Appetising food is made with seasonal ingredients from nearby villages.

Tramerka (☎ 701 707; Andrije Mohorovičića 15; mains from 30KN) Locals in the know flock to the stonewall interior of this *konoba* named after an uninhabited island in the Zadar archipelago. Expect creatively prepared and well-priced seafood dishes.

Le Mandrać (☎ 701 357; Supilova Obala 10; mains from 60KN) The forward-thinking Mediterranean food is innovative and full of flavour, though the overdesigned, swank interior is a tad intimidating. Splurge on a tasting menu (270KN to 490KN).

KRK ISLAND
pop 16,400

Croatia's largest island, 409-sq-km Krk (Veglia in Italian) is also one of the busiest in the summer. It may not be the lushest or most beautiful island in Croatia – in fact, it's largely overdeveloped and stomped over – but its decades of experience in tourism make it an easy place to visit, with good transport connections and well-organised infrastructure.

The picturesque Krk town makes a good base for exploring the island. Baška, on a wide, sandy bay at the foot of a scenic mountain range, is the island's prime beach destination.

GETTING THERE & AWAY

The Krk toll bridge links the northern part of the island with the mainland, and a regular car ferry links Valbiska with Merag on Cres (17KN per passenger, 113KN per car, 30 minutes). Another ferry by Split Tours operates between Valbiska and Lopar (37KN, 1½ hours) on Rab four times daily.

Krk is also home to **Rijeka airport** (www.rijeka-airport.hr), the main hub for flights to the Kvarner region, which consist mostly of low-cost and charter flights during summer.

About 14 buses per weekday travel between Rijeka and Krk town (50KN, one to two hours). There are 10 daily buses to Baška from Krk town (27KN, 45 minutes). All services are reduced on weekends.

Six daily buses run from Zagreb to Krk town (163KN to 183KN, three to four hours). Note that some bus lines are more direct than others, which will stop in every village en route.

Krk Town

Krk town clusters around a medieval walled centre and, spreading out into the surrounding coves and hills, a modern development that includes a port, beaches, camping grounds and hotels. From the 12th to 15th centuries, Krk town and the surrounding region remained semi-independent under the Frankopan Dukes of Krk, an indigenous Croatian dynasty, at a time when much of the Adriatic was controlled by Venice. This

history explains the various medieval sights in Krk town, the ducal seat.

The bus from Baška and Rijeka stops at the station (no left-luggage office) by the harbour, a few minutes' walk from the old town. The **seasonal tourist office** (☎ 220 226; www.tz-krk.hr, in Croatian; Obala Hrvatske Mornarice bb; ☼ 8am-9pm Jun-Sep) distributes brochures and materials, including a map of hiking paths. Out of season, go to the nearby **main tourist office** (☎ 220 226; Vela Placa 1; ☼ 8am-3pm Mon-Fri). You can change money at any travel agency (there are 13 in town); there are numerous ATMs around town.

Sights include the Romanesque **Cathedral of the Assumption** and the fortified **Kaštel** (Trg Kamplin) facing the seafront on the northern edge of the old town. The narrow cobbled streets that make up the pretty old quarter are worth a wander.

SLEEPING

There is a range of accommodation in and around Krk, but many hotels only open between April and October. Private rooms can be organised through any of the agencies, including **Autotrans** (☎ 222 661; www.autotrans-turizam.com; Šetalište Svetog Bernardina 3; ☼ 8am-9pm Mon-Sat, 9am-1.30pm & 6-9pm Sun) in the bus station. Expect to pay between 210KN and 250KN for a double room in high season.

Marina (☎ 221 357; www.hotelikrk.hr; Obala Hrvatske Mornarice 6; s 760KN, d 1168KN; P ✖ ☐) The most recent overhaul boosted this old-town hotel to four stars. Now each of the 10 deluxe units sports sea vistas and modern trappings like LCD TV.

Bor (☎ /fax 220 200; www.hotelbor.hr; Šetalište Dražica 5; low-high s 152-369KN, d 231-564KN; P) The rooms are modest and without trimmings at this low-key hotel, but the seafront location amidst pine forests makes it a worthwhile stay.

Autocamp Ježevac (☎ 221 081; camping@valamar.com; Plavnička bb; adult/site 44/56KN; ☼ mid-Apr–mid-Oct) This beachfront ground offers shady sites and places to swim. It's the closest campsite to town, a 10-minute walk southwest.

EATING & DRINKING

There are a number of restaurants along the harbour.

Konoba Nono (☎ 222 221; Krčkih Iseljenika 8; mains from 40KN) Savour local specialities like *šurlice* (homemade noodles) topped with goulash or scampi, just a hop and a skip from the old town.

Casa del Padrone (Šetalište Svetog Bernardina bb) Krk partygoers crowd the two floors of this faux-Renaissance bar-club, which hosts DJs on summer weekends. Daytime fun consists of lounging on the seaside tables as you nibble cakes and sip espresso.

Jungle (☎ 221 503; Stjepana Radića bb; ☼ May–Sep) The only veritable club in town draws a youngish set to its tropically themed dance floor where house music is king. The cocktail bar outside is more low-key.

Baška

At the southern end of Krk Island, Baška has its most beautiful beach, a 2km-long crescent set below a dramatic, barren range of mountains. There's one caveat should you visit in summer – tourists are spread towel-to-towel and what's otherwise a pretty pebble beach turns into a fight for your place under the sun. The 16th-century core of Venetian townhouses is pleasant enough for a stroll, but what surrounds it is a bland tourist development of apartment blocks and restaurants.

The bus stops at the top of a hill on the edge of the old town, between the beach and the harbour. The main street is Zvonimirova, which overlooks the harbour; the beach begins at the western end of the harbour, continuing southwards past a big, sprawling hotel complex. The **tourist office** (☎ 856 817; www.tz-baska .hr; Zvonimirova 114; ☼ 7am–9pm Mon-Sat & 8am–1pm Sun Jun–mid-Sep, 8am-3pm Mon–Fri mid-Sep–May) is just down the street from the bus station.

Most hotels and the two camps are managed by **Hoteli Baška** (☎ 656 111; www.hotelibaska .hr). Private accommodation can be arranged by most agencies in town, such as **PDM Guliver** (☎/fax 856 004; www.pdm-guliver.hr; Zvonimirova 98; ☼ 7am-9pm Mon-Sat & 8am-1pm Sun Jun–mid-Sep, shorter hr rest of yr). There's a four-night minimum stay in summer (or a hefty surcharge).

Popular trails include an 8km walk to **Stara Baška**, a restful little village on a bay surrounded by stark, salt-washed limestone hills.

RAB ISLAND

Rab (Arbe in Italian) is the most enticing island in Kvarner when it comes to the diversity of its landscapes. The more densely populated southwest is pockmarked with pine forests, beaches and coves, while the northeast tip is taken over by the Lopar Peninsula, with the island's best sandy beaches. The cultural and historical showcase is the enchanting Rab

town, characterised by four elegant bell towers rising from the ancient stone streets. Even at the peak of the summer season, when the island is overrun with visitors, you can still escape to nearly deserted beaches just a quick boat ride away.

GETTING THERE & AWAY

The Split Tours ferry between Valbiska on Krk and Lopar (37/225KN per passenger/car, 1½ hours, four daily) operates all year. In summer, a car ferry by Rapska Plovidba shuttles nonstop between Mišnjak on the island's southeastern edge and Jablanac on the mainland (15/105KN per passenger/car, 15 minutes).

Jadrolinija has a daily catamaran service between Rijeka and Rab (40KN, two hours); it continues on to Novalja on Pag, from where you can proceed to Zadar.

The most reliable way to come and go is on one of the two daily buses between Rab and Rijeka (120KN, three hours). In the high season there are three direct buses from Zagreb to Rab (188KN, four to five hours).

Rab Town
pop 592

Medieval Rab town is among the northern Adriatic's most spectacular sights. Crowded onto a narrow peninsula, its four instantly recognisable bell towers rise like exclamation points from a red-roofed huddle of stone buildings. Uphill from the harbour leads a maze of streets dotted with richly endowed churches and lovely lookout points as a treat at the top.

Highlights of the old town include the chapel of **St Christopher** (Svetog Kristofora), which houses a small collection of ancient stones in its **lapidarium** (donation; ☼ 10am-12.30pm & 7.30-9pm Mon-Sat, 7.30-9pm Sun summer only); the 13th-century **Holy Cross church** (Svetog Križa), which is the venue for summer concerts during Rab Musical Evenings; and the town's tallest **tower** (admission 5KN; ☼ sporadic), dating back to the 13th century and positively one of the most beautiful on the entire Croatian coast. Also, don't miss a walk around the beautifully landscaped **Komrčar Park** just to the west of the old town, bordered by the town beaches.

ORIENTATION & INFORMATION

The old town lies directly across the bay from the marina. Narrow side streets climb up from the three main streets parallel to the harbour –

CROATIA

Donja, Srednja and Gornja Ul (literally, lower, middle and upper roads). Trg Municipium Arba by the harbour is the old town's focal point. A five-minute walk north of the old town is the new commercial centre.

The main source of information is the **tourist office** (☎ 771 111; www.tzg-rab.hr; Trg Municipium Arba 8; ☼ 8am-10pm Jul-Sep, to 9pm May-Jun & Oct, to 2pm Mon-Fri Nov-Apr), which gives out plentiful maps and brochures. The **bus station** (Mali Palit bb) in the commercial centre has **left-luggage facilities** (per hr 0.70KN; ☼ 5.30am-7.30pm). **Erste Banka** (Mali Palit bb) nearby changes money and has an ATM.

SIGHTS & ACTIVITIES

In addition to beaches, Rab is crisscrossed with 100km of marked hiking and 80km of biking trails, several of which can be accessed from Rab town. Pick up the map from the tourist office. Diving sites include various submarine caves and tunnels as well as a protected amphora field off the cape of Sorinj. You can arrange to dive or take a course at **Mirko Diving Centre** (☎ 721 154; www.mirkodivingcenter .com; Barbat 710) in nearby Barbat.

Most travel agencies – try **Numero Uno** (☎ / fax 724 688; www.numero-uno.hr; Šetalište Markantuna Dominisa 5; ☼ 6am-midnight Mon-Sat, 8am-11pm Sun), which also rents bikes (55KN per half-day) – offer boat tours (100KN to 200KN), with swim stops around Rab and at nearby islands like Sveti Grgur and Goli Otok. Alternatively, take one of the taxi boats that depart from the harbour outside Hotel Istra and opposite Trg Municipium Arba.

FESTIVALS & EVENTS

For a few days each summer, Rab goes back to the Middle Ages during **Rab Fair** (Rapska Fjera), when residents dress in period garb and the town comes alive with drumming, processions, fireworks, medieval dancing and crossbow competitions. Celebrated between 25 and 27 July, this tradition commemorates Rab's liberation from Venetian rule in 1364 and honours its patron saint, St Christopher.

SLEEPING

Everything from camping to expensive hotels can be found in and around Rab town. Most of the hotels and camping grounds on the island are managed by **Imperial** (www.imperial .hr). Any travel agency can organise private rooms, with prices starting at 145KN (and up to 245KN) per double in high season. There's a surcharge for stays of fewer than three nights in summer.

Hotel Arbiana (☎ 724 444; www.arbianahotel.com; Obala Kralja Petra Krešimira 12; s 876KN, d 978-1300KN; ⓅⓍ☐) Understated luxury seekers get lucky with this recently refurbished boutique hotel on the harbour. Most of the 28 colourful rooms and suites have balconies; each boasts wireless, LCD TV and bathrobes. There's a slow-food restaurant on site.

Hotel Istra (☎ 724 134; www.hotel-istra.hr; Šetalište Markantuna Dominisa bb; low-high s 300-420KN, d 458-696KN; Ⓟ) From the outside this freshly painted yellow building looks inviting, but inside the outdated rooms need a facelift. The location, right on the harbour, is a serious bonus, though.

Hotel Imperial (☎ 724 522; www.imperial.hr; Palit bb; low-high s 370-505KN, d 560-760KN; Ⓟ) Set back from town in shady Komrčar Park, some newer rooms here have air-con, others balconies with sea views. The cafe terrace is lovely, bar the cheesy piano tunes.

Campsite Padova III (☎ 724 355; www.rab-camping .com; Banjol bb; adult/tent 43/30KN; ☼ Apr-Oct) To sleep cheap, carry your tent around the bay and walk south along the waterfront to this camping ground about 2km from the old town. It's right on a sandy beach and has extensive facilities.

EATING

Rab cuisine revolves around fresh fish, seafood and pasta. The quality and prices are generally uniform, with restaurants catering mainly to summer tourists.

There's a supermarket at the entrance to town on Šetalište Markantuna Dominisa and another one in the basement of the Merkur department store in the commercial centre, where there's also a fruit and vegetable market.

our pick **Konoba Rab** (☎ 725 666; Kneza Branimira 3; mains from 65KN; ☼ closed lunch Sun) Some of the scrumptious specialities at this cosy *konoba*, such as lamb baked under *peka*, must be ordered in advance. Others not, like *rapska grota*, beef steak with cheese and prosciutto in a sweet fruit sauce (190KN for two).

Paradiso (☎ 771 109; Stjepana Radića 1; mains 70-130KN) Bundle art, wine and good food, offer it all in an ancient stone townhouse and you're close to paradise. This art gallery–wine boutique–restaurant-cafe has a patio in the back and a Venetian loggia up front. Try the dentex fish fillet in Traminac wine.

Konoba Riva (☎ 725 887; Biskupa Drage 3; mains 40-90KN) Riva has tables on the harbour, an at-

---

WORTH THE TRIP: LOŠINJ & CRES ISLANDS

Separated by only an 11m-wide canal, these two serpentine islands in the Kvarner archipelago are often treated as a single entity. Although their topography is different, the islands' identities are blurred by a shared history and close transportation links. The 31-km-long Lošinj is the more populated and developed. Stretching 68km from tip to tip, Cres is more on the wild side, an island where you can wander around primeval forests, swim in hidden coves and visit ageing hilltop towns.

On lush Lošinj, with 1100 plant species and a profusion of fragrant pine forests, visit the pretty old town of **Mali Lošinj**, with its stately sea captains' houses and the verdant bays of Čikat and Sunčana Uvala nearby. In the smaller fishing village of **Veli Lošinj**, just 4km to the northwest, stop by the **Lošinj Marine Education Centre**, a project of **Blue World** (www.blueworld.org) dedicated to sensitising visitors to the local marine life, particularly its endangered population of bottlenose dolphins. For accommodation, turn to **Lošinj Hotels & Villas** (www.losinj-hotels.com), which manages the majority of hotels and resorts on the island.

On Cres Island, wander around the sun-drenched **Cres town**, with its pastel-coloured townhouses and Venetian mansions around the medieval harbour. Stop by **Ruta** (www.ruta-cres.hr), a local collective that promotes the island's cultural and ecological identity by preserving old traditions such as felting of sheep wool. At the heart of the Tramuntana region on the island's northern tip, with virgin forests, abandoned villages, lone chapels and myths of good elves, is the ancient hilltop town of Beli, home to **Eco-Centre Caput Insulae** (www.caput-insulae.com), part nature park, part sanctuary for the endangered Eurasian griffon. While here, be sure to hike one of the seven educative eco-trails through Tramuntana's forests. **Cresanka** (☎ 571 161; www.cresanka.hr) in Cres town is the best source of private accommodation on the island.

The islands are connected to the mainland by various **Jadrolinija** (www.jadrolinija.hr) ferries and catamarans. There are also daily buses departing from Rijeka; it takes just over four hours to get to Veli Lošinj, the last stop on the islands.

---

mospheric terrace covered with fish nets and a small stone interior. The menu features fish and seafood, with some meat dishes thrown in.

ENTERTAINMENT

San Antonio (www.sanantonio-club.com; Trg Municipium Arba 4) It has tables on the square filled with daytime crowds sipping cocktails and a popular bar that stays open till 6am.

Santos Beach Club (www.sanantonio-club.com; Pudarica Beach; ☯ 10am dawn Jul & Aug) The owners of San Antonio are behind this seasonal beach-club affair about 10km from Rab town near Barbat (shuttles run at night). It's reminiscent of Zrće on Pag, with DJs spinning tunes to a party crowd.

Lopar

The tourist development on Lopar Peninsula, occupying the northern tip of Rab Island, has little charm, but there is a compelling reason to come here – a series of 22 sandy beaches that fringe the cape, bordered by shady pine groves. Central European families flock here in droves in the summer months, as the sea is shallow and perfect for small children, particularly on the 1500m-long **Paradise Beach** (Rajska Plaža) on Crnika Bay right at the heart of town. As the island's most famous beach, it gets crowded, so head to nearby **Livačina Beach** for a quieter option.

If you wish to strip out of your bikini, **Sahara Beach** is a popular nudist spot in a delightful northern cove. It's accessible along a marked trail through pine forests; pass the San Marino hotel complex and pick up the trail from there. The beach is pretty remote – it takes about 45 minutes to get there. A closer nudist option is **Stolac Beach**, a 15-minute walk from Paradise Beach.

The unattractive settlement centred on Crnika Bay is comprised of **Camping San Marino** (☎ 775 133; www.imperial.hr; Lopar bb; adult/tent 43/30KN; ☯ Apr-Oct), fronting Paradise Beach, the San Marino Hotel complex, a small commercial centre, and several cookie-cutter restaurants. Should you wish to stay, book a room at **Epario Hotel** (☎ 777 500; www.epario.net; Lopar 456a; low-high s 160-232KN, d 362-593KN; P ⊠ ▢), within spitting distance of Paradise Beach, where there are clean, comfy rooms with wi-fi; most have balconies.

CROATIA

lonelyplanet.com

The town centre has a **tourist office** (☎ 775 508; www.lopar.hr; Lopar bb; ⏰ 8am-9.30pm Jul & Aug, to 8pm Mon-Sat, to 2pm Sun Sep & Jun), which can furnish you with information. For private accommodation, go to **Sahara Tours** (☎ 775 444; www.sahara-tours.hr; Lopar bb), which has double rooms from 230KN and two-person apartments from 360KN in high season. The ferry from Valbiska stops 1km from the town centre; there's a small train for foot passengers (adult/child 10/5KN).

DALMATIA

Roman ruins, historic cities, spectacular beaches, old fishing ports, medieval architecture and unspoilt offshore islands make a trip to Dalmatia (Dalmacija) unforgettable. Occupying the central 375km of Croatia's jagged Adriatic coast, Dalmatia offers a matchless combination of hedonism and history.

Split is the largest city in the region and a hub for bus and boat connections along the Adriatic, as well as home to the late-Roman Diocletian's Palace. Nearby are the early Roman ruins in Solin. Zadar has yet more Roman ruins and a wealth of churches. The architecture of Hvar and Korčula recalls the days when these places were outposts of the Venetian empire. None can rival majestic Dubrovnik, a cultural and aesthetic jewel.

The dramatic coastal scenery is due to the rugged Dinaric Alps, which form a 1500m-long barrier that separates Dalmatia from BiH. After the last ice age, part of the coastal mountains was flooded, creating the sort of long, high islands seen in the Kvarner Gulf. The deep, protected passages between these islands are a paradise for sailors and cruisers.

ZADAR
☎ 023 / pop 72,700
It's hard to decipher the mystery of why Zadar (ancient Zara), the main city of northern Dalmatia, is an underrated tourist destination. Is it because it has a compact, marble, traffic-free old town that follows the old Roman street plan and contains Roman ruins and medieval churches? Or could it be that it's recently been dubbed Croatia's 'city of cool' for its clubs, bars and festivals run by international music stars? Perhaps it's the lively street life, one of Dalmatia's best markets, the busy cafes and good food? Or maybe it's the unusual attrac-

tions like the incredible Sea Organ and the Sun Salutation, a pair of sights – and sounds – that need to be seen and heard to be believed.

Zadar is a city to behold on the Dalmatian coast – its cultural and entertainment offerings are growing by the year, and with one of Europe's biggest budget airlines (Ryanair) starting to fly into its airport, it's safe to say that Zadar is not going to remain off the beaten track for much longer.

History
In the past 2000 years Zadar has escaped few wars. Its strategic position on the Adriatic coast made it a target for the Romans, the Byzantine, Venetian and Austro-Hungarian empires, and Italy. Although it was damaged by Allied bombing raids in 1943–44 and Yugoslav rockets in 1991, this resilient city has been rebuilt and restored, retaining much of its old flavour. Don't forget to sample Zadar's famous maraschino cherry liqueur.

Orientation
The adjacent train station and **bus station** (☎ 211 035) are 1km southeast of the harbour and old town. From the stations, Zrinsko-Frankopanska leads northwest to the town and harbour. Buses marked 'Poluotok' run from the bus station to the harbour. Narodni trg is the heart of Zadar.

Information
Aquarius Travel Agency (☎ /fax 212 919; www .jureskoaquarius.hr; Nova Vrata bb) Books accommodation and excursions.
Garderoba (per day 15KN) bus station (⏰ 7am-9pm Mon-Fri); Jadrolinija dock (⏰ 7am-8pm Mon-Fri, to 3pm Sat); train station (⏰ 24hr)
Hospital (☎ 315 677; Bože Peričića 5) Emergency services are available 24 hours.
Internet Spot (Varoška 3; per hr 30KN)
Main post office (Poljana Pape Aleksandra III) You can make phone calls here.
Miatours (☎ /fax 212 788; www.miatours.hr; Vrata Sveti Krševana) Books accommodation and excursions. (Vrata Sveti Krševana is an extremely tiny passage through the walls that contains little more than the travel agency.)
Tourist office (☎ 316 166; www.tzzadar.hr; Mihe Klaića 5; ⏰ 8am-8pm Mon-Sat, to 1pm Sun Jun-Sep, to 6pm Mon-Sat Oct-May)

Sights & Activities
Most attractions are near **St Donatus church** (Sveti Donat; ☎ 250 516; Šimuna Kožičića Benje; admis-

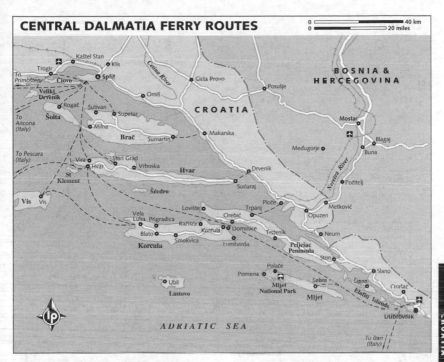

CENTRAL DALMATIA FERRY ROUTES

sion 10KN; 9.30am-1pm & 4-6pm Mar-Oct), a circular 9th-century Byzantine structure built over the **Roman forum**. Slabs from the ancient forum are visible in the church and there's a Roman-era pillar on the northwestern side. In summer ask about the musical evenings here (featuring Renaissance and early baroque music). The outstanding **Museum of Church Art** (Trg Opatice Čike bb; adult/student 20/10KN; 10am-12.30pm daily, plus 6-8pm Mon-Sat), in the Benedictine monastery opposite St Donatus, offers three floors of elaborate gold and silver reliquaries, religious paintings, icons and local lacework.

The 13th-century Romanesque **Cathedral of St Anastasia** (Katedrala Svete Stošije; Trg Svete Stošije; Mass only) has some fine Venetian carvings in the 15th-century choir stalls. The **Franciscan Monastery** (Franjevački Samostan; Zadarskog Mira 1358; admission free; 7.30am-noon & 4.30-6pm) is the oldest Gothic church in Dalmatia (consecrated in 1280), with lovely interior Renaissance features and a large Romanesque cross in the treasury, behind the sacristy.

The most interesting museum is the **Archaeological Museum** (Arheološki Muzej; Trg Opatice Čike 1; adult/student 10/5KN; 9am-1pm & 6-9pm Mon-Fri, 9am-1pm Sat), across from St Donatus, with an extensive collection of artefacts from the neolithic period through the Roman occupation to the development of Croatian culture under the Byzantines. Some captions are in English and you are handed a leaflet in English when you buy your ticket.

Less interesting is the **National Museum** (Narodni Muzej; Poljana Pape Aleksandra III; admission 10KN; 9am-1pm & 5-7pm Mon-Fri), just inside the port gate, featuring photos of Zadar from different periods, and old paintings and engravings of many coastal cities. The same admission ticket will get you into the **Art Gallery** (Galerija; Smiljanića; 9am-noon & 5-8pm Mon-Fri, 9am-1pm Sat). One church worth a visit is **St Šimun church** (Crkva Svetog Šime; Šime Budinića; 8am-1pm & 6-8pm Jun-Sep), which has a 14th-century gold chest.

Zadar's incredible (and world's only) **Sea Organ** (Morske Orgulje), designed by local architect Nikola Bašić, is bound to be one of the more memorable sights you'll see in Croatia. Set within the perforated stone stairs that descend into the sea is a system of pipes and whistles that exudes wistful sighs when the

ZADAR

INFORMATION	
Aquarius Travel Agency	1 D2
Garderoba	2 D2
Internet Spot	3 C3
Main Post Office	4 C2
Miatours	5 C2
Tourist Office	6 D3

SIGHTS & ACTIVITIES	
Archaeological Museum	7 C2
Art Gallery	8 D3
Cathedral of St Anastasia	9 C2
Franciscan Monastery & Church	10 B2
Museum of Church Art	11 C2
National Museum	12 C2
Roman Forum	13 C2
St Donatus Church	14 C2
St Šimon Church	15 D3
Sea Organ	16 A2
Sun Salutation	17 A1

SLEEPING	
Venera Guest House	18 C4

EATING	
Foša	19 D4
Kornat	20 B1
Market	21 D2
Trattoria Canzona	22 C3

DRINKING	
Galerija Đina	23 C3
Kult Caffe	24 C3
Maya Pub	25 B1

ENTERTAINMENT	
Arsenal	26 B1
Garden	27 B1

TRANSPORT	
Croatia Airlines	28 C1
Jadrolinija	29 B1
Jadrolinija Stall	30 C1

movement of the sea pushes air through the pipes.

Right next to it is the newly built **Sun Salutation** (Pozdrav Suncu), another wacky and wonderful Bašić creation. It's a 22m circle cut into the pavement and filled with 300 multilayered glass plates that collect the sun's energy during the day; powered by the same wave energy that makes the sound of the Sea Organ, it produces a trippy light show from sunset to sunrise, meant to simulate the solar system.

You can swim from the steps off the promenade and listen to the sound of the Sea Organ. There's a **swimming area** with diving boards, a small park and a cafe on the coastal promenade off Zvonimira. Bordered by pine trees and parks, the promenade takes you to a beach in front of Hotel Kolovare and then winds on for about a kilometre up the coast.

Tours

Any of the many travel agencies around town can supply information on tourist cruises to the beautiful **Kornati Islands** (Kornati National Park is an archipelago of 147 mostly uninhabited islands), and river rafting.

Festivals & Events

Major annual events:

Garden Festival (www.thegardenzadar.com) In nearby Petrčane from 4 to 6 July, this is fast becoming one of the most beloved dance-music festivals in Croatia.

Zadar Dreams (Zadar Snova; www.zadarsnova.hr)
Theatrical festival takes over Zadar's parks and squares
from 7 to 14 August with offbeat theatrical happenings.
Full Moon Festival On the night of the full moon in
August; the quays are lit up with torches, and boats
become floating fish markets.

Sleeping

Most visitors head out to the 'tourist settlement' at Borik, 3km northwest of Zadar, on
the Puntamika bus (6KN, every 20 minutes
from the bus station). Here there are hotels,
a hostel, a camping ground, big swimming
pools, sporting opportunities and numerous
sobe (rooms) signs; you can arrange a private
room through a travel agency in town. Expect
to pay from €22 to €50 for a room, depending
on the facilities.

ourpick Villa Hrešć (☎ 337 570; www.villa-hresc
.hr; Obala Kneza Trpimira 28; low-high s 550-650KN, d 750-
850KN; P ⊠ ⛱) Zadar's plushest choice is in
a cheery pink building on a bay. The stylish
rooms are in pastel colours, the beds are luxurious dreaming spots, and as you lounge by
the swimming pool you can admire views of
the Old Town. The suites are excellent value,
some with massive terraces. It's within walking distance of Zadar's restaurants, sights
and nightlife.

Venera Guest House (☎ 214 098; www.hotel-venera
-zd.hr; Šime Ljubića 4a; low-high d 300-450KN) Venera –
also known as the Jović Guesthouse – is the
centre's only option. The rooms are minuscule and have oversized wardrobes and no
numbers on the doors, but all have en suite
bathrooms, the beds are good and the atmosphere is pretty relaxed. The price doesn't include breakfast. If you can't reach Gojko, the
owner, you can book through Aquarius Travel
Agency (p220).

Zadar Youth Hostel (☎ 331 145; zadar@hfhs.hr;
Obala Kneza Trpimira 76; per person €13; ⌨) A great
option for backpackers, with plain but clean
rooms – some have wooden floors that creak
comfortingly. Many were renovated in 2006
and are quite modern. The service is friendly
and multilingual, and Borik beach is minutes away. There's internet access at 5KN for
15 minutes.

Autocamp Borik (☎ 332 074; low-high per adult
36-53KN, per site 90-135KN; ⌨ May-Oct) Steps away
from Borik beach, the campsite is shaded by
tall pines and has decent facilities. It's a better option than Zaton if you want to savour
city pleasures.

Eating

Zadar's **market** (⌨ 6am-3pm) is one of Croatia's
best.

ourpick Kornat (☎ 254 501; Liburnska Obala 6; mains
from 80KN) This is without a doubt Zadar's best
restaurant. It's elegant, with wooden floors
and modern furnishings, and the service is excellent, but it's the food that's the real knockout. There's smooth Istrian truffle monkfish,
and creamy squid and salmon risotto (70KN),
and the fresh fish (around 350KN per kilogram) is prepared with simple ingredients to
maximum deliciousness.

ourpick Foša (☎ 314 421; Kralja Dmitra Zvonimira 2;
mains from 80KN) Foša looks out over the narrow
channel that runs alongside the city walls and
takes its name from it. There is fantastic fish,
and the small stone terrace is one of Zadar's
most gorgeous places to eat. The interior is
slick and elegant and the service attentive
and discreet.

Trattoria Canzona (☎ 212 081; Stomorića 8; mains
40KN) A great little trattoria in the old town,
with red-and-white chequered tablecloths,
friendly waiters and tonnes of locals who love
the menu of daily specials. Try the delicious
pašticada that comes with a bunch of juicy
gnocchi, and accompany it with a crunchy
green salad.

Niko (☎ 337 888; www.hotel-niko.hr; Obala Kneza
Domagoja 9; mains from 60KN) A real Zadar institution,
Niko is loved for its daily fresh-fish menu –
grilled and sprinkled with smooth, aromatic
olive oil – long wine list, and pasta and seafood dishes. The large terrace overlooks the
shimmering Adriatic. Niko is on Puntamika,
in Borik.

Zalogajnica Ljepotica (☎ 311 288; Obala Kneza
Branimira 4b; mains from 35KN) The cheapest place
in town prepares three to four dishes a day
at knockout prices in a setting that would
fit well in a Kaurismaki movie – you know,
a rugged, lonesome diner and a pot-bellied
chef-waiter who brings you a steaming dish
with a somnolent look on his face. The food
is great and home cooked, and the dishes are
usually squid-ink risotto, tomato and seafood
pasta, plus something meaty.

Drinking

In summer the many cafes along Varoška and
Klaića place their tables on the street; it's great
for people watching.

ourpick Arsenal (☎ 253 833; www.arsenalzadar
.com; Trg 3 Bunara 1) A large renovated shipping

warehouse now hosts this brilliant cultural centre, with a large lounge bar–restaurant–concert hall in the centre, that has a small stage for live music and shows.

Galerija Đina (Varoška 2) Just off the main square, Djina's is an arty hang-out that serves good cocktails to a trendy crowd. It's electro music all the way, and a great place to start the night.

Kult Caffe (Stomorića 4) The Kult Caffe draws a young hip-hop, heavy metal, rock-and-roll, hippie, punk – you name it – crowd, who hang out on the shady terrace outside.

Maya Pub (☎ 251 716; Liburnska Obala 6) This is a real chill-out bar, with 'ethnic' decor and quiet electro music in the background.

Entertainment

our pick Garden (☎ 450 907; www.thegardenzadar.com; Bedemi Zadarskih Pobuna; ☽ late May-Oct) One of the reasons many of Croatia's youngsters rate Zadar as 'a really cool place' is basically because it has the Garden. It's owned and run by UB40's producer Nick Colgan and drummer James Brown. Daytime here is relaxed, while night time is when the fun really begins. Don't miss it if you're in town.

our pick Barbarella's (☎ 450 907; www.thegarden zadar.com; Punta Radman Put 8, Petrčane) Opened in May 2008, this more ambitious and spacious project for the owners of the Garden serves as the setting for the Garden Festival (p222) and lots of beach clubbing all through summer.

Getting There & Away

AIR
Zadar's airport, 12km east of the city, is served by **Croatia Airlines** (☎ 250 101; Poljana Natka Nodila 7) and **Ryanair** (www.ryanair.com). A Croatia Airlines bus meets all flights and costs 15KN; it goes from the airport to the main bus and train station. A taxi into town costs around 175KN.

BOAT
The **Jadrolinija** (☎ 254 800; Liburnska Obala 7) office is on the harbour and has tickets for all local ferries, or you can buy ferry tickets from the Jadrolinija stall on Liburnska Obala.

For information on boat connections to Italy, see p444.

BUS & TRAIN
The **bus station** (☎ 211 035; www.liburnija-zadar.hr, in Croatian) is a 10-minute walk from the centre and has daily buses to Zagreb (100KN to 140KN, 3½ to seven hours, 20 daily). The **train station** (☎ 212 555; www.hznet.hr; Ante Starčevića 3) is adjacent to the bus station. There are five daily trains to Zagreb: two fast trains (150KN, seven hours) and three slower ones (134KN, 9¾ hours).

AROUND ZADAR
Plitvice Lakes National Park
☎ 053

This **park** (☎ 751 015; www.np-plitvicka-jezera.hr; adult/student 110/50KN Apr-Oct, 70/35KN Nov-Mar; ☽ 7am-8pm) lies midway between Zagreb and Zadar. The 19.5 hectares of wooded hills enclose 16 turquoise lakes, which are linked by a series of waterfalls and cascades. Wooden footbridges follow the lakes and streams over, under and across the rumbling water for an exhilaratingly damp 18km. In 1979 Unesco proclaimed the Plitvice Lakes a World Heritage site, and the lakes and forests are carefully regulated to ensure their continuing preservation.

There's no bad time to visit: in spring the falls are flush with water, in summer the surrounding hills are greener, and in autumn there are fewer visitors and you'll be treated to the changing colours of the leaves.

The lake system is divided into the upper and lower lakes. The upper lakes, lying in a dolomite valley, are the most impressive, while the lower lakes are smaller and shallower. Most of the water comes from the White and Black rivers (Bijela and Crna Rijeka), which join south of Prošćansko Lake, but the lakes are also fed by underground springs.

The upper lakes have encrusted plants growing on top of each other, forming travertine barriers and creating waterfalls. The lower lakes were formed by cavities created by the water of the upper lakes. This unique interaction of water, rock and plant life has continued more or less undisturbed since the last ice age.

The colours of the lakes change constantly: from azure to bright green, deep blue or grey; the colours depend upon the quantity of minerals and organisms in the water, and whether it has been raining.

The luxuriant vegetation of the national park is a delight. The northeastern section is covered with beech forests, while the rest of it is covered with beech, fir spruce and white pine dotted with patches of whitebeam, hornbeam and flowering ash, which change colour in autumn.

WILDLIFE

Animal life flourishes in the unspoilt conditions. The stars of the park are bears and wolves, but there are also deer, boar, rabbits, foxes and badgers. There are over 120 different species of bird such as hawks, owls, cuckoos, thrushes, starlings, kingfishers, wild ducks and herons. You might occasionally see black storks and ospreys, and flocks of butterflies flutter throughout the park.

ORIENTATION & INFORMATION

The **tourist office** (☎ 751 015; www.np-plitvicka-jezera .hr; 7am-8pm) has its main entrance on Plitvička Jezera and a secondary entrance at Velika Poljana, near the hotels. At the main entrance you can pick up brochures and a map to walk you around the lakes. There are well-marked trails throughout the park and a system of wooden walkways that allows you to appreciate the beauty of the landscape without disturbing the environment. The admission ticket includes the boats and buses you need to see the lakes.

The post office is near the hotels and there's an ATM near the Hotel Bellevue. Luggage can be left at the tourist office or at one of the hotels.

SIGHTS

The lower lakes string out from the main entrance and are rich in forests, grottoes and steep cliffs. **Novakovića Falls** is nearest the entrance and is followed by **Kaluđerovac Lake**, near two caves: the Blue Cave and Šupljara. Next is **Gavanovac Lake**, with towering waterfalls, and last is **Milanovac Lake**, notable for colours that are variously azure or emerald green.

Kozjak is the largest lake and forms a boundary between the upper and lower lakes. Three kilometres long, it's surrounded by steep, forested slopes and contains a small oval island, composed of travertine. Past the hotels, you'll see **Gradinsko Lake**, bordered by reeds that often harbour nesting wild ducks. A series of cascades links Gradinsko to **Galovac Lake**, considered the most beautiful of all. An abundance of water has formed a series of ponds and falls. A set of concrete stairs over the falls, constructed long ago, has eventually been covered by travertine, forming even more falls in a spectacular panorama. Several smaller lakes are topped by the larger **Okrugljak Lake**, supplied by two powerful waterfalls. Continuing upward you'll come to **Ciginovac Lake** and finally **Prošćansko Lake**, surrounded by thick forests.

SLEEPING & EATING

The Zagreb buses drop you off just outside the camping ground, while the hotels are clustered on Velika Poljana overlooking Kozjak Lake. There are many *sobe* signs along the road from Korana village to the national park. The tourist office in the park or its branch in Zagreb (p184) can refer you to rooms in the neighbouring villages, the closest of which is about 400m from the entrance. Expect to pay about 225KN for a double. Hotels can be booked through the tourist office website.

Hotel Jezero (☎ 751 400; jezero@np-plitvicka-jezera .hr; Velika Poljana; low-high s €61-83, d €86-118; ⓟ ⓡ) This is by far the most comfortable and best-appointed hotel in the park, though it's by no means a boutique delight. There's a sauna and a swimming pool.

Hotel Plitvice (☎ 751 100; Velika Poljana; low-high s €50-72, d €65-96; ⓟ) A comfortable, modern hotel with spacious, well-equipped rooms, each with a TV, phone and minibar. There are more expensive rooms that are larger and have views.

Korana (☎ 751 015; per adult all incl €9; May-Oct) This is a large, well-equipped autocamp about 6km north of the main entrance on the main road to Zagreb.

Lička Kuća (☎ 751 024; meals from 70KN; Ⓥ) Just across from the main entrance, this sprawling place is usually crowded with tourists who come for the local sausages and roasted-meat dishes. Vegetarians will appreciate the *djuveč*, a stew of rice, carrots, tomatoes, peppers and onions, and the fine local cheese.

GETTING THERE & AWAY

The Zagreb–Zadar buses that don't use the new motorway (ie the ones that drive between Zagreb and Zadar in over three hours) stop at Plitvice (check www.akz.hr for more details). The journey takes three hours from Zadar (80KN) and 2½ hours from Zagreb (60KN).

ŠIBENIK
pop 41,012

Despite, or perhaps because of, the fact that Šibenik often gets overlooked by visitors to northern Dalmatia, the city has really been coming into its own in the last few years. There are exciting new sights, restaurants and bars are opening every year and the town is abuzz with new energy. Find a place to stay in town – and avoid the restaurants and hotels scattered among the tourist complexes along the coast – and stroll along the harbour and explore the steep back streets and alleys. Šibenik has one of the most remarkable cathedrals in Croatia and a network of curving streets and sunny squares from the 15th and 16th centuries.

History

Unlike many other Dalmatian coastal towns, Šibenik was settled first by Croat tribes, not Illyrians or Romans. The city was conquered by Venice in 1116 but was tossed back and forth among Venice, Hungary, Byzantium and the Kingdom of Bosnia until Venice seized control in 1412 after a three-year fight. The city suffered from Venetian rule until it passed into the hands of Austria in 1797, where it remained until 1918.

Šibenik fell under attack in 1991 from the Yugoslav federal army, and was subject to shelling until 1995. The town has started to make a serious comeback in the past few years.

Orientation

The city spreads like an amphitheatre from the harbour up to the surrounding hills. The main road is Kralja Zvonimira and the old town lies between it and the harbour. The main commercial street is Ante Starčevića (which becomes Ante Šupuka east of the old town), with the train station lying southeast.

Information

Hospital (☎ 334 421; Stjepana Radića 83)
NIK Travel Agency (☎ /fax 338 540; www.nik.hr; Ante Šupuka 5; ✆ 9am-6pm Mon-Fri, to noon Sat) The largest travel agency in town. It finds private accommodation and sells international bus and air tickets.
Post office (Vladimira Nazora 51; ✆ 8am-7pm Mon-Fri, 9am-noon Sat) You can make calls and change money here.
Tourist information centre (☎ 214 441; www .sibenik-tourism.hr; Obala Franje Tuđmana 5; ✆ 8am-9pm Mon-Sat, to 2pm Sun mid-Jun–mid-Sep, to 3pm Mon-Fri mid-Sep–mid-Jun)

Sights & Activities

The **Cathedral of St James** (Katedrala Svetog Jakova; Trg Republike Hrvatske; ✆ 8am-noon & 6-8pm daily May-Oct, Mass only Nov-Apr) is Juraj Dalmatinac's masterpiece. The crowning glory of the Dalmatian coast, the cathedral, a World Heritage site, is worth a considerable detour to see. Its most unusual feature is the frieze of 71 heads on the exterior walls of the apses. These portraits in stone are vivid character studies of ordinary 15th-century citizens. Placid, annoyed, proud or fearful, their expressions convey the timelessness of human emotion through the centuries.

The cathedral was constructed entirely of stone quarried from the islands of Brač, Korčula, Rab and Krk, and is reputed to be the world's largest church built completely of stone without brick or wood supports. The unusual domed-roof complex was completed after Dalmatinac's death by Nikola Firentinac, who continued the facade in a pure Renaissance style. The church was completed in 1536.

The hottest new attraction in town, the **Medieval Garden of St Lawrence's Monastery** (Vrt Svetog Lovre; ☎ 212 515; www.cromovens.hr; Trg Republike Hrvatske 4; admission 15/10KN; ✆ varies) was fully restored after an entire century, and opened in late 2007. The garden has medicinal plant patches, water fountains and pretty pathways.

The town has a wealth of beautiful churches, such as the Gothic-Renaissance **Church of St Ivan** (Crkva Svetog Ivana; Trg Ivana Paula II), and the **Franciscan Church & Monastery** (Franjevački Samostan; Ćulinovića), with an array of Venetian baroque paintings.

You can climb to the top of **St Ana fortress** in the northeast for a magnificent view over Šibenik and the surrounding region.

Sleeping & Eating

Most private accommodation is in neighbouring villages such as Primošten, Tribunj and Vodice along the coast, easily reached by bus from Šibenik. In July and August you may be met by women at the bus or train station offering *sobe* at much lower prices.

Hotel Jadran (☎ 212 644; www.rivijera.hr; Obala Oslobođenja 52; low-high s 380-470KN, d 760-940KN) This modern hotel conveniently located along the harbour is the only one in town. It's somewhat impersonal but in excellent condition and rooms are equipped with satellite TV.

Camp Solaris (☎ 364 450; www.solaris.hr; Solaris; adult/ site 42/75KN; ✆ mid-Mar–Oct; ⚐) This elaborate camping ground comes complete with a seawater pool, sports facilities and restaurants.

our pick Pelegrini (☎ 485 055; Palih Omladinaca 2; mains from 60KN) Sitting on the top of the Bunari Museum and opened in 2007, this is the most suave new restaurant in Šibenik. The interior is stylish and Mediterranean minimalist, while the menu is full of creamy risottos and perfectly prepared pasta.

Penkala (☎ 219 869; Fra Jeronima Milete 17; mains from 25KN; ☾ closed Sun) Popular with the locals and very good, this neighbourhood spot serves up homespun cooking with a focus on hearty meat stews.

Self-caterers can stock up at the **supermarket** (Kralja Zvonimira) or the **fruit and vegetable market** (btwn Ante Starčevića & Stankovačka).

Getting There & Away

Šibenik is well connected by bus to local and international destinations. There are buses to Dubrovnik (217KN, six hours, eight daily), Zadar (60KN, 6½ hours, 48 daily), Split (80KN, 1¾ hours, 24 daily) and Zagreb (160KN, 6½ hours, 15 daily), as well as other destinations.

Jadrolinija (☎ 213 468; Obala Franje Tuđmana 8; ☾ 9am-6pm Mon-Fri) has tickets for ferry sailings.

SPLIT
☎ 021 / pop 188,700

The second-largest city in Croatia, Split (Spalato in Italian) is a great place to see Dalmatian life as it's really lived. Free of mass tourism and always buzzing, this is a city with just the right balance of tradition and modernity. Just step inside Diocletian's Palace – a Unesco World Heritage site and one of the world's most impressive Roman monuments – and you'll see dozens of bars, restaurants and shops thriving amid the atmospheric old walls where Split life has been going on for thousands of years. Split's unique setting and exuberant nature make it one of the most delectable cities in Europe. The dramatic coastal mountains are the perfect backdrop to the turquoise waters of the Adriatic and you'll get a chance to appreciate the gorgeous Split cityscape when making a ferry journey to or from the city.

History

Split achieved fame when Roman emperor Diocletian (AD 245–313), noted for his persecution of the early Christians, had his retirement palace built here from 295 to 305. After his death the great stone palace continued to be used as a retreat by Roman rulers. When the neighbouring colony of Salona was abandoned in the 7th century, many of the Romanised inhabitants fled to Split and barricaded themselves behind the high palace walls, where their descendants continue to live to this day.

Orientation

The main bus station, train station and ferry terminal are adjacent on the eastern side of the harbour, a short walk from the old town. The seafront promenade, Obala hrvatskog narodnog preporoda, better known as Riva, is the best central reference point.

Information

Change money at travel agencies or the post office. You'll find ATMs around the bus and train stations.

Algoritam (Map p230; Bajamontijeva 2) A good English-language bookshop.

Atlas Travel Agency (Map p230; ☎ 343 055; Nepotova 4) The town's Amex representative.

Daluma Travel (Map p230; ☎ /fax 338 484; www .daluma.hr; Obala Kneza Domagoja 1) Finds private accommodation and has information on boat schedules.

Garderoba (Map p230; per hr/day 2.20/20KN) main bus station (Map p230; ☾ 6am-10pm); train station (Obala Kneza Domagoja 6; ☾ 7am-9pm) The train station's left-luggage office is about 50m north of the station.

KBC Firule (Map p229; ☎ 556 111; Spinčićeva 1) Split's hospital. Emergency services are available 24 hours.

Main post office (Map p230; Kralja Tomislava 9; ☾ 7.30am-7pm Mon-Fri, 8am-noon Sat) There's also a telephone centre (open 7am-9pm Monday to Saturday) here.

Mriža (Map p230; ☎ 321 320; Kružićeva 3; per hr 20KN) Internet access.

Turist Biro (Map p230; ☎ /fax 342 142; turist-biro -split@st.t-com.hr; Obala hrvatskog narodnog preporoda 12; ☾ 9am-7pm Mon-Fri, to 4pm Sat) Arranges private accommodation; sells guidebooks and the Split Card (see the boxed text, below).

Turistička Zajednica (Map p230; ☎ /fax 342 606; www.visitsplit.com; Peristil; ☾ 9am-8.30pm Mon-Sat, 8am-1pm Sun) Has information on Split; sells the Split Card.

SPLIT CARD

Not a bad deal at all – get the Split Card for 36KN (€5) for one day and you can use it for three days without paying anything extra. You get free access to most of the city's museums, half-price discounts to many galleries, and tonnes of discounts on car rental, restaurants, shops and hotels.

Sights

DIOCLETIAN'S PALACE

The old town is a vast open-air museum and the new information signs at the important sights explain a great deal of Split's history. **Diocletian's Palace** (Map p230), facing the harbour (entrance on Obala hrvatskog narodnog preporoda 22), is one of the most imposing Roman ruins in existence. It was built as a strong rectangular fortress, with walls measuring 215m from east to west, 181m wide at the southernmost point and reinforced by square corner towers. The imperial residence, mausoleum and temples were south of the main street, now called Krešimirova, connecting the east and west palace gates. Don't expect a palace, though, or a museum – this is the living heart of the city, and its often ragged labyrinthine streets are packed with people (locals and tourists alike), bars, shops and restaurants. The narrow streets hide passageways and courtyards, some deserted and eerie, others thumping with music from bars and cafes, while the residents hang their washing to dry overhead, kids play football amid the ancient walls, and grannies sit in their windows watching the action below. It's an enchanting place.

Enter through the central ground floor of the palace. On the left are the excavated **Basement Halls** (Map p230; 10am-6pm), empty but impressive. Go through the passage to the **Peristil** (Map p230), a picturesque colonnaded square with a neo-Romanesque cathedral tower rising above. The **Vestibule** (Map p230), an open dome above the ground-floor passageway at the southern end of the Peristil, is grand and cavernous. A lane off the Peristil opposite the cathedral leads to the **Temple of Jupiter** (Map p230), now a baptistery.

On the eastern side of the Peristil is the **Cathedral** (Map p230), originally Diocletian's mausoleum. The only reminder of Diocletian in the cathedral is a sculpture of his head in a circular stone wreath, below the dome which is directly above the baroque white-marble altar. The Romanesque wooden doors (1214) and stone pulpit are notable. For a small fee you can climb the tower.

In the Middle Ages the nobility and rich merchants built their residences within the old palace walls; the Papalic Palace is now the **Town Museum** (Gradski Muzej; Map p230; ☎ 341 240; Papalićeva ul 5; adult/concession 10/5KN; 9am-noon & 5-8pm Tue-Fri, 10am-noon Sat & Sun Jun-Sep, 10am-5pm Tue-Fri, to noon Sat & Sun Oct-May). It has a tidy collection of artefacts, paintings, furniture and clothes from Split; captions are in Croatian.

OUTSIDE THE PALACE WALLS

The **East Palace Gate** (Map p230) leads to the market area. The **West Palace Gate** (Map p230) opens onto medieval Narodni trg, dominated by the 15th-century Venetian Gothic **Old Town Hall** (Map p230).

Go through the **North Palace Gate** (Map p230) to see Ivan Meštrović's powerful 1929 **statue of Gregorius of Nin** (Map p230), a 10th-century Slavic religious leader who fought for the right to perform Mass in Croatian. Notice that his big toe has been polished to a shine; it's said that touching it brings good luck.

OUTSIDE CENTRAL SPLIT

The **Archaeological Museum** (Arheološki Muzej; Map p229; ☎ 318 720; Zrinjsko-Frankopanska 25; adult/student 20/10KN; 9am-2pm Tue-Fri, to 1pm Sat & Sun), north of town, is a fascinating supplement to your walk around Diocletian's Palace, and to the site of ancient Salona (modern-day Solin). The history of Split is traced from Illyrian times to the Middle Ages, in chronological order, with explanations in English.

The finest art museum in Split is **Meštrović Gallery** (Galerija Meštrović; ☎ 358 450; Šetalište Ivana Meštrovića 46; adult/student 30/15KN; 9am-9pm Tue-Sun Jun-Sep, 9am-4pm Tue-Sat, 10am-3pm Sun Oct-May). You'll see a comprehensive, well-arranged collection of works by Ivan Meštrović, Croatia's premier modern sculptor.

From the Meštrović Gallery it's possible to hike straight up **Marjan Hill** (Map p229). Go up Tonča Petrasova Marovića on the western side of the gallery and continue straight up the stairway to Put Meja. Turn left and walk east of the gallery to Put Meja 76. The trail begins on the western side of this building. Marjan Hill offers trails through the forest to lookouts and old chapels.

Festivals & Events

February Carnival Traditional carnival in the old town.
Feast of St Duje 7 May.
Flower show May.
Festival of Popular Music End of June.
Split Summer Festival Mid-July to mid-August. Features open-air opera, ballet, drama and musical concerts.

Sleeping

Good budget accommodation is quite thin on the ground in Split, unless you're looking to

SPLIT

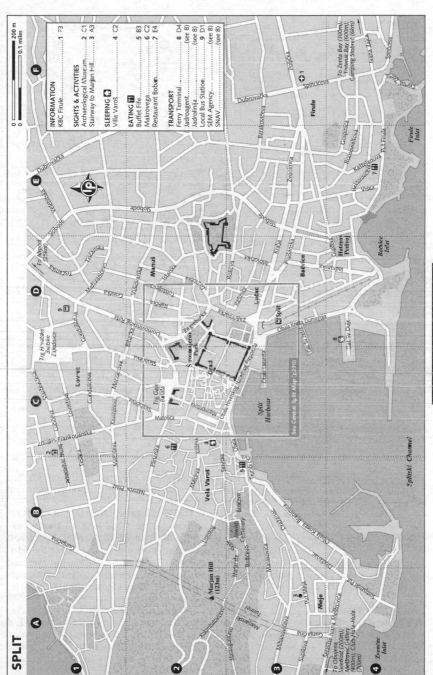

CROATIA

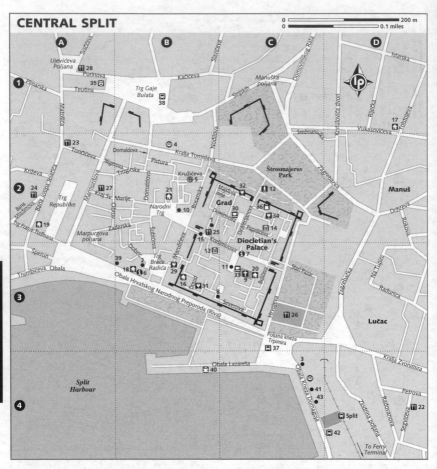

CENTRAL SPLIT

CROATIA

sleep in dorms. Private accommodation is the best option; in summer you may be deluged at the bus station by women offering *sobe*. Make sure you're clear about the exact location of the room or you may find yourself several bus rides from the town centre. The best thing to do is book through the Turist Biro (p227). Expect to pay between 145KN and 220KN for a double where you will probably share the bathroom with the proprietor.

DIOCLETIAN'S PALACE

our pick **Hotel Peristil** (Map p230; ☎ 329 070; www .hotelperistil.com; Poljana Kraljice Jelene 5; low-high s 700-1000KN, d 900-1200KN; 🔀 🖳) The loveliest hotel in Split also has the best location – it overlooks the bell tower of the cathedral. The rooms

are absolutely gorgeous – all have wooden floors, antique details, smooth linen and good views.

our pick **B&B Kaštel 1700** (Map p230; ☎ 343 912; www.kastelsplit.com; Mihovilova Širina 5; low-high s 290-510KN, d 400-660KN; 🔀 🖳) Among Split's best value for money places, it's near the bars, overlooks Trg Braće Radića, and has sweet and tidy rooms and friendly, efficient service.

Split Hostel Booze & Snooze (Map p230; ☎ 342 787; www.splithostel.com; Narodni Trg 8; dm low-high 110-180KN; 🔀) A great new addition to Split's backpacker scene, this hostel is run by Aussie Croats and does exactly what it says on the tin – it's a party place, with 23 beds to snooze in and a nice terrace, and it's right in the centre of town.

OUTSIDE THE PALACE WALLS

our pick Villa Varoš (Map p229; ☎ 483 469; www.villa
varos.hr; Miljenka Smoje 1; d high-low 400-500KN; 🖳)
Owned by a New Yorker Croat, Villa Varoš
is central, the rooms are simple, bright and
airy, the three apartments are excellent (with
a well-equipped kitchen), and the price is
most commendable.

Hostel Split Mediterranean House (Map p230;
☎ 0989871312; www.hostel-split.com; Vukasovićeva 21;
dm from 100KN; 🖳) It's a 10-minute walk from
the North Palace Gate to this friendly, family-
run hostel, set in a lovely old stone building.
There are two six-bed dorms and some newer
en suite three-bed dorms.

Hotel Bellevue (Map p230; ☎ 345 644; www.hotel-belle
vue.hr; Bana Josipa Jelačića 2; low-high s 513-610KN, d
703-830KN) The Bellevue is an atmospheric old
classic that has surely seen more polished
days but remains one of the more dreamy
hotels in town. It's all regal patterned wallpaper here, dark-brown wood, art deco elements, billowing gauzy curtains and faded but
well-kept rooms.

Hotel Adriana (Map p230; ☎ 340 000; www.hotel
-adriana.com; Obala Hrvatskog Narodnog Preporoda 9; low-
high s 550-650KN, d 750-900KN; 🖳) Good value, excellent location. The rooms are not massively
exciting, with their navy curtains and beige
furniture, but some have sea views, which is
a real bonus in Split's old town.

Camping Stobreč (off Map p229; ☎ 325 426; www
.campingsplit.com; Sv Lovre 6, Stobreč; low-high per adult
€3.60-4.60, site €2.90-4.50; 🕑 Apr-Nov) A great place
to pitch your tent and enjoy Split and Solin

(around 6km away from each), as well as the
beach. It's a well-equipped place, with two
beaches (one sandy and great for kids), three
bars, a restaurant, a shop, an internet cafe,
you name it.

Eating

our pick Konoba Trattoria Bajamont (Map p230;
☎ 0912537441; Bajamontijeva 3; mains from 50KN) A
one-room joint with four or five tables on one
side and a heavily leaned-on bar on the other;
there's no sign above the door and the menu
is written out in marker pen and stuck in an
inconspicuous spot by the entrance. The food is
excellent and the menu usually features things
like small fried fish, squid-ink risotto, *brujet*
(fish/seafood stew with wine, onions and herbs,
served with polenta) and octopus salad.

Konoba Hvaranin (Map p230; ☎ 0917675891; Bana
Mladenova 9; mains from 70KN) A mother-father-son
business that feeds Split's journalists and writers, the Hvaranin is a long-standing favourite
of the city's creatives. Mum and dad cook
great fish and seafood, bake their own bread
and stew their own tomato sauce, and the
regulars adore their traditional basics like
pašticada and risotto. This is a good place to
try the *rožata* (Croatian crème brûlée) – it's
fresh and homemade.

Noštromo (Map p230; ☎ 0914056666; www.restoran
-nostromo.hr; Kraj Sv Marije 10; mains from 80KN) Sitting
on the side of the fish market, Noštromo is
one of Split's poshest restaurants. The locals
love it because it prepares fish bought daily
at the market.

CROATIA

Galija (Map p230; Tončićeva 12; pizzas from 26KN) Galija has been the most popular place on Split's pizza scene for several decades now. It's the sort of joint that the locals take you to for an unfussy but good lunch or dinner, and where everyone relaxes on the wooden benches with the leftovers of a *quattro staggioni* or a margherita in front of them.

Buffet Fife (Map p229; ☎ 345 223; Trumbićeva Obala 11; mains around 40KN) Dragomir presides over a motley crew of sailors and misfits who drop in for the simple home cooking (especially the *pašticada*) and his own brand of grumpy but loving hospitality.

Restaurant Boban (Map p229; ☎ 543 300; Hektorovićeva 49; mains from 60KN) Split's favourite restaurant since 1973, and you'll know why when you sink your teeth into the fresh seafood and juicy fish that's seared and served with some imaginative sauces. It's a family-run place that likes to innovate and keep its reputation high. In the Firule area.

Black Cat (Map p230; ☎ 490 284; Segvićeva 1; mains from 20KN) If you get tired of Croatian food and crave a taco, quesadilla or any other Mexican delight, head straight for this little bistro, five minutes' walk away from the seafront and main bus station.

Makrovega (Map p229; ☎ 394 440; www.makrovega.hr; Leština 2; mains from 40KN; ☽ 9am-7pm Mon-Fri, to 4pm Sat; Ⓥ ✕) A meat-free haven with a clean, spacious (nonsmoking!) interior, a delicious buffet and à la carte food that alternates between macrobiotic and vegetarian.

Self-catering options:

Market (Map p230; ☽ 6am-2pm) Outside the East Palace Gate; has a wide array of fresh local produce.

Supermarket (Map p230; Svačićeva 1) The vast delicatessen here has a wide selection of meat and cheese for sandwiches.

Drinking

Split is great for nightlife, especially (or more so) during the spring and summer months. The palace walls are generally throbbing with loud music on Friday and Saturday night, and you can spend the entire night going around the mazy streets, discovering new places. The entertainment complex of Bačvice (Map p229) has a multitude of open-air bars and clubs which stay open till the wee hours.

Le Porta (Map p230; Majstora Jurja) is renowned for its cocktails. On the same square – Majstora Jurja – are Kala, Dante, Whisky Bar and Na

Kantunu, all of which end up merging into one when the night gets busy.

Puls 2 (Map p230; Mihovilova Širina) and **Café Shook** (Map p230; Mihovilova Širina) are pretty much indistinguishable late on Friday or Saturday night, when the dozen steps that link these two bars are chock-a-block with youngsters. It's an area that's hard to miss if you enter the palace from the Riva, and its popularity hasn't waned in a decade. Great for people watching and cocktail drinking.

Galerija (Map p230; Dominisova 9) Parallel to Majstora Jurja is Dominisova, another street that's full of fun bars. Galerija is quieter than others, catering to smooching lovers or those wanting to catch up with friends without blasting music drowning out the conversation. The interior is granny-chic.

Ghetto Club (Map p230; ☎ 346 879; Dosud 10) Head for Split's most bohemian bar, on an intimate courtyard with chairs amid flowerbeds and a trickling fountain, great music and friendly atmosphere.

Luxor Bar (Map p230; Kraj Sv Ivana 11) Having coffee in this courtyard may be the most touristy thing to do, but it's also one of the best: little cushions are laid out on the steps, you've got the cathedral on the one side and the Peristil on the other, people are snapping photos all round, and the locals are going about their business.

Entertainment

Croatian National Theatre (Map p230; Trg Gaje Bulata; best seats about 60KN) During winter, opera and ballet are presented here. Erected in 1891, the theatre was fully restored in 1979 in its original style; it's worth attending a performance for the architecture alone.

Club Hula-Hula (off Map p229; ☎ 398 589; Uvala Zvončac; ☽ Jun-Sep) There's a never-ending string of events here, including live music on weekends with local groups.

Obojena Svjetlost (off Map p229; ☎ 358 280; Šetalište Ivana Meštrovića 35) Tonnes of live and DJ music, a wide seafront terrace and a massive interior. It's by Kasuni beach so you can watch the sunrise whilst dipping your toes in the sea.

Shopping

The Diocletian's Palace walls are packed with shops – small boutiques and international chains like Diesel alike. Marmontova street is equally popular for shopping among the locals.

BUS SERVICES FROM SPLIT

Destination	Price (KN)	Duration (hr)	Daily departures
Dubrovnik	105-166	4½	12
Makarska	60	1½	every half-hour
Međugorje*	120	3	5
Mostar*	120	2-4	4
Pula	331	10	1
Rijeka	250-380	7½	10
Sarajevo*	200	7	11
Zadar	120	3	8
Zagreb	195	5-9	27

*BiH destinations

Zlatna Vrata (Map p230 ☎ 360 122; Carrarina Poljana 1) Antiques and junk lovers will delight in the knick-knacks at Zlatna Vrata – old Yugoslav clocks, antique ceramics, vintage socialist phones and who knows what else can be found with a bit of digging around.

Diocletian's Cellars (Map p230; ☒ 10am-6pm) Part of the palace basement halls, this is a market for crafted jewellery, reproductions of Roman busts, silver cigarette cases, candlestick holders, wooden sailing ships, leather goods and other odds and ends.

Getting There & Away
AIR
The country's national carrier, **Croatia Airlines** (Map p230; ☎ 062-777 777; Obala Hrvatskog Narodnog Preporoda 8), operates flights between Zagreb and Split (170KN to 350KN, 45 minutes) up to four times every day. Rates are lower if you book in advance. There's also **Easyjet** (www.easyjet.com).

BOAT
You can buy tickets for passenger ferries at the **Jadrolinija stall** (Map p230; Obala Kneza Domagoja). There are also several agents in the large ferry terminal (Map p229) opposite the main bus station that can assist with boat trips from Split: **Jadroagent** (Map p229; ☎ 338 335) represents Adriatica Navigazione for its connections between Split and Ancona; **Jadrolinija** (Map p229; ☎ 338 333) handles all car-ferry services that depart from the docks around the ferry terminal; **SEM agency** (Map p229; ☎ 060 325 523) handles tickets between Ancona, Split and Hvar; **SNAV** (Map p229; ☎ 322 252) has a four-hour connection to Ancona and Pescara.

For more details on connections to/from Italy see p444.

BUS
Advance bus tickets with seat reservations are recommended. For services from the **main bus station** (Map p230; ☎ 060 327 327; www.ak-split.hr, in Croatian), see the table, above.

Touring (Map p230; ☎ 338 503; Obala Kneza Domagoja 10), near the main bus station, represents Deutsche Touring and sells tickets to German cities.

Bus 37 to Solin, Split airport and Trogir leaves from a **local bus station** (Map p229; Domovinskog Rata) 1km northeast of the city centre.

TRAIN
From the train station there are three fast trains (138KN, six hours) and three overnight trains (138KN, 8½ hours) between Split and Zagreb. From Monday to Saturday there are six trains a day between Šibenik and Split (33KN, two hours) and four trains on Sunday.

Getting Around
There's an airport bus stop on Obala Lazareta 3 (see Map p230). The bus (30KN, 30 minutes) leaves about 90 minutes before flight times, or you can take bus 37 from the local bus station on Domovinskog Rata (11KN for a two-zone ticket).

Buses run about every 15 minutes from 5.30am to 11.30pm. A one-zone ticket costs 9KN for one trip in central Split. You can buy tickets on the bus and the driver can make change.

SOLIN (SALONA)
The ruins of the ancient city of Solin (known as Salona by the Romans), among the vineyards at the foot of mountains 5km

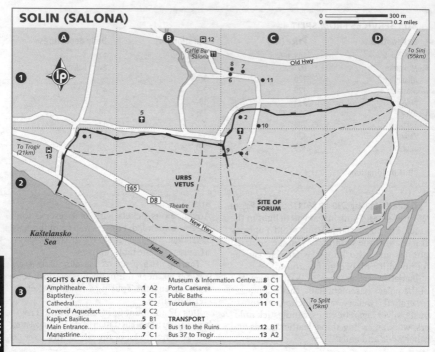

SOLIN (SALONA)

SIGHTS & ACTIVITIES
Amphitheatre	1	A2
Baptistery	2	C1
Cathedral	3	C2
Covered Aqueduct	4	C2
Kapljuč Basilica	5	B1
Main Entrance	6	C1
Manastirine	7	C1
Museum & Information Centre	8	C1
Porta Caesarea	9	C2
Public Baths	10	C1
Tusculum	11	C1

TRANSPORT
Bus 1 to the Ruins	12	B1
Bus 37 to Trogir	13	A2

northeast of Split, are the most interesting archaeological site in Croatia. Salona was the capital of the Roman province of Dalmatia from the time Julius Caesar elevated it to the status of colony. It held out against the barbarians and was only evacuated in AD 614 when the inhabitants fled to Split and neighbouring islands in the face of Avar and Slav attacks. Solin is the site of a summer **Ethnoambient** (www.ethnoambient.net) music festival each August.

Sights

A good place to begin your visit is at the main entrance, near Caffe Bar Salona. There's a small **museum and information centre** (admission 10KN; ☑ 9am-6pm Mon-Sat Jun-Sep, to 1pm Mon-Sat Oct-May) at the entrance, which also provides a helpful map and some literature about the complex.

Manastirine, the fenced area behind the car park, was a burial place for early Christian martyrs before the legalisation of Christianity. Excavated remains of the cemetery and the 5th-century basilica are highlights, although this area was outside the ancient city itself.

Overlooking Manastirine is **Tusculum**, with interesting sculptures embedded in the walls and in the garden.

The Manastirine-Tusculum complex is part of an archaeological reserve that can be freely entered. A path bordered by cypress trees runs south towards the northern **city wall** of Salona. Note the **covered aqueduct** along the inside base of the wall. The ruins in front of you as you stand on the wall were the early Christian cult centre, which include the three-aisled, 5th-century **cathedral** and a small **baptistery** with inner columns. **Public baths** adjoin the cathedral on the eastern side.

Southwest of the cathedral is the 1st-century east city gate, **Porta Caesarea**, later engulfed by the growth of Salona in all directions. Grooves in the stone road left by ancient chariots can be seen at this gate.

Walk west along the city wall for about 500m to **Kapljuč Basilica** on the right, another martyrs' burial place. At the western end of Salona you'll find the huge 2nd-century **amphitheatre**, which was destroyed in the 17th century by the Venetians to prevent it from being used as a refuge by Turkish raiders.

Getting There & Away

The ruins are easily accessible on Split city bus 1 direct to Solin every half-hour from the city bus stop at Trg Gaje Bulata (Map p230).

From the amphitheatre at Solin it's easy to continue to Trogir by catching a westbound bus 37 from the nearby stop on the adjacent new highway. If, on the other hand, you want to return to Split, use the underpass to cross the highway and catch an eastbound bus 37 (buy a four-zone ticket in Split if you plan to do this).

Alternatively, you can catch most Sinj-bound buses (15KN, 10 daily) from Split's local bus station to take you to Solin.

TROGIR

☎ 021 / pop 600

Gorgeous and tiny Trogir (formerly Trau) is beautifully set within medieval walls, its streets knotted and mazy. It's fronted by a wide sea-side promenade that's lined with bars and cafes and luxurious yachts docking in the summer. Trogir is unique among Dalmatian towns for its profuse collection of Romanesque and Renaissance architecture (which flourished under Venetian rule), and this, along with its magnificent cathedral, earned it its status as a World Heritage site in 1997.

Trogir is an easy day trip from Split and a relaxing place to spend a few days, taking a trip or two to nearby islands.

The heart of the Old Town is a few minutes' walk from the bus station. After crossing the small bridge near the station, go through the north gate. Trogir's finest sights are around Narodni trg to the southeast.

Atlas travel agency (☎ 881 374; www.atlas-trogir .com; Zvonimira 10) finds private accommodation, books hotels and runs excursions.

The glory of the three-nave Venetian **Cathedral of St Lovre** (Trg Ivana Pavla II; adult/child 15KN/ free; ☺ 9.30am-noon yr-round, plus 4.30-7pm daily summer) is the Romanesque portal of *Adam and Eve* (1240) by Master Radovan, the earliest example of the nude in Dalmatian sculpture. Enter the building via an obscure back door to see the perfect Renaissance Chapel of St Ivan and the choir stalls, pulpit, ciborium (vessel used to hold consecrated wafers) and treasury. You can even climb the cathedral tower, if it's open, for a great view. Also located on the square is the renovated **Church of St John the Baptist**, with a magnificent carved portal and an interior showcasing a *Pietà* by Nicola Firentinac.

ourpick **Hotel Pašike** (☎ 885 185; www.hotel pasike.com; Sinjska bb; low-high s 550-600KN, d 700-800KN; ✷ ☐), the most gorgeous hotel in Trogir (and wider Dalmatia), has eight rooms full of 19th-century furniture, while the hotel itself is in a 15th-century house. The rooms are painted in vivid colours, some with tur-quoise walls that set off the heavy walnut and wrought-iron beds (covered with antique knitted gloves) beautifully. The **restaurant** (mains from 50KN) is also good, serving local specialities.

In Split, city bus 37 leaves from the local bus station on Domovinskog Rata. It runs between Trogir and Split every 20 minutes (15KN, one hour) throughout the day, with a short stop at Split airport en route. There's also a ferry (11KN, 2½ hours) once a week from Split to Trogir.

Southbound buses from Zadar (130km) will drop you off in Trogir, as will most north-bound buses from Split going to Zadar, Rijeka, Šibenik and Zagreb.

MAKARSKA

☎ 021 / pop 15,000

Makarska is a pretty port town, with a lime-stone centre that turns a peachy orange at sunset. It's an active place – there's an abundance of hiking, climbing, windsurf-ing and swimming – and it has a spectacu-lar natural setting, backed by the gorgeous Mt Biokovo (1762m). There's a long peb-bly town beach offering a feast of activities from beach volleyball to screaming children's games. Makarska is favoured by tourists from neighbouring BiH, who descend upon the town in huge numbers during the July and August holidays.

Being the largest town in the region, Makarska has very good transport connec-tions, making it a good base for exploring the coast and BiH. Don't miss venturing up Mt Biokovo.

Orientation

The bus station on Ante Starčevića is about 300m uphill from the centre of the old town. Take Kralja Zvonimira from the bus station downhill to Obala Kralja Tomislava and you'll be on the main promenade of the old town, with travel agencies, shops and restaurants.

The beach stretches from Sveti Petar park at the beginning of Obala Kralja Tomislava northwest along the bay.

CROATIA

Information

Hospital (☎ 612 033; Stjepana Ivičevića 2) Emergency services are available 24 hours.

Post office (Trg 4 Svibnja 533) You can change money, make phone calls or withdraw cash on MasterCard here.

Turistička Zajednica (☎/fax 612 002; www.makarska .com; Obala Kralja Tomislava 16; ☒ 7am-9pm daily Jun-Sep, to 2pm Mon-Fri Oct-May) It distributes the useful *Official City Guide*, which you can pick up here or at any travel agency.

Zagrebačka Banka (Trg Tina Ujevića 1) Has an ATM.

Sights & Activities

Makarska is more renowned for its natural beauty than its cultural highlights. Visit the **Franciscan monastery** (Franjevački Samostan; Franjevački Put 1; ☒ Mass only), built in 1400 and restored in 1540 and 1614. The monastery's single-nave church is worth visiting for the **shell collection** (☎ 611 256; admission 10KN; ☒ 11am-noon) in the cloister and a painting of the Assumption (1760) by the Flemish artist Pieter de Coster. The 18th-century **St Mark's church** (Crkva Svetog Marka; ☎ 611 365; Kačićev trg; ☒ Mass only) features a baroque silver altar from 1818 and a marble altar from 18th-century Venice.

Mt Biokovo offers wonderful **hiking** opportunities. The Vošac peak (142m) is the nearest target for hikers, only 2.5km from the city. From St Mark's church in Kačićev trg, you can walk or drive up Put Makra, following signs to the village of Makar, where a trail leads to Vošac (one to two hours). From Vošac a good marked trail leads to Sveti Jure, the highest peak at 1762m (two hours). Take plenty of water.

Biokovo Active Holidays (☎ 679 655; www.biokovo .net; Kralja Petra Krešimira IV 7b; ☒ 9am-7pm Mon-Fri, to 2pm Sat) is an excellent source of hiking and other information about Mt Biokovo. For scuba diving, try **More Sub** (☎ 611 727, 098265241; Hotel Dalmacija, Kralja Krešimira bb).

Sleeping & Eating

All of the travel agencies listed earlier can find private rooms. Count on spending from €14 for a simple double with shared bathroom to €25 for better digs with private facilities.

Hotel Biokovo (☎ 615 244; www.hotelbiokovo.hr; Obala Kralja Tomislava bb; low-high s €60-96, d €90-134; P ☒) The swankiest hotel in town in the postwar years, Biokovo is still regarded as one of its better hotels. The rooms are spacious, the beds comfortable, and all have balconies. It's right in the centre, on the promenade.

Hotel Porin (☎ 613 744; www.hotel-porin.hr; Marineta 2; d low-high €90-117; P ☒) A decent choice in the town centre. The soundproofed rooms have good beds and satellite TVs, though little in the way of cosiness or decoration. The price goes down around 10% for stays over two nights.

Baško Polje (☎ 612 329; adult/tent 40/60KN; ☒ May-Oct) Between Makarska and Baška Voda, this is a lovely autocamp, close to town and on the beach, amid thick pines.

Riva (☎ 616 829; Obala Kralja Tomislava 6; mains 40-90KN) A lovely restaurant just off the main drag, in a quiet leafy courtyard. The food is decent, with the usual choice of fish, seafood and meat. Some of the pasta dishes can be too creamy and heavy, so try a risotto or a fish and seafood platter.

Ivo (☎ 611 257; Starčevića 41; mains around 60KN) Away from the main drag and the beach, Ivo is a true find. Fish and meat dishes are cooked to perfection and expertly seasoned.

Susvid (☎ 612 732; Kačićev Trg; meals from 45KN; Ⓥ) Right on the main square and massively popular, Susvid has excellent vegetarian and fish dishes.

Entertainment

Art Cafe (☎ 615 808; Don M Pavlinovića 1) A former disco, Art Cafe now holds a changing series of concerts, exhibits and events. It's one of the best hang-outs on the coast.

Grotta (☎ 0915694657; Sv Petar bb) On Sveti Petar Peninsula just after the port, this popular disco tucked into a cave welcomes local DJs plus an array of jazz, blues and rock bands.

Getting There & Away

In summer there are three to five ferries a day between Makarska and Sumartin on Brač (23KN, 30 minutes), reduced to two a day in winter.

There are 10 buses daily from the **bus station** (☎ 612 333; Ante Starčevića 30) to Dubrovnik (129KN, three hours), 11 buses daily to Split (64KN, 1¼ hours), two buses daily to Rijeka (307KN, nine hours) and two buses daily to Zagreb (110KN to 150KN, six hours). The **Jadrolinija stall** (☎ 338 333; Obala Kralja Tomislava) is near the Hotel Biokovo.

There's also a daily bus to Sarajevo (160KN, six hours).

AROUND MAKARSKA
Brela

The town of Brela, 14km northwest of Makarska, is surrounded by the longest and

VIS & BRAČ ISLANDS

Of all the Croatian islands, **Vis** is the most mysterious. It spent much of its recent history serving as a military base for the Yugoslav National Army, cut off from foreign visitors from the 1950s all the way until 1989. The isolation preserved the island from tourist development but, as has happened with impoverished islands across the Mediterranean, this has become its very draw as a tourist destination.

Vis town sits in the northeast and Komiža in the southwest, at the foot of two large bays. The rugged coast is dotted with gorgeous coves, caves and a couple of sand beaches. The island's remnants of antiquity, displayed in the Archaeological Museum and around Vis town, are a fascinating additional insight into the complex character of this tiny place. Stay at **Villa Nonna** (☎ 098380046; www.villa-nonna.com; Ribarska 50; d low-high €35-70; ﹡) in Komiža, a lovely old townhouse with seven renovated apartments, each with wooden floors and kitchens, and eat at **Bako** (☎ 713 008, Gundulićeva 1; mains from 50KN; ﹡ dinner only Sep-Jun) with its fabulous seaside terrace and excellent lobster stew.

our pick **Natural Holiday** (☎ 0981731673; www.bisevo.org; Salbunara Bay; per bungalow per week low-high €466-728) is an eco-friendly and luxury campsite on the tiny islet of Biševo, off Vis. It doesn't feature tents but has bungalows of sorts, with supercomfy beds, an outdoor area and a private bathroom with 50L of water per shelter.

Brač is famous for two things: its radiant white stone, which has built Diocletian's Palace in Split and the White House in Washington DC (oh, yes!), and Zlatni Rat, the long pebbly beach at Bol that sticks out lasciviously into the Adriatic and adorns 90% of Croatia's tourism posters. It's the largest island in central Dalmatia, with two towns, several sleepy villages and a dramatic Mediterranean landscape of steep cliffs, inky waters and pine forests. The two main centres, Supetar and Bol differ greatly from one another – Supetar takes on the appearance of a transit town, while luxurious Bol revels in its more exclusive appeal. Stay at **Hotel Kaštil** (☎ 635 995; www.kastil.hr; Riva Frane Radića 1; low-high s 330-710KN, d 480-1040KN; P ﹡), where all rooms have sea views, and eat at **Taverna Laguna** (☎ 635 692; Ante Starčevića 9; mains from 65KN), a romantic spot next to a quiet lagoon.

Vis and Brač are best reached by daily car ferries from Split (see www.jadrolinija.hr). In July and August there are boats to Vis (47KN, two hours 20 minutes) departing at 9am on Friday, Saturday and Sunday, coming back at 6pm. Other days the ferry leaves at 9.30am from Split but doesn't come back in the afternoon. Out of high season, a day trip is not viable.

There are 13 car ferries a day between Split and Supetar in summer (30KN, one hour) and seven a day at other times of the year. There's a Jadrolinija catamaran in summer between Split and Bol (50KN, 50 minutes).

loveliest coastline in Dalmatia. Six kilometres of pebble beaches curve around gentle coves thickly forested with pine trees. A shady, paved promenade winds around the coves, the sea is crystal clear and there are convenient outdoor showers on some beaches.

ORIENTATION & INFORMATION

The bus stop (no left-luggage office) is behind Hotel Soline. From here it's a short walk downhill to Obala Kneza Domagoja, the harbour street and town centre.

Turistička Zajednica (☎ 618 455, 618 337; www.brela .hr; Obala Kneza Domagoja bb; ﹡ 8am-9pm mid-Jun–mid-Sep, to 2pm Mon-Fri mid-Sep–mid-Jun) provides a town map and a cycling map for the region, and **Bonavia travel agency** (☎ 619 019; www.bonavia-agency.hr; Obala Kneza Domagoja 18) finds private accommodation, changes money and books excursions.

SIGHTS & ACTIVITIES

Beaches and coves are on both sides of the town, but the longest stretch is the 4km coast west of the town centre. The best is **Punta Rata**, a stunning pebble beach about 300m southwest of the town centre where there are showers and changing rooms.

SLEEPING & EATING

The closest camping is available at Baško Polje (opposite). For private accommodation you'll pay from €13 to €16 per person per day.

The four large hotels are managed by **Brela Hotels** (☎ 603 190; www.brelahotels.com).

CROATIA

Hotel Soline (☎ 603 207; low-high s 316-750KN, d 544-1368KN; P) A four-star luxury hotel with plush, spacious rooms overlooking the beach. There's a fragrant wellness centre, and if you're here in the winter you can swim in the indoor pool. Soline is close to the centre.

Hotel Marina (☎ 608 608; low-high s 287-625KN, d 442-1088KN; P) The Marina is the most affordable of the Blue Sun Hotels, with basic but comfortable rooms and a wall of pine trees that separates the hotel from the luxuriant Brela beach.

Konoba Feral (☎ 618 909; Obala Kneza Domagoja 30; mains from 40KN) Every Dalmatian place has its *konoba*, and this is Brela's local. It's friendly, with wooden tables and good seafood and fish. The line-caught squid (280KN per kilogram) is deliciously grilled with garlic and parsley.

DRINKING

our pick **Southern Comfort Beach Bar** (Ikovac Beach) Apart from fabulous beaches, Brela hides one of Croatia's best beach bars too. Southern Comfort prepares killer cocktails – the margaritas are divine – plays good music, has comfy chairs by the sea (torches are lit after dark), and stays open pretty much all day and night. To get here, walk past Hotel Berulia, towards Baska Voda, around 200m down.

CROATIA

GETTING THERE & AWAY

All buses between Makarska and Split stop at Brela, making it an easy day trip (1½ hours, 40KN) from either town.

HVAR ISLAND

☎ 021 / pop 12,600

Hvar is the number one carrier of Croatia's superlatives: it's the most luxurious island, the sunniest place in the country (2724 sunny hours each year) and, along with Dubrovnik, the most popular tourist destination. Hvar is also famed for its verdancy and its lavender fields, as well as other aromatic herbs such as rosemary and heather.

Hvar Town

The island's hub and busiest destination, Hvar town is estimated to draw around 30,000 people a day in high season. It's odd that they can all fit in the small bay town, but fit they do. Visitors wander along the main square, explore the sights on the winding stone streets, swim on the numerous beaches or pop off to nudist Pakleni Islands. There are several good restaurants and a number of great hotels, as well as a couple of hostels.

ORIENTATION

Car ferries from Split deposit you in Stari Grad, but local buses meet most ferries in summer for the trip to Hvar town. The town centre is Trg Sv Stjepana, 100m west of the bus station. Passenger ferries tie up on Riva, the eastern quay, across from Hotel Slavija.

INFORMATION

Atlas travel agency (☎ 741 670) On the western side of the harbour.

Clinic (☎ 741 300; Sv Katarina) About 200m from the town centre, it's past the Hotel Pharos. Emergency services are available 24 hours.

Garderoba (per day 15KN; 7am-midnight) The left-luggage office is in the bathroom next to the bus station.

Internet Leon (☎ 741 824; Riva; per hr 42KN; 8am-9pm Mon-Fri, to 10pm Sat, to 6pm Sun) Internet access next to the Hotel Palace.

Pelegrini Travel (☎ /fax 742 250; pelegrini@inet.hr) Also finds private accommodation.

Post office (Riva) You can make phone calls here.

Tourist office (☎ /fax 742 977; www.tzhvar.hr; 8am-1pm & 5-9pm Mon-Sat, 9am-noon Sun Jun-Sep, 8am-2pm Mon-Sat Oct-May) In the arsenal building on the corner of Trg Sv Stjepana.

SIGHTS & ACTIVITIES

The full flavour of medieval Hvar is best savoured on the backstreets of the old town. At each end of Hvar is a monastery with a prominent tower. The Dominican **Church of St Marko** at the head of the bay was largely destroyed by Turks in the 16th century, but you can visit the local **Archaeological Museum** (admission 10KN; 10am-noon Jun-Sep) in the ruins. If it's closed you'll still get a good view of the ruins from the road just above, which leads up to a stone cross on a hilltop offering a picture-postcard view of Hvar.

At the southeastern end of Hvar you'll find the 15th-century Renaissance **Franciscan Monastery** (10am-noon & 5-7pm Jun-Sep, Christmas & Holy Weeks), with a great collection of Venetian paintings in the church and adjacent **museum** (admission 15KN; 10am-noon & 5-7pm Mon-Sat Jun-Sep), including *The Last Supper* by Matteo Ingoli.

Smack in the middle of Hvar is the imposing Gothic **arsenal**, and upstairs is Hvar's prize, the first **municipal theatre** in Europe (1612) – both under extensive renovation at the time of research. On the hill high above Hvar town is a **Venetian fortress** (1551), and it's worth the climb up to appreciate the lovely, sweeping panoramic views. The fort was built to defend Hvar from the Turks, who sacked the town in 1539 and 1571.

There is a small town beach next to the Franciscan monastery, but the best beach is in front of the Hotel Amphora, around the western corner of the cove. Most people take a launch to the offshore islands that include the naturist Pakleni Islands of Jerolim and Stipanska and lovely Palmižana.

In front of the Hotel Amphora, **Diving Centar Viking** (☎ 742 529; www.viking-diving.com) is a large operation in Podstine that offers a certification course, dives (€30) and hotel packages.

SLEEPING

Accommodation in Hvar is extremely tight in July and August: reservations are highly recommended. For private accommodation, try Pelegrini Travel (see opposite). Expect to pay from 160/280KN per single/double with bathroom in the town centre.

our pick **Hotel Adriana** (☎ 750 200; www.suncani hvar.hr; Riva bb; per person from €300; ❄ 🔲 🖩) Opened in June 2007, this is Croatia's only Leading Small Hotel of the World, and that's only an inkling of the world of comfort you'll find in this place. There's a comprehensive spa, a gorgeous rooftop pool (heated), and the rooms are simply magnificent.

Hotel Riva (☎ 750 750; www.suncanihvar.hr; Riva bb; low-high s €176-380, d €187-391; ❄ 🔲) Now the luxury veteran on the Hvar town scene, the Riva is a 100-year-old hotel that's a picture of modernity. The location is right on the harbour, perfect for watching the yachts.

Hotel Croatia (☎ 742 400; www.hotelcroatia.net; Majerovica bb, per person low high 245-575KN; ℗) Only a few steps from the sea, this medium-sized, rambling 1930s building is among gorgeous, peaceful gardens. The rooms are simple and fresh, many with balconies overlooking the gardens and the sea.

Jagoda & Ante Bracanović Guesthouse (☎ 741 416, 0915203796; www.geocities.com/virgilye/hvar-jagoda .html; Poviše Škole; low-high s 100-120KN, d 190-220KN) The Bracanović family has turned a traditional stone building into a small *pansion*. Rooms come with balconies, bathrooms and kitchen access, and the family goes out of its way for guests.

Green Lizard Hostel (☎ 742 560; www.greenlizard.hr; Lučića bb; dm 110KN, d per person 135KN; ❄ Apr-Nov) This privately run hostel is a welcome and most necessary budget option on Hvar. Rooms are

simple and immaculately clean, there's a communal kitchen, and there are a few doubles with private and shared facilities.

EATING

The pizzerias along the harbour offer predictable but inexpensive eating. The **grocery store** (Trg Sv Stjepana) is a viable restaurant alternative, and there's a morning market next to the bus station.

Konoba Menego (☎ 742 036; mains from 70KN; ⓥ) This is a rustic old house decked out in Hvar antiques, and the staff wear traditional outfits. Try the cheeses and vegetables, prepared the old-fashioned Dalmatian way.

Luna (☎ 741 400; mains from 70KN) Climb the 'stairway to heaven' (you have to guffaw) to the rooftop terrace. Luna has dishes like gnocchi with truffles and seafood and wine pasta.

Yakša (☎ 277 0770; www.yaksahvar.com; mains from 80KN) A top-end restaurant where many come not just for the food but also for its reputation as the place to be seen in Hvar. There is a lovely garden at the back and the food is excellent, with lobster (250KN) being a popular choice.

ENTERTAINMENT

Hvar has some of the best nightlife on the Adriatic coast, and it's mainly famous for **Carpe Diem** (☎ 742 369; www.carpe-diem-hvar.com; Riva), the mother of all Dalmatian clubs. The music is smooth, there're drinks aplenty, and there's lots of dancing on the tables in bikinis.

Veneranda (🕙 from 9.30pm) A former fortress on the slope above Hotel Delfin, Veneranda alternates star DJs with live bands while the punters dance on a floor surrounded by a pool.

GETTING THERE & AWAY

The Jadrolinija ferries between Rijeka and Dubrovnik stop in Stari Grad before continuing to Korčula. The **Jadrolinija agency** (☎ 741 132; Riva) sells boat tickets. Car ferries from Split call at Stari Grad (42KN, one hour) three times daily (five daily in July and August). A speedy catamaran (22KN, one hour) goes five times a day between Split and Hvar town in the summer months. The **Jadrolinija agency** (☎ 741 132; www.jadrolinija.hr) is beside the landing in Stari Grad. There're at least 10 shuttle ferries (less in low season) running from Drvenik, on the mainland, to Sućuraj on the tip of Hvar island (13KN, 25 minutes).

Buses meet most ferries that dock at Stari Grad in July and August, but if you come in

CROATIA

low season it's best to check at the tourist office or at Pelegrini to make sure the bus is running. A taxi costs from 150KN to 200KN. **Radio Taxi Tihi** (☎ 098338824) is cheaper if there are a number of passengers to fill up the mini-van. It's easy to recognise with the photo of Hvar painted on the side.

It's possible to visit Hvar on a (hectic) day trip from Split by catching the morning Jadrolinija ferry to Stari Grad, a bus to Hvar town, then the last ferry from Stari Grad directly back to Split.

KORČULA ISLAND
☎ 020 / pop 16,200

Rich in vineyards and olive trees, the island of Korčula was named Korkyra Melaina (Black Korčula) by the original Greek settlers because of its dense woods and plant life. As the largest island in an archipelago of 48, it provides plenty of opportunities for scenic drives, particularly along the southern coast.

Swimming opportunities abound in the many quiet coves and secluded beaches, while the interior produces some of Croatia's finest wine, especially dessert wines made from the *grk* grape cultivated around Lumbarda. Local olive oil is another product worth seeking out.

Korčula Town

On a hilly peninsula jutting into the Adriatic sits Korčula town, a striking walled town of round defensive towers and red-roofed houses. Resembling a miniature Dubrovnik, the gated, walled old town is crisscrossed by narrow stone streets designed to protect its inhabitants from the winds swirling around the peninsula. Korčula Island was controlled by Venice from the 14th to the 18th centuries, as is evident from the Venetian coats of arms adorning the official buildings. If you don't stop in Korčula, one look at this unique town from the Jadrolinija ferry will make you regret it.

ORIENTATION

The big Jadrolinija car ferry drops you off either in the west harbour next to the Hotel Korčula or the east harbour next to Marko Polo Tours. The old town lies between the two harbours. The large hotels and main beach lie south of the east harbour, and the residential neighbourhood Sveti Nikola (with a smaller beach) is southwest of the west harbour. The town bus station is 100m south of the old town centre.

INFORMATION

There are ATMs in the town centre at HVB Splitska Banka and Dubrovačka Banka. You can change money there, at the post office or at any of the travel agencies. The post office, hidden next to the stairway up to the old town, also has telephones.

Atlas travel agency (☎ 711 231; Trg Kralja Tomislava) Represents Amex, runs excursions and finds private accommodation. There's another office nearby.

Eterna (☎ 716 538; eterno.doo@du.t-com.hr; Put Sv Nikola bb; per hr 25KN) Finds private accommodation and offers internet access.

Hospital (☎ 711 137; ul 59, Kalac) It's south of the old town, about 1km past the Hotel Marko Polo. Emergency services are available 24 hours.

Marko Polo Tours (☎ 715 400; marko-polo-tours @du.t-com.hr; Biline 5) Finds private accommodation and organises excursions.

Tino's Internet (☎ 0915091182; ul Tri Sulara; per hr 30KN) Tino's other outlet is at the ACI Marina; both are open long hours.

Tourist office (☎ 715 701; tzg-korcule@du.t-com.hr; Obala Franje Tudjmana bb; 🕑 8am-3pm & 5-9pm Mon-Sat, 8am-3pm Sun Jun-Sep, 8am-1pm & 5-9pm Mon-Sat Oct-May) An excellent source of information, located on the west harbour.

SIGHTS

Other than following the circuit of the former city walls or walking along the shore, sightseeing in Korčula centres on Trg Sv Marka. The Gothic **St Mark's Cathedral** (Katedrala Svetog Marka; 🕑 10am-noon & 5-7pm Jul & Aug, Mass only rest of yr) features two paintings by Tintoretto (*Three Saints* on the altar and *Annunciation* to one side).

The **Town Museum** (Gradski Muzej; ☎ 711 420; Trg Sv Marka; admission 10KN; 🕑 10am-1pm Nov-Mar, 10am-2pm Apr-May, 10am-2pm & 7-9pm Jun & Oct, 10am-9pm Jul & Aug), in the 15th-century Gabriellis Palace opposite the cathedral, has exhibits of Greek pottery, Roman ceramics and home furnishings, all with English captions. The **treasury** (☎ 711 049; Trg Sv Marka; admission 15KN; 🕑 9am-2pm & 5-8pm May-Oct), in the 14th-century Abbey Palace next to the cathedral, is also worth a look. It's said that Marco Polo was born in Korčula in 1254; you can visit what is believed to have been his **house** (De Polo; admission 10KN; 🕑 10am-1pm & 5-7pm Mon-Sat Jul & Aug) and climb the tower.

There's also an **Icon Museum** (Trg Svih Svetih; admission 7.50KN; 🕑 9am-2pm & 5-8pm May-Oct) in the old town. It isn't much of a museum, but visitors are let into the beautiful old **All Saints Church**.

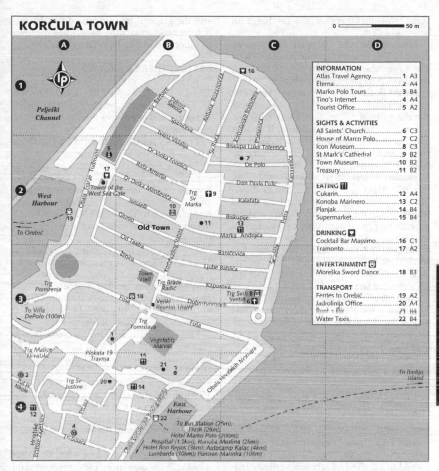

KORČULA TOWN

0 _____ 50 m

INFORMATION	
Atlas Travel Agency	**1** A3
Éterna	**2** A4
Marko Polo Tours	**3** B4
Tino's Internet	**4** A4
Tourist Office	**5** A2

SIGHTS & ACTIVITIES	
All Saints' Church	**6** C3
House of Marco Polo	**7** C2
Icon Museum	**8** C3
St Mark's Cathedral	**9** B2
Town Museum	**10** B2
Treasury	**11** B2

EATING	
Cukarin	**12** A4
Konoba Marinero	**13** C2
Planjak	**14** B4
Supermarket	**15** B4

DRINKING	
Cocktail Bar Massimo	**16** C1
Tramonto	**17** A2

ENTERTAINMENT	
Moreška Sword Dance	**18** B3

TRANSPORT	
Ferries to Orebić	**19** A2
Jadrolinija Office	**20** A4
Rent a Đir	**21** B4
Water Taxis	**22** B4

In the high summer season, water taxis at the east harbour collect passengers to visit various points on the island, as well as **Badija Island**, which features a historic 15th-century Franciscan monastery in the process of reconstruction, plus **Orebić** and the nearby village of **Lumbarda**, which both have sandy beaches.

TOURS
Both Atlas travel agency and Marko Polo Tours offer a variety of boat tours and island excursions.

SLEEPING & EATING
The big hotels in Korčula are overpriced, but there is a wealth of guesthouses that offer clean, attractive rooms and friendly service.

Atlas and Marko Polo Tours arrange private rooms, charging from 200KN to 220KN for a room with a bathroom, and starting at about 400KN for an apartment.

Pansion Marinka (☎ 712 007, 098344712; marinka .milina-bire@du.t-com.hr; low-high d 150-230KN) This is a working farm and winery situated in Lumbarda, in a beautiful setting within walking distance of the beach. The owners turn out excellent wines and liqueurs, catch and smoke their own fish, and are happy to explain the processes to their guests.

Villa DePolo (☎ /fax 711 621; tereza.depolo@du.t-com .hr; low-high d 240-290KN; ❄) In a residential neighbourhood close to the old town and 100m west of the bus station, this guesthouse has four modern, clean rooms, some with sea views. Note that there's a 30% surcharge on one-night stays.

Autocamp Kalac (☎ 711 182; fax 711 146; per person/site €5.40/8.20) This attractive ground is behind Hotel Bon Repos, about 4km from the west harbour, in a dense pine grove near the beach.

Konoba Maslina (☎ 711 720; Lumbarajska cesta bb; mains from 50KN) It's well worth the walk out here for the authentic Korčulan home cooking. The multibean soup is a standout. It's about a kilometre past the Hotel Marko Polo on the road to Lumbarda, but you can often arrange to be picked up or dropped off in town.

Konoba Marinero (☎ 711 170; Marka Andrijića; mains from 50KN) Right in the heart of the medieval old town, the family-run and marine-themed Marinero has the sons catch the fish and the parents prepare it according to a variety of traditional recipes.

Planjak (☎ 711 015; Plokata 19 Travnja; mains from 50KN) Meat lovers should head here for the mixed grill and proper Balkan dishes, served on a covered terrace.

Fresh (☎ 0917992086; www.igotfresh.com; 1 Kod Kina Liburne; snacks from 20KN) Right across from the bus station, Fresh is fab for breakfast smoothies, lunch wraps or beers and cocktails in the evening.

Cukarin (☎ 711 055; Hrvatske Bratske Zajednice; cakes from 10KN) You've got to try Korčula's pastries such as *cukarini* (sweet biscuit), *klajun* (walnut pastry), *amareta* (round, rich cake with almonds) and *harubica* (carob biscuit).

DRINKING

Cocktail Bar Massimo (Šetalište Petra Karnevelića) It's original, you have to grant them that: it's lodged in a turret and accessible only by ladder; the drinks are brought up by pulley. You also get lovely views.

Fresh (☎ 0917992086; www.igotfresh.com; 1 Kod Kina Liburne; snacks from 20KN) A party atmosphere develops at this little kiosk in the evenings, when happy hours and two-for-one offers kick in.

Tramonto (☎ 0981921048; Ismaelli 12) Fantastic sunsets are to be savoured as you sip cocktails at this terrace bar. It's popular with locals, tourists and yachters alike. The music is relaxed and the vibe easygoing.

ENTERTAINMENT

Between June and October there's **moreška sword dancing** (tickets 100KN; ☼ shows 9pm Thu) by the old town gate; performances are more frequent during July and August. The clash of swords

and the graceful movements of the dancer-fighters make an exciting show. Atlas, the tourist office and Marko Polo Tours sell tickets.

GETTING THERE & AROUND

Transport connections to Korčula are good. There's one bus every day to Dubrovnik (87KN, three hours), one to Zagreb (195KN, 12 hours), and one a week to Sarajevo (165KN, eight hours).

There's a **Jadrolinija office** (☎ 715 410) about 25m up from the west harbour.

There's a regular afternoon car ferry between Split and Vela Luka (35KN, three hours), on the island's western end, which stops at Hvar most days. Six daily buses link Korčula town to Vela Luka (28KN, one hour), but services from Vela Luka are reduced at the weekend.

The daily fast boat running from Split to Hvar and Korcula is great for locals working in Split but not so great for tourists, who find themselves leaving Korčula at 6am. Nevertheless, you can go quickly from Korčula to Hvar (33KN, 1½ hours) and to Split (55KN, 2¾ hours). Get tickets at Marko Polo.

From Orebić, look for the passenger launch (15KN, 15 minutes, at least five times daily on weekdays), which will drop you off near Hotel Korčula below the old town's towers. There's also a car ferry to Dominče (10KN, 15 minutes) that stops near the Hotel Bon Repos, where you can pick up the bus from Lumbarda (10KN) a few times a day or a water taxi to Korčula town. For international connections, see p444.

Next to Marko Polo, **Rent a Đir** (☎ 711 908; www.korcula-rent.com) hires cars, scooters and small boats.

MLJET ISLAND

☎ 020 / pop 1111

Of all the Adriatic islands, Mljet (Meleda in Italian) may be the most seductive. Over 72% of it is covered by forests and the rest is dotted by fields, vineyards and small villages. Created in 1960, **Mljet National Park** occupies the western third of the island and surrounds two saltwater lakes, Malo Jezero and Veliko Jezero. Most people visit the island on excursions from Korčula or Dubrovnik, but it is now possible to take a passenger boat from Dubrovnik or come on the regular ferry from Dubrovnik and stay a few days for hiking, cycling and boating.

Orientation & Information

The island is 37km long, and has an average width of about 3km. The main points of entry are Pomena and Polače, two tiny towns about 5km apart. Tour boats from Korčula and the Dubrovnik catamarans arrive at Polače wharf in high season. Pomena is the site of the island's only conventional hotel, Hotel Odisej. There's a good map of the island posted at the wharf. Jadrolinija ferries stop only at Sobra, but catamarans from Dubrovnik and Korčula stop at Polače.

Goveđari, the national park's entry point, is just between Pomena and Polače. The **national park** (adult/concession 90/30KN) measures 54 sq km; the entry price includes a bus and boat transfer to the Benedictine monastery. If you stay overnight on the island you only pay the park admission once.

The **tourist office** (☎ 744 186; www.mljet.hr; ☼ 8am-8pm Mon-Sat, to 1pm Sun Jun-Sep, 8am-1pm & 5-8pm Mon-Fri Oct-May) is in Polače and there's an ATM next door. There's another ATM at the Hotel Odisej in Pomena.

The administrative centre of the island is at Babino Polje, 18km east of Polače, where there is another **tourist office** (☎ /fax 745 125; www.mljet .hr; ☼ 9am-5pm Mon-Fri) and a post office.

Sights & Activities

From Pomena it's a 15-minute walk to a jetty on **Veliko Jezero**, the larger of the two lakes. Here you can board a boat to a lake islet and have lunch at a 12th-century **Benedictine monastery**, which now houses a restaurant.

You can catch an early boat back to the main island and spend a couple of hours walking along the lakeshore before taking the late-afternoon excursion boat back to Korčula or Dubrovnik. There's a small landing on the main island opposite the monastery where the boat operator drops off passengers on request. It's not possible to walk right around Veliko Jezero, because there's no bridge over the channel that connects the lakes to the sea.

Mljet is good for cycling; several restaurants along the dock in Polače and the Odisej hotel in Pomena hire bicycles (10/100KN per hour/half-day). If you plan to cycle between Pomena and Polače be aware that the two towns are separated by a steep mountain. The bike path along Veliko Jezero is an easier pedal, but it doesn't link the two towns.

The island offers some unusual opportunities for **diving**. There's a Roman wreck dating from the 3rd century in relatively shallow water. The remains of the ship, including amphorae, have calcified over the centuries and this has protected them from pillaging. There's also a German torpedo boat from WWII and several walls to dive. Contact **Kronmar diving** (☎ 744 022; Hotel Odisej).

Sleeping & Eating

The Polače tourist office arranges private accommodation at 200KN per double in summer, but it's essential to make arrangements before arrival in peak season. There are more *sobe* signs around Pomena than Polače, but practically none at all in Sobra.

Stermasi (☎ 0989390362; Saplunara; low-high per apt €30-45; ❂) An excellent choice for those wanting to self-cater and get away from it all – seven well-equipped, bright apartments sleep two to four people. Saplunara is pretty isolated, though, on the eastern side of the island, but you are near the only sandy beaches on Mljet. There's also an excellent restaurant attached, where you can eat octopus and kid under the bell (200KN and 260KN respectively; book two hours in advance), possibly the most delicious, sticky, aromatic and juicy way of preparing them. Alternatively, you can just turn up and order the spaghetti with lobster (280KN).

Soline 6 (☎ 744 024; www.soline6.com; Soline; low-high d €45-75) This hotel is a more interesting choice. It's the only accommodation within the national park and is designed with waterless toilets, solar heating and organic waste composting. You'll have to do without electricity, though.

Odisej (☎ 744 022; Pomena; s/d from €62/88; ❂) Rooms are pleasant enough here, plus you are right on the port, and you can hire bicycles, snorkelling equipment etc.

Melita (☎ 744 145; www.mljet-restoranmelita.com; St Mary's Island, Veliko Jezero; mains from 60KN) A more romantic (and touristy) spot can't be found on the island – this is the restaurant attached to the church on the little island in the middle of the big lake.

Getting There & Away

Jadrolinija ferries stop only at Sobra (32KN, two hours), but the **Melita catamaran** (☎ 313 119; www.gv-line.hr; Vukovarska 34) goes to Polače (70KN) after Sobra (50KN) in the summer months, leaving Dubrovnik at 9.45am daily and returning from Polače at 4.55pm, making it ideal for a day trip from Dubrovnik. From Sobra, you can get to Pomena on a bus (1½ hours), and from Polače you can either cycle or walk there.

Tickets are sold in the **tourist office** (Map p245; ☎ 417 983; Obala Stjepana Radića 27) in Gruž or on board, but it's wise to buy in advance as the boat fills up quickly.

DUBROVNIK
☎ 020 / pop 43,770

No matter whether you are visiting Dubrovnik for the first time or if you're returning again and again to this marvellous city, the sense of awe and beauty when you set eyes on the Stradun never fades. It's hard to imagine anyone, even the city's inhabitants, becoming inured to its marble streets and baroque buildings, or failing to be inspired by a walk along the ancient city walls that once protected a civilised, sophisticated republic for five centuries and that now look out onto the endless shimmer of the peaceful Adriatic.

History

Founded 1300 years ago by refugees from Epidaurus in Greece, medieval Dubrovnik (Ragusa until 1918) shook off Venetian control in the 14th century, becoming an independent republic and one of Venice's more important maritime rivals, trading with Egypt, Syria, Sicily, Spain, France and later Turkey. The double blow of an earthquake in 1667 and the opening of new trade routes to the east sent Ragusa into a slow decline, ending with Napoleon's conquest of the town in 1806.

The deliberate shelling of Dubrovnik by the Yugoslav army in 1991 sent shockwaves through the international community but, when the smoke cleared in 1992, traumatised residents cleared the rubble and set about repairing the damage. Reconstruction has been extraordinarily skilful.

After a steep postwar decline in tourism, Dubrovnik has become a major tourist destination once again.

Orientation

The Jadrolinija ferry terminal and the bus station are a few hundred metres apart at Gruž, several kilometres northwest of the old town, which is closed to cars. The main street in the old town is Placa (better known as Stradun). Most accommodation is on the leafy Lapad Peninsula, west of the bus station.

Information

You can change money at any travel agency or post office. There are numerous ATMs in town, near the bus station and near the ferry terminal.

Algoritam (Map p246; Placa) Has a good selection of English-language books, including guidebooks.

Atlas travel agency Obala Pape Ivana Pavla II (Map p245; ☎ 418 001; Obala Pape Ivana Pavla II 1); Sv Đurđa (Map p245; ☎ 442 585; Sv Đurđa 1) In convenient locations, this agency is extremely helpful for general information as well as finding private accommodation. All excursions are run by Atlas.

Garderoba (Map p245; ⏰ 5.30am-9pm) At the bus station.

Hospital (Map p245; ☎ 431 777; Dr Roka Mišetića bb) Emergency services are available 24 hours.

Lapad post office (Map p245; Šetalište Kralja Zvonimira 21)

Main post office (Map p246; cnr Široka & Od Puča)

Netcafé (Map p246; ☎ 321 125; www.netcafe.hr; Prijeko 21; per hr 30KN; ⏰ 9am-11pm) A wonderfully friendly cafe with a fast connection and good services.

Tourist office (www.tzdubrovnik.hr) bus station (Map p245; ☎ 417 581; Obala Pape Ivana Pavla II 24; ⏰ 8am-8pm daily Jun-Sep, 8am-3pm Mon-Fri, 9am-2pm Sat, closed Sun Oct-May); Gruž harbour (Map p245; ☎ 417 983; Obala Stjepana Radića 27; ⏰ 8am-8pm daily Jun-Sep, 8am-3pm Mon-Fri, 9am-2pm Sat, closed Sun Oct-May); Lapad (Map p245; ☎ 437 460; Šetalište Kralja Zvonimira 25; ⏰ 8am-8pm daily Jun-Sep, 8am-3pm Mon-Fri, 9am-2pm Sat, closed Sun Oct-May); old town (Map p246; ☎ 323 587; Široka 1; ⏰ 8am-8pm daily Jun-Sep, 8am-3pm Mon-Fri, 9am-2pm Sat, closed Sun Oct-May); old town 2 (Map p246; ☎ 323 887; Sv Dominika 7; ⏰ 8am-8pm daily Jun-Sep, 8am-3pm Mon-Fri, 9am-2pm Sat, closed Sun Oct-May); Pile Gate (Map p246; ☎ 427 591; Branitelja Dubrovnika 7; ⏰ 8am-8pm daily Jun-Sep, 8am-3pm Mon-Fri, 9am-2pm Sat, closed Sun Oct-May) Maps, information and the indispensable *Dubrovnik Riviera* guide.

Sights
OLD TOWN

You will probably begin your visit of Dubrovnik's World Heritage–listed old town at the city bus stop outside **Pile Gate** (Map p246). As you enter the city, Dubrovnik's wonderful pedestrian promenade, Placa, extends before you all the way to the **clock tower** (Map p246) at the other end of town.

Just inside Pile Gate is the huge 1438 **Onofrio Fountain** (Map p246) and **Franciscan monastery** (Muzej Franjevačkog Samostana; Map p246; ☎ 426 345; ⏰ 9am-5pm) with a splendid cloister and the third-oldest functioning **pharmacy** (Map p246;

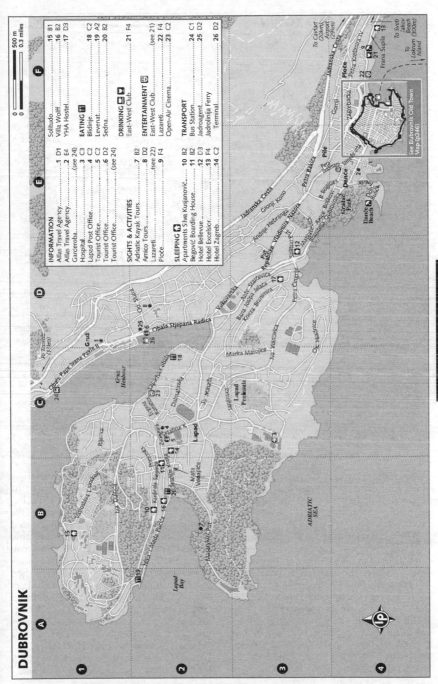

DUBROVNIK

0 — 500 m
0 — 0.3 miles

INFORMATION
Atlas Travel Agency.....................1 D1
Atlas Travel Agency.....................2 E4
Garceroba............................(see 24)
Hospital.................................3 C3
Lapad Post Office......................4 C2
Tourist Office...........................5 C2
Tourist Office...........................6 D2
Tourist Office........................(see 24)

SIGHTS & ACTIVITIES
Adriatic Kayak Tours...................7 B2
Amico Tours.............................8 D2
Lazareti.............................(see 22)
Ploce..................................9 F4

SLEEPING 🛏
Apartments Silva Kusjanović.........10 B2
Begović Boarding House..............11 B2
Hotel Bellevue.........................12 D3
Hotel Excelsior.........................13 F4
Hotel Zagreb...........................14 C2

Solitudo................................15 B1
Villa Wolff.............................16 B2
YHA Hostel.............................17 D3

EATING 🍴
Blidinje................................18 C2
Levenat................................19 A2
Sedna.................................20 B2

DRINKING 🍷 ▯
East-West Club.........................21 F4

ENTERTAINMENT ▯
East-West Club......................(see 21)
Lazareti...............................22 F4
Open-Air Cinema......................23 C2

TRANSPORT
Bus Station............................24 C1
Jadroagent............................25 D2
Jadrolinija Ferry
Terminal..............................26 D2

CROATIA

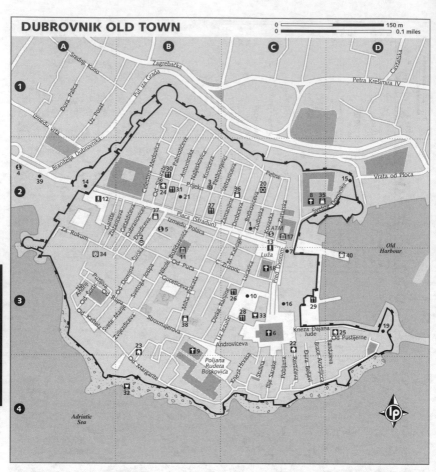

DUBROVNIK OLD TOWN

9am-5pm) in Europe; it's been operating since 1391. The **church** (Map p246; 7am-7pm) has recently undergone a long and expensive restoration to startling effect. The **monastery museum** (Map p246; adult/concession 20/10KN; 9am-5pm) has a collection of liturgical objects, paintings and pharmacy equipment.

In front of the clock tower at the eastern end of Placa (on the square called Luža) is the 1419 **Orlando Column** (Map p246) – a favourite meeting place. On opposite sides of the column are the 16th-century **Sponza Palace** (Map p246) – originally a customs house, later a bank, and which now houses the **State Archives** (Državni Arhiv u Dubrovniku;p246 321 032; admission free; 8am-3pm Mon-Fri, to 1pm Sat) – and **St Blaise's Church** (Map p246), a lovely Italian baroque

building built in 1715 to replace an earlier church destroyed in the 1667 earthquake. At the end of Pred Dvorom, the wide street beside St Blaise, is the baroque **Cathedral of the Assumption of the Virgin** (Map p246). Located between the two churches, the 1441 Gothic **Rector's Palace** (Map p246; Knežev Dvor; 426 469; adult/student 35/15KN; 9am-2pm Mon-Sat Oct-May, to 6pm daily Jun-Sep) houses a museum with furnished rooms, baroque paintings and historical exhibits. The elected rector was not permitted to leave the building during his one-month term without the permission of the senate. The narrow street opposite opens onto Gundulićeva Poljana, a bustling **morning market** (Map p246). Up the stairs south of the square is the 1725 **Jesuit monastery** (Map p246; Poljana Ruđera Boškovića).

INFORMATION	Pile Gate.....................**14** A2	Lokanda Peskarija....................**29** C3
Algoritam...................**1** C2	Ploče Gate....................**15** D2	Nishta......................**30** B2
Main Post Office.................**2** B2	Rector's Palace....................**16** C3	Smuuti Bar......................**31** B2
Netcafé.................**3** B2	Sponza Palace....................**17** C2	
Tourist Office...................**4** A2	St Blaise's Church....................**18** C3	**DRINKING** 🍸 🍷
Tourist Office.................**5** B2	St John Fort.....................**19** D3	Buža....................**32** B4
	State Archives........................(see 17)	Troubadur..........................**33** C3
SIGHTS & ACTIVITIES	Synagogue....................**20** C2	
Cathedral of the Assumption of the	War Photo Limited....................**21** B2	**ENTERTAINMENT** 🎭
Virgin.....................**6** C3		Open-Air Cinema.............. **34** A3
Church....................(see 8)	**SLEEPING** 🛏	Sloboda Cinema...................(see 17)
Clock Tower.....................**7** C3	Apartments Amoret....................**22** C3	
Dominican Monastery.............**8** C2	Fresh Sheets.....................**23** B3	**SHOPPING** 🛍
Franciscan Monastery &	Hotel Stari Grad....................**24** B2	Maria......................**35** C2
Museum....................(see 8)	Karmen	Photo Gallery
Jesuit Church................**9** B3	Apartments....................**25** D3	Carmel......................**36** C2
Monastery Museum..............(see 8)	Pucić Palace........................(see 26)	Sheriff & Cherry....................**37** B2
Morning Market....................**10** C3		Đardin......................**38** B3
Museum of Orthodox Church...**11** B3	**EATING** 🍴	
Onofrio Fountain....................**12** A2	Defne.......................**26** C3	**TRANSPORT**
Orlando Column.....................**13** C3	Fresh......................**27** B2	Croatia Island Airlines.............. **39** A2
Pharmacy........................(see 8)	Kamenice.....................**28** C3	Lokrum Ferry Dock................**40** D3

As you proceed up Plaça, make a detour to the **Museum of the Orthodox Church** (Muzej Pravuslavne Crkve; Map p246; ☎ 426 260; Nikole Božidaverića; adult/concession 10/5KN; ☻ 9am-1pm Mon-Fri) for a look at a fascinating collection of 15th- to 19th-century icons.

By now you'll be ready for a leisurely walk around the **city walls** (Map p246; adult/child 50/20KN; ☻ 9am-7pm), which has entrances just inside Pile Gate, across from the Dominican monastery and near St John Fort. Built between the 13th and 16th centuries, these powerful walls are the finest in the world and Dubrovnik's main claim to fame. They enclose the entire city in a protective veil 2km long and up to 25m high, with two round and 14 square towers, two corner fortifications and a large fortress. The views over the town and sea are great – this walk could be the high point of your visit.

Whichever way you go, you'll notice the 14th-century **Dominican monastery** (Muzej Dominikanskog Samostana; Map p246; ☎ 426 472; adult/child 20/10KN; ☻ 9am-6pm) in the northeastern corner of the city, whose forbidding fortress-like exterior shelters a rich trove of paintings from Dubrovnik's finest 15th- and 16th-century artists.

Dubrovnik has many other sights, such as the unmarked **synagogue** (Sinagoga; Map p246; ☎ 412 219; ul Žudioska 5; admission 10KN; ☻ 10am-1pm Mon-Fri) near the clock tower, which is the second-oldest synagogue in Europe. The uppermost streets of the old town below the north and south walls are pleasant to wander along.

One of the better photography galleries you're likely to come across, **War Photo Limited** (Map p246; ☎ 326 166; www.warphotoltd.com; Antuninska 6; admission 30KN; ☻ 9am-9pm daily May-Sep, 10am-4pm Tue-Sat, 10am-2pm Sun Oct & Apr, closed Nov-Apr) has changing exhibitions that are curated by gallery owner and former photojournalist Wade Goddard. It's open summer only, and has up to three exhibitions over that period, relating to the subject of war and seen from various perspectives.

BEACHES

Ploče (Map p245), the closest beach to the old city, is just beyond the 17th-century **Lazareti** (Map p245), a former quarantine station, outside **Ploče Gate** (Map p246). Another nearby, good, local beach is **Sveti Jakov**, a 20-minute walk down Vlaho Bukovac street or a quick ride on bus 5 or 8 from the northern end of the old town. Another excellent place for swimming is underneath Buža bar (p250), on the outside of the city walls. Diving is off the rocks, there are steps to help you get in and out, and there's some cemented space between the rocks for sunbathing. There's not much shade here, so bring a hat and strong sun protection. There are also hotel beaches along the **Lapad Peninsula** (Map p245), which you are able to use without a problem. The largest is outside the Hotel Kompas.

An even better option is to take the ferry that shuttles half-hourly in summer to lush **Lokrum Island** (see the boxed text, p250).

Activities

Adriatic Kayak Tours (Map p245; ☎ 312 770; www.kayak croatia.com; Frankopanska 6) offers a great series of kayak tours for experienced and beginning kayakers. Tours cover Lokrum Island and the Elafiti Islands, but you can also go white-water rafting on the Tara River canyon and kayaking in Kotor Bay in Montenegro.

Tours

Amico Tours (Map p245; ☎ 418 248; www.amico-tours .com; Od Skara 1) offers day trips to Mostar and Međugorje (390KN), Montenegro (390KN), Albania (990KN), Korčula and Pelješac (390KN), and the Elafiti Islands (250KN), as well as numerous kayaking, rafting and jeep safari day trips (590KN).

Festivals & Events

Feast of St Blaise 3 February.
Carnival February.
Dubrovnik Summer Festival Mid-July to mid-August.
A major cultural event, with over 100 performances at different venues in the old town.

Sleeping

Private accommodation is generally the best option in Dubrovnik, but beware of the scramble of private owners at the bus station or Jadrolinija wharf. Some offer what they say they offer, others are rip-off artists. The owners listed below meet you at the station if you call in advance. Otherwise, head to any of the travel agencies or the Turistička Zajednica. Expect to pay about €28 to €50 per room in high season.

OLD TOWN

ourpick Karmen Apartments (Map p246; ☎ 323 433, 098619282; www.karmendu.com; Bandureva 1; apt €55-145; ▣) Set inside an old stone house in the middle of the old town, the four apartments are beautifully decorated with original artwork and imaginative use of recycled materials. There are small, one- to two-person apartments, as well as two for three and four people. Book well in advance because it all gets snapped up by June.

ourpick Hotel Bellevue (Map p245; ☎ 330 000; www .hotel-bellevue.hr; Petra Čingrije 7; d from €250; ▣ ▣ ▣) Although not strictly speaking within the borders of the old town but a five-minute walk west from Pile Gate, Hotel Bellevue's location – on a cliff overlooking the open sea and the lovely bay underneath – is pretty much divine. The rooms are beautifully designed, the balconies taking in that marvellous water view. Its restaurant, Vapor, is top-notch too, with

excellent seasonal products, fish, meat and a wide range of Croatian wines.

Fresh Sheets (Map p246; ☎ 0917992086; beds@igot fresh.com; Sv Šimuna 15; per person €25; ▣) A brand new place, this is a collection of four individually decorated apartments – Lavender, Rainforest, Sunshine, Heaven – each sleeping two to four people (plus a sofa), and one double room. The location is excellent – in the heart of the old town – and you get free internet and wi-fi, and, when the Fresh bar's kitchen is open, a free smoothie every day.

Pucić Palace (Map p246; ☎ 326 222; www.thepucic palace.com; Od Puča 1; low-high s €206-315, d €290-505; ▣ ▣) Right in the heart of the old town and inside what was once a nobleman's mansion, this five-star hotel is Dubrovnik's most exclusive and hottest property. There are only 19 rooms, all exquisitely decorated and featuring Italian mosaics, Egyptian cotton and baroque beds.

Apartments Amoret (Map p246; ☎ 0915304910; www .dubrovnik-amoret.com; Dinke Ranjine 5 & Restićeva 2; apt €50-120; ▣) Six artistically appointed apartments and rooms are tucked away within two old townhouses (Amoret 1 and Amoret 2) that date to the 16th century. Each is different but all are lovingly decorated to create some of Dubrovnik's most charming accommodation.

Hotel Stari Grad (Map p246; ☎ 322 244; www.hotel starigrad.com; Palmotićeva; low-high s 650-1180KN, d 920KN-1580KN; ▣) Staying in the heart of the old town in a lovingly restored stone building is an unmatchable experience. The eight rooms are elegantly and tastefully furnished to feel simple and luxurious at the same time.

OUTSIDE THE OLD TOWN

ourpick Villa Wolff (Map p245; ☎ 438 710; www.villa -wolff.hr; Nika i Meda Pucića 1; low-high s 1533-1879KN, d 1606-1898KN; ▣ ▣ ▣) A gorgeous boutique hotel right on the lovely seaside promenade, Villa Wolff has only six rooms, all beautifully outfitted, bright and airy. There is a verdant garden that the guests use for sunbathing.

ourpick Hotel Zagreb (Map p245; ☎ 430 930; www .hotels-sumratin.com; Šetalište Kralja Zvonimira 27; low-high s 400-660KN, d 700-1060KN; ▣) This stylish hotel is set inside a lovely, salmon-coloured 19th-century building. The rooms are large, with marine motifs and large bathrooms.

Hotel Excelsior (Map p245; ☎ 353 353; www.hotel -excelsior.hr; Frana Supila 12; s/d from 1640/1890KN; ▣ ▣ ▣) This is possibly Dubrovnik's biggest hotel extravaganza – after a €10-million refit and much bated breath, the legendary

Excelsior reopened in 2008. The adjacent boutique villa, Villa Odak, is gorgeously understated. There's also an indoor and outdoor swimming pool and a palm-tree terrace.

Hotel Uvala (Map p245; ☎ 433 580; www.hotelimaestral.com; Masarykov Put 6; d €120-170; P 🐾 🏊) A newly renovated four-star hotel that's decked out with a lovely reception, indoor and outdoor pools and a comprehensive spa. It's unfortunate, however, that the rooms are a bit of a let-down with their glum browns and whites. The service is friendly and it's a comfortable place, very close to the beach.

Vila Micika (Map p245; ☎ 437 332; www.vilamicika.hr; Mata Vodopića; low-high s 150-210KN, d 300-420KN; P) A simple, well-run establishment with rooms painted in soft and pleasant colours and equipped with TVs and modern bathrooms. There's a pleasant outdoor terrace, and it's only 200m to the Lapad beaches.

Apartments Silva Kusjanović (Map p245; ☎ 435 071, 098244639; silva_dubrovnik@yahoo.com; Kardinala Stepinća 62; per person 100KN) Sweet Silva has four large apartments that can hold four to eight beds. All have terraces with gorgeous views and barbecues.

Begović Boarding House (Map p245; ☎ 435 191; http://begovic-boarding-house.com; Primorska 17; low-high dm €14-19, s €25-32, d €32-40) A long-time favourite with our readers, this friendly place in Lapad has three rooms with shared bathroom and three apartments. There's a terrace out the back with a good view. Breakfast is an additional 30KN.

YHA Hostel (Map p245; ☎ 423 241; dubrovnik@hfhs.hr; Vlnka Sagrestana 3; low-high per person B&B 85-120KN) Basic in decor, the YHA hostel is clean and, as travellers report, a lot of fun. If you're allowed to choose a bed (rare), the best dorms are rooms 31 and 32, for their 'secret' roof terrace with a refreshingly lovely view.

Solitudo (Map p245; ☎ 448 200; www.camping-adriatic.com; per person/site €5.40/10.20) This pretty and renovated camping ground is within walking distance of the beach.

Eating
OLD TOWN
Weed out tourist traps and choose carefully, and you'll find fabulous food in the old town.

our pick Lokanda Peskarija (Map p246; ☎ 324 750; Ribarnica bb; mains from 40KN) Located on the Old Harbour right next to the fish market, this is undoubtedly one of Dubrovnik's best eateries. The quality of the seafood dishes is unfaltering, the prices are good, and the location is gorgeous. The locals queue along with the tourists for the wonderful baby squid, the substantial risottos and the juicy mussels.

Defne (Map p246; ☎ 326 200; Od Puča 1; mains from 70KN) Pucić Palace's top-floor restaurant, this is one of the old town's classiest. Try the octopus *carpaccio* starter, served with black tagliolini and truffle – a slice of heaven in your mouth – or the gorgeous lobster with white risotto. The wine list is impeccable.

Kamenice (Map p246; ☎ 421 499; Gundulićeva Poljana 8; mains from 40KN) It's been here since the 1970s and not much has changed: the socialist-style waiting uniforms, the simple interior, the massive portions of mussels, grilled or fried squid and griddled anchovies, and *kamenice* – oysters – too. The terrace is on one of Dubrovnik's most gorgeous squares.

Fresh (Map p246; ☎ 0918967509; www.igotfresh.com; Vetranićeva 4; wraps from 20KN) A mecca for young travellers, who gather here for the smoothies, wraps and other healthy snacks, as well as drinks and music in the evening.

Nishta (Map p246; ☎ 0918967509; Prijeko 30; mains from 30KN; V) When this unprecedented-in-Dubrovnik, 100%-vegetarian restaurant opened, baffled locals asked the owners what it served. 'Everything except meat,' the owners said, and the locals concluded, 'Well, then you're serving nothing.' Hence the name 'Nishta', which means 'Nothing' in Croatian. Alas, you're in the Balkans, what do you expect? Head here for a refreshing gazpacho, a heartwarming miso soup, Thai curries, veggies and noodles, and many more veggie delights.

Smuuti Bar (Map p246; ☎ 0918967509; Palmotićeva 5; smoothies 18-25KN) Perfect for breakfast smoothies and nice big mugs of coffee (at a bargain 10KN).

LAPAD
our pick Levanat (Map p245; ☎ 435 352; Nika i Meda Pucića 15; mains 45-120KN) One of the best spots in the whole city, Levanat overlooks the sea from the pine-laden hill between Lapad Bay and Babin Kuk. The food is equally gorgeous, and it innovates with seafood and unusual sauces, fresh ingredients and delicious vegetarian options.

Blidinje (Map p245; ☎ 358 794; Lapadska Obala 21; mains from 70KN) A great local that's not frequented by many tourists, Blidinje has fabulous views of Gruž harbour from its terrace. The food is aimed primarily at carnivores, so use the opportunity to taste lamb or veal slow cooked under hot coals – but make sure you ring and order at least two hours in advance.

Sedna (Map p245; ☎ 352 000; www.hotel-kompas .hr; Petra Čingrije 7; omelettes 30-35KN, pizzas from 26KN) The Hotel Kompas bar-pizzeria is a great and unpretentious spot for breakfast, lunch or dinner. You can sit on a terrace overlooking the beach and Lapad Bay while the locals buzz around, drinking coffee and chatting on sunny mornings and afternoons.

Drinking

our pick **Buža** (Map p246; Ilije Sarake) The Buža is just a simple place on the outside of the city walls, facing onto the open sea, with straightforward drinks and blissful punters.

EastWest Club (Map p245; ☎ 412 220; Frana Supila bb) By day this outfit on Banje beach rents out beach chairs and umbrellas and serves drinks to the bathers. When the rays lengthen, the cocktail bar opens.

Troubadur (Map p246; ☎ 412 154; Bunićeva Poljana 2) Come to this legendary Dubrovnik venue for live jazz concerts in the summer.

Entertainment

The summer months are chock-full of concerts and folk dancing. The tourist office has the full schedule.

EastWest Club (Map p245; ☎ 412 220; Frana Supila bb) A great chill-out bar with cocktails on the beach.

Lazareti (Map p245; ☎ 324 633; Frana Supila 8) Dubrovnik's best art and music centre, Lazareti hosts club nights, live music, masses of concerts and pretty much all the best things in town. Free art-film seasons are hosted by a group of local film enthusiasts throughout the year. International and local films are projected onto the 19th-century walls of the Lazareti complex, once a quarantine barracks.

Open-Air Cinema Lapad (Map p245; Kumičića); old town (Map p246; Za Rokom) In two locations, the cinema's open nightly in July and August, with screenings starting after sundown (9pm or 9.30pm); ask at Sloboda Cinema for the schedule.

Shopping

You'll find souvenir stores all over Stradun, selling Dalmatian marine details, stripy tops, anchors and the like.

Maria (Map p246; ☎ 321 330; www.maria-dubrovnik .hr; ul Sv Dominika bb) Take a few deep breaths before you step into this shop, for you are sure to swoon at the sight of soft Miu Miu leather bags, lacquered Alexander McQueen shoes and gorgeous Marni dresses. The prices are international, of course, and the service is friendly, too, which is always a pleasant surprise.

Sheriff & Cherry (Map p246; ☎ 324 888; www.sheriff andcherry.com; Đorđićeva 4; ☺ 10am-5pm Mon-Fri, to 3pm

DAY TRIPS FROM DUBROVNIK

Cavtat is a small town that curves around an attractive harbour bordered by nice beaches. Don't miss the memorial chapel to the Račič family designed by Ivan Meštrović. Bus 10 to Cavtat runs often from Dubrovnik's bus station (Map p246; 15KN, 45 minutes) and there are three daily boats during summer (40KN). A ferry (Map p246) shuttles half-hourly in summer to lush **Lokrum Island** (80KN return), a Unesco-protected national park. It's a beautiful, peaceful place, with a rocky nudist beach (marked FKK), a **botanical garden** and the ruins of a **medieval Benedictine monastery.**

A day trip to one of the islands in the archipelago northwest of Dubrovnik makes a perfect escape from the summer crowds. The most popular islands are **Koločep**, **Lopud** and **Šipan**, which are accessible by daily **Jadrolinija** (www.jadrolinija.hr) car ferry. From Dubrovnik you can take a fast boat to Koločep (11KN, 20 minutes), Lopud (11KN, 35 minutes) or Šipan (16.50KN, 1¼ hours) on Saturday morning.

Only 13km northwest of Dubrovnik sits **Trsteno**, a verdant haven that once served as Dubrovnik's aristocratic gardening grounds. Trsteno really came into its own during the 16th century, when Ivan Gučetić, a Dubrovnik aristocrat, planted the first seeds of his garden, now an **arboretum** (☎ 751 019; admission 12KN; ☺ 8am-8pm summer, to 5pm rest of yr) with a Renaissance layout and tonnes of gorgeous plants. Don't miss the two **plane trees** at the entrance – each is over 400 years old.

To get to Trsteno, take any bus bound for Split from Dubrovnik's main bus station. Buses stop at the plane trees.

BUS SERVICES FROM DUBROVNIK

Destination	Price (KN)	Duration (hr)	Daily departures
Korčula	95	3	1
Mostar*	100	3	2
Orebić	80	2½	1
Rijeka	400	13	2
Sarajevo*	200	5	1
Split	120	4½	14
Zadar	250	8	7
Zagreb	250	11	7-8

*BiH destinations

Sat) One of the few 'urban-clothes' boutiques in town, this Zagreb-based shop stocks all the major fashion labels like Paul & Joe, Cheap Mondays, Anya Hindmarch and Dries Van Noten, among many, many others.

Photo Gallery Carmel (Map p246; ☎ 0915777157; www.photogallerycarmel.com; Zamanjina 10; ☼ 9am-4pm Mon-Sat) This newly opened photography gallery hosts work by local and international artists. Prints are for sale.

Đardin (Map p246; ☎ 324 744; Miha Pracata 8; ☼ 9.30am-6pm Mon Fri, to 12.30pm Sat) A sprawling jewellery shop where you can get lost for hours.

Getting There & Away

AIR
Daily flights to/from Zagreb are operated by **Croatia Airlines** (Map p246; ☎ 413 777; Brsalje 9). The fare runs from 400KN one way, higher in peak season; the trip takes about an hour.

There are also nonstop flights to Rome, London and Manchester between April and October.

BOAT
In addition to the **Jadrolinija** (Map p245; ☎ 418 000; Gruž) coastal ferry north to Hvar, Split and Rijeka (Rijeka–Split 12½ hours, Split–Hvar 1¾ hours, Hvar–Korcula 3¾ hours, Korcula–Dubrovnik 3¼ hours), there's a local ferry that leaves Dubrovnik for Sobra on Mljet Island (50KN, 2½ hours) throughout the year. There are several ferries a day year-round to the outlying islands of Šipan, Suđurađ, Lopud and Koločep. See the map, p221.

Jadroagent (Map p245; ☎ 419 009; fax 419 029; Radića 32) handles ticketing for most international boats from Croatia.

For information on international connections, see p444.

BUS
For services from Dubrovnik, see the table, above. There's a daily 11am bus to the Montenegro border, from where a Montenegro bus takes you to Herceg Novi (80KN, two hours) and on to Kotor (120KN, 2½ hours) and Bar (150KN, three hours). In the busy summer season and at weekends buses out of Dubrovnik can be crowded, so book a ticket well before the scheduled departure time.

Getting Around
Čilipi international airport is 24km southeast of Dubrovnik. The Croatia Airlines airport buses (25KN, 45 minutes) leave from the main **bus station** (Map p245; ☎ 357 088) 1½ hours before flight times. Buses meet Croatia Airlines flights but not all others. A taxi costs around 200KN.

Dubrovnik's buses run frequently and generally on time. The fare is 10KN if you buy from the driver but only 8KN if you buy a ticket at a kiosk.

CROATIA DIRECTORY

ACCOMMODATION
Accommodation listings in this guide have been arranged in order of preference. Many hotels and camping grounds issue their prices in euros, but some places have stuck with the kuna. Although you can usually pay with either currency, we have listed the primary currency the establishment uses in setting its prices.

Along the Croatian coast accommodation is priced according to three seasons, which tend to vary from place to place. Generally

CROATIA

PRACTICALITIES

- Electrical supply is 220V to 240V/50Hz to 60Hz. Croatia uses the standard European round-pronged plugs.

- Widely read newspapers include *Vecernji List*, *Vjesnik*, *Jutarnji list* and *Slobodna Dalmacija*. The most popular weeklies are *Nacional* and *Globus*.

- The radio station HR2 broadcasts traffic reports in English every hour on the hour from July to mid-September; Croatian Radio broadcasts news in English on 88.9, 91.3 and 99.3FM.

- Croatia uses the metric system.

October to May are the cheapest months and June and September are midpriced; count on paying top price during peak season, which runs for six weeks in July and August. Prices quoted in this chapter do not include 'residence tax' (7.50KN per person per night). Note that prices for rooms in Zagreb are pretty much constant all year and that many hotels on the coast close in winter. Some places offer half board, which is bed and two meals a day, usually breakfast and one other meal.

Camping

Nearly 100 camping grounds are scattered along the Croatian coast. Opening times generally run from mid-April to September, give or take a few weeks. The exact times change from year to year, so it's wise to call in advance if you're arriving at either end of the season.

Many camping grounds, especially in Istria, are gigantic 'autocamps' with restaurants, shops and row upon row of caravans. Expect to pay up to 100KN for a campsite at some of the larger establishments but half that at most other camping grounds, in addition to 38KN to 48KN per person.

Nudist camping grounds (marked FKK) are among the best because their secluded locations ensure peace and quiet. However, bear in mind that freelance camping is officially prohibited. A good site for camping information is www.camping.hr.

Hostels

The **Croatian YHA** (☎ 01-48 47 472; www.hfhs.hr; Dežmanova 9, Zagreb) operates youth hostels in Dubrovnik, Zadar, Zagreb and Pula.

Nonmembers pay an additional 10KN per person daily for a stamp on a welcome card; six stamps entitle you to membership. Unless otherwise stated, prices in this chapter are for July and August; prices fall the rest of the year. The Croatian YHA can also provide information about private youth hostels in Krk, Zadar, Dubrovnik and Zagreb.

Hotels

Hotels are ranked from one to five stars, with most in the two- to three-star range. Features such as satellite TV, direct-dial phones, high-tech bathrooms, minibars and air-con are standard in four- and five-star hotels, and one-star hotels have at least a bathroom in the room. Many two- and three-star hotels offer satellite TV, but you'll find better decor in the higher categories. Unfortunately, the country is saddled with too many 1970s concrete-block hotels, built to warehouse package tourists, but there are more and more options for those looking for smaller and more personal establishments. Unless otherwise stated, prices in this chapter are for the mid-July to August period, during which some hotels may demand a surcharge for stays of fewer than four nights. This is usually waived during the rest of the year, when prices drop steeply.

Breakfast is included in the prices quoted for hotels in this chapter, unless stated otherwise.

Private Rooms

Private rooms or apartments are the best accommodation in Croatia. Service is excellent and the rooms are usually extremely well kept. You may very well be greeted by offers of *sobe* as you step off your bus or boat, but rooms are most often arranged by travel agencies or the local tourist office. Booking through an agency is somewhat more expensive but at least you'll know who to complain to if things go wrong.

The most expensive rooms are three star and have private bathrooms, in establishments resembling small guesthouses. Some of the better ones are listed in this chapter. It's best to call in advance, as the owners will often meet you at the bus station or ferry dock. In a two-star room, the bathroom is shared with one other room; in a one-star room, the bathroom is shared with two other rooms or with the owner, who is usually an elderly widow. Breakfast is usually not included but can sometimes be arranged for an additional 30KN; be sure to clarify whether the price agreed upon is per person or per room. If you're travelling in a small group it may be worthwhile to get a small apartment with cooking facilities, which are widely available along the coast.

It makes little sense to price-shop from agency to agency since prices are fixed by the local tourist association. Whether you deal with the owner directly or book through an agency, you'll pay a 30% surcharge for stays of fewer than four nights and sometimes 50% or even 100% more for a one-night stay, although you may be able to get them to waive the surcharge if you arrive in the low season. Prices for private rooms in this chapter are for a four-night stay in peak season.

ACTIVITIES
Diving
The clear waters and varied underwater life of the Adriatic have led to a flourishing diving industry along the coast. Cave diving is the real speciality in Croatia; night diving and wreck diving are also offered and there are coral reefs in some places, but they are in rather deep water. You must get a permit for a boat dive: go to the harbour captain in any port with your passport, certification card and 100KN. Permission is valid for a year. If you dive with a dive centre, they will take care of the paperwork. Most of the coastal resorts mentioned in this chapter have dive shops. See **Diving Croatia** (www.diving-hrs.hr) for contact information.

Hiking
Risnjak National Park at Crni Lug, 12km west of Delnice between Zagreb and Rijeka, is a good hiking area in summer. Hiking is advisable only from late spring to early autumn. The steep gorges and beech forests of Paklenica National Park, 40km northeast of Zadar, also offer excellent hiking.

Kayaking
There are countless possibilities for anyone carrying a folding sea kayak, especially among the Elafiti and Kornati islands. Lopud makes a good launching point from which to explore the Elafiti Islands; there's a daily ferry from Dubrovnik. Sali on Dugi Otok is close to the Kornati Islands and is connected by daily ferry to Zadar.

Rock Climbing
The karstic stone of Croatia's coast provides excellent climbing opportunities. Paklenica National Park has the widest range of routes – nearly 400 – for all levels of experience. Spring, summer and autumn are good seasons to climb, but in winter you'll be fighting the fierce *bura* (cold northeasterly wind). Other popular climbing spots include the rocks surrounding Baška on Krk Island, which can be climbed year-round (although if you come in summer, you can combine climbing with a beach holiday). Brela on the Makarska riviera also allows climbing and beach-bumming, but in winter there's a strong *bura*. Also on the Makarska riviera is the wall from Baška Voda to Makarska on Mt Biokovo, with 200m to 400m routes. For more information, contact the **Croatian Mountaineering Association** (☎ /fax 01-48 24 142; http://hps.inet.hr; Kozaričeva 22, 10000 Zagreb).

Yachting
There's no better way to appreciate the Croatian Adriatic than by boat. The long, rugged islands off Croatia's mountainous coast all the way from Istria to Dubrovnik make this a yachting paradise. Fine, deep channels with abundant anchorage and steady winds attract yachties from around the world. Throughout the region there are quaint little ports where you can get provisions, and yachts can tie up right in the middle of everything.

There are 40 marinas along the coast, some with more facilities than others. Every coastal town mentioned in this chapter has a marina, from little Sali on Dugi Otok to the large marinas in Opatija, Zadar, Split and Dubrovnik. Most marinas are open throughout the year, but it's best to check first. A good source of information is **Udruženje Nautičkog Tourism** (Association of Nautical Tourism; ☎ 051-209 147; fax 051-216 033; Bulevar Oslobođenja 23, 51000 Rijeka), which represents all Croatian marinas. You could also try the **Adriatic Croatia International** (ACI; ☎ 051-271 288; www.aci-club.hr; ul Maršala Tita 51, Opatija), which represents about half the marinas.

Although you can row, motor or sail any vessel up to 3m long without authorisation, for larger boats you'll need to get authorisation from the harbour master at your port of entry, which will be at any harbour open to international traffic. Come equipped with a boat certificate, documents proving your sailing qualifications, insurance documents and money.

Yachting enthusiasts may wish to charter their own boat. Experienced sailors can charter a yacht on a 'bareboat' basis or you can pay for the services of a local captain for a 'skippered' boat. **Sunsail** (☎ in UK 0870 777 0313, in USA 888 350 3568; www.sunsail.com) is an international operator with offices in the UK and the USA. It offers bareboat and skippered charters from Pula and Rogoznica near Trogir. In the UK, you could also try **Cosmos Yachting** (☎ 0800 376 9070; www.cosmosyachting.com), which offers charters out of Dubrovnik, Pula, Rovinj, Split, Trogir and Zadar, or **Nautilus Yachting** (☎ 01732-867 445; www.nautilus-yachting.com), which offers rentals from Pula and Split. The price depends upon the size of the boat, the number of berths and the season.

An interesting option for sailing enthusiasts is **Katarina Line** (☎ 051-272 110; www.katarina-line.hr; ul Maršala Tita 75, Opatija), which offers week-long cruises from Opatija to Krk, Rab, Dugi Otok, Lošinj and Cres, or cruises from Split to Dubrovnik that pass the Kornati Islands. Prices run from €370 to €490 a week per person depending on the season and cabin class and include half board. For specific tours in individual regions, see Tours in the destination sections.

BOOKS

Lonely Planet's *Croatia* is a comprehensive guide to the country. There's also Zoë Brân's *After Yugoslavia,* part of the Lonely Planet Journeys series, which recounts the author's return to a troubled region.

As Croatia emerges from the shadow of the former Yugoslavia, several writers of Croatian origin have taken the opportunity to rediscover their roots. *Plum Brandy: Croatian Journeys* by Josip Novakovich is a sensitive exploration of his family's Croatian background. *Croatia: Travels in Undiscovered Country* by Tony Fabijančić recounts the life of rural folks in a new Croatia. *Café Europa* is a series of essays by a Croatian journalist, Slavenka Drakulić, which provides an inside look at life in the country since independence. Marcus Tanner's *Croatia: A Nation Forged in War* provides an excellent overview of Croatia's history.

BUSINESS HOURS

Banking and post office hours are 7.30am to 7pm on weekdays and 8am to noon on

Saturday. Many shops are open 8am to 7pm on weekdays and until 2pm on Saturday. Along the coast life is more relaxed; shops and offices frequently close around noon for an afternoon break and reopen around 4pm. Restaurants are open long hours, often noon to midnight, with Sunday closings outside peak season. Cafes are generally open 10am to midnight, bars 9pm to 2am. Internet cafes are also open long hours, usually seven days a week.

CUSTOMS

Travellers can bring their personal effects into the country, along with 1L of liquor, 1L of wine, 500g of coffee, 200 cigarettes and 50mL of perfume. The import or export of kuna is limited to 15,000KN per person.

EMBASSIES & CONSULATES

The following addresses are in Zagreb (area code ☎ 01):
Albania (☎ 48 10 679; Jurišićeva 2a)
Australia (☎ 48 91 200; www.auembassy.hr; Kaptol Centar, Nova Ves 11) North of the centre.
Bosnia & Hercegovina (☎ 46 83 761; Torbarova 9) Northwest of the centre.
Bulgaria (☎ 48 23 336; Novi Goljak 25) Northwest of the centre.
Canada (☎ 48 81 200; zagreb@dfait-maeci.gc.ca; Prilaz Đure Deželića 4)
Czech Republic (☎ 61 77 239; Savska 41)
France (☎ 48 93 680; consulat@ambafrance.hr; Hebrangova 2)
Germany (☎ 61 58 105; www.deutschebotschaft-zagreb .hr, in German; ul grada Vukovara 64) South of the centre.
Hungary (☎ 48 22 051; Pantovčak 128/I) Northwest of the centre.
Ireland (☎ 66 74 455; Turinina 3)
Montenegro (☎ 45 73 362; 4th fl, Trg Nikole Šubića Zrinjskog 1)
Netherlands (☎ 46 84 880; nlgovzag@zg.t-com.hr; Medveščak 56) North of the centre.
New Zealand (☎ 61 51 382; Trg Stjepana Radića 3) Southwest of the centre.
Poland (☎ 48 99 444; Krležin Gvozd 3)
Romania (☎ 45 77 550; roamb@zg.t-com.hr; Mlinarska ul 43) North of the centre.
Serbia (☎ 45 79 067; Pantovčak 245) Northwest of the centre.
Slovakia (☎ 48 48 941; Prilaz Đure Deželića 10)
Slovenia (☎ 63 11 000; Savska 41)
UK (☎ 60 09 100; I Lučića 4) East of the centre.
USA (☎ 66 12 200; www.usembassy.hr; Ul Thomasa Jeffersona 2) South of the centre.

FESTIVALS & EVENTS

In July and August there are summer festivals in Dubrovnik, Split, Pula and Zagreb. Dubrovnik's summer music festival emphasises classical music with concerts in churches around town, while Pula hosts a variety of pop and classical stars in the Roman amphitheatre and also hosts a film festival. Mardi Gras celebrations have recently been revived in many towns, with attendant parades and festivities, but nowhere is it celebrated with more verve than in Rijeka.

GAY & LESBIAN TRAVELLERS

Homosexuality has been legal in Croatia since 1977 and is tolerated, but not welcomed with open arms. Public displays of affection between members of the same sex may be met with hostility, especially outside major cities. Exclusively gay clubs are a rarity outside Zagreb, but many of the large discos attract a mixed crowd. Raves are also a good way for gay people to meet.

On the coast, gay people gravitate to Rovinj, Hvar, Split and Dubrovnik and tend to frequent naturist beaches. In Zagreb, the last Saturday in June is Gay Pride Zagreb day, an excellent opportunity to connect with the local gay scene.

Most Croatian websites devoted to the gay scene are in Croatian only, but a good starting point is the English-language www.touristinfo .gay.hr, which has articles on the gay scene and links to other relevant websites.

HOLIDAYS

New Year's Day 1 January
Epiphany 6 January
Easter Monday March/April
Labour Day 1 May
Corpus Christi 10 June
Day of Antifascist Resistance 22 June; marks the outbreak of resistance in 1941
Statehood Day 25 June
Victory Day and National Thanksgiving Day 5 August
Feast of the Assumption 15 August
Independence Day 8 October
All Saints' Day 1 November
Christmas 25 & 26 December

INTERNET ACCESS

Internet cafes are springing up everywhere. The going rate is about 25KN per hour, and connections are usually good. They can be busy, especially with kids playing online games.

INTERNET RESOURCES

Croatia Homepage (www.hr.hr) Hundreds of links to everything you want to know about Croatia.
Croatia Traveller (www.croatiatraveller.com) All ferry schedules, flights, forums, accommodation, sightseeing and travel planning.
Dalmatia Travel Guide (www.dalmacija.net) All about Dalmatia, including reservations for private accommodation.
Find Croatia (www.findcroatia.com) More Croatia links, with an emphasis on tourism and outdoor activities.

MONEY
Credit Cards

Amex, MasterCard, Visa and Diners Club cards are widely accepted in large hotels, stores and many restaurants, but don't count on cards to pay for private accommodation or meals in small restaurants. ATMs accepting MasterCard, Maestro, Cirrus, Plus and Visa are available in most bus and train stations, airports, all major cities and most small towns. Many branches of Privredna Banka have ATMs that allow cash withdrawals on an Amex card.

Currency

The currency is the kuna. Banknotes are in denominations of 500, 200, 100, 50, 20, 10 and five. Each kuna is divided into 100 lipa in coins of 50, 20 and 10.

Moneychangers

Many places exchange money, all with similar rates. Exchange offices may deduct a commission of 1% to change cash or travellers cheques, but some banks do not. Hungarian currency is difficult to change in Croatia and Croatian currency can be difficult to exchange in some neighbouring countries.

Tax

A 22% VAT is imposed upon most purchases and services, and is included in the price. If your purchases exceed 500KN in one shop you can claim a refund upon leaving the country. Ask the merchant for the paperwork, but don't be surprised if they don't have it.

CROATIA

Tipping

If you're served well at a restaurant, you should round up the bill, but a service charge is always included. (Don't leave money on the table.) Bar bills and taxi fares can also be rounded up. Tour guides on day excursions expect to be tipped.

POST

Mail sent to Poste Restante, 10000 Zagreb, Croatia, is held at the **main post office** (Branimirova 4; ☟ 24hr Mon-Sat, 1pm-midnight Sun) next to the Zagreb train station. A good coastal address to use is c/o Poste Restante, Main Post Office, 21000 Split, Croatia. If you have an Amex card, most Atlas travel agencies will hold your mail.

TELEPHONE
Mobile Phones

Croatia uses GSM 900/1800 and the two mobile networks are T-Mobile and VIP. If your mobile is compatible, SIM cards are widely available and cost about 400KN.

Phone Codes

To call Croatia from abroad, dial your international access code, ☎ 385 (Croatia's country code), the area code (without the initial zero) and the local number. When calling from one region to another within Croatia, use the initial zero. Phone numbers with the prefix 060 are sometimes free and other times charged at a premium rate, while numbers that begin with 09 are mobile numbers (and are quite expensive). When in Croatia, dial ☎ 00 to speak to the international operator.

Phonecards

To make a phone call from Croatia, go to the town's main post office. You'll need a phonecard to use public telephones, but calls using a phonecard are about 50% more expensive. Phonecards are sold according to *impulsa* (units), and you can buy cards of 25 (15KN), 50 (30KN), 100 (50KN) and 200

EMERGENCY NUMBERS

- Ambulance ☎ 94
- Fire service ☎ 93
- Police ☎ 92
- Roadside assistance ☎ 987

(100KN) units. These can be purchased at any post office and most tobacco shops and newspaper kiosks.

TOURIST INFORMATION

The **Croatian National Tourist Board** (Map pp182-3; ☎ 45 56 455; www.htz.hr; Iblerov trg 10, Importanne Gallerija, 10000 Zagreb) is a good source of information with an excellent website. There are regional tourist offices that supervise tourist development, and municipal tourist offices which have free brochures and good information on local events. Some arrange private accommodation.

Tourist information is also dispensed by commercial travel agencies such as **Atlas** (www.atlas-croatia.com), Croatia Express, Generalturist and Kompas, which also arrange private rooms, sightseeing tours and so on. Ask for the schedule for coastal ferries.

Croatian tourist offices abroad:

UK (☎ 020-8563 7979; info@cnto.freeserve.co.uk; Croatian National Tourist Office, 2 Lanchesters, 162-164 Fulham Palace Rd, London W6 9ER)

USA (☎ 212-279 8672; cntony@earthlink.net; Croatian National Tourist Office, Ste 4003, 350 Fifth Ave, New York, NY 10118)

TRAVELLERS WITH DISABILITIES

Because of the number of wounded war veterans, more attention is being paid to the needs of travellers with disabilities. Public toilets at bus stations, train stations, airports and large public venues are usually wheelchair accessible. Large hotels are wheelchair accessible, but very little private accommodation is. The bus and train stations in Zagreb, Zadar, Rijeka, Split and Dubrovnik are wheelchair accessible, but the local Jadrolinija ferries are not. Note that the steep streets in the old towns, such as in Dubrovnik, are restrictive for travellers with walking difficulties and those in wheelchairs. For further information, get in touch with **Savez Organizacija Invalida Hrvatske** (☎ /fax 01-48 29 394; Savska cesta 3, 10000 Zagreb).

VISAS

Visitors from Australia, Canada, New Zealand, the EU and the USA do not require a visa for stays of less than 90 days. For other nationalities, visas are issued free of charge at Croatian consulates. Croatian authorities require all foreigners to register with the local police when they first arrive in a new area of the country, but this is a routine matter that is normally handled by your hotel, hostel or camping ground, or the agency that organises your private accommodation.

TRANSPORT IN CROATIA

GETTING THERE & AWAY

Connections into Croatia are in a constant state of flux, with new air and boat routes opening every season. Following is an overview of the major connections into Croatia, but you should refer to the regional transport chapter, p439, for more detail.

Air

Major airports in the country:

Dubrovnik (code DBV; ☎ 020-773 377; www.airport-dubrovnik.hr)

Pula (code PUY; ☎ 052-530 105; www.airport-pula.com)

Rijeka (code RJK; ☎ 051-842 132)

Split (code SPU; ☎ 021-203 506; www.split-airport.hr)

Zadar (code ZAD; ☎ 023-313 311; www.zadar-airport.hr)

Zagreb (code ZAG; ☎ 01-62 65 222; www.zagreb-airport.hr)

In addition to domestic connections to Zagreb, Pula has direct flights to London (Gatwick) and Manchester, while Split has direct flights to Amsterdam, Frankfurt, Manchester, London (Gatwick and Heathrow), Lyon, Munich, Paris, Prague, Rome (Fiumicino) and Vienna.

Dubrovnik has direct flights to Manchester, London (Gatwick), Glasgow, Nottingham, Paris, Frankfurt, Rome, Tel Aviv and Vienna, as well as flights to Zagreb and Split. Many of the International connections to the coast are available only from April or May to September or October.

Zagreb is connected domestically to Dubrovnik, Split, Pula, Rijeka and Zadar and internationally to all European capitals plus Milan, Munich, Frankfurt, Istanbul and Sarajevo.

Zadar receives domestic flights from Zagreb only.

Major airlines flying into the country:

Adria Airways (code JD; ☎ 01-48 10 011; www.adria-airways.com) Hub Ljubljana.

Aeroflot (code SU; ☎ 01-48 72 055; www.aeroflot.ru) Hub Moscow.

Air Canada (code AC; ☎ 01-48 22 033; www.aircanada.ca) Hub Toronto.

Air France (code AF; ☎ 01-48 37 100; www.airfrance.com) Hub Paris Charles de Gaulle.

Alitalia (code AZ; ☎ 01-48 10 413; www.alitalia.it) Hub Milan.

Austrian Airlines (code OS; ☎ 062 65 900; www.aua.com) Hub Vienna.

British Airways (code BA; www.british-airways.com) Hub London.

Croatia Airlines (code OU; ☎ 01-48 19 633; www.croatiaairlines.hr; Zrinjevac 17, Zagreb) Hub Zagreb. Croatia's national carrier has recently stepped up its service to serve many more routes.

ČSA (code OK; ☎ 01-48 73 301; www.csa.cz) Hub Prague.

Delta Airlines (code DL; ☎ 01-48 78 760; www.delta.com) Hub Atlanta.

KLM-Northwest (code KL; ☎ 01-48 78 601; www.klm.com) Hub Amsterdam.

LOT Polish Airlines (code LO; ☎ 01-48 37 500; www.lot.com) Hub Warsaw.

Lufthansa (code LH; ☎ 01-48 73 121; www.lufthansa.com) Hub Frankfurt.

Malév Hungarian Airlines (code MA; ☎ 01-48 36 935; www.malev.hu) Hub Budapest.

Turkish Airlines (code TK; ☎ 01-49 21 854; www.turkishairlines.com) Hub Istanbul.

Land

BUS

Bosnia & Hercegovina

There are daily connections from Sarajevo (€18, five hours, daily), Medugorje (€18, three hours, two daily) and Mostar (€15, three hours, two daily) to Dubrovnik; from Sarajevo to Split (€19, seven hours, five daily), which stop at Mostar; and from Sarajevo to Zagreb (€18, eight hours, three daily) and Rijeka (€35, 10 hours, daily).

Montenegro

The border between Montenegro and Croatia is open to visitors, allowing Americans, Australians, Canadians and Brits to enter visa free. There's a daily bus from Kotor to Dubrovnik (120KN, 2½ hours) that starts at Bar and stops at Herceg Novi.

Serbia

There are six daily buses from Zagreb to Belgrade (€20, six hours). At Bajakovo on the border, a Serbian bus takes you on to Belgrade.

CAR & MOTORCYCLE

The main highway entry/exit points between Croatia and Hungary are Goričan (between Nagykanisza and Varaždin), Gola (23km east of Koprivnica), Terezino Polje (opposite Barcs) and Donji Miholjac (7km south of

Harkány). There are dozens of border crossings into BiH, Serbia and Montenegro, including the main Zagreb to Belgrade highway. Major destinations in BiH, such as Sarajevo, Mostar and Međugorje, are accessible from Zagreb, Split and Dubrovnik.

Motorists require vehicle registration papers and the green insurance card to enter Croatia. Bear in mind that if you hire a car in Italy, many insurance companies will not insure you for a trip into Croatia. Border officials know this and may refuse you entry unless permission to drive into Croatia is clearly marked on the insurance documents. Most car-hire companies in Trieste and Venice are familiar with this requirement and will furnish you with the stamp. Otherwise, you must make specific inquiries.

See opposite for road rules and more info.

TRAIN
Bosnia & Hercegovina
There's a daily train service to Zagreb from Sarajevo each morning (260KN, eight hours), a daily train to Osijek (113KN, 8½ hours) and a daily service to Ploče (310KN, 10 hours) via Mostar, Sarajevo and Banja Luka.

Serbia
Five daily trains connect Zagreb with Belgrade (€25, seven hours).

Sea
Regular boats from several companies connect Croatia with Italy. See p444 for information about ferries back and forth. All of the boat-company offices in Split are located inside the ferry terminal.

GETTING AROUND
Air
Croatia Airlines is the one and only carrier for flights within Croatia. The price of flights depends on the season, and you get better deals if you book ahead. Seniors and people aged under 26 get discounts.

Bicycle
Cycling is a great way to see the islands and bikes are fairly easy to hire in most tourist spots. Many tourist offices have helpful maps of cycling routes. Bike lanes are nearly unknown in Croatia, however; you'll need to exercise extreme caution on the many narrow two-lane roads.

FLIGHT-FREE TRAVEL

To learn how to get to Zagreb from London without having to fly, log on to www .seat61.com and search 'Croatia'. You'll get instructions on how to get to Zagreb from the UK capital via bus and rail (it gives you departure times and all!).

Boat
Year-round Jadrolinija car ferries operate along the Bari–Rijeka–Dubrovnik coastal route, stopping at Zadar, Split and the islands of Hvar, Korčula and Mljet. Services are less frequent in winter. The most scenic section is Split to Dubrovnik, which all Jadrolinija ferries cover during the day. Ferries are a lot more comfortable than buses, though somewhat more expensive. From Rijeka to Dubrovnik the deck fare is €26/31 in low/high season, with high season running from about the end of June to the end of August; there's a 20% reduction on the return portion of a return ticket. With a through ticket, deck passengers can stop at any port for up to a week, provided they notify the purser beforehand and have their ticket validated. This is much cheaper than buying individual sector tickets but is only good for one stopover. Cabins should be booked a week ahead, but deck space is usually available on all sailings.

Deck passage on Jadrolinija is just that: *poltrone* (reclining seats) are about €6 extra and four-berth cabins (if available) begin at €48.50/58 in low/high season from Rijeka to Dubrovnik. You must buy tickets in advance at an agency or the Jadrolinija office as they are not sold on board. Cabins can be arranged at the reservation counter aboard the ship, but advance bookings are recommended if you want to be sure of a place. Bringing a car means checking in at least two hours in advance, more in the summer.

Local ferries connect the bigger offshore islands with each other and the mainland. Some of the ferries operate only a couple of times a day and, once the vehicular capacity is reached, the remaining motorists must wait for the next available service. During summer the lines of waiting cars can be long, so it's important to arrive early.

Foot passengers and cyclists should have no problem getting on, but you must buy your tickets at an agency before boarding since they are not sold on board. You should bear in mind that taking a bicycle on these services will incur an extra charge, which depends on the distance.

Bus

Bus services are excellent and relatively inexpensive. There are often a number of different companies handling each route so prices can vary substantially, but the prices in this book should give you an idea of costs (and unless otherwise noted, all bus prices are for one-way fares). Generally, the cheaper fares are on overnight buses.

It's generally best to call or visit the bus station to get the complete schedule. Larger companies:

Autotrans (☎ 051-660 360; www.autotrans.hr) Based in Rijeka with connections to Istria, Zagreb, Varaždin and Kvarner.

Brioni Pula (☎ 052-502 997; www.brioni.hr, in Croatian) Based in Pula with connections to Istria, Trieste, Padua, Split and Zagreb.

Contus (☎ 023-315 315; www.contus.hr) Based in Zadar with connections to Split and Zagreb.

At large stations bus tickets must be purchased at the office; book ahead to be sure of a seat. Tickets for buses that arrive from somewhere else are usually purchased from the conductor. Buy a one-way ticket only or you'll be locked into one company's schedule for the return. Most intercity buses are air-conditioned and make rest stops every two hours or so. Some of the more expensive companies charge extra for a video system that allows you to watch Croatian soap operas during your trip. If you plan to catch a nap, bring earplugs since there's bound to be music playing. Luggage stowed in the baggage compartment under the bus costs extra (10KN per piece, including insurance).

On schedules, *vozi svaki dan* means 'every day' and *ne vozi nedjeljom ni praznikom* means 'not Sunday and public holidays'. Check www .akz.hr (in Croatian) for information on schedules and fares to and from Zagreb.

Car & Motorcycle

You have to pay tolls on the motorways around Zagreb, to use the Učka tunnel between Rijeka and Istria, the bridge to Krk Island, and the road from Rijeka to Delnice and from Zagreb to Split. Tolls can be paid in foreign currencies. The motorway connecting Zagreb and Split has cut travel time to the coast to around four hours. Tolls add up to about 160KN. Over the next few years, look for completion of the final leg running from Split to Dubrovnik. For general news on Croatia's motorways and tolls, see www.hac.hr.

DRIVING LICENCE

Any valid driving licence is sufficient to legally drive and hire a car; an international driving licence is not necessary. **Hrvatski Autoklub** (HAK; Croatian Auto Club; www.hak.hr; Avenija Dubrovnik 44) offers help and advice, plus there's the nationwide **HAK road assistance** (vučna služba; ☎ 987).

FUEL

Petrol stations are generally open 7am to 7pm and often until 10pm in summer. Petrol is Eurosuper 95, Super 98, normal or diesel. See www.ina.hr for up-to-date fuel prices.

HIRE

The large car-hire chains represented in Croatia are Avis, Budget, Europcar and Hertz. Throughout Croatia, Avis is allied with the Autotehna company, while Hertz is often represented by Kompas.

Independent local companies are often much cheaper than the international chains, but Avis, Budget, Europcar and Hertz have the big advantage of offering one-way rentals that allow you to drop the car off at any one of their many stations in Croatia free of charge.

Prices at local companies begin at around €40 a day with unlimited kilometres. Shop around as deals vary widely and 'special' discounts and weekend rates are often available. Third party public-liability insurance is included by law, but make sure your quoted price includes full collision insurance, called collision damage waiver (CDW). Otherwise your responsibility for damage done to the vehicle is usually determined as a percentage of the car's value. Full CDW begins at 50KN a day extra (compulsory for those aged under 25), theft insurance is 15KN a day and personal accident insurance another 40KN a day.

Sometimes you can get a lower car-hire rate by booking the car from abroad. Tour companies in Western Europe often have fly-drive packages that include a flight to Croatia and a car (two-person minimum).

ROAD RULES

Unless otherwise posted, the speed limits for cars and motorcycles are 50km/h in the

CROATIA

urban zones, 90km/h outside urban zones, 110km/h on main highways and 130km/h on motorways. On any of Croatia's winding two-lane highways, it's illegal to pass long military convoys or a line of cars caught behind a slow-moving truck. The maximum permitted amount of alcohol in the blood is – none at all! It is also forbidden to use a mobile phone while driving. Drive defensively, as some local drivers lack discipline, to put it mildly.

Hitching

Hitching is never entirely safe, and we don't recommend it. Hitchhiking in Croatia is unreliable. You'll have better luck on the islands, but in the interior cars are small and usually full.

Local Transport

Zagreb and Osijek have well-developed tram systems as well as local buses, but in the rest of the country you'll only find buses. In major cities such as Rijeka, Split, Zadar and Dubrovnik buses run about every 20 minutes, less often on Sunday. Small medieval towns along the coast are generally closed to traffic and have infrequent links to outlying suburbs.

Taxis are available in all cities and towns, but they must be called or boarded at a taxi stand. Prices are rather high (meters start at 25KN).

Train

Train travel is about 15% cheaper than bus travel and often more comfortable, although slower. The main lines run from Zagreb to Rijeka, Zadar and Split and east to Osijek. There are no trains along the coast. Local trains usually have only unreserved 2nd-class seats. Reservations may be required on express trains. 'Executive' trains have only 1st-class seats and are 40% more expensive than local trains.

On posted timetables in Croatia, the word for arrivals is *dolazak* and for departures is *odlazak* or *polazak*. For train information check out **Croatian Railway** (www.hznet.hr).

Dramatic Ostrog Monastery (p364), Montenegro

BEST OF THE BALKANS

There's a lot to see in the Western Balkans, but don't plan to do too much. We suggest you aim to experience the best of the region but allow for some spontaneous diversions. Culinary aficionados and party people are in for urban escapades offering the spectrum of flavours and round-the-clock thrills. Or you can commit to the countryside to discover villages so remote we've never heard of them, and arduous adventures in valleys, canyons and mountains. Culture junkies – wherever you go – will get more hits than you can handle.

City Life

For many people, city life is a euphemism for nightlife. For others, it denotes the culinary creativity offered by both rustic and world-class restaurants. Or it's the architectural montage that evolved from warring worlds in urban hubs. For us, it's all of the above.

1 Pristina

Pristina (p273) is a chaotic post-conflict collage. Visitors to Kosovo's self-declared capital will see it evolve before their eyes as local and international players strive to get things in order.

2 Mostar

Mill-house restaurants tucked into a surreally picturesque little valley and canyonside cafes overlooking the gorgeous Unesco-listed bridge make dining in Mostar (p131) one of Hercegovina's most memorable experiences.

3 Belgrade

Belgrade (p301), Serbia, is the clubbing capital of the Balkans. It's also here that you'll have some of the most eclectic meals and conversations to be found in the region.

4 Podgorica

After dark, the cafe-bars of Podgorica's Nova Varoš quarter (p362), in Montenegro, are the only place to be.

5 Tirana

What happens when an artist gets into politics? In the case of Albania's capital (p62), the town gets painted red (and yellow, and purple...).

6 Zadar

An up-and-coming city destination, Croatia's Zadar (p220) has one of Dalmatia's prettiest old town centres, with marble, traffic-free streets. Zadar's Roman ruins and medieval churches dazzle, as does the nightlife.

7 Skopje

Macedonia's capital, Skopje (p289), is fascinating for its merrily coexisting dualities: Ottoman and Byzantine shrines, Yugoslav and ultramodern architecture, Zastavas and Land Rovers on the streets, traditional tea houses and chic modern bars.

4

Great Outdoors

Dalmatian dreams in the buff on Croatia's coast, skiing and summertime walks in Serbia, a ferry ride in Albania, rafting in Bosnia and Hercegovina (BiH), paddling in glassy lakes in Macedonia, hiking in national parks…these outdoors are beyond great. The only thing missing is the crowds that flock to the rest of the continent.

1 Zlatibor
Serbia's gentle region of Zlatibor (p414) is beloved for its easy ski slopes, but it's summertime walks through hospitable villages and lush countryside that will make you fall in love with it.

2 Mavrovo National Park
This pristine park (p298) offers rich forests, Mt Korab (at 2764m, Macedonia's highest peak), the tranquil heritage village of Galičnik, stunning Sveti Jovan Bigorski monastery, and great skiing and hiking.

3 Tara Canyon
With sheer rock walls extending up to 1300m at their highest, BiH's amazing Tara Canyon (p146) is best seen while floating through on a raft.

4 Durmitor National Park
Boasting 48 peaks over 2000m, Montenegro's Durmitor range (p365) still harbours bears and wolves in its most remote reaches.

5 Naturism
Yes, you read it right. Edward VIII and Wallis Simpson went skinny-dipping here in the '30s, so Croatia has a venerable naturist history. Istria (p199) is Croatia's top destination for going starkers – look for the FKK signs!

6 Lake Koman
When the communists dammed the river and created Lake Koman (p91) back in the '70s for hydro-electricity, little did they know that they'd given Albania a spectacular, world-class ferry route.

7 Kopaonik
The secret about Kopaonik (p413) is getting out. Lots of slopes for not many euro in a well-facilitated national park make this the prime ski resort in Serbia.

Cultural Life

The legacy of colliding cultures in the Western Balkans is borne out in the region's eclectic architectural terrain and in the diversity of its people. Orthodox monks rub shoulders with trend-setting restaurateurs and pace-setting DJs. Traditional life has endured for centuries, but edgy cultural movements continually evolve in urban hubs.

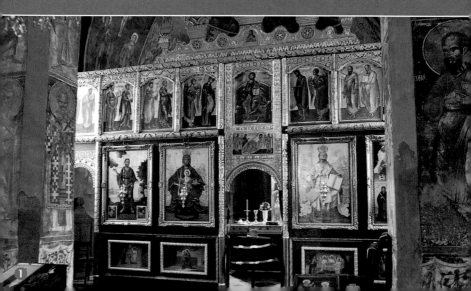

① Fruška Gora

Fruška Gora (p402) isn't just a national park; home to 16 of the country's monasteries, it's also a repository of Serbia's cultural heritage. Monastic life has endured for centuries in these ancient hills.

② Macedonian Festivities

The fun loving Macedonians are always up for a good time, whether it be lakeside techno parties, traditional weddings (p299) or raucous events like the costumed winter carnivals of Strumica (p326) and Vevčani (p300).

③ Kosovo

Kosovo (p269) not only is home to a proud populace of ethnic Albanians, but also harbours some cultural treasures of Serbian Orthodoxy and architectural treasures of Islam.

④ Castles

Explore BiH's impressive yet little-known medieval fortress ruins, from picture-perfect Počitelj (p141; pictured) to idyllic Vranduk (p151), powerful Jajce (p154) and dramatic Srebrenik (p149).

⑤ Theth

With blood feuds a slightly distant memory, the people of Theth (p92), Albania, are putting their energy into providing tourists with hot showers and never-ending supplies of sheep cheese, drinking yoghurt and warm milk.

⑥ Trogir

Pocket-sized Trogir (p235) brims with Romanesque and Renaissance architecture and has one of the loveliest cathedrals on the Croatian coast; its illustrious history has left it with a fantastic Venetian heritage.

⑦ Cetinje

The museums of Cetinje (p358), the former capital, celebrate Montenegro's independent spirit.

Church on rocky mountain above the town of Kotor (p345), Montenegro

Kosovo

Kosovo doesn't leap to mind as a travel destination: it has the weakest economy in Europe, half the population is unemployed, and the innards of buildings stripped to their skeletons still lie strewn across smashed-up sidewalks. But though the wounds of the past are visible, the future is coming on quickly. In towns set against snowcapped mountains and endless green fields lush with promise, buildings are being transformed into shiny new shopping centres, and apartment blocks are shooting up from the razed earth. Though not universally recognised, Kosovo claimed ownership of all this activity by declaring itself independent in early 2008.

The capital, Pristina, is a montage of everywhere that's had a hand in its past and vies to play a role in its future. The centre is a *Who's Who* of international organisations. Tucked between them are restaurants with waiters offering you a choice of languages alongside the wine list. Incongruous images abound; burgers on Bulevardi Bil Klinton, *burek* and Istanbul hair salons, and blood-red Albanian flags flapping next to the benign blue of the UN and the EU.

Nothing is more than a few hours from Pristina; you can visit Unesco-recognised Serbian Orthodox monasteries in Prizren or barter in Peja's Turkish-style bazaar and be back in Pristina for dinner. Kosovo is a complicated country, but interesting places are rarely simple.

FAST FACTS

- **Area** 10,887 sq km
- **Capital** Pristina
- **Currency** euro (€); US$1 = €0.76; UK£1 = €1.10; A$1 = €0.51
- **Famous for** being the world's newest self-declared country
- **Key phrases** *tungjatjeta* (hello), *mirupafshim* (goodbye), *ju lutem* (please), *faleminderit* (thank you), *me falni* (excuse me), *më vjen keq* (I'm sorry)
- **Official language** Albanian
- **Population** 1.8 million to 2.4 million
- **Telephone codes** country code ☎ 381; international access code ☎ 00
- **Visas** not required; see p280
- **Land boundaries** 702km
- **Number of kitsch film clips played during an hour-long bus ride** Too many
- **GDP per capita** US$1800
- **Population living below poverty line** 37%
- **Google hits** 35,500,000 (July 2008)
- **Unemployment rate** 43%
- **Cost of living** Half of Kosovars live on less than €3 per day

TRAVEL ADVISORY

Government travel advisories strongly warn against visiting certain areas of Kosovo. At the time of writing, areas of North Mitrovica and northern municipalities of Leposavic, Zubin Potok and Zvecan (all northwest of Pristina) were no-go zones after police and border posts were attacked following Kosovo's declaration of independence. Unrest in border areas between Serbia and Kosovo make travelling overland between them ill-advised. Check the situation before attempting to do so.

There is a heavy Kosovo Force (KFOR) presence in Serbian enclaves and sites of potential tension (border areas and heritage buildings at risk of vandalism). Carry your passport at all times to present to KFOR. Stay clear of protests and roadblocks, which can erupt into violence.

HIGHLIGHTS

- **Kaljaja Fort** (p277) Fine views over the former medieval capital of 'Old Serbia', Prizren.
- **Pristina** (p273) Culinary cosmopolitanism in the new capital.
- **Gadimë** (p276) Cave explorations.
- **Peja** (p276) Goat cheese of every texture and shade of white in the town's farmers market.
- **Patriachate of Peç** (p277) See it at the last KFOR checkpoint before Montenegro.

ITINERARIES

- **Two to three days** Fine dining and sightseeing in Pristina (p273) and a day trip to Gračanica Monastery (p276).
- **One week** The above, then loop to Prizren (p277) for mosques and churches, and Peja (p276) for monasteries and markets.

CLIMATE & WHEN TO GO

There is no tourist season to contend with, but winter can be cold. Ski season stretches from December until the end of April, if things are running again. Summers sit comfortably in the mid-20s.

HISTORY

In the 12th century, Kosovo was the heart of the Serbian empire. This Serbian golden age under Stefan Dušan saw construction of many Orthodox churches until the Turkish triumph at the pivotal 1389 Battle of Kosovo ushered in 500 years of Ottoman rule. The number of Serbs drastically fell, and Albanians and Muslims came to dominate the region's ethnic and religious make-up.

In the 1912 Balkan Wars, Serbia regained control and Serbs settled vacated land. In WWII the territory was incorporated into Italian-controlled Albania and liberated in October 1944 by Albanian partisans. Tito wanted Albania united with Kosovo in the new Yugoslavia, but it never happened. After decades of neglect, Yugoslavia granted Kosovo de facto self-governing status in 1974. Despite increased economic aid, the standard of living in Kosovo remained a quarter of the Yugoslav average.

In 1987, Slobodan Milošević rallied Kosovo Serbs to speak out against alleged hostilities from the majority Kosovo Albanian population; in 1989 the autonomy Kosovo enjoyed under the 1974 constitution was suspended and a state of emergency was declared. Ethnic Albanian leaders declared independence from Serbia in 1990; Belgrade responded by replacing some 115,000 Albanians in government and media with Serb loyalists.

In 1992, war broke out; the same year Ibrahim Rugova was elected president of the self-proclaimed republic of Kosovo. Ethnic conflict heightened and the Kosovo Liberation Army (KLA) was formed in 1996. In March 1999, a US-backed plan to return Kosovo's autonomy was rejected by Serbia, which moved to empty the

HOW MUCH?

- **Short taxi ride** €2
- **One-hour bus ride** €1
- **Internet access** €1 per hour
- **Coffee** €1
- **Independent Republic of Kosovo Passport Cover** €2

LONELY PLANET INDEX

- **Litre of petrol** €1.20
- **Litre of water** €0.30
- **Half-litre of Peja beer** €0.50 to €1
- **Souvenir T-shirt** €5
- **Street snack (burek)** €0.50 to €1

province of its non-Serbian population. Nearly 850,000 Kosovo Albanians fled to Albania and Macedonia. After Serbia ignored demands to desist, NATO began a bombing campaign in March 1999. In June, Milošević agreed to withdraw troops from Kosovo, the air strikes ceased, the KLA agreed to disarm and the NATO-led KFOR took over. From June 1999, Kosovo was administered as a UN-NATO protectorate.

In February 2002, Ibrahim Rugova became president of the coalition government. In March 2004, violence broke out in Mitrovica; 19 people were killed, 600 homes were burnt and 29 monasteries and churches were destroyed in the worst ethnic violence since 1999. KFOR was criticised for its slow response. The elections in 2004 (boycotted by most Serbs) saw President Rugova triumph. Former rebel commander Ramush Haradinaj resigned as prime minister in March 2005 following his indictment to the Hague for alleged war crimes; he was given a hero's welcome after his acquittal in April 2008. President Rugova died of lung cancer in early 2006 and was succeeded by Fatmir Sejdiu.

UN-sponsored talks on the status of Kosovo began in February 2006. In October, Serbians voted in favour of a new constitution declaring Kosovo an integral part of Serbia. Hasim Thaci became president of Kosovo in November 2007 and the following February declared Kosovo independent. Several countries recognised Kosovo's independence, but Serbian prime minister Vojislav Kostunica dismissed the declaration, stating that 'As long as the Serb people exist, Kosovo will be Serbia.'

In June 2008 a new constitution transferred power from the UN to the government of Kosovo. Kosovo Serbs established their own assembly in Mitrovica.

PEOPLE
Census estimates for the population of Kosovo range from 1.8 million to 2.4 million; 88% of the population is Albanian and 7% are Serbs. The remaining 5% comprise Bosniaks, Gorani, Roma, Turk, Ashkali and Egyptians. The minority Serb population mostly lives in KFOR-protected enclaves.

RELIGION
Muslims are mostly Albanians and Orthodox Christians mostly ethnic Serbs. There is a

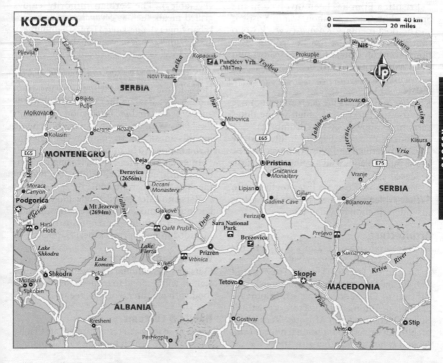

Roman Catholic minority. Roma often identify as Muslims.

There are concerns about extremist elements, but the vast majority of Islam practised
is liberal and progressive.

ARTS
Literature
Former president Ibrahim Rugova was significant in the literary scene; his presidency
of the Kosovo Writers' Association was a step
towards his presidency of the nation.

Eqrem Basha, Ali Podrimja and Sabri Hamiti
are recognised amongst Kosovo's greatest
poets. Works of Sali Bashota have been translated into English, German and Romanian.

Feminist writer Flora Brovina is largely
concerned with the freedom of individuals
and peoples. She has received several international awards.

Cinema
Isa Qosja's 2005 film *The Kukum* is a step
towards reviving the film industry, as is the
establishment of a film school by award-
winning filmmakers including Isa Qosja.

Prishtina Film has been involved in the
Spanish film *Guerreros* about war in Kosovo.

The documentary *Kosovo* (www.kosovo
film.com) follows the trials of young local
filmmaker Luli Hoti as he makes a short film
portraying postwar Kosovo.

Music
Kosovar music bears the deep imprint of five
centuries of Turkish rule; high-whine flutes
carry tunes above goat-skin drumbeats.

Modern music is heavily influenced by
Albanian, Serbian and Western music scenes.
Roma music blends it all together with a dash
of Macedonian.

To hear what Kosovars listen to, tune in to
Radiotelevision (www.rtklive.com), or catch a bus
for indoctrination by video-clip.

Architecture
Architectural styles are a mix of Byzantine/
Orthodox, Islamic and vernacular.

Gračanica (p276), Dečani (p277) and
Patrijaršija Monasteries are enormously significant to Orthodox Serbs. An important
example of Ottoman architecture is Pristina's
Sultan Mehemit Fatih Mosque. Vernacular
architecture refers to traditional houses (*kul-
las* and *konaks*) and other structures.

The aesthetic deprivation of communism,
neglect under Milošević and war damage has
placed Kosovo's cultural heritage in a fragile
state. Architecture enthusiasts will enjoy the
Kosovar Stability Initiative's heritage map of
Pristina (www.iksweb.org/publications.php).

Visual Arts
In the late 1980s and early 1990s, artistic ex-
pression was repressed when ethnic Albanians
were removed from artistic institutions. The
arts scene is re-emerging, symbolised by Fisnik
Ismajli's outdoor sculpture on Pristina's rr
Luan Haradinaj: 3m-high metal letters read
'New Born'. Exhibitions are held at Kosovo
Art Gallery (see p274).

FOOD & DRINK
Staples & Specialities
'Traditional' and 'local' food is generally
Albanian. Stewed and grilled meat (especially
lamb and veal) and fish feature prominently.
Kos (yoghurt made from goat cheese) is eaten
on its own and accompanies almost anything.
Turkish kebabs are widely available, particularly in Pristina, as is *đuveč* (baked meat and
vegetables). The Serbian minority enjoys
grilled meats such as *ćevapčići* (grilled spicy
kebab fingers), *pljeskavica* (spicy hamburger),
and *ražnjići* (pork or veal kebabs).

The local beer is Peja (from Peja).

Where to Eat & Drink
Holes-in-the-wall filled with men who look as
though they haven't moved since independence was declared are often good choices for
local fare. Women can be thin on the ground,
but this doesn't mean you won't be welcome
if you happen to be one.

International presence has brought a variety of world cuisines to Pristina; pork is about
the only thing hard to come by.

Bars and cafes are often one and the same;
late-night 'drinks' aren't necessarily alcohol.

With a couple of exceptions, breakfast
included in hotel prices is best skipped.

Vegetarians & Vegans
Outside international restaurants in Pristina,
waiters will respond to requests for vegetarian
food with laughter. For tips, see p44.

Habits & Customs
Some sit so long at a restaurant or cafe that it's
hard to know which meal they're there for, if

not all three. Lunch is a more leisurely affair than breakfast. Dinner out usually happens after 8pm.

For a list of Albanian eating and drinking words, see p45.

ENVIRONMENT

Kosovo lies among the Dinaric Alps, land-locked by borders with Serbia (352km), Montenegro (79km), Albania (112km) and Macedonia (159km). It's broadly flat, averaging between 400m and 700m above sea level, surrounded by impressive mountains. The highest is Đeravica (2656m) in the west

There are an estimated 46 mammal species in Kosovo; larger animals include bears, lynxes, wildcats, wolves, foxes, wild goats, roebucks and deer. Small mammals include weasels and the endangered river otter. Around 220 bird species live in or visit Kosovo, including eagles and falcons. Water-bird numbers have declined in recent decades; waterfowl have stopped visiting and birds of prey have almost disappeared.

Most of Kosovo's protected area is in Šara National Park, created in 1986 to protect Balkans and Mediterranean flora and fauna. There is momentum creating the Balkans Peace Park shared by Montenegro, Kosovo and Albania. See the boxed text, p61.

Pollutants emitted from infrastructure hit by NATO bombs impacted Kosovo's biodiversity. Fires and overharvesting of wood threaten forests. Aquatic ecosystems have been damaged by sand and gravel mining, dumping and industrial pollution. Construction is causing rapid urbanisation and straining natural habitats. These problems are exacerbated by inadequate enforcement of laws concerning natural resources.

PRISTINA

☎ 038 / pop 200,000

Pristina looks like a torn-apart town crudely reassembled by differences of opinion, but look closer and you'll notice its pride at being a newly declared capital. It's a great base for day trips to Peja and Prizren.

ORIENTATION

The main artery is bulevardi Nëna Terezë, which converges with Agim Ramadani near the government buildings. Parallel is Luan Haradinaj. From bulevardi Nëna Terezë, bul-

evardi Bil Klinton runs southwest past the bus station and airport (18km) on the way to Peja.

INFORMATION

Air Kosova (☎ 246 510; www.airkosova.biz; rr UÇK 54; ☺ 8am-7pm Mon-Sat)

Barnatorja Pharmacy (☎ 224 245; bul Nëna Terezë; ☺ 7.30am-8pm Mon-Sat, 9am-5pm Sun)

Bookstalls (bul Nëna Terezë) Along bulevardi Nëna Terezë, just north of the Grand Hotel. Maps and copies of Noel Malcolm's *Kosovo: A Short History*.

Kino ABC (☎ 243 117; www.kinoabc.info; rr Rexhep Luci, nr 1; ☺ 8am-midnight) Recent blockbusters in English.

Library Dukagjini (☎ 248 143; bul Nëna Terezë 20; ☺ 8am-8pm Mon-Sat) Maps, language, history and novels.

MCM Travel (☎ 242 424; sr Lidhja e Pejës E12; www .mcmtravel.net; ☺ 9am-8pm) Agent for Austrian and other airlines.

Police station (☎ 504 604 6666; www.kosovopolice .com; rr Luan Haradinaj)

ProCredit Bank (www.procreditbank-kos.com; rr Skenderbeu; ☺ 9am-5.30pm Mon-Fri, to 2pm Sat) Guarded ATM.

PTK (www.ptkonline.com) Agim Ramadan (☺ 8am-10pm Mon-Sat; rr UÇK 66 (☺ 8am-8pm Mon-Sat)

Raiffeissen Bank (☎ 222 222; www.raiffeisen-kosovo .com; rr UÇK 51; ☺ 8am-5pm Mon-Fri, 10am-2pm Sat)

Reisebüro Pristina (Turist Kosovo, ☎ 232 999, 237 777; www.turistkosova.net; bul Nëna Terezë 25a; ☺ 8am-7pm Mon-Fri, to 1pm Sat)

SIGHTS
Bazaar Area

Reminiscent of a Turkish bazaar, the area is home to some of Pristina's key attractions.

Kosovo Museum (☎ 249 964; Sheshi Adam Jashari; admission €1; ☺ 9.30am-5.30pm Tue-Fri, 11am-3pm Sun) has an Austro-Hungarian exterior that you might find yourself staring at, in a futile wait for it to open. Some 1247 pieces of the museum's collection sent to Belgrade for safekeeping in 1998 are yet to return.

In front is the 15th-century **Carshi Mosque**. **Sultan Mehmet Fatih Mosque** (the 'Big Mosque') was built by its namesake around 1461, converted to a Catholic church during the Austro-Hungarian era and refurbished again during WWII.

Nearby is the 26m **clock tower** and the **Great Hamam**, which was being renovated at the time of writing. Next to the clock tower is **Jashar Pasha Mosque**; its vibrant interiors exemplify Turkish baroque style. Nearby, the lovely

KOSOVO

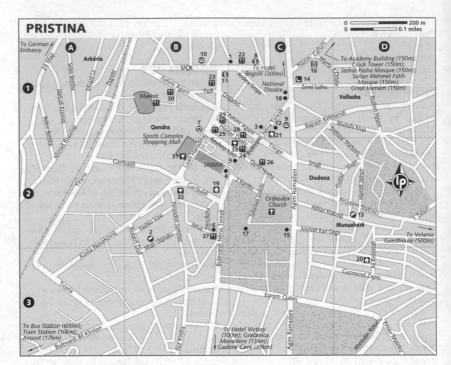

PRISTINA

Balkan-style **Academy Building** is occupied by the Academy of Science and Arts.

Centre

Southeast of the Grand Hotel, a green patch joins bulevardi Nëna Terezë and Agim Ramadani. In the centre, the **National Library** (www.biblioteka-ks.org), completed in 1982 by Croatian architect Andrija Mutnjakovic, must be seen to be believed (think of gelatinous eggs wearing armour).

East towards Agim Ramadani, **Kosovo Art Gallery** (www.kosovart.com) shows works of local artists; opening hours and admission prices vary by exhibition.

The gates of the government buildings (at the northern end of bulevardi Nëna Terezë) are a stark reminder of how recently Pristina was in turmoil; they bear **photos** of locals who went missing during the conflict.

SLEEPING
Budget
Velania Guesthouse (Guesthouse Professor; ☎ 531 742, 044167455; www.guesthouse-ks.com; Velania 4/34; s/d €13/18; 🖳) Run by a jovial professor of engineering,

Velania is the long-term budget choice for anyone missing the social atmosphere of hostels, or their granddad. Rooms are private and homely, and have satellite TV and cable internet. Some have bathrooms, but shared facilities are comfortable. Velania is a €2 taxi ride or 10-minute walk east of the centre.

Midrange
our pick **Hotel Begolli** (☎ 044308093, 049308093; www.hotel-begolli.pizco.com; rr Maliq pash Gjinolli nr 8; s/d €30/35, ste €50-60, apt €80-100; 🖳) Begolli offers twice what you need and charges half what it could (the catch: no internet and dull breakfast). Standard rooms are unremarkable (some lack windows), but suites come in every size, furniture configuration and jacuzzi-to-occupant ratio. Opt for a room at the front of the building rather than the smaller carpeted ones. Diligent staff treat all 23 rooms with shoes-off respect.

Hotel Iliria (☎ 224 275; bul Nëna Terezë; s/d €25/50, without bathroom €20/40) Past its use-by date but central, Iliria seems kitted out in everything cracked or stained, but all is actually clean. Warm service takes the chill out of the dark, lonely corridors.

Top End

Hotel Afa (☎ 225 226; www.hotelafa.com; Ali Kelmendi nr 15; s/d €65/75; ✗ 🖳) A shining needle in a haystack of hotchpotch buildings, Afa is one of the greats. Rooms are spotless and spacious, with free soft drinks in the minibar. The breakfast buffet stretches further than others and there's a garden.

Hotel Victory (☎ 543 267, 543 277; www.hotel-victory .com; bul Nëna Terezë; s/d/ste €80/100/120; ✗ 🖳) Even standard rooms here offer stretch-out space. Interiors are appealing, but for faux-Grecian toilets. Victory, pitched at business clientele, tries to stand out with its 6m-high rooftop Statue of Liberty.

Grand Hotel (☎ 220 210; www.grandhotel-pr.com; bul Nëna Terezë; s €50-90, d €120, s/d ste €300/350, presidential ste €800/1000; 🖳) Included here only so you don't get lured into staying (and to forewarn those who have the misfortune of being prebooked),

this institution is deservedly mocked for its ironic name.

EATING

Restaurants line rr Luan Haradinaj and the narrow streets between it and bulevardi Nëna Terezë. Competition is sprouting up along rr UÇK and rr Fehmi Agani. For local fare, try Bulevardi Nëna Terezë south of rr Garibaldi. For groceries, head to **Maxi supermarket** (Rexhep Luci; ⊙ 7am-midnight).

our pick de Rada Brasserie (☎ 222 622; rr UÇK nr 50; mains €7; ⊙ 8am-midnight Mon-Sat, 6pm-midnight Sun) The sort of place you wish you could afford in Paris: chandeliers, candlelight and cigars brought down to earth by lounge-room ambience and a soundtrack of Sinatra, Piaf and Winehouse. Start with tomato wrapped in aubergine (€3.50) or gorgonzola-stuffed mushrooms (€3.70).

Pishat (☎ 245 333; rr Qamil Hoxha 11; mains €6; ⊙ 8am-11pm Mon-Sat, noon-11pm Sun) A favourite since it opened its terrace, Pishat is popular with expats and discerning locals. Sample Albanian dishes (€5) or sensationally stewy vegetables in a pot (€3).

Tiffany (☎ 244 040; mains €6; ⊙ 8am-11pm Mon-Sat, 6-11pm Sun) Everyone knows Tiffany, despite her efforts to remain mysterious. There's no menu, but the chefs grill up a treat. The restaurant's off rr Fehmi Agani, opposite the stadium.

Renaissance-2 (☎ 044118/96; meals €15; ⊙ 6-11pm) You only pay for your chair at Renaissance-2. Warm traditional atmosphere (complete with piano) is a surprising thing to find down an alleyway off bulevardi Nëna Terezë (follow the signs to Caffe PikNik opposite Radio Kosovo).

Restaurant Ex (☎ 044157039, 044557700; rr Fehmi Agani nr 3/8; mains €6; ⊙ 8am-11pm Mon-Sat, 4-11pm Sun) The easy-to-miss entrance of Restaurant Ex opens into an elegant eatery lit with ambient streetlights. The menu changes regularly; if it still features, try the rich red curry (€4.50).

Home (☎ 244 041, 044336336; home@pristinanet.com; mains €7; ⊙ 7am-11pm Mon-Sat, 11am-11pm Sun; Ⓥ) Ambient lighting and an ambitious veal-laden menu (dishes €6.50 to €7) pitched at expats. Vegetarians opt for the tasty eggplant tower (€6.50). Book ahead for the three-course weekend brunch (€7.90).

Restaurant Pizzeria XIX (☎ 044300022, 248 022; www.xixonline.com; rr Luan Haradinaj 2; ⊙ 7am-midnight Sun-Thu, to 2am Fri & Sat) This rugged place gets good mileage from its pizza oven, which bakes

KOSOVO

sandwiches (€1.50 to €2.50) as well as pizzas (€2.50 to €6). Full English breakfast with coffee costs €4.

DRINKING

Strip Depot (☎ 222 888; rr Rexhep Luci; ☺ 8am-midnight Mon-Sat, 9am-midnight Sun) Nothing to do with stripping but lots to do with conversation and cocktails, this place is the lounge room of Pristina's philosophers and their sycophants.

Blue Sky Caffe (☎ 377 44 411 117, 377 44 373 177; www.blueskycaffe.com; rr Luan Haradinaj; ☺ 9am-midnight) Buried in the shopping centre behind the UN, Blue Sky is a hip hang-out where staff have as much fun as patrons. Light streams through the roof during the day, and at night there's often a DJ.

Publicco (☎ 044627927; www.gizzigroup.com/publico; rr Garibaldi nr 7; ☺ 8am-1am) This suave bar has cool stone walls, leather-look lounges, and attentive but laid-back staff.

GETTING THERE & AWAY
AIR
For details of airlines flying to and from Kosovo, see p280.

To/From the Airport
There are supposedly regular buses (€3, 30 minutes, 18km, every two hours between 5am and 11pm) between the airport and Hotel Grand, but the timetable is unreliable. At the airport, ask at the information booth on your right when you exit the arrivals hall. Official taxis charge €20 to €25, unofficial taxis (a guy with a car) €10 to €12.

Bus
The major **bus station** (Stacioni i Autobusëve; ☎ 550 011; rr Lidja e Pejes) is 2km northwest of the centre off bulevardi Bil Klinton.

GETTING AROUND
Bus
Small kombis (minibuses) can be pulled over anywhere. Rides cost between €0.30 and €0.50, but taxis are so cheap it's unlikely you'll need them.

Taxi
Kosovar taxi drivers are honest folk who generally flick on the meter unprompted. Local trips are rarely more than a few euros; the meter starts at €1.50. Operators include **Radio Taxi** (☎ 044111999) and **VIP taxi** (☎ 044333444), and

queues are everywhere. Unofficial operators must be negotiated with, but generally the price starts fairly.

AROUND PRISTINA

The following gems are but a €1 bus ride from Pristina.

GRAČANICA MONASTERY
Dusty gold fingers of sunlight pierce the darkness of this **monastery** (☺ 6am-5pm), completed in 1321 by Serbian King Milutin. Admission is free, but you may pay the price of feeling generally unwelcome by resident nuns. The enchanting place is guarded by KFOR soldiers; bring your passport. Here you can buy a copy of *Crucified Kosovo*, showing Serbian sites damaged or destroyed in conflicts, coded by flags to show on whose watch it happened.

The only thing hinting at potential unrest in this sleepy Serbian enclave is the regular patrols of benign but heavily armed Swedish KFOR soldiers.

From Pristina, take a Gjilan-bound bus (€0.50, 15 minutes, every 30 minutes). Ask to be let out in Gračanica.

GADIMË CAVE
This **cave** (admission €2.50; ☺ 9am-7pm) is an underground marvel discovered in 1969 by Ahmet Diti (who was home-renovating) and opened for visitors in the mid-'70s. Famed for curly stalagmites, the cave can only be visited with a guide, who will crank up the generator and enthusiastically point out shapes like a hand, an elephant head and various body parts which only the most active (male) imagination can see. You may be more comfortable with companions (and a jumper – it's about 15ºC).

Buses go to Gadimë (€1, 30 minutes, every half-hour) via Lipjan. On Sunday your best bet is a Ferizaj-bound bus. Ask to be dropped at the Gadimë turn-off and walk the 3km to town.

PEJA (PEĆ)
☎ 039
Pressed against the lush border region shared by Montenegro and Albania, Peja is flanked by sites vital to Orthodox Serbians and has a Turkish-style bazaar at its heart. The Lumbardhi River flows through town.

ORIENTATION & INFORMATION

From Hotel Royal Arda, follow the river towards the mountains past a catalogue of eateries. Diagonally opposite it, the brown-and-orange Bankosi building is near eateries and ATMs. **Raiffeisen Bank** (☑ 8am-6pm Mon-Fri, 10am-2pm Sat) is between here and the bazaar.

SIGHTS

The bustling **bazaar** around Bajrakli mosque makes you feel as though you've turned left into Istanbul. Of note are traditional carved wooden *djepi* (cradles). On Saturday morning, generations of farmers fill the area with wooden vats of goat cheese. Follow your nose from Bajrakli mosque.

The **Patriachate of Peć** (☎ 044150755; ☑ 9am-6pm) is a slice of Serbian Orthodoxy. Multilingual Mrs Dobrilla (☎ 044150755) may be able to show you around, or purchase a booklet (€5) inside. A taxi from town costs €2. Alternatively, follow the river until the road bends inland to the KFOR checkpoint.

About 15km south of Peja, **Dečani monastery** (☎ 377 44 158 326; decani@gmx.net, RI Ul 5t Manastirit, ☑ 11am-1pm & 4-6pm) is an oasis from everything disorganised outside its walls. Services on Thursday at 8pm fall outside visiting hours; residents won't mind your attendance if you contact them beforehand.

Bring your passport to both monasteries.

SLEEPING & EATING

Hotel Gold (☎ 434 571; Ellot Engl 122/2; s/d €40/50; 🖵) Halfway between the bus station and the centre, Hotel Gold has well-furnished rooms; the corner ones afford street views.

Hotel Peja (☎ 044406777; hotel_peja@hotmail.com; Pjetro Marko; s/d €30/40; 🍴) The Peja has lovely rooms, though the bathroom may be so small you have to sit side-saddle on the toilet. Follow the laneway right of the Bankosi building.

Tiffany (☎ 044778190; pizzas €3.50; ☑ 7am-midnight) A stone's throw from Hotel Peja, Tiffany proffers dishes where flavours are full and servings are enormous. *Arrabiatta* macaroni costs €2.50 and Greek salad €2.50.

Fortuna! Club (☑ 8am-11pm) This waterfront watering hole has stone walls, glass windows, and big plans to make the food eclectic. Follow the road along the river towards the mountains from Hotel Royal Arda; it's in a busy laneway lined with eateries on your right.

Semitronix Centre (☎ 432754; semitronix3@yahoo.com; Mbretëresha Teutë; meals €4; ☑ 7am-11pm) The rooftop restaurant here, halfway between the bus station and the centre, offers average food but splendid views, particularly during daylight.

GETTING THERE & AROUND

Frequent buses serve Peja (€3, 90 minutes, every 15 to 20 minutes) from Pristina.

From Peja, several buses go to Dečani (€0.80, 30 minutes, every 20 minutes) on their way to other destinations, such as Gjakovë. It's a pleasant 2km walk from where the bus drops you. Keep to the roads – KFOR warns of unexploded ordnance (UXO) in the area.

PRIZREN

☎ 029 / pop 70,000

Laneways bustle around picturesque Prizren, shining with post-independence euphoria, but burnt-out buildings hang over the macchiato-sipping centre like a bad conscience. A heavy presence of KFOR troops protecting vandalised Orthodox churches evokes Edith Durham's comment on Prizren in 1909: 'Of one thing the populace is determined: that is, that never again shall the land be Serb.'

ORIENTATION & INFORMATION

From abandoned Hotel Theranda at the centre, across the road is Hotel Tirana, across the river is the Shadrvan (old cobbled centre), upriver is the museum, up the hill is Kalaja fortress and next door is the post office. At the centre of the Shadrvan is **Raiffeissen Bank** (☑ 8am-5pm Mon-Fri, 10am-2pm Sat) and a drinking fountain.

SIGHTS

Prizren's centrepiece, the 15th-century **Ottoman bridge**, has been superbly restored. Nearby is **Sinan Pasha Mosque** (1561), closed for renovations at the time of writing. **Gazi Mehmed Pasha Baths** were also closed, but you can admire exteriors, featuring frequently on postcards.

Opposite the post office is a marooned **minaret**, a remnant of Arasta mosque (destroyed in 1963).

Unesco site the **Orthodox Church of the Virgin of Leviša** is wrapped with barbed wire and signs threatening the use of force to dissuade would-be vandals.

The 2nd floor of the **Ethnological Museum** (admission €1; ☑ 11am-7pm Tue-Sun) is a repository of Prizren's history, with portraits and busts of

KOSOVO

past heroes. The actual building is perhaps more interesting: the Prizren League (for Albanian autonomy) organised itself here in 1878.

At the 11th-century **Kalaja fortress** there is naught to see but the stunning 180-degree view over Prizren. From here you trace the gorges for a few kilometres to the ruins of **Holy Archangels monastery**. On the way to the fortress, **St Savoir church** is hollow behind its front facade and heavily guarded by KFOR, a reminder of the fragility of Prizren's remaining relics.

SLEEPING & EATING
Upstream on the Shadrvan side of the river is a vibrant strip of bars and eateries (near the ugly bridge).

Hotel Tirana (☎ 230 818, 044216155; tirana_ho telpz@yahoo.com; rr Adem Jashari 14; s/d/tr €30/30/45) The German-speaking Tirana pulls off comfort without any attempt to coordinate decor.

Family Restaurant Besimi (average main €4; ☯ 6am-1am) At this popular option in the Shadrvan the food and people-watching position compensate for service too busy to break a smile.

GETTING THERE & AWAY
Prizren is well connected to Pristina (€3, 90 minutes, every 10 to 25 minutes), Peja (€3, 90 minutes, six daily) and Gjakovë (€2, 40 minutes, every 30 minutes).

KOSOVO DIRECTORY

ACCOMMODATION
What you pay here for a spacious room with wi-fi and a radio-playing shower would get you a cell in central Europe. Options generally fall within the midrange category; top-enders and hostels are missing from the spectrum.

Don't be lured into timeworn hotels on main roads; newer gems hide down laneways.

ACTIVITIES
Ski lifts at Brezovica (60km from Pristina) ground to a halt after independence was declared. Hopefully, skiers will return, but for the moment it's an isolated Serbian enclave with heavy KFOR presence.

Seek KFOR's advice about unexploded ordnance (UXO) before exploring nature.

BOOKS
Noel Malcolm's *Kosovo: A Short History* is authoritative. Tim Judah's *Kosovo: What Everyone Needs to Know* takes in the February 2008 independence declaration.

Ismail Kadare's *Elegy for Kosovo* revolves around the 1389 Kosovo battle (the centre of antagonism between Serbs and Albanians). Also see p22.

BUSINESS HOURS
Banks are open from 8am to 5pm Monday to Friday and 8am to 2pm Saturday, shops for around an hour longer. Restaurants close around 11pm and bars as late as the last person standing.

DANGERS & ANNOYANCES
Keep an eye on (and apply a grain of salt to) government travel advisories. Kosovo's February 2008 independence declaration led to a spate of Serb-Albanian conflict, making northern municipalities no-go zones at the time of writing.

Always carry your passport to present to KFOR soldiers.

There's still some UXO; seek KFOR advice before venturing off beaten tracks.

Organised-crime groups have bigger fish to fry than low-profile travellers.

Make sure your insurance covers travel in Kosovo, and reconsider driving. See p280.

EMBASSIES & CONSULATES
At the time of writing, the following embassies were coming into being in Pristina.

Albania (☎ 248 208; mission.kosova@mfa.gov.al; Qyteza Pejton, rr Mujo Ulqinaku 18)

Germany (☎ 254 500; www.konsulate.de/kosovo _e.php; Azem Jashanica 17)

PRACTICALITIES

■ The *Koha Ditore* (Daily Times) newspaper is widely read.

■ KFOR Radio 96.6FM broadcasts safety information (www.radiokfor.com).

■ RTK public service broadcaster is available at www.rtklive.com/eng/index.php.

■ Stay posted with UNMIK's Division of Public Information, www.unmikonline .org/pio.htm.

■ The system used for weights and measures is metric.

■ Kosovo uses standard European electricity (220V to 240V/50Hz to 60Hz).

Switzerland (☎ 248 088/089/090 (Visa); www.eda.admin.ch/pristina; Adrian Krasniqi 11; ⏲ 8.15am-noon & 2-3pm Mon-Fri)
UK (☎ 254 700; www.britishembassy.gov.uk; Ismail Qemajli 6; ⏲ 8.30am-5pm Mon-Thu, to 1.30pm Fri)
USA (☎ 5959 3119; http://pristina.usembassy.gov; Arberia, Nazim Hikmet 30; ⏲ 8am-5pm Mon-Fri)

In the absence of consular representation, contact embassies in Skopje (p328).

FESTIVALS & EVENTS

Funds permitting, **Pristina Jazz Festival** (www.jazzprishtina.com) is held each November. **Skena Up** (www.skenaup.com) is an international student film and theatre festival held annually since 2003, in late November.

GAY & LESBIAN TRAVELLERS

Discrimination on the grounds of sexual orientation is illegal, but the gay scene remains deep underground.

The **Centre for Social Emancipation** (www.qesh.org) is a good contact point. Albanian-speakers should visit www.gaykosova.org.

HOLIDAYS

Official public holidays are up in the air. Kosovo's declaration of independence may earn February 17 the status. Flag Day is traditionally marked on 28 November, but this may change. Traditional Islamic holidays will likely be marked.

INTERNET RESOURCES

Department of Tourism (www.visitkosova.org)
Kosovo Government (www.ks-gov.net)
Kosovo: The Land of the Living Past (www.kosovo.net) Kosovo's culture and heritage from a Serbian perspective.
Kosovo Tourism Association (www.kotas-ks.org)
North Atlantic Treaty Organization Kosovo Force (KFOR) (www.nato.int/kfor/)
Pristina in Your Pocket (www.inyourpocket.com/city/pristina.html) Download this guide (or buy one at Library Dukagjini; see p273)
UN Interim Administration in Kosovo (UNMIK) (www.unmikonline.org)

LANGUAGE

Kosovar Albanians speak the Gheg dialect of Albanian, while Tosk is generally used for print media. Serbian is spoken in Serb enclaves, but it's not wise to use it unless absolutely sure your audience will appreciate it. Some people speak English and German. See also p454.

MAPS

International Travel Maps' *Kosovo* is a decent topographical map. KFOR maps are downloadable at www.nato.int/kfor/media/maps.htm.

MONEY

The official currency is the euro; try to arrive with small denominations. ATMs are common in Pristina, Peja and Prizren, and established businesses accept credit cards.

POST

Posting postcards anywhere costs €0.50. Letters cost between €0.70 and €2.50. Parcel postage is generally reliable; sending a kilogram costs €25 within Europe.

TELEPHONE

Small offices offer competitive calling rates, but internet calls are cheaper.

Given that the official dialling code (☎ 381) was used by the former Yugoslavia and now Serbia, there's talk of Kosovo getting its own code.

Phonecards

Vala (www.valamobile.com) SIM cards are effectively free; the €5 you initially pay includes €5 worth of credit. Recharge cards are bought from PTK and street vendors. Rates vary from around €0.50 the first minute and €0.12 each minute thereafter to €7.80 the first minute and €1.95 thereafter.

TOURIST INFORMATION

Though they primary deal with airline bookings, travel agents may offer basic information. For useful websites, see left.

TRAVELLERS WITH DISABILITIES

Travellers with disabilities should be warned that even visitors without mobility difficulties can have trouble on smashed-up pavements.

EMERGENCY NUMBERS

- Ambulance ☎ 94
- Emergency ☎ 541 644 (from Vala phones ☎ 112)
- Fire service ☎ 93
- Police ☎ 92

VISITING KOSOVO FIRST

Because Serbia doesn't consider Kosovo's entry and exit points to be official international borders, attempts to enter Serbia may be futile unless you initially entered Kosovo from Serbia.

Wheelchair access is virtually nonexistent, but help is always at hand.

VISAS

Kosovo has no visa requirements. Upon arrival, you get an UNMIK 90-day entry stamp; longer stays require police permission. There's no problem entering as a tourist, though it may raise eyebrows.

Also see the Visiting Kosovo First boxed text, above.

WOMEN TRAVELLERS

Travelling is as hassle-free in Kosovo as elsewhere in Europe. The majority of women do not wear headscarves. Conservative dress is appropriate for both sexes in places of worship of any denomination.

TRANSPORT IN KOSOVO

This section addresses travel to, from and around Kosovo. For travel throughout the Western Balkans, see p439.

GETTING THERE & AWAY
Air

Pristina International Airport (☎ 038-5958 123; www.airportpristina.com) is 18km from Pristina. Telephone numbers below are in Pristina (☎ 038).

Adria Airways (airline code JP; ☎ 543 411, 543 285; www.adria-airways.com) Hub Ljubljana.

Albanian Airlines (airline code LV; ☎ 542 056; www.albanianairlines.com) Hub Tirana.

Austrian Airlines (airline code OS; ☎ 548 435, 502 456; www.aua.com) Hub Vienna.

British Airways (airline code BA; ☎ 548 661; www.britishairways.com) Hub London Heathrow.

German Wings (☎ 355 1 526 7005; www.germanwings.com) Hub Cologne.

Germania Airlines (airline code ST; www.gexx.de) Hub Berlin.

Kosova Airlines (airline code KOS; ☎ 249 185; www.kosovaairlines.com) Hub Pristina.

Malév (Hungarian Airlines; airline code MA; ☎ 535 535, 260 026; www.malev.hu) Hub Budapest.

Meridiana (airline code IG; ☎ 5859 123; www.meridiana.it) Hub Olbia.

SAS Scandinavian Airlines (airline code SK; www.flysas.com) Hub Copenhagen.

Turkish Airlines (airline code TK; ☎ 247 711, 247 696; www.turkishairlines.com) Hub Istanbul.

Bus

Sample international fares from Pristina include Serbia's Belgrade (€19, six hours) and Novi Pazar (€5, three hours), the latter also reachable from Peja (€5, three hours) and Prizren (€10, six hours). Other international destinations include Skopje, Macedonia (€5, 1½ hours); Linz, Austria (€50, 14 hours); Podogorica, Macedonia (€15, seven hours); and Istanbul, Turkey (€30, 20 hours, 2pm).

GETTING AROUND

Street names are relatively new; it's more effective to ask directions to landmarks.

You'll occasionally see road signs bearing pictures of animals; this is KFOR's politically neutral way of navigating ('turn right at Cat Rd').

Bus

Bus services linking towns and villages are excellent. Bus stops are distinctly marked by blue signs, but buses can be flagged down anywhere. Tickets are bought on board.

Car

Check whether your insurance allows you to bring your car into Kosovo. There are several rental-car agencies in Kosovo, including **Europcar** (☎ 038-594 101; www.auto-shkodra.com), and glitzy petrol stations line major roads. It's unwise to bring in Serbian-plated cars; we've had reports about them attracting hostility.

Hard-to-spot potholes make road conditions far from safe.

It's possible to hire taxis for excursions from Pristina.

Train

The train system was stretching itself to routes including Pristina–Peja (€3, 1½ hours, 5.30pm) and Pristina–Skopje (€4, three hours, 6.24pm). Check the moderately useful and slightly apologetic website (www.kosovorailway.com), or do what locals do –get the bus.

Macedonia Македонија

With vast lakes ringed by Byzantine churches, thickly forested mountains, inexhaustible archaeological riches and endless vineyards bursting with grapes, Macedonia is truly a land of plenty. Still largely unexplored, it's also somewhat mysterious for outsiders. Yet, as the locals fondly attest, Macedonia is a little country with a big heart. This is felt in its gracious hospitality, the merry creativity of its carnivals and feasts, and in Macedonians' close ties to their faith, family and traditions. Indeed, being relatively ignored by outsiders, the country has happily retained an authenticity missing elsewhere in Europe.

Aside from Skopje and some small cities, Macedonia is all natural. Bountiful agricultural plains are intersected with rugged mountain ranges, many peaks topping 2500m. Rivers and ancient tectonic lakes dot this country where the continental and Mediterranean climate zones merge. Diverse ecosystems, with endemic flora and fauna, enhance its natural beauty.

The other main draw is history: Macedonia boasts everything from Ottoman mosques, Roman baths and antique theatres to traditional village houses, medieval castles and neolithic observatories. The prime tourist destination, Ohrid, has numerous historical attractions and an atmospheric old town, all set against a sublime and unforgettable lake.

Of course, not everything's perfect – the economy is sluggish, while littering, and insufficient flights to important destinations, still vex. Nevertheless, curious and open-minded visitors will be amply rewarded here.

FAST FACTS

- **Area** 25,713 sq km
- **Capital** Skopje
- **Currency** Macedonian denar (MKD); US$1 = 46.56MKD; UK£1 = 67.85MKD; €1 = 61.66MKD; A$1 = 31.38MKD
- **Famous for** Lake Ohrid, Byzantine monasteries, name dispute with Greece
- **Key phrases** *zdravo* (hello), *blagodaram/ fala* (thanks), *molam* (please), *prijatno* (goodbye)
- **Official language** Macedonian
- **Population** 2 million
- **Telephone codes** country code ☎ 389; international access code ☎ 00
- **Visas** not necessary for most visitors; see p330

MACEDONIA

HIGHLIGHTS

- **Ohrid** (p301) Macedonia's spiritual heart, this ethereal place is rich in cultural treasures and set against a magnificent lake.
- **Skopje** (p289) A blend of Ottoman architecture, Byzantine flourishes and Yugoslav concrete excess, with great food, cafe culture and nightlife.
- **Mariovo** (p314) Macedonia's southern-border badlands are rich in legends, mountain rivers and ghost villages.
- **Strumica** (p325) This good-natured place, in Macedonia's eastern agricultural heartland, boasts a fantastic carnival and nightlife, mountain waterfalls, Roman baths and gorgeous Byzantine churches.
- **Tikveš wine region** (p318), With its Mediterranean climate and enviable soil, the region offers winery tours, historical sites and outdoor activities.

HOW MUCH?

- **Hotel room in Skopje** 2750MKD
- **Ohrid-area private accommodation** 500MKD
- **Loaf of bread** 25MKD
- **Souvenir icon** 800MKD
- **Shot of rakija** 60MKD
- **Short taxi ride** 50MKD

LONELY PLANET INDEX

- **Litre of petrol** 71MKD
- **Litre of bottled water** 20MKD
- **Skopsko beer in shop/bar** 35/100MKD
- **Souvenir T-shirt** 450MKD
- **Street snack (burger, pizza or toasted sandwich)** 90MKD

ITINERARIES

- **One week** Explore Skopje (p289) for two days: see its *čaršija* (old-town bazaar), churches, Ottoman mosques and shops, and Kale Fortress, then unwind in its cafes. Day-trip over to Lake Matka (p297), with its idyllic canyon and cave churches. Then spend two days in Ohrid (p301) exploring its old town and beaches. Finish in fashionable Bitola (p311) and see traditional villages Dihovo (p314) and Malovište (p315).
- **Two weeks** After two nights in Skopje (p289), hire a car and stay in a Mavrovo National Park (p298) ski lodge, on the way seeing the Sufi monastery and Painted Mosque at Tetovo (p297). From Mavrovo, visit idyllic Galičnik (p299), and then Sveti Jovan Bigorski Monastery (p298), along the back road to Ohrid (p301). Spend three days there to absorb the ambience and nightlife, and boat over to Sveti Zaum church (p307) and Sveti Naum monastery (p307). Make a day trip to tranquil Elšani (p308) in Galičica National Park, or see Struga (p300) and always-entertaining Vevčani (p299). Next, hit Bitola (p311) for two days, visiting ancient Heraclea Lyncestis (p313), and tackle Mariovo (see the boxed text, p314) by jeep. Continuing through Prilep (p317), see Treskavec monastery (p318) or King Marko's Towers (p317); spend

two days in the Tikveš wine region (p318) touring wineries. Head east to Strumica (p325) for one night, seeing the Veljusa and Vodoča Byzantine churches (p326), and a mountain waterfall at Smolare or Kolešino (p327). Finally, cross the Maleševski mountains to placid Berovo (p324), finishing with the Ottoman stone towers and bridges of Kratovo (p323).

CLIMATE & WHEN TO GO

Macedonia's hot, dry summers, sustained by warm Aegean winds, exceed 40°C. In winter, temperatures may sink to -30°C in the mountains. Snowfall in high mountain areas continues from November until as late as May.

Macedonia's best between May and September. It's hectic (in Ohrid especially) in July and August.

For a Skopje climate chart, see p429.

HISTORY

The historical or geographical Macedonia is now divided between the Republic of Macedonia (38%), Greek Macedonia (51%) and Bulgaria's Pirin Macedonia (11%). For its people, their history's a source of great pride but also a heavy burden. The post-Yugoslav experience has been one of existential pressure from neighbours, constantly challenging their right to an identity. Macedonia's history is too complex for simple truths or answers; remember that many people have strong opinions.

Ancient Macedonians & Romans

As a powerful Macedonian dynasty emerged, King Philip II (r 359–336 BC) compelled the Greeks and other powers to submit. His son, Alexander the Great, spread the empire to India before suddenly dying in 323 BC. The empire soon dissolved amidst infighting. In 168 BC, Rome conquered Macedonia; its position on key trade routes (the Via Egnatia from Byzantium to the Adriatic, and the Axios from Thessaloniki up the Vardar Valley) kept cities prosperous. Today's Vlach minority, whose language derives from Latin (Aromanian), possibly descend from Romans based here.

With the preaching of the Apostle Paul, Christianity arrived in Macedonia and was soon solidified. With the Roman Empire's division in AD 395, Macedonia came under Constantinople and Greek-influenced Orthodox Christianity. During this early Byzantine period, Macedonia remained significant and was the birthplace of Emperor Justinian (r 527–565).

The Coming of the Slavs & the Macedonian Cars

The 7th-century Slavic migrations intermingled Macedonia's various peoples. In 862, two Thessaloniki-born monks, St Cyril and St Methodius, were dispatched by the Byzantine emperor to spread orthodoxy and literacy among the Slavs of Moravia (in the modern-day Czech Republic). Their disciple, St Kliment of Ohrid, would modify their Glagolitic script to create the Cyrillic alphabet. With St Naum, he propagated literacy in Ohrid – the first Slavic university – in the late 9th century.

Byzantium and the Slavs shared a religion, but sharing political power was impossible. Numerous wars unfolded between Constantinople and an expansionist Bulgarian state led by Car Simeon (r 893–927) and subsequently Car Samoil (r 980–1014). Prespa and Ohrid in Macedonia became their strongholds, until Byzantine emperor Basil II defeated Samoil at the Battle of Belasica (near today's Strumica, in eastern Macedonia) in 1014. According to legend (probably only that), he blinded 14,000 of Samoil's men in this battle.

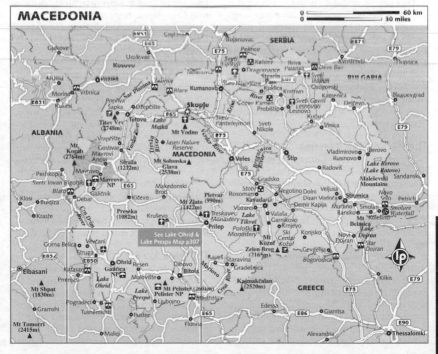

After Belasica, the Byzantines annexed Macedonia. The sack of Constantinople by Latin knights in 1204, and the rise of the Serbian Nemanjić dynasty, allowed Serbia to briefly expand into Macedonia, where it built several important churches. However, after Emperor Stefan Dusan (r 1331–1355) died, Serbian power waned. The Ottoman Turks soon arrived, and Macedonia would remain theirs until 1913.

Ottoman Rule

The Ottomans introduced Islam and Turkish settlers to Macedonia. Christians were essentially second-class citizens; some, especially Albanians, began converting to Islam for social benefits. However, the Turks allowed the Orthodox Macedonians to preserve their culture, though some restrictions (particularly regarding church building) applied. After the 1492 Spanish Inquisition, the sultan took in Sephardic Jews forced from Spain, and Macedonian towns such as Bitola became major centres of Balkan Jewish life.

The Macedonians adapted to Turkish rule, as resistance was futile. Skopje became a trade centre, and the Turks built beautiful mosques, hamams and forts. However, even though the Turks were in charge, Greeks wielded considerable behind-the-scenes power. In 1767, Greek intriguing led to the abolition of the seven-centuries-old Ohrid archbishopric. Greek priests started opening schools and building churches in Macedonia, to the resentment of the Macedonians. Bulgaria and Serbia also sought Macedonia. The lines were drawn.

The Macedonian Question

In Macedonia, Western European ethnic nationalism collided violently with the Ottomans' organisation of citizens by religion, not ethnicity. Europe's great powers got involved after the Russo-Turkish War of 1877–78, when the Treaty of San Stefano awarded Macedonia to Bulgaria. However, with Western powers fearful of Russia, the ensuing Treaty of Berlin reversed the decision; the enmities this inspired fuelled 40 years of conflict.

After the Berlin treaty, Macedonia remained Ottoman, but the 'Macedonian question' persisted. With the Turks' days in Europe numbered, various Balkan powers sponsored revolutionary groups. Greek *Makedonomahi* ('Macedonia fighters') emerged and, in 1893,

the Internal Macedonian Revolutionary Organisation (in Macedonian, Vnatrešna-Makedonska Revolucionerna Organizacija, or VMRO) was formed. VMRO was fatally divided, however, between 'Macedonia for the Macedonians' propagandists and a pro-Bulgarian wing.

The Ottoman army, and especially the *bashibazouks* (gangs of Turkish and Albanian Muslim irregulars) conducted massacres of Macedonian peasants. In the Ilinden (St Elijah's Day) Uprising (2 August 1903), Macedonian revolutionaries declared the first Balkan republic in Kruševo; the Turks crushed it 10 days later. Although nationalist leader Goce Delčev had died months earlier, he's considered Macedonia's national hero today.

Turkish atrocities played big in the European press, and an 'advisory' mission in Macedonia, the Murzsteg Reform Programme, was implemented from 1902 to 1908. However, this ineffectual program merely saw European powers jostle for influence, and the chaos continued. A reformist secret society, the Young Turks, penetrated the Ottoman military and in July 1908 a pro–Young Turk military detachment in Resen, near Lake Prespa, marched on Constantinople, demanding Sultan Abdulhamid reinstate the Ottoman Constitution of 1876. He did, but tensions grew.

In 1912 the Balkan League (Greece, Serbia, Bulgaria and Montenegro) declared war on Turkey: in this, the First Balkan War, Macedonia was the prime battleground. The Turks were expelled, but Bulgarian dissatisfaction led Sofia to declare war on its former allies in 1913 (the Second Balkan War). Bulgaria was soon defeated, but quickly allied with Germany and Austria in WWI and then reoccupied Macedonia. The trenches separating them from the British, Greeks, French and Serbs to the south essentially conform to today's Macedonia–Greece border. Macedonia's population was again beset by rivals demanding their allegiance, and further divided.

The Yugoslav Experience

The end of WWI saw Bulgaria defeated and Macedonia divided between Greece and the new Kingdom of Serbs, Croats and Slovenes (Royalist Yugoslavia). The Belgrade authorities banned the name Macedonia and the Macedonian language. Disgruntled VMRO elements helped Croat nationalists assassinate

Serbian king Aleksandar in 1934. During WWII, resistance to the Bulgarian-German occupation was led by Josip Broz Tito's Partisans. He promised Macedonians republican status within a communist Yugoslavia but had no interest in the Macedonian people or their goals; Macedonian Partisans pushing to fight for Greek-controlled Macedonia were shot as an example to the rest. Nevertheless, the Greek communists got many Macedonians there to fight the Royalists in the 1946–49 Greek Civil War. Their defeat forced thousands of Macedonians, many of them children (known as the *begalci,* or refugees) to flee Greece. The Athens government conducted a policy of assimilation on those left behind.

After WWII the communists redistributed Macedonia's wealth, as in other Yugoslav republics. Nationalisation of property and industry ruined villages, with farmers soon deprived of their flocks. Tito's concrete monstrosities sheltered the newly urbanised populations. Nevertheless, some nation-building overtures were made: a Macedonian grammar was released in 1952 and the Macedonian Orthodox Church was created in 1967 – the 200th anniversary of the Ohrid archbishopric's abolition.

Macedonia After Independence

In a referendum on 8 September 1991, 74% of Macedonians voted to split from Yugoslavia. In January 1992 the Republic of Macedonia declared full independence. Macedonian president Kiro Gligorov negotiated a peaceful withdrawal of the Yugoslav army – the only such withdrawal in any of the Yugoslav republics.

The Greeks, however, were enraged. Macedonia's first flag bore the Vergina star – the ancient Macedonian royal symbol – and Greece argued that use of the Macedonian name implied territorial claims on northern Greece, something the Macedonian side has continually denied.

Vigorous Greek lobbying thus forced Macedonia to accept a 'provisional' name, the Former Yugoslav Republic of Macedonia (FYROM), to gain UN admission in April 1993. When the USA (following six EU countries) recognised the country as FYROM in February 1994, Greece retaliated with an economic embargo. In November 1995 Greece relented when Macedonia changed its flag and agreed to further name negotiations.

Macedonia's first independent years were ruled by the Social Democrats, led by Branko Crvenkovski, later president from 2004 to 2009. As in other transition countries, new oligarchs arose amidst shady privatisations, deliberate bankrupting of state-owned firms and dubious pyramid schemes. Public disgust was manifest in 1998, when the nationalist VMRO-DPMNE – self-declared successors to the VMRO revolutionaries of 1893 – won elections.

However, tensions were simmering with Macedonia's ethnic Albanians, who complained of ill treatment. Macedonians considered their ethnic neighbours provocateurs, as when an Albanian-speaking university was illegally created in Tetovo in 1995. During the 1999 NATO bombing of Serbia, Macedonia sheltered over 400,000 Kosovo Albanian refugees; despite this, emboldened separatist leaders from the Ushtria Çlirimtare Kombëtare (UÇK; National Liberation Army) attacked it in early 2001. The conflict lasted six months, until the Ohrid Framework Agreement was signed, granting more minority rights for languages and national symbols, along with quota-based public-sector hiring.

In 2002 the Social Democrats, together with the erstwhile Albanian rebels, won elections. Implementing the Framework Agreement was difficult, though, especially when it came to power decentralisation and municipal re-districting. The agreement stipulated more rights for local minorities comprising 20% of the population; through political horse trading, the coalition partners were accused of gerrymandering new municipal boundaries to meet Albanian wishes, disadvantaging other ethnic groups. In the future, this 'solution' might effectively mean a bi-ethnic (not multi-ethnic) Macedonia.

Towards Europe

Macedonia is enacting EU-membership reforms and has restructured its army to NATO standards, participating in peacekeeping missions abroad. However, Greece blocked Macedonia's NATO invitation in April 2008, citing the unresolved name issue – a stance that frustrated not only Macedonians but also many foreign leaders. Greece said it would block Macedonia's future NATO – and EU – membership, and nationalism surged in both countries. In summer 2008, Macedonian prime minister Nikola Gruevski reminded world leaders of Greece's failure to recognise its Macedonian minority, prompting Athens to accuse Skopje of meddling in its internal affairs. Western countries pressured both sides to resolve their differences.

Through all of this turbulence, Macedonians today try to stay optimistic. Although the economy remains slow, things are improving: more cash is circulating and the government is working on economic development. Ethnic tensions have dissipated. EU membership seems distant, but unpopular EU-ordered laws (for example, restrictions on smoking) are already here. Still, for many Macedonians, joining the EU simply means the ability to travel and work without visas.

PEOPLE
Macedonia's population of 2,022,547 people (in 2004) was divided thus: Macedonians (66.6%), Albanians (22.7%), Turks (4%), Roma (2.2%), Serbs (2.1%) and others (2.4%). Most Serbs live near the Serbia border, while most Albanians live in the northern and western towns nearest to Kosovo and Albania. The ancestral villages of the Vlachs, long assimilated into Macedonianness, surround Bitola. Ottoman holdovers like the Yörük Turks inhabit eastern villages between Strumica and Radoviš. Turks also live between Debar and Tetovo, in Skopje, and elsewhere. The disadvantaged Roma are mostly urban, surviving through begging and odd jobs.

Ethnic Macedonians live most everywhere, with eastern Macedonia especially having few other ethnic groups. An interesting recent twist is the Bulgarian government's offer to grant passports to any Macedonian who could 'prove' their Bulgarian ancestry – not particularly difficult, considering Bulgaria doesn't recognise the Macedonian identity. So far over 3000 people have been granted citizenship, though it's clear that their interest has less to do with Bulgarian affinity than with having an EU passport.

RELIGION
Most Macedonians are Orthodox Christians, with a few Macedonian-speaking Muslims (the so-called Torbeši and Gorani, in western Macedonia). Albanians are predominantly Muslim, though Catholics exist (Mother Teresa grew up here as Agnes Gonxha Bojaxhiu, in an Albanian Catholic family). A Jewish community of about 200 people is descended from Sephardic Jews who fled Spain. Before WWII they were prominent, but in March 1943 the Bulgarian occupation army deported 7200 Jews – 98% of Macedonia's entire Jewish population – to the Treblinka concentration camp. However, some heroic Macedonian families sheltered Jews or helped them to escape. Today, the community retains its traditions, and holds a Holocaust commemoration ceremony every 11 March.

With post-communist property denationalisation, religious groups have sought reparations. The Islamic community has complained of insufficient reimbursement, though many new mosques have been built.

The Macedonian Orthodox Church was created in 1967, but neighbouring Orthodox countries (Serbia, Bulgaria and Greece) don't recognise it. The church has become more prominent in recent years, and church-building and restoration work has increased, with over 70 monasteries and convents reoccupied. Although Macedonians don't attend church services often, you'll see them stop by church to light a candle, kiss icons and pray.

ARTS
Architecture
Macedonia is famous for stonemasonry. Traditional village dwellings are boxy stone structures intersected with thick timber; red terracotta roofs adorn both village homes and townhouses. Ohrid's distinctive traditional mansions are white, multilevel houses with overhanging wood balconies, brown trim and red-tiled roofs. The upper floor is always wider than the one below it. Bitola has some gorgeous architecture, dating from the late Ottoman period. These colourful buildings have lovely curving balconies, ornate edges and narrow windows.

Cinema
Macedonia's leading filmmaker, Milčo Mančevski, highlighted interethnic relations in the Oscar-nominated *Before the Rain* (1994). In it, a Macedonian monk falls for an ethnic Albanian girl accused of murder. Mančevski's next film, *Dust* (2001), was an Ilinden Uprising–era cowboy classic that riled the Greeks (see p284). In 2007 Mančevski released *Semki* (Shadows) a racy urban love story with supernatural overtones. In it, an elderly female speaking an 'Aegean'

Macedonian dialect intones the film's recurring line – 'give back what is not yours'. The Greeks were infuriated; Mančevski insisted it was not a nationalistic reference.

Music & Dance

In 2006, near Veles, Macedonians discovered a 6000-year-old object with three small holes: a neolithic flute, producing an eerie, melancholic sound, that is among the world's oldest known instruments.

Macedonian folk instruments include the *gajda*, a single-bag bagpipe, played solo or accompanied by a large drum, the *tapan*, which is played with different sticks for different tones. The *kaval* (flute) and/or *tambura* (small lute with two pairs of strings) are other instruments, as is the Turkish-inherited *zurla* (a double-reed horn, also accompanied by the *tapan*). The *Čalgija* music form, involving clarinet, violin, *darabuk* (hourglass-shaped drum) and *đoumbuš* (banjo-like instrument) is representative. Macedonian music employs the 7/8 time signature.

Traditional bands play at weddings and on holidays, and at festivals like Ohrid's Balkan Festival of Folk Dances & Songs (p305) and the Galičnik Wedding (p299).

Macedonian traditional folk dancing includes the *oro*, a simple Balkan circle dance. The real show-stopper, the male-only *Teškoto oro* (difficult dance), accompanied by the *tapan* and *zurla*, is performed in traditional Macedonian costume. The *Komitsko oro* symbolises the anti-Turkish struggle, while the *Tresenica* is a women's dance.

The Ministry of Culture website (www .culture.in.mk) lists dates and venues for performances. Try to see the national folk-dance ensemble, **Tanec** (☎ 1 021; www.tanec.com .mk; Vinjamin Macukovski 7, Skopje).

FOOD & DRINK
Staples & Specialities

Macedonia's specialities combine Ottoman flavours with central European tastes. Condiments include *ajvar*, a sweet red-pepper sauce, and *lutenica*, like *ajvar* but with hot peppers and tomatoes. The national salad, *šopska salata*, features tomatoes and cucumbers topped with *sirenje* (white cheese). *Čorba* (soup) is popular, as is *tavče*

KNOW YOUR WINE

If you want to truly appreciate Macedonia's wines, take a minute to learn about what makes them so special. Besides the usual French varieties (merlot, chardonnay, pinot noir and cabernet sauvignon), the country's 240,000 tons of grapes grown annually are used to produce several others unique to the region.

Vranec, a hearty Balkan red that gets better with age, is Macedonia's signature style. The most famous vranec is T'ga Za Jug, made by Tikveš Winery in Kavadarci and named after Macedonia's favourite national poem (see p300). With its intense ruby-red colour, taste of forest fruits and subtle sweetness, it's been compared to a Californian barbera.

Temjanika, Macedonia's most popular white, is a dry, semisweet wine with remarkable freshness, best by itself or with dessert. The gold-toned traminec has a more complex taste, involving fruits, spices and even lavender. It's also a good dessert wine.

Stanošina, however, is most beguiling. An indigenous variety grown only in Macedonia, this delicate rosé carries hints of strawberry and raspberry. Stanošina grapes ripen very late, but the wine itself is best drunk young.

Winery tasting tours should be organised in advance, through travel agencies or the wineries themselves. Most cost from €10 to €20 per person and include seeing the winery's facilities and tasting several wines accompanied by meats, cheeses and sometimes chocolates or fruit.

If you haven't time to visit the Tikveš wine region (see p318) and want to find some good winemakers in the Skopje area, three favourites are **Skovin** (☎ 02-3175 107; info@skovin.com.mk; 15th Korpus, No 3), **Chateau Kamnik** (☎ 02-252 352; contact@chateaukamnik.com) and **Kartal** (☎ 02-2461 700; info@kartal.com.mk).

For more information, visit Macedonia's wine portal (www.winemk.com), the informative www .macedonianwineroute.com or www.mkwineriesguide.com.mk. And remember these words: *degustacija na vino* (Macedonian for wine tasting)!

gravče (oven-cooked white beans). Tetovo and Prespa are famous for beans, the latter also for apples.

Skara (grilled meat), prepared as spare ribs, beef *kebapci* (kebabs) and *uviač* (rolled chicken or pork stuffed with yellow cheese), is hugely popular. Eastern Macedonian speciality *pastrmajlija* is a bit like Turkish *pide*, with pork chunks and egg. *Selsko meso* ('village meat') is pork and mushrooms simmered in brown sauce in a ceramic pot.

For breakfast, try *burek* (cheese, spinach or minced meat in filo pastry) accompanied by drinking yoghurt or *kiselo mleko* (sour milk, like yoghurt).

The strong, bitter Skopsko Pivo is Macedonia's leading beer, followed by the lighter Zlaten Dab. The national firewater, *rakija*, is a strong grape spirit, delicious when served hot with sugar in winter. *Mastika*, like ouzo, is also popular. Macedonians enjoy making homemade brandies from cherries and plums. The Tikveš region produces excellent wines. (p318).

Where to Eat & Drink

Burek are found at the *burekdžilnica* (*burek* shop), sweets at the *slatkarnica*. Grill joints serving kebabs are *kebapčilnici*. Many eateries call themselves 'restoran', with no specialisation mentioned. The older term *kafana* suggests a restaurant with traditional food accompanied by live music, while a *gostilnica* indicates a simple soup-and-meat place. The words *kafič* and *kafeteria* both mean cafe.

For a list of Macedonian eating and drinking words, see p45.

ENVIRONMENT
The Land

Macedonia's 25,713 sq km is mostly plateau (600m to 900m above sea level), though over 50 mountain peaks top 2500m. It's also where the continental and Mediterranean climate zones converge, and alpine climates exist. The Vardar River passes Skopje and runs into the Aegean near Thessaloniki. Ohrid and Prespa Lakes, in the southwest, are two of the oldest tectonic lakes (around three million years old); at 300m, Ohrid is the Balkans' deepest lake. Lining the borders are mountains, including Šar Planina, near Kosovo in the northwest; Mt Belasica, in the southeast, bordering Greece; and the Osogovski and Maleševski ranges, in the west, abutting Bulgaria. Macedonia's highest peak, Mt Korab (Golem Korab; 2764m), borders Albania near Mavrovo.

Wildlife

Macedonia belongs to the eastern Mediterranean and Euro-Siberian vegetation region. Upper slopes are pine clad, while the lower mountains feature beech and oak. Vineyards dominate the central plains. Endemic fauna includes the molika tree, a subalpine pine unique to Mt Pelister, and the very rare *foja* tree on Golem Grad island in Lake Prespa.

Macedonia's alpine and low Mediterranean valley zoological zones contain forest fauna such as bears, wild boars, wolves, foxes, chamois and deer. The rare lynx inhabits Šar Planina. Blackcaps, grouse, white Egyptian vultures, royal eagles and forest owls inhabit woodlands, while lake birds include Dalmatian pelicans, herons and cormorants.

OHRID TROUT: JUST OPT OUT

Macedonia's most famous fish, the Ohrid trout, is a denizen of long standing, having inhabited the lake since before the last ice age. Unfortunately, modern humans may end this historic run. Overfishing and the destruction of the reed belts that compose the fish's natural habitat are taking their toll, and this dappled wonder of nature has become an endangered species.

Although the Macedonian government has declared a fishing moratorium, many continue to hook the trout. And, as a quick peek at many restaurant menus reveals, people continue to eat it.

Why? Ohrid trout is much more expensive than other local trout varieties, and it's considered a delicacy. Still, this may be one culinary experience conscientious travellers can postpone till the trout's stock rises.

So if you'd like some good fish while in Macedonia, go for a *mavrovska, kaliforniska* or *rekna* (river) trout instead – they're just as tasty, and you'll save money and help Macedonia's ecological situation too.

A SUSTAINABLE FUTURE

Suffering from low visibility abroad, little Macedonia must try extra hard to highlight what it has to offer. Dragi Pop-Stojanov, executive director of the Macedonian Tourism Chamber and backer of the eco-tourism initiative in Brajčino (see p310), is optimistic. 'We don't have a sea coast,' he says. 'So we must concentrate on what we have – pristine mountains, history and authentic traditional villages, a very special combination.' Dragi looks to alternative activities such as outdoor-adventure tourism, yoga tourism, monastery tourism and wine tourism. 'But the key is to make tourism sustainable,' he says, 'or we cannot succeed in the long term.'

A man who has taken the vision of environmental sustainability to heart is the gracious Boris Trajanov, one of the world's top opera singers. Wanting to create 'a better future for all of our citizens', Boris led a remarkable initiative to plant two million trees in a single day – on 11 March 2008 – a huge undertaking involving thousands of volunteers.

Then, at the end of November, Trajanov's volunteers beat this record by planting a staggering six million trees in one day – and looked forward to 11 March 2009, when they plant 20 million more.

With the widespread forest fires of summer 2007 unfortunately repeating in August 2008, Macedonia will need all the trees it can get. Trajanov, an official Unesco Artist for Peace, considers his initiative a small step to help Macedonia's environment, and something that might inspire neighbouring countries to join forces on similar initiatives 'for a sustainable common future'. The Den na Drvoto (Day of the Tree) is to be repeated annually on 11 March, in tandem with neighbouring countries.

Storks (and their huge nests) are visible. Macedonia's national dog, the *šar planinec*, is a 60cm tall sheepdog that will fight bears and wolves.

Lakes Ohrid, Prespa and Dojran are separate fauna zones, due to territorial and temporal isolation. Ohrid, which boasts 146 endemic species, is a living museum of the fossil age. Ohrid's endemic trout predates the last ice age. Ohrid also has whitefish, gudgeon and roach, plus a 30-million-year-old snail genus, and the mysterious Ohrid eel, which arrives from the Sargasso Sea to live for 10 years before returning to breed and die; its offspring restart the cycle. Lake Tikveš catfish reach 200kg.

National Parks

Macedonia's national parks are Pelister (near Bitola; see p315), Galičica (between Lakes Ohrid and Prespa; see p308) and Mavrovo (between Debar and Tetovo; see p298). Pelister and Galičica are part of a tri-border protected area involving Albania and Greece. Hiking in summer and skiing at Mavrovo in winter are fantastic. All parks are accessible by road; none requires tickets or permits.

Environmental Issues

Despite strict new laws, littering continues and recycling is rare.

SKOPJE СКОПЈЕ

☎ 02 / pop 640,000

Don't let the drab Yugoslav-era architecture fool you   Skopje's a lively town, and one with more to it than meets the eye. It's both an outgoing place where shopkeepers shout greetings across cobbled lanes and lithe young in-line skaters blaze by, and a conspiratorial one where political apparatchiks and foreign diplomats crouch over their coffees – a place where everyone knows something about everyone else.

While much of what makes Skopje tick will be lost on the first-time visitor, there's also much to enjoy. Crossing the Vardar River on the 15th-century Stone Bridge (Kamen Most) leads into the Čaršija (old Turkish bazaar), with its enduring Ottoman attractions. Here, the handsome mosques and Turkish baths renovated into art galleries are interspersed with shops where skilled craftsmen fashion silver, gold and clothing. Above it looms Tvrdina Kale (the city fort), still yielding up archaeological treasures.

Skopje also offers great cafes and night-life. Its clubs are pumping and there's always something on, from jazz and classical to opera, theatre and rock. It might not make many lists of top European capitals, but then again, Skopje might surprise you.

MACEDONIA

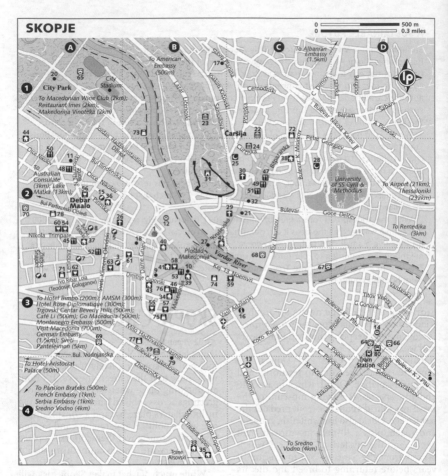

SKOPJE

HISTORY

From 148 BC, Roman law and culture reigned in the Paionian-founded Scupi. With the empire's division in AD 395, Scupi and Macedonia became Byzantine. After an earthquake in 518, local son and Byzantine emperor Justinian rebuilt it further north. However, 7th-century Slavic invaders destroyed it, resettling on present-day Skopje, and calling it thus.

Skopje passed through Bulgarian, Byzantine and Serbian hands before being captured by Turks in 1392. An important Ottoman commercial centre, it was damaged by an earthquake in 1555. Then, in 1689, Austrian general Piccolimini burned Skopje during a war with Turkey.

After the Ottomans and WWI, Macedonia entered Royalist and subsequently communist Yugoslavia. Skopje grew, but an earthquake destroyed much of it on 26 July 1963. More than 1000 people were killed and 120,000 made homeless. Afterwards, Yugoslav president Tito brought in workers, new residents and architects. Except for Ottoman and Byzantine sites, Skopje's classic architecture had disappeared; concrete communist constructions replaced it.

ORIENTATION

The Vardar River, spanned by the Stone Bridge and other bridges, divides Skopje. North of it is the Čaršija and south is the new town, where a pedestrianised central zone

INFORMATION			
Ajvar Internet	1 B2	Soboren Hram Sveti Kliment	
Atlantis Travel	2 D4	Ohridski	26 A2
British Embassy	3 A3	Stone Bridge	27 B2
Bulgarian Embassy	4 A3	Sultan Murat Mosque	28 C2
Canadian Embassy	5 A2	Sveti Dimitrija	29 C2
City Hospital	6 B3	Sveti Spas	30 C2
Contact Café	(see 74)	Trvdina Kale Fortress	31 B2
Dutch Embassy	7 A3	Čifte Amam	32 C2
Greek Embassy	8 A2		
Ikona Bookstore	9 B3	SLEEPING	
Knizharnica Tri	(see 74)	Art Hostel	33 B4
Kultura Bookstore	10 B3	Best Western Hotel Turist	34 B3
Macedonia Travel	11 A2	Hostel Hostel	35 B4
Main Post Office	12 B2	Hotel Ambasador	36 A2
Menuvačnica Euro	(see 74)	Hotel Ani	37 A2
Neuromedica	13 C4	Hotel Arka	38 C2
Post Office	14 D3	Hotel Dal Met Fu	39 B3
Post Office	(see 74)	Hotel Jadran	40 B2
Post Office	(see 77)	Hotel Square	41 B3
Russian Embassy	15 A2	Hotel Stone Bridge	42 B2
Telephone Centre	(see 12)	Hotel TCC Plaza	43 B3
Tourist Information Centre	16 C3	Tim's Apartments	44 A1
Visit Macedonia	17 B1		
World Press Shop	18 B2	EATING	
		Amiri Miei	45 A2
SIGHTS & ACTIVITIES		Burekdžilnica Rekord	46 B3
Bit Pazar	(see 72)	Dal Met Fu Restaurant	(see 39)
City Art Gallery	(see 21)	Destan	47 C2
City Museum	19 B3	Idadija	48 A2
City Park	20 A1	Kapan An	49 C2
Daud Paša Baths	21 C2	Papu	50 A2
Kuršumli An	22 C1	Pivnica An	51 C2
Museum of		Slatkarnica Stella	52 A3
Contemporary Art	23 B1	Wine Restaurant Nana	53 B3
Museum of Macedonia	24 C2		
Mustafa Paša Mosque	25 C2	DRINKING	
		Aja	54 A2

Barcelona	55 B3	ENTERTAINMENT	
Bastion	56 A2	Club Castro	64 D3
Café di Roma	57 B3	Colosseum (summer location)	65 A1
Café Trend	58 B3	Colosseum (winter location)	66 D3
La Bodeguito Del Medio	59 C3	Element	(see 20)
Lezet	60 A2	Hard Rock	67 D3
Mr Jack	61 B3	Kino Milenium	(see 74)
New Age	62 A3	Kino Ramstore	(see 77)
Piazza Liberta	63 A3	Macedonian National Theatre	68 C3
		Multimedia Centre Mala	
		Stanica	69 A3
		Universal Hall	70 A2
		SHOPPING	
		Beershop	71 A3
		Bit Pazar	72 C1
		Djelo	73 B1
		Gradski Trgovski Centar	74 B3
		Ikona	75 B3
		Lithium Records	(see 74)
		Militaria Makedonika	76 B3
		Ramstore Mall	77 B3
		Trgovski Centar Bunjakovac	78 A2
		TRANSPORT	
		Budget Car Rental	79 B4
		Bus Station	80 D3

spans main square Ploštad Makedonija, the Gradski Trgovkl Centar city mall, and ul Makedonija, featuring many cafes. The adjoining train and bus stations are a 10-minute walk from the square.

Maps
Get the Trimaks *New Skopje City Map* (200MKD) at **Kultura Bookstore** (Ploštad Makedonija bb).

INFORMATION
Bookshops
Ikona Bookstore (☎ 3065 312; Dimitrije Čupovski) Travel books, including Lonely Planet guides, and English-language novels.

Knizharnica Tri (Gradski Trgovski Centar) Colourful, English-language art and architecture books.

> ### STREET ADDRESSES
> Addresses given ending in 'bb' mean *bez broj* (no number). 'Lok' means the office number in a specific building.

Kultura Bookstore (☎ 3235 862; Ploštad Makedonija bb) Maps, guides and Macedonia-related books.

World Press Shop (☎ 3298 082; Vasil Glavinov 3) Foreign-language print media.

Internet Access
Skopje has many wi-fi hotspots and internet cafes, including at the train station.

Ajvar Internet (27 Mart bb; per hr 40MKD; ☺ 9am-10pm) Simple net cafe.

Contact Café (Gradski Trgovski Centar; per hr 120MKD; ☺ 9am-10pm) Central but pricier.

Media
The **World Press Shop** (Vasil Glavinov 3) has English- and European-language newspapers. Cable-TV companies carry international channels.

Medical Services
City hospital (☎ 3130 111; 11 Oktomvri 53; ☺ 24hr)

Neuromedica private clinic (☎ 3133 313; 11 Oktomvri 25; ☺ 24hr)

Remedika (☎ 2603 100; XVI Makedonska Brigada; ☺ 24hr)

MACEDONIA

SKOPJE IN TWO DAYS

Catch the morning sun while sipping an espresso at **Café di Roma** (p295) on pedestrianised ul Makedonija, before crossing the **Stone Bridge** (below) into the old town. See modern paintings at the **Daud Paša Baths** (below) and **Čifte Amam** (below). Wander the **Čaršija** (below) and savour beef kebabs at **Destan** (p294). Next, see the magnificent wood-carved iconostasis at **Sveti Spas Church** (opposite) and visit **Mustafa Pasa Mosque** (opposite). Climb Ottoman fortress **Kale** (opposite) for panoramic views. Back in the new town, watch the action at **Dal Met Fu Restaurant** (p294). By night, tackle a whisky bar like **Mr Jack** (p295), or go Cuban at **La Bodeguito Del Medio,** (p295).

On day two, visit **Lake Matka** (p297), outside Skopje, for hiking, climbing and relaxing. See Byzantine frescos at **Sveti Pantelejmon monastery** (opposite) on Mt Vodno. Have succulent *skara* (barbecued meat) at **Idadija** (p294) and dessert at **Slatkarnica Stella** (p294).

Money

ATMs and *menuvačnici* (exchange offices) abound. Try **Menuvačnica Euro** (Gradski Trgovski Centar; ☺ 9am-8.30pm Mon-Sat).

Post & Telephone

Post offices exist opposite the train station, in the Gradski Trgovski Centar and in Ramstore mall.

The train-station branch houses the telephone centre. Kiosks (newsagents) have private telephones, and display the price and sell cards for public phones.

Main post office (☎ 3141 141; Orce Nikolov 1; ☺ 7am-7.30pm Mon-Sat, 7.30am-2.30pm Sun) About 75m northwest of Ploštad Makedonija.

Tourist Information

City of Skopje Bureau for Tourism and Information (☎ 070812882; www.skopje.mk; Vasil Adzilarski bb; ☺ 8.30am-4.30pm Mon-Fri) The friendly official city tourism office offers free info on Skopje and other places in Macedonia.

Travel Agencies

Atlantis Travel (☎ 2400 941; skopje@atlantis.com.mk; Bojmija 1, lok I7m; ☺ 9am-5pm) City maps, accommodation information and in-country tours. Opposite the train station, 50m east of Cosmofon Bldg.

Go Macedonia (☎ 3232 273; www.gomacedonia.com .mk; Trgovski Centar Beverly Hills lok 32, Naroden Front 19) Arranges hiking, biking, caving and winery tours.

Macedonia Travel (☎ 3112 408; www.macedonia travel.com; Orce Nikolov 109/1, lok 3) Tours, including trips to the hard-to-access Jasen Nature Reserve, and discounted air tickets.

Visit Macedonia (☎ /fax 3071 614; www.visitmace donia.com.mk; Newdelhi 4, lok 1) Many trips, including history and archaeology tours.

SIGHTS
Ploštad Makedonija & the South Bank

Ploštad Makedonija is your orientation point. Stroll the south bank along the riverside path, or relax in one of numerous river-facing cafes jutting from the Gradski Trgovski Centar. More cafes line pedestrianised ul Makedonija, which crosses ul Dimitrije Cupovski, ending at the **City Museum** (☎ 3114 742; Mito Hadživasilev Jasmin bb; admission free; ☺ 9am-3pm Tue-Sun), which has interesting temporary exhibitions. It's in the old train station; the fingers of its stone **clock** were frozen in time at 5.17am on 27 July 1963, the moment the great earthquake struck.

The austere **Soboren Hram Sveti Kliment Ohridski** (bul Sveti Kliment Ohridski bb; admission free; ☺ 7am-8pm) is Skopje's main Orthodox cathedral. It's full on holidays and sees daily visitors who light candles in its dark, icon-rich confines. Cross over to **Debar Maalo**, with its tree-lined streets and old architecture. Follow bulevar Ilindenska to the **city park**, where kids can run around and chase the ducks and geese.

North Bank & Čaršija

From Ploštad Makedonija cross the **Stone Bridge** and enter the **Čaršija**, where Skopje's Ottoman past lingers. On the left is **Sveti Dimitrija** (☺ 9am-6pm), a handsome, three-aisled Orthodox church from 1886. Across from it rise the double domes of the **Daud Paša Baths** (1466), once the Balkans' largest Turkish bath. The building houses the **City Art Gallery** (☎ 3133 102; Kruševska 1a; admission 100MKD; ☺ 9am-3pm Tue-Sun), where modern art occupies seven rooms, illuminated by rays of sunlight coming through the domed ceiling's tiny holes.

Another beautiful old bath-turned–art gallery, **Čifte Amam** (admission 50MKD; ☺ 9am-4.45pm

MACEDONIA

Mon-Fri, to 3pm Sat, to 1pm Sun) preserves an original feel, one room left unplastered and walls revealing exposed brickwork, stone arches and old clay heating pipes.

From the Čaršija's small shops and tea houses, take ul Samoilova to **Sveti Spas** (admission 100MKD; 🕐 8am-3pm Tue-Sun). It was built underground, as the Turks didn't allow churches to be taller than mosques. The wood-carved iconostasis is 10m wide and 6m high, built by early-19th-century master craftsmen Makarije Frčkovski and the brothers Petar and Marko Filipovski. See the **Tomb and Museum of Goce Delčev**, leader of VMRO and national hero, killed by Turks in 1903.

Back in Čaršija, the **Museum of Macedonia** (🕿 3116 044; Čurčiska 86; admission 50MKD; 🕐 9am-3pm Tue-Sun) documents neolithic through communist times. The ethnographical exhibition has old costumes and traditional house models. The museum's highlights, however, are its icons and wood-carved iconostases. Archaeological items decorate the lovely **Kuršumli An** (1550), once an Ottoman caravanserai (inn).

The Čaršija ends at **Bit Pazar**, a big, busy vegetable market also selling bric-a-brac and household goods. North of the Vardar, the Albanian presence is very strong. Being Muslims as well, the Turks tend to blend in with them, though you can discern the different languages and peoples. Crossing bul Goce Delčev from Bit Pazar, you'll see **Sultan Murat mosque** (1436), with its distinctive, red-tipped clock tower and Ottoman madrassa (Islamic school) remains.

Kale & Around

Above Sveti Spas, the 1492 **Mustafa Paša mosque** (Samoilova bb) is a magnificent example of Ottoman architecture, with a lovely lawn, rose garden and fountain.

Opposite it, ascend the **Tvrdina Kale fortress**, a lengthy set of Ottoman ramparts and towers, originally built in the 6th century. Restoration and archaeological investigations continue; six layers of civilisation have been discovered, with neolithic pottery and ancient Macedonian, Roman, Bulgarian and Byzantine coins and ceramics discovered here. There are great views too.

Further up, the **Museum of Contemporary Art** (🕿 3117 735; Samoilova bb; admission 100MKD; 🕐 9am-3pm Tue-Sun) displays works by Macedonian artists and paintings by Piccasso, Hans Hortung and Andre Masson.

Mt Vodno Водно

Framing Skopje to the south, **Mt Vodno** is popular with hikers and picnickers. Topping it is the 66m-high **Millennium Cross** (2002), the world's largest, illuminated at night. Taxis drive to Sredno (Middle) Vodno (about 120MKD).

Further west along Vodno, in the Gorno Nerezi suburb-village, the **Sveti Pantelejmon monastery** (1164) has very important Byzantine frescos. Some, such as the *Lamentation of Christ*, depict a previously unseen pathos and realism that predate the Renaissance by two centuries. The church is 20 minutes by taxi (120MKD).

FESTIVALS & EVENTS

The **Skopje Jazz Festival** (🕿 3131 090; www.skopje jazzfest.com.mk; Maksim Gorki 5), held in October, is always big. Past headliners have included Tito Puente, Ray Charles, Ornette Coleman and McCoy Tyner. The organisers stage the **Off-Fest** (www.offest.com.mk) in May, combining world music and DJ events. There's also the **May Opera Evenings** (🕿 3114 691).

In December, the ever-more-popular **Taxirat Festival** (🕿 2775 430; www.lithiumrecords.com.mk; Gradski Trgovski Centar) rocks Skopje. Art exhibitions, performances and concerts compose the summertime **Skopsko Leto** (🕿 3165 064; www.dku.org.mk; bul Sveti Kliment Ohridski 58) festival.

SLEEPING

In summer or during special events, book ahead if possible. Online resources like www .allmacedoniahotels.com do hotel bookings. Macedonia Travel (see opposite) offers good-value flight-hotel combos.

Budget

Art Hostel (🕿 070233336; www.art-hostel.com.mk; Tome Arsovski 14; dm/s/d €12/25/40) This cheerful place in a residential suburb is a 20-minute walk from both the central square and the bus/train stations. There are six-bed dorms and small private rooms. All bathrooms are clean and new but shared. The hostel has a relaxed vibe, with a billiards table and low-lit outdoor balcony with couches. A similar feel prevails at smaller sister Hostel Hostel (🕿 3222 321; Ognjen Pricev 18; dorm beds/singles/doubles €12/25/40), a five-minute walk away.

MACEDONIA

Hotel Square (☎ 3225 090; 6th fl, Nikola Vapcarov 2; s/d/tr incl breakfast €45/50/75) Well situated overlooking the Ploštad, this place offers great value for location. The cosy rooms are well-kept and modern, and the balcony cafe offers lovely views.

Hotel Bimbo (☎ 321 4517; 29 Noemvri 63; s/d incl breakfast €35/50) Rooms are basic but clean, and there's a cosy breakfast nook. It's in a residential area near the centre.

Hotel Ambasador (☎ 3215 510; Pirinska 36; s/d incl breakfast €57/84) Skopje's only place for lava mud–wrap massages, the Ambasador has slightly dated but pleasant rooms. Staff are well informed and helpful.

Hotel Ani (☎ 3222 193; Borka Taleski 5; s/d/tr/apt €36/47/59/72) Fairly central, opposite the Greek embassy, Ani has decent though slightly musty rooms and helpful staff.

Pansion Brateks (☎ 3176 606; Aco Karamanov 3; s/d 1920/3200MKD) This well-kept B&B 20 minutes from downtown enjoys the clean, posh air below Mt Vodno, in a quiet, upscale neighbourhood.

Midrange

ourpick **Hotel Dal Met Fu** (☎ 3239 584; www.dalmetfu.com.mk; Ploštad Makedonija; s/d/apt from €59/65/85) A trendy, discreet boutique hotel above the eponymous restaurant, this central address offers well-designed modern rooms with flair.

Hotel Rose Diplomatique (☎ 3135 469; Roza Luksemburg 13; s/d from €65/90) This B&B has eight charming rooms and a garden. Staff are attentive.

Hotel Aristocrat Palace (☎ 3133 978; www.aristocratpalace.com.mk; Elisie Popovski 59; d/apt €80/99) This relaxing, friendly new hotel is a 15-minute walk from downtown, in the posh Vodno neighbourhood. The handsome rooms feature all mod cons, including jacuzzis in the bathrooms. There's restaurant, bar and terrace too.

Tim's Apartments (☎ 3237 650; Orce Nikolov 120; s/d/apt €69/89/110) Near the park, friendly Tim's has 10 classy rooms and seven apartments with kitchenettes.

Hotel Jadran (☎ 3118 427; 27 Mart bb; s/d €45/75) Service is a bit gruff and some of the fixtures are a bit antiquated, but the Jadran is very central and the rooms have an old-style charm, with high, lengthy ceilings.

Top End

Hotel TCC Plaza (☎ 3111 807; Vasil Glavinov 12; s/d/ste €95/115/144; 🖳) This central five-star hotel offers spacious, nicely lit rooms and suites; the spa centre includes swimming pool, fitness and massage (from 600MKD).

Best Western Hotel Turist (☎ 3289 111; Gjuro Strugar 11; s/d/ste €133/155/166) This four-star international chain hotel with all expected amenities is centrally located on ul Makedonija.

Hotel Arka (☎ 3230 603; www.hotel-arka.com.mk; Bitpazarska 90/2; s/d/ste from €88/120/157) Near Bit Pazar, the Arka is a glossy, upmarket place. Gaze down on the Čaršija through the 7th-floor pool bar's big windows.

Hotel Stone Bridge (☎ 324 900; Kej Dimitar Vlahov 1; s/d/apt €138/159/259) Near the bridge, this deluxe hotel has sophisticated rooms with stylised Ottoman furnishings – great if you can afford it.

EATING

The Čaršija has *kebapčilnici* – the classic is **Destan** (kebabs 120MKD; ⏰ 7am-11pm), with Skopje's best kebabs, accompanied by seasoned grilled bread – plus Turkish *doner* kebab and *lahmacan* (a spicy sort of pizza) places, as well as fancier joints. Several eateries are tucked inside the shaded old-town courtyard of **Kapan An** (Čaršija; mains 160-400MKD), behind Čifte Amam; it's good for *kebapci* and alfresco dining. Ploštad Makedonija has both fast-food and chic eateries, while leafy Debar Maalo is clustered with good *skara* spots.

Burekdžilnica Rekord (Dimitrije Čupovski 5; burek 45MKD; ⏰ 6am-midnight) One of Skopje's best-known *burek* joints; though tiny, it's known as a landmark.

Slatkarnica Stella (bul Sveti Kliment Ohridski 56; cakes 70-90MKD; ⏰ 7am-11pm) Hands down Macedonia's best cakes-and-pastries shop, Stella has comfortable couches, an aquarium and garden seating.

Idadija (Rade Koncar 1; mains 180-250MKD; ⏰ 8am-midnight) In Debar Maalo's *skara* corner, Idadija has been serving excellent grills for 80 years.

Amici Miei (Nikola Trimpare 6; mains 350-500MKD; ⏰ 11am-midnight) Before opening, owner Alessio Zuccarini imported his Tuscan parents to train the chefs; the frequent visits of Italian diplomats attest to the results.

Wine Restaurant Nana (Ploštad Makedonija; mains 250-450MKD; ⏰ 9am-1am) This slightly highbrow bistro has subtle decor, inventive cosmopolitan fare, and over 100 wines and spirits.

Dal Met Fu Restaurant (Ploštad Makedonija; mains 280-350MKD; ⏰ 7.30am-midnight) It might strike tourists as, well, touristy, but Dal Met Fu is appreciated by locals for its light pastas, cheerful waitresses and preening position behind big windows. The chocolate soufflé topped with ice cream is divine.

Papu (Djuro Djakovic 63; mains 220-400MKD) The tastes and decor of old Kruševo are preserved with style at this lovely place in Debar Maalo, studded with stone arches, antiques and the sounds of cascading water.

Pivnica An (☎ 3212 111; Čaršija; mains 300-500MKD; ☯ 9am-midnight) You're paying for the ambience, primarily, at this 'beerhouse' located in the sumptuous courtyard of a restored Ottoman building (while tasty, the food is overpriced).

Restaurant Imes (☎ 3061 367; Ilindenska 138a; mains 350-520MKD; ☯ 9am-midnight) This banquet-hall restaurant hosts the Macedonian Wine Club's monthly tastings (see right).

DRINKING

Cafes and bars stay open until 1am on Friday and Saturday night, till midnight the rest of the week. After that, only late-licence nightclubs can operate. Note that grocery shops and kiosks can't sell alcohol after 7pm.

ourpick La Bodeguito Del Medio (Kej 13 Noemvri; ☯ 9am-1am) Known as 'the Cuban', this gregarious riverfront place does do Cuban food – but it's best at night, when the long bar's lined with carousers and cocktails.

Café di Roma (Makedonija; ☯ 8am-1am) Italian expats swear Skopje's best espresso is served at this place, which has a stylish clientele and 150 different drinks.

Aja (Nikola Trimpere 8; ☯ 9am-1am) This glittering, ceramic-tiled cafe plays ambient house music for a laid-back young crowd.

Lezet (Nikola Trimpere 8a; ☯ 9am-1am) Next to Aja, this Ottomanesque cafe cluttered with amphorae, curtains and gurgling fountains exudes atmosphere.

Barcelona (cnr Makedonija & Luj Paster; ☯ 8am-1am) This popular cafe and night bar – with glass floors and great cocktails – plays pop, house and retro.

Bastion (Pirinska 43; ☯ 8am-1am) Bohemian Bastion is a Skopje classic, popular day and night.

Café Li (Ankarska 23; ☯ 8am-midnight) Arty Li offers speciality coffees, juices and cocktails.

New Age (Kosta Šahov 9; ☯ 9am-midnight) A hippie hangout even a pasha would love, laid-back New Age has plush floor cushions, chaise longues and weathered wood fixtures.

Café Trend (Ploštad Makedonija; ☯ 8am-1am) Aspiring socialites mix with (and gossip about) local celebrities at this slick Ploštad place.

Piazza Liberta (Veljko Vlahovic 24; ☯ 8am-1am) This beer hall has long wooden benches and floors become covered with peanut shells as the night progresses.

Mr Jack (bul Partizanski Odredi 3; ☯ 8am-1am) This rockin' night bar with 50 whiskies, draught Guinness and live bands has a mixed Macedonian international clientele.

Vinoteka Temov (Gradishte 1a; ☯ 9am-midnight) Tucked right under the church of Sveti Spas in the Čaršija, this warm and inviting wine bar has great ambience. More than 15 types of Macedonian wine can be sampled here, accompanied by fruit and cheese. There's relaxed music, plus smoking and nonsmoking floors.

ENTERTAINMENT

Little Skopje gets many international DJs; see www.skopjeclubbing.com.mk.

Colosseum (www.colosseum.com.mk; City Park summer, under train station winter) is Skopje's biggest and most popular club, along with **Element** (www.element.com.mk; City Park). When major international DJs appear, tickets run 250MKD to 500MKD.

Multimedia Center Mala Stanica (Zhelezhnička 18; ☯ 9am-midnight) Featuring arty, ornate decor, the cafe of the National Art Gallery hosts temporary exhibitions, live jazz and rock.

Club Castro (train station; ☯ 8pm-4am) This student favourite under the train station gets going late with live rock, reggae and ska.

Hard Rock (Kej Dimitar Vlahov bb; ☯ 10pm-4am) A very popular late-night place, Hard Rock features mostly DJ parties and sometimes live bands.

Macedonian Wine Club (mwc.org.mk; Ilindenska 138a; tasting 300MKD) Monthly wine tastings involve sampling from four different wineries and a *skara*-and-salads buffet at Restaurant Imes – Skopje's cheapest gourmet experience. All are welcome, but dress smart; you'll be rubbing shoulders with foreign diplomats.

Universal Hall (☎ 3224 158; bul Partizanski Odredi bb; tickets 100-200MKD) Classical, jazz, pop and even kids' performances happen here.

Macedonian National Theatre (☎ 3114 060; Kej Dimitar Vlahov bb; tickets 100-400MKD) In a communist-era building, the theatre hosts opera, ballet and classical music.

Kino Milenium (☎ 3111 111; Gradski Trgovski Centar; tickets 60-120MKD) The Kino is Skopje's largest modern cinema; Ramstore shopping mall has another.

SHOPPING

The Čaršija sells jewellery, carpets, dresses and more, while Bit Pazar sells fruit, vegetables and anything random. The **Gradski Trgovski Centar** (11 Oktomvri; ☯ 9am-8pm) is a modern mall, like the slicker **Ramstore** (Mito Hadživasilev Jasmin bb; ☯ 8am-8pm) by the City Museum. **Trgovski Centar Bunjakovec** (bul Partizanski; ☯ 9am-7pm), and **Trgovski Centar Beverly Hills** (☯ 9am-7pm) are smaller.

Ikona (☎ 3215 330; Luj Paster 19; gifts 300-7000MKD; ☯ 9am-9pm Mon-Fri, 9am-4pm Sat) 'Traditional' souvenirs, including Orthodox icons, archaeological replicas, pottery, painted boxes and folk dolls, are on offer here.

Lithium Records (Gradski Trgovski Centar; ☯ 8.30am-8pm Mon-Sat) Lithium sells CDs (Macedonian traditional and contemporary, plus major artists) and tickets for concerts and festivals in Macedonia and abroad, including Serbia's Exit Festival (see the boxed text, p401).

Djelo (Čaršija; ☯ 9am-6pm) Master filigree craftsman Xheladin Asani has long created silver and gold jewellery, boxes and pens at this tiny shop.

Makedonska Vinoteka (Ilindenska 138a; ☯ 9am-6pm) The Macedonian Wine Club's official shop, in Restaurant Imes.

Beershop (Teodosije Gologanov 47; ☯ noon-7pm, closed Sun) One of the Balkans' biggest selections (over 200 different brews!) is available here.

Militaria Makedonika (Veljko Vlahovic 5; ☯ 11am-7pm) In the market for a WWI helmet, Turkish scimitar or Yugoslav medallions? Robert Mitevski, an English-speaking military historian, explains and provides necessary certificates to accompany such loot. It's behind Burekdzilnica Rekord.

GETTING THERE & AWAY
Air
Alexander the Great Airport (Aerodrom Aleksandar Veliki; ☎ 3148 333; www.airports.com.mk) is 21km east of Skopje and handles flights from major European cities. Flying into Thessaloniki with a budget carrier and then getting a train, bus or vehicle transfer into Macedonia is often cheaper.

Bus
Skopje's **bus station** (bul Jane Sandanski; ☎ 2466 011) adjoins the train station. English is spoken, and there's an exchange office.

Buses to Ohrid go via Kičevo (three hours, 167km) or Bitola (four to five hours, 261km). In summer, book ahead. For details of domestic routes, see the table, below; for international routes, see the table, p331.

Train
The train station (Zheleznička Stanica) serves Negotino (135MKD, two hours, three daily), Prilep (170MKD, three hours, three daily) and Bitola (200MKD, four hours, three daily). The north–south line hugging the Vardar connects Skopje with Thessaloniki via Veles,

DOMESTIC BUS SERVICES FROM SKOPJE

Destination	Price (MKD)	Duration	Departures
Berovo	380	3hr	9 daily
Bitola	430	2½hr	10 daily
Brajčino	500	4hr	1 daily
Kavadarci	240	1½hr	9 daily
Kratovo	220	2hr	5 daily
Kriva Palanka	200	2hr	10 daily
Kruševo	330	3hr	3 daily
Kumanovo	100	40min	18 daily
Mavrovo	170	1½hr	4 daily Mon-Fri
Negotino	310	2hr	5 daily
Ohrid	450	3-4hr	11 daily
Prilep	330	2hr	13 daily
Probištip	250	2hr	5 daily
Resen	460	3½hr	2 daily
Strumica	360	2½hr	13 daily
Tetovo	100	40min	18 daily
Vevčani	450	4hr	2 daily

MACEDONIA

Negotino and Gevgelija (185MKD, 2½ hours, three daily) and Belgrade via Kumanovo (60MKD, 40 minutes, four daily). For international train info, see p330. Three daily trains serve Kičevo (150MKD, two hours).

GETTING AROUND
To/From the Airport
There's no airport bus. Taxi prices should be signposted; they're around 800MKD.

Bus
Skopje city buses cost 25MKD to 35MKD.

Car
Daily rental prices start at 2600MKD. Try **Budget Car Rental** (☎ 3290 ???; Mito Hadživasilev Jasmin bb; ☿ 9am-5pm).

Taxi
Skopje's taxi base rate is 50MKD, and drivers use their meters. Central destinations cost 50MKD to 100MKD. **Pulstar** (☎ 15177) and **Vardar** (☎ 15165) are two fair and reliable taxi companies, but generally any cab displaying a five-digit number starting with 151 is OK. Don't take a bus-/train-station taxi unless you're seeking an opportunity to swear in Macedonian. Walking 50m towards the centre and hailing a passing cab is better.

AROUND SKOPJE

For possible day trips from Skopje, see p322.

LAKE MATKA ЕЗЕРО МАТКА
Some 30 minutes from Skopje, tranquil Lake Matka sits beneath the steep Treska Canyon – created by damming the Treska River – amidst verdure concealing Byzantine cave churches. Try hiking, rock climbing, or boating to canyon caves (€10). Restaurants along the dam serve excellent fish; the best is **Manastirska Pestera** (Monastery Cave; ☎ 02-2052 512; mains 350-600MKD), dug into the rock.

Matka means womb in Macedonian; the link with the Virgin Mary is accentuated by unusual grotto shrines like **Sveta Bogorodica**, below the wall. From here a steep path leads to **Sveti Spas**, **Sveti Trojica** and **Sveta Nedela** – the last, a 90-minute walk away. In these caves hermits once meditated and Macedonian revolutionaries hid from Turks.

The **Church of Sveti Nikola** is beyond the dam, across the bridge, and the **Church of Sveti Andrej** (1389), with important frescos, is after it. Next door, the mountaineering hut **Matka** (☎ 02-3052 655; per bed 500MKD) offers guides, climbing gear and accommodation.

From Skopje drive, take a taxi (350MKD), or catch bus 60 along bul Partizanski Odredi (50MKD, 40 minutes, hourly).

WESTERN MACEDONIA

TETOVO ТЕТОВО
☎ 044 / pop 86,580
Macedonia's biggest northwestern town, Tetovo sits dramatically beneath the steep Šar Planina mountain range. Despite boasting magnificent Ottoman monuments, as a city it's a work in progress, with nonstop construction, ongoing roadworks and a surging population giving it an acrid, gritty air. Macedonia's largest Albanian-majority town, Tetovo is surrounded by heavily Albanian villages too. Despite past problems, however, the Albanians, Macedonians, Serbs and Turks of this border region coexist. Nevertheless, officialdom could be more active in the tourism arena, considering the value of sadly neglected Popova Šapka ski centre.

Tetovo's bus station is on its northeastern edge (ul Vasil Kidrič), a 10-minute walk from downtown. If coming by bus, disembark opposite the Vero supermarket and follow bul Maršal Tito. At the square, this street meets bul Ilindenska; turn left towards the Pena River (500m). Cross it, and you'll see the truly sublime 1459 **Painted Mosque** (Šarena Dzamija). The mosque is highly unusual for having floral paintings rather than ceramic tile decoration. Over 30,000 eggs were used to make the paint and glaze. Photos are allowed.

About 2km southwest stands the **Baba Arabati tekke** (1538), the finest surviving Bektashi monastery in Europe (for information about this mystical Islamic sect see the boxed text, p57). The sprawling complex features flowered lawns, prayer rooms, dining halls, lodgings and a great marble fountain inside a wooden pavilion, mostly dating from the 18th century. Tombs of several Bektashi saints are preserved.

In 1992 Shiite Bektashi dervishes reoccupied the *tekke*, but in 2002 armed Albanian Sunni hotheads invaded and made a mosque in one building. Photos and graffiti glorifying

MACEDONIA

ALL LUBED UP & READY TO RUMBLE

If you fancy the sight of ruddy country lads oiled up and heaving each other around in the grass, **Vrapčiste** is the place for you. With over 3000 inhabitants, this hamlet northwest of Gostivar is Macedonia's largest Turkish village. Each June, villagers organise the **Days of Culture of Vrapčiste** (for information, contact Alinadir Karabatak on ☎ 070582338). The festivities include traditional cuisine, costumes and handcrafted goods – but let's face it, what the punters really want to see is a good, hard body slam.

With some help from the Macedonian Wrestling Federation, the Vrapčiste fest preserves the ancient Turkish sport of *pelivan* (oil wrestling). Slathered in oils, combatants duel inside an open circle framed by their cheering supporters. Once the Ottoman Empire's national sport, *pelivan* goes back to the ancient Persians. If you want to witness 'the mother of all sports', visit Vrapčiste to see some greasy punishment doled out.

From Gostivar, kombis (minibuses) to Vrapčiste (40MKD) leave often. Or take a taxi (150MKD). In Gostivar itself, visit sweet shop **Rekord** (☎ 042-217 369; Borce Jovanovski 82; per piece/kg 15/350MKD; ✆ 9am-6pm) for authentic Turkish baklava: it's so good the Turkish ambassador in far-off Skopje sometimes sends for a few kilograms.

---

the Albanian UCK (National Liberation Army) from the 2001 conflict were displayed. The damage caused by these events is now being repaired. Walk (15 minutes) or take a taxi (60MKD) to get there.

Sleeping & Eating

Hotel Tivoli (☎ 352 379; bul Ilirija 19; s/d/apt incl breakfast €45/60/70) This modern, central hotel has a restaurant and piano bar.

Restaurant Bella Mia (Goce Delčev 108; meals 300-450MKD; ✆ 9am-1am) Traditional specialities are on offer here.

Restaurant Kaj Stole (Dimo Gavrovski-Kara; mains 150-250MKD) This old-timer's place serves *skara* and Macedonia's bean speciality, *tavče gravče*, made with Tetovo's famous beans.

Getting There & Away

BUS

Buses from Tetovo's **bus station** (☎ 334 194) serve Skopje (100MKD, 40 minutes, 18 daily); Ohrid (430MKD, 2½ hours, three daily) and Struga (400MKD, five daily) via Gostivar and Kičevo; Priština (Kosovo; €7, two hours, nine daily) and Tirana (Albania; €20, seven hours).

MAVROVO NATIONAL PARK
МАВРОВО НАЦИОНАЛЕН ПАРК
☎ 042

Macedonians equate Mavrovo with skiing, and it indeed boasts the country's biggest resort. However, the rarefied air and stunning vistas make Mavrovo great year-round. It comprises 73,088 hectares of birch and pine forest, gorges, karst fields and waterfalls, and features Macedonia's highest peak, Mt Korab (2764m). The park contains the must-see Sveti Jovan Bigorski monastery and rustic villages like Galičnik, famous for its traditional wedding (see opposite).

Located off a road near Gostivar, the park and its remote villages are tough to navigate without a car. Hotels populate the resort area south of Lake Mavrovo, though buses only reach Mavrovi Anovi, on the north bank. This artificial lake sponsors the Mavrovska trout – eat it, and spare the endangered Ohrid trout (see the boxed text, p288).

Sights & Activities

The **Zare Lazarevski ski centre** (☎ 489 002; www .zarelaz.com) is Macedonia's top ski resort and, though small, is quite good, with average snow cover of 70cm and slopes from 1860m to 2255m. Ski rental is 600MKD, lift tickets 700MKD/3500MKD per day/week). There's also a ski school. Hotel Bistra (see opposite) runs the show. Mavrovo's also a good base for summer **hiking**, when hotel prices drop.

Visiting **Sveti Jovan Bigorski monastery**, off the Debar road, is mandatory. From Mavrovo, drive; if bussing in from Skopje or Tetovo, any bus transiting Debar for Ohrid or Struga will stop by the monastery's entrance point.

Built in 1020 on the spot where an icon of Sveti Jovan Bigorski (St John the Forerunner, ie St John the Baptist) miraculously appeared, the monastery has been rebuilt often since – the miraculous icon occasionally reappearing.

MACEDONIA

The monastery complex contains an ossuary (charnel house), a defensive tower, living quarters for monks and guests (you can stay in self-catering dorms here; see right), and an impressive church boasting – dogma instructs – the forearm of the saint himself. But what really makes it equal to any world religious shrine is its iconostasis. The final of just three iconostases carved by 19th-century local master craftsmen Makarije Frčkovski and the brothers Filipovski between 1829 and 1835, this colossal work depicting biblical scenes is enlivened with 500 tiny human and 200 animal figures. Gazing up at this enormous, intricate masterpiece will take your breath away. After finishing this stupendous work, the story goes, the carvers flung their tools into the nearby Radika River – ensuring that the secret of their artistic genius would be washed away forever.

Lying 17km southwest of Mavrovo, up a winding, tree-lined road ending in rocky moonscape, idyllic, almost depopulated **Galičnik** survives, its houses rising steeply out of the mountainside. Galičnik's villagers were once wealthy, but Tito's nationalisation program ended their shepherding livelihood and they migrated to Skopje or abroad. Nevertheless, their **traditional homes** are preserved by descendents for summer holidays. The road's snowed in by November, meaning that after that, if you're in, you're in.

Galičnik's national significance survives with the traditional **Galičnik Wedding** (12 to 13 July), for which couples must enter a lottery. This is a responsibility (the order of events is rigid and the bridal dress alone weighs 30kg) but also a great honour. Everyone's welcome: attending unites you with 3000 happy Macedonians (and a few bemused foreigners) and involves much eating and drinking. It's also your best chance to experience traditional Macedonian folk dancing and music in their natural setting.

Sleeping & Eating
For Galičnik Wedding visits, book early for Mavrovo hotels. Alternatively, Go Macedonia (see p292) arranges Galičnik Wedding trips including transport, guided activities, local accommodation and monastery tours.

Hotel Bistra (☎ 489 007; Mavrovo; s/d €65/90; ⛷) The big Bistra has comfortable, clean rooms and everything required (atmospheric restaurant, bar, pool, fitness centre, sauna) to cultivate that ski-lodge glow, including jacuzzis in the deluxe rooms. Prices fall in summer. In season, the Bistra runs the simpler Hotel Ski Škola and Hotel Mavrovski (singles/doubles €20/40); guests have access to the Bistra's facilities.

Hotel Srna (☎ 388 083; s/d/apt €20/40/60; Mavrovo) The smaller Srna, 400m from the chairlifts, has a cosy ambience and breezy, clean rooms. Apartments come with balconies.

Sveti Jovan Bigorski (☎ 478 675; per person €5) The monastery has dormitories with self-catering facilities.

Hotel Neda (☎ 070596114; Galičnik; r 800MKD) The ageing Neda isn't always open, so call.

Getting There & Away
Buses pass through Mavrovo Anovi (2km away) heading south to Debar (120MKD, seven daily), or north to Tetovo (140MKD, five daily) and Skopje (180MKD, three daily).

VEVČANI ВЕВЧАНИ
It's impossible not to like offbeat Vevčani, a traditional Macedonian village nestled in the folds of the Jablanica mountains and surrounded by Muslim villages some 14km northwest of Struga. With around 2500 inhabitants, it's one of the few ethnic Macedonian villages where the locals are keen to stay put. Indeed, the stubbornness of the Vevčani, as they're known, has manifested itself often. In 1987, the Belgrade authorities wanted to tap Vevčani's precious mountain springs and pipe water to Struga. Like hell, the villagers said. They built barricades to block construction, even using grandmas as 'human shields'. Belgrade wisely backed down.

After Macedonia declared independence in 1991, locals countered by declaring an independent Republic of Vevčani. They never followed through, but they did have some fun with it, creating their own flag, passports and currency. The villagers' priorities are clearly displayed on the money, known as ličnici; politics, in the form of the mayor's visage, occupies the lowest-value note, whereas the highest is decorated with the naked female form.

With its church, old houses, mountain springs and great eats, Vevčani can be a day trip or overnight destination. Its famous carnival, a raucous three-day costumed binge, attracts a few thousand onlookers each January.

Orientation & Information

Vevčani has a lower and an upper half. The main entrance road leads to the Struga–Debar road, the other through Oktisi, a Muslim village 800m south. From the central square, where the bus stops, leave the grand municipal building to your right and walk uphill for the (signposted) church and springs. A sign lists Vevčani's most historic houses. The small tourist information office is on the square.

Sights & Activities

Below the main square lie some **19th-century church ruins** discovered accidentally in 2005, during construction of the small **amphitheatre** adjacent. It dates from the time of Sultan Abdulhamid (r 1876–1909), notorious for his massacres of Macedonians.

Convivial priest Zoran will show you Vevčani's well-kept 18th-century **Church of Sveti Nikola** (☎ 798 133; ☽ 8am-5pm), which contains many fine icons. Don't miss the giant, rocket-shaped candles for sale near the entrance.

Vevčani's wooded **mountain springs** are criss-crossed by little bridges and steps. It's very relaxing, and the trails are illuminated at night. Two small **chapels** line the paths. Do drink the refreshing ice-cold water. The springs are particularly impressive in March-April, when the mountain-snow run-off thunders down. **Hiking** in these mountains is enjoyable.

Vevčani's major claim to fame, however, is the **Vevčani Carnival**, held annually from 12 to 14 January (over Orthodox New Year). It attracts around 3000 Macedonians (and others), who come to witness some villagers don elaborate costumes, ride livestock and pontificate from homegrown floats. The flames are as real as the thrusting pitchforks, but the real killer is satire: themes chosen by individual or group participants usually mock politicians and social developments, or exaggerate stereotypes. The newly 'commercialised' opening night features Macedonian pop and rock performances. The carnival parade occurs the next morning, with traditional music and dancing later. Throughout, people visit one another's homes, where food and hot *rakija* are served for anyone and everyone; do join in.

Sleeping & Eating

Vevčani has private rooms. Staying during carnival time requires advance bookings, or stay in Struga or Ohrid.

our pick Pansion Kutmičevica (☎ 798 399, 070249197; kutmicevica@yahoo.com.mk; d €30) This superbly relaxing, family-run guesthouse has a great ambience, with its traditional decor and big, comfortable beds. There are just two rooms, so call ahead. The Kutmičevica's restaurant is excellent (try the succulent pork ribs). It's in the upper town, with views to Lake Ohrid. Turn right at the church (it's signposted) and walk about 70m.

Domakinska Kukja (☎ 790 505; mains 350MKD; ☽ noon-10pm Wed-Sun) This traditional restaurant has garden seating and an interior decorated with folk implements and rugs. It's signposted on the left after the church. It also rents out traditional-style rooms (doubles/apartments €50/60).

Hotel Premier (☎ 071380295; s/d 1600/2400MKD) Not particularly traditional, this small hotel opposite the municipal building has clean, modern rooms and a restaurant.

Restoran vo Izvori (mains 230-350MKD; ☽ noon-11pm) Before the springs, this place serves *skara* and salads.

Restoran Via Egnatia (mains 300-350MKD; ☽ 10am-midnight) This banquet-style restaurant 500m down on the Oktisi road offers great national cuisine.

Getting There & Away

An hourly bus connects Vevčani with Struga (30MKD, 20 minutes), stopping at Struga's bus stop for the villages. From pedestrian street ul Maršal Tito, turn northwards on ul Proleterski Brigada; confusingly, it's opposite the bus shelter. Some minibuses here serve Vevčani. Alternatively, take a taxi (300MKD). Taxis from Ohrid are expensive. Connect in Struga first if starting from there.

From Skopje, twice-daily buses serve Vevčani (450MKD, four hours).

STRUGA СТРУГА

☎ 046 / pop 33,376

Situated along a sandy beach at Lake Ohrid's northern end, where the Crn Drim River comes tumbling out, Struga has a long-attested romantic appeal. It was immortalised by beloved 19th-century Macedonian poet Konstantin Miladinov, who intones his wish to desert cold northern climes for warm, inviting Struga in his most famous poem, 'T'ga za Jug' (Longing for the South). In his honour, an international poetry festival is celebrated each August (and a wine has been named after the poem; see the boxed text, p287).

Struga is quieter than Ohrid, 15km away, and has a different feel. Its stone pedestrian street and old architecture are evocative, though Miladinov, were he alive today, might no longer be moved to verse by it. Long-time visitors concede that Struga is looking somewhat scruffy and kitsch. Nevertheless, it does have sandy beaches and some fascinating local sights.

Unlike Ohrid, Struga has a large Albanian Muslim population, something that has caused tensions. Nevertheless, it remained peaceful during the 2001 conflict, and Macedonians and Albanians live amicably enough here today.

Orientation

Struga is bisected by the Crn Drim, which flows from Lake Ohrid to the south. About four blocks in from this, Struga's major pedestrian street, ul Maršal Tito, crosses the river. Struga's older part, where the best restaurants and cafes are, is on the river's western bank. The bus station's 1.5km north, on the Debar road.

Sights & Activities

Strolling Struga's riverside and the old pedestrian mall is relaxing. The water is warm at Struga's two sandy **beaches** – oddly enough, they're known as *mazhki* (male) and *zhenski* (female), out of respect for the Muslim modesty of the local Albanians. The former is located east of the river, near Hotel Drim, and is somewhat shabby, while the latter is more relaxed and cleaner.

The **Struga Poetry Nights** (www.svp.org.mk) have been held since 1963. From 23 to 28 August, around 200 poets gather for readings and vie for the coveted Golden Wreath. Many literati have attended, including Allen Ginsberg, Seamus Heaney, Pablo Neruda and Ted Hughes. There's a nice buzz when the festival's on, so enjoy if you're here.

Just outside Struga, along the western coast road, lie several medieval **cave churches**. Little **Radožda**, a traditional fishing village 9km from town (and the best place to eat the fabled Ohrid eel), has arguably the best, the 13th-century **Cave Church of St Michael the Archangel**, with vivid frescos.

Sleeping & Eating

Hotel Drim (☎ 785 800; www.drim.com.mk; Boris Kidrič bb; s/d €39/49/78) The friendly, lakefront Drim is Struga's best-known hotel. Its grand foyer suggests Yugoslav origins; the rooms are similarly dated but acceptable.

Restoran Sveti Nikola (Goce Delčev 88; mains 250-350MKD; ☽ 7am-midnight) This classic *skara* restaurant lies along the western riverbank.

Pizza Restoran Angela (Dimitar Vlahov 2; mains 200-300MKD; ☽ 9am-midnight) Good pizzas are served here. Go west on ul Maršal Tito, turn left on ul Proleterski Brigada and it's one block away on the right.

Getting There & Away

Struga is 10km from **St Paul the Apostle Airport** (☎ 252 820; www.airports.com.mk), served by four airlines and summer charters. Buses to Ohrid (50MKD, 15km) leave every 30 minutes. Five daily buses serve Skopje (400MKD, three hours) via Debar or Tetovo.

OHRID ОХРИД

☎ 046 / pop 55,749

If you haven't seen Ohrid, you haven't seen Macedonia – it's as simple as that. The country's most popular destination boasts an atmospheric old town with beautiful churches stacked up a graceful hill, all topped by a medieval castle overlooking serene, 32km-long Lake Ohrid. Nearby, mountainous Galičica National Park offers pristine nature, while secluded beaches dot the lake's lush coast.

In summer, the town and big beaches are packed; full-on nightlife and the summer festival will keep you entertained. For more tranquillity, but still warm weather, try June or September.

At 300m deep and three million years old, this lake, shared by Macedonia (two-thirds) and Albania (one-third), is one of Europe's very deepest and most ancient. Usually Ohrid is calm, but during storms its steely-grey whitecaps evoke the sea.

History

The 4th-century BC city of Lychnidos ('city of light' in Ancient Greek, reflecting the lake's translucent clarity) hugged the Roman Via Egnatia connecting Byzantium with the Adriatic. It thus became a key trade and cultural centre and, with the early Byzantine expansion of Christianity, an ecclesiastic one as well.

The Slavic migrations in Macedonia opened a new period. They rechristened Lychnidos as Ohrid (from *vo rid*, or 'city on the hill'). Bulgarian Slavs arrived in 867, and the Ohrid

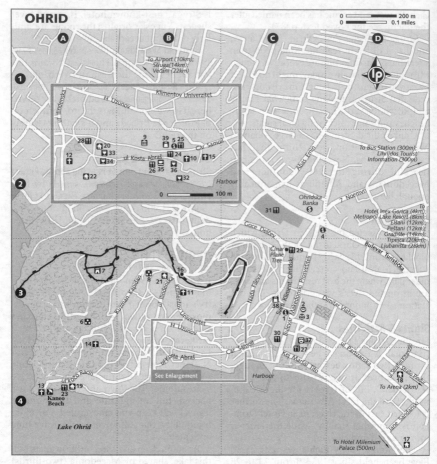

literary school – the first Slavic university any-where – was established by St Kliment and St Naum in the late 9th century. Their work ex-pedited Macedonia's Christian development and Slavic literacy in general, with Kliment's creation of the Cyrillic alphabet. Ohrid be-came the stronghold of Cars Simeon (r 893–927) and Samoil (r 997–1014). However, the latter's 1014 defeat by the Byzantines led to Ohrid's demotion from patriarchate to archbishopric.

The Turks conquered in the late 14th century, ruining Ohrid's period of great-ness. Due to Greek meddling, the Ottomans abolished the archbishopric in 1767 – a long-lasting grievance for both Macedonians and Bulgarians. Despite damage from the

revolutionary period and both world wars, many historical structures have survived.

Orientation & Information

The compact old town is hemmed in south and east by the lake and the pedestrian mall ul Sveti Kliment Ohridski. The bus station is about 1.5km east of the centre.

Danijel Medaroski (☎ 070836074; dmedaroski @gmail.com) Witty, erudite philologist, certified tour guide and Ohrid native Danijel leads city tours (€10) and trips to intriguing lake-area spots on foot, or by vehicle or boat.

Internet Café Inside (Amam Trgovski Centar, bul Makedonski Prosvetiteli; per hr 60MKD; ☺ 9am-1am) One of four internet cafes in a mall near Ploštad Sveti Kliment Ohridski. Phone cabins and friendly service.

Lihnidos Tourist Information (☎ 230 940; 7 Noemvri; ☎ 8am-8pm) At the bus station; information and accommodation advice.

Ohrid.com (www.ohrid.com.mk) Municipal website.

Post office (bul Makedonski Prosvetiteli; ☼ 7am-8pm Mon-Sat)

Telephone centre (bul Makedonski Prosvetiteli; ☼ 7am-8pm Mon-Sat)

Tina Tours (☎ 254 665; bul Turisticka 66; ☼ 9am-6pm) Full-service travel agency opposite Ohridska Banka.

Tourist Bureau Biljana (☎ 070684428; www.beyond ohrid.com; Car Samoil 38; ☼ 10am-midnight) General info and accommodation help. Specialises in activities: mountain-bike rental (€8 per day); guided hiking tours (€25 per person); paragliding on Mt Galičica (€80 per person); scuba diving (€60 per person including equipment).

Sights

The massive, turreted walls overshadowing Ohrid enclose the 10th-century **Car Samoil's Castle** (admission 30MKD; ☼ 9am-6pm, closed Mon). Ascend the narrow stone stairways to the ramparts for fantastic views of the lake, Galičica National Park and Ohrid town.

Near the old town's **Upper Gate** (Gorna Porta) stands the impressive **Classical Amphitheatre**. Originally built for theatre, the Romans later retrofitted it by yanking out the first 10 rows to accommodate the gladiators. It hosts the Summer Festival's most important performances (see p305).

CHURCHES

Ohrid's Byzantine-era **churches** (admission 100MKD) are its jewels. The 11th-century **Sveta Sofija Cathedral** (Car Samoil bb; ☼ 10am-8pm), lined with columns, is Ohrid's grandest church, modelled after Constantinople's St Sophia. Its elaborate

frescos were preserved under Ottoman-era wall plastering. Sveta Sofija's superb acoustics mean it's also used for concerts. Once part of a larger complex, the church has remnants of the archbishop's palace, with wall frescos, beneath it. The complex's ruins are extensive; however, nearby houses sit on top of them.

The graceful domes of the 13th-century **Church of Sveti Jovan at Kaneo**, high on a cliff against the lake, are Ohrid's most sublime image. It's quite possibly Macedonia's most photographed structure, and a wonderful place to relax. Peer down into the azure waters and you'll see why medieval monks found spiritual inspiration here. The small church has some original frescos behind the altar. The tiny chapel of **Mala Bogorodica** is tucked into the cliff's base below.

The church of **Sveti Kliment i Pantelejmon**, or Plaošnik (☼ 9am-6pm; admission free), is Ohrid's most unusual church. Originally a 5th-century basilica, it was modified during Slavic and Byzantine times, and then the Ottomans got to work on it. However, in 2002 a project led by archaeologist Pasko Kuzman (see the boxed text, p304) rebuilt Plaošnik according to its Byzantine architectural design – an almost unprecedented feat. This multidomed church with facing clock tower has glass floor segments revealing original foundations. It also houses St Kliment's relics. Several intricate 5th-century mosaics are outside.

Across from Plaošnik, **4th-century church** foundations, replete with early Christian mosaics of flora and bird and animal life, stand under a protective roof. A warren of trenches and mounds between the two structures keeps yielding exciting new finds.

MACEDONIA

Before St Kliment's bones were transferred to Plaošnik they had lived in the 13th-century Sveti Kliment Church, now renamed **Sveta Bogorodica Perivlepta** (admission 100MKD; ☺ 9am-1pm & 4-8pm). The church features vivid biblical frescos and has an intriguing **icon gallery** (☺ 9am-2pm & 5-8pm, closed Mon).

Two other 14th-century churches stand in the old town, **Sveta Bogorodica Bolnička** and **Sveti Nikola Bolnički**. *Bolnica* means hospital in Macedonian; during plagues, visitors faced 40-day quarantines here. The churches boast delicate frescos.

MUSEUMS

Superb 19th-century Macedonian architecture is preserved in the 1827 **National Museum** (Car Samoil 62; admission 50MKD; ☺ 9am-4pm & 7-11pm Tue-Sun) buildings. The **Robev Residence** houses an archaeological display including ancient epigraphy, and the **Urania Residence** opposite has an ethnographic display.

Walking Tour

Note that many sites are closed on Monday.

First, walk or take a taxi (50MKD to 80MKD) to the **Upper Gate (1**; p303). Turn left to **Sveta Bogorodica Perivlepta (2**; left). See its frescos, and the **icon gallery**. Return to the splendid **Classical Amphitheatre (3**; p303), site of concerts and theatrical performances. Backtrack to the Upper Gate, veering uphill to **Car Samoil's Castle (4**; p303), a five- to 10-minute walk, and gaze from the ramparts.

A forested path leads downhill towards the ruins of a **4th-century church (5**), and **Sveti Kliment i Pantelejmon (6**; p303). Back on the pine-ringed path, prepare for the stunning image of **Sveti Jovan at Kaneo (7**; p303) rising over the lake. Relax in its flowering grounds and enjoy the superlative views.

Next, veer down towards the water on the small right-hand path to the chapel of **Mala Bogorodica (8**; p303), tucked into the cliff base. Continue along narrow, stone-filled **Kaneo beach (9)**, busy in summer, with a bohemian feel and great splashes of colour coming from its bronzed bathers, painted caiques, and umbrella-clad cafes and fish restaurants. Stop for a quick dip, coffee or lunch. Tired walkers can return to port from here by water-taxi (50MKD).

Next, take the stepped pathway that twists uphill, joining ul Kočo Racin. Admire the

---

HUNTING FOR HIDDEN TREASURE

With over 4000 known archaeological sites, Macedonia has a wealth of historical relics. Exciting archaeological discoveries are made every day; unfortunately, however, most aren't reported. Poor farmers seduced by lucre are recruited by Europe's 'antiquities mob', who spirit away priceless treasures to the private auction market.

However, the bad guys can't always win, as the sheer volume of treasure is just too great. And the most important artefacts may just be immovable. In October 2008, archaeologists began excavating **Cyclops Hill** (Kiklopski Rid), a large hill 5km north of Ohrid. Since there's a proving ground of long standing nearby, the army's presence has prevented looting. Leading archaeologists such as Pasko Kuzman and Nikola Kiselinov, both of Ohrid, believe it may conceal a lost ancient Macedonian structure – if so, a monumental find.

Could they be on to something? Says Kiselinov, 'The dimensions of the fortress wall's stones are 1m by 2m, and each weighs up to 2.5 tons. These blocks are so precisely counterbalanced, no plastering was needed.' And building here would make sense; whoever controlled the Cyclops Hill and Ohrid vantage points controlled the Via Egnatia. The prospect of what lies beneath the hill has even led some Macedonians to speculate that the long-lost body of Alexander the Great may be here.

The merry, white-bearded Pasko Kuzman, National Director for Protection of Cultural Heritage, is the boss when it comes to Macedonian archaeology. In 2008 the government trebled his budget for excavations, allowing him to concentrate on several 'mega-projects' in Ohrid, Skopje, Heraclea and Stobi.

This largesse has left the effusive archaeologist feeling like a kid in a candy store. 'I'm the only archaeologist who lives in a country with every major civilisation represented, and now I get to dig all of them,' Kuzman says, a twinkle in his eye. 'It's a very exciting feeling – both for me, and for the future of Macedonian archaeology.'

MACEDONIA

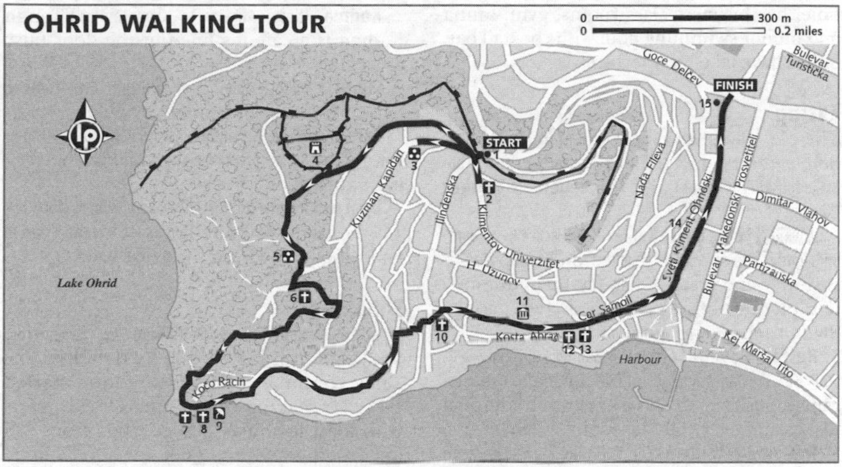

traditional architecture, and walk down to **Sveta Sofija** (**10**; p303) and see its magnificent frescos. On summer evenings, concerts are held – an opportunity to experience the church's amazing acoustics.

Now follow ul Car Samoil through the old town to visit the **National Museum** (**11**; opposite). **Sveti Bogorodica Bolnička** (**12**; opposite) and **Sveti Nikola Bolnički** (**13**; opposite) are soon visible.

Exiting the old town, hit pedestrian street **ul Sveti Kliment Ohridski (14)**. Grab a cafe table for people watching. Continue to the fountained square and **Činar (15)**, an enormous, geriatric plane tree 600 to 1000 years old.

Festivals & Events

July's five-day **Balkan Festival of Folk Dances & Songs** draws regional folkloric groups. The mid-July to mid-August **Ohrid Summer Festival** (☎ 262-304; www.ohridsummer.com.mk) features classical and opera concerts, theatre and dance. Ohrid's **swimming marathon** is a 30km race from Sveti Naum to Ohrid, usually in June.

Each August, a three-week **Macedonian language course** (€850) attracts students from all over. The course includes language lessons, cultural excursions and accommodation and is by all accounts great fun. See the SS Cyril & Methodius University website (www.ukim.edu.mk/smjlk).

Sleeping

BUDGET

Private rooms or apartments (per person €5-10) are available anywhere you see the sign *sobi* (rooms) – search, or ask Tourist Bureau Biljana (p303), which finds private accommodation.

Villa Lucija (☎ 265 608; lucija@mtnet.mk; Kosta Abraš 29; s/d/apt €15/25/40) The old-town Lucija has fantastic ambience and lovingly decorated, breezy rooms with balconies right over the lake.

Stefan Kanevče Rooms (☎ 234 813; apostolanet @yahoo.co.uk; Kočo Racin 47; per person €10) Near Kaneo beach, this atmospheric 19th-century house boasts carved wooden ceilings and good hospitality.

Mimi Apartments (☎ 250 103; mimioh@mail.com .mk; Strašo Pindur 2; r incl breakfast 800MKD) These centrally located private rooms are spacious and equipped with fridge and satellite TV.

MIDRANGE & TOP END

Vila Sofija (☎ 254 370; www.vilasofija.com.mk; Kosta Abraš 64; s/d €35/60, ste €80-120) This opulent getaway combines traditional furnishings with chic modern bathrooms. It's in an old Ohrid mansion near Sveta Sofija church. Book ahead.

Villa Forum (☎ 267 060; www.villaforumohrid.com .mk; Kuzman Kapidan 1; s/d/apt €45/60/80) New and luxurious, this Upper Gate hotel has well-furnished, comfortable rooms with sparkling bathrooms. Book ahead.

Hotel Tino (☎ 261 665; www.hoteltino.com.mk; Kej Maršal Tito 55; s/d €39/49) This lakeside place has nice air-conditioned rooms, plus a good ground-floor restaurant.

Hotel Millenium Palace (☎ 263 361; www.milleniumpalace.com.mk; Kej Maršal Tito bb; s/d/ste/apt €49/70/99/149;) This southern waterfront hotel has business-class rooms, gym, sauna and indoor swimming pool with cocktail bar. Suites have lake-view terraces.

Eating

The old town has Ohrid's best restaurants. Self-caterers have **Tinex supermarket** (bul Makedonski Prosvetiteli) and the **vegetable market** (Kliment Ohridski).

our pick **Letna Bavča Kaneo** (Kočo Racin 43; 8am-midnight) The 'summer terrace' on Kaneo beach is simple and great. A fish fry-up of diminutive plasnica, plus salad, feeds two people. Swim from the restaurant's dock.

Restoran Sveta Sofija (Car Samoil 88; mains 300-500MKD; 9am-midnight) This upscale restaurant opposite Sveta Sofija has great traditional dishes and over 100 Macedonian wines.

Restoran Belvedere (Kej Maršal Tito 2; 8am-2am) Excellent *skara* is the speciality here, where outdoor tables extend under a leafy canopy. When it's busy at night, the overworked staff can be forgetful, though.

Pizzeria Leonardo (Car Samoil 31; pizzas 200-350MKD; 9am-midnight) This old-town joint has Ohrid's best pizza.

Restaurant Antiko (Car Samoil 30; mains 350-600MKD; 9am-midnight) Set in an old Ohrid mansion, the famous Antiko has great traditional ambience and (pricey) food.

Restaurant Dalga (Kosta Abraš bb) Another popular old-town restaurant, the Dalga has good fish and grills, and great lake views.

Star Činar (pl Činar; mains 250-450MKD; 9am-midnight) This *skara*-and-beer restaurant is opposite the plane tree.

Drinking & Entertainment

The old town's bars are packed with carousing vacationers in summer. Entertainment runs from bars and clubs to the Summer Festival (see p305).

our pick **Jazz Inn** (070304737; Kosta Abraš 74; 10.30pm-4am) Charismatic owner Vilijam Hristovski lets the funk flow at low-lit Jazz Inn, one of Ohrid's most storied bars. This jazzy hipster hangout gets roaring after midnight; famous visitors have included Lenny Kravitz's touring band.

Liquid (Kosta Abraš 17; 9am-1am) This hip, chill-out place has a lakefront patio.

Aquarius (Kosta Abraš bb; 10am-1am) Near Liquid, always-popular Aquarius was Ohrid's original lake-terrace cafe and it remains cool.

Kadma (Kosta Abraš; 10am-1am) Though Kadma is a cafe it's line-out-the-door busy as a club.

Cuba Libre (Kosta Abraš; 10pm-4am) This festive bar-cum-club is perennially popular.

Arena (cnr Jane Sandanski & Karpoš Vojvoda; 10pm-4am) Sweaty, packed pop-rock nightclub Arena is 1.5km out of town.

Dom na Kultura (Grigor Prličev; admission 50-100MKD) The House of Culture holds cultural events and is home to Ohrid's movie theatre.

Shopping

Bisera (Kliment Ohridski 60; pearls from €25; 9am-1pm & 6-10pm) From his little shop, friendly Vane Talev continues a family tradition started in 1924: making the unique Ohrid pearls with local formulas. Prices range from €25 for a simple piece to €600 for an elaborate necklace.

National Workshop for Hand Made Paper (Car Samoil 60; prints 200-600MKD; 10am-10pm) The workshop sells old-town prints, small boxes and copies of illuminated manuscripts.

Getting There & Away

AIR

Four airlines serve Ohrid's **St Paul the Apostle Airport** (252 820; www.airports.com.mk), 10km north. JAT flies to Belgrade via Skopje on Monday and Friday. Charter flights from the Netherlands and Israel also operate. Take a taxi to reach it (300MKD).

BUS

From the **bus station** (260 339; 7 Noemvri bb), 1.5km east of the centre, buses serve Skopje, either via Kičevo (450MKD, three hours, seven daily) or (the longer route) via Bitola; for Bitola itself, 10 daily buses run (300MKD, 1¼ hours). Buses to Struga (50MKD, 14km) leave every 30 minutes. Book ahead for Skopje buses in summer. Some kombis (minibuses) and taxis wait outside Tina Tours for intercity destinations.

International buses serve Belgrade (Serbia), at 1pm (via Bitola, 2050MKD, 12 hours) and 5.30pm (via Kičevo, 1820MKD, 10 hours). A daily bus at 7pm serves Sofia (Bulgaria; 1450MKD, eight hours). For Albania, take a bus to Sveti Naum (110MKD, 29km). Cross the border and take a cab (€5) 6km to Pogradeci. Ohrid to Sveti Naum by taxi costs 900MKD.

LAKE OHRID EASTERN SHORE
☎ 046

The coast road first passes several waterfront hotels. The masses congregate on the beaches closest to Ohrid. In summer, frequent buses and kombis serve everywhere up to Gradište; further destinations like Trpejca, Ljubaništa and Sveti Naum are served less frequently.

For people watching and luxuriating, **Cuba Libre Beach** and **Corali** (one of the 10 **Lagadin** beaches), 2km from Ohrid, are packed summer spots with chilled-out music and cocktails. Water clarity improves at **Peštani** (12km from Ohrid), the last coastal village, with ATM, health centre, police station and night bars, but no sights.

Gradište Градиште
Just 2km further, Gradište is a wooded campsite with beaches ranging from placid lagoons and hidden coves to full-on beach bar action, connected by wooden bridges running below a sheer cliff. Young hedonists pitch their tents for weeks here, where days spent sunbathing are followed by beachside DJ parties at night.

Gradište's soon-to-be-opened **Neolithic Settlement Museum**, on the campsite's southernmost beach, contains artefacts from a 4000-year-old neolithic settlement. They were found underwater by scuba-diving archaeologists, led by local legend Pasko Kuzman (see the boxed text, p304). The new museum recreates the actual neolithic houses, built on stilts over the lake, and will display discovered artefacts.

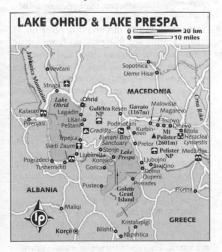

LAKE OHRID & LAKE PRESPA

Trpejca Трпејца
With one foot in the door of tourism and the other kicking a tardy donkey laden with sticks, Trpejca is a 500-strong fishing hamlet cupped between a sloping hill and a tranquil bay. The last Ohrid village of its kind, it features cluttered white houses with terracotta roofs, finishing at a white-pebble beach where painted caiques bob on aquamarine waters. In high season it's busy, but otherwise it's serene. At night, the sounds of crickets and frogs fill the air.

Trpejca has few restaurants and shops, and there's limited public transport. Nevertheless, those looking for laid-back rustic charm can do worse than spend a few days here. The superb waters offer excellent swimming, and the forested Mt Galičica's just opposite. Visit the upper **Church of Sveti Nikola** for views.

Another church, **Sveta Bogorodica Zahumska** (usually called by its shorter name, Sveti Zaum) is only accessible by water. It's located some 2.5km south of Trpejca on a wooded beach. This church was first built by Sveti Naum and rebuilt in 1361. Its unusual frescos, such as one of the bare-breasted Mary suckling the infant Christ, and another of Christ and Mary in royal garments, date from that time.

Visiting Sveti Zaum requires a boat; for information on arranging a trip, see p308.

Ljubanište Љубаниште
A quieter campsite than Gradište is **Ljubaniste**, 27km from Ohrid. In summer, Tourist Bureau Biljana (p303) operates an informative eco-tourism centre here.

Sveti Naum Свети Наум
Splendid **Sveti Naum monastery**, 29km south of Ohrid, lies just before the Albania border. Built by Naum, a contemporary of Sveti Kliment's, the monastery became a leading educational centre. Naum built the Church of the Holy Archangels (900), replaced by the 16th-century **Church of Sveti Naum**; this multidomed, Byzantine-style structure, surrounded by roses and peacocks and set on a grassy clifftop, boasts fine 16th- and 19th-century **frescos**.

When inside, drop an ear to the **tomb of Sveti Naum** to hear his muffled heartbeat. Outside, there's a deep **wishing well** for spare denars. The surrounding woods and glassy pond, where the ice-cold Crn Drim River rushes into the

MACEDONIA

lake, are beautiful. The river maintains its co-hesion underwater, tumbling out 34km later in Struga. Sveti Naum gets crowded in sum-mer; it has one of Ohrid's few sandy beaches.

Galičica National Park
Галичица Национален Парк

The rippling, rock-crested Mt Galičica sepa-rates Lake Ohrid from Lake Prespa. A national park since 1958, Galičica's peaks top 2000m. It comprises 22,750 hectares of territory, and features endemic plants and trees, caves, and hiking, mountain biking and paragliding; from above, there are spectacular views of both lakes. For more views, drive through Galičica to Lake Prespa, via the snaking mountain road starting near Trpejca.

Galičica's best village, idyllic **Elšani**, is 10km from Ohrid. It's totally tranquil compared to the coast, 2.5km below, and Peštani's beach is still only a 15-minute walk down the trail. Elšani makes a great base for out-door activities, but the lake views alone make it worthwhile.

Elšani's small square houses a **photographic gallery** of unique nature photos, while at the time of research a **village museum** of traditional garments and implements was shortly due to open. The 19th-century **Church of Sveti Ilias** occupies Elšani's top spot: a high bluff with kaleidoscopic views over the lake. The church-yard is also the village cemetery; the slanted gravestones studding the hill, with nothing but beautiful blue lake and sky behind them, make for a moving, melancholy sight.

Activities

The coast offers **water sports**, while **hiking**, **cycling** and **paragliding** are great on Galičica. Paddle boats, kayaks, and caiques (plus skip-per) are rented.

For swimmers, Ohrid's southeastern coast offers crystal-clear water, with umber cliffs and Mediterranean verdure for scenery. Two recommended **swimming** routes include Peštani to Gradište (2.2km) and Gradište to Trpejca (5km), passing hidden beaches and rocky outcroppings. Since beaches are stony, wearing aqua-socks might be good.

Boat trips from Ohrid include the Ohrid–Sveti Naum day trip (350MKD return). At Sveti Naum, an organised half-hour cruise crosses the Crn Drim lagoons (100MKD). Boating itineraries are flexible. Try the ebul-lient Danijel Medaroski (p302), an Ohrid

tour guide and boatsman with knowledge of history and hidden beaches. **B&B/Apartments Lale** (☎ 285 511; www.lale-pestani.com; Peštani) ar-ranges boating, kayak rental (600MKD) and paragliding, as does Ohrid's Tourist Bureau Biljana (p303).

For more **mountain activities** in Galičica, see Risto at **Risto's Guest House** (☎ 285 464, 075977930; elshani@mt.net.mk; Elšani). His hikes range from easy walks to tough treks, and along the way he'll inform you about Galičica's unique flora, fauna and history. Tours include a traditional lunch prepared by Risto's charming wife, Anita, who runs **traditional cooking classes**.

Sleeping

Most coastal accommodation and restaurants shut down after summer – low-season travel-lers should call ahead to check. In summer, **private accommodation** (per person 300-600MKD) is plentiful, and you can usually find some-thing on the spot. Quality standards vary; shop around.

Campers can try the waterfront **Gradište Camping** (☎ 285 920; Gradište; per tent 1000MKD; ☺ May-Oct), 14km from Ohrid, which attracts party-minded youngsters. Families and solitude seekers might prefer **Camping Ljubaništa** (☎ 283 240; per tent 800MKD; ☺ May-Oct), 27km from Ohrid. Despite a nice beach, however, its facilities are dated and hot water's very limited, as is public transport. Both campsites have shops and eateries.

our pick **Risto's Guest House** (☎ 285 464, 075977930; elshani@mt.net.mk; Elšani; s/d/tr incl breakfast €15/24/32) Friendly young couple Risto and Anita Stojoski run this relaxing place on Mt Galičica. Ring for free pick-up from Ohrid. Rooms are spacious and clean, and most have shared bathrooms. All have lake-view balco-nies. Anita's excellent home-cooked meals (€12 per person) are all natural; there's no Coca-Cola here, only delicious homemade juices and wines.

B&B/Apartments Lale (☎ 285 511; www.lale-pest ani.com; Naum Ohridski 83, Peštani; s/d/ste €15/20/28; ☒) Signposted on Peštani's main road, Lale of-fers four rooms with shared bathrooms, plus studios with kitchens and bathrooms (behind the garden swimming pool). It gets booked out early, so confirm ahead.

Apartmeni Bašoski (☎ 285 431; Naum Ohridski 96, Peštani; d/tr/apt €20/30/55) The new rooms have fridge, TV and balcony, though bathrooms are small. There's maid service and common kitchens. Look for the lawn pagoda 50m past Lale.

Hotel Lagadin (☎ 261 448; Lagadin; s/d/tr €20/40/51) Opposite Lagadin beach, this family-run hotel has clean, good-sized rooms, a restaurant and a bar.

Vila DeNiro (☎ 070212518; Trpejca; d/apt €25/50) Trpejca's only modern place is this yellow mansion, located exactly where the main walkway downhill branches off. The DeNiro has three double rooms, plus one apartment with gleaming kitchenette.

Hotel Sveti Naum (☎ 283 080; Sveti Naum; s/d/ste from €37/74/116) This fancy hotel with restaurant in the Sveti Naum monastery works year-round. The stylish rooms are luxurious; note lake-view rooms cost €20 extra.

Vila Boris (☎ 070227701; www.villaboris.com.mk; Peštani; d/apt €50/65) On Peštani's beach, this chic mini-hotel has breezy rooms and sparkling bathrooms. For beach access and comfort, it's unbeatable. Take ul Turistička (by the police station) to the last house.

Metropol Lake Resort (☎ 203 001; www.metropol-ohrid.com.mk/apt incl breakfast from €63/80/112; 🛒) This three-hotel resort has the expected amenities, though rooms aren't spectacular. It's been home to numerous visiting heads of state, local celebrities and foreign rock stars. There's a fitness and spa centre, a patio bar, a swimming pool and a 600m-long beach.

Inex Gorica Hotel (☎ 277 521; www.inexgorica.com.mk; s/d/apt €99/158/189) The coast's best lake views may be here. Rooms are spacious and well kept, though furnishings and common areas are showing age. Like the Metropol, the exterior architecture is tragically communistic. However, a new deluxe spa centre may persuade.

Eating

There are good fish restaurants and *skara* places, most open summer only. Fish is usually cheaper here than in town. Hotel restaurants are many though not spectacular.

Restoran Galeo (Peštani; mains 300-500MKD; 🕐 10am-1am) This little Peštani restaurant has a leafy courtyard and very tasty and reasonably priced Mavrovska trout. Macedonia's bluesy music of yesteryear, *staro gradsko* ('old city style') plays.

Restoran Ribar (Trpejca; fish per person 300-600MKD; 🕐 9am-midnight) Right on the Trpejca waterfront, Ribar is one of Ohrid's best fish restaurants.

BUS & TAXI FARES FROM OHRID		
Destination	**Bus fare (MKD)**	**Taxi fare (MKD)**
Elšani	40	300
Gradište	60	400
Lagadin	30	200
Ljubaništa	90	600
Peštani	50	300
Sveti Naum	110	900
Trpejca	70	500

Restoran St Tropez (Trpejca; mains 200-350MKD; 🕐 8am-midnight) Also on Trpejca's waterfront, the St Tropez is fine for a lazy coffee or good *skara* lunch.

Getting There & Away

Frequent buses and kombis ply the Ohrid–Sveti Naum route in summer; however, most reach only Gradište's campsite and beaches. Services are less frequent to Trpejca, Ljubaništa and Sveti Naum further on. In Ohrid, wait for kombis by Tina Tours (p303), opposite Ohridska Banka. Buses operate in summer until 2am.

Taxis are expensive. During summer they may charge bus-ticket rates when filling up fast (check with the driver).

For bus and regular taxi fares from Ohrid, see the table, above. Boat travel from Ohrid includes the daily 30km tour to Sveti Naum on a big cruising vessel (350MKD return), starting from Ohrid's port. Rates for boat trips from villages vary.

LAKE PRESPA & AROUND
☎ 047

Macedonia's 'other' tectonic lake, Prespa, sits east of Lake Ohrid, beyond Mt Galičica. Macedonians lament how Prespa – much shallower than Ohrid at only 30m – is steadily receding. Global warming and subterranean tectonic grinding have both been blamed. Nevertheless, the warm, shallow waters and sandy beaches make humble Prespa good for small children.

The lake shelters over 200 bird species, making birdwatching excellent; it also hosts Golem Grad, Macedonia's only island (see the boxed text, p310). This wild, unpopulated haven for snakes and birds is one of Macedonia's true oddities. Prespa also features evocative villages, churches and hiking.

MACEDONIA

FEAR & LOATHING ON THE ISLAND OF SNAKES

Macedonia's weirdest attraction is without doubt **Golem Grad**, an uninhabitable jungle land huddled ominously in Lake Prespa. Part of Galičica National Park, the island is a protected zone and home to thousands of snakes (most not dangerous), as well as lake birds whose droppings have both canvassed the boxy facing boulders in white, like some infernal Cubist painting, and snowed over the already half-dead *foja*, a brittle sort of pine found almost nowhere else around.

Remarkably, the island was inhabited until the 15th century, as church ruins attest, and then given over to serpents. Nevertheless, in Yugoslavia's glory days of the 1960s, hordes of day trippers braved the snakes to venture onto Golem Grad's rocky, forested shores. A 1967 mongoose-importing project meant to eradicate the reptiles failed when the plucky little hunters didn't survive the Macedonian winter. The snakes have had the run of the place since.

Clambering around on Golem Grad, located just before the invisible, aqueous tri-border division with Greece and Albania, is definitely one of the coolest experiences you can have in Macedonia. There's nothing to worry about from the skitterish snakes, but wear hiking boots and bring water and snacks. Along with the ruins, there's one reconstructed church and numerous unsettling views through the demented trees hanging over the lake.

Local fisherman can take you from Dolno Dupeni (€50), Pretor (€50) or Stenje (€40). The price includes a two- or three-hour guided tour. Alternatively, come on a day trip or multiday adventure trip through Bitola's Baloyannis Tours (opposite).

Western Shore

Prespa's provincial capital, **Resen**, lies on the Bitola–Ohrid road. It's not outstanding, but if travelling by bus, transfer here. Taxis and minibuses also wait at the bus station.

Resen's 15 minutes came in July 1908, when it became the launching pad for an Ottoman military uprising against the sultan (see p284).

Southwest of Resen the **Ezerani Bird Sanctuary**, established in 1996, shelters 200 bird species; cormorants, Dalmatian pelicans and herons are common sights. It has two elevated bird-watching stations.

The coast road ends at **Stenje**, framed by Mt Galičica. A 5km dirt road continues to **Konjsko**, a secluded spot with a lovely spit of sand for sunbathers. Stenje itself is somewhat unkempt, with wild grasses and bulls snorting on the long sandy beach, but offers accommodation, eating and boating opportunities, such as an expedition to the uninhabited island of Golem Grad (see the boxed text, above).

Eastern Shore

Turning south off the Resen–Bitola road, you'll see apple orchards on the left and, on the right, reeds and bushes rising in ungainly splendour all the way down to the water's edge. In **Podmočani**, stop at the signposted **Ethnological Museum** (☎ 489 260; admission 60MKD; ☺ daylight hours), a lovely display of traditional clothing, implements and household goods.

Next, turn for **Kurbinovo**, a few kilometres west, and continue 1km through it to the Byzantine **Church of Sveti Gjorgji**. Its rare and vivid frescos, from 1191, preserve late Comnenian art. The images on Macedonia's 50-denar note come from these frescos. Go with an informed local or on an organised day trip, as only one (hard-to-find) villager has the key.

Back on the main road, continue to **Pretor**, which has a 2km-long sandy beach. Once a popular tourist destination, Pretor's now rather glum though still visited in summer. The water's recession has been dramatic here, and you'll have a memorable experience when your leg is swallowed by the mud upon entering the water.

Prespa's most photogenic villages, Ljubojno, Brajčino and Dolno Dupeni, are clustered before the Greece border. Their distinctive stone houses, some a century old, have ornate facades and columns. As with other Prespa villages, many locals here emigrated, with only a few hundred people remaining here year-round.

While **Ljubojno** has arguably the best architecture, the most developed is **Brajčino**, which won foreign funding to develop eco-tourism. Its winding streets and stone houses, tucked into Pelister National Park, make it an atmospheric place. Visit the **Monastery of Sveta Petka**, 300m above the centre, which contains 16th-century frescos. On 7 August, the eve of Sveta

Petka's feast day, 2000 visitors congregate here for traditional food and drink, followed by music in town.

A 17km, six-hour **hike** into Pelister begins in Brajčino, passing mountain springs before reaching a lakeside **mountain hut** (☎ 070497751) with 25 beds.

Placid **Dolno Dupeni**, with houses dating to 1913, is the last village. Go 2km further to its **beach**; a tranquil sandy stretch reserved for escapists, it's within swimming distance of Greek territorial waters, in case you're plotting a really daring escape.

Sleeping & Eating

Summer-only private accommodation is available. Just show up, or contact the Ohrid-based Tourist Bureau Biljana (p303).

Monastery of Sveti Petka (Brajčino; r 100MKD) Simple, clean shared rooms are on offer here.

Rooms Divna Kostovska (☎ 070507367; Brajčino; s/d incl breakfast 800/1600MKD) Divna Kostovska has five well-done rooms with spiffy wooden floors and shared bathrooms.

Villa Vasilica (☎ 482 342; vdinevski@yahoo.com; Brajčino; s/house 800/5000MKD) This family house can be rented whole or by the room. Although somewhat dated for the price, it's comfortable and good for self-caterers.

Martin Hotel (☎ 480 444; viktor_martin@t-home .mk; Pretor; s/d from 1300/2000MKD; 🖳) Pretor's modern beachfront hotel offers handsome rooms with lake-view balconies, plus swimming pool, restaurant, and coffee bar with a view of the lake.

Hotel Riva (☎ 484 165; Stenje; s/d/apt incl breakfast 650/1300/1800MKD) Stenje's brand-new Riva, with eight breezy, inviting rooms and two apartments, has a good restaurant and lakefront cafe terrace.

Raskrsnica (☎ 482 322; Brajčino; mains 300-420MKD; 🕒 8am-midnight) Owner Milka Popjanevska and family serve local specialities, wines and liqueurs at this restaurant surrounded by lawns, trees and a flowing fountain. At the time of research accommodation was planned.

Restaurant Kruna (Pretor; mains 120-250MKD; 🕒 8am-1am) The beachfront Kruna has a big lake-view patio and does tasty *skara*.

Getting There & Away

Ten daily Ohrid–Bitola buses pass through **Resen bus station** (☎ 451756), from where regular buses serve Prespa's villages. Buses leave Resen at 6am, 9am, 11am, 2.30pm and 3.30pm for Kurbinovo (90MKD, 20 minutes), Pretor (90MKD, 25 minutes), Ljubojno (110MKD, 30 minutes), Brajčino (110MKD, 35 minutes) and Dolno Dupeni (110MKD, 40 minutes). Buses head east towards Oteševo and Stenje (100MKD, 30 minutes) at 6.20am, 10.45am, 2.30pm and 6pm.

CENTRAL MACEDONIA

BITOLA БИТОЛА
☎ 047 / pop 95,385

With some of Macedonia's most elegant buildings and most beautiful people, elevated Bitola (660m) has a taste for sophistication inherited from its days as the Ottoman 'City of Consuls' over a century ago. An important commercial and political centre before WWI, Bitola was always marked by its unique mixture of peoples, including Macedonians, Turks, Greeks, Sephardic Jews and the dark-eyed Vlachs, who herded sheep through the passes of Mt Pelister, rising gracefully to the south.

Bitola is considered one of Macedonia's most patriotic cities, with over 600 traditional Macedonian songs singing its praises. Its colourful 18th- and 19th-century townhouses, Ottoman mosques, and vibrant cafe culture make it the most intriguing and liveable of Macedonia's big towns. Its sophisticated new hotels aspire to emulate the Bitola of old.

Orientation & Information

The adjoining train and bus stations stand beside the park; from here, it's a 15-minute walk downtown. Cafes and neoclassical architecture line the major pedestrian street, ul Maršal Tito, commonly known as Širok Sokak (Wide Street in Turkish).

The Širok Sokak is a wi-fi hotspot, and internet cafes are nearby.

Baloyannis Tours (☎ 220 204, 075207273; Solunska 118; 🕒 8am-6pm Mon-Sat) Bitola's oldest and best travel agency, providing city tours and adventure trips in the region (see p312).

Tourist information centre (☎ 241 641; bitola -tourist-info@t-home.mk; Sterio Georgiev 1; 🕒 9am-6pm Mon-Sat) This friendly place finds accommodation and provides maps, travel timetables and general information.

Sights & Activities

Bitola's 16th-century **Yeni mosque**, **Isak mosque** and **Yahdar-Kadi mosque**, all between the Dragor River and the Stara Čaršija (Old Bazaar),

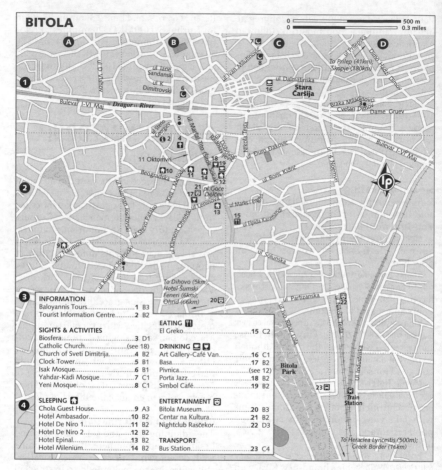

BITOLA

0   500 m
0   0.3 miles

testify to its Ottoman past, as does the enormous **Clock Tower** (Saat Kula) nearby.

One great pleasure here is strolling Bitola's winding lanes, parks and grand streets, lined with ornate old architecture. Despite considerable WWI-era damage, Bitola has retained its character and preserved distinctive townhouses. Ornate, narrow balconies, often bedecked with bright flowers, jut from grand facades, their windows shuttered neatly. The ever-changing interplay of sunlight and shadow accentuates Bitola's charm for photographers. The tourist information centre arranges guided three-hour **architecture sightseeing tours** (per group €30).

During Ottoman times, the **Stara Čaršija** boasted around 3000 clustered artisans' shops;

though much smaller today, about 70 different trades are still conducted, and cheaply (250MKD for shoe repairs).

The **Church of Sveti Dimitrij** (11 Oktomvri bb; 7am-6pm), near the Clock Tower, is a grand structure dating from 1830, with rich frescos, ornate lamps and a huge iconostasis. Bitola's **Catholic church** is staid but has a strikingly conspicuous placement amidst the multicoloured facades of the Širok Sokak. Enjoy the **cafe life** here, and sip a coffee while the beautiful people promenade past; it's an essential Bitola experience.

If it's adventure you crave, see outdoorsman Gorki Baloyannis, the friendly owner of Baloyannis Tours (p311). The 'Macedonian Military Trail' trip includes **boating** down Lake

Tikveš, followed by **hiking** the Crna River canyon and crossing wild Mariovo to Bitola, while the 'Via Egnatia Trail' involves hiking through Pelister National Park to Lake Prespa and crossing the mountain to Ohrid.

Eco-tourism NGO **Blosfera** (☎ 234 973; http://biosfera.org.mk; Dimo Hadzi Dimov 3), led by environmentalist Nesad Azenovski, arranges local hiking and **birdwatching** trips.

Festivals & Events

The **Bit Fest** (June to August) features concerts, literary readings and art exhibits. The **Ilinden festival** (2 August), honouring the Ilinden Uprising of 1903, is celebrated with food and music.

The **Manaki Brothers Film Festival** (www.manaki.com.mk), from late September to early October, screens independent foreign films. It honours Milton and Ianachia Manaki, the first Balkan filmmakers (around 1905). It's followed by the **Inter Fest**, with classical-music performances in the Centar na Kultura and Bitola Museum.

Sleeping & Eating

Chola Guest House (☎ 224 919; guesthouse_chola @hotmail.com; Stiv Naumov 80; s/d €12/20) Bitola's best budget option is this quiet place in an old mansion. The pretty rooms are clean and well kept and have colourful modern bathrooms. If going by taxi, ask for Video Club Dju (directly across from the Chola).

Hotel Milenium (☎ 241 001; h.milenium@t-home.mk; Maršal Tito 48; s/d/ste/apt €39/66/80/99) Atriums with splashes of stained glass, smooth marble opulence and historical relics channel old Bitola. The spacious rooms have all mod cons and sparkling bathrooms. Great value for quality, and right on the Širok Sokak too. The hotel has a superior restaurant.

Hotel De Niro (☎ 229 656; www.hotel-deniro.com; Kiril i Metodij 5; s/d/ste €35/50/80) The central yet discreet De Niro has two locations: one has snazzy, old Bitola–style rooms and an Italian restaurant, while the other has slick minimalist fixtures and a happening pub below.

Hotel Epinal (☎ 224 777; www.hotelepinal.com; Maršal Tito bb; s/d €49/69; 🏊) The ageing Epinal rises unpromisingly over central Bitola but is actually quite nice – especially factoring in the swimming pool, jacuzzi and gym.

Hotel Ambasador (☎ 225 623; www.hotelambasadorbitola.com; Beogradska 2; s/d/apt 1750/3500/6000MKD)

This handsomely furnished business hotel is central and has all the expected amenities.

Hotel Šumski Feneri (☎ 293 030; sfeneri@mt.net.mk; Trnovo; s/d/apt €30/45/60) In Mt Pelister's Trnovo village, 4km from Bitola, this hotel has snug rooms and four good-sized apartments. The restaurant has a nice outdoor terrace. A taxi from Bitola costs 250MKD.

El Greko (crnr Maršal Tito & Elipda Karamandi; mains 180-320MKD; ☽ 10am-1am) This Širok Sokak taverna and pizzeria has great beer-hall ambience.

Drinking & Entertainment

Simbol Café (Maršal Tito 65; ☽ 8am-midnight), on the Širok Sokak, has an old-Bitola feel. The nearby **Porta Jazz** (Maršal Tito; ☽ 8am-midnight) is popular, and Pivnica, the subterranean bar at Hotel De Niro (left), is a fun nightspot.

Art Gallery-Café Van (Dalmatinska 29; mains 250MKD; ☽ 10am-11pm) Over in the Stara Čaršija, this cafe has eclectic decor such as Orthodox icons, oil paintings and photos of old Bitola to complement the coffee.

Basa (☽ 10pm-2am) Get your groove on at this dark-lit bar on a side street off ul Leninova, behind Centar na Kultura. It plays house music and Serbian, Macedonian and Western pop.

Nightclub Rasčekor (☽ 10pm-4am) The best Bitola nightclub is the smooth, sleek and trendy Rasčekor, near the train station. Macedonian and international DJs play; it's line-out-the-door on weekends.

Getting There & Away

The **bus station** (☎ 231 420; Nikola Tesla) and the **train station** (☎ 237 110; Nikola Tesla) are adjacent, about 1km south of the centre. Buses serve Skopje (480MKD, four hours, 10 daily) via Prilep (120MKD, one hour); Kavadarci (280MKD, two hours, four daily); Strumica (480MKD, four hours, one daily); and Ohrid (300MKD, 1¼ hours, 10 daily).

For Greece, take a taxi to the border (450MKD) and then catch a Greek cab to Florina, or find a Bitola cab driver who will take you (3000MKD).

Three daily trains (3.49am, 1.39pm and 6.50pm) serve Skopje (210MKD) via Prilep (66MKD) and Veles (154MKD).

AROUND BITOLA
Heraclea Lyncestis

The mandatory local visit here is to **Heraclea Lyncestis** (admission 100MKD, photos 500MKD; ☽ 9am-3pm winter, to 5pm summer), one of Macedonia's most significant ancient sites, 1km south of Bitola. You can drive, or take a taxi (70MKD); a city-park extension will make it a 30-minute walk from Bitola.

Founded by Philip II, Heraclea became an important commercial city. The Romans conquered in 168 BC, but Heraclea's position on the Via Egnatia kept it prosperous. In the 4th century it became an episcopal seat, and the best ruins date from this period. In the 5th and 6th centuries, Goths and then Slavs sacked Heraclea, and it waned.

The site is fairly compact, though excavations are continuing. The Roman baths, portico and amphitheatre are remarkable, but most striking are the two early Christian basilica ruins and adjoining episcopal palace, with beautiful, well-preserved floor mosaics. Along with their early Christian themes, which absorbed pagan motifs, they're unique in depicting trees and animals endemic to the

area. A cafe inside the site's museum provides relief from the summer heat.

Dihovo Дихово
☎ 047

Get here while it's still a secret – the mountain hamlet of Dihovo, only 5km from Bitola, is a world away in terms of ambience, with some of Macedonia's best rustic digs. Crisp, 830m-high Dihovo is also a base for Pelister hikes, or for simply relaxing in a forested setting where the sounds of a rushing river and crickets complement the clear starry skies at night.

Unlike nearby villages, Dihovo is of Macedonian, not Vlach, origins. Its founders originally came from Brajčino, across Mt Pelister, and were thus dubbed Prespani (Prespa people). See Dihovo's stone houses, and the **Church of Sveti Dimitrije** (1830), 500m from the centre, near the Sapungica River.

MAGICAL MARIOVO

If there's one place name in Macedonia that still connotes mystery, it's Mariovo. The southern-border badlands region hums with the disconcerting energy of another time, still resonating in its rugged mountains, deep river-canyons and strange plateaus dotted with deserted villages.

Mariovo is bounded to the west and north by the Pelagonian Plain, which runs from Prilep to Bitola, and to the east melds with the mountains south of Lake Tikveš and west of Gevgelija. It's bounded to the south by the fearsome Kajmakčalan (2520m), the peak of a range that runs along the Greece border. Mariovo's major river, the Crna, was called the Erigon in antiquity. The only European river that flows in all four directions, it runs a meandering course into Lake Tikveš and the Vardar.

For centuries, the 25 Mariovo villages were wealthy sheep-herding centres. However, the wars (and later Tito's nationalisation program) killed them. During wildfires, the muffled boom of buried WWI ordnance exploding can occasionally be heard in this former front-line zone. But it's the promise of buried treasure – gold and century-old French Cognac left by the troops – that draws a few adventurers today. Foreigners with crumbling maps, and Macedonians with metal detectors, pass through what is now the solitary dominion of shepherds telling tales of quaffing the priceless French elixir.

Mariovo's traditional villages are now mostly deserted. Still, hiking or touring the area by car and admiring the faded beauty of traditional Macedonian architecture is a great pleasure. The area astonishes too with its diverse nature: wild orchids and carnations peek out of thick forests that conceal icy-clear, gold-specked rivers, full of freshwater crabs and trout. Weird cratered hills rise like gravestones out of the mists, studded with pink quartz, granite and shale.

When coming from Bitola, Mariovo's major villages include pretty **Rapeš**, **Staravina** and five-centuries-old **Gradesnica**, the largest today, with 80 inhabitants. They're easily accessible by road, but for off-the-beaten-track adventures, go with an experienced guide. The rough dirt tracks branch off into bewildering dead ends, or pass completely through dense jungle, making getting lost inevitable. And, though mountain huts exist, they're not always open, so plan ahead.

Various **hiking trips**, **jeep safaris**, **village tours** and **mountain-climbing trips** to Kajmakčalan's peak are organised in Bitola. Try the experienced Gorki Baloyannis at Baloyannis Tours (p311) or environmentalist Nesad Azenovski at Biosfera (p313).

Painted in lovely eggshell blue, the church has an icon collection that includes a dark depiction of the Crucifixion, dating from 1785.

Dihovo's outdoor **swimming pool** (basically, a very large conduit for mountain-spring waters) is a popular summer hang-out for young Bitolans. Chill at the cafe, or chill still more in the ice-cold water.

Hiking trips in Pelister National Park are led by the hale Petar Cvetkovski of Villa Dihovo (see below). Among several routes is the 3½-hour hike to the glacial lakes atop Mt Pelister (€40) and the 6½-hour hike across Pelister to Brajčino (€80). It's a steep walk, so take good boots and stamina. There's a mountain hut to stay in. Alternatively, Petar can explain local trails and river walks you can tackle independently.

From Bitola, a taxi costs 150MKD.

SLEEPING & EATING

our pick **Villa Dihovo** (☎ 070544744; persafizicko@yahoo .com; pay as you like) One of the most extraordinary guesthouses anywhere, Villa Dihovo offers three perfectly decorated traditional rooms in the 80-year-old home of former professional footballer and ski instructor Petar Cvetkovski, his family and their enormous, fluffy white Siberian Samoyed. It's inside the first long driveway after the village centre's restaurant, and has a big flowering lawn that's great for kids. The only fixed prices are for the homemade wine and *rakija*; all else, room price included, is your choice.

Villa Patricia (☎ 239 977; s/d 900/1440MKD) Another new family-run guesthouse with lawn, this friendly place is a 10-minute walk from the centre, on the road towards the pool. The rooms and kitchen are spacious and well maintained by attentive owners Nevenka and Sasa.

Restoran Idela (☎ 293 033; mains 250-400MKD; ☻ 6am-midnight) This nourishing restaurant has a hunting-lodge feel and does great sausages and grilled *sirenje* (white cheese), plus specialities such as snails and river trout. It's furnished with traditional rugs and other accoutrements; a giant pagoda seats 20 out the back.

PELISTER NATIONAL PARK
ПЕЛИСТЕР НАЦИОНАЛЕН ПАРК

Macedonia's oldest national park (1948) covers 12,500 hectares of forest on the country's third-highest mountain range, the quartz-filled Baba massif. Eight peaks top 2000m, crowned by Mt Pelister (2601m). Two glacial

lakes, known as Pelisterski Oči (Pelister's Eyes), provide cool relief for tired hikers.

Pelister's 88 tree species include the rare five-leafed Molika pine. The mountain also hosts endemic Pelagonia trout, deer, wolves, chamois, wild boars and eagles. Bears frequently travel, apparently without visas, across the mountain to Greece.

A tiny, one-lift **ski area** operates, sometimes, by Hotel Molika (below). With waning snowfall and confusion over ownership, it's not dependable; nevertheless, if there's snow, ski rental is cheap. If the lift isn't working, build character by skiing down and walking up.

Malovište Маловиште

This lovely old Vlach village has great rustic ambience and some of Macedonia's best-preserved traditional architecture. However, the elderly villagers have proven totally uninterested in tourism and, despite many well-intended efforts, Malovište thus remains a nice place to visit with nowhere to stay.

Malovišta's little Šemnica River is spanned by precarious wooden bridges. The rough cobblestone laneways require good shoes. See the grand **Church of Sveta Petka** (1856), brimming with frescos and icons that reveal bygone wealth. A 30-minute hike accesses the **Church of Sveta Ana**, in a secluded beech forest.

To reach Malovišta from Bitola, drive 4km west towards Resen, and turn off at Kazani. Take the first left, and then another left through a tunnel and proceed straight.

Magarevo Магарево

Laid-back Magarevo (literally, 'Donkey Village') is another Pelister hamlet, 900m up the slopes. It was once the wealthiest and most populous of all the Vlach villages, with factories for textiles and cheeses, and seas of sheep; however, in WWI the Bulgarian and German occupying forces made it their headquarters, and it thus suffered considerable French and Serbian shelling from the ridgeline above.

Nowadays, people come to relax and take village walks in the clear mountain air. Find **private accommodation** (per person 900MKD) through Baloyannis Tours (p311) in Bitola. Rooms are simple but well maintained and clean, and home cooking is offered.

Hotel Molika (☎ 047-229 406; s/d €28/46) is up at 1420m, 12km from Bitola. The setting is great, the facilities worn. Still, despite the cramped rooms and uninventive cuisine, watching the stars glimmer on a snowy winter's night here is perfect.

A taxi from Bitola costs 400MKD.

KRUŠEVO КРУШЕВО
☎ 048 / pop 6000

For Macedonian history and identity there's no place like Kruševo. The Ilinden Uprising broke out here on 2 August 1903 and, though it was brutally suppressed by the Turks 10 days later, it's still celebrated annually nationwide – especially in Kruševo. The town has recently also become close to the Macedonian heart as the hometown of Toše Proeski (see the boxed text, below), the talented and compassionate singer who died tragically at the age of 26 on 16 October 2007. You'll appre-

ciate his importance to the Macedonians by visiting his memorial and the monastery he helped fund above the town.

Kruševo also boasts traditional houses nestled together along winding streets. At 1350m, it's the Balkans' most elevated town.

Sights & Activities

Admire Kruševo's old **traditional houses**, including a 250-year-old family mansion that's now the **Gallery Nikola Martinovski** (☎ 477 197; Nikola Gurkevič bb; ☯ 9am-4pm Tue-Sun), displaying the works of this very distinguished painter. Born on 18 August 1903, just after the Turks suppressed the Ilinden Uprising, Martinovski vividly captured Kruševo's daily life and heroic past. His most famous work, *Doilka* (The Wetnurse), depicts a woman

A SAINT IS BORN

If there's one name you should know when visiting Macedonia, it's Toše Proeski. Although he lived only 26 years, this handsome singer with a booming, operatic voice and seductive smile won the hearts of an entire nation with his music and compassionate spirit. At the time of his untimely passing in a car crash in Croatia on 16 October 2007, Toše was beloved across the Balkans. And, given the popularity of his first English-language album, released posthumously, it's clear that the young singer from Kruševo was on course for even greater global popularity.

Toše was 'discovered' at age 12 at a children's music festival, and had pop hits four years later. The charismatic singer became a teen heart-throb, and each successive album topped the charts. He was named a Unicef Goodwill Ambassador in 2004, singing before audiences of 30,000. Toše represented Macedonia at the Eurovision Song Contest, entertaining guests and media with his charm and phenomenal voice.

Toše was also a favourite with little children, who were allowed to come up on stage during his concerts and shyly give him a hug and a teddy bear or flowers. He donated money to support children's hospitals and schools, becoming known for his humanitarian work as much as for his singing. It's no exaggeration to say that Toše's passing was felt with as much grief by the Macedonians as the deaths of Princess Diana and John Lennon put together for the British.

In the last years of his life, Proeski became increasingly spiritual and introspective. He was determined to complete a long-planned monastery above Kruševo. After his death, those close to him recalled cryptic statements that suggested he had some mysterious foreknowledge of his own death. In the intense period of national mourning and media attention immediately after it, his last telephone call to friends about needing to go 'up there' (ostensibly, to Croatia) seemed to take on a more heavenly meaning.

While official sanctification is a difficult process, Macedonians are already treating Toše like a saint, with iconlike photos placed in shrines and private prayers for a young man they now call an angel looking down over them. When in Macedonia, you'll hear Toše's music played everywhere, especially in his hometown of Kruševo. Visit the Toše Proeski Memorial there to appreciate his significance, and if you're there on 16 October, the anniversary of Toše's death, expect massive and tearful ceremonies. On 5 October 2008, the first anniversary of Proeski's last performance, a concert featuring musicians from Macedonia and the whole Balkans was held in his honour in Skopje before 40,000 fans – this too is expected to become an annual event.

with baby, her eyes following yours wherever you move, like an Orthodox icon.

The museum holds original rugs, implements and artefacts. Martinovski's niece, the lively Viktorija Peti, speaks Macedonian, Greek and French.

The grandiose **Church of Sveti Nikola** (1905) boasts nice icons, as does the nearby **Church of Sveti Jovan** (1897). There's also a fascinating **icon gallery**.

On the northern hill looking over Kruševo, in the **cemetery** devoted to its national heroes, stands the **Toše Proeski Memorial**. This very moving open shrine to the late singer, bedecked with flowers, pictures and children's gift such as teddy bears and hearts, sees a constant stream of visitors, many in tears, from all over the Balkans.

Some 12km beyond the nearby **Memorial to the Ilinden Uprising**, the new **Monastery of Preobraženie** (Monastery of the Transfiguration) stands on a cliff. Endowed by Proeski before his death, the austere church has numerous icons and expansive views down into Kruševo's valley from outside. The idea that love can indeed move mountains is well attested to on the way here by the asphalt road blasted out of the rock in a matter of months – almost unheard of in a country where many main roads have languished unrepaired for decades. However, given Toše's popularity, and the fact that special events related to him will be held here for as long as there are Macedonians, the road had to be capable of holding two tour buses passing at the same time.

In winter, Kruševo has **skiing**, though slopes are more modest than those of Mavrovo. Nevertheless, it's cosy and good for beginners. In summer, conditions are good for **hiking** and **mountain biking**.

Sleeping & Eating

Hotel Montana (☎ 477 121; Hotelska zona bb; s/d 1740/2140MKD; ☒) The clifftop Montana offers great views of Kruševo's clustered roofs. However, facilities are dated, the dining hall disconsolate. Still, an indoor pool, a fitness centre, and marked hiking and mountain-biking trails nearby (bikes are available) provide action. Prices rise in ski season.

Restoran Sape (Ilindenska bb; mains 120-250MKD; ☒ 9am-midnight) Good grills are done at this fixture known for traditional sausages.

Getting There & Away

For the best travel experience, get to Kruševo from Bitola, and then continue to Prilep. From Bitola, you pass placid **Demir Hisar** (Iron Castle in Turkish) and then wind upwards through beautiful greenery. Leaving Kruševo, below you emerges the legendary Pelagonian Plain.

From Skopje, a bus serves Kruševo (330MKD, three hours, three daily).

PRILEP ПРИЛЕП

☎ 048 / pop 76,768

The tobacco town of Prilep sits along the Pelagonian Plain, surrounded by weird, jagged rock formations. It's a dusty, hard-working town, with some decent eating and drinking. Its main attractions are the craggy castle of 14th-century Macedonian king Marko, and the magnificent Treskavec monastery nearby.

Orientation & Information

Prilep's train station is 20 minutes' walk from the centre; at the time of research the bus station was being moved alongside it. The action is centred on the connected main squares. Internet cafes are in the Trgovski Centar off the square.

Sights & Activities

Some 2km from town, **King Marko's Tower** (Markovi Kuli) rises from a sharp cliff. This defensive position, largely a natural formation, was fortified in ancient times. Today's remains date from 14th-century King Marko (r 1371–1395), a semi-autonomous despot acknowledged in folk songs. The windswept site offers great views.

Prilep's old marketplace, the **Čaršija**, houses traditional artisans' shops. The **clock tower** above is from Ottoman times.

Locals stroll well-lit **Mogila Park**, on Prilep's southern edge, on summer evenings. It's a moving place, with communist-era memorials to fallen Macedonian soldiers.

Prilep's **theatre festival** (June to July) stages performances in the Dom na Kultura. The mid-August **beer festival** is good fun.

Sleeping

Hotel Breza (☎ 423 683; Moša Pijade 24a; s/d 840/1680MKD) The Breza has good renovated rooms near the centre and friendly service.

Hotel Sonce (☎ 401 800; Aleksandar Makedonski 4/3a; s/d 1040/2080MKD' ⚄) Five minutes beyond the Breza, the Sonce has decent rooms, a restaurant and an outdoor swimming pool.

Hotel Crystal Palace (☎ 418 000; Leninova 184; s/d/tr €35/59/83) Near the train station, Prilep's four-star institution has well-appointed rooms with amenities.

Eating & Drinking

Pizzeria Leone (Goce Delcev 30; ☯ 8am-1am) This central place is very popular for pizza and drinks.

Porta Club Restaurant (Republikanska 84; mains 300-450MKD; ☯ 9am-1am) A spacious, nicely lit bistro, the Porta Club does fancy grills and cheap fish (Mavrovska trout is 600MKD per kilogram). It's under nightclub Tabu.

Bankok Oriental (☎ 425 027; Marksova 212; mains 250-440MKD; ☯ noon-1am) Macedonia's only Thai restaurant is run by the beaming Pichet Siangdang and his Macedonian wife, Biljana. Both the cooking and the colourful decor are authentic.

Entertainment

our pick **Virus** (Borka Taleski bb; ☯ 8am-1am) Pop, house and live rock are frequently played at this very popular place. Its classic touches include weathered wooden stairs, ornate print wallpaper, old paintings and little balcony tables.

Aporea (Orde Tuteski 66; ☯ 9am-1am) Rock with Prilep's underground set at this no-frills bar. Live bands appear on Sunday.

Tabu (Republikanska 84; ☯ 9am-1am) This stylish, slickly lit rooftop club-bar is near the clock tower.

Getting There & Away

From Prilep buses serve Skopje (420MKD) via Negotino and Veles, some turning for Strumica (400MKD, four hours); Bitola (120MKD, 11 daily), a few continuing to Ohrid (380MKD); and Kavadarci (190MKD, 1½ hours, two daily). Prilep is also on the Bitola–Skopje train line (three daily trains).

AROUND PRILEP
Treskavec Monastery
Манастир Тресқавец

This 13th-century monastery 10km above Prilep rises from Mt Zlato (1422m), a bare massif replete with twisted rock formations.

Its vivid frescos, including a rare depiction of Christ as a boy, line the 14th-century **Church of Sveta Bogorodica**, itself built over a 6th-century basilica. Earlier Roman remains are visible inside, along with graves, inscriptions and monks' skulls.

The monastery has suffered due to neglect, but in July 2008 the Macedonian government announced investment of €320,000 to repair some of the damaged structures.

Treskavec offers basic **accommodation** (☎ 070918339; per person 200MKD), and food.

GETTING THERE & AWAY
A paved road is planned; till then, drive from Prilep to the end of the paved road, unless you have a 4WD for the final few rocky kilometres. If going by jeep, start from Prilep's cemetery and look for the sign marked 'Manastir Sveta Bogorodica, Treskavec'. Head straight up.

Alternatively, to hike there, drive or take a taxi to Dabnica village and follow the cobbled track up towards Mt Zlato; after the fountain, continue on a straight path, and you'll arrive (two hours total).

TIKVEŠ WINE REGION
Macedonia's winery heartland, Tikveš is a place of rolling vineyards, serpentine lakes, deep caves and mountains, as well as world-class archaeological sites and churches. It's especially beautiful at dusk, when the fading sunlight suffuses soft hills laden with millions and millions of grapes.

The Tikveš wine region stretches from Rosoman and Negotino to Kavadarci and Demir Kapija. Vintners both local and foreign venerate its unique soil, with apocryphal tales of Frenchmen sighing in despair over not having such fertile earth back home. In any case, the climatic conditions mean that very little rain is necessary. Tikveš local grapes generally retain an ideal sugar concentration (17% to 26%).

Wine's been made here since the 4th century BC, continuing under the Romans and Byzantines. Under communism the industry was nationalised, lowering quality and upping bulk exports. Nowadays, Macedonian wine is finally getting some well-deserved attention (see the boxed text, opposite).

Skopje travel agencies arrange wine tastings; alternatively, contact the wineries themselves (advance reservations required).

FOR THE LOVE OF WINE

It's no surprise that Macedonians are wont to wax eloquent about their beloved wines; now, however, discerning foreign visitors are also head over heels for them.

In fact, Dutchman Dave Vlam was enthused enough to start a wine club in Skopje; its monthly tastings now represent key social events for cultivated locals and foreign dignitaries alike (see p295). An indefatigable wine lover, Dave gushes that 'some Macedonian wines are even better than French wines'.

Others agree, such as Norway's ambassador to Macedonia, Carl Schiotz Wibye. 'During my four years in Macedonia, I have enjoyed a number of excellent wines from professional producers,' he attests. 'I believe that Macedonian wines will be competitive in any market.'

Another committed wine aficionado is American consultant Jason Miko, a longtime visitor to Macedonia. The adjectives fly from his tongue when describing Macedonian wines, which he compares to Californian and South African wines. 'Within the next 10 years,' he adds, 'Macedonia could well become known for producing some of the best handcrafted wines in Europe.'

Handcrafted is the key for Kire Ristov, winemaker at Disan Hills Winery (see p322). Considered a winemaking prodigy, this 29-year-old has already won four consecutive first-place awards for his wine at Negotino's annual competition. He's benefited, of course, from some good advice (Kire's father worked for 30 years at the large Povardarije Winery). Says Kire, 'I love my job, so even though hand-picking the grapes to use only the best is hard work, it's part of the joy of making the best wine.'

Macedonia's newfound winemaking success has been enhanced by modern technology and equipment, in which Disan Hills has invested heavily. Yet there are some stubborn iconoclasts, like friendly old Nikola Velkov, grandson of the man who started the original Tikveš Winery in 1885. 'I'm not against new technology,' he says, 'but the secret to making great wine is in the wood barrels.' For Nikola, and for many other locals, 'the spirit of Kavadarci is wine. Without wine, you can do nothing.'

The Macedonian Wine Club in Skopje occasionally holds tasting tours here (see p295). The informative www.tikveswineregion .com website offers geographic, cultural and historical information.

Kavadarci Кавадарци
☎ 043 / pop 38,741

Fittingly dusty and agricultural, the Tikveš hub of Kavadarci is starting to improve its services and attractions, the top one being Tikveš Winery, southeastern Europe's biggest and oldest. Kavadarci's gregarious locals have one humorous peculiarity probably lost on outsiders: their good-natured profanity. Basic greetings are heavily soaked in swearing, apparently for its own sake – so don't blush when someone greets you by saying *dojdi da t'ebam* (literally, 'come here so I can screw you'!).

SIGHTS & ACTIVITIES

The **Kavadarci Museum** (☎ 413 470; 7 Septembri 58; admission free; ⊙ 8.30am-4.30pm, closed Sun) contains ancient finds, some depicting divine wine bacchanalia.

Massive **Tikveš Winery** (☎ 414 204; www.tikves .com.mk; 29 Noemvri 5) was created in 1885 and produces 29 wines, including T'ga Za Jug, an agreeable red considered the Macedonian classic (see the boxed text, p287). New technology and foreign expertise have transformed Tikveš into an elite vintner. Winery tours involve seeing the facilities, followed by a tasting.

The central **Vinoteka David** (cnr Cano Pop Ristov & Ilindenska; ⊙ 8am-1pm & 5-7pm) has regional wines.

Harvest season opens with the **Kavadarci Wine Carnival** (5 to 7 September), and its costumed parade, public wine tasting and merrymaking.

SLEEPING & EATING

our pick Hotel Uni Palas (☎ 419 600; Edvard Kardelj bb; s/d incl breakfast €36/56) This comfortable modern hotel has well-appointed rooms with hydromassage showers, and a popular cafe-bar.

MACEDONIA

Restoran Exclusive (☎ 411 561; bul Makedonija 66; ☽ 8am-midnight) About 100m from the hotel, Kavadarci's best wine restaurant serves Macedonian and international dishes.

GETTING THERE & AWAY

From Kavadarci buses serve Skopje (240MKD, eight daily), Prilep (190MKD, one hour, two daily) and Bitola (300MKD, four daily). For Negotino, use local buses (30MKD, 15 minutes, six daily), or take a taxi (200MKD).

Around Kavadarci

Lying 3km southwest of Kavadarci, past **Vataša**, the **Monastery of Sveti Nikola** sits prettily amidst forests alongside a river. Its tiny church boasts rare 16th-century frescos. In the 18th century it was a theological school and protected books salvaged from abandoned monasteries.

Continuing south, **Grkov Winery** (☎ /fax 400 565; pericajovevski@urbaninvest.com.mk; Krnjavo) enjoys a spectacular vineyard setting in **Krnjavo** (26km from Kavadarci). Organised tours and tastings are held. It's challenging to reach; after **Garnikovo** village, turn at the large yellow road-sign with many printed destinations onto the small left-hand road. Continue straight, and turn on a dirt road leading uphill to the winery. If you reach the settlement below, you've missed this road.

Returning to Vataša, stop for some homemade wine at **Badev Winery** (☎ 071250693; Blažo Itsev 10, Vataša). This family establishment is planning organised tours and accommodation.

Lake Tikveš Тиквешко Езеро

If you've been to Lake Ohrid and are looking for something weirder but just as wet, get off the beaten track and onto the dynamited one at **Lake Tikveš**. Created in 1968 by damming the Crna River, the lake's surrounded by scrubland and stark cliffs, dotted with medieval hermitage frescos, and circled by eagles and hawks. Being artificial, it has no endemic species, though it seems the monster catfish – weighing in at up to 200kg – have been pretty territorial since Comrade Tito first dispatched them into the 100m depths.

The 32km-long lake lies 11km southwest of Kavadarci; turn south at **Vozarci**, then pass **Resava** to reach the small **beach**. The strange slanted stones above it are said to be 11th-century **Byzantine graves**, part of a now mostly underwater cemetery.

In Kavadarci, **Saško Atanasov** (☎ 071250810; atanasov.sasko@yahoo.com) arranges half-day **boat trips** with skippers and English-speaking guide. Large groups use the 40-seater boat (4000MKD per group), while small groups use a regular fisherman's caique (1800MKD).

The tour navigates the lake's widest stretches for 20km, visiting the 14th-century **Pološki Monastery** (also called Polog Monastery). The monastery's **Church of Sveti Gijorgji** is a single-nave construction built by Serbian emperor Stefan Dušan (r 1331–55). His brother, Dragutin, is buried in the church's portico. Note the unusually expressive **frescos**, like that of the Dormition of the Virgin, which presents Christ stooping to kiss the dying Mary. Emperor Dušan and his wife, Empress Jelena, are depicted in frescos facing you when entering. Eat at the shaded picnic tables outside.

Ringed by rugged cliffs, the lake is good for **birdwatching** (look for the royal eagle, bearded vulture and white Egyptian vulture). Sometimes **fishing** is possible, though reeling in the obese catfish from the muddy depths might require a hydraulic lift. Go **swimming**, from boat or shore, but remember that Tikveš's strange currents sometimes run counter to the prevailing flow, so don't stray far.

Mt Kozuf & Ski Centar Kozuf

Mt Kozuf, 30km west of Gevgelija, preserves pristine wilderness filled with endemic flora. Here the brand-new **Ski Centar Kozuf** (Kavadarci office ☎ /fax 400 635; www.skikozuf.com.mk; Edvard Kardelj bb; Skopje office ☎ 02-3290 603; III Makedonska Brigada) seeks to rival Mavrovo. In Kavadarci, its office is inside Hotel Uni Palas (see p319). From Skopje to Kozuf via Gevgelija is 200km.

The ski centre opened in 2007 with 10 trails (12km total). Base lifts start at 1480m, reaching Zelen Breg peak (2160m); 60km of trails will be finished by 2010. Daily lift tickets cost 1000MKD. A ski school operates. Extensive cross-country trails exist here as well. In summer, enjoy **hiking**, **climbing** and **caving** on Mt Kozuf with guides (ask at the ski centre). At the time of research a smart modern hotel, self-catering apartments and a restaurant were shortly to open; check before you arrive.

Hunting Lodge Mili Sin (☎ 071361198; Mt Kozuf; r incl breakfast from €35) is located 18km southeast of the ski centre, ensuring skiers don't have to worry about Roger Moore–style chases while skiing. The lodge is well organised for would-be assassins of deer, martins and wild boars. It'll arrange hunting permit, guide, gun, attack dog and taxidermist. In summer, prices drop and hikers can stay.

Vataša's Monastery of Sveti Nikola has basic rooms (100MKD per person) set amidst forests. Staying at Lake Tikveš's Položski Monastery requires advance preparations. If interested, consult ahead with whoever is organising your trip. **Grkov Winery** (☎ /fax 400 565; pericajovevski@urbaninvest.com.mk; Krnjavo) has an ideal vineyard setting and a few rooms, but arrange in advance.

Negotino Неготино
☎ 043 / pop 19,212

Negotino is small, but big on wine. It's on the north–south E75 highway and railway line, 90 minutes from Skopje. In the 8th century BC, the Paeonian city of Antigonea stood nearby. It and Stobi, just further north, were important cities under the ancient Macedonians and Romans.

A tourist information centre, planned for near the municipal building, will offer town and winery information.

SIGHTS & ACTIVITIES
For ambience, visit the **Čaršija** and Ottoman **clock tower** (1821). The **Negotino Museum** (☎ 361 712; Maršal Tito 119; ☼ 8.30am-4.30pm) boasts finds from the 8th century BC through to communist times; these include immaculately preserved gold coins of Philip II and Alexander the Great, discovered in August 2008. Wine-related artefacts, including a touching 2nd-century-BC gravestone depicting a Macedonian family tending their vineyards under the Antigonean sun, live at the new **wine museum** adjacent. It displays old winemaking implements, has historical background on Tikveš winemaking, and offers tastings.

The pacific **Monastery of Sveti Gjorgji** (☎ 360 091) occupies a wooded hill 3km east of Negotino. Built in the 14th century, it was rebuilt in 1860 and features numerous faded frescos; near them stand vivid new ones. Down a hill, there's a fountain and a path lined with 20 tiny **chapels**, each dedicated to

a different saint, filled with icons and run through with spring water. Locals visit these sacred grottoes to pray. To get here, take a taxi (90MKD).

With a reputation for excellence, **Bovin Winery** (☎ 365 322; www.bovin.com.mk; Industriska bb) has been awarded at international competitions since it opened in 1998. Tours include extensive tastings.

Negotino's square offers free tastings and fun during the **Week of Wine** (8 to 14 February), honouring Sveti Trifun, patron saint of vintners.

SLEEPING & EATING
Monastery of Sveti Gjorgji (☎ 360 091; per person 150MKD) There are 50 clean and decent shared rooms in this tranquil location; however, there's no air-con and most rooms share a bathroom. One private room (600MKD) has its own bathroom.

Hotel Havana (Industriska; s/d 1200/1500MKD) Well-kept rooms with wooden floors, air-con and spacious bathrooms are found at this curious place set between a gas station and an enormous pool – Negotino's top summer nightclub – on the main road passing town.

Restoran Chardak (Straso Pindzur 46; mains 200-400MKD; ☼ 8am-1am) Negotino's top restaurant, Chardak has traditional Macedonian food and myriad Macedonian wines.

GETTING THERE & AWAY
Local buses serve Kavadarci (30MKD, 15 minutes, six daily); a taxi there is 200MKD. Buses from the **bus station** (☎ 361 744; Industriska bb) serve Skopje (220MKD, 1½ hours, nine daily), Strumica (210MKD, 1½ hours, three daily), Prilep (230MKD, 1½ hours,five daily) and Bitola (310MKD, two hours, four daily). Two summer-only buses reach Ohrid (480MKD, four hours) and Struga (510MKD, 4½ hours).

Trains from the **train station** (☎ 363 950), serve Skopje (135MKD, two hours, three daily) and Gevgelija (82MKD, one hour, three daily). One Gevgelija-bound train continues to Thessaloniki, Greece (900MKD, three hours).

Other Wineries
Winery Dudin (☎ 043-368 506; www.dudinwinery.com.mk; Aco Adzi Ilov 5; Krivolak), 7km northwest of Negotino in Krivolak, offers tours. Its traditional-style

MACEDONIA

tasting room has a great ambience for imbibing. To get here, you'll cross the main E75 highway; turning south on it leads to Demir Kapija, located near the magnificent **Demir Kapija Gorge**.

At Demir Kapija, visit **Elenov Winery** (☎ 02-367 232; vinarija_elenov@t-home.com.mk; Ivo Lola Ribar bb; Demir Kapija), on the right-hand side before entering the village. Dating from 1928, it was Serbian king Aleksandar's official wine cellar. Elenov also organises tastings.

Also in Demir Kapija is **Popova Kula Winery** (☎ 02-3228 781; Demir Kapija), which has great views over vineyards and the gorge from its tasting room, decorated with traditional rugs and fixtures. Rooms were being prepared here at the time of research (check ahead). Entering town, turn right past the cemetery up an 800m dirt road to reach the winery.

Just 5km south of Negotino, **Disan Hills Winery** (☎ 043-362 520, 070384325; ristov@mt.net .mk; Dolni Disan) is set amidst rolling vineyards, and run by people who put their heart and soul into crafting limited quantities of high-quality wine. From here you can enjoy fantastic views over the fields and lively little **Dolni Disan**, sustained for decades by its large-scale grape collective, and run by wine-dark elders. A decrepit Ottoman mosque and oak tree here are both around 300 years old. Families here descend from Macedonians who fled Greece during the 1912–13 Balkan Wars.

Beyond Dolni Disan the asphalt road ends with the much more sparsely populated **Gorni Disan**; from here you can reach Ski Centar Kozuf, if travelling by jeep. Near this village, Dolni Disan locals claim, once stood an ancient church; razed by the Turks, it has disappeared, except for a **secret tunnel**. A very few villagers claim to have crawled through the tunnel – together with the enormous snakes that inhabit it – for 1km before turning back in fear; no one knows for sure how long the tunnel is, why it was created, or what might lie at the end.

At the time of research Disan Hills Winery was preparing traditional rooms overlooking rolling vineyards (check ahead); it can also arrange rooms in private homes 500m away in Dolni Disan. Drink at the iconoclastic Pensioner's Club, or at the local *kafana*, where elders may surprise you with homemade *kiselo mleko*, fried dough and organic cheese.

Stobi Стоби
The ruins of Roman Stobi occupy a valley beside the E75 highway, 9km northwest of Negotino. The **site** (admission 100MKD; ◷ 9am-5pm), discovered in 1861, is organised, with running descriptions of the major ruins. There's a patio with snack bar and gift shop selling replicas and wines.

Stobi was built in the 7th century BC, and grew under the Macedonians and Romans, who developed this strategically set city on the north–south Axios trade route. Stobi's ancient Jewish population is attested to by synagogue foundations beneath those of a Christian basilica. Stobi became an early Byzantine archbishopric, yet a Gothic sacking in 479 and an earthquake in 518 portended doom, and depopulation occurred by the 13th century.

Start at the **Roman amphitheatre** (on the left) and clamber up past it; from here, you'll see Stobi's best **mosaics**. The path continues past several well-marked ruins, including **ancient sanctuaries** to gods. At the end, turn right to the enormous **city walls**. Excavations continue.

EASTERN MACEDONIA

The major northeastern sites are all fairly contiguous, making Skopje day trips easy. **Kumanovo** is Macedonia's third-biggest city, but unfortunately is getting ragged and run-down. However, some 4km north, **Staro Nagoričane** village boasts the lovely **Church of Sveti Gjorgji**. Built in 1071 by the Byzantines, the church was rebuilt by Serbian king Milutin (1313), who commissioned its rich **frescos**, now considered among the country's most important Byzantine paintings.

To get there, head north of the E871 Kumanovo–Sofia highway, turn left at the Prohor Pčinski sign, again left at the T-intersection and then take the next right. Staro Nagoričane is 1km off the main road. Ask the local police station to find the keyholder if the church is closed.

Carry on to the isolated, jagged peak of Taticev Kamen, and the **Kokino megalithic observatory**, built around 1815 BC to measure solar and lunar movements. Artefacts exist, but it's not a grand structure like Stonehenge. Nevertheless, the peak's calibrated marks and niches were definitely used to mark the solstices and equinoxes, along with the moon's four annual positions (with an accuracy experts find astonishing today) for determining optimal times to harvest different crops. After Kokino's observatory status was confirmed in 2002, it entered NASA's charts at number four, behind Abu Simbel in Egypt, Stonehenge and Cambodia's Angkor Wat – not bad company.

To reach Kokino, head north 5km from Staro Nagoričane on the main road, turning right to Dragomance. Head northeast for 15km past Stepanče; a small left-hand sign points uphill about 200m. The final climb (20 to 30 minutes) up to Kokino's volcanic ridge is steep, though safe.

One of Macedonia's largest monasteries is the **Monastery of Sveti Joakim Osogovski**, near the E871 highway and the Bulgaria border, at **Kriva Palanka**. Skopje buses serve Palanka via Kumanovo (200MKD, two hours, 10 daily). Services are limited, though decent eateries exist. The monastery occupies a wooded valley 3km from town; drive there (five minutes), walk (30 minutes), or go by taxi (100MKD).

The monastic complex includes a large bell tower, charnel house, three-storey dormitory, guardhouse and two churches, the small, 12th-century **Church of Sveta Bodorodica** and the larger, multidomed, 19th-century **Church of Sveti Joakim Osogovski**. Its door and 12 roof cupolae, representing the twelve apostles, feature vivid frescos. The monastery is especially busy on 29 August – Sveti Joakim's feast day.

Accommodation in the old monks' quarters (300MKD) or modern pilgrims' lodge (600MKD) is available, though phone reservations are required (☎ 031-375 063) – despite the place having 80 rooms. Ask a Macedonian speaker to call for you, as no English is spoken. Along with spiritual solitude, sleeping here is a useful and inexpensive option for those travelling to Bulgaria.

KRATOVO КРАТОВО

Kratovo is one of Macedonia's best-kept secrets. An ancient mining town within a volcanic crater, its medieval stone towers overlook three rivers spanned by stone bridges. A secret tunnel labyrinth connects the town underneath. Near town, hiking, bizarre rock formations and prehistoric cave art abound.

From Roman through Ottoman times, Osogovski mountain iron, gold and silver

deposits enriched Kratovo, justifying its fortress-like construction. The town is also associated with Macedonian revolutionary Petre Vojnički Karpoš. In 1689, with Austrian soldiers advancing on Skopje, Karpoš launched the first Macedonian uprising. However, the feckless Austrians withdrew, the uprising was crushed, and Karpoš was beheaded by the Turks. Today, his head has been returned, in a sense, with the sculpted bust you'll see displayed in his last stronghold.

Friendly Stevče Donevski of the **Rock Art Centre** (☎ 481 572; Planinska 1; ✆ 8am-8pm) does walking tours (€60 per group) covering Kratovo's traditional architecture, and explains the cave paintings and sculptures discovered in the nearby mountains. (He also offers tours to the cave-art sites and the observatory.)

Sights

One of the town's six 18th-century **bridges**, the **Radin Bridge** – the most beautiful – connects Kratovo's two major parts. Kratovo's six surviving 14th-century **towers** were used for safeguarding gold, silver and citizens during sieges. The best preserved, the **Watch Tower**, features massive walls and gunholes. It houses a small **museum**, which preserves some interesting historical artefacts.

Unfortunately, Kratovo's **secret tunnels** are closed. Built to hide or evacuate the citizenry during sieges, this astonishing feat of medieval architectural ingenuity can be partially appreciated in the only open tunnel entrance, under the **Emin Beg Tower**, Enter through Restoran Aleksandrija (see p324), and watch for the puddles.

The exciting **prehistoric rock art** discoveries made in the nearby Osogovski mountains include sculpted stone and clay figurines of prehistoric gods and 30,000-year-old cave paintings. There's also the astonishing neolithic **Cocev Kamen Observatory** – like Kokino, it was possibly used for making astronomical calculations – containing the Balkans' only known neolithic paintings. The site is hard to find, hard to understand without a guide and, with its narrow neolithic stone cliff-stairs, definitely for the sure-of-foot only. Happily, the Rock Art Centre does guided observatory tours and rock-art cave tours (both €60 per group) to these remote areas. It also arranges local **hiking** and other outdoor trips.

Sleeping & Eating
At the time of writing, Stevče Donevski from the Rock Art Centre was planning to open a central, restored old townhouse with antique flourishes – check in advance.

Hotel Kratis (☎ 481 201; Goce Delčev bb; s/d 800/1600MKD). Those seeking the worn, unfriendly communist experience can try the Yugoslav-era Hotel Kratis.

Restoran Aleksandrija (☎ 481 289; Josip Daskalov 35; mains 150-300MKD; ✹ 9am-midnight) Near Emin Beg Tower, Aleksandrija does good *skara* and conceals Kratovo's only tunnel entrance, now home to the restaurant's tiny wine cellar.

Shopping
Rock Art Centre (☎ 481 572; Planinska 1; ✹ 8am-8pm) Gems, strange stones and other local artefacts are displayed here. Traditional souvenirs include Kratovo salt (about 100MKD) – a delicious substance involving 13 ingredients.

Getting There & Away
Kratovo lies 18km south of the E871 highway, after you turn off at the Stracin Pass. From Skopje, there are five daily buses (220MKD, two hours).

AROUND KRATOVO
Just 12km northwest of Kratovo, down a dirt road, is **Kuklica** – the 'Valley of the Stone Dolls'. Bizarre rock formations resembling various human and animal forms, these sand-toned pinnacles have inspired countless legends. Note that climbing around on them erodes and damages these soft rock formations.

There's no Kuklica bus, and the dirt road's rough. The Rock Art Centre (p323) arranges trips.

The magnificent **Monastery of Sveti Gavril Lesnovski**, 12km south of Kratovo, has a beautiful church, one of only three to have an iconostasis carved by the Frčkovski–Filipovski team. Lesnovski was a 12th-century literary centre, producing beautiful illuminated manuscripts. The large church (1341) was built over an 11th-century one. Its vivid frescos include an unusual depiction of the 12 zodiac signs.

Since the monastery hasn't accommodation, sleep in nearby Probištip; try **Hotel Crešovo Topče** (☎ 032-484 683; pl Leninov bb; Probištip; s/d incl breakfast 850/1700MKD), with bright, clean rooms and a restaurant.

The monastery is not well signposted, and the road up contains hairpin turns. Skopje has five daily buses to Probištip (250MKD, two hours). A taxi from here to Lesnovski costs 250MKD.

BEROVO БЕРОВО
☎ 033 / pop 7,000
Tucked up at 850m in the heavily forested Maleševski mountains near Bulgaria, placid Berovo is essentially a weekend getaway for city dwellers. Its traditional Macedonian architecture and churches are worth seeing, its pine-ringed lake a tranquil place for contemplation. The Maleševski range is largely uninhabited.

Sights
The living **Monastery of Sveti Arhangel Mihail** is distinguished by its octagonal bell tower, set on a stone base. This 19th-century convent became an important educational centre. The wood-and-stone convent quarters have a nice garden, and the main chapel, with large wooden portico, is elegant.

Pretty **Lake Berovo**, 4km from town, is a meditative, pine-flanked place (though cold for swimming). There's a hotel and restaurant in front.

Visiting local **mountain villages** is entertaining. **Rusinovo** is a traditional weaving centre, while nearby **Vladimirovo** is full of rugged individuals telling apocryphal tales of epic, *mono-i-mono* battles with wolves. Berovo's villages and mountains feature slant-roofed, Swiss-style wooden houses; when it snows, try **cross-country skiing**.

Sleeping & Eating
Loven Dom (☎ 470 454; r from €25) The forested lodge has airy, comfortable rooms and restaurant.

Maleševo Recreation Centre (☎ 471 212; www.malesevo.com.mk; cabin 1400MKD) Simple cabins are on offer at this lakeside place. The nearby restaurant has outdoor seating and good *skara* (200MKD to 350MKD).

Getting There & Away
From Skopje, take a bus (350MKD, three hours, nine daily). Eastern towns like Kratovo, Probištip and Berovo aren't well connected, though taxis are inexpensive. If driving south, the 47km road to Strumica

across the Maleševski mountains is wonderful; the numerous curves and horse-drawn carts means you'll be taking it slow and enjoying the views. A Berovo–Strumica taxi costs 1500MKD.

To enter Bulgaria from Berovo, head 25km north to Delčevo (120MKD, three daily buses). Crossing from Delčevo to the yeah-baby university town of Blagoevgrad requires a taxi (€25).

STRUMICA СТРУМИЦА

☎ 034 / pop 54, 676

Mention Strumica to a Macedonian and you might get a knowing grin: not only the country's agricultural powerhouse, it's renowned for good-natured excess, which includes great nightlife and a huge costumed carnival. For travellers, lush mountain waterfalls, gorgeous Byzantine churches and Roman ruins also entice.

History

Documents dating from 181 BC first mention Strumica as Astraion, but the Romans renamed it Tiberiopolis and so it was known until the Slavs arrived in the 7th century. Strumica's strategic position, on a fertile plain near the Belasica range, made it militarily significant in the Byzantine-Bulgarian wars of the 10th and 11th centuries. In fact, the Battle of Belasica – in which, according to legend, the forces of Basil II Voulgaroktonos (Basil the Bulgar-Slayer in Greek) blinded 14,000 Bulgarian soldiers – was fought on the plain east of Strumica in July 1014. In the mid-14th century, Serbian emperor Stefan Dušan ruled over Strumica; however, by 1383 the Ottomans had annexed it.

When the Turks were expelled during the Balkan Wars of 1912–13, Strumica was contested ground; the 1913 Treaty of Bucharest awarded it to Bulgaria.

In WWI, Bulgaria lost, and Strumica, and Macedonia, became part of Royalist Yugoslavia. In WWII, Bulgaria again occupied the area but was again defeated, and Strumica became part of communist Yugoslavia. Nevertheless, for reasons of geographical and cultural proximity, the local Strumički dialect has a bit of a Bulgarian flavour – another detail other Macedonians note with a chuckle.

Orientation & Information

Walk from the bus station to the centre (10 minutes) or take a taxi (40MKD). Across the street from the station, ul Bratstvo Edinstvo reaches bul Maršal Tito after 800m. The main square and pedestrian street (ul Leblebigiska) are to the right.

Ace Stojanov (☎ 075513222; acestojanov@yahoo.com) Go Macedonia (see p292) local guide for tours to Kolešino and Smolare Waterfalls, Bansko's Roman baths, and the Veljusa and Vodoča Byzantine churches.

Atlantis Travel (☎ 346 212; www.atlantis.com.mk; Dimitar Vlahov 18; ◷ 9am-7pm) Run by the helpful Saško Dončovski, this agency near the municipality has branches nationwide and provides local information. Also arranges tours, local outdoor activities, flights, and ground transport to Greece and Bulgaria.

Sights & Activities

In 1913, the occupying Greek army torched Strumica, destroying 1900 buildings. Little classic architecture thus remains, though **Arsovi House** (Toše Arsov) is one interesting 19th-century townhouse that survived, as is **Adzitosevi House** (1820), a grand, square construction with arching windows. It's 100m from the **Church of Sveti Kiril i Metodij** in southwestern Strumica. The nearby **Strumica Museum** (77 Mart 2; ◷ 8am-4pm) preserves thousands of artefacts from neolithic to modern times; here, enthusiastic young archaeologist Zoran Rujak provides good background.

The modern **Church of the 15 Holy Martyrs of Tiberiopolis** (Slavčo Stojmensko bb; ◷ 5am-9pm) conceals some older treasures. Named for 15 Christians banished here by Julian the Apostate (the offbeat Roman emperor who tried to revive paganism between 361 and 363), it was originally a basilica and preserves original mosaic fragments. The church's **icon gallery** houses icons from the 15th century.

Strumica's Ottoman past survives in the **Orta mosque** (1613), on the road to Veljusa village. It was built over a 6th-century church, and archaeologists have found artefacts from both here. The former **Turkish post office** is opposite.

On a jagged, windswept peak overlooking Strumica from the southwest stand the **Czar's Towers** (Carevi Kuli). Inhabited since neolithic times, the site's dominated by two grand towers and offers great views over Strumica and its plain. From the centre, it's a brisk 15-minute walk (400m) uphill.

MACEDONIA

Strumica's large **city park** offers **swimming** in two adjacent outdoor **pools** (admission 80MKD; 🕙 10am-6pm), and **tennis** on clay **courts** (per hr 200MKD; 🕙 May-Oct). Borrowing a racquet is free.

Festivals & Events

At the beginning of Lent, the annual **Strumica Carnival** comes roaring to life. Drawing upwards of 30,000 visitors from Macedonia and abroad, the carnival involves five days of drinking, debauchery and costumed merrymaking. Its pagan roots as a promoter of fertility and protector against evil spirits are undeniable, as the behaviour of the participants reveals. The well-organised proceedings include a masked ball, a special children's day, door-to-door parading and the awarding of cash prizes for the sophisticated costumes and floats.

Sleeping & Eating

Hotel Sirius (☎ 345 141; Kliment Ohridski 110; s/d incl breakfast 1500/2580MKD; 🏊) This relaxing place 2km from town has modern, airy rooms. The outdoor pool is very popular with locals. The restaurant does good grills and breakfasts. Taxis from downtown cost 70MKD.

Hotel Ilinden (☎ 348 000; Goce Delčev bb; s/d/tr incl breakfast 1200/2000/2500MKD) This cosy, central hotel has air-conditioned, modern rooms and a restaurant.

Hotel Studio Inn (☎ 071205851; Kliment Ohridski; s/d 1240/2180MKD) Above a banquet hall, Studio Inn has new rooms. It's 1km from downtown, by Pilikatnik fish restaurant.

Restoran Dukat (cnr Leblebigiska & Maršal Tito; mains 200-320MKD; 🕙 7am-midnight) This local favourite is a *skara* restaurant, 50m up from Select Café-Bar.

Pilikatnik Riben Restoran (Kliment Ohridski 110; mains 250-400MKD; 🕙 8am-midnight) Grilled trout, carp and catfish are specialities at this classic fish joint.

Drinking & Entertainment

Strumica's nightlife is legendary. On summer evenings the streets and bars are full of fashionable young people until late.

Select Café-Bar (☎ 343-000; JJ Svestarot bb; 🕙 8am-3am) This pumping three-floor cafe, bar and nightclub always delivers Strumica's best night out.

Getting There & Away

From Strumica's **bus station** (☎ 346 030; Kliment Ohridski bb), buses serve Skopje (360MKD,

2½ hours, 13 daily), Negotino (220MKD, two hours, three daily), Prilep (420MKD, three hours, three daily), Bitola (480MKD, four hours, two daily) and Ohrid (650MKD, five hours, one daily). Kombis also serve Skopje (500MKD).

A bus from Strumica to Bulgaria leaves Monday through Saturday. After the Novo Selo border crossing, it stops in Sandanski and Blagoevgrad before Sofia (600MKD, four hours). Alternatively, take a taxi to Sandanski (€35).

AROUND STRUMICA
Bansko Банско

The bubbling geothermal waters of Bansko, 12km east of Strumica, have revitalised bathers since antiquity, as the well-preserved **Roman baths** there show. The 3rd-century site, discovered accidentally in 1978, is extensive; to ensure the doors will be open, find archaeologist Zoran Rujak (☎ 075288666) at the Strumica Museum (p325). The 10-room baths used hot and cold mineral waters. The spring that feeds the baths (and now the communist-era hotel nearby) is 50m below.

Churches

About 4km west of Strumica, **Vodoča** village hosts the intriguing **Monastery of Sveti Leontij-Vodoča**. The Byzantines modified this 5th-century basilica in 1018, four years after Car Samoil's forces were defeated at the Battle of Belasica, fought outside Strumica. Additions continued through the 12th century, when Sveti Leontij was a major regional monastery. Valuable 11th-century frescos survive, and the macabre **necropolis** holds over 1000 tombs, from the 14th to the 20th century. A few nuns live here.

Lying 3km further, **Veljusa** village boasts the gorgeous **Monastery of Sveta Bogorodica-Eleusa** (1080) a secluded oasis of Byzantium, surrounded by flowering lawns. Some original floor mosaics and a marble iconostasis have survived. The vivid frescos date from 1085, 1164 and the 19th century, and include a rare depiction of Christ as a child. Unfortunately, when they burnt Strumica in 1913, the Greek army also burnt Eleusa and took its precious manuscripts. The Bulgarians also left with some valuable loot when they pulled out later. Eleusa's now inhabited by kindly, English-speaking nuns.

Waterfalls

Mt Belasica is home to the 39m-high **Smolare Waterfall**, Macedonia's largest, tumbling from a forested cliff 29km east of Strumica. A 580m trail, complete with wooden bridges, leads up from **Smolari** village (a 20-minute walk). The agile can clamber down from the viewing bridge and cavort in the falls' ice-cold reservoir. Another waterfall, 17km east of Strumica above **Kolešino**, is essentially a series of large mountain streams. The **Kolešino Waterfalls** require some dexterity, as the trail's narrow and sometimes slippery, and involves leap-frogging rocks and logs. Nevertheless, it's worth the exertion to enjoy the fresh, moist air of Belasica's forests. Driving up, you'll pass a tourist information centre with information about local flora and fauna.

In Kolešino, stop to marvel at **Kolid market**, the biggest watermelon depot in the Balkans. In summer this huge parking lot is full of tanned and sweating farmers hoisting melons into trucks; the 18-wheelers, coming from as far away as Serbia and Croatia, attest to Strumica's agricultural greatness.

Lake Dojran Дојранско Езеро

Humble Lake Dojran is severed by the Greece border, 25km southeast of Strumica. Despite chronic water loss caused by Greek farmers siphoning off water for crops, the Macedonian government's replenishment program has helped the lake survive. Of course, it's not Ohrid, but Dojran's waters do have therapeutic qualities, they say, for everything from skin ailments to arthritis. A warm, shallow lake, Dojran is a good and safe spot for children.

In summer, Dojran sees families, local weekenders and cross-border guests. While today's Hellenes come for Dojran's casino, those of longer memory know the lake differently: the great Herodotus himself recorded Dojran's **cormorant fishing**, in which fishermen on stilted huts send birds to drive fish into their nets. Known only here and in China, this fishing is still practised in winter.

Sleeping & Eating

Podgorski An (☎ 351 100; Kolesino; s/d incl breakfast 700/1400MKD) New rooms adorn a restaurant considered the Strumica area's most atmospheric. The traditional fare is tasty and good value. The rooms, while clean and new, are not traditional.

Hotel Istatov (☎ 225 234; Novi Dojran; s/d/apt 1200/2400/3000MKD; 🏊) This Novi Dojran village hotel has modern rooms with amenities, a sports centre, a swimming pool, a fitness centre and a hearty restaurant.

Restoran Fuk-tak (☎ 225 320; Marsal Tito 15, Star Dojran; mains 200-400MKD) Who could resist a place with a name like this? Great Dojran carp and traditional Macedonian specialities, not Chinese, are done well here.

Getting There & Away

Except for Dojran, Strumica-area sites are not far apart. If without transport, however, try a personalised tour: contact guide Ace Stojanov (p325) or Atlantis Travel (p292).

Veljusa and Vodoča churches require a car or taxi (200MKD to 300MKD). For Smolare Waterfall, drive east, and turn right after Novo Selo to Smolari. Continue past the enormous tree, and park before the path. For Kolešino Waterfalls, head east, but turn right after 2km for Murtino and continue past it and Bansko to Kolešino. If coming from Novo Selo, head south for Mokrievo, and continue to Kolešino.

Bansko, Kolešino and Smolari are served by kombis (50MKD to 100MKD), which wait near Strumica's post office. Taxis to Kolešino and Smolari cost 150MKD and 400MKD respectively.

There's no Strumica–Dojran bus; a taxi costs 700MKD.

MACEDONIA DIRECTORY

ACCOMMODATION

Accommodation listings are ordered by preference. Skopje's hotels are expensive; agencies find private rooms. Ohrid and villages have budget and midrange choices; book ahead for July-August, Orthodox Christmas (7 January), and Orthodox Easter, and during major festivals or carnivals elsewhere.

ACTIVITIES

Zare Lazarevski ski centre in Mavrovo National Park is Macedonia's premier resort, followed by Ski Centar Kozuf, near Gevgelija. Pelister National Park's one-lift centre sometimes works. Popova Šapka ski centre, near Tetovo, will hopefully resume operations – check locally.

PRACTICALITIES

■ Print media is politically aligned. Sensationalism and scandal prevail. *Dnevnik, Večer* and *Vest* are popular Macedonian-language dailies; *Forum* is a well-regarded weekly news-and-views magazine. Albanian-language newspapers include *Fakti* and *Koha Ditore*. Roma and Turkish papers exist. *Politika* (Belgrade) sells in smaller numbers.

■ A1 is popular among many Macedonian-language TV stations for news; its A2 channel has top films. Macedonian National TV operates in Macedonian (MTV1) and Albanian (MTV2). Albanian-language Alsat TV is popular. Cable-access international channels exist. FM radio stations include City Radio (94.7), Radio Antenna 5 (95.5) and Jazz FM (100.8).

■ Electricity is standard European (220V to 240V/50Hz to 60Hz).

■ The metric system is used.

■ Macedonia uses the PAL video system.

Hiking is spectacular in Mavrovo, Galičica and Pelister National Parks, and in Bitola-area Mariovo. Strumica-area waterfalls in the southeast make nice wooded walks, as does Lake Matka near Skopje. **Zoran 'Max' Stamboliski** (☎ 075292928; zoke_madmax@yahoo.com) is a very experienced guide who leads a variety of tours and trips including hiking, caving, canyoning, paragliding and horseback riding in some of Macedonia's most beautiful spots.

Lake Ohrid is perfect for swimming and boating. Birdwatch on Lake Prespa and Lake Tikveš. Paragliding's great on Mt Galičica near Ohrid and in Kruševo.

Travel agencies run outdoors tour; see p292. In Bitola, try Baloyannis Tours (p311) or Biosfera (p313); in Ohrid, contact Tourist Bureau Biljana (p303). Macedonia's biggest mountaineering association, **Korab Mountain Club** (www.korab.org.mk/indexen.html) details 14 mountain routes online.

BOOKS

Who Are the Macedonians? by Hugh Poulton offers good background.

For Balkans and Macedonian travel literature, see p22. For language resources, see opposite.

BUSINESS HOURS

Businesses operate 8am to 8pm weekdays and 8am to 2pm Saturday. Post offices operate 6.30am to 4pm, banks 7am to 5pm Monday to Friday.

CUSTOMS

Customs checks are cursory. One litre of alcohol and 200 cigarettes are allowed in. The limit for nondeclarable cash is €10,000.

DANGERS & ANNOYANCES

Macedonia's Albanian villages near Kosovo and Albania don't see tourists, and outsiders may be suspiciously scrutinised (sheepdogs are usually more dangerous, however, and the locals friendly enough). Avoid Skopje's avaricious bus/train station taxis. Some visitors are alarmed by Roma children's begging and occasional pickpocketing attempts. Littering still vexes, but for many it's the new 'Europeanising' law forbidding sale of alcohol in shops and kiosks after 7pm that represents Macedonia's greatest annoyance.

EMBASSIES & CONSULATES

All missions below are in Skopje (see the map, p290; area code ☎ 02).
Albania (☎ 2614 636; ambshqip@mt.net.mk; HT Karpoš 94a)
Australia (☎ 3061 114; austcon@mt.net.mk; Londonska 11b)
Bulgaria (☎ 3229 444; bgemb@unet.com.mk; Ivo Ribar Lola 40)
Canada (☎ 3225 630; honcon@unet.com.mk; bul Partizanski Odredi 17a)
France (☎ 3118 749; www.ambafrance-mk.org; Salvador Aljende 73)
Germany (☎ 3093 900; dt.boskop@mol.com.mk; Lerinska 59)
Greece (☎ 3219 260; grfyrom@unet.com.mk; Borka Taleski 6)
Montenegro (☎ 3227 277; mail@montenegroembassy .org.mk; Vasil Stefanovski 7)
Netherlands (☎ 3129 319; www.nlembassy.org.mk; Leninova 69-71)
Russia (☎ 3117 160; embassy@russia.org.mk; Perinska 44)
Serbia (☎ 3129-298; yuamb@unet.com.mk; Pitu Guli 8)
UK (☎ 3299 299; beskopje@mt.net.mkl; Dimitrie Čupovski 26)

USA (☎ 3116 180; www.skopje.usembassy.gov; Samoilova bb)

FESTIVALS & EVENTS

The Ohrid Summer Festival (p305) is Macedonia's best cultural event, the springtime Strumica Carnival (p326) its most fun. Visit Vevčani's raucous Carnival (12 to 14 January; p300) or Ohrid's captivating Balkan Festival of Folk Dances & Songs (July; p305).

The Galičnik Wedding is a beloved traditional event in gorgeous nature (12 to 13 July; p299). Skopje's music festivals include the wintertime Taxirat Festival (p293) and the Skopje Jazz Festival (October; p293).

HOLIDAYS

New Year 1 & 2 January
Orthodox Christmas 7 January
International Women's Day 8 March
Orthodox Easter Week March/April
Labour Day 1 May
SS Cyril and Methodius Day 24 May
Ilinden Day 2 August
Republic Day 8 September
1941 Partisan Day 11 October

INTERNET RESOURCES

Balkanalysis (www.balkanalysis.com) Politics and current events, with archive covering Macedonia and other Balkan countries.
Beyond Ohrid (www.beyondohrid.com) Ohrid-Prespa alternative outdoor activities.
Skopje Online (www.skopjeonline.com.mk) Updated city info, plus nightclub listings.
Culture in Macedonia (www.culture.in.mk) Cultural info and festival listings.
Exploring Macedonia (www.exploringmacedonia.com) Useful travel website.
FAQ Macedonia (http://faq.macedonia.org) General Macedonia-interest portal.
Macedonian Wine Route (www.macedonian wineroute.com) Macedonian wineries information.
Tikves Wine Region (www.tikveswineregion.com) More information on Macedonia's wine country.

LANGUAGE

Macedonia's official national language is Macedonian, though minority languages such as Albanian, Vlach, Romany and Serbian are also used officially. Albanian is the most extensively used minority language. Macedonian's a south-Slavic language, closely related to Bulgarian, with regional dialects. The literary language is based on the Veles central dialect. Macedonian Cyrillic is official, but Latin script is also used. Macedonian and Bulgarian are the only non-inflected Slavic tongues, and the only to use infixed direct articles. Knowing Serbian, Croatian or Bulgarian is helpful. Try Lonely Planet's *Eastern Europe Phrasebook* or Christina Kramer's *Macedonian: A Course for Beginning and Intermediate Students.*

Cyrillic was created by 9th-century Macedonian monks Kliment and Naum of Ohrid, who modified the Glagolitic script of their mentors (SS Cyril and Methodius) with Greek. To learn Cyrillic, identify the Latin-identical letters, then isolate the others. The Language chapter (p454) lists useful Macedonian words and phrases.

MONEY

There are Macedonian denar (MKD) 10, 50, 100, 500, 1000 and 5000 notes, and 1-, 2- and 5-denar coins. Denars are nonconvertible abroad. Euros are usually accepted. Some hotels quote rates in euros, but payment in denars is always accepted.

Macedonian exchange offices (*menuvačnici*) work commission-free. ATMs are widespread, except in villages. Avoid travellers cheques. Credit cards aren't always accepted; carry cash.

POST

Mail to Europe and North America takes seven to 10 days. Certified mail (*preporačeno*) is more expensive. The small green form you fill out should be kept as proof. Letters to the USA cost 38MKD, to Australia 40MKD and to Europe 35MKD. Skopje has global shipping companies.

TELEPHONE & FAX

Internet cafes offer cheap international digital phone service. Public-telephone cards sold in kiosks or post offices in units of 100

EMERGENCY NUMBERS

- Ambulance ☎ 194
- Highway and roadside assistance ☎ 196
- Police ☎ 192

MACEDONIA

(200MKD), 200 (300MKD), 500 (650MKD) or 1000 (1250MKD) offer good value for domestic calls. Drop the initial zero in city codes and mobile prefixes (three-digit numbers starting with ☎ 07) when calling from abroad.

Macedonia's largest provider is T-Mobile, followed by Cosmofon and VIP.

Major post offices do international faxing, though lawyers' offices do it more cheaply.

TOURIST INFORMATION

Travel agencies are best, though some towns have information offices; see the information section of specific towns.

TRAVELLERS WITH DISABILITIES

City streets' random holes can challenge the wheelchair-bound, and most historical sites and old quarters aren't handicapped-friendly. Expensive hotels may provide ramps. Buses and trains have no disabled access.

VISAS

Passport holders from Australia, Canada, the EU, Iceland, Israel, New Zealand, Norway, Switzerland, Turkey and the USA do not need a visa and can stay for three months. Visas are required for most others. Visa fees average US$30 for a single-entry visa and US$60 for a multiple-entry visa. Check www.mfa.gov .mk for updated information.

TRANSPORT IN MACEDONIA

GETTING THERE & AWAY

This section covers travel options to and from countries covered in this book. For information on getting to Macedonia from, say, Greece or Bulgaria, see the Transport chapter (see p439).

Air

Macedonia flights mostly arrive at/depart from **Alexander the Great Airport** (☎ 02-3148 651), 21km from Skopje. Ohrid's **St Paul the Apostle Airport** (☎ 046-252 820) sees little action. See www.airports.com.mk for information, including timetables and weather conditions. Exchange offices and hotel-booking and car-rental services are at Skopje's airport.

Airlines flying to/from Macedonia within the Western Balkans:

Adria Airways (airline code JP; ☎ 02-117 009; www .adria.si) Hub Ljubljana.

Croatia Airlines (airline code OU; ☎ 02-3115 858; www.croatiaairlines.hr) Hub Zagreb.

JAT (airline code JU; ☎ 02-3116 532; www.jat.com) Hub Belgrade.

Macedonian Airlines (MAT; airline code IN; ☎ 02-3292 333; www.mat.com.mk) Hub Skopje.

Land

This section covers travel between countries covered in this book, but Macedonia also borders Greece and Bulgaria. Access to/from all neighbouring states is unrestricted.

BORDER CROSSINGS

Albania

The two most-used of four border crossings to Albania are along Lake Ohrid: Kafasan/Qafa e Thanës, 12km southwest of Struga, is busiest, followed by Sveti Naum/Tushëmishti, 29km south of Ohrid. There's also Blato, 5km northwest of Debar, and Stenje, on Lake Prespa's southwestern shore.

Serbia & Kosovo

Tabanovce is the major border crossing for Serbia (both road and rail). Pelince, about 25km northeast, is used infrequently. For Kosovo, the Blace border crossing is 20 minutes north from Skopje. Another crossing point is Tetovo's Jazince.

BUS

Regular buses serve all Balkan cities. See the table, opposite, for details of international services from Skopje.

CAR & MOTORCYCLE

A green card endorsed for Macedonia is required.

TRAIN

The north–south train line serving Macedonia starts in Thessaloniki, Greece. There's one daily Skopje–Thessaloniki train (700MKD, five hours). The line continues through Serbia to Belgrade (1300MKD, eight to 10 hours, two daily), and then Zagreb (Croatia) and Ljubljana (Slovenia). Another international line goes from Skopje to Pristina (Kosovo). However, at present, only a ticket to the border (100MKD, two hours) is sold; buy another one after entering Kosovo.

Find international-route timetables on the Macedonian Railways (Makedonski Zheleznici) website (www.mz.com.mk /patnichki/timetable.htm), and on the Euro Railways website (www.eurorailways .com).

GETTING AROUND
Bicycle
Cycling is popular, and out of cities traffic is light, though mountains and reckless drivers are common.

Bus
Skopje is well connected to domestic destinations. Buses vary from old and rickety to new and air-conditioned. During summer, book ahead for Ohrid buses. (For service details, see the table, p296.) Baggage fees (10MKD) are encountered. People ship parcels or letters by bus, paying the driver about 100MKD. The recipient waits to retrieve the item upon the bus's arrival.

Car & Motorcycle
Police at checkpoints randomly stop cars. If you have the correct documentation and aren't violating laws, don't worry.

AUTOMOBILE ASSOCIATIONS
AMSM (Avto Moto Soyuz na Makedonija; ☎ 02 3181 181; www.art.com.mk; Ivo Ribar Lola 51, Skopje) offers road assistance, towing services and information (in German, English and Macedonian), and has branches nationwide.

DRIVING LICENCE
National driving licences are respected, though an international driving permit is best.

FUEL & SPARE PARTS
Petrol stations are prevalent except in rural areas, where they often close after dark. Unleaded and regular petrol cost about 60MKD per litre, while diesel costs around 44MKD per litre. Spare parts and sometimes service are available at the fantastically named 'vulkanizer' shops.

HIRE
Skopje's rental agencies include international biggies and local companies. Ohrid has many agencies, other cities fewer. Sedans average €50 daily, including insurance. Bring passport, driving licence and credit card.

INSURANCE
Rental agencies provide insurance (€15 to €25 a day, depending on vehicle type; the non-waivable excess is €1000 to €2500). Green-card insurance is accepted; third-party insurance is compulsory.

ROAD CONDITIONS
Major roads are safe and maintained. Secondary rural roads are more run-down and feature livestock, tractors and horse drawn carts. Minor mountain roads can be narrow and slippery; ascertain conditions locally. Signage is hit and miss. Skopje drivers are particularly selfish; some consider long, straight boulevards like bul Partizanski Odredi and bul Jane Sandanski to be Formula One racecourses.

ROAD RULES
Drive on the right. Speed limits are 120km/h (motorways), 80km/h (open road) and 50km/h to 60km/h (in towns). Speeding fines start from 1500MKD. Seat belts and headlights are compulsory. Cars must carry replacement bulbs, two warning triangles, a first-aid kit

INTERNATIONAL BUS SERVICES FROM SKOPJE

Destination	Price (MKD)	Duration (hr)	Departures
Belgrade	1400	9	13 daily
Istanbul	2560	12	5 daily
Ljubljana	3770	14	1 daily
Pristina	350	2	8 daily
Sofia	850	5½	3 daily
Thessaloniki	1280	4	Mon, Wed & Fri
Tirana	1300	7	2 daily
Zagreb	3150	12	1 daily

MACEDONIA

and (15 November to 15 March) snow chains. Motorcyclists and passengers must wear helmets. Police are vigilant on speeding, drink driving and headlights. Fines are payable immediately. The legal blood-alcohol limit is 0.05%.

Taxi

Macedonian taxis are inexpensive. Skopje base rates are 50MKD, in smaller cities 30MKD to 40MKD. For intercity routes, some taxis wait to fill up with four people before going – the individual cost is barely more than the bus-ticket rate.

Train

Macedonia's trains are living museums, and hopefully the government won't follow through on its threat to modernise them. Macedonian Railways' website has timetables (www.mz.com.mk/patnichki/timetable.htm).

The major lines are Tabanovce (on the Serbia border) to Gevgelija (on the Greece border), via Kumanovo, Skopje, Veles, Negotino and Demir Kapija; and Skopje to Bitola, via Veles and Prilep. Smaller Skopje–Kičevo and Skopje–Kočani lines exist.

Trains from Skopje serve Negotino (135MKD, two hours, three daily), Prilep (170MKD, three hours, three daily), Bitola (200MKD, four hours, three daily), Gevgelija (185MKD, 2½ hours, three daily), Kumanovo (60MKD, 40 minutes, four daily) and Kičevo (150MKD, two hours, three daily).

Montenegro Црна Гора

Imagine a place with sapphire beaches as spectacular as Croatia's, rugged peaks as dramatic as Switzerland's, canyons nearly as deep as Colorado's, palazzos as elegant as Venice's and towns as old as Greece's and then wrap it up in a Mediterranean climate and squish it into an area two-thirds of the size of Wales and you start to get a picture of Montenegro.

Going it alone is a brave move for a nation of this size – its entire population of 678,000 would barely fill a medium-sized city – but toughing it out is something with which this gutsy people has had plenty of experience. Their national identity is built around resisting the Ottoman Empire for hundreds of years in a mountainous enclave much smaller than its current borders.

Given Montenegro's natural assets, tourism is vitally important to its future. In that respect it's done spectacularly well in filling its tiny coast with Eastern European sunseekers for two months of each year, while serving up the rest of the country as bite-sized day trips. The upshot for intrepid travellers is that you can easily sidestep the border in the rugged mountains of Durmitor, the primeval forest of Biogradska Gora or in the many towns and villages where ordinary Montenegrins go about their daily lives. This is, after all, a country where wolves and bears still lurk in forgotten corners.

Montenegro, Crna Gora, Black Mountain: the name itself conjures up romance and drama. There are plenty of both on offer as you explore this perfumed land, bathed in the scent of wild herbs, conifers and Mediterranean blossoms. Yes, it really is as magical as it sounds.

FAST FACTS

- **Area** 13,812 sq km
- **Capital** Podgorica
- **Currency** euro (€); US$1 = €0.76; UK£1 = €1.10; A$1 = €0.51
- **Famous for** being really beautiful
- **Key phrases** zdravo (hello), doviđenja (goodbye), hvala (thanks)
- **Official language** Montenegrin
- **Population** 678,000 (2008 estimate)
- **Telephone codes** ☎ 382; international access code ☎ 00
- **Visas** not necessary for Australian, British, Canadian, New Zealand or US passport holders or most EU citizens (see p371 for more information)

HIGHLIGHTS

- **Bay of Kotor** (p341) Marvel at the bay's majesty and explore the historic towns hemmed in by its limestone cliffs.
- **Lovćen National Park** (p357) Drive the vertiginous route from Kotor to the Njegoš Mausoleum at the top of the national park.
- **Sveti Stefan** (p353) Enjoy the island's iconic views while lazing on its sands.
- **Ostrog Monastery** (p364) Seek the spiritual at this peaceful place.
- **Tara Canyon** (p365) Float through paradise on a rafting trip between the canyon's kilometre-plus walls.

ITINERARIES

- **Ten days** Spend a night in Herceg Novi (p341), then base yourself in Kotor (p345) for two nights. Drive through Lovćen (p357) to Cetinje (p358), then the next day stop for lunch in Rijeka Crnojevića (p361) before continuing to Šćepan Polje (see p366) via Ostrog Monastery (p364). Go rafting the following morning and spend the night in Podgorica (p362). Head to Virpazar (p361) for a boat tour of Lake Skadar (p360) and then take the scenic road to Ulcinj (p356) via the southern shore. Finish with two nights in Ulcinj and two nights in Sveti Stefan (p353).
- **Two to three weeks** As above, but allow another night in Kotor and Cetinje. From Šćepan Polje head instead to Žabljak (see p365) and then Biogradska Gora (p367) before continuing to Podgorica. Spend a night on Lake Skadar before filling up your remaining days on the beaches of Ulcinj and Sveti Stefan.

CLIMATE & WHEN TO GO

Like most of the Mediterranean, the coast enjoys balmy summers and mild winters. The warmest months are July and August, when the temperature ranges from 19°C to 29°C (average lowest to average highest). The coldest is January, ranging from 4°C to 12°C. The sea temperature ranges from a chilly but hardly frigid 13°C in January and February to 25°C in August.

In the mountainous interior the temperatures are considerably cooler, with the exception of the plain around Podgorica, which sizzles in summer. January temperatures range from -7°C to 2°C, while even in August, the warmest month, the average minimum temperature is a nippy 9°C, although the maximum is around 23°C. Spectacular afternoon thunderstorms are common in summer.

Montenegrin tourism is hung up with the idea of 'the Season', which in most places is July and August. Wherever possible, these months should be avoided, as prices skyrocket, accommodation options dry up, traffic snarls along the coastal road, insanely loud music thumps through the streets at night and hordes of tourists blanket the beaches. Worse still, some coastal areas experience water shortages.

The best months are May, June, September and October. You'll still get plenty of sunshine, and the average water temperature is over 20°C. The downside of avoiding 'the Season' is that you will find some places closed (especially camping grounds and beachside bars and restaurants) and activities harder to track down.

The ski season is roughly from December to March. Winter can be a lovely time to visit the coast if you relish peace and quiet and the opportunity to hang out with locals in the few cafes that remain open. Many hotels close their doors also, but accommodation shouldn't be difficult to find.

HISTORY

For a small and little-known country, Montenegro packs a great deal of history into its rugged terrain.

HOW MUCH?

- Short taxi ride €5
- Internet access €1 per hour
- Cup of coffee €1
- Bottle of local wine €2.50
- Postcard €0.50

LONELY PLANET INDEX

- Litre of petrol €1.23
- Litre of water €1
- Half-litre of beer €1.50
- Souvenir T-shirt €12
- Street snack (burek) €1

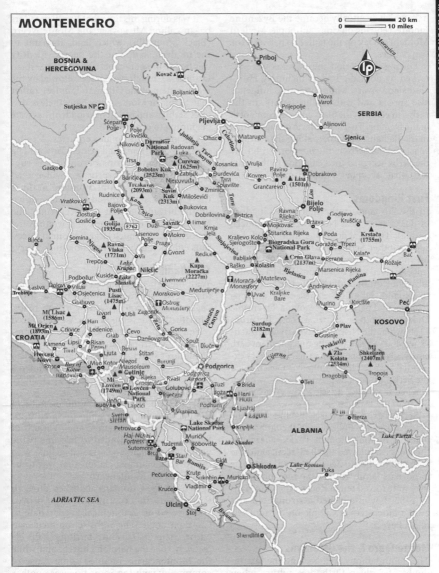

MONTENEGRO

Before the Slavs

Historians record the Illyrians inhabiting the region by 1000 BC, establishing a loose federation of tribes across much of the Balkans. Maritime Greeks created colonies on the sites of some Illyrian settlements around 400 BC, and when Illyrian Queen Teuta attacked the Greeks in 229 BC, the Greeks asked for Roman protection.

The Romans subdued the Illyrians and by AD 10 had absorbed the Balkans into their provinces, establishing roads and trade networks. The most important Roman town in what is now Montenegro was Doclea near present-day Podgorica. In 395 the Roman Empire was split into two halves, the Western half retaining Rome as capital, and the Eastern half, which eventually became the Byzantine Empire, centring on Constantinople. Modern Montenegro lay on the fault line between the two entities.

During this period the Balkans were attacked by nomadic raiders including Huns, Goths and Avars, while Byzantine influence also spread and with it Christianity. In the early 7th century, the Slavs arrived from north of the Danube. Two main Slavic groups settled in the Balkans, the Croats along the Adriatic coast and the Serbs in the interior. With time the Serbs accepted the Orthodox faith, while the Croats accepted Catholicism.

First Kingdoms

In the 9th century the first Serb kingdom of Raška arose near Novi Pazar (in modern Serbia). This kingdom was short lived, but soon another Serb state, Duklja, sprang up on the site of the Roman town of Doclea. Initially allied with Byzantium, Duklja eventually shook off Byzantine influence and began to expand, taking in Pelješac (in modern Croatia) and parts of Hercegovina. Over time Duklja came to be known as Zeta, but from 1160, when the Nemanjič dynasty was established, Raška again became the dominant Serb entity. Over two centuries the Nemanjičs expanded Serb territory. Emperor Dušan ruled the Serb empire at its greatest extent, when it reached from the Adriatic to the Aegean and north to the Danube.

Serbian expansion was halted in 1389 at the battle of Kosovo Polje, where the Serbs were defeated by the Ottoman Turks. Thereafter the Turks swallowed up the Balkans and the Serb nobility fled to Zeta, on Lake Skadar. The Crnojevići family rose to the fore, but when they were forced out of Zeta by the Ottomans in 1480 they established a stronghold and built a monastery at Cetinje on the foothills of Mt Lovćen.

Montenegro & the Ottomans

This mountainous area became the last redoubt of Serbian Orthodox culture when all else fell to the Ottomans. Over time the Montenegrins attempted to fight back and established a reputation as fierce and fearsome warriors. The Ottomans opted for pragmatism, and largely left them to their own devices. Meanwhile Kotor, Budva and much of the Adriatic coast were controlled by the Venetians.

It was during this time that Venetian sailors began calling Mt Lovćen the Monte Negro (Black Mountain), which lends its name to the modern state. For the people, identity was tied to the notion of tribe and the Serbian Orthodox Church (which was allowed by the *millet* system of the Ottoman Empire), rather than Serbia or Montenegro. Nonetheless, distinct Serbian and Montenegrin identities were beginning to evolve.

During the Ottoman centuries, Montenegrin society remained geared for war. The land the Montenegrins occupied was rugged and desolate. Poverty was widespread and banditry and raiding common. At times the Ottomans attempted to clamp down on the brigandage that was occurring. The Montenegrins fought back and won several victories against much larger Ottoman forces, thus enhancing their reputation for bravery.

The Vladikas

With the struggle against a common enemy, the previously highly independent tribes began to work collaboratively by the 1600s. This further developed a sense of shared Montenegrin identity and the *vladikas,* previously a metropolitan position within the Orthodox Church, began mediating between tribal chiefs. As such, the *vladika* assumed a political role, and *vladika* became a hereditary title: the prince-bishop.

In 1697 Metropolitan Danilo established the Petrović dynasty. Danilo declared himself the 'Vladika of Cetinje and Warlord of Serbia'. Danilo continued to take the battle up to the Ottomans and established links with the Russians, an association that was to be significant for Montenegro.

In 1766 the Ottomans abolished the Serb Patriarchate in Peć (in modern Kosovo) and created an Ecumenical Patriarchate in Constantinople. The Serbs set up their own patriarchate in Habsburg territory. This effectively split the Serbian church, and while the Montenegrins retained some sense of community with the Serbs this was another factor in the divergent experience and evolution of a separate national consciousness for Montenegro.

While Serbia remained under Ottoman control, the Montenegrins under Petar I began to expand their territory in the late 18th century. The Montenegrins took the region known as Brda; in 1820 they defeated the Ottomans at Morača, and under Petar II Njegoš they defeated a much larger Ottoman force at Grahovo in 1858. In the space of little over 50 years they had doubled their territory.

Meanwhile, in 1797 Napoleon snuffed out the Venetian Republic, thus removing a rival for power in the Adriatic. The Habsburgs were given control of the Bay of Kotor and land north of Cetinje. Following further shenanigans Napoleon took these Habsburg territories in 1805. Later, however, the Montenegrins captured Kotor with naval support from the British. For the first time the Montenegrins had access to the sea, but it was shortlived, as Kotor was returned to the Habsburgs soon after.

Petar II Njegoš made further unsuccessful attempts to gain access to the sea. In other aspects of nation-building Njegoš was more successful. He increased the role of government and developed a system of taxation for Montenegro. While Njegoš made significant territorial gains, the Serbs and Montenegrins remained separated by a strip of Ottoman territory. However, Njegoš made contacts with the Serbs and first mooted the idea of a south Slavic state.

Freedom from the Ottomans

A rebellion against Ottoman control broke out in Bosnia and Hercegovina (BiH) in 1875. Both Serbs and Montenegrins joined the insurgency, Montenegrins, under Nikola Petrović, again excelling themselves and making significant territorial gains. At the Congress of Berlin in 1878 Montenegro and Bosnia achieved independence. Montenegro also won control of upland territories in Nikšić, Podgorica and Žabljak, territory around Lake Skadar, and the port of Bar.

It was at this time that the Montenegrins acquired a certain celebrity in Western Europe. Their achievements in the face of perceived Ottoman thuggishness were extolled as the feats of a 'race of heroes'. The Serbs, meanwhile, were suspicious of Montenegrin intentions, and the expansionist Austrians annexed Bosnia, thus stymying any further Montenegrin expansion to the north.

In the early years of the 20th century there were increasing calls for union with Serbia and rising political opposition to the Petrović dynasty. The Serbian Petar Karađorđević attempted to overthrow King Nikola Petrović,

and Montenegrin-Serbian relations reached their historical low point.

The Balkan Wars of 1912–13 saw the Montenegrins joining the Serbs, Greeks and Bulgarians in an effort to throw the Ottoman Turks out of southeastern Europe. Montenegro gained Bijelo Polje, Berane and Plav and joined their territory with that of Serbia. The idea of a Serbian-Montenegrin union gained more currency. In the elections of 1914, many voters opted for union. King Nikola pragmatically supported the idea on the stipulation that both the Serbian and Montenegrin royal houses be retained.

The Two Yugoslavias

Before the union could be realised WWI intervened. The Serbs entered the war on the side of the great powers, and the Montenegrins followed in their footsteps. Austria-Hungary invaded Serbia shortly afterwards and swiftly captured Cetinje, sending King Nikola into exile in France. In 1918 the Serbian army reclaimed Montenegro, and the French, keen to implement the Serbian-Montenegrin union, refused to allow Nikola to leave France. The following year Montenegro was incorporated into the Kingdom of the Serbs, Croats and Slovenes, the First Yugoslavia.

Throughout the 1920s some Montenegrins, peeved at the loss of their sovereignty, put up spirited resistance to the union with Serbia. This resentment was increased by the abolition of the Montenegrin church, which was absorbed by the Serbian Orthodox Patriarchate.

During WWII the Italians occupied the Balkans. Tito's Partisans and the Serbian Chetniks engaged the Italians, sometimes lapsing into fighting each other. Ultimately, Tito's Partisans proved the best organised and the most successful at resisting invading powers. With the diplomatic and military support of the Allies, the Partisans entered Belgrade in October 1944 and Tito was made prime minister. Once the communist federation of Yugoslavia was established, Tito decreed that Montenegro have full republic status and the border of the modern Montenegrin state was set.

In 1948 Tito fell out with Stalin and broke off contacts with Soviet Russia. This caused some consternation in Montenegro, given its historical links with Russia. Of all the Yugoslav states, Montenegro had the highest per-capita membership of the communist party and it was highly represented in the armed forces.

The Union & Independence

With the collapse of communism, Slobodan Milošević used the issue of Kosovo to whip up a nationalist storm and ride to power on a wave of Serbian nationalism. The Montenegrins largely supported their Orthodox co-religionists. In 1991 Montenegrin paramilitary groups were responsible for the shelling of Dubrovnik and parts of the Dalmatian littoral. In 1992, by which point Slovenia, Croatia and BiH had opted for independence, the Montenegrins voted overwhelmingly in support of a plebiscite to remain in rump Yugoslavia with Serbia. Admittedly, there was some Montenegrin edginess about their place within 'greater Serbia' and Montenegrins raised the issue of the Montenegrin autocephalous church in 1993. By 1997 Milo Djukanović was in charge of Montenegro and he broke with Milošević. In doing so he immediately became the darling of the West, which was now trying to isolate and bring down the Milošević regime. As the Serbian regime became an international pariah, Montenegrins increasingly wanted to re-establish their distinct identity.

In 2000 Milošević lost the election in Serbia. Meanwhile, Vojislav Kostunića came to power in Montenegro. With Milošević now toppled, Kostunića was pressured to vote for a Union of Serbia and Montenegro. In theory this union was based on equality between its two members; however, in practice Serbia was such a dominant partner that the union proved unfeasible from the outset. This rankled, given the Montenegrins' historic self-opinion as the 'best of the Serbs'. In May 2006 the Montenegrins voted for independence. Since then the divorce of Serbia and Montenegro has proceeded relatively smoothly. Montenegro has rapidly opened up to the West – in particular, welcoming many holidaymakers – and has instituted economic, legal and environmental reforms with a view to becoming a member of the EU.

PEOPLE

In the last census (2003) 43% of the population identified as Montenegrin, 32% as Serb, 8% as Bosniak (with a further 4% identifying as Muslim), 5% as Albanian, 1% as Croat and 0.4% as Roma. Montenegrins are the majority along most of the coast and in the centre of the country, while Albanians dominate in the southeast (around Ulcinj), Bosniaks in the far west (Rožaje and Plav), and Serbs in the north and Herceg Novi.

To get an idea of the displacement of the recent wars you need only look at changes since the 1981 census, when Montenegrins made up 69% of the population and Serbs only 3%.

RELIGION

Religion and ethnicity broadly go together in these parts. Over 74% of the population is Orthodox (mainly Montenegrins and Serbs), 18% Muslim (mainly Bosniaks and Albanians) and 4% Roman Catholic (mainly Albanians and Croats). Protestants barely register (0.06%) and only 12 people identify as Jewish.

In 1993 the Montenegrin Orthodox Church (MOC) was formed, claiming to revive the autocephalous church of Montenegro's bishop-princes, which was dissolved in 1920 following the annexation of Montenegro by Serbia in 1918. Furthermore, it claims that all church property predating 1920, and any churches built with state funds since, should be returned to it. The Serbian Orthodox Church (SOC) doesn't recognise the MOC and neither does mainstream Orthodoxy. The SOC still controls most of the country's churches and monasteries.

ARTS

Literature

Towering over Montenegrin literature is Petar II Petrović Njegoš (1813–51) – towering so much, in fact, that his mausoleum overlooks the country from the top of the black mountain itself (p358). This poet-prince-bishop produced the country's most enduring work of literature, *Gorski vijenac* (The Mountain Wreath), a verse play depicting the brutal lengths taken to maintain Orthodox Christianity as it faced the Ottoman threat.

An acclaimed writer of the Yugoslav period, Danilo Kiš was born in Serbia to a Montenegrin mother and Hungarian Jewish father, and raised in Montenegro. Several of his books are available in English, including *A Tomb for Boris Davidovich*.

Cinema

In the few years since independence, Montenegrin cinema has yet to set the world alight. Someone that's working hard to change that is Marija Perović, who's credited with being the country's first female film and TV director. She followed up her 2004 debut, *Opet pakujemo majmune* (Packing the Monkeys, Again!), with *Gledaj me* (Look At Me) in 2008.

Montenegro's biggest Hollywood success is cinematographer Bojan Bazeli, whose titles include *King of New York* (1990), *Kalifornia* (1993), *Mr & Mrs Smith* (2005) and *Hairspray* (2007).

Ironically, the movie that springs to most people's minds when they think of Montenegro is the 2006 Bond flick *Casino Royale*; the Montenegrin scenes were actually shot in the Czech Republic. Serbian Dušan Makavejev directed the Golden Palm–nominated *Montenegro* (1981), set in Sweden.

Music & Dance

If anyone doubts the relevance of the Eurovision Song Contest they should travel through Montenegro. Montenegrins love their local pop, particularly if it's a gut-wrenching power ballad or a cheesy ditty played loud and accompanied by a thumping techno beat. Popular artists include Sergej Ćetković, Vlado Georgiev and up-and-coming pretty boy Bojan Marović.

In the 1990s the excruciatingly named Monteniggers carried the torch for home-grown hip-hop. Continuing the unfortunate name theme, Rambo Amadeus is Montenegro's answer to Frank Zappa. He's been releasing albums since the late 1980s, flirting with styles as diverse as turbo folk, hip-hop and drum and bass.

Jumping back in time, Archbishop Jovan of Duklja was producing religious chants in the 10th century, making him the earliest-known composer in the region. The first reference to secular musical instruments is contained in 12th-century military instructions outlining tactics to create an illusion of greater numbers in battle. Traditional instruments include the flute and the one-stringed *gusle*, used to accompany epic poetry.

The unusual *oro* is a circle dance accompanied by the singing of the participants as they tease each other and take turns to enter the circle and perform a stylised eagle dance. For a dramatic conclusion, the strapping lads form a two-storey circle, standing on each other's shoulders.

Architecture

Traditional Montenegrin houses are sturdy stone structures with small shuttered windows and terracotta-tiled pitched roofs. In the mountainous regions a stone base is topped with a wooden storey and a steeply pitched cut-gable roof designed to let the winter snow slide off. The *kula* is a blocky towerlike house built for defence that's most common in the country's far-eastern reaches. They're usually three storeys tall with no windows on the lowest floor, and they sometimes have ornate overhanging balconies in wood or stone.

The influence of Venice is keenly felt in the walled towns of the coast, while Cetinje's streets feature late-19th-century mansions and palaces.

It's easy to be dismissive of the utilitarian socialist architecture of the Yugoslav period, yet there are some wonderfully inventive structures dating from that time. It's easy to imagine James Bond settling in with a martini beneath the sharp angles and bubbly light fixtures of some of the 1970s hotels. It would be a shame if those that haven't already been bowled over or modernised aren't restored to their period-piece glory.

Visual Arts

Montenegro's artistic legacy can be divided into two broad strands: religious iconography and Yugoslav-era painting and sculpture.

The nation's churches are full of wonderful frescos and painted iconostases. A huge number were produced by members of the Dimitrijević-Rafailović clan from Risan on the Bay of Kotor, which turned out 11 painters between the 17th and 19th centuries.

Of the modern painters, an early great was Petar Lubarda (1907–74), whose stylised oil paintings included themes from Montenegrin history. Miodrag (Dado) Đurić is now in his seventies but still creates accomplished surrealist musings. Other names to look out for include Milo Milunović, Filip Janković, Jovan Zonjić, Vojo Stanić, Dimitrije Popović and sculptor Risto Stijović. The best places to see the works of these and others are at Cetinje's Art Museum (p358) and the Podgorica Museum & Gallery (p362).

Of the contemporary crop, one to watch is Jelena Tomašević, whose paintings and video installations have been exhibited in New York, Berlin and Venice.

FOOD & DRINK

Loosen your belt, you're in for a treat. Eating in Montenegro is generally an extremely pleasurable experience. By default, most of the food is local, fresh and organic, and hence very seasonal.

The food on the coast, especially around the Bay of Kotor, is virtually indistinguishable from Dalmatian cuisine: lots of grilled seafood, garlic, olive oil and Italian dishes. Inland it's much more meaty and Serbian-influenced.

The only downside is a lack of variety. Restaurants tend to come to in three types: traditional (serving the aforementioned fish or meat grills), pizza and pasta joints, or a mixture of the two. By the time you've been here a week, menu déjà vu is likely to have set in.

Staples & Specialities

The village of Njeguši in the Montenegrin heartland is famous for its *pršut* (dried ham) and cheese. Anything with Njeguški in its name is going to be a fair-dinkum Montenegrin dish and stuffed with these goodies; this might be pork chops, veal, steak or spit-roasted meat *(Njeguški ražanj)*.

In the mountains, meat roasted *ispod sača* (under a metal lid covered with hot coals) comes out deliciously tender. Lamb is also slowly cooked in milk. You might eat it with *kačamak,* a cheesy, creamy cornmeal or buckwheat dish – heavy going but comforting on those long winter nights.

On the coast, be sure to try the fish soup, grilled squid (served plain or stuffed with *pršut* and cheese) and black risotto (made from squid ink). Whole fish are often presented to the table for you to choose from and sold by the kilogram.

Montenegro's domestic wine is eminently drinkable and usually the cheapest thing on the menu. Vranac is the indigenous red grape, producing excellent, full-bodied wines. Locally produced whites include chardonnay, sauvignon blanc and the native krstač.

Nikšićko *pivo* (try saying that after a few) is the local beer and a good thirst quencher. Many people distil their own *rakija* (brandy), made out of just about anything (grapes, pears, apples etc). They all come out tasting like rocket fuel, although the plum variety *(šljivovica)* is the most lethal.

The coffee is universally excellent. In private houses it's generally served Turkish style, 'black as hell, strong as death and sweet as love'. If you want anything other than herbal teas (camomile or hibiscus), ask for Indian tea.

Where to Eat & Drink

Fast-food outlets and bakeries *(pekara)* serving *burek* (meat- or spinach-filled pastries), pizza slices and *palačinke* (pancakes) are easy to find. American chains have yet to infest Montenegro.

Anywhere that attracts tourists will have a selection of restaurants and *konoba* (small family-run affairs). Most hotels will have a decent eatery and many offer full or half board.

There's usually no distinction between a cafe and a bar.

Vegetarians & Vegans

Eating in Montenegro can be a trial for vegetarians and almost impossible for vegans. Pasta, pizza and salad are the best fall-back options.

Habits & Customs

Lunch has traditionally been the main family meal but, with Western working hours catching on, this is changing. Bread is served free with most meals. It's perfectly acceptable to use your hands to pick out the bones of small fish.

For a list of Montenegrin eating and drinking words, see p45.

ENVIRONMENT

'Wild Beauty' crows Montenegro's enduring tourism slogan and indeed it's right to highlight the nation's extraordinary natural blessings. A lot of focus is placed on the clear coastal waters, but journey into the mountainous interior and you'll still find pockets of virgin forest and large mammals long since hunted out of existence on most of the continent.

The Land

Montenegro is comprised of a thin strip of Adriatic coast, a fertile plain around Podgorica and a whole lot of mountains. The highest peak is Zla Kolata (2534m) in the Prokletije range near the Albania border. Most of the mountains are limestone and karstic in nature and they shelter large swaths of forest and glacial lakes. Rivers such as the Tara, Piva and

Morača have cut deep canyons through them. The oddly shaped Bay of Kotor is technically a drowned river canyon, although it's popularly described as a fjord. Lake Skadar, the largest in the Balkans, spans Montenegro and Albania in the southeast.

Wildlife
Among the mammals that live in Montenegro are otters, badgers, roe deer, chamois, foxes, weasels, moles, groundhogs and hares. Bears, wolves, lynxes and jackals are a much rarer sight. Tortoises, lizards and snakes are easier to find and you might spot golden and imperial eagles, white-headed vultures and peregrine falcons above the peaks. The rare Dalmatian pelican nests around Lake Skadar, along with pygmy cormorants, yellow herons and whiskered terns.

National Parks
Sometime during the lifetime of this book it's possible that Montenegro will declare a section of the Prokletije mountains bordering Albania its fifth national park. This area holds the country's highest peak and is part of the proposed cross-border Balkans Peace Park (see the boxed text, p61).

Montenegro's first three parks were declared in 1952: Lovćen (p357), Durmitor (p365) and Biogradska Gora (p367). In 1983 Lake Skadar (p360) joined them as the country's first nonmountainous national park. In total they cover an area of 90,070 hectares.

Environmental Issues
For a new country, especially one recovering from a recent war, Montenegro has made some key moves to safeguard the environment, not least declaring itself an 'ecological state' in its constitution. Yet in the rush to get bums on beaches the preservation of the nation's greatest selling point sometimes plays second fiddle to development.

Water shortages continue to affect the coast and in 2008 high salinity levels rendered Tivat's supply undrinkable. A new desalination plant has been constructed near Budva, but these operations are notoriously energy-intensive.

The country currently imports 40% of its electricity; ideas mooted for increasing supply have included new hydro projects, requiring the flooding of river canyons, and potentially nuclear energy.

There's little awareness of litter as a problem. It's not just the ubiquitous practice of throwing rubbish out of car windows; we've seen waitresses clear tables by throwing refuse straight into a river and we've heard reports of train employees doing the same. It's particularly bad in places such as Rožaje and Plav, where the rivers are clogged with household refuse. Along the coast, fly-tipping of rubble from building sites is a problem. On an encouraging note, recycling is being trialled in Herceg Novi.

An invasive form of Red Sea algae that has blanketed large sections of the Mediterranean has started to establish itself in Montenegrin waters. But by and large the water quality for swimming is good.

BAY OF KOTOR (BOKA KOTORSKA) БОКА КОТОРСКА

Coming from Croatia the Bay of Kotor starts simply enough, but as you progress through fold upon fold of the bay and the surrounding mountains get steeper and steeper, the beauty meter gets close to bursting. It's often described as southern Europe's most spectacular fjord, and even though the label's not technically correct (see left) the sentiment certainly is

HERCEG NOVI ХЕРЦЕГ НОВИ
☎ 031 / pop 12,739
It's easy to drive straight through Herceg Novi without noticing anything worth stopping for, especially if you've just come from Croatia with visions of Dubrovnik dazzling your brain. However, just below the uninspiring roadside frontage hides an appealing old town with ancient walls, sunny squares and a lively atmosphere. The water's cleaner here near the mouth of the bay, so the pebbly beaches and concrete swimming terraces are popular.

Orientation
Herceg (pronounced *hertz*-egg) Novi sprawls along the coast, absorbing former villages on either side of the old town. Pedestrian-friendly Šetalište Pet Danica runs along the waterfront, lined with summer bars and shops. The main shopping strip is Njegoševa, which

ends just outside the old town's walls at Trg Nikole Đurkovića.

Information

There's a cluster of banks with ATMs around Trg Nikole Đurkovića.

Pizzeria Una Storia (☎ 322 844; Njegoševa bb; internet per hr €1) Has two internet terminals and two scarily well-patronised poker machines.

Post office (Njegoševa 31)

Tourist office (☎ 350 820; www.hercegnovi.travel; Jova Dabovica 12; ♥ 8am-3pm Mon-Fri) On the 1st floor above a house.

Sights

Herceg Novi is extremely hilly and the fastest way from the highway to the beach is via one of numerous sets of stairs. Charming as the stairways are, they make Herceg Novi one of the most challenging towns in Montenegro for the mobility impaired.

The big fort visible from the main road is the **Bloody Tower** (Kanli-Kula; admission €1; ♥ 8am-midnight), a notorious prison during Turkish rule (roughly 1482–1687). You can walk around its sturdy walls and enjoy views over the town. The bastion at the town's seaward edge, **Fortemare**, was rebuilt by the Venetians during their 110-year stint as overlords.

The elegant crenulated **clock tower**, built in 1667, was once the main city gate. Just inside the walls is Trg Herceg Stjepana (commonly called Belavista Sq), a gleaming white piazza that's perfect for relaxing, drinking and chatting in the shade. At its centre is the Orthodox **Archangel Michael's Church** (built 1883–1905), its lovely proportions capped with a dome and flanked by palm trees. The archangel is pictured in mosaic above the door under an elegant rose window. Its Catholic counterpart, **St Jerome's** (1856), is further down the hill, dominating Trg Mića Pavlovića.

From its hillside location in the town's eastern fringes, **Savina monastery** (☎ 345 300; Manastirska 21; ♥ 6am-8pm) enjoys wonderful coastal views. This peaceful complex is dominated by the elegant 18th-century Church of the Dormition, carved from pinkish stone from Korčula, Croatia. Inside there's a beautiful gilded iconostasis, but you'll need to be demurely dressed (no shorts, singlets or bikinis) to enter. The smaller church beside it has the same name but is considerably older (possibly 14th-century) and has the remains of frescos. The monastery is well signposted from the highway.

Apart from the building itself (a fab bougainvillea-shrouded baroque palace with absolute sea views), the highlight of the **Regional Museum** (☎ 322 485; www.rastko.org .yu/rastko-bo/muzej/; Mirka Komnenovića 9; admission €1.50; ♥ 9am-6pm Mon-Sat winter, to 8pm Tue-Sun summer) is its impressive icon gallery.

High above the town, on the other side of the main road, is the **Španjola fortress**, which was started and finished by the Turks but named after the Spanish (yep, in 1538 they had a brief stint here as well). If the graffiti and empty bottles are anything to go by, it's now regularly invaded by local teenagers.

Activities

Herceg Novi is shaping up as the best base for arranging active pursuits, largely due to a network of expats running professional, customer-focused, environmentally aware businesses. A good place to start is **Black Mountain** (☎ 321 968; www.montenegroholiday.com; Šetalište Pet Danica 41), an agency that can arrange pretty much anything, including diving, rafting, hiking and paragliding. It offers mountain-bike tours (about €20 per person) and hires bikes (€15). There's a second office at the bus station.

Another excellent outfit, run by British expats, **Kayak Montenegro** (☎ 067887436; www .kayakmontenegro.com; Šetalište Pet Danica bb; hire 1-/4-/8hr €5/15/25) rents kayaks and offers paddling tours across the bay (€45 including equipment), as well as day trips to explore Lake Skadar from Rijeka Crnojeviča (price on application). In October it works with Black Mountain to stage the Adventure Race Montenegro (p369).

From May to September **Diving Center Marina** (☎ 069637915; www.dcmarina.com) organises dives to about 20 sites in the vicinity of the bay and Budva, including various wrecks and caves. A two-dive trip costs €55 including tanks, weights and the boat trip.

Yachting Club 32 (☎ 069333011; Šetalište Pet Danica) offers parasailing (single/double €40/60 per 10 minutes) and hires jet skis (€50 per 20 minutes), paddleboats (per hour €8) and mountain bikes (per hour/three hours/day €3/6/15).

The Coastal Mountain Traversal hiking path (see p368) starts from Herceg Novi.

Festivals & Events

Running from late January until March, the **Mimosa Festival** is a mash of yellow blooms, marching majorettes, concerts and a swimming

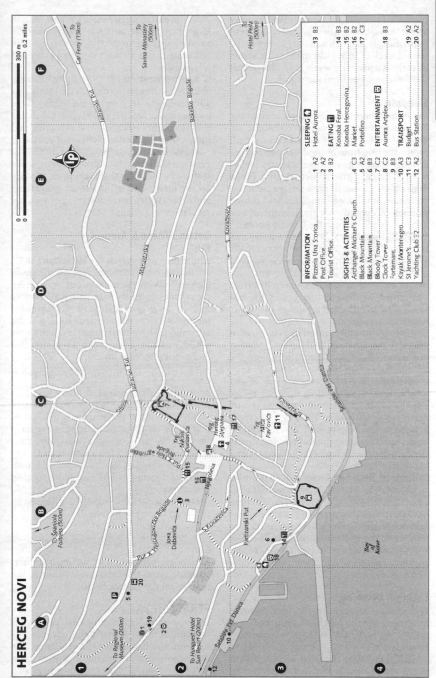

HERCEG NOVI

0 300 m
0 0.2 miles

INFORMATION		
Pizzeria Una S'orica	1	A2
Post Office	2	A2
Tourist Office	3	B2

SIGHTS & ACTIVITIES		
Archangel Michael's Church	4	C3
Black Mountain	5	A2
Black Mountain	6	B3
Bloody Tower	7	C2
Clock Tower	8	C2
Fortemare	9	B3
Kayak Montenegro	10	A3
St Jerome's	11	C3
Yachting Club 2	12	A2

SLEEPING		
Hotel Aurora	13	B3

EATING		
Konoba Feral	14	B3
Konoba Hercegovina	15	B2
Market	16	B2
Portofino	17	C3

ENTERTAINMENT		
Aurora Artplex	18	B3

TRANSPORT		
Budget	19	A2
Bus Station	20	A2

carnival. The three-day **Sunčane Skale** (Sunny Steps) music competition, a kind of low-rent Eurovision, is held in the Bloody Tower in the second week of July. Held in the same venue in early August, the week-long **film festival** showcases movies from the region.

Sleeping

In summer there are often people around the bus station touting private accommodation. Black Mountain (p342) can fix you up with rooms starting from around €15 per person, although most of its apartments are at a higher level. If skyclad is your preferred attire, **Zelena Banja** (☎ 684 559; www.full-monte.com) is a clothing-optional complex of campsites and cabins planned to open during the lifetime of this book in woodland near the Croatia border.

ourpick **Hotel Aurora** (☎ 321 620; www.auroramon tenegro.com; Šetalište Pet Danica 42; low-high tw €70-100, d €80-100, tr €105-120; ⊠) You'd never suspect that this handsome stone building was once the railway station, especially given its prime waterfront location at the foot of the old town. Oscar-nominated filmmaker Emir Kusturica was behind its loving transforma-tion into a chic and comfortable eight-room boutique hotel, hence the three tiny cinemas of the Aurora Artplex (admission €3) on the ground floor.

Hotel Perla (☎ 345 700; www.perla.cg.yu; Šetalište Pet Danica 98; low-high s €61-104, d €76-130, tr €111-189, apt €140-210; ⊠) It's a fair stroll from the centre, but if it's beach you're after, Perla's possie is perfect. The helpful staff speak excellent English and the front rooms of this medium-sized modern block have private terraces and sea views.

Hunguest Hotel Sun Resort (☎ 355 000; www .hunguesthotels.hu; Sveta Bubala bb; low-high s €62-196, d €96-252, apt €106-280; ⊠ ☜) A Hungarian chain has taken over this sprawling seaside resort and, while the facilities have been lifted to four stars, the attitude of some of the staff still belongs to an earlier era. There's secure parking, a tennis court, a large outdoor pool and a spa centre.

Eating & Drinking

If you want to take on the local women in a tussle for the best fresh fruit and veg-etables, get to the **market** (Trg Nikole Đurkovića) by around 8am.

ourpick **Portofino** (Trg Herceg Stjepana; breakfast €2.50-5, mains €6-16) Its blissful location in Herceg Novi's prettiest square makes it tempting to linger here all day, which is exactly what the town's expat community seems to do. The Italianate menu features creamy pastas and juicy steaks.

Konoba Hercegovina (☎ 322 800; Trg Nikole Đurkovića; mains €2-6) A firm favourite with the locals, this all-year-long eatery serves everything from burgers and *čevapčići* (grilled spicy kebab fin-gers) to traditional meat and fish grills and more exotic dishes like Hungarian goulash.

Konoba Feral (Šetalište Pet Danica 47; mains €7.50-15) *Feral* is a local word for a ship's lantern, so it's seafood not wild cat that takes pride of place on the menu. The grilled squid is amazing and comes with a massive serving of seasonal vegetables and salads.

Getting There & Around

BUS

At the time of research the **bus station** (☎ 321 225; Jadranski Put; ⊙ 6am-9pm) was on the main highway above the centre, but there were plans afoot to move international services to the western approach to town. Hopefully, through services will continue to stop at the old station. There are frequent buses to Kotor (€3.50, one hour), Budva (€5, 1¾ hours) and Podgorica (€9, three hours).

CAR

A tortuous, often gridlocked, one-way system runs through the town, so you're best to park on the highway. If you're driving to Tivat or Budva it's usually quicker to take the ferry (motorcycle/car/passenger €1.50/4/free), run-ning 24 hours a day, from Kamenari (15km northeast of Herceg Novi) to Lepetane (north of Tivat). Queues can be horrendously long in summer.

Budget (☎ 321 100; www.budget.com; Njegoševa 90) rents cars from €68 for one day.

For a taxi, call **Taxi More** (☎ 9730).

BOAT

Taxi boats ply the coast during summer, charging about €10 for a one-way trip to the beaches on the Luštica Peninsula.

PERAST ПЕРАСТ

Looking as though a chunk of Venice has floated down the Adriatic and anchored it-self onto the bay, Perast's streets hum with melancholy memories of the days when it was rich and powerful. This tiny town boasts 16 churches and 17 formerly grand palazzos, one of which has been converted into the **Perast Museum** (☎ 373 519; admission €2.50; ☼ 9am-6pm Mon-Sat, to 2pm Sun) and showcases the town's proud seafaring history.

The 55m bell tower belongs to **St Nicholas' Church**, which also has a **museum** (admission €1; ☼ 10am-6pm) containing bits of saints and beautifully embroidered vestments. The church itself is unfinished and, given that it was commenced in the 17th century and the bay's Catholic community has declined markedly since then, one suspects it will remain so.

Just offshore are two peculiarly picturesque islands. The smaller **St George's Island** rises from a natural reef and houses a Benedictine monastery shaded by cypresses. Its big sister, **Lady of the Rock Island** (Gospa od Škrpjela), was artificially created in the 15th century and every year on 22 July the locals row over with stones to continue the task. Its magnificent church was erected in 1630. Boats regularly go to the island for around €1.

Perast makes an atmospheric and peaceful base from which to explore the bay. Several houses rent rooms or you can try the **Hotel Conte** (☎ 032-373 687; www.hotel-conte.com; apt low-high €90-250; ❄), a series of deluxe studio to two-bedroom sea-view apartments (with wi-fi) in historic buildings scattered around St Nicholas' Church. Its wonderful restaurant, **Conte Nautilus** (mains €6.50-14), serves fresh fish with lashings of romance on its waterside terrace.

Not far from Perast, Risan is the oldest town on the bay, dating to at least the 3rd century BC. Signposts point to some superb **Roman mosaics** (admission €2; ☼ 8am-8pm 15 May-15 Oct), discovered in 1930.

KOTOR КОТОР
☎ 032 / pop 13,510

Those prone to operatic outbursts may find themselves launching into Wagner at their first glimpse of this dramatically beautiful town, wedged between brooding mountains and a moody corner of the bay. Its sturdy walls – started in the 9th century and tweaked until the 18th – arch steeply up the slopes behind it. From a distance they're barely discernable from the mountain's grey hide but at night they're spectacularly lit, reflecting in the water to give the town a golden halo. Within those walls lie labyrinthine marbled lanes where churches, shops, bars and restaurants surprise you on hidden piazzas.

In July and August people pour into Kotor and the yachts of the super-rich fill the marina, but this town never gets quite as Eurotrashy as the coast – this sheltered arm of the bay just isn't as appealing for swimming. But anyone with a heart for romance, fine food, history and architecture will find Kotor a highlight of their Montenegrin travels.

History

It's thought that Kotor began as Acruvium, part of the Roman province of Dalmatia. Its present look owes much to nearly 400 years of Venetian rule, when it was known as Cattaro. In 1813 it briefly joined with Montenegro for the first time, but the great powers decided to hand it back to Austria, where it remained until after WWI. There's a strong history of Catholic and Orthodox cooperation in the area, although the number of Catholics has dropped from 51% in 1900 to 13% today. Croats now number only 8% of the population.

Orientation

Kotor's funnel-shaped old town sits between the bay and Mt Sv Ivan, which is part of the lower slopes of Mt Lovćen (p357). Newer suburbs surround the town, linking to the old settlements of Dobrota to the north, Muo to the west and, beyond this, Prčanj. The main road to Tivat and Budva turns off the waterfront road at a baffling uncontrolled intersection south of the old town and heads through a long tunnel.

Information

You'll find a choice of banks with ATMs and the post office on the main square, Trg od Oružja.

A&E Clinic (Dom Zdravlja; ☎ 334 538; Jadranski Put, Dobrota) Accident and emergency.

Apoteka Aesulap (☎ 334 699; Jadranski Put, Dobrota; ☼ 7am-11pm) Pharmacy next to the A&E clinic.

Dr Oliver Prvulović (☎ 068738067) English-speaking doctor who works in Kotor and Budva.

Forza (☎ 304 352; Trg od Oružja; ☼ 7am-midnight) Internet access (€2 per hour), bookshop, cake shop, ice-cream parlour and sleek cafe.

Information booth (☎ 325 950; www.kotor.travel; ☼ 8am-8pm) Tourist and private accommodation information, maps, and brochures; outside the Sea Gate.

Sights

The best thing to do in Kotor is to let yourself get lost and found again in the maze of streets. You'll soon know every corner, since the town is quite small, but there're plenty of old churches to pop into and many coffees to be drunk in the shady squares.

The main entrance is the **Sea Gate** (Vrata od Mora), constructed in 1555 when the town was under Venetian rule (1420–1797). Look out for the winged lion of St Mark, Venice's symbol, as you wander around the town. Above the gate the date of the city's liberation from the Nazis is remembered with a communist star and a quote from Tito. As you pass through the gate, look out for the 15th-century stone relief of the Madonna and Child, flanked by St Tryphon and St Bernard.

Stepping through onto Trg od Oružja (Square of Arms) you'll see the strange stone pyramid in front of the **clock tower** (1602) that was used as a pillory to shame wayward citizens.

Kotor has a proud history as a naval power and the **Maritime Museum** (☎ 069045447; Trg Bokeljske Mornarice; admission incl audioguide €4; ☼ 8am-11pm Jul-Aug, 8am-7pm Mon-Sat & 9am-1pm Sun Apr-Jun & Sep, 8am-2pm Mon-Sat & 9am-1pm Sun Oct-Mar) celebrates it with three storeys of displays housed in a wonderful early-18th-century palace.

The town's most impressive building is the Catholic **St Tryphon's Cathedral** (Trg Sv Tripuna; admission €1.50; ☼ 8.30am-7pm), originally built in the 12th century but reconstructed after several earthquakes. When the entire frontage was destroyed in 1667 the baroque bell towers were added; the left one has never been finished. The cathedral's gentle-hued interior is a masterpiece of Romanesque-Gothic architecture with slender Corinthian columns alternating with pillars of pink stone, thrusting upwards to support a series of vaulted roofs. Its gilded silver-relief altar screen is considered Kotor's most valuable treasure. Up in the reliquary chapel are some lovely icons, a spooky wooden crucifix (1288) and, behind the grill, assorted body parts of saints including St Tryphon. The early martyr's importance to both the Catholic and Orthodox Churches makes him a fitting patron for the city.

Sweet little **St Luke's Church** (Trg Sv Luke) speaks volumes about the history of Croat-Montenegrin relations in Kotor. It was constructed in 1195 as a Catholic church but from 1657 until 1812 a Catholic and Orthodox altar stood side by side, with each faith taking turns to celebrate their Masses here. It's now solely Orthodox. Fragments of 12th-century frescos

still survive, along with two wonderful painted iconostases: a 17th-century one in the main church and another from the 18th century in the side chapel of St Spiridon, another saint venerated by both churches.

Breathe in the smell of incense and beeswax in the relatively unadorned 1909 Orthodox **St Nicholas' Church** (Trg Sv Luke). The silence, the iconostasis with its silver bas-relief panels, the dark wood against bare grey walls, the filtered light through the dome and the simple stained glass conspire to create a mystical atmosphere.

Tucked in the quiet northern corner of town is the parklike **Trg od Drva** (Wood Sq), hidden behind the Catholic **St Mary Koleđata church** (1221). As it's not usually open you'll probably have to content yourself with admiring the bas-reliefs on the modern bronze doors. Nearby is the 1540 **North Gate**, where a moat is formed by the clear mountain water of the bubbling Škurda River.

Fewer tourists make it to the southern end of town, where the houses narrow into a slim corridor leading to the **South Gate**, parts of which date from the 12th century, and the drawbridge over the Gurdić spring. Without the crowds it's easy to imagine yourself transported to an earlier time.

Activities

The energetic can make the 1200m ascent via 1350 steps up the **fortifications** (May-Sep €2, Oct-Apr free) for unforgettable views and a huge sense of achievement. There are entry points near the North Gate and Trg od Salata.

Looming above Kotor is Mt Lovćen. The journey to this ancient core of the country is one of the world's great drives. Take the road heading towards the Tivat tunnel and turn right just past the graveyard (there's no sign). After 5km, follow the sign to Cetinje on your left near the fort. From here there's 17km of good but narrow road snaking up 25 hairpin turns, each one revealing a vista more spectacular than the last. Take your time and keep your wits about you; you'll need to pull over and be prepared to reverse if you meet oncoming traffic. From the top the views stretch over the entire bay to the Adriatic. You can stop for a coffee at the entrance to Lovćen National Park (p357) before heading back; allow two hours for the return trip. Otherwise, continue straight ahead for the shortest route to Cetinje (p358) or turn right and continue the spectacular drive on the scenic route through the park.

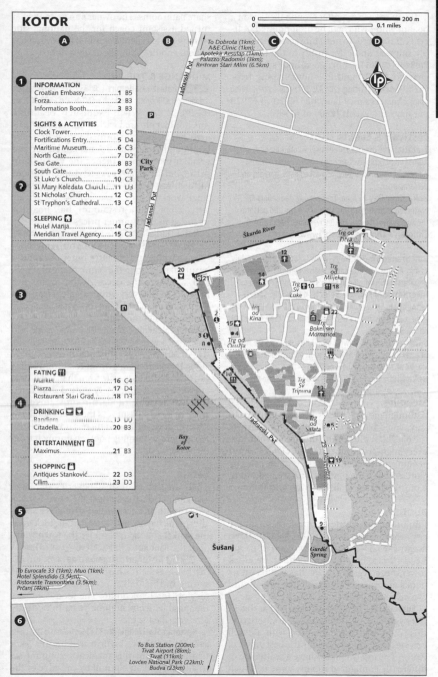

KOTOR

0 _____ 200 m
0 _____ 0.1 miles

INFORMATION
Croatian Embassy.................1 B5
Forza...............................2 B3
Information Booth...............3 B3

SIGHTS & ACTIVITIES
Clock Tower........................4 C3
Fortifications Entry..............5 D4
Maritime Museum...............6 C3
North Gate.........................7 D2
Sea Gate...........................8 B3
South Gate.........................9 C5
St Luke's Church................10 C3
St Mary Koledata Church....11 D3
St Nicholas' Church...........12 C3
St Tryphon's Cathedral.......13 C4

SLEEPING
Hotel Marija.....................14 C3
Meridian Travel Agency......15 C3

EATING
Market.............................16 C4
Piazza.............................17 D4
Restaurant Stari Grad.........18 D3

DRINKING
Bandiera..........................19 D5
Citadella..........................20 B3

ENTERTAINMENT
Maximus..........................21 B3

SHOPPING
Antiques Stanković............22 D3
Čilim...............................23 D3

To Dobrota (1km);
A&E Clinic (1km);
Apoteka Aesulap (1km);
Palazzo Radomiri (3km);
Restoran Stari Mlini (6.5km)

City Park

Jadranski Put

Škurda River

Trg od Drva

Trg od Mlijeka

Trg Sv Luke

Trg od Kina

Trg od Oružja

Trg Bokeljske Mornarice

Trg Sv Tripuna

Trg od Salata

Jadranski Put

Bay of Kotor

Šušanj

Gurdić Spring

To Eurocafe 33 (1km); Muo (1km);
Hotel Splendido (3.5km);
Ristorante Tramontana (3.5km);
Prčanj (4km)

To Bus Station (200m);
Tivat Airport (8km);
Tivat (11km);
Lovćen National Park (22km);
Budva (23km)

If you're keen to potter around the bay on a boat of your own you'll be disappointed. A licence is required, so most hire companies supply skippers and cater firmly to the top end. **ProRent** (☎ 305 194) offers two-hour speedboat charters (€150) and five-hour fishing trips (€250). **Avel Yachting** (☎ 325 207; info@avel-yachting .com) charters fancy launches (€720 to €7920 per day) and yachts (€500 to €1190).

Festivals & Events

Traditional Kotor Carnival (www.kotorkarneval .com) End of February. Carrying on the Venetian Renaissance tradition with a week of masked balls, parades and performances.

Boka Navy Day 26 June. Traditionally clad sailors are presented with the flag and keys of the city and perform the *kolo* (wheel dance). The festival dates back to 1420.

Children's Theatre Festival (www.kfest.cg.yu) Early July.

Don Branko's Music Days (www.kotorart.com) Mid-July to mid-August. Classical-music festival featuring international artists performing in Kotor's squares and churches.

International Fashion Selection Late July. Some seriously big names (including Romeo Gigli in 2008) send their collections down the catwalk in front of the cathedral on Trg Sv Tripuna.

Summer Carnival (www.kotorkarneval.com) Late July or early August. A condensed version of the main carnival staged at a more tourist-friendly time.

Boka Night Mid-August. Decorated boats take to the bay.

Sleeping

Although the old town is a charming place to stay, you'd better pack earplugs. In summer the bars blast music onto the streets until 1am every night, rubbish collectors clank around at 6am and the chattering starts at the cafes by 8am. Some of the best options are just out of Kotor in quieter Dobrota, Muo and Prčanj.

BUDGET

Enquire about private accommodation at the city's information booth (p345). **Meridian Travel Agency** (☎ 323 448; www.tameridian.cg.yu; ☘ 9am-3pm & 6-9pm Mon- Sat), in the lane behind the clock tower, near Trg od Oružja, has rooms on its books at around €15 to €30 per person and can also book hotels.

Eurocafe 33 (☎ 069047712; lemaja1@cg.yu; Muo 33; r per person €20-25; ☒) On the Muo waterfront, this traditional stone building with a small private beach enjoys possibly the best views of Kotor. The top two floors have a scattering of differently configured rooms, some of which

share bathrooms. The owner's an ex-footballer turned assistant coach for the national side who speaks excellent English. If there are a few of you, enquire about booking a floor.

MIDRANGE & TOP END

our pick **Palazzo Radomiri** (☎ 333 172; www.palazzo radomiri.com; Dobrota; low-high s €60-160, d €100-200, ste €60-280; ☒ ☒) Wi-fi. Exquisitely beautiful, this honey-coloured early-18th-century palazzo has been transformed into a first-rate boutique hotel. Some rooms are bigger and grander than others (hence the variation in price), but all 10 have sea views and luxurious furnishings. Guests can avail themselves of a small workout area, a sauna, a pool, a private jetty, a bar and a restaurant; half board is included in the summer prices.

Hotel Marija (☎ 325 062; hotel.marija.kotor@cg.yu; s/d/tr/q €65/90/103/130; ☒) Did you remember those earplugs? This little hotel occupies a beautiful palazzo in the centre of the old town and, although the decor of the rooms is a little dated, it's very comfortable, clean and bordering on grand. One room has a balcony for those Juliet moments.

Hotel Splendido (☎ 301 700; www.splendido-hotel .com; Prčanj; low-high s €65-116, d €93-166, apt €119-199; ☒ ☐ ☒) Wi-fi. Negotiating the 4km drive along the narrow waterfront road from Kotor can be stressful but, aside from that, Splendido is *magnifico*. Completely gutted and fitted with comfortable modern rooms, this large stone palazzo still surveys the bay as solidly as it's ever done, although there's now a blissful terrace and swimming pool separating it from the water's edge.

Eating

There are tonnes of small bakeries and takeaway joints on the streets of Kotor. For the sweet-toothed, cherry-filled strudel is a speciality of the region. Self-caterers can stock up at the **market** (☘ 7am-2pm) under the town walls, or at the **Pantomart** (Jadranski Put; ☘ 6am-11pm).

our pick **Ristorante Tramontana** (☎ 301 700; Prčanj; mains €4-16) It's hard to top the romantic setting of this Italian restaurant on the terrace of Hotel Splendido. The food is equally memorable, from sublime pasta to perfectly tender grilled squid.

Restoran Stari Mlini (☎ 333 555; Jadranski Put, Ljuta; meals €11-21) It's well worth making the 7km trip to Ljuta for this magical restaurant set in and around an old mill by the edge of the bay. If you've got time to spare and don't mind picking out bones, order the Dalmatian fish stew with polenta for two. The steaks are also excellent, as are the bread, wine and service.

Restaurant Stari Grad (☎ 322 025; Trg od Mlijeka; mains €8-18; **V**) Head straight through to the stone-walled courtyard, grab a seat under the vines and prepare to get absolutely stuffed full of fabulous food – the serves are huge. Either point out the fish that takes your fancy or order from the traditional a la carte menu.

Piazza (☎ 069205720; Trg Bokeljske Mornarice; mains €2.50-7.50 🕑 8am-late) Serves sandwiches, pancakes and excellent pizza with thin bases and perfectly measured toppings – great for snacks or an inexpensive sit-down meal.

Drinking & Entertainment

Kotor's full of cafe-bars that spill into the squares and during the day are abuzz with conversation. All chit-chat stops abruptly in the evening, when speakers are dragged out onto the ancient lanes and the techno cranked up to near ear-bleeding volumes. On summer nights it's hard to escape it, not that the dolled-up teenagers that pour into town would want to.

Bandiera (ul 29 Novembra) Tourists don't tend to venture down this darker end of town, where you'll find Che Guevara on the wall and rock music on the stereo.

Citadella (☎ 311 000) This large terrace bar on top of the fortifications near Trg od Oružja is fairly touristy, but you can't beat the views of the bay, town and mountains.

Maximus (☎ 334 342; admission €2-5; 🕑 11pm-5am Thu-Sat, nightly in summer) Montenegro's most pumping club comes into its own in summer, hosting big-name international DJs and local starlets.

Shopping

Indulge your inner Montenegrin at Cilim, near Trg od Mlijeka, which stocks embroidered folk shirts, knitted socks and locally woven carpets.

Antiques Stanković (☎ 069071819; Trg Bokeljske Mornarice) A treasure trove of socialist medals, Roman coins, antique jewellery, traditional garb and other interesting stuff.

Getting There & Away

The **bus station** (☎ 325 809; 🕑 6am-9pm) is to the south of town, just off the road leading to the Tivat tunnel. Buses to Herceg Novi (€3.50, one

hour), Budva (€3, 40 minutes) and Podgorica (€7, two hours) are at least hourly.

A taxi to Tivat airport (8km away through the tunnel) costs around €8.

Azzurra Line ferries connect Kotor with Bari, Italy (p444).

TIVAT ТИВАТ
☎ 032 / pop 9467

Big things are planned for this town, which isn't a bad thing as Tivat doesn't have a lot to lose from development. At present it's the airport that's the drawcard, although there are a lot of sweet villages and beaches to explore on the coast between here and Kotor and on the Luštica Peninsula. The helpful **tourist office** (☎ 671 324; www.tivat.travel; Palih Boraca 8; 🕑 8am-3pm Mon-Sat, to 2pm Sun) can point you in the direction of some terrific walks.

If you've got an early flight, the **Hotel Villa Royal** (☎ 675 310; www.hotelvillaroyal.cg.yu; Kalimanj bb; low-high s €42-65, d €68-102, apt €102-141; 🍴 🖥) is a bright, modern block with clean rooms and friendly staff.

From the **bus station** (Palih Boraca bb) there are frequent buses to Budva (€2) via the airport (€0.50) as well as services to Kotor (€1, six daily) and Herceg Novi (€3, seven daily).

Tivat airport is 3km south of town. Airport minibuses leave when full and head to Budva (€3.50) and Herceg Novi (€8).

ADRIATIC COAST

Much of Montenegro's determination to reinvent itself as a tourist mecca has firmly focused on this gorgeous stretch of beaches. In July and August it seems that the entire Serbian world and a fair chunk of its Orthodox brethren can be found crammed onto this less-than-100km stretch of coast. Avoid those months and you'll find a charismatic set of small towns and fishing villages to explore, set against clear Adriatic waters and Montenegro's mountainous backdrop.

BUDVA БУДВА
☎ 033 / pop 10,098

The poster child of Montenegrin tourism, Budva – with its atmospheric old town and numerous beaches – certainly has a lot to offer. Yet the child has quickly moved into a difficult adolescence, fuelled by rampant development that has leeched much of the charm from the place. In the height of the season the sands are blanketed with package holidaymakers from Russia and the Ukraine, while the 'novorich' park their multimillion-dollar yachts in the guarded marina. By night you'll run a gauntlet of glorified strippers attempting to cajole you into the beachside bars.

It's the buzziest place on the coast, so if you're in the mood to party, bodacious Budva will be your best buddy.

Orientation

The Adriatic highway, Jadranski Put, runs straight through Budva. The old town isn't visible from the road but juts into the sea near the Tivat approach to town. The marina is immediately north of it and beyond this Slovenska Beach begins. The main beachside promenade is pedestrianised Slovenska Obala. Apart from the old town, hardly any streets have names and fewer have signs.

Information

There are clusters of banks on and around ulica Mediteranska.

Apoteka Sv Vrači (☎ 453 813; Jadranski Put bb; 🕑 8am-10pm) Pharmacy.

Dr Oliver Prvulović (☎ 068738067) English-speaking doctor who works in Budva and Kotor.

Internet (Slovenska Obala bb; per 30min €2) Terminals are set up in tents in summer.

Police (☎ 451 183)

Post office (☎ 402 564; ul Mediteranska bb)

Tourist office (☎ 452 750; Njegoševa bb; 🕑 9am-9pm May-Oct) Brochures on sights and accommodation.

Sights

Budva's best feature and star attraction is the old town – a mini Dubrovnik with marbled streets and Venetian walls rising from the clear waters below. Much of it was ruined in two earthquakes in 1979, but it's since been completely rebuilt and now houses more shops, bars and restaurants than residences. At its seaward end, the **citadel** (admission €2; 🕑 8am-midnight May-Nov) offers striking views, a small museum and a library full of rare tomes and maps. Nearby is the **entry to the town walls** (admission €1; 🕑 9am-5pm Mon-Sat).

In the square in front of the citadel is a cluster of interesting churches. Frescos cover the walls and ceiling of the **Church of the Holy Trinity** (Sv Trojica; 🕑 8am-noon & 5-8pm summer, 8am-noon & 4-7pm winter). Built in 1804 out of stripes of pink and honey-coloured stone, this Orthodox church is the only one that's regularly open. The Catholic **St John's Church** (Sv Ivan), parts of which possibly date from the 9th century, houses the *Madonna of Budva* – a 12th-century icon venerated by Catholic and Orthodox Budvans alike. Tiny **St Mary's in Punta** dates from 804 and **St Sava's** from the 14th century, but they're rarely open.

The **Archaeological Museum** (☎ 453 308; Petra I Petrovića 11; adult/child €2/1; 🕑 9am-10pm) shows off the town's ancient and complicated history – dating back to at least 500 BC – over three floors of exhibits. There's an impressive collection of Greek and Roman jewellery, ceramics and glassware (how it survived in a town so prone to earthquakes and war is anyone's guess), and an ancient helmet with holes in the back that suggest that the former owner had at least one very bad day.

Also in the old town is the **Museum of Modern Art** (☎ 451 343; Cara Dušana 19; admission free; 🕑 8am-2pm & 5-8pm), an attractive gallery staging temporary exhibitions.

With so much construction going on, you might find yourself being lulled by the sound of concrete mixers rather than waves on Budva's beaches – that's if you can find a spot with no Euro-disco blaring. Little **Stari Grad beach**, immediately south of the old town, has the ancient walls as an impressive backdrop. If you wander around the headland you'll find quieter, double-bayed **Mogren beach**. There's a spot near here where the fearless or foolhardy leap from the cliffs.

Heading in the opposite direction is the long sweep of **Slovenska beach**, the town's main beach. A short drive further will bring you to **Bečići**, a broad crescent of sand, much of which is attached to the large resort-style hotels that line it. The blue waters and coarse sands of **Jaz beach**, just off the road to Tivat, have been the backdrop to recent concerts by the Rolling Stones and Madonna.

The small island of **St Nikola**, locally known as Hawaii, is an uninhabited green spot a nautical mile offshore where locals head for the beaches and the fish restaurant (there's only one). Boats run to and from the island from all along the coast during the summer.

Activities

Run by yet another Brit, this one a qualified senior paragliding instructor, the **Montenegro Adventure Centre** (☎ 067580664; www.montenegrofly.com; Lapčići) offers plenty of action from its perch

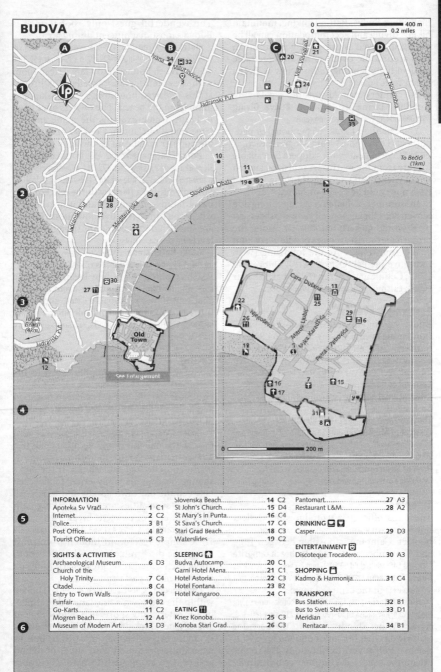

BUDVA

0   400 m
0   0.2 miles

INFORMATION

Apoteka Sv Vrači	**1**	C1
Internet	**2**	C2
Police	**3**	B1
Post Office	**4**	B2
Tourist Office	**5**	C3

SIGHTS & ACTIVITIES

Archaeological Museum	**6**	D3
Church of the Holy Trinity	**7**	C4
Citadel	**8**	C4
Entry to Town Walls	**9**	D4
Funfair	**10**	B2
Go-Karts	**11**	C2
Mogren Beach	**12**	A4
Museum of Modern Art	**13**	D3

Slovenska Beach	**14**	C2
St John's Church	**15**	D4
St Mary's in Punta	**16**	C4
St Sava's Church	**17**	C4
Stari Grad Beach	**18**	C3
Waterslides	**19**	C2

SLEEPING

Budva Autocamp	**20**	C1
Garni Hotel Mena	**21**	C1
Hotel Astoria	**22**	C3
Hotel Fontana	**23**	B2
Hotel Kangaroo	**24**	C1

EATING

Knez Konoba	**25**	C3
Konoba Stari Grad	**26**	C3

Pantomart	**27**	A3
Restaurant L&M	**28**	A2

DRINKING

Casper	**29**	D3

ENTERTAINMENT

Discoteque Trocadero	**30**	A3

SHOPPING

Kadmo & Harmonija	**31**	C4

TRANSPORT

Bus Station	**32**	B1
Bus to Sveti Stefan	**33**	D1
Meridian Rentacar	**34**	B1

high above Budva. Rafting, hiking, mountain biking, diving and accommodation can all be arranged, as well as paragliding from launch sites around the country. An unforgettable tandem flight landing 750m below at Bečići beach costs €65.

For underwater adventures try Diving Center Marina (p342) or **Budva Diving** (☎ 069060416; www.budvadiving.com).

You can hire a kayak (€5 per hour) or paddle boat (€6 per hour) from Mogren beach. A huge range of boats with skippers is available for hire from the marina. A midsized launch might charge €400 for a day's fishing, while a flash one could be €1200 or more.

In summer a **funfair** sets up alongside Slovenska Obala, as well as **waterslides** (per ride €0.40) and **go-karts** (per 10min €7). Along the promenade tourist agencies peddle every kind of day tour, including the following (with indicative prices): Ostrog (€17); Dubrovnik (€30); Cetinje and Lovćen (€23); Lake Skadar (€35); rafting on the Tara River (€60).

Festivals & Events

Budva's going all out to develop a reputation for big events, having hosted the Rolling Stones in 2007 and a Powerboat Grand Prix, Lenny Kravitz and Madonna in 2008. An annual beer festival is mooted for June.

Carnival of Budva Early May. Venetian masked hijinks.

International Folklore Festival Early June.

Busker Fest Mid-June.

Theatre Town Mid-June to mid-August.

Festival of Mediterranean Song Late June. Three-day song competition; Julio Iglesias made an appearance in 2008.

Days of Širun First Saturday in October. A one-day celebration of wine, fish and song.

Sleeping

The tourist office (p350) produces an excellent hotel directory and private-accommodation booklet. Camping is possible between June and September at swampy **Jaz beach campsite** (☎ 463 545; adult/child €2.50/1, tent & car €2.50) and at **Budva Autocamp** (☎ 069062759; Velji Vinogradi bb; tent & 2 people €8) in the centre of town.

Hotel Astoria (☎ 451 110; www.hotelastoria.cg.yu; Njegoševa 4; low-high s €130-190, d €170-230, ste €180-380; ✗ ▣) Water shimmers down the corridor wall as you enter this chic boutique hotel hidden in the old town's fortifications. The rooms are on the small side, but they're beautifully furnished; the sea-view suite is spectacular.

The wonderful guest-only roof terrace is Budva's most magnificent dining area.

Hotel Kangaroo (☎ 458 653; www.kangaroo.cg.yu; Velji Vinogradi bb; low-high s €29-69, d €39-69, tr €59-104; ✗ ▣) Wi-fi. Bounce into a large, clean room with desk, terrace and excellent bathroom at this midsized hotel that's a hop, skip and jump from the beach. The owners once lived in Perth, which explains the name and the large mural of Captain Cook's *Endeavour* in the popular restaurant below.

Hotel Fontana (☎ 452 153; fontana.lekic@cg.yu; Slovenska Obala 23; s low-high €72-114, d low-high €90-142, tr low-high €122-192, q low-high €162-256; ✗) Wi-fi. Sitting pretty in a park by the beach, Fontana has a holiday-home feel and a terrace cafe where you can chat with fellow guests. Rooms are smallish but fine, and most on the upper levels have sea views.

Garni Hotel Mena (☎ 459 310; www.hotelmena .co.me; Velji Vinogradi; low-high s €25-40, d €50-80; ✗) Peach coloured and peachy keen, little Mena has a laid-back attitude to breakfast and checkout times, reasonable rates, and nicely furnished rooms. The only downers are all shower related: raspy towels, no soap and tiny hot-water cylinders.

Eating

If you're looking for supplies, head to the **Pantomart** (☎ 452 523; Mediteranska 1; ✗ 6am-midnight) near the old town. For cheap fast food and delicious gelato you need only stroll along Slovenska Obala.

Konoba Stari Grad (☎ 454 443; Njegoševa 14; mains €3-12) The small interior looks and smells like an Italian mama's kitchen, with a cosy atmosphere and checked tablecloths. If the sun's shining, head for the sunny terrace sandwiched between the old town's walls and beach. All the local specialities are served, along with ham-and-eggs or omelette breakfasts.

Restaurant L&M (☎ 451 468; 13 Juli bb; mains €5-12) A simple restaurant hidden from most except the discerning locals who all seem to know each other. It's a great place to fill up on inexpensive pasta and salads.

Knez Konoba (Mitrov Ljubiše bb; mains €9-15) Hidden within the old town's tiny lanes, this atmospheric eatery only sports two outdoor tables and a handful inside. Try the black risotto – it's more expensive than most (€10) but it's beautifully presented with slices of lemon and orange along with tomato, cucumber and olives.

Drinking & Entertainment

Casper (Petra I Petrovića bb) Chill out under the pine tree in this picturesque old-town cafe-bar. From July DJs kick off, spinning everything from jazz to drum and bass.

Discoteque Trocadero (☎ 069069086; ul Mediteranska 4; admission €3-8; ✆ 10pm-4am) DJs hit the decks every night except Saturday, which is folk night.

Shopping

Kadmo & Harmonija (☎ 068553699; citadel) Named after Budva's mythical founders, this gallery-like shop sells antiquities, traditional filigree jewellery and beautiful painted icons in silver filigree frames. If you're not a Russian oligarch you may find the prices a little steep (up to €4000).

Getting There & Away

The **bus station** (☎ 456 000; Ivana Milutinovića bb) has regular services to Herceg Novi (€5, 1¾ hours), Kotor (€3, 40 minutes) and Cetinje (€3, 40 minutes).

You can flag down the Olimpia Express (€1.50) from the bus stops on Jadranski Put to head to Bečići (five minutes) or Sveti Stefan (20 minutes). They depart every 30 minutes in summer and hourly in winter.

Meridian Rentacar (☎ 454 105; www.meridian-rent acar.com; Mediteranski Sportski Centar) Opposite the bus station; one-day hire from €45.

Taxi Association (☎ 9715)

Terrae-Taxi (☎ 9717) Advertises set fares to the following airports: Tivat (€15), Podgorica (€40), Ćilipi/Dubrovnik (€90).

SVETI STEFAN СВЕТИ СТЕФАН

033

Impossibly picturesque Sveti Stefan, 5km south of Budva, provides the biggest 'wow' moment on the entire coast. From the 15th century to the 1950s this tiny island, connected to the shore by a narrow isthmus and crammed full of terracotta-roofed dwellings, housed a simple fishing community. That was until someone had the idea to buy the whole thing and turn it into a luxury hotel. It became a big hit with both Hollywood and European royalty – guests included Sofia Loren, Doris Day and Queen Elizabeth II – but as with so many other things in the former Yugoslavia, it lost its appeal during the 1990s.

The island is a slice of Mediterranean heaven, with oleanders, pines and olives scenting the air and little houses looking straight at the sea. Over the last few years tradesmen have replaced screen goddesses on its exclusive streets, but the resort will reopen during the lifetime of this book, more bizarrely glamorous than ever. When it does, it's likely that a day rate will once again be charged for mere mortals to wander around. In the meantime, make the most of the lovely beaches gazing at the island while they're comparatively uncrowded.

Sveti Stefan is also the name of the new township that's sprung up onshore. From its slopes you get to look down at that iconic view all day – which some might suggest is even better than staying in the surreal enclave below.

From the beach there's a very pleasant walk north to the cute village of Pržno, where there are some excellent restaurants and another attractive beach.

Sleeping & Eating

Not only does the charming, helpful owner of **Levantin Travel Agency** (☎ 468 200, www.geocities .com/levantin88/levantin; Vukice Mitrović 3) bear a striking likeness to Michael Palin c Life of Brian, he can sort you out with private accommodation, apartments and other travel arrangements.

our pick **Vila Drago** (☎ 468 477; www.viladrago.com; Slobode 32, low-high d €34-68, tr €58 100, apt €103-170; ✷) The only problem with this place is that you may never want to leave your terrace as the views are so sublime. Try for room 5, a spacious double with two terraces; rooms 1, 2 and 6 are cheaper but have limited views. The super-comfy pillows and fully stocked bathrooms are a nice touch, especially at this price. Watch the sunset over the island from the grapevine-covered terrace restaurant (mains €4 to €11) and enjoy specialities from the local Paštrovići clan, like roast suckling pig (€15 per kilogram).

Getting There & Away

Olimpia Express buses head to and from Budva (€1.50, 20 minutes) every 30 minutes in summer and hourly in winter, stopping on ulica Slobode near Vila Drago.

PETROVAC ПЕТРОВАЦ

033

The Romans had the right idea, building their summer villas on this lovely bay. If only the new crop of developers had a scrap

MONTENEGRO

of their classic good taste. Still, once you get down to the pretty beachside promenade where lush Mediterranean plants perfume the air and a 16th-century **Venetian fortress** guards a tiny stone harbour, the aberrations up the hill are barely visible. This is one of the best places on the coast for families: the accommodation's reasonably priced, the water's clear, and kids roam the esplanade at night with impunity.

In July and August you'll be lucky to find an inch of space on the town beach, but wander south and there's cypress and oleander-lined **Lučice beach**, with a kids' waterslide on its far end. Continue over the leafy headland for another 30 minutes and the 2.5km-long sweep of **Bulgarica beach** comes into view, most of which is blissfully undeveloped.

Information

This seaside village has no street signs.

A&E Clinic (Zdravstvena Stanica; ☎ 461 055) At the top of town; follow the road from the bus station.

Apoteka Lijek (☎ 462 350; ☽ 8am-9pm Mon-Sat, 8am-1pm & 5-9pm Sun) Pharmacy opposite the A&E clinic.

Internet Café (per hr €2; ☽ 10am-midnight) At the side of the gallery on the promenade.

Komercijalna Bank At the side of the large Hotel Palas; no ATM outside.

Post office (☎ 461 010) In the very centre of town.

Sleeping

Mornar Travel Agency (☎ 461 410; www.mornar-travel .com; ☽ 8am-8pm summer, to 2pm winter) An excellent local agency offering private accommodation from €23 per person.

Hotel W Grand (☎ 461 703; www.wgrandpetrovac .com; low-high s €41-71, d €54-94, tr €81-141; ☒ ☐) Wi-fi. The colour scheme simulates the effect of waking up inside an egg yolk, but this modern midsized hotel has roomy accommodation with comfy beds and puts on a brilliant breakfast buffet on its view-tastic terrace.

Eating & Drinking

The esplanade is lined with fast-food joints, ice-cream stands, restaurants and cafe-bars.

Konoba Bonaca (☎ 069084735; mains €8-15) Set back slightly from the main beach drag, this traditional restaurant focuses mainly on seafood, but the local cheeses and olives are also excellent. Grab a table under the grapevines on the terrace and gaze out to sea.

Castello (☎ 067614423; terrace/club free/€2; ☽ terrace from 6pm, club from midnight) Sip a cocktail and enjoy gorgeous views over the parapets of the Venetian fortress. DJs spark up both on the terrace and inside on summer nights.

Getting Around

Petrovac's **bus station** (☎ 068838184) is near the top of town. Regular services head to Budva and Bar (both €2, 30 minutes).

BAR БАР

☎ 030 / pop 13,790

Dominated by Montenegro's main port and a large industrial area, Bar is unlikely to be anyone's highlight but is a handy transport hub, welcoming trains from Belgrade and ferries from Italy. More interesting are the ruins of Stari Bar in the mountains behind.

Orientation & Information

Bar's centre is immediately east of the marina and ferry terminal. Beaches stretch north from here, while the port and industrial area are to the south. There are several banks with ATMs around ulica Maršala Tita and ulica Vladimira Rolovića.

A&E Clinic (☎ 124; Jovana Tomeševića 42)

Police (☎ 311 222; Maršala Tita 18)

Post Office (☎ 301 300; Jovana Tomeševića bb)

Tourist Information Centre (☎ 311 633; Obala 13 Jula bb; ☽ 7am-9pm Jul & Aug, to 2pm Mon-Fri Sep-Jun) Helpful staff with good English; stocks useful brochures listing sights and private accommodation.

Sights

With a large industrial port and marina on its doorstep, Bar's **city beach** isn't the most appealing option for swimming. Heading north, **Šušanj** is popular with Serbian holidaymakers. A succession of rocky coves follows, perfect for snorkelling and secluded swimming.

Presenting an elegant facade to the water, **King Nikola's Palace** (☎ 314 079; Šetalište Kralje Nikole; admission €1; ☽ 8am-3pm) has been converted into a museum housing a collection of antiquities, folk costumes and royal furniture. Its impressive gardens contain plants cultivated from seeds and cuttings collected from around the world by Montenegro's sailors.

STARI BAR СТАРИ БАР

Impressive **Stari Bar** (Old Bar; adult/child €1/0.50; ☽ 8am-8pm), Bar's original settlement, stands on a bluff 4km northeast off the Ulcinj road. A steep cobbled hill takes you past a cluster of old houses and shops to the fortified

TAKING THE BAR EXAM

One of the legacies of Yugoslavia's communist years is a rigorous education system. We asked English teacher Daniela Đuranović to teach us a thing or two about her home town and country.

Where's a good place to begin? First swim in the sea. Bar's most beautiful beaches are a little out of town. For me, Montenegro's best beach is Pržno (see p353) near Sveti Stefan. I think that God when he made that place said 'wow, this is one beautiful place'.

What about cultural pursuits? Definitely visit Bar Museum (opposite) and Stari Bar (opposite). I think there are some artists still living there and it comes alive with performances during the summer festival.

What else shouldn't be missed? You must visit the mountains. They're beautiful in summer, but I like them in winter covered in snow. I don't ski, though. I just drink coffee and tea and enjoy the nature.

You were born and raised in Bar. How has it changed over the years? Bar has developed a lot. One thing I don't like is that they have cut down the trees that gave the centre of town its name: Topolica. In this park (behind the museum) there are some very interesting trees. King Nikola asked sailors to bring them from all around the world.

You seem to have a good life here. I see TV programs about Provence, talking about the nature, the cheese, the produce. I can eat that food every day. I wouldn't change that. In summer I have everything I need here.

entrance, where a short, dark passage pops you out into a large expanse of vine-clad ruins and abandoned streets overgrown with grass and wild flowers.

Findings of pottery and metal suggest that the Illyrians founded the city in around 800 BC. In the 10th century, the Byzantine town was known as Antibarium as it's opposite the Italian city of Bari. It passed in and out of Slavic and Byzantine rule until the Venetians took it in 1443 (note the lion of St Mark in the entryway) and held it until it was taken by the Ottomans in 1571. Nearly all the 240 buildings now lie in ruins, a result of Montenegrin shelling when they captured the town in 1878.

A small **museum** just inside the entrance explains the site and its history. The northern corner has an 11th-century **fortress** with views showcasing the isolated setting amid mountains and olive groves. Nearby are the foundations of the **Cathedral of St George**, Bar's patron saint. Originally a Romanesque church, it was rebuilt as a mosque by the Turks in the 17th century, but the unlucky spot was yet again in ruins after an accidental explosion of gunpowder. Around the corner is a **Turkish bathhouse** from the 17th or 18th century – a solid, charming building. In the western part of the town are the remains of the **St Nicolas' Church**, offering glimpses of Serbo-Byzantine frescos.

Buses marked Stari Bar depart from the centre of new Bar every hour (€1).

Sleeping & Eating

Decent sleeping and eating options are extremely limited, but Bar has plenty of bars.

Hotel Princess (☎ 300 100; www.hotelprincess-montenegro.com; Jovana Tomaševića 59; low-high s €80-140, d €100-200, apt €150-450; 🅿 🖳 🖵) Wi-fi. It's pricey and generic, but this resort-style hotel is the only decent option in town. Get your money's worth at the private beach, pool and spa centre.

Ciao (Šetalište Kralje Nikole; breakfast €2-4, mains €4.50-10) A pleasant place for an omelette, pizza or pasta on the waterfront.

Konoba Spilja (☎ 340 353, Stari Bar bb; mains €3-15) So rustic you wouldn't be surprised if a goat wandered through, this is a terrific spot for a traditional meal after exploring Stari Bar.

A PEACEFUL OBSERVER

At Mirovica near Stari Bar is a living witness that has stood and mutely waved symbols of peace while the armies of consecutive empires have swept through this land. At 2000 years of age, **Stara Maslina** (old olive tree) is possibly the oldest tree in continental Europe and one of the oldest of its species in the world. A ring of white stone protects its personal space from tree-huggers, and there's a nominal charge to visit (adult/child €1/0.50), but it can be admired nearly as well from the road. You'll find it well signposted from the road to Ulcinj.

Konoba Kod Džema (☎ 067888405; mains €4-10) This atmospheric stone-walled restaurant is an air-conditioned haven midway between the train and bus stations. Nibble on delicious *pršut* and bread straight off the griddle while you're waiting for your connection.

Shopping
Opal II Filigren (☎ 340 634; Stari Bar bb) An excellent place to buy silver-filigree jewellery – its been perfecting its craft over a hundred years.

Getting There & Away
From Bar the fastest route to Podgorica is via a toll road (€2.50 each way) that leaves the highway past Sutomore, northwest of Bar.

The **bus station** (☎ 346 141) and adjacent **train station** (☎ 301 622; www.zeljeznica.cg.yu) are 1km southeast of the centre. Destinations include Podgorica (€5, seven daily) and Ulcinj (€2.50, six daily). Trains to Podgorica (€3, one hour, 14 daily) also stop at Virpazar (€2).

Ferries to Bari and Ancona in Italy (p444) leave from the **ferry terminal** (Obala 13 Jula bb) near the centre. You can book your Montenegro Lines ferry tickets here and there's a post office and ATM. Azzura Line can be booked at **Mercur** (☎ 313 617; Vladimir Rolovića bb).

In summer you can hail a taxi boat from the marina or beach for a short trip up the coast (€2 for Sutomore).

ULCINJ УЛЦИЊ
☎ 030 / 10,838
If you want a feel for Albania without actually crossing the border, buzzy Ulcinj's the place to go. The population is 72% Albanian and in summertime it swells with Kosovar holidaymakers for the simple reason that it's a hell of a lot nicer than any of the Albanian seaside towns. The elegant minarets of numerous mosques give Ulcinj a distinctly oriental feel, as does the music echoing out of the kebab stands around Mala Plaža (Small Beach).

Orientation & Information
You're unlikely to find a single street sign in most Montenegrin towns, but in Ulcinj you'll sometimes find three different ones per street: a Montenegrin and an Albanian version of the Yugoslav-era name as well as a new Albanian name. Thus the main boulevard leading east–west at the top of town is either Maršala Tita or Gjergj Kastrioti Skënderbeu,

and the main street heading down to the beach is either ul 26 Novembra or rr Hazif Ali Ulqinaku. In this text we've used the name that was most prominently displayed at the time of research (usually the new Albanian name), but be aware that there is a push to return to the old names.

You'll find banks, internet cafes, supermarkets, pharmacies and the post office on rr Hazif Ali Ulqinaku.

Sights & Activities
The ancient old town overlooking Mala Plaža is still largely residential and somewhat dilapidated – a legacy of the 1979 earthquake. A steep slope leads to the **Upper Gate**, where there's a small **museum** (☎ 421 419; admission €1; ☉ 6am-noon & 5-9pm) containing Roman and Ottoman artefacts just inside the walls.

Mala Plaža may be a fine grin of a cove, but it's hard to see the beach under all that suntanned flesh in July and August. You're better to stroll south, where a succession of rocky bays offers a little more room to breathe. **Ladies' beach** (admission €1.50) has a strict women-only policy, while a section of the beach in front of Hotel Albatross is clothing-optional.

The appropriately named **Velika Plaža** (Big Beach) starts 4km southeast of the town and stretches for 12 sandy kilometres. Sections of it sprout deckchairs, but there's still plenty of space to lose yourself. To be frank this large, flat expanse isn't as picturesque as it sounds and the water is painfully shallow – great for kids but you'll need to walk a fair way for a decent swim.

On your way to Velika Plaža you'll pass the murky **Milena canal**, where the local fishermen use nets suspended from long willow rods attached to wooden stilt houses. The effect is remarkably reminiscent of Southeast Asia. There are more of these contraptions on the banks of the **Bojana River** at the other end of Velika Plaža.

Divers wanting to explore various wrecks and the remains of a submerged town should contact the **D'olcinium Diving Club** (☎ 067319100; www.uldiving.com; intro dive €30, 2 dives incl equipment €40). It also hires snorkelling (€3) and diving (€15) gear.

Sleeping
The strangely named **Real Estate Travel Agency** (☎ 421 609; www.realestate-travel.com; Hazif Ali Ulqinaku bb; ☉ 8am-9pm) has obliging English-speaking

PIRATES OF THE MEDITERRANEAN

Listen up, me hearties, to a swashbuckling tale of murder, theft and slavery. Even before the Venetians took over in 1405, Ulcinj had a reputation as a pirates' lair. That didn't change when the Ottomans wrested control (nominally at least) in 1571. Quite the opposite, in fact. By the end of the 16th century as many as 400 pirates, mainly from Malta, Tunisia and Algeria, made Ulcinj their main port of call – wreaking havoc on passing vessels and then returning to party up large on Mala Plaža.

Legendary leaders became celebrities across the eastern Mediterranean, with stories of the Karamindžoja brothers, Lika Ceni, Ali Hodža and the like fuelling the imaginations of avid listeners. Legendary Spanish writer Cervantes was one victim; he's said to have spent five years in the vaults by the main square before being ransomed. The story goes that he appropriated the town's name for his character Dulcinea in *Don Quixote*. Others were less lucky, like the pilgrims bound for Mecca robbed then drowned by Lika Ceni – an act which outraged the sultan and landed him a hefty price on his head.

Along with their usual business of pirating, Ulcinj's crews had a lucrative sideline in slavery. Ulcinj became the centre of a thriving trade, with people – mainly from North Africa and some as young as two or three – paraded for sale on the town's main square.

staff who can help you find private rooms (from €10 per person), apartments or hotel rooms. It also rents cars, runs tours and sells maps of Ulcinj.

Hotel Dolcino (☎ 422 288; www.hoteldolcino.com, Hazif Ali Ulqinaku bb; s/d/q/ste €40/50/60/70; ✻) You can't quibble over the exceptionally reasonable prices of this modern business-oriented mini hotel in the centre of town. The quieter rooms at the back have spacious terraces, although the small front balconies are great for watching the passing parade.

Dvori Balšića & Palata Venecija (☎ 421 457; www .realestate-travel.com; s/d/q/apt €75/100/140/190; ✻) Wi-fi. If you've ever fancied being king of the castle, these grand stone palazzos in the old town should satisfy the urge. The sizeable rooms all have kitchenettes, romantic sea views, and stucco and dark-wood interiors.

Eating & Drinking

OURPICK Riblja Čorba (☎ 401 720; Bojana River; mains €6-10) Not actually in Ulcinj but well worth the 14km drive, this memorable fish restaurant is one of several that jut over the Bojana River just before the bridge to Ada Bojana. The name means fish soup and the broth is indeed sublime: thick with rice and served in a metal pot that will fill your bowl twice over.

Restaurant Pizzeria Bazar (☎ 421 639; Hazif Ali Ulqinaku bb; mains €4-10) An upstairs restaurant that's a great idling place when the streets below are heaving with tourists. People watch in comfort as you enjoy a plate of *lignje na žaru* (grilled calamari), the restaurant's speciality.

Rock (Hazif Ali Ulqinaku bb) A worthy attempt at an Irish pub with dark wood and electric candles adding to the atmosphere.

Getting There & Away

The **bus station** (☎ 413 225) is on the northeastern edge of town just off Bulevar Vёllazerit Frashёri. Services head to Bar (€2.50, 30 minutes, six daily), Podgorica (€7, one hour, daily) and Shkodra (€4.50, 90 minutes, daily).

Minibuses head to Shkodra at 9am and 3pm (or when they're full) from the carpark beside Ulcinj's market (about €5).

CENTRAL MONTENEGRO

The heart of Montenegro – physically, spiritually and politically – is easily accessed as a day trip from the coast, but it's well deserving of longer exploration. Two wonderful national parks separate it from the coast and behind them lie the two capitals, the ancient current one and the newer former one.

LOVĆEN NATIONAL PARK ЛОВЋЕН

Directly behind Kotor is **Mt Lovćen** (1749m), the Black Mountain that gave Crna Gora (Montenegro) its name (*crna/negro*/black; *gora/monte*/mountain). This locale occupies a special place in their hearts of all Montenegrins. For most of its history it represented the entire nation – a rocky island of Slavic resistance in an Ottoman sea. The old capital of Cetinje nestles in its foothills.

The national park's 6220 hectares are home to 85 species of butterflies, 200 species of birds (including regal birds of prey) and mammals including brown bears and wolves. It's criss-crossed with well-marked hiking paths that can be accessed from Kotor, Budva or Cetinje, and the new Coastal Mountain Traversal (p368) runs straight through it.

The **National Park Office** (☎ 033-761 128; www .nparkovi.cg.yu; Ivanova Korita bb; ☼ 9am-5pm Apr-Oct, shorter hr winter) is near its centre and offers accommodation in four-bed bungalows (€40). If you're planning some serious walking, buy a copy of the 1:25,000 *Lovćen Mountain Touristic Map*, available from the office and park entrances.

Lovćen's star attraction is the magnificent **Njegoš Mausoleum** (admission €3) at the top of its second-highest peak, Jezerski Vrh (1657m). Take the 461 steps up to the entry, where two granite giantesses guard the tomb of Montenegro's greatest hero (see p337). Inside, under a golden mosaic canopy, a 28-tonne Petar II Petrović Njegoš rests in the wings of an eagle, carved from a single block of black granite by Croatian sculptor Ivan Meštrović. The actual tomb lies below; a path at the rear leads to a dramatic circular viewing platform providing the same spectacular views that caused George Bernard Shaw to exclaim, 'Am I in paradise or on the moon?' A photographer stationed near the entrance has a stash of folk costumes and a computer set up to print out instant quirky souvenirs (€5).

If you're driving, the park can be approached from either Kotor or Cetinje (entry fee €2). The back route between the two shouldn't be missed (see p346).

CETINJE ЦЕТИЊЕ
☎ 041 / pop 15,137

Rising from a green vale surrounded by rough, grey mountains, Cetinje is an odd mix of former capital and overgrown village where single-storey cottages and stately mansions share the same street. Several of those mansions – dating from times when European ambassadors rubbed shoulders with Montenegrin princesses – have become museums or schools for art and music.

Orientation & Information

Cetinje's main street is pretty Njegoševa, a partly pedestrianised thoroughfare lined with interesting buildings including the **presidential** palace and various former embassies marked with plaques (check out the unusual **former French embassy** at the corner of ulica Jovana Tomaševica). Everything of significance is in the immediate vicinity, including banks and the **post office** (☎ 232 026; Njegoševa bb).

A&E Clinic (Hitna Pomoć; ☎ 233 002; Vuka Mićunovića 2)

Tourist Information (☎ 078-108 788; Novice Cerovića bb; ☼ 8am-8pm Mon-Sat, 9am-5pm Sun) No English spoken, but you can buy souvenirs and Cetinje guidebooks (€10).

Sights
MUSEUMS

The **National Museum of Montenegro** (Narodni muzej Crne Gore; all museums adult/child €8/4; ☼ 9am-5pm, last admission 4.30pm) is actually a collection of five museums housed in a clump of important buildings. A joint ticket will get you into all of them or you can buy individual tickets.

Two are housed in the former parliament (1910), Cetinje's most imposing building. The fascinating **History Museum** (Istorijski muzej; ☎ 230 310; Novice Cerovića 7; adult/child €3/1.50) is very well laid out, following a timeline from the Stone Age to 1955. There are few English signs, but the enthusiastic staff will walk you around and give you an overview before leaving you to your own devices. Bullet holes are a theme of some of the museum's most interesting relics: there are three in the back of the tunic that Prince Danilo was wearing when assassinated; Prince Nikola's standard from the battle of Vučji Do has 396; and in the communist section there's a big, gaping one in the skull of a fallen comrade.

Upstairs is the equally excellent **Art Museum** (Umjetnički muzej; adult/child €3/1.50). There's a small collection of icons, the most important being the precious 9th-century *Our Lady of Philermos*, which was traditionally believed to have been painted by St Luke himself. It's spectacularly presented in its own blue-lit 'chapel', but the Madonna's face is only just visible behind its spectacular golden casing, mounted with diamonds, rubies and sapphires. Elsewhere in the gallery all of Montenegro's great artists are represented, with the most famous (Milunović, Lubardo, Dado etc) having their own separate spaces. Expect a museum staff member to be hovering as you wander around.

While the hovering at the Art Museum is annoying, the **King Nikola Museum** (Muzej kralja

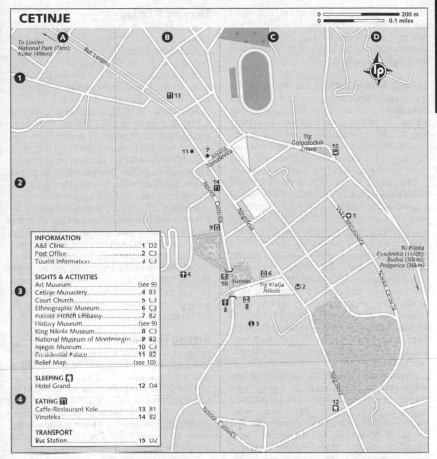

CETINJE

0 _____ 200 m
0 _____ 0.1 miles

To Lovćen
National Park (7km);
Kotor (49km)

Trg
Golootockih
Zrtava

To Rijeka
Crnojevica (13km);
Budva (30km);
Podgorica (36km)

Trg Kralja
Nikole

INFORMATION
A&E Clinic.....................................1 D2
Post Office...................................2 C3
Tourist Information.......................3 C3

SIGHTS & ACTIVITIES
Art Museum.............................(see 9)
Cetinje Monastery.......................4 B3
Court Church...............................5 C3
Ethnographic Museum.................6 C3
Former French Embassy................7 B2
History Museum.......................(see 9)
King Nikola Museum....................8 C3
National Museum of Montenegro...9 B2
Njegos Museum........................10 C3
Presidential Palace.....................11 B2
Relief Map..............................(see 10)

SLEEPING
Hotel Grand..............................12 D4

EATING
Caffe-Restaurant Kole................13 B1
Vinoteka..................................14 B2

TRANSPORT
Bus Station...............................15 D2

Nikole; ☎ 230 555; Trg Kralja Nikole; adult/child €5/2.50) can be downright infuriating. Entry is only by guided tour, which the staff will only give to a group, even if you've prepaid for a ticket and they've got nothing else to do. Still, this 1871 palace of Nikola I, last king of Montenegro, is worth the hassle. Although it was looted during WWII, enough plush furnishings, stern portraits and taxidermied animals remain to capture the spirit of the court.

Opposite the National Museum, the castle-like **Njegoš Museum** (Njegošev muzej; ☎ 231 050; Trg Kralja Nikole; adult/child €3/1.50) was the residence of Montenegro's favourite son, prince-bishop poet Petar II Petrović Njegoš. The hall was built and financed by the Russians in 1838 and housed the nation's first billiard table, hence the museum's alternative name, Biljarda. The bottom floor is devoted to military costumes, photos of soldiers with outlandish moustaches, and exquisitely decorated weapons – these people clearly loved their guns. Upstairs are displayed Njegoš's personal effects, including his bishop's cross, garments, documents, fabulous furniture and, of course, the billiard table.

When you leave the museum turn right and follow the walls to the glass pavilion housing a fascinating large-scale **relief map** (adult/child €1/0.50) of Montenegro created by the Austrians in 1917. If it's closed you can peer through the windows.

Occupying the former Serbian embassy, the **Ethnographic Museum** (Etnografski muzej; Trg Kralja

Nikole; adult/child €2/1) is the least interesting of the five, but if you've bought a joint ticket you may as well check it out. The collection of costumes and tools is well presented and has English notations.

CETINJE MONASTERY МАНАСТИР ЦЕТИЊЕ

It's a case of three times lucky for the **Cetinje monastery** (☎ 231 021; ☽ 8am-6pm), having been repeatedly destroyed during Ottoman attacks and rebuilt. This sturdy incarnation dates from 1785, with its only exterior ornamentation being the capitals of columns recycled from the original building founded in 1484.

The chapel to the right of the courtyard holds the monastery's proudest possessions: a shard of the true cross (the *pièce de résistance* of many of Europe's churches) and the mummified right hand of St John the Baptist. The hand's had a fascinating history, having escaped wars and revolutions and passed through the hands of Byzantine emperors, Ottoman sultans, the Knights Hospitalier, Russian tsars and Serbian kings. It's now housed in a bejewelled golden casket by the chapel's window, draped in heavy fabric and with an icon of the Baptist at its, ahem, foot. The casket's only occasionally opened for veneration, so if you miss out you can console yourself that it's not a very pleasant sight.

The monastery **treasury** (admission €2; ☽ 8am-4pm) is only open to groups, but if you're persuasive enough and prepared to wait around, you may be able to get in. It holds a wealth of fascinating objects that form a blur as you're shunted around the rooms by one of the monks. These include jewel-encrusted vestments, ancient handwritten texts, icons (including a lovely Syrian Madonna and Child), royal crowns and a copy of the 1494 *Oktoih* (Book of the Eight Voices), the first book printed in Serbian.

If your legs, shoulders or cleavage are on display you'll either be denied entry or given a smock to wear.

COURT CHURCH

Built in 1886 on the ruins of the original Cetinje monastery, the cute little **Court Church** (Dvorska crkva; Novice Cerovića bb) has a lovely gilded iconstasis, but its main claim to fame is as the burial place of Cetinje's founder, Ivan Crnojević, and Montenegro's last king and queen. Nikola I and Milena died in exile in Italy and were only interred in these white-marble tombs in 1989.

Sleeping & Eating

Cetinje seems to expect its visitors to flit in and out on tour buses. Accommodation is limited and there are only a few proper restaurants. Come the weekend, competing sound systems blast the cobwebs from the main street. If war broke out on a Saturday night you probably wouldn't hear it.

Hotel Grand (☎ 242 400; hotelgrand@cg.yu; Njegoševa 1; s €45-60, d €64-80, apt €120) Fading Grandeur would be a more accurate description, but aside from a few pigeons roosting in the walls, Cetinje's only hotel is a pleasant place to stay. The comfy beds, new linen and spongy carpet strips certainly help. Locals glam it up for afternoon drinks on the leafy terrace.

Vinoteka (☎ 068555771; Njegoševa 103; mains €2.20-5) The wood-beamed porch looking onto the garden is such a nice spot that the excellent and reasonably priced pizza and pasta feel like a bonus – the decent wine list even more so.

Caffe-Restaurant Kole (☎ 069035716; bul Lenjina 12; mains €3-8) They serve omelettes, pizza and pasta at this snazzy modern eatery, but what's really great are the local treats. Try the *Njeguški ražanj* stuffed with *pršut* and cheese.

Getting There & Away

Cetinje's on the main highway between Budva and Podgorica and can also be reached by a glorious back road from Kotor via Lovćen National Park (p346). The **bus station** (Trg Golootočkih Žrtava) is only two blocks from the main street, but it doesn't have a timetable, a ticket counter or even a phone. Buses leave every 30 minutes for Podgorica (€3) and hourly for Budva (€3).

LAKE SKADAR NATIONAL PARK
СКАДАРСКО ЈЕЗЕРО

The Balkans' largest lake, dolphin-shaped Skadar has its tail and two-thirds of its body in Montenegro and its nose in Albania. Covering between 370 sq km and 550 sq km (depending on the time of year), it's one of the most important reserves for wetland birds in Europe. The endangered Dalmatian pelican nests here, along with 256 other species, while 48 known species of fish lurk beneath its smooth surface. On the Montenegrin side, an area of 400 sq km has been protected by a national park since 1979. It's a blissfully pretty area encompassing steep mountains, hidden villages, historic churches, clear waters and floating meadows of waterlilies.

The main **National Park Visitors' Centre** (☎ 020-879 100; www.skadarlake.org; Vranjina bb; admission €2; ⏲ 8am-4pm) is on the opposite side of the causeway heading to Podgorica from Virpazar. This modern facility has excellent displays about all the national parks, not just Lake Skadar, and sells park entry tickets (€4 per day) and fishing permits (€5 per day).

In the busy months various tour operators set up kiosks in the vicinity. **Kings Travel** (☎ 020-202 800) hires rowboats (€25/100 per hour/day) and speedboats with driver (€60/300 per hour/day). The complex also includes **Restoran Jezero** (☎ 020-879 106; mains €5-9), a reputable traditional restaurant with beautiful lake views that's owned by the Plantaže wine company. This is Montenegro's main wine region; stock up at the **Plantaže store** (⏲ 9am-4pm), built into a cave by the car park, or look out for roadside stalls.

Just along the causeway are the remains of the 19th-century fortress **Lesendro**. The busy highway and railway tracks prevent land access to the site.

Rijeka Crnojevića Ријека Црнојевића

The northwestern end of the lake thins into the serpentine loops of the Rijeka Crnojevića (Crnojević River) and terminates near the pretty village of the same name. When Montenegro was ruled from Cetinje, this is where the royals came to escape the Black Mountain's winter. It's a charming, tucked-away kind of place, accessed by side roads that lead off the Cetinje–Podgorica highway.

The village's main feature is the photogenic arched stone bridge constructed by Prince Danilo in 1854. Occupying four wooden huts that jut out over the river on stilts is a **National Park Visitors' Centre** (admission €1; ⏲ 8am-4pm) that features a historical display.

Kayak Montenegro's day trips from Herceg Novi take to the water here and paddle along the river to the lake (see p342).

If you fall under Rijeka Crnojevića's spell, there are rooms available at **Kuća Perjanik** (☎ 067478440; r €30), one house back from the bridge. The garrulous owner has returned from Melbourne to fix up his ancestral home and, although it's still a work in progress, the simple rooms are clean and tidy and should have en suites by the time this book is published. You can grab a simple meal and a cold beer downstairs.

You wouldn't expect it, but this sleepy place is home to one of Montenegro's best restaurants. **Stari Most** (Old Bridge; ☎ 033-239 505; fish €25-45 per kg, 5-course set menu €40-50) is well located on the marble riverside promenade, looking to the old bridge from which it derives its name. Fish, particularly eel, is the speciality here and the fish soup alone is enough to justify a drive from Podgorica.

Virpazar Вирпазар

This sweet little town is what passes for the big smoke in these parts and serves as the main gateway to the national park. It's centred on a pretty town square and a picturesque stone bridge across a river blanketed with waterlilies and, disappointingly, litter. Looking over the town are two testaments to its bloody past: the ruins of **Besac castle**, the scene of a major battle with the Turks in 1702, and a striking **bronze sculpture** atop a watchtower memorialising the Partisans who lost their lives in WWII.

Most of the boat tours of the lake depart from here, so the tranquillity is briefly shattered at around 10.30am when the tour buses from the coast pull in. There's a national park kiosk by the marina that sells entry tickets and fishing permits but doesn't offer much information.

The **Pelikan Hotel** (☎ 020-711 107; pelikanzec@cg.yu; r €52-75; ✱) is a well-run one-stop shop offering accommodation, an excellent traditional restaurant (mains €5 to €12) and 2½-hour boat tours that explore the lake's northern reaches (€30). The rooms are clean and have nice views over the square, but some of them are tiny.

Virpazar doesn't have a bus station, but buses on the Bar–Podgorica route stop here. The decrepit **train station** (☎ 020-441 435) is off the main road, 800m south of town. There are regular services to Bar (€2) and Podgorica (€2.50).

Murići Мурићи

The southern edge of the lake is the most dramatic, with the Rumija mountains rising precipitously from the water. From Virpazar there's a wonderful drive following the contours of the lake through the mountains towards the border before crossing the range and turning back towards Ulcinj. About halfway, a steep road descends to the village of Murići.

This is one of the lake's best swimming spots. The water's clear, if a little weedy in places, and swarms of little fish follow your feet as you kick up the nutrients beneath. Local boatmen offer trips to the monasteries on the nearby islands for around €10 per hour. Keen hikers can start the Coastal Mountain Traversal from here (p368).

The **Murići Vacation Resort** (☎ 069688288; www .nacionalnipark-izletistemurici.com; per person €35) is, thankfully, more school camp than Club Med. Simple log cabins nestle within an olive grove and share a decent ablutions block with a separate bath and shower. The price includes a bed plus three meals in the shady outdoor **restaurant** (mains €5-9). It also organises **lake tours** (€16) that visit the islands and Virpazar. If you don't have transport to Murići, jump on the boat at Virpazar.

PODGORICA ПОДГОРИЦА
☎ 020 / pop 136,473

Podgorica's never going to be Europe's most happening capital, but if you can get past the sweltering summer temperatures and concrete apartment blocks you'll find a pleasant little city with lots of green space and some decent galleries, restaurants and bars. If you've got limited time it's probably not worth a special trip, but, given that it's a major transport hub, why not leave your bags at the bus station and wander around for the day?

Orientation
Podgorica sits at the confluence of two rivers. West of the broad Morača is what passes for the business district. The smaller Ribnica River divides the eastern side in two. To the south is Stara Varoš, the heart of the Ottoman town, where you'll find a Turkish **clock tower** (Trg Bećir-Bega Osmanagića), a **mosque** (ul Nemaljića) and the **ruins of fortifications** where the rivers meet. North of the Ribnica is Nova Varoš, an attractive, mainly low-rise precinct of late-19th- and early-20th-century buildings housing a lively mixture of shops and bars. At its heart is the attractive main square, Trg Republika.

Information
A&E clinic (Hitna Pomoć; ☎ 124; Vaka Djurovića bb)
IPS (☎ 664 202; Njegoševa 28; 9am-9pm) The best selection of English-language books in the country, which isn't saying much.
Lijek Apoteka (☎ 623 994; Mitra Bakića bb; 7am-9pm) Pharmacy.
Montenegro Adventures (☎ 202 380; www.monte negro-adventures.com; Moskovska 63-64) The commercial wing of the nonprofit Centre for Sustainable Tourism

Initiatives (www.cstimontenegro.org), with whom it shares an office. It organises tours, accommodation and the like.
Prva Banka CG (Luka Karadžića bb) One of many bank branches with 24-hour ATMs in the central city.
Tourist Organisation Podgorica (TOP; ☎ 667 535; www.podgorica.travel; Slobode 47) Information on local sights, accommodation and services.
www.club (Bokaška 4; per hr €1.50; 8am-2am) Decent cafe-bar with internet terminals.

Sights
Despite Cetinje having nabbed most of the national endowment, the new capital's well served by the **Podgorica Museum & Gallery** (☎ 242 543; Marka Miljanova 4; adult/child €5/1; 9am-8pm). There's an interesting section on the city's history, which had its start around the time of Christ as the Roman town of Doclea. The gallery features local big hitters such as Dado Đurić and Petar Lubarda, whose large canvas *Titograd* (1956) takes pride of place in the foyer.

The Centre for Contemporary Art operates two galleries in Podgorica. The bottom two floors of the former royal palace **Dvorac Petrovića** (☎ 243 513; Kruševac bb; 8am-2pm & 4-9pm Mon-Fri & 10am-4pm Sat summer, 8am-8pm Mon-Fri, to 2pm Sat winter) are given over to high-profile exhibitions, while the top floor has an oddball collection of miscellanea (Indonesian batik, a metal palm tree from Iraq) that have the look of diplomatic gifts. The lovely grounds contain interesting sculpture, a tiny church and a small exhibition space in the former guardhouse (Perjanički Dom). Temporary exhibitions are also staged in the small **Galerija Centar** (☎ 665 409; Njegoševa 2; admission free; 9am-2pm & 5-9pm Mon-Fri, 10am-2pm Sat).

For a city formerly known as Titograd there is an inordinate number of royal sculptures dotted around its many parks. The most imposing is the huge bronze **statue of Petar I Petrović Njegoš** standing on a black-marble plinth on the Cetinje edge of town. You won't find Tito anywhere, but there's a spectacularly cheesy sculpture of Russian singer **Vladimir Visockij** near the **Millennium Bridge**, pictured shirtless with a guitar and a skull at his feet.

An indicator of the healthy state of Orthodoxy in Montenegro is the immense **Temple of Christ's Resurrection** (Hram Hristovog Vaskrsenja; Bul Džordža Vašingtona). It's still incomplete after 15 years' construction, but its large dome, white-stone towers and gold crosses are a striking addition to Podgorica's skyline.

Sleeping

Most visitors to Podgorica are here for business, either commercial or government-related. Hotels set their prices accordingly and private accommodation isn't really an option.

Hotel Evropa (☎ 623 444; www.hotelevropa.cg.yu; Orahovačka 16; s €55-70, d/tr €90/120; ❷ 🖵) Wi-fi. It's hardly a salubrious location, but Evropa is handy to the train and bus stations and offers clean rooms with comfortable beds, writing desks and decent showers. Despite its diminutive size there's a sauna, a fitness room and ample parking.

Hotel Eminent (☎ 664 646; eminent@cg.yu; Njegoševa 25; s/d/tr €80/130/160, apt €90-140; ❷) Wi-fi. Given its location and excellent facilities, the Eminent seems to be set up for businesspeople keen on an after-work tipple. The front rooms can be noisy, but the funky mezzanine apartments open on to a covered verandah at the back.

Hotel Podgorica (☎ 402 500; www.hotelpodgorica.cq.yu; bul Sv Petra Cetinjskog 1; s €115-145, d €160-170, tw 170, ste €175-185; ❷) Wi-fi. A wonderful showcase of 1960s Yugoslav architecture, the Podgorica has been luxuriously modernised yet retains its period charm – the pebblecrete exterior blending into stone the shade of Montenegro's mountains. The best rooms have terraces facing the river.

Eating

Head to the **little market** (Moskovska bb) or the **big market** (Bratstva Jedinstva bb) for fresh fruit and vegetables, and the large **Maxi** (Braće Zlatić Ana bb; ❷ 7am-midnight Mon-Sat, 7.30am-3.30pm Sun) supermarket for other cooking supplies.

our pick **Leonardo** (☎ 242 902; Svetozara Markovića bb; mains €4-13; Ⓥ) Leonardo's unlikely position at the centre of a residential block makes it a little tricky to find, but the effort's well rewarded by accomplished Italian cuisine. The pasta dishes are delicious and reasonably priced, given the upmarket ambience, while the €4 pizzas should leave even those on a budget with a Mona Lisa smile.

Laterna (☎ 232 331; Marka Miljanova 41; mains €4-13; ❷ 9am-midnight Mon-Sat; Ⓥ) Farm implements hang from the rough stone walls, creating a surprisingly rustic ambience for the centre of the city. A selection of meat and fish grills is offered, but it's hard to go past the crispy-based pizza – it's quite possibly Montenegro's best.

Linea (☎ 254 456; Trg Republika 22; mains €4.50-13; Ⓥ) This attractive indoor-outdoor cafe serves decent breakfasts (omelettes, bacon and eggs), substantial sandwiches (€2.40) and all the usual pasta, pizza and steak selections. The pear and walnut salad with gorgonzola makes a tasty change from grilled meat.

Drinking & Entertainment

Buda Bar (☎ 067344944; Stanka Dragojevića 26; ❷ 8am-2am) A golden Buddha smiles serenely as you meditate over your morning coffee or search for the eternal truth at the bottom of a cocktail glass. This is one slick watering hole; the tentlike semi-enclosed terrace is the place to be on balmy summer nights.

Living Room (Njegoševa 37) There are loads of tables on the street, but if you can handle the volume, the leather couches and chandeliers of the raised 'living area' are pretty cool.

Nice Vice (Slobode 84) Step through a wonky picture frame to a wine bar looking something like an English gentleman's library.

Greenwich (Njegoševa 29; ❷ 8am-3am) A pseudo-London pub where everyone ends up in the wee hours.

Kino Kultura (IV Proleterske Brigade 1; admission €2.50) The screenings aren't as regular as you might expect for the city's only cinema, but you might luck upon an English-language movie with Montenegrin subtitles.

Shopping

RV Rakočević (☎ 067840802; Njegoševa 23; ❷ 8am-9pm Mon-Sat) If you're in the mood for a spot of *oro* (see p339) here's where you'll find your fancy folk threads. A beautifully hand-embroidered, uniquely Montenegrin shirt will set you back €60 to €150.

Getting There & Away

BUS

Podgorica's **bus station** (☎ 620 430; Trg Golootočkih Žrtava; ❷ 5am-10pm) has a left-luggage service, a post office, an ATM, a restaurant and regular services to all major towns, including Nikšić (€3, one hour), Herceg Novi via Cetinje (€9, three hours), Kotor (€7, two hours), Bar (€7) and Ulcinj (€7, one hour).

TRAIN

Don't expect any English or a lot of help from the information desk at the **train station** (☎ 441 211; www.zeljeznica.cg.yu; Trg Golootočkih Žrtava 13; ❷ 5am-11pm). Luckily, timetables are posted and fairly straightforward. Destinations include Bar (€3, one hour, 14 daily), Virpazar

(€2.50, 40 minutes, 14 daily), Kolašin (90 minutes, three daily) and Belgrade (€22, 7½ hours, four daily).

CAR

Avis (www.avisworld.com), **Europcar** (☎ 606 310; www.europcarcg.com), **Kompas** (☎ 244 117; www.kompas-car.com), **Rokšped** (☎ 620 000; www.roksped.com) and **Sixt** (www.sixt.com) all have counters at Podgorica airport. Excellent local agency **Meridian** (☎ 234 944, 069316666; bul Džordža Vašingtona 85) also has a city office.

Getting Around

It's not difficult to get around town on foot, but if you fancy trying a local bus they cost €0.60 for a short journey. **Podgorica airport** (☎ 872 016) is 9km south of the city. Montenegro Airlines runs a shuttle bus (€3) between the airport and Trg Republika, timed around their flights. Airport taxis have a standard €15 fare to the centre, but ordinary taxis should only charge about €8; try to grab one as they drop off passengers. Taxi companies:

Alo Taxi (☎ 9700)
City Taxi (☎ 9711)
PLL Taxi (☎ 9705)

OSTROG MONASTERY
МАНАСТИР ОСТРОГ

Resting in a cliff face 900m above the Zeta valley, the gleaming white Ostrog monastery is the most important site in Montenegro for Orthodox Christians. Even with its masses of pilgrims, tourists and trashy souvenir stands, it's a strangely affecting place.

Leaving the main Podgorica–Nikšić highway 19km past Danilovgrad, a narrow road twists uphill for 7km before it reaches the **lower monastery** (1824). In summer you'll be greeted with sweet fragrances emanating from the mountain foliage. The church has vivid frescos and behind it is a natural spring where you can fill your bottles with deliciously fresh water and potentially benefit from an internal blessing as you sup it.

From here the faithful, many of them barefoot, plod up another two steep kilometres to the main shrine. Nonpilgrims and the pure of heart may drive to the upper car park. Halfway up, the beautiful stone walls of the little domed **Church of St Stanko the Martyr** gleam golden in the sunset.

The **upper monastery** (the really impressive one) is dubbed St Vasilije's miracle, because

no one seems to understand how it was built. Constructed in 1665 within two large caves, it gives the impression that it has grown out of the very rock. St Vasilije (Basil), a bishop from Hercegovina, brought his monks here after the Ottomans destroyed Tvrdos monastery near Trebinje.

Pilgrims queue to enter the atmospheric shrine where the saint's fabric-wrapped bones are kept. To enter you'll be wearing a long skirt or trousers (jeans are fine) and cover your shoulders. Most women also cover their head with a scarf. It's customary to back out of the doorways and you'll witness much kissing of lintels and making of signs of the cross from the devout.

This idyllic place isn't without controversy. Radovan Karadžić christened his grandson here and several reports suggest that the monastery sheltered the former Bosnian Serb leader and alleged war criminal during his lengthy spell as a fugitive. This has always been strenuously denied; perhaps the matter will be settled now that Karadžić has finally been arrested.

One of the only nonsmoking establishments in the country, the **guesthouse** (☎ 067405258; dm €4; ✗) near the lower monastery offers tidy single-sex dorm rooms, while in summer many pilgrims lay sleeping mats in front of the upper monastery.

There's no public transport, but numerous tour buses head here from all of the tourist hot spots. Expect to pay about €15 to €20 for a day trip from the coast.

MONTENEGRO'S MOST EXTRAORDINARY DRIVES

- The Bay of Kotor
- Kotor to Cetinje via Lovćen National Park
- Virpazar to Ulcinj along the southern edge of Lake Skadar
- Podgorica to Kolašin along the Morača canyon
- Kolašin over the mountains to Andrijevica and on to Plav
- Mojkovac to Žabljak along the Tara River
- Nikšić to Šćepan Polje along the Piva canyon

NORTHERN MOUNTAINS

This really is the full monty: soaring peaks, hidden monasteries, secluded villages, steep river-canyons and a whole heap of 'wild beauty', to quote the tourist slogan. Parts may look remote on the map, but don't underestimate how tiny Montenegro is. Plenty of tours head clear across the country from the coast to the Tara River for a day's rafting. It's well worth hiring a car for a couple of days to get off the beaten track – some of the roads are truly spectacular.

DURMITOR NATIONAL PARK & TARA CANYON
ДУРМИТОР И КАЊОН ТАРЕ
☎ 052 / pop 4900

Magnificent scenery ratchets up to the stupendous in this national park, where ice and water have carved a dramatic landscape from the limestone. Some 18 glacial lakes known as *gorske oči* (mountain eyes) dot the Durmitor Range, with the largest, **Black Lake** (Crno Jezero), a pleasant 3km walk from Žabljak. The rounded mass of the **Bear** (Međed, 2287m) rears up behind the lake, flanked by others of the park's 48 peaks over 2000m, including the highest, **Bobotov Kuk** (2523m). In winter (December to March) Durmitor is Montenegro's main ski resort; in summer it's a popular place for hiking, rafting and other active pursuits.

The park is home to enough critters to cast a Disney movie as well as purportedly the greatest variety of butterflies in Europe. The golden eagle is the king of the 163 species of bird, and about 50 types of mammals roam the woodlands. It's very unlikely you'll spot the bears and wolves, which is either a good or a bad thing depending on your perspective. We're assured that the wolves are only dangerous during mating season (December) or if they're really starving at the end of a long winter.

Orientation & Information
Durmitor National Park includes the Durmitor Range and a narrow branch heading east along the Tara River. West of the park, the Tara forms the border with BiH, joining the Piva River near Šćepan Polje.

Žabljak, at the eastern edge of the range, is the park's principal gateway and the only town within its boundaries. It's not very big and nor is it attractive, but it has a supermarket, a post office, a bank, hotels and restaurants, gathered around the parking lot that masquerades as the main square.

Durmitor National Park Visitor Centre (☎ 360 228; www.nparkovi.cg.yu; ☺ 7am-2pm autumn & spring, 8am-6pm winter & summer) On the road to Black Lake, this centre includes a wonderful micro museum focusing on the park's flora and fauna. The knowledgable English-speaking staff answer queries and sell local craft, fishing permits (river/lake €15/10), maps (€8) and hiking guides.

Internet (Božidara Žugića bb, Žabljak) In an unmarked wooden hut next to Restaurant Durmitor.

Summit Travel Agency (☎ 361 502; anna.grbovic @cg.yu; Njegoševa bb, Žabljak) Owner Anna Grbović speaks good English and can arrange 4WD tours (€100 for up to three people), rafting trips (p366) and mountain-bike hire (€2/10 per hour/day).

Žabljak Tourist Centre (Trg Durmitorskih Ratnika) This wooden hut in the car park below Hotel Žabljak may be able to help out with maps and advice in winter, but when we visited in the height of the summer season there was no sign of life.

Sights & Activities
TARA RIVER & CANYON
РИЈЕКА ТАРА И КАЊОН

Slicing through the mountains at the northern edge of the national park as though they were made from the local soft cheese, the **Tara River** forms a canyon that drops to 1300m at its deepest point. Colorado's Grand Canyon is only 200m deeper. A **rafting** jaunt along the river is one of the sure-fire things that enduring Montenegro memories are made of.

This is one of the country's most popular tourist activities, with various operators running trips daily between May and October. The river has a few rapids, but don't expect an adrenalin-fuelled white-water experience. You'll get the most excitement in May when the last of the melting snow revs up the flow.

The 82km section that is raftable starts from Splavište, south of the impressive 150m-high Tara Bridge, and ends at Šćepan Polje on the BiH border. The classic two-day trip heads through the deepest part of the canyon on the first day, stopping overnight at Radovan Luka. Most of the day tours from the coast traverse only the last 18km – this is outside the national park and hence avoids hefty fees. You'll miss out on the canyon's depths, but it's still a beautiful stretch including most of the rapids. The buses follow a spectacular road along the Piva River, giving you a double dose of canyon action.

At Šćepan Polje you'll find rafting operators set up along the river. If you've got your own wheels you can save a few bucks and avoid a lengthy day tour by heading directly here. **Tara Tour** (☎ 069086106; www.tara-tour.com) offers an excellent half-day trip (€30/40 with/without breakfast and lunch) and has a cute set of wooden chalets with squat toilets and showers in a separate block; accommodation, three meals and a half-day's rafting costs €55. Another good operator is **Kamp Grab** (☎ 083-200 598; www.tara-grab.com), with lodgings blissfully located 18km upstream at Brstanovica.

Summit (p365) offers a range of tours from Žabljak starting from Splavište (€50/110/200 for a half-/one-/two-day tour). The park fees bump up the price, but you'll get to see the heart of the canyon. If you can find nine friends, a two-day trip on a wooden raft can be arranged (€3000).

If you'd rather stay dry and admire the canyon from afar, the best view is from the top of **Ćurevac** (1625m). It's unsignposted and pretty hard to find without a local in tow, but a taxi from Žabljak should get you there for €10 (one way).

HIKING
Durmitor is one of the best-marked mountain ranges in Europe. Some suggest it's a little too well labelled, encouraging novices to wander around seriously high-altitude paths that are prone to fog and summer thunderstorms. However, as the national park staff point out, the longest walks can be done in a (lengthy) day and there shouldn't be a problem if you're sensibly prepared. That means checking the weather forecast before you set out, sticking to the tracks and preparing for sudden drops in temperature.

You'll be charged €2 per day to enter the park, and paths can be as easy as a 40-minute stroll around Black Lake. A more substantial hike is to the two **Škrka lakes**, in the centre of a tectonic valley, where you can stay overnight in a mountain hut (opposite) and enjoy magnificent scenery.

Durmitor and the Tara Canyon by Branislav Cerović (€12 from the National Park Office) is an excellent resource for mountaineers and serious hikers.

SKIING & SNOWBOARDING
On the slopes of **Savin Kuk** (2313m), 5km from Žabljak, you'll find the main ski centre. Its 3.5km run starts from a height of 2010m and is best suited to advanced skiers. Even in the height of summer Savin Kuk wears a pocket of snow. On the outskirts of town near the bus station, **Javorovača** is a gentle 300m slope that's good for kids and beginners. Shortly due to reopen at the time of research was a third centre at **Mali Štuoc** (1953m), with terrific views over Black Lake, Međed and Savin Kuk and slopes to suit all levels of experience.

One of the big attractions for skiing here is the cost: day passes are around €15, weekly passes €70, and ski lessons between €10 and €20. You can rent ski and snowboard gear from **Sport Trade** (☎ 069538831; Vuka Karadžića 7, Žabljak) for €10 per day.

The season runs from December to March, peaking in the new year.

DOBRILOVINA MONASTERY
Near the eastern boundary of the national park, 28km from Mojkovac, this 17th-century monastery has an idyllic setting in lush fields hemmed in by the mountains and Tara River. If you knock, a black-robed nun will unlock the church but only if she's satisfied that you're appropriately attired. Dedicated to St George, it has some lovely frescos.

Sleeping
ŽABLJAK ЖАБЉАК
Summit Travel Agency (p365) can help you source private accommodation starting from around €10 per person. Most of the giant Yugoslav-era hotels either were closed for renovations when we visited or deserved to be.

Autokamp Mlinski Potok Mina (☎ 069497625; sites per person €3, beds €10) With a fabulously hospitable host (there's no escaping the *rakija* shots), this campsite above the national park office is an excellent option. When we visited the toilet block was a work in progress, but the six showers and clean sit-down toilets are already a step up from most Montenegrin camping options. The owner's house can sleep 12 guests in comfortable wood-panelled rooms and he has another house sleeping 11 by Black Lake.

Hotel Javor (☎ 361 337; vladoprof@hotmail.com; Božidara Žugića 8; s/d/tr €26/52/78) There's not a lot of English spoken, but you'll find eight cosy rooms with TVs, minibars and en suites.

MB Hotel (☎ 361 601; www.mb-hotel.com; Tripka Đakovića bb; s/d/villas €30/57/100) Wi-fi. In a quiet backstreet halfway between the town centre and the bus station, this little hotel offers modern rooms, English-speaking staff, and an attractive restaurant and bar. The restaurant even has a nonsmoking section – something even less likely to be seen in these parts than wolves.

ELSEWHERE

The staff at the National Park Visitor Centre (p365) should be able to give you information about mountain huts. There's a 20-bed hut between the large and small Škrćka lakes (€5) and another near Sušićko lake; don't expect electricity or running water. You can pitch a tent nearby, or indeed anywhere appropriate within the park (€3/5 per small/large tent).

our pick Eko Oaza Suza Evrope (☎ 067511755; eko-oaza@cg.yu; Dobrilovina; cottages €50) Situated 25km west of Mojkovac at the beginning of the arm of the park that stretches along the Tara River, this 'eco-oasis' consists of four comfortable wooden cottages, each sleeping five. From here you can hike up the mountain and stay overnight in a hut near the glacial lake Zabojsko Jezero (1477m).

Eating & Drinking

Restaurant Durmitor (☎ 069657316; Božidara Žugića bb, Žabljak; meals €2-9; ⏱ 7am-11pm) Offers home cooking at its best in what's just a small wooden hut seating 20. At this size a cosy winter atmosphere is guaranteed.

National Eco Restaurant (☎ 361 337; Božidara Žugića 8, Žabljak; mains €3-10) A great place to try traditional mountain food, such as lamb or veal roasted 'under the pan' (€24 per kilogram). It's all locally sourced and hence organic without trying very hard.

Čudna Šuma (Vuka Karadžića bb) Somehow managing to be rustic and hip at the same time, this is easily Žabljak's best cafe-bar.

Getting There & Away

All of the approaches to Durmitor are spectacular. The most reliable road to Žabljak follows the Tara River west from Mojkovac. In summer this 70km route takes about 90 minutes. If you're coming from Podgorica the quickest route is through Nikšić and Šavnik, but the road can be treacherous in winter. The main highway north from Nikšić follows the dramatic Piva canyon to Šćepan Polje.

There's a petrol station near the **bus station** (☎ 361318) at the southern end of Žabljak on the Nikšić road. Buses head to Belgrade (€25, nine hours, two daily) and Podgorica (€9.50, 3½ hours, three daily). In summer the Podgorica

buses go through Nikšić, while in winter they take the Mojkovac–Kolašin route.

BIOGRADSKA GORA NATIONAL PARK
БИОГРАДСКА ГОРА

Nestled in the heart of the Bjelasica mountain range, this pretty national park has as its heart 1600 hectares of virgin woodland – one of Europe's last three remaining primeval forests. King Nikola is to thank for its survival; on a visit in 1878 he was so taken by the beauty of Biogradska Lake that the locals gifted him the land and he ordered it to be preserved.

The main entrance to the park is between Kolašin and Mojkovac on the Podgorica–Belgrade route. After paying a €2 entry fee you can drive the further 4km to the lake. It really is exquisitely pretty and oh so green. If you're knowledgable about such things you should be able to spot beech, fir, juniper, white ash, maple and elm trees. Occasional tour buses pull in, but a 10-minute stroll should shake the masses and quickly return you to tranquillity.

Most of the busloads head straight to **Restoran Biogradsko Jezero** (mains €5.50-9.20). It has a wonderful terrace where you can steal glimpses of the lake through the trees as you tuck into a traditional lamb or veal dish.

You can hire boats (€5 per hour) and buy fishing permits (€20 per day) from the **park office** (☎ 020-865 625; www.nparkovi.cg.yu) by the car park. If you're planning to tackle the excellent hiking tracks it's worth buying a copy of the *Mountains of Bjelasica* booklet (€3). Nearby there's a campsite with basic squat toilets (€3/5 per small/large tent) and a cluster of 11 new log cabins, each with two beds (€20). The ablutions block for the cabins is much nicer.

If you don't have a car, the nearest bus stop is an hour's walk away at Kraljevo Kolo and the nearest train station is a 90-minute walk at Štitarička Rijeka. The next major town with decent hotels and an excellent **tourist office** (☎ 020-865 110; Trg Borca 2; ⏱ 8am-4pm) is Kolašin, 15km south of the park entrance.

MONTENEGRO DIRECTORY

ACCOMMODATION

A tidal wave of development has seen hotels large and small spring up in the popular destinations. Prices are very seasonal, peaking in

MONTENEGRO

PRACTICALITIES

- *Vijesti* (The News), *Dan* (The Day), *Republika* (The Republic) and *Pobjeda* (Victory) are all daily newspapers. *Monitor*, a weekly news magazine, joins local-language versions of international titles on the newsstands.

- RTCG (Montenegrin Radio TV) is the state broadcaster, with a radio station and two TV channels. In total there are four national free-to-air TV channels and eight regional channels.

- There are dozens of independent radio stations based around the country.

- Montenegro uses standard European electricity (220V to 240V/50Hz to 60Hz). Plugs are of the round two-pin variety that is the norm for continental Europe.

- The video system in Montenegro is PAL.

- The metric system is used for weights and measurements (see conversion chart on the inside front cover).

July and August on the coast. Where the prices vary according to the season, we've listed a range from the cheapest low-season price through to the most expensive high-season rate for each room category. Unless otherwise mentioned the rooms have en suite bathrooms and the tariff usually includes breakfast.

The cheapest option is private accommodation and apartment rentals. These can be arranged through travel agencies or, in season, you may be approached at the bus stop or see signs hanging outside houses. Some local tourist offices publish handy guides. Private rooms shouldn't be hard to find, but some places will require minimum stays in high season.

Facilities at camping grounds tend to be basic, often with squat toilets and limited water. The national parks have cabin-style accommodation.

An additional tourist tax (less than €2 per night) will be added to the rate for all accommodation types.

ACTIVITIES

Hooking up with activity operators can be challenging due to language difficulties, lack of permanent offices and out-of-date websites. Luckily, there are some excellent travel agencies that will do the legwork for you:

Black Mountain (p342)

Montenegro Adventures (p362)

So Montenegro (☎ 44-20-3039 5651; www.somonte negro.co.uk) London-based agency that can construct a customised action-packed tour.

The National Tourist Office, in association with the mountain clubs, has developed *Wilderness Hiking & Biking*, which outlines

five magical routes for each (downloadable from www.montenegro.travel/xxl/en/bro chures/index.html). One of the most exciting is the Coastal Mountain Traversal, a 138km hiking route from Herceg Novi to Lake Skadar that can also be accessed from Kotor and Budva. The tourist office has also produced the pamphlet *Wilderness Biking Montenegro* (downloadable from www .montenegro.travel/xxl/en/brochures/index .html). It outlines five 'top trails' and the mother of all mountain tracks, the 14-day, 1276km Tour de Montenegro, which circles the entire country.

Other activities and their prime locations:

- **Boating** – Kotor (p348), Budva (p352), Lake Skadar (p360)
- **Diving** – Herceg Novi (p342), Budva (p350), Ulcinj (p356)
- **Kayaking** – Herceg Novi (p342), Budva (p352), Rijeka Crnojevića (p361)
- **Paragliding** – Budva (p350)
- **Rafting** – Tara River (p365)
- **Skiing** – Durmitor (p366)

BOOKS

Try the following to get you in the Montenegro mood.

- *Life and Death in the Balkans: A Family Saga in a Century of Conflict* by Bato Tomašević (2008)
- *Realm of the Black Mountain: A History of Montenegro* by Elizabeth Roberts (2007)
- *Nikola & Milena, King & Queen of the Black Mountain: The Rise & Fall of Montenegro's Royal Family* by Marco Houston (2003)

- *Montenegro: A Novel* by Starling Lawrence (1997) for turn-of-the-20th-century politics, bloodshed and romance
- *Black Lamb & Grey Falcon* by Rebecca West (1941), a wordy but often hilarious travelogue providing wry observations on the peoples and politics of Yugoslavia before WWII

BUSINESS HOURS

Business hours in Montenegro are a relative concept. Even if hours are posted on the doors of museums or shops, don't be surprised if they're not heeded. Banks are usually open 8am to 5pm Monday to Friday and until noon Saturday. Shops in busy areas often start at around 8am or 9am and close at a similar time in the evening. Sometimes they'll close for a few hours in the late afternoon. Restaurants open at around 8am and close around midnight, while cafe-bars may stay open until 2am or 3am.

CUSTOMS

In a bid to stop tourists from neighbouring countries bringing all their holiday groceries with them, Montenegro now restricts what food can be brought into the country, but the odd chocolate bar isn't going to be an issue.

It's not permitted to take more than €2000 out of the country. If you're entering with a big wad of cash or travellers cheques and think you might have more than €2000 left when you leave, you're best to complete a currency declaration form on arrival or you may find your money confiscated.

DANGERS & ANNOYANCES

Montenegro's towns are generally safe places. You'll see children playing unsupervised on the streets and young women walking alone at night or even hitchhiking (not to say that we suggest these things).

Montenegro's roads, on the other hand, can be treacherous. They're generally in good condition, but many are narrow and have sheer drops on one side. The main hazard is from other motorists who have no qualms about overtaking on blind corners while talking on their mobile phones or stopping in the middle of the road without warning. There's plenty of random tooting – don't let it faze you. You're best to keep your cool and stick to the speed limit, as the traffic police are everywhere.

Chances are you'll see some snakes if you're poking around ruins during summer.

Montenegro has two types of venomous viper, but they'll try their best to keep out of your way. If bitten you will have time to head to a medical centre for the antivenom. Water snakes are harmless.

Check with the police before photographing any official building they're guarding.

A major annoyance is the time it takes to pay your bill in restaurants and cafes. For every week spent in Montenegro expect to spend at least seven hours waiting for waiters.

Virtually everyone smokes and they do it pretty much everywhere except churches and (usually) buses.

EMBASSIES & CONSULATES

For a full list, see www.vlada.cg.yu/eng/mininos/. The following are all in Podgorica unless otherwise stated.

Albania (☎ 020-652 796; Zmaj Jovina 30)
BIH (☎ 020-618 105; Atinska 58)
Croatia Podgorica (☎ 020-269 760; Vladimira Ćetkovića 2); Kotor (Map p347; ☎ 032-323 127; Šušanj 248)
France (☎ 020-655 348; Atinska 35)
Germany (☎ 020-667 285; Hercegovačka 10)
Italy (☎ 020-234 661; bul Džordža Vašingtona 83)
Serbia (☎ 020-402 500; Hotel Podgorica, bul Svetog Petra Cetinjskog 1)
UK (☎ 020-205 460; bul Svetog Petra Cetinjskog 149)
USA (☎ 020-225 417; Ljubljanska bb)

FESTIVALS & EVENTS

Most of the coastal towns host summer festivals and the former Venetian towns have a tradition of masked carnivals.

Active types should enter the awesome **Adventure Race Montenegro** (www.adventureracemontenegro.com; 1-/2-day entry €120/200). This two-day event in early October combines outdoor pursuits (kayaking, mountain biking, trekking and orienteering), brilliant scenery, environmental awareness and fundraising for local charities.

FOOD

We haven't always listed per-kilogram prices for fish restaurants, but a standard portion is around 200g to 250g; ask for a rough price before you choose a fish if you're unsure. Budget mains can be had for less than €5, while midrange mains should be less than €10. See p340 for more details.

GAY & LESBIAN TRAVELLERS

Where's the party? The answer's nowhere. Although homosexuality was decriminalised in 1977, you won't find a single gay or lesbian venue in Montenegro. Don't be fooled by all the men walking arm-in-arm or hand-in-hand in the Albanian areas. Attitudes to homosexuality remain hostile and life for gay people is extremely difficult, exacerbated by the fact that most people are expected to live at home until they're married.

Many gay men resort to online connections (try www.gayromeo.com) or take their chances at a handful of cruisy beaches. These include Njevica near Herceg Novi, Jaz beach near Budva (far left-hand side), Pržno near Tivat (far left-hand side) and below the ruins of Ratac near Bar.

HOLIDAYS

Public holidays in Montenegro:

New Year's Day 1 January
Orthodox Christmas 7 and 8 January
Orthodox Easter Monday Date varies, usually April
Statehood Day 27 April
Labour Days 1 and 2 May
Victory Day 9 May
Republic Day 29 November

INTERNET RESOURCES

Destination Montenegro (www.destination-monte negro.com)
Montenegro Times (www.themontenegrotimes.com)
National Tourist Organisation (www.montenegro .travel)
Visit Montenegro (www.visit-montenegro.com)

LANGUAGE

Montenegrin is now the official name for the language of Montenegro, although it's virtually indistinguishable from Serbian (which is what many still call it) and extremely close to Bosnian and Croatian. Both the Cyrillic and Latin alphabets are used. Albanian is widely spoken around Ulcinj. See the language chapter (p454) for useful phrases and the Cyrillic alphabet.

MAPS

Unless you're planning on doing a lot of driving, the maps in this book should be adequate. Magic Map's *Montenegro Road Map* (1:370,000) is widely available and has enlargements of the coast and major towns.

MONEY

Montenegro uses the euro and all prices quoted in this chapter are in that currency. You'll find banks with ATMs in all the main towns, most of which accept Visa, MasterCard, Maestro and Cirrus. ATMs tend to dish out big notes, which can be hard to break. Don't rely on restaurants, shops or smaller hotels accepting credit cards. **Western Union** (www .westernunion.com) transfers can be made at most banks and major post offices.

Tipping isn't expected, although it's common to round up to the nearest euro.

POST

Every town has a post office that locals use for paying their bills, so be prepared for horrendous queues. Parcels should be taken unsealed for inspection. You can receive mail, addressed poste restante, in all towns for a small charge. International postal services are slow.

SHOPPING

Montenegro offers plenty of potential liquid souvenirs: vranac or krstač wine and various types of *rakija*. Other specifically Montenegrin ideas include filigree jewellery, religious icons and embroidered folk costumes.

TELEPHONE

Montenegro has recently been given its own country code (382) and a new set of local codes. Partly because of the changes, many businesses advertise their mobile numbers (starting with 06) instead of land lines.

The international access prefix is 00 or + from a mobile phone. Press the 'i' button on public phones for dialling commands in English. Post offices are the best places to make international calls; phonecards don't give enough time for a decent call.

Local SIM cards are a good idea if you're planning a longer stay. The main providers are T mobile, M:tel and Promonte; they have storefronts in most towns.

TOURIST INFORMATION

Official tourist offices are hit and miss (see the individual towns for details). Some have wonderfully helpful English-speaking staff and a

---

EMERGENCY NUMBERS

- Ambulance ☎ 124
- Fire service ☎ 123
- Police ☎ 122

good supply of free material, while others have none of the above. Thankfully, the national office is more switched on and its website (www .montenegro.travel) is a great resource.

TRAVELLERS WITH DISABILITIES

The mobility-impaired will find the country's cobbled lanes and numerous stairways extremely challenging. There are very few specific facilities for either travellers or residents with disabilities. Some of the top-end hotels have wheelchair-accessible rooms.

VISAS

Visas are not required for citizens of most European countries, Australia, New Zealand, Canada and the USA. In most cases this allows a stay of up to 90 days.

WOMEN TRAVELLERS

Other than a cursory interest shown by men towards solo women travellers, travelling is hassle-free and easy. In Muslim areas a few women wear a headscarf but most adopt Western fashions.

TRANSPORT IN MONTENEGRO

This section deals with travel connections between Montenegro and the other countries in this book. For more details about getting here from outside the Western Balkans, see p439.

GETTING THERE & AWAY
Air

Both **Tivat** (TIV; ☎ 032-617 337) and **Podgorica** (TGD; ☎ 020-872 016) have airports, and Dubrovnik's Ćilipi (p251) is very near the border. Airlines flying between Montenegro and Western Balkans destinations:

Adria Airlines (airline code JP; ☎ 020-201 201; www .adria-airways.com; Ivana Vujoševića 46, Podgorica) Hub Ljubljana. Flies from Podgorica to Ljubljana and Sarajevo.
Croatia Airlines (airline code OU; ☎ 020-201 201; www.croatiaairlines.com; Ivana Vujoševića 46, Podgorica) Hub Zagreb. Flies from Tivat to Zagreb and from Podgorica to Skopje and Zagreb.
JAT Airways (airline code JU; www.jat.com) Budva (☎ 033-451 641; Mediteranska 2); Podgorica (☎ 020-664 750; Njegoševa 25) Hub Belgrade. Flies from Tivat to Belgrade and Niš and from Podgorica to Belgrade.

Montenegro Airlines (airline code YM; www.monte negroairlines.com) Budva (☎ 033-454 900; Slovenska Obala bb); Podgorica (☎ 020-664 411; Slobode 23) Hub Podgorica. Flies from Tivat to Belgrade and Niš and from Podgorica to Ljubljana and Skopje.

Land
BORDER CROSSINGS
Albania

There are two main crossings, linking Shkodra to Ulcinj (Sukobin) and to Podgorica (Hani i Hotit).

Bosnia & Hercegovina

Two major checkpoints link Nikšić to Trebinje (Dolovi) and to Srbinje (Šćepan Polje). There's a more remote crossing halfway between the two at Vratkovići and another in the Kovač mountains in the far north.

Croatia

Expect delays at this busy checkpoint on the Adriatic highway between Herceg Novi and Dubrovnik.

Kosovo

There's only one crossing here, on the road between Rožaje and Peć.

Serbia

The busiest crossing is north of Bijelo Polje near Dobrakovo, followed by the checkpoint northeast of Rožaje and another east of Pljevlja.

BUS

There's a well-developed bus network linking Montenegro with the major cities of the region. Podgorica is the main hub but buses stop at many coastal towns as well. From Herceg Novi, for example, there are buses to Dubrovnik (€8, two hours, two daily), Sarajevo (€22, seven hours, four daily), Belgrade (€30, 13 hours, nine daily) and Skopje (€36, daily).

From Ulcinj there's a daily bus to Shkodra (€4.50, 90 minutes) and three to Pristina (€22.50, eight hours). Minibuses head to Shkodra at 9am and 3pm from the carpark beside Ulcinj's market (about €5).

CAR & MOTORCYCLE

Drivers need an international driving permit and vehicles need green-card insurance or insurance must be bought at the border.

MONTENEGRO

TRAIN

Montenegro's only working passenger train line starts at Bar and heads into Serbia (see right). Four trains depart Podgorica for Belgrade every day (€22, 7½ hours).

GETTING AROUND
Bicycle

Cyclists are a rare species, even in the cities. Don't expect drivers to be considerate. Wherever possible, try to get off the main roads. The National Tourist Office has been developing a series of wilderness mountain-biking trails (see p368).

Bus

The local bus network is extensive and reliable. Buses are usually comfortable and air-conditioned and they're rarely full. It's slightly cheaper to buy your ticket on the bus rather the at station, but a station-bought ticket theoretically guarantees you a seat. Luggage carried below is charged at €1 per piece.

Car & Motorcycle

Independent travel by car or motorcycle is an ideal way to gad about and discover the country; some of the drives are breathtakingly beautiful (see the boxed text, p364). Traffic police are everywhere, so stick to speed limits and carry an international driving permit. Allow more time than you'd expect for the distances involved, as the terrain will slow you down. You'll rarely get up to 60km/h on the Bay of Kotor road, for instance.

FUEL & SPARE PARTS

Filling up is no problem in any medium-sized town, but don't leave it until the last drop as there are few late-night petrol stations. Spare parts for major makes will be no problem in the cities, and mechanics are available everywhere for simple repairs.

HIRE

The major European car-hire companies have a presence in various centres, but **Meridian Rentacar** (☎ 033-454 105; www.meridian-rentacar.com), which has offices in Budva, Bar and Podgorica, is a reliable local option; one-day hire starts from €45.

Train

Željeznica Crne Gore (☎ 020-441 211; www.zeljeznica.cg.yu) runs the only passenger train line, heading north from Bar. The trains are old and stiflingly hot in summer, but they're priced accordingly and the route through the mountains is spectacular. Useful stops include Virpazar, Podgorica and Kolašin.

Serbia Србија

Newsflash: Serbia is no longer the Bad Boy of the Balkans. Some former territory has stepped out on its own in recent years, but what remains has much to offer independent travellers who want to form their own opinion of this misunderstood and misrepresented state.

Serbia has been a melting pot of colliding and complementary cultures for centuries. Up north, Hungarian influences have crossed the border into the Vojvodinian region; the art nouveau town of Subotica is as much Hungarian as it is Serbian. The town of Novi Sad, presided over by the Petrovaradin Citadel, hosts an edgy music festival that reverberates through all of Europe, except perhaps the nearby pocket of Fruška Gora National Park, where monastic life has endured unaltered for generations.

Pressed against the southern border of Bosnia and Hercegovina (BiH), the Zlatibor region, with village traditions and sincere hospitality, is one of the most special places in the country. Below the mountainous ski resort of Kopaonik is the eclectic town of Novi Pazar, where Ottoman stylings show how modern day Islam evolved from Turkish rule in the Sandzak region.

Beating at the heart of all this is Belgrade. Once dismissed as drab, this dynamic capital is now hailed as a Balkan highlight. Vivid museums, creative restaurants and nightlife of every pace for every taste make this all-hours town a visitors' playground.

After years of isolation and repression, this soulful state has emerged bruised but determined to launch itself into a future with Europe.

FAST FACTS

- **Area** 77,474 sq km
- **Capital** Belgrade
- **Currency** Serbian dinar (DIN); US$1 = 69.59DIN; UK£1 = 101.38DIN; €1 = 92.14DIN; A$1 = 46.89DIN
- **Famous for** triumphing in the Eurovision Song Contest and tennis (think Ana Ivanovic, Monica Seles, Novak Djokovic, Jelena Jankovic…)
- **Key phrases** zdravo (hello), doviđenja (goodbye), hvala (thanks)
- **Official language** Serbian
- **Population** 7.5 million
- **Telephone codes** country code ☎ 381; international access code ☎ 00
- **Visas** not required for most visitors; see p420

HIGHLIGHTS

- **Kalemegdan Citadel** (p383) A mighty backdrop to Belgrade's eclectic culinary offerings.
- **Novi Sad** (p399) This quiet town morphs into the State of Exit (see the boxed text, p401) every July.
- **Novi Pazar** (p410) Contrasting architecture and cultural fusions in this Turkish-toned town in southern Serbia.
- **Subotica** (p404) The town's art nouveau architecture is one of the splendid surprises bursting from the Vojvodinian plains.
- **Best Activities** (p417) Winter skiing and summer wandering in the gently rolling plains of Zlatibor (p414) or the steeper slopes of Kopaonik (p413).

ITINERARIES

- **One week** Two days of cultural and culinary exploration in Belgrade (p381), then on to Novi Sad (p399) for day trips into Fruška Gora (p402).
- **Two to three weeks** The above then north to Hungarian-influenced Subotica (p404), before slicing south for mountain air in Zlatibor (p414) on your way to Ottoman-influenced Novi Pazar (p410).

CLIMATE & WHEN TO GO

The north has a continental climate with cold winters and humid summers. Hottest months

---

HOW MUCH?

- **Short taxi ride** 150DIN
- **Internet access** 80DIN to 150DIN per hour
- **Cup of coffee** 100DIN
- **Bottle of plum brandy** 500DIN
- **Postcard** 30DIN
- **Postcard postage** 40DIN

LONELY PLANET INDEX

- **Litre of petrol** 100DIN
- **Litre of water** 80DIN
- **Half-litre of beer (Lav/Jelen)** 80DIN
- **Souvenir T-shirt** 600DIN
- **Street snack (burek)** 60DIN

---

are July and August. Ski season is generally December to March. Local festivals and events can make accommodation scarce. See p430 for a Belgrade climate chart.

HISTORY
Medieval History

Celts supplanted the original inhabitants of the region, the Illyrians, from the 4th century BC; the Romans arrived in the 3rd century BC. In AD 395 Theodosius I divided the empire, passing Serbia to the Byzantine Empire.

During the 6th century, Slavic tribes crossed the Danube and occupied much of the Balkan Peninsula. In 879 SS Cyril and Methodius converted the Serbs to Christianity.

Serbian independence briefly flowered from 1217, with a golden age during Stefan Dušan's reign (1346–55). After Stefan's death Serbia declined; its defeat by the Turks at the pivotal Battle of Kosovo in 1389 ushered in 500 years of Ottoman rule.

Ottoman Era

Turkish Islamic rule led to extreme oppression of Serbian Christians; many were forced into slavery in Constantinople and family units were fractured as people fled urban centres and rural areas.

There were several revolts. In 1804 a national uprising against Turkish rule gained momentum and support from Montenegro and Russia. After two years of fighting, a severely battered Belgrade was liberated. Russia's withdrawal of support contributed to the instability that followed; Russia signed treaties with the Turks to return Serbia to Ottoman rule. Belgrade (and many Serbians along the way) was lost again in 1813.

Another uprising in 1815 lead to de facto Serbian independence. Despite remaining conflicts, an era of great progress and innovation followed. The last vestiges of the Ottoman Empire disappeared until Serbia achieved complete independence in 1878.

WWI & WWII

On 28 June 1914 Austria-Hungary used the assassination of Archduke Ferdinand by a Bosnian Serb as a pretext (albeit a tenuous one) to invade Serbia, sparking WWI. Almost 30% of the Serbian population was lost during the war.

Afterwards, Croatia, Slovenia, BiH, Vojvodina, Serbia and its Kosovo province,

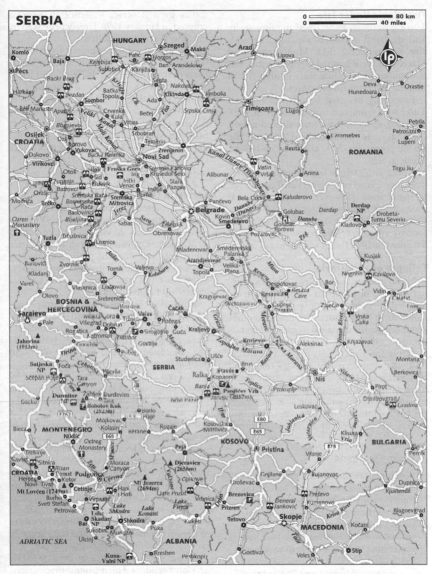

Montenegro and Macedonia formed the Kingdom of Serbs, Croats and Slovenes which in 1929 was renamed Yugoslavia – land of the south Slavs.

Pressured from all sides, Yugoslavia joined the fascist Tripartite Alliance in March 1941. This sparked a military coup, to which Germany responded by bombing Belgrade in April. Nazi occupation and the horrors that came with it prompted strong resistance from pro-Serbian, anti-communist Chetniks led by Dragoljug Mihailović and pro-communist Partisans led by Josip Broz Tito. The latter (with an enormous cost of lives along the way) ultimately gained power in 1945.

Yugoslavia Under Tito

Tito's government abolished the monarchy and declared a federal republic. Serbia's size was reduced; BiH, Montenegro and Macedonia were granted republic status, but Kosovo and Vojvodina were denied it and became autonomous provinces.

Favouring his own brand of socialism, Tito broke from communist Stalin in 1948 and Yugoslavia became a nonaligned nation (belonging to neither the USA nor the USSR power blocks), albeit bolstered by Western aid.

Under Tito's strong leadership, Yugoslavia held together over the years and prospered in many ways. However, growing regional inequalities heightened tensions; Slovenia, Croatia and Kosovo demanded greater autonomy to counter Serbian dominance. When Tito died in 1980 things started to fall apart.

Collapse of Yugoslavia

By 1986 Serbian nationalists were espousing the idea of a Greater Serbia, a doctrine adopted by Slobodan Milošević, the Serbian Communist Party leader. This horrified other republics, which managed to gain independence by 1992.

While the violent collapse of Yugoslavia resulted in wars in neighbouring Croatia and BiH, Serbia and Montenegro formed the 'third' Yugoslav federation in April 1992. The new constitution made no mention of 'autonomous provinces', infuriating Albanians in Kosovo, who were stripped of their autonomous

---

MONEY MATTERS

During the 1990s, economic sanctions and gross economic mishandling led to the highest hyperinflation in European history; it became cheaper to paper walls with banknotes than to buy wallpaper. In 1993 a 500 billion (500,000,000,000DIN) banknote was printed, making every Serb an instant multimillionaire.

Many state industries were unable to pay employees, instead paying in kind or by issuing worthless company shares. When a multinational bought the local brewery in the small town of Apatin, locals found their shares suddenly worth a fortune. Apatin is now one of the richest municipalities per capita in Serbia.

---

status by Milošević. Violence in Kosovo erupted in January 1998, largely provoked by the federal army and police.

This incited a storm of protest from the international community and an arms embargo. Paris peace talks in March 1999 failed when Serbia rejected a US-brokered peace plan. In reply to resistance in Kosovo, Serbian forces moved to ethnically cleanse the country of its Albanian population. Hundreds of thousands fled into Macedonia and Albania, galvanising NATO into a 78-day bombing campaign. On 12 June 1999 Serbian forces withdrew from Kosovo.

Serbia in the 21st Century

In the September 2000 federal presidential elections, the opposition – led by Vojislav Koštunica – declared victory, a claim denied by Milošević. Opposition supporters took over the streets and stormed parliament. When Russia recognised Koštunica's presidency, Milošević's last support evaporated and his leadership finally toppled.

Koštunica restored ties with Europe, acknowledged Yugoslav atrocities in Kosovo and rejoined the UN. In April 2001 Milošević was arrested for misappropriating state funds and extradited to the Hague. He was found dead in his cell in March 2006.

In April 2002 Yugoslavia was replaced by a loose union of Serbia and Montenegro. The EU-brokered deal was intended to stabilise the region by settling Montenegrin demands for independence and preventing further changes to Balkan borders.

In March 2003 Serbia's first democratically elected prime minister since WWII, Zoran Đinđić, was assassinated. Đinđić had been instrumental in handing Milošević to the Hague and had been trying to purge politics and business of crime and corruption. In May 2007, 12 people (several of whom were former members of the paramilitary wing of the state security police) were found guilty of the murder.

At the end of his term in January 2003, Serbian president Milan Milutinović surrendered to the Hague to plead not guilty to charges of crimes against humanity. Between 2003 and 2004 three attempts to elect a new president failed due to low voter turnout. Parliamentary elections in December 2003 were inconclusive but saw the resurgence of nationalism, worrying the rest of Europe. A series of power-sharing deals installed Koštunica as head of a centre-right coalition that now relies on the support of Milošević's Socialist Party. Finally, in June 2004, Serbia and Montenegro gained a new president in the pro-European Boris Tadić. Tadić was re-elected in February 2008.

In May 2006, 55% of Montenegrins voted for independence from Serbia, which was formally declared the following month. Kosovo declared its independence in February 2008, a move which Serbia held to be illegal. The coalition government remains fractured over how this issue impacts on Serbia's future with the EU. Early elections were held in May 2008. Tadić won 102 seats in Serbia's 250-member parliament, reaffirming Serbia's pro-European future.

PEOPLE

The outside world often can't see Serbians through the fog of their history. Differences in language, religion and ethnicity haven't always led to happy endings, but the interacting identities of the people at the heart of it all make for a wondrously diverse bunch.

A 2002 census revealed that the population comprised 7.5 million people. These figures included Serbs (82.9%), Hungarians (3.9%), Bosniaks (1.8%), Roma (1.4%) and others (8.9%, including 0.8% Albanians). Almost 1.1% of the population attempted to subvert this ethnic headcount by identifying as Yugoslav.

Vojvodina is the most ethnically diverse region, with more than 30 minority groups, 4% of whom are Hungarians. This part of the population is influential; Hungarian is even taught in some schools.

Migration flows of the minority Roma population reflect the region's turbulent history; many fled into Serbia following ethnic cleansing by Kosovar Albanians. Despite the increased efforts of the Serbian government, Roma living standards still fall below those of the rest of the population.

Though numbers of Vlach minority have decreased as they are absorbed into the mainstream population, the language (a dialect of Romanian) and many traditions are still alive. In the 2002 census, 40,054 people (0.53%) identified as 'Valachian', while 54,818 people declared themselves native speakers of the Vlach language.

The Sandžak region on the southwest border with Montenegro and Kosovo comprises six regions in Serbia. Within this region, the majority identified in the 2002 census as Bosniaks (almost 57%) or Serbs (almost 38%), while 3.5% stated their nationality as Muslim and 0.4% as Montenegrin.

RELIGION

Religion and ethnicity often relate; around 85% of the population identify as Serbian Orthodox. The 5% Roman Catholic population are generally Vojvodinian Hungarians. Muslims comprise around 3% of the population; they are Albanians and Slavic Muslims. Protestantism appeals to 1% of the population, and the rest is a diverse mix of every and no belief.

The fall of Yugoslavia (which imposed restrictions on the Serbian Orthodox Church) lead to a resurgence in Orthodoxy.

The Serbian Orthodox Church became an independent branch of Christian Orthodoxy in 1219 when ecclesiastical independence was negotiated with Constantinople. The location of many significant Orthodox churches in Kosovo is a key reason for Serbian opposition to Kosovo's declaration of independence.

ARTS

Though it was the Ukranian drag queen who dropped the jaws of the continent, Serbia's Marija Šerifovi brought home the blue ribbon from the 2007 Eurovision Song Contest. The 23-year-old was given a heroine's welcome for lifting the nation's spirits, while the media went into a frenzy analysing how the contest acts as a peaceful forum for countries of the former Yugoslavia to come together. Between 10 and 25 May 2008, Belgrade was abuzz hosting the event, seizing the opportunity to show Serbia off to the world. Whether or not the Eurovision Song Contest counts as art, it certainly highlights the fact that Serbians are passionate about their creative scene.

The survival and active rebellion of artistic expression throughout dark periods of history is a source of pride among the people. Creative juices flow thick and strong, with films spawning idyllic villages (see p416), art sold in cocktail bars and music performed in restaurants.

Literature

The oral tradition of epic poetry was the most important way of recording historical events and figures in Serbia (and other parts of former Yugoslavia) for centuries.

Singers composed as they performed, rigidly confined to 10 or eight syllables per line. Accompanying it was the *gusle*, a one-stringed instrument held upright like a cello. Poems depicted brave battles or tragic love stories. For more, see p38.

A significant figure in late-19th-century Serbian literature was Jovan Jovanović Zmaj (1833–1904), who wrote poetry, fiction and essays. Contemporary writers include Vasko Popa, whose poems have been translated into many languages. Other interesting reads are *In the Hold* by Vladimir Arsenijević, *Words Are Something Else* by David Albahari, *Petrija's Wreath* by Dragoslav Mihailović and *Fear and Its Servant* by Mirjana Novaković.

More and more Serbian writers are crossing the language divide and launching their work into the English-speaking world. Bosnian-born former Belgrade resident Ivo Andrić was awarded the Nobel Prize for a body of work including *The Bridge on the Drina*. Excellent works of Danilo Kiš are available in English, including *A Tomb for Boris Davidovich* (2001). Slobodan Selenić's novels illuminate the post-WWII journey of Belgrade. Belgrade-based Zoran Zivkovic's *Hidden Camera* layers intricate elements to spell-binding affect. Internationally acclaimed word wizard Milorad Pavić writes in many dimensions; his novel *The Inner Side of the Wind* can be read from the back or the front. *Last Love in Constantinople: A Tarot Novel for Divination* is interwoven with tarot symbolism, while *Landscape Painted with Tea* can be approached as a crossword puzzle. Choose your own ending in *Unique Item* and choose between male and female editions of Pavić's lyrical lexicon *Dictionary of the Khazars*. For books about Serbia, see p417.

Cinema

Oscar-nominated 1969 WWII classic *The Battle of Neretva* (directed by Veljko Bulajic and with a star-studded cast including Yul Brynner and Orson Welles) is still declared one of the greatest films hailing from Yugoslavia. But cinema has come a long way in Serbia.

World-renowned director Emir Kusturica sets the bar with his raucous approach to storytelling. Sarajevo-born Kusturica is famed for telling tragic stories with enormous humour and affection. Titles to look out for include *Underground* (1995), the surreal tale of seemingly never-ending Balkans conflicts; *Time of the Gypsies* (1989) about a telekinetic Roma boy lured into crime; *Black Cat, White Cat* (1998) about the arranged marriage between the son of a petty criminal and the daughter of a gangster; *Zavet* (2007) about a country boy searching for a wife in the city; and *Life Is a Miracle* (2004) about an optimistic Serbian engineer working on the Mokra Gora railway (p416). Kusturica became a Unicef National Ambassador for Serbia in 2002 and has festival aspirations; see p416.

For more recent Serbian insights try black comedies such as *The Optimist* (2007) by Goran Paskaljevic, or *Seven and a Half* (2006) by director Miroslav Momcilovic, which weaves seven tales of the city with seven mortal sins, or romantic *Tomorrow Morning* (2006) by Oleg Novkovic.

Other titles to look out for include Slobodan Sijan's *Ko to tamo peva?*, which puts an unlikely cast of characters together in a bus, and Branco Baletic's *Balkan Express*. Srdjan Dragojevic's award-winning *Rane* (The Wounds) tells the tale of two youths who become Belgrade gangsters in a context of increasing ethnic conflict. Stevan Filipovićs confronting *Haircut* (Skinning, 2008) explores neo-Nazi gang culture.

Music

Like everything else about it, Serbia's music is eclectic. Traditionally, the *kolo* folk dance is performed in a circle to accordions, flutes and fiddles. *Blehmuzika* (brass music influenced by Turkish and Austrian military music) is the national music, commonly played by Roma at weddings or funerals. A popular example is the soundtrack to the film *Underground* and albums by the trumpet player Boban Marković. There's also an annual festival at Guča (see the boxed text, p414).

Cross ethnic folk music with techno and you get 'turbofolk'; controversial during the Milošević era for nationalist overtones, it's now more mainstream fun – and hard to avoid. The long-reigning queen of turbofolk is sultry Svetlana Ražnatović 'Ceca', the controversial, heavy-bosomed wife of the late war criminal Arkan.

Modern music covers anything from wild Roma music to house, techno, blues, jazz, drum and bass, and hip-hop. Nightlife follows suit, offering every type of soundtrack from funk, soul and reggae to rock, metal and gothic.

Serbia's favourite rock groups include Eyesburn, Bajaga i Instruktori, iconic Darkwood

Dub and Van Goh, chosen as Best Adriatic Act at the 2007 MTV Europe Music Awards. An imprint has been left on the alternative scene by Rambo Amadeus – a colourful Montenegrin-born, Belgrade-based character.

Home-grown hip-hop emerged in the mainstream in the late 1990s with groups like Bad Copy, and survived the war to come back throwing punches, like those from politically vocal Beogradski Sindikat.

Eurovision is a source of enormous pride since Marija Šerifovi won in 2007, giving Serbia the honour of hosting the event in 2008. Serbia and Montenegro entered the Eurovision hall of fame by coming second in 2004 with a haunting love ballad that effectively blended Serbian and Turkish influences. Also head to Novi Sad's Exit Festival (see the boxed text, p401).

Architecture

Architecture is a living record of who has been and gone. Ottoman, Austro-Hungarian, and Serbian-Byzantine styles have fought for dominance, often over the same buildings, which have been stripped, redressed and modified over the years depending on who is in power.

Orthodox churches comprise a sparse central prayer area where the congregation stands under a dome. Churches are often tall and lit only by sunlight, which enters from high windows. The walls beneath are adorned with ornate frescos, a distinctive mark of Serbian Orthodox churches. Sites selected for churches and monasteries were deliberately remote, enabling residents to worship safely and without distractions or temptations. Serbian architecture from the 12th to 14th centuries is a product of the Raška school and bears the indelible marks of Byzantine and Romanesque style. Particular examples can be seen in the churches of Studenica (p412). The late 13th and early 14th centuries ushered in a more purely Byzantine era. Contributions of King Milutin's rule (in what came to be known as Serbian-Byzantine style) are evident in Kosovo's Gračanica (p276) and the hallowed Patriarchate of Peć (p277).

Architecture of the Moravian school eventuated from the Serbian retreat into the valley of Morava in the Battle of Kosovo. This style is showcased widely throughout the country, particularly at Manasija monastery (p407).

The Ottomans brought their own architects, who built mosques and converted existing places of worship. This was a volatile time for the frescos of earlier years, which offended

Islamic sensibilities; much medieval work was covered or destroyed. Towns in the south bear a Turkish imprint; the Ottoman influence is evident in the bustling centre of Novi Pazar (p410), and Niš still has an eerie Tower of Skulls (p408). For more on Ottoman-style architecture, see p39.

In northern Vojvodina, 19th-century imperial Austro-Hungarian style dominates. The monasteries of Fruška Gora (p402) reveal that the Habsburgs were here, and there are some magnificent examples of Hungarian Secessionism in Subotica (p404).

On top of all of this is the concrete layer of linear post-WWII buildings.

Visual Arts

The ubiquitous works of Croatian sculptor Ivan Meštrović (1883–1962) appear in several places around Belgrade, most notably the *France* and *Messenger of Victory* statues in the Kalemegdan Citadel and the war memorial in Avala (p390)

Munich-educated impressionist painter Nadežda Petrović (1873–1915) produced some wonderfully energetic portraits. Her earthy Serbian period (1903–10) shows a change in perception from the earlier, more impassioned Munich period (1898–1903). Her final and perhaps most accomplished paintings come from the Parisian period (1910–12) shortly before she died of typhoid, contracted in a Serbian WWI hospital where she volunteered as a nurse. Her paintings are displayed in Belgrade's (temporarily closed) National Museum (p383).

Michael Collin notes that during the Balkan Wars, 'art was used as a political tool to promote the insular, backward-looking state mentality'. Modern artists who grew up in artistic isolation are now emerging to define a new creative scene in Serbia. One interesting example is Ivan Grubanov, who fuses various media in works contextualised by his history as a young artist surviving the Milošević era.

Belgrade-based artist Dobri Stojanović has displayed his whimsical works in more than 80 international exhibitions and won several awards. Some of his works hang in Belgrade's National Museum and Museum of Contemporary Art (both closed for renovation at the time of research).

FOOD & DRINK
Staples & Specialities

The ubiquitous snack is *burek*, a filo-pastry pie made with *sir* (cheese), *meso* (meat), *krompir* (potato) or occasionally *pečurke* (mushrooms), most commonly consumed with yoghurt. It's a great breakfast, especially if made *ispod sača* (baked on hot coals, in a covered tray).

Serbia is famous for grilled meats such as *ćevapčići* (kebab), *pljeskavica* (spicy hamburger) and *ražnjići* (pork or veal kebabs). Another speciality is Karađorđe's schnitzel, a long tubular roll of veal stuffed with *kajmak* (curdled, salted milk). *Đuveč* is grilled pork cutlets with spiced stewed peppers, courgettes and tomatoes on rice.

For less meaty meals try *musaka* (layers of aubergine, potato and minced meat), *sarma* (minced meat and rice rolled in sour-cabbage leaves), *kapama* (stewed lamb, onions and spinach with yoghurt) and *punjene tikvice* (courgettes stuffed with minced meat and rice).

Regional cuisines range from spicy Hungarian goulash in Vojvodina to Turkish kebab in Novi Pazar.

Pivo (beer) is universally available; Lav and Jelen are popular brews. Many people distil their own *rakija* (brandy) from grapes or plums *(šljivovica)*. There are other varieties such as *orahovača* (walnut), *kruškovača* or *viljamovka* (pear), or *jabukovača* (apple). If you ask for *domaća rakija* in a restaurant, you'll be offered homemade *rakija* made with a choice of fruit.

A traditional Serbian dessert wine is *bermet* – try it in Vojvodina, where family recipes have been passed down for generations. Sremski Karlovci is a good place to buy it. Monasteries in the Fruška Gora region also brew their own wines.

A bittersweet aperitif popular in Belgrade is the herbal liquor *pelinkovac*. A more upmarket, less bitter version is German Jägermeister.

Superb espresso and cappuccino can be found in larger towns, but Serbian coffee is the local drink of choice. Pretend it's not so, but Serbian coffee is actually Turkish coffee.

Where to Eat & Drink

Hole-in-the-wall counters, kiosks and bakeries offer *burek,* pizza, *ćevapčići* or sandwiches. Small restaurants offer cheap and satisfying but limited menus. Many can be found around bus and train stations. Hotel restaurants also figure in providing fine food.

The distinction between cafes, bars and restaurants is blurred. Cafes usually sell alcohol and offer an extensive menu, and more upmarket ones serve cocktails.

For assistance finding new favourite foods, turn to p45.

Vegetarians & Vegans

Waiters are looking less baffled at requests for vegetarian food these days. Restaurants in larger cities offer vegetarian options or variations on meat dishes. Outside large cities, things are harder (and impossible for vegans). There's always the ubiquitous vegetarian pizza. Satisfying salads are *Srpska salata* (Serbian salad) of raw peppers, onions and tomatoes, seasoned with oil, vinegar and maybe chilli, and *šopska salata* (chopped tomatoes, cucumber and onion, topped with grated soft white cheese). Also try *gibanica* (cheese pie), *zeljanica* (cheese pie with spinach) or *pasulj prebranac* (a dish of cooked and spiced beans). There are plenty of fish restaurants.

Habits & Customs

People generally skimp on breakfast and catch something on the go. Work hours are usually 7.30am to 3.30pm, when lunch starts, pushing dinner to between 8pm and 10pm.

ENVIRONMENT
The Land

Serbia proper comprises 77,474 sq km of land. At 2169m, Midzor is its highest mountain. Zlatibor (p414) and Kopaonik (p413) are winter playgrounds.

Vojvodina is pancake-flat agricultural land. South of the Danube the landscape rises through rolling green hills, which crest where the eastern outpost of the Dinaric Alps slices southeastwards across the country.

Serbia is landlocked. The Danube arrives in Vojvodina from Hungary, defines the Croatia border and passes through Novi Sad and Belgrade (where it meets the Sava) on its way to the 'Iron Gate' gorge separating Serbia from Romania. The Morava River – which meets the Danube near Smederevo – divides at Niš, heading south to Thessaloniki and east to Sofia and Istanbul.

Wildlife

There are around 360 bird species in Serbia, about 40% of which are of European Conservation Concern (SPECS). More than 120 bird species can be spotted in Belgrade alone, including bee-eaters, sparrowhawks, Syrian woodpeckers and nightingales. The golden eagle and crossbill are rare birds. Bird enthusiasts can find out more from the **League for Ornithological Action of Serbia** (www.ptica.org).

Among Serbia's mammals are wild boars, wildcats, beavers, otters, susliks, lynxes, and mouflons. Among its 70 reptile species, the uncommon viviparous lizard crawls around Kopaonik. If you're (un)lucky you may encounter brown bears, wildcats and chamois, which all live in its woods.

National Parks

Serbia is proud of its four national parks, 20 nature parks and 120 nature reserves.

Đerdap National Park in eastern Serbia stretches over almost 64,000 hectares along the Romania border. Its *pièce de résistance* is the 'Iron Gate'; an immense 100km gorge.

The 12,000-hectare Kopaonik National Park, in southern Serbia, is a prime skiing site. The mountainous area is sliced with canyons of the Ibar, Jošanica, Toplica and Brzeća rivers. Kopaonik houseleek, Kopaonik violet and Pančić cuckoo flower are endemic species of flora.

In western Serbia, Tara National Park spreads over 20,000 hectares between altitudes of 250m and 1500m. Mountain peaks and deep river gorges make for spectacular and dramatic scenery. The gorge of the Drina River is the park's main waterway. Pančić spruce and locust are endemic species here.

Fruška Gora National Park in Vojvodina stretches over 10,000 hectares of orchards, vineyards and plains, taking in maple, oak and linden forests – and 16 Orthodox monasteries. Bird species include imperial eagles, booted eagles, woodpeckers and ravens as well as several songbirds. Mammals include wildcats, badgers, weasels and bats.

Environmental Issues

Serbia faces air pollution around Belgrade, rubbish dumping in the countryside and dumping of industrial waste into the Sava.

Some remnants of the 1999 NATO bombings are ecological hazards, such as the destruction of the petrol factory in Novi Sad and factories outside Belgrade. Destroyed bridges over the Danube have also caused heavy river pollution.

The Serbian-only website www.naturepro tection.org.yu keeps its finger on the pulse of environmental issues in Serbia.

BELGRADE БЕОГРАД

☎ 011 / pop 1.58 million

Belgrade is rarely described as beautiful. All at once, it is edgy, adventurous, dignified and audacious.

The city evolves before your eyes; for centuries cultures and opinions have mingled and collided to create what is quickly becoming known as a Balkans melting pot. This chaos shows in the architecture; socialist blocks are squeezed between art nouveau masterpieces, and remnants of the Habsburg legacy contrast with Ottoman relics. Administrative buildings destroyed by the NATO bombings of 1999 are overlooked in the buzz of new development as the urban sprawl continues boldly beyond the Sava River, with stark skyscrapers giving rise to Novi Beograd (New Belgrade).

It is here where the Sava River meets the Danube that East meets West, where old-world culture gives way to new-world nightlife. The pedestrian street of Knez Mihailova is lined with chic cafes and flanked by fascinating historical buildings all the way to ancient Kalemegdan Citadel, crowning the city. Deeper in Belgrade's bowels are museums guarding the country's cultural, religious and military heritage. Josip Broz Tito and other ghosts of the past have been laid to rest here.

The cafe culture is second to none; grandiose coffee houses, funky sidewalk ice-creameries and tatty smoky dens all have a place here. Party pilgrims from around the world are starting to find their way to nightclubs that continually explore and invent new paces and spaces in apartment blocks, underground dens or floating barges.

'Beograd' means 'White City', but this colourful capital is anything but.

HISTORY

As its mishmash of architecture shows, Belgrade has been destroyed and rebuilt countless times in its 2300-year history. The Celts first settled on the lumpy hill at the confluence of the Sava and Danube rivers. The Romans came in the 1st century and stayed for around 400 years. Havoc was wreaked by Goths and Huns until the area was colonised by Slavic tribes in the 6th century. In 1403 Hungary gave Belgrade to Despot Stefan Lazarević, making it the Serbian capital. The 1400s saw waves of Turkish attacks; Sultan Suleyman the

SERBIA

Magnificent (and 300,000 soldiers) conquered Belgrade in 1521 and shipped its population to Istanbul. Belgrade continued to be fought over by Austrians, Turks and Serbs themselves. The Karađorđević dynasty began in 1807 when Belgrade was liberated from the Turks. The Obrenović dynasty followed when Miloš Obrenović staged the second Serbian uprising and ordered the murder of Karađorđe. Turkey finally relinquished control in 1867. In 1914, the Austro-Hungarian Empire captured Belgrade but was soon driven out, returning more triumphantly with German help in 1915 and staying for three years. In 1918, Belgrade became the capital of Yugoslavia after Serbs, Croats and Slovenes united into one state. Belgrade was bombed by both Nazis and Allies during WWII, triggering the emergence of two Serbian resistance movements. One successfully liberated Belgrade with the help of the Red Army, ushering in the era of Tito.

In the 1990s, Belgrade became the stage for strong resistance to Slobodan Milošević, both underground and in the open – protestors took to the streets on numerous occasions. In 1999, NATO forces bombed Belgrade for three months after Milošević refused to cease the ethnic cleansing of Albanians. Belgrade's power of protest was displayed in 2000, when citizens stormed parliament in a show against Milošević's electoral fraud. People took to the streets again in 2008 in opposition to Kosovo's declaration of independence. Hundreds of thousands of Serbs staged peaceful demonstrations throughout the city, while smaller groups became violent, leading to diplomatic controversy about damage caused to the US embassy.

ORIENTATION

The central train station and two adjacent bus stations are on the southern side of the centre. A couple of blocks northeast is Terazije, the heart of modern Belgrade. Knez Mihailova, Belgrade's lively pedestrian boulevard, runs northwest through the old town from Terazije to the Kalemegdan Citadel at the confluence of the Sava and Danube rivers. Novi Beograd and Zemun are west of the central train station, over the Sava River.

INFORMATION

Bookshops

Guidebooks, English novels and some CDs and DVDs are available at the following:

IPS (Map p386; ☎ 328 1859; Trg Republike 5; ☺ 9am-9pm Mon-Fri, 10am-5pm Sat)
Mamut (Map p386; ☎ 0645152248; cnr Knez Mihailova & Sremska; ☺ 9am-10pm Mon-Sat, noon-10pm Sun)
Plato (Map p386; ☎ 262 4751; Knez Mihailova 48; ☺ 9am-midnight Mon-Sat, noon-midnight Sun)

Internet Access

Click 011 (Map p386; ☎ 263 0024; Rajićeva 14; per hr 100DIN; ☺ 9am-9pm Mon-Fri, 11am-7pm Sat & Sun) Basement internet cafe.
Mamut (Map p386; ☎ 0645152248; cnr Knez Mihailova & Sremska; per hr 100DIN; ☺ 9am-10pm Mon-Sat, noon-10pm Sun) Top-floor internet cafe. Wireless (BYO laptop) is free.
Net Hol (Map p386; ☎ 323 9853; Nušićeva 3; per hr 100DIN; ☺ 10am-2am) Late-night internet cafe off passageway behind Kasina Hotel.

Internet Resources

Belgrade City (www.beograd.org.yu)
Belgrade in Your Pocket (www.inyourpocket.com /serbia/city/belgrade.html)
Tourist Organisation of Belgrade (www.tob.co.yu)

Left Luggage

Central train station (Map p386; Savski Trg 2; per piece per day 110DIN)

Medical Services

Boris Kidrič Hospital Diplomatic Section (Map p386; ☎ 643 839; Miloša Porcerca Pasterova 1; ☺ 7am-7pm Mon-Fri)
Klinički Centar (Map p386; ☎ 361 7777; Miloša Porcerca Pasterova 2; ☺ 24hr) Medical clinic.
Prima 1 (Map p386; ☎ 361 0999; Nemanjina 2; ☺ 24hr) All-hours pharmacy.

Money

There is an ATM, an exchange office or a Western Union–equipped bank on every corner in Belgrade.
Banca Intesa (Map p386; ☎ 310 8888; www .bancainesabeograd.com; Knez Mihailova 30; ☺ 8am-8pm Mon-Fri, 9am-3pm Sat)
Erste Bank (Map p386; Knez Mihailova 36; ☺ 8am-6pm Mon-Fri, 9.30am-1.30pm Sat)
Raiffeisen (Map p386; www.raiffeisenbank.co.yu; Terazije 27; ☺ 8am-7pm Mon-Fri, 9am-3pm Sat) In the walkway linking Terazije with Trg Nikole Pašića.

Post

Central post office (Map p386; ☎ 633 492; Takovska 2; ☺ 8am-7pm Mon-Sat)

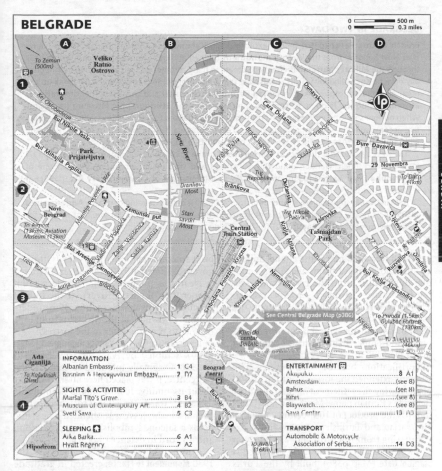

BELGRADE

0 — 500 m
0 — 0.3 miles

SERBIA

INFORMATION
Albanian Embassy..............................1 C4
Bosnian & Hercegovinian Embassy......2 D2

SIGHTS & ACTIVITIES
Maršal Tito's Grave..........................3 B4
Museum of Contemporary Art.............4 B2
Sveti Sava..5 C3

SLEEPING
Arka Barka......................................6 A1
Hyatt Regency.................................7 A2

ENTERTAINMENT
Akapulko.......................................8 A1
Amsterdam..................................(see 8)
Bahus...(see 8)
Kihis..(see 8)
Blaywatch...................................(see 8)
Sava Centar..................................10 A3

TRANSPORT
Automobile & Motorcycle
Association of Serbia........................14 D3

Telephone & Fax

Post offices often incorporate call centres and fax facilities. See p419.

Mamut (Map p386; ☎ 0645152248; cnr Knez Mihailova & Sremska; per min 25DIN; ☼ 9am-10pm Mon-Fri, noon-10pm Sun) Internet calls; on the top floor.

Tourist Information

Tourist Organization of Belgrade (Map p386; www .tob.co.yu; Terazije underpass (☎ 635 622; fax 635 343; ☼ 9am-8pm Mon-Fri, to 5pm Sat); central train station (☎ 361 2732; ☼ 9am-8pm Mon-Fri, 9am-5pm Sat, 10am-4pm Sun); Makedonska (☎ 334 3460; Makedonska 5; ☼ 9am-9pm Mon-Fri, 10am-4pm Sat & Sun) Cheery and friendly with useful brochures, city maps and events listings.

Travel Agencies

Bas Turist (Map p386; ☎ 265 8759; www.bas .co.yu; BAS bus station; ☼ 7am-8pm Mon-Sat, to 4pm Sun) International bus tickets.

KSR Beograd Tours (Map p386; ☎ 641 258; fax 687 447; Nemanjina 4/14; ☼ 8am-8pm Mon-Fri, to 8pm Sat) Train tickets at station prices.

Lasta (Map p386; Milovana Milovanovića (☎ 264 1251; www.lasta.co.yu; Milovana Milovanovića 1; ☼ 6am-8pm Mon-Sat, to 6pm Sun); Lasta bus station (☎ 263 9769; www.lasta.co.yu; ☼ 7am-8pm Mon-Fri, 8am-4pm Sat) International bus tickets.

SIGHTS

Kalemegdan Citadel Калемегдан
Approaching Kalemegdan (Map p386) from Knez Mihailova, past trinket sellers and

BELGRADE IN TWO DAYS

Brunch at **Que Pasa?** (p393) before exploring the **Kalemegdan Citadel** (p383). Admire views over Novi Beograd from the **Victory monument** (below) and get a sense of the past with a walk through the **Military Museum** (below). Ice cream in hand, promenade leisurely down architecturally eclectic Knez Mihailova. Stop at **Russian Tsar** (p394) for opulent coffee and cake. Soak up the meeting-point atmosphere at nearby **Trg Republike** (opposite) and check whether the **National Museum** (opposite) is open, or spend the afternoon in the **Ethnographic Museum** (opposite). When hunger sets in, wander through cobblestoned **Skadarska** (p388) to enjoy traditional Serbian fare accompanied by energetic Roma violins. Leave bohemia behind and return to 'real' Belgrade with a live gig at **Akademija** (p396) or a cocktail at **Ben Akiba** (p394).

The next day, ponder the past at **Maršal Tito's grave** (p390) before heading to **Zemun** (p397) for a seafood lunch. Wander along the waterfront and stop for an afternoon drink on one of the **Danube River barges** (p396) on your way to the **Museum of Contemporary Art** (p390) – if it's open after renovations.

Back in the big smoke, enjoy dinner at historical **?** (p393) before heading to nearby **Anderground** (p395) for a heady Belgrade-style clubbing experience. If clubbing's not for you, opt instead for a leisurely meal at **Little Bay** (p392) for fine dining and live opera.

ice-cream vendors, makes the citadel appear as little more than a prime place for a picnic. But coming from the river, its imposing form gives a stronger sense of its past. This large fortification is perched on a site overlooking the confluence of the Sava and Danube rivers, with central Belgrade sprawling behind. Some 115 battles have been fought over Kalemegdan.

Fortifications began in Celtic times. The Romans extended the fortress onto the flood plains during the settlement of 'Singidunum', Belgrade's Roman name. Much of what stands today is the product of 18th-century Austro-Hungarian and Turkish reconstructions.

Entering from Knez Mihailova brings you to the Upper Citadel. The main entrance is **Stambol Gate** (Map p386), built by the Turks around 1750. Through Stambol Gate you'll find yourself in the firing line of cannons and tanks; welcome to the **Military Museum** (Map p386; ☎ 334 4408; adult/child 100/50DIN; ☺ 10am-5pm Tue-Sun), a large complex presenting a complete military history of the former Yugoslavia right up to the 1999 NATO bombings. Captured Kosovo Liberation Army (KLA) weapons and bits of a downed American stealth fighter are on display as successful 'catches'. Outside is a number of bombs and missiles dropped by NATO and a line-up of old guns and tanks, some quite rare.

Crossing through Clock-Tower Gate just by the museum, look up at the **Clock Tower**, built during the 18th-century Austrian occupation. Further on is the **mausoleum of Damad Ali-Paša**, built to commemorate the vizier (Ottoman governor) killed at Petrovaradin in 1716.

Nearby is the **Great Well**, 62m deep (10m deeper than the Sava River), at the foot of a double stairway descending 30m underground. It was built by the Austrians from 1721 to 1731 to provide water to the fortress.

Look up to see the **Victory monument** (Map p386), sculpted by Ivan Meštrović (p379) in 1928. Originally intended to stand in the city centre, it was placed here after comlaints about its nudity. It now stands pointing its privates towards Novi Beograd, where people are presumably less easily offended. The statue holds a falcon, symbolising Slavic freedom, and a sword in defence of peace.

Another of Meštrović's legacies is the 1930 **Monument to France**, erected in gratitude to French soldiers who fought and died in Belgrade during WWI.

On the northeastern side is **Despot Gate**, the main medieval entrance and the best-preserved fortification of that period. Next to it is the 15th-century **Dizdar Tower**, built where the citadel was entered by a drawbridge.

Nearby is **Dungeon Gate**, with two impressive round towers on each side, used as a prison during medieval times. Below is the **Rose Church of Our Lady**, originally an arsenal, then a military chapel before its restoration in 1925. The original church is said to have been destroyed by the Turks in the 16th century.

The **City Zoo** (Map p386; ☎ 262 4526; adult/child 300/200DIN; ☺ 8am-8pm) is further down towards the street. It's not a prime attraction by global standards, but it's proud of its white lions. And it comes with an interesting anecdote reminiscent of *Twelve Monkeys*: Nazi bombs damaged several enclosures, allowing some of its dangerous occupants to freely wander the streets of Belgrade.

The Lower Citadel can be viewed from the northernmost walls of the fortress. One of its few remaining sites is the 15th-century **Nebojša Tower**. Initially built to protect the harbour (playing a key role in the 1521 siege), it later became a torture chamber under the Ottomans.

Old Town

South of the citadel is the old town. The jigsaw of architecture covers two centuries, beginning when Belgrade was snatched from the dying Ottoman Empire and given a boost by the Habsburgs. Pedestrian **Knez Mihailova** (Map p386), the first street in Belgrade with an official name, is where cafes spill onto pavements and people promenade in their multitudes.

Knez Mihailova has some fine buildings, such as the elegant pink-and-white, neo-Renaissance **School of Fine Arts** (Map p386), on the corner with Rajićeva. Further down is the **Serbian Academy of Arts & Sciences** (Map p386), an early-20th-century art nouveau–style building, with the goddess Nike at its helm crowning Industry and Trade with two wreaths.

At the other end of Knez Mihailova is Trg Republike (Republic Sq), a popular meeting point and outdoor exhibition space. On the square is the **National Museum** (Map p386; ☎ 330 6000; www.narodnimuzej.org.yu; Trg Republike 1a). At the time of writing the museum could only be admired from the outside; costly renovations are taking their time.

A few blocks away, the **Ethnographic Museum** (Map p386; ☎ 328 1888; Studentski Trg 13; admission 60DIN; ☽ 10am-5pm Tue-Sat, 9am-2pm Sun) contains traditional costumes, living spaces and working utensils. The exhibition dedicated to *ćilim* carpets is an interesting primer to the southern Serbian town of Pirot (p409). The 2nd floor displays historical living conditions and 19th-century mountain-village interiors. It's interesting to compare this with the almost 'real' thing in the open-air museum village of Sirogojno (p416).

The 1831 **Palace of Princess Ljubica** (Map p386; ☎ 263 8264; Kneza Sime Markovića 8; adult/child 100/50DIN;

☽ 10am-5pm Tue, Wed, Fri & Sat, noon-8pm Thu, 10am-2pm Sun) is a Balkans-style palace built for the wife of Prince Miloš. Rooms are filled with period furniture, and Pirot *ćilim* (carpets). The most authentic area is the hamam (Turkish bath) where Ljubica would have been steamed and massaged.

West of the palace is the 19th-century **Saborna church** (Orthodox cathedral; Map p386), a mixture of late-baroque and neo-classical styles. The church holds the tombs of Prince Miloš Obrenović and his two sons. Vuk Karadžić, the man responsible for phoneticising the Serbian language, is buried in the church's graveyard. Opposite is the Patriarchate (Patrijaršija) building, containing the five-room **Museum of the Serbian Orthodox Church** (Map p386; ☎ 263 8875; Kralja Petra 5; adult/child 50/20DIN; ☽ 8am-3pm Mon-Fri, 9am-noon Sat, 11am-1pm Sun). Objects here were passed between many hands (including those of its first collector, St Sava) before finally being displayed together here in the 1940s. Valuable items include robes of King Milutin (12th and 14th century), Ivan the Terrible's cup, and various icons, prints and engravings.

Opposite the church, on Kralja Petra, is **?** (p393), Belgrade's oldest inn in a traditional *kafana*. Built in 1823 as Ećim Toma's Café-Restaurant, it later changed its name to Cathedral Café because of its location. Church authorities protested that this 'desecrated the name of God's temple'. Baffled by all the hoo-ha, the owner of the tavern relabelled it with an honest '?'. The complaints stopped and the question mark stayed.

For some quality art exhibitions, pop into **Akademija Fine Arts Gallery** (Salon Muzeja Savremene Umetnosti; Map p386; ☎ 328 2800; www.fluc.org; Pariška 16; admission free; ☽ 10am-7pm Mon-Fri, to 3pm Sat). This faculty of fine arts gallery hosts temporary art exhibitions by high-profile artists. At the time of research it was exhibiting pieces of the temporarily closed Museum of Contemporary Art.

Dorćol Дорћол

Named from the Turkish *dört yol* ('four roads'), Dorćol stretches from Studentski Trg (Student Sq) to the Danube, and from Skadarska to Kalemegdan. Once upon a time, Turks, Greeks, Jews, Germans, Armenians and Vlachs filled these streets. Christmas, Passover and Ramadan were celebrated side by side and merchants bartered in a mix

SERBIA

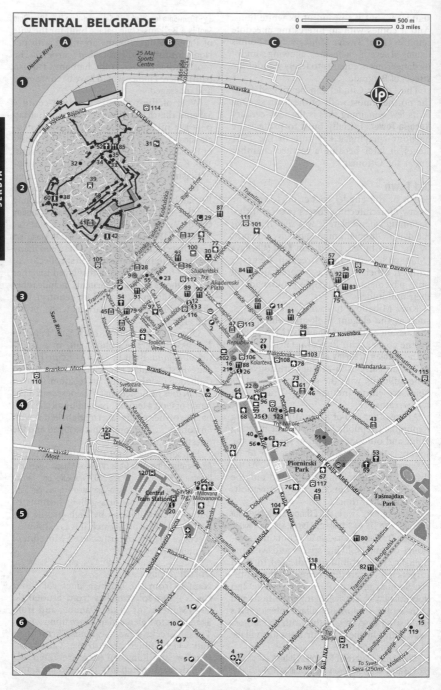

CENTRAL BELGRADE

of languages. These days Dorćol is a pleasant residential area, but little remains of its former cosmopolitanism.

The area has been nipped and tucked by tug-of-war over the years; the Turks gave it the oriental characteristic of cobbled winding streets, the Austrians 'straightened' them between 1717 and 1739, and then the curves came back with the Turks in 1739.

One of the few remaining pieces of oriental architecture is the 18th-century **Burial Chamber of Sheikh Mustafa** (Map p386; cnr Braće Jugovića & Višnjićeva), a dervish sheikh from Baghdad. The last remaining mosque in Dorćol – and indeed Belgrade – is the **Bayrakli mosque** (Map p386; cnr Kralja Petra & Gospodar Jevremova). Dating back to the 17th century, the mosque is being reconstructed after it was damaged in the March

2004 riots (a backlash against the anti-Serb pogroms in Kosovo at the time) and is now guarded to prevent further retaliation.

The **St Aleksandar Nevski church** (Cara Dušana) is the first Christian place of worship to have been built in the area. Roma bands often play outside the church for Saturday-afternoon wedding festivities.

Opened in 1953, the **Gallery of Frescos** (Map p386; ☎ 262 1491; www.narodnimuzej.org.yu; Cara Uroša 20; admission free; ☼ 10am-5pm Tue, Wed, Fri & Sat, noon-8pm Thu, 10am-2pm Sun) was built on the site of an old synagogue. The vast collection gives a good idea of Byzantine Serbian church art from the end of the 11th century to the beginning of the 15th century, with full-size replicas (and some originals) of church and monastery paintings. Replicas are exact down to the last detail, even reproducing scratches and wear.

Skadarska Скадарска

Skadarska (Map p386), or 'Skadarlija', is Belgrade's bohemian heartland. East of Trg Republike this surprising cobblestoned strip has been sliced straight out of Montmartre. At the turn of the 20th century, bohemianism was authentic; Skadarska was a gathering point for Belgrade's creative community. Old-fashioned charm remains, but it's more forced these days; having said that, you may find yourself dining next to a writer, poet, philosopher or film star. The thing to do here is drop your cynicism and enjoy Serbian cuisine while roving Roma bands provide the ambience.

In the 1830s this area was a collection of abandoned trenches outside Belgrade's defensive walls populated by the city's Roma community. Later the Roma shantytown was removed and houses were built for craftsmen and poorer civil servants. The street got its name in honour of the Albanian city of Skadar (Shkodra).

Further up, off Skadarska, is the Association of Serbian Writers, with a famous restaurant (the Writers' Club; see p393) where Belgrade's men and women of the pen met and ate during socialist times.

Skadarska is at its best in summer, when outdoor performances enliven meals.

Central Belgrade

Belgrade hustles and bustles along **Terazije**. The jewel in this crown is the **Hotel Moscow** (p392), with a fountain out the front built in honour of the return of Prince Miloč. Built between 1906 and 1907 as a hotel and office building for a Russian insurance company, the Moscow is one of the few architecturally interesting buildings that aren't lost in the busy blur of traffic.

From the Hotel Moscow towards the Sava River (downhill from the Balkan Hotel), you come across the partly covered **Zeleni Venac market** (Map p386; ☼ 7am-4pm), a place of trade since the 19th century. The market lost much of its messy character when it was redeveloped in 2007 but still sells everything from clothes to DVDs and food. This area is a hub for city buses, including those to Zemun and Ada Ciganlija.

Back on Terazije, the charming art nouveau **Smederevo Bank** (Map p386; Terazije 39) is a slim construction built in 1912 for a local merchant. Opposite is another art nouveau building, now the **Zvezda cinema** (Map p386; Terazije 40) but originally the studio of portrait photographer Milan Jovanović. The wall of the building on the left-hand side features a reproduction of one of Jovanović's elegant photographs, called *A Girl with a Parasol*.

A fine example of a neo-baroque style house on Terazije is **Krsmanović House** (Map p386; Terazije 34), where the Kingdom of Serbs, Croats and Slovenes was first pronounced in 1918.

The tall, modernist **Albania building** (Map p386) marks the point where Terazije meets Knez Mihailova. The building's underground passage hides shops and a tourist information office.

From Terazije, walk through to adjacent Trg Nikole Pašića and the **Museum of the History of Serbia** (Map p386; ☎ 328 7242; Trg Nikole Pašića; adult/child 100/50DIN; ☼ noon-6pm Tue-Sat). At the time of research, slow-going renovations meant only a small space was open to the public. The partly audiovisual exhibition concerns the assassinations of Prince Đorđe Petrovic Karađorđe, Prince Mihailo Obrenović III and King Aleksandar Obrenović and Queen Draga. It even includes bloodstained clothes worn by victims at the time of their assassination and some weapons used by assassins. With someone explaining what you're looking at, it's enthralling (without, it's obscure).

Across Trg Nikole Pašića is **parliament** (Map p386), images of which were beamed around the world when it was stormed by anti-Milošević protestors in 2000.

Across Kneza Miloša is the grandiose 1938 **post office building** (Map p386), constructed to accompany the 1908 **old telephone building** (Map p386), a good example of Serbian-Byzantine style.

Southwest down Kneza Miloša are stark reminders of how recently the NATO bombs fell. Two destroyed administrative buildings at the corner of Nemanjina make the 1999 bombings seem as though they just happened.

Behind the post office is **Sveti Marko church** (Map p386; ☎ 323 1940; bul Kralja Aleksandra 17), based on the design of the Gračanica monastery in Kosovo. It's five-domed, with a bell tower above the main entrance. The church contains the grave of Emperor Dušan (1308–55). Behind is the tiny white **Russian church** (Map p386), erected by Russian refugees who fled the October Revolution.

Surrounding these two churches is **Tašmajdan park** (Map p386), a former quarry and the location of the Belgrade cemetery. The park, laid out behind the post office, once served as an extension of the Belgrade racetrack.

If vehicles are your thing, the **Museum of Automobiles** (Map p386; ☎ 303 4625; Majke Jevrosime 30; adult/child 100/80DIN; ☼ 11am-7pm) is a compelling collection of cars and motorcycles, many still in working order. The pick for our garage would be the '57 Cadillac convertible: only 25,000km and one careful owner – President Tito.

For film buffs, the **Yugoslav Film Archives Museum** (Map p386; ☎ 324 8250; www.kinoteka .org.yu; Kosovska 11) has more than 90,000 films, stills, books and magazines illustrating the technical development of film. The collection includes invaluable historical footage from coronations to assassinations. Keep an eye out for interesting screenings.

One of the capital's best museums is the **Nikola Tesla Museum** (Map p386; ☎ 243 3886; www .tesla-museum.org; Krunska 51; admission 200DIN; ☼ 10am-6pm Tue-Fri, to 1pm Sat & Sun), where you can meet the man on the 100DIN note. As well as a well-organised (and English-captioned) collection of documents, books and models, and Nikola Tesla's ashes, the museum has some wondrously interactive elements that you'll enjoy most with a guide. For more on Tesla and his inventions, see the boxed text, below.

NIKOLA TESLA: AN ELECTRIC LIFE

You couldn't invent Nikola Tesla. The embodiment of mad professor, minus the wild hair, the moustachioed Serb was about as influential in the world of physics and electronic engineering as Einstein. Tesla invented the rotating magnetic field and produced and distributed electrical energy based on alternate currents. For you and me that means he invented motors and generators; without him, you'd be starting your car with a wind-up mechanism.

Born in northern Croatia in 1856, Tesla studied in Graz and Prague before moving to Paris in 1882 to work for Edison's Continental Company, where he made the prototype of the induction motor. Two years later he moved to New York and started playing with X-rays and wireless power transmission. He invented the first neon light tube and forever changed the look of American streets. He also came up with a way to transmit electricity over long distances, and generated hydro-electricity from Niagara Falls. The cables stretching across many a country's landscape are also thanks to him. He toyed with remote controls and electric motor ignition, both of which are integral today, and was an early starter at radio astronomy, trying for many years to talk to Mars. His more idiosyncratic inventions like the 'electric laxative' somehow never became household items.

Unfortunately, Tesla was often tricked out of money and credit for his work by more shrewd businessmen, and ended up dying half-forgotten in the New Yorker hotel in Manhattan in 1943. A few months later, the US Supreme Court finally credited Tesla as the inventor of radio, though it was Guglielmo Marconi who won the Nobel Prize in 1911.

Years after his death Tesla finally achieved the recognition he deserved. Unesco and the governments of Serbia and Croatia declared 2006 the Year of Nikola Tesla, a monument was unveiled at Niagara Falls, and Belgrade's airport was named after him. Perhaps it's dubious respect, but the same year, David Bowie played Tesla in *The Prestige*.

Robert Lomas's book *The Man Who Invented the Twentieth Century: Nikola Tesla* is a detailed account of this fascinating man's life.

SERBIA

Outer Belgrade

South down Kraja Milana and across Trg Slavija is the enormous Orthodox church of **Sveti Sava** (Map p383; Svetog Save). This is Serbia's biggest Orthodox church, a fact that's entirely obvious looking at the city skyline from a distance or up at the church's dome from within. The church is built where the Turks apparently burnt relics of St Sava, the youngest son of a 12th-century ruler and founder of the independent Serbian Orthodox Church. In front is **Karađorđe park**, graced by a statue of legendary Karađorđe himself. This area was the site of peaceful protests against Kosovo's declaration of independence in early 2008. The church has been a work in progress since 1894, with wars continually interrupting construction. It's still not finished, but it's open for you to gawp at.

Further south, don't miss **Maršal Tito's grave** (25th of May Museum, or Kuća Cveća, or House of Flowers; Map p383; ☎ 367 1485; bul Mira; admission free; ⊗ 10am-5pm Tue-Sat, to 1pm Sun), with an interesting museum of gifts presented to him over the years, including the Rolls Royce from Queen Elizabeth, a writing set from JFK and a bowl given 'with great admiration and affection' by Elizabeth Taylor and Richard Burton. The silver gifts are presented in the building in front of the mausoleum, and the rest sprawls in the long building just beyond it. Next to the grave is a room containing an impressive baton collection. Getting here is a cinch; take trolleybus 40 or 41 at the south end of parliament on Kneza Miloša. It's the second stop after it turns into bul Mira.

Aircraft enthusiasts should head to the **Aviation Museum** (off Map p383; ☎ 267 0992; Suračin; admission 400DIN; ⊗ 8.30am-6.30pm summer, 9am-3pm winter, closed Mon) at the airport. It contains some rare planes and a strong WWII collection including a Hurricane, a Spitfire and a Messerschmitt from WWII, and bits of the infamous American stealth fighter shot down in 1999.

The **Museum of Contemporary Art** (Muzej Savremene Umetnosti; Map p383; ☎ 311 5713) is in Novi Beograd, on the banks of the Danube River, and like many of Belgrade's gems is closed for renovation. The permanent collection covers three periods: impressionist (1900–18); expressionist, constructivist and surrealist (1918–41); neosurrealist, modern and contemporary (1945 to the present day). There's also a 20th-century sculpture collection. When it opens again, get there by bus 15, 84, 704E or 706 from Zeleni Venac

market. In the meantime, parts of its collection are sporadically shown at **Akademija Fine Arts Gallery** (p385) and in the gallery windows along Knez Mihailova.

ACTIVITIES

The Victory monument at Kalemegdan Citadel looks towards the Sava River and Veliko Ratno Ostrvo (Great War Island; Map p383). This is a renowned birdwatching area.

Belgrade's summer retreat is **Ada Ciganlija** (Map p383; www.adaciganlija.co.yu), an island park on the Sava River. Between June and September you can cycle around the park, swim, kayak, row or water ski in the 4.2km-long artificial lake, or get your kit off in the naturist zone 1km upstream. There are several sporting facilities, nine holes of golf, paintball and a 55m bungee platform. Take bus 53 or 56 from Zeleni Venac market.

Košutnjak (off Map p383) is a park on Belgrade's southwestern outskirts. Follow exercise instructions along the 'health path', a leftover from when the social government adopted the slogan 'A healthy spirit is in a healthy body' to get the masses jogging. Get bus 53 from Zeleni Venac market – or jog the 9km for an extra-healthy spirit.

Another popular summer spot is **Avala** (off Map p383) mountain 16km south of Belgrade. There are water springs and walking opportunities here, as well as WWI and WWII monuments, the most famous being Ivan Meštrović's Monument to the Unknown Hero, a tomb for a Serbian soldier with eight granite female figures symbolising the Yugoslav peoples.

COURSES

For information, see p418.

TOURS

Putnik Travel Agency (Map p386; ☎ 324 5642; www .putnik.com; Trg Nikole Pašića 1; ⊗ 8am-8pm Mon-Fri, 9am-3pm Sat) Excursions in and beyond Belgrade.
Romantika (www.serbianrailways.com) Steam-hauled train to Austro-Hungarian Sremski Karlovci. Contact KSR Beograd Tours (p383).
Tourist Organization of Belgrade (p383) Guided bus tours. The 90-minute bus trip (10am Sunday from Trg Nikole Pašića 12) is an enlightening introduction to Belgrade.

FESTIVALS & EVENTS

FEST film festival (www.fest.org.yu) International and local films from February to March, with talks by directors.

In Vino (www.invino.co.yu) Wine festival at the Sava Centar (p396) in May.

Beer Festival (www.belgradebeerfest.com) Live music and beer in August.

BITEF international theatre festival (www.bitef .co.yu) September festival originating in the avant-garde '60s and '70s, now showcasing global thespian talent.

BEMUS Music Festival (www.bemus.co.yu) Classical and contemporary music at the Sava Centar (p396) in October.

SLEEPING

Accommodation in Belgrade is the worst value for money in the country. The spectrum of crumbling midrange to newer high-end options is covered, but few stand out as well priced for what you get. Thankfully, more hostels are starting to get with it and some of the older classics are considering renovations.

City Centre

Options below are east of the Sava River, effectively within the tram 2 loop.

BUDGET

The **Youth Hostel organisation** (Ferijalni Savez Beograd; Map p386; ☎ 324 8550; www.hostels.org .yu; 2nd fl, Makedonska 22; ◷ 9am-5pm) does deals with local hotels. You need HI membership (500/700DIN under/over 26 years old) or an international student card.

At the time of writing, **Hotel Splendid** (Map p386; ☎ 323 5444; www.splendid.co.yu; D Jovanovića 5) was about to close for renovations. Cross your fingers that it reopens in this price category.

Hostel City Center (Map p386; ☎ 264 4055; www .hostelcitycenterbelgrade.com; Savski trg 7; dm 850-1020DIN, s/d from 2460/3280DIN, without bathroom from 1890/2520DIN, apt 3925DIN) Immediately opposite the central train station, this one's perfect for late arrivals or early departures. Rooms range from hostel to hotel style; those without toilets have a private sink and are airy, though perhaps a little loud.

UniTurs Hostel (Map p386; ☎ 334 6241; www .uni-turs.com; Andrićev Venac 12/3; dm 800-960DIN, tw per person 1200DIN; 🖳) Here's a clean-as-a-whistle surprise in an otherwise gloomy building. Floors are fresh parquet, large cupboards are lockable, computers are available, the kitchen is breezy, and the shower has an inbuilt radio. It's at the southern tip of Piornirski Park.

Yellowbed Hostel (Map p386; ☎ 262 8220; www .yellowbed.net; Višnjećeva 3; dm from 1000DIN) A cosy place with space for 15 lucky buggers. Balconies, wireless internet, a light terrace,

good-humoured staff and a central location behind Studentski Trg make this a great budget base.

Hotel Royal (Map p386; ☎ 263 4222; www.hotel royal.co.yu; Kralja Petra 56; s/d 2640/3600DIN; 🖳) Royal books up quickly because it covers the four 'c's: cheap, clean, central and has character. Rooms are pleasant and tidy, staff are friendly, the reception buzzes with action around a bizarre glass-mosaic staircase, and live music in the basement restaurant offers some folk fun.

Hotel Astoria (Map p386; ☎ 360 5100; www .astoria.co.yu; Milovana Milovanovića 1; s/d 2970/4620DIN, d with shared bathroom 2970DIN, d with air-con 5170DIN) Astoria offers light and airy rooms with cable TV and minibar. Linen is crisp and fresh, staff are helpful, and the location is close enough to the train station for convenience but far away enough for quiet.

MIDRANGE

Hotel Palace (Map p386; ☎ 263 7222; www.palace hotel.co.yu; Topličin Venac 23; s/d/ste €70/105/130; 🖳) A grand oldie that's kept up with the times more than the competition, the Palace books up quickly. The lobby is dolled up with a water feature and the freshly furnished rooms have large bathrooms and wireless internet. There's a good city view from the upstairs Panorama restaurant.

Hotel Excelsior (p386; ☎ 323 1381; www.hotel excelsior.co.yu; Kneza Miloša 5; s/d from €33/50; 🖳) Though not for the detail-oriented, Excelsior offers great value relative to others that jack up prices but not facilities. Rooms are spacious and have cable TV. Some offer balcony views over Piornirski Park. All have character. Despite the dubious advertisement for the downstairs nightclub, this authentic oldie has an evocative history; former guests include Ivo Andrić, Josephine Baker and German staff during WWII. The wireless internet and the lift work when they feel like it.

Kasina Hotel (Map p386; ☎ 323 5575; www.kasina .stari-grad.co.yu; Terazije 25; standard/comfort s €42/€81, d €81/103; 🖾 🖳) Vying for attention near the Moscow and Balkan hotels, Kasina offers pleasant albeit overpriced rooms. Depending on your choice of 'comfort' or 'standard' you get air-con and minibar, or neither and a slightly darker room. Compensate in the latter situation by requesting a room with a view of the square.

Hotel Prag (Map p386; ☎ 361 0422; www.hotel prag.co.yu; Kraljice Natalije 27; s/d with air-con 4700/6500DIN, without air-con 4100/5900DIN; 🛇 🖵) Not particularly bright but decent value next to the competition. Dark-brown rooms with new parquet floors are more pleasant than the smaller carpeted ones. There's wireless in the foyer.

Hotel Union (p386; ☎ 324 8022; www.hotelun ionbelgrade.com; Kosovska 11; s/d from €49/79; 🛇 🖵) Overpriced given that the only change in recent years has been the addition of large-screen TVs, the Union offers advantages like wireless in rooms and a quiet but central location. Check rooms before you commit – some are larger than others and some windows open to neighbouring walls.

TOP END

ourpick Hotel Moscow (Hotel Moskva; Map p386; ☎ 268 6255; hotelmoskva@absolutok.net; Balkanska 1; s/d from €100/143; 🛇 🖵) This art nouveau building has been a source of city pride since 1906, but the Moscow has rested on its old-world-character laurels and not made moves to modernise. Reminiscent of but more tasteful than novelty underwear, the carpets in the lifts are changed daily according to the day of the week written on them. It isn't perfect; some of the singles make you feel persecuted for not being a double and some communal areas waste space. But despite this and the fact that prices mock the common man, this is the place to scribble out your Balkan memoirs at a big old desk.

Le Petit Piaf (Map p386; ☎ 303 5252; www .petitpiaf.com; Skadarska 34; ste €120-170; 🛇 🖵) Since it opened in 2004, the Petit Piaf has fit right into Skadarska – Belgrade's answer to Montmartre. Rooms (named after French landmarks and clichés) are elegant affairs with tastefully toned furniture. The more expensive loft rooms evoke true Parisian apartments, with split levels and sloping ceilings.

Aleksandar Palas (Map p386; ☎ 330 5300; www .aleksandarpalas.com; Kralja Petra 13-15; apt €250; 🛇 🖵) One of the most exclusive places but with an unpretentious vibe, Aleksandar Palas offers nine suites with separate living rooms and bedrooms, and king-size beds overlooking the DVD-equipped home cinema system. Showers offer bathing bling. Prices drop by €30 on Friday and €60 on weekends.

Balkan Hotel (Map p386; ☎ 363 6000; www.bal kanhotel.net; Brankova Prizrenska 2; s/d from 9020/10,660DIN, ste 12,000-18,400DIN; 🛇 🖵) Renovations have made modern rooms incongruous amid the old-world exterior. Standard rooms are small for this price, but comfort rooms and suites

offer light, airy space with splendid views. The attached Orient Express cafe with a summer terrace is an asset.

Outer Belgrade

Arka Barka (Map p383; ☎ 0642004445; www.arkabarka .net; bul Nikole Tesle bb; per person €15; 🛇 🖵) Arka Barka is a character-flooded prime hostel, so long as you don't mind a long walk or a short bus ride (15 or 84) to the centre. Floating on the water off Usće Park (within stumbling distance of the Danube River barges), Arka Barka offers Ikea-fresh furniture, wireless internet, and cafe-style chairs on the verandah to enjoy the breeze. There are a couple of private rooms with loft beds for up to four people.

Hyatt Regency (Map p383; ☎ 301 1234; www.belgrade .regency.hyatt.com; Milentija Popovića 5; s/d from €275/295; 🛇 🖵 ♿) A convenient location for events at the Sava Centar, this stately standard hotel (across the Sava River in Novi Beograd) offers all the mod cons, luxury shops and restaurants you'd expect.

EATING

Belgrade offers fabulous fine dining; don't skimp on meals. Options range from traditional to modern and quaint to quirky. The choice is overwhelming along Knez Mihailova, 29 Novembra and Makedonska. If you like your meal with a side of music, head to Skadarska. For floating food experiences, head for restaurants along the Danube.

Post- or pre-clubbing munchies can be satiated at Trg Republike for under 100DIN.

Restaurants

ourpick Little Bay (Map p386; ☎ 328 4163; www .little-bay.co.uk; Dositejeva 9a; average meal 400DIN; ☺ 9am-1am) Little Bay is the best of Europe in the heart of Belgrade. The grandeur of an opera house fills a tiny space; sit in a private box, under the marquee roof or on the tree-lined street. Start with beef cappaccio with blue-cheese mousse and mustard pear (240DIN) or dive straight into a lamb steak (480DIN), roasted aubergine (295DIN) or traditional roast (295DIN). Things couldn't get better, until an opera singer takes a swig of water and belts out Puccini. You're wondering where the catch is, when the bill reveals you've just had one of the best-value meals in town, and been to the opera. What the…?!

Iguanaćošku (Iguana at the Corner; Map p386; ☎ 744 8690; www.iguanacosku.com; Beogradska 37; meals 800-

1200DIN; ☻ noon-11am Mon-Sat, 1-5pm Sun) After 15 years in Melbourne, husband-and-wife team Goran and Bata brought the best of Australian fusion food back to Belgrade. Sit at a white linen-clothed table or in a cosy booth to enjoy Thai, French and Indian highlights with class and kick. Try tequila-marinated chicken with pink-grapefruit salad (580DIN), or a salmon steak with sweet-chilli sauce and coconut milk (880DIN). For dessert, there's homemade sticky date pudding (250DIN).

? (Map p386; ☎ 635 421; Kralja Petra 6; meals 250-500DIN; ☻ 8am-midnight) The dining experience can be hit and miss, but eating here is essential for the fact that it has remained an old-style Serbian tavern both in atmosphere and in flavour. Tender lamb or veal *ispod saća* is mouth-watering (and more enticing than the young bull's sex glands on offer). For more on the quizzical name, see p385.

Que Pasa? (Map p386; ☎ 330 5377, www.ale ksandarpalas.com; Kralja Petra 13-15; meals 600-700DIN; ☻ 10am-2am Tue-Sat, to 1am Sun & Mon) Attached to Aleksandar Palas hotel, Que Pasa? pulls in high rollers from the 30+ age bracket. Like the music, the menu leans decidedly towards Mexico (though the ice cream is imported from Italy). It's spacious, luminous and chic, with a menu showing the calorie cost next to the price. Have a burrito brunch with multi-vitamin juice (420DIN). Later in the day, try the turkey in hazelnut sauce (720DIN, 912 calories) or 'Steak My Love' (1250DIN, 1066 calories).

Trattoria Košava (Map p386; ☎ 262 7344; www .trattoriakosava.com; Kralja Petra 36; meals 400-800DIN; ☻ 8am-1am Mon-Fri, noon-1am Sat & Sun) Popularity hasn't let Trattoria Košava get complacent. Sit upstairs in warm, lamp-lit surrounds graced with nostalgic music and charming touches (like a window painted on the ceiling) and enjoy an enormous plate of wildberry pancakes (250DIN).

Jevrem (Map p386; ☎ 328 4746; www.restoran -jevrem.com; Gospodar Jevremova 36; average meal 800DIN; ☻ 11am-1am Mon-Sat) In a lovingly restored Dorćol house, Jevrem is decorated to 1920s tastes with plush armchairs and white umbrellas in the courtyard. A full roast costs 2200DIN, or there's even a burger (590DIN). Live music (Thursday to Saturday) starts at 8pm.

Writers' Club (Klub Književnika; Map p386; ☎ 262 7931; Francuska 7; meals 400-600DIN; ☻ 8pm-2am) This legendary institution was once frequented by the state-approved literati of the Tito era. Locals still come to reminisce about stuffed courgettes and roast lamb with potatoes, both of which have kept their cult status. The busiest time is around 10pm.

Dačo (off Map p383; ☎ 278 1009; Patrisa Lumumbe 49; meals 250-700DIN; ☻ 10am-midnight, closed Mon) Dačo is a Serbian village experience on steroids. Chillies hang from ceilings, wooden chairs and folksy bits and bobs clutter walls, waiters wear traditional garb, and roving musicians entice diners into singalongs. Entrées – *kajmak*, cheeses, *pršuta* (prosciutto) and other cold meats and salads – are the speciality. It's a haul from the centre; get going before you get hungry.

Priroda (☎ 241 1890; sneskapriroda@yahoo.com; Batutova 11; meals 25-400DIN; ☻ noon-7pm; **V**) Despite odd opening hours, quirky Priroda deserves a medal for overcoming adversity: it's a superb vegetarian restaurant in a land of carnivores. Even meat eaters will appreciate the break from traditional Serbian cuisine. The macrobiotic cake is a mouth stunner. Priroda is about 6km east of the central train station.

Peking Restaurant (Map p386; ☎ 181 931; Vuka Karadžića 2; meals 600-700DIN; ☻ 11am-midnight Mon-Sat, 1-11pm Sun; **V**) Red lanterns, Chinese decor and the tinkling tunes of the Orient don't hide the fact that there isn't an Asian to be found in this two-floor Chinese restaurant. But the menu offers exciting choices – like duck with walnuts – and sweet relief for vegetarians in the vegetarian dish (180DIN).

Kalemegdanska Terasa (Map p386; ☎ 328 3011; Kalemegdan bb; meals 400-900DIN; ☻ 9am-late) This slick, peach-coloured restaurant in the grounds of Kalemegdan Citadel could serve stale bread and not deter view-seeking clients. Thankfully, it doesn't; the menu consists of grilled meats and cutlets (whose prices seem to carry a location tax). Summer dining should happen alfresco on the terrace, but the faux-ancient interior is also a fitting choice for a citadel meal.

Plato (Map p386; ☎ 658 863; Akademski Plato 1; average meal 650DIN; ☻ 9am-midnight) Plato (*plar*-to) is a restaurant, cafe, bar and live-music venue. It's mostly Italian food in a relaxed atmosphere where you can eat, drink and listen to jazz or Cuban rhythms.

allo allo (Map p386; ☎ 323 8888; Svetozara Markovića 19a; meals 350-600DIN; ☻ 9am-midnight) If you're sick of *šopska*, come here for a more nuanced salad like rocket- and pine-nut-laden 'Le Cler'

SERBIA

(550DIN) or sesame-sprinkled 'Lili' (350DIN). Pizzas aren't the cheapest but are up there with the best. Black-tie waiters will bring a blanket if you get chilly on the terrace.

Šešir Moj (My Hat; Map p386; ☎ 322 8750; Skadarska 21; meals 300-500DIN; ☽ 9am-2am) Roma bands swirl past your alcove playing heart-tugging music as you hoe into *punjena bela vešalica* (pork fillet stuffed with *kajmak*). Finish with coffee and a piece of *orašnica* (walnut cake).

Guli (Map p386; ☎ 323 7204; Skadarska 13; meals 400-800DIN; ☽ noon-11pm Mon-Sat, 2-11pm Sun) A modern rebel in an old-world area, Guli couldn't be more different from its neighbours. The pizza and pasta is acclaimed by the A-list clientele, and there's a pleasing international wine selection.

Also recommended for hearty doses of food and live music in Skadarska:

Ima Dana (There Are Days; Map p386; ☎ 323 4417; www.visnjica.co.yu; Skadarska 38; meals 300-800DIN; ☽ 11am-1am)

Tri Šešira (Three Hats; Map p386; ☎ 324 7501; Skadarska 29; meals 300-460DIN; ☽ lunch & dinner)

Quick Eats & Self-Catering

Belgrade has numerous supermarkets.

Loki (Kralja Petra; 100-200DIN; ☽ 24hr) For late-night or early-morning munchies, head to this renowned fast-food kiosk. Its exquisite *pljeskavica* is responsible for the 1am queue.

Pekara Toma (Map p386; Kolarčeva 10; ☽ 24hr) The smell wafting from this place could make you hungry after a three-course meal. Drop in for freshly baked pizzas, pastries and bread, or salads.

Zeleni venac market (Map p386; cnr Brankova Prizrenska & Narodnog Fronta; ☽ 7am-4pm) This is a scrounging ground for DIY food; fruit and veg sell out in the early morning.

DRINKING

There's a fine line between a cafe, a bar, and even a club in Belgrade. A quiet cafe during the day will morph into a drinking den at night and a thumping club in the early hours. All are open daily from early morning to at least midnight, with a later start on Sunday. In spring and summer, action spills onto terraces and pavements.

Cafes

Hot Spot Café (Map p386; ☎ 263 9205; Studentski Trg 2; ☽ 8am-1am Mon-Fri, 9am-1am Sat & Sun) Glass-fronted and elegantly furnished with soft

---

SILICON VALLEY

Trendy Strahinjića Bana (aka Silicon Valley) in Dorćol is nicknamed for the assets of trophy girlfriends coming here to accompany or acquire well-endowed boyfriends. By day it's a quiet street with a string of fashionable bars, but during the pumpkin hour there's nowhere to park and hardly anywhere to walk. The only thing to do is sit back, enjoy the show and think about alternative nicknames for the place (Peroxide Promenade, Solarium City, Botox Block...).

---

seats, this is a great (hot) spot for breakfast/ brunch or coffee during the day, or something harder during the night.

Russian Tsar (Ruski Car; Map p386; ☎ 633 628; Obilićev Venac 28; ☽ 8am-1am) Recently renovated to look as though it hasn't changed for 100 years; grand gold trimmings and dripping chandeliers add dollars to decadent cakes, but the ambience on the leafy summer terrace is lovely. If you can't decide which sweet treat to choose, grab the surprise dessert (325DIN).

Greenet (Map p386; ☎ 323 8474; Nušićeva 3; ☽ 8am-midnight) You'll probably hear more than once that Greenet is *the* place for coffee connoisseurs. You can take away your hot beverage, but it's better enjoyed in the green and brown tones draped over the width of Nušićeva. Linger over a mocha – the local favourite.

Tema (Map p386; ☎ 337 3859; Makedonska 11-13; ☽ 8am-midnight) A subtly lit modern bar welcoming both young and old. It does a pleasant line in coffees with a spirit kick.

Bars

our pick **Federal Association of Globe-Trotters** (Map p386; ☎ 324 2303; www.aur.org.yu; bul Despota Stefana 7/1; ☽ 1pm-midnight Mon-Fri, 3pm-late Sat & Sun) Through the big black gate, past the lazy cats and down the dingy staircase is an oasis of eclectic cool. Trust us. If you sent a photo of this home to friends, they wouldn't be able to guess where you are. Tables are anything from a piano to an old sewing machine. Exotic lamps, glitter balls and fairy lights adorn the courtyard. Have a cocktail (250DIN) and enjoy wireless internet.

Ben Akiba (Map p386; ☎ 323 7775; Nušićeva 8; ☽ 9am-late) You're not supposed to know about this exclusive place, but everyone will tell you. Belgrade's worst-kept secret is a converted 1st-floor flat which began as a haven for liberals to drink and deplore Milošević. Now Belgrade's chic come for hard cocktails and light conversations. Walls often exhibit the work of local artists.

Pastis Bistro (☎ 328 8188; Strahinjića Bana 52b; ☽ 8am-late) In style in Silicon Valley (see the boxed text, opposite), Pastis is the place to go if you're feeling sociable. The mood is mild, the tunes smooth and the people suave, yet despite it all Pastis is free of the pretensions of many of its neighbours. This cosy French-influenced bistro-style bar fills up early and stays that way until morning; get here quick to claim your bar stool inside or leaning table outside.

Kandahar (☎ 0643343970; Strahinjića Bana 48; ☽ 8am-late) Also on the Silicon Valley beat, this lounge bar is Arabic in theme with gentle drapes hanging overhead and soft reclining cushions. Apart from cocktails (200DIN to 300DIN), there are exotic teas (150DIN) and coffee blends (160DIN to 190DIN).

Movie Bar (Map p386; ☎ 262 3818; moviebar @prototim.com; Kolarčeva 6; ☽ 4.30pm-late) A long white room with a longish bar and many long drinks under the Albania building, this is a cool oasis during the summer heat and a cool jazz joint at night.

Three Carrots (Map p386; ☎ 683 748; www.three carrots.co.yu; Kneza Miloša 16; ☽ 9am-1am) Belgrade's obligatory Irish pub is a worthy offering, thankfully erring towards minimalism rather than being overly Leprechaun-laden. Its two-level wooden interior is a mellow retreat during the day. At night, fast-flowing Guinness and occasional live music pulls in cosmopolitan crowds.

Crveni Petao (Map p386; ☎ 262 0050; Cara Lazara 16; ☽ 9am-2am) The place where locals come for their post-week wind-down and pre-weekend rev-up, Crveni Petao is an outdoor bar pleasantly plonked where two streets intersect. DJs and live music regularly feature.

ENTERTAINMENT

The club scene in Belgrade is only limited by imagination and hours in the day. Every night is Saturday night, and every mood and pace can be found in the city. Or under it. Or above it. The music is a smorgasbord of well-known European and local DJs playing house, R&B, hip-hop, drum and bass, or Balkans beats of turbofolk or lurid tones of jazz. It's all here.

If you'd rather take it easy, cinemas screen films in English (with Serbian subtitles) and concerts are held at the Sava Centar (p396).

Clubs
CITY CLUBS

Andergraund (Underground; Map p386; ☎ 063407070; www.andergraund.com; Pariška 1a; ☽ 10am-4am) The city's most famous nightspot is on a tiered terrace on the citadel walls and underneath in an old cavern where sweaty crowds gyrate. Regular local DJs include Acim, Dejan Milecevic and Kinetic Vibe. Global guests spin on Saturday.

White (Map p386; ☎ 063308039; Pariška 1a; ☽ 11am-4am) Next to Andergraund, White offers a markedly different atmosphere. Its entrance is white, its waiters wear white, and its clientele is…colourful. Perhaps less eclectic than Andergraund, White pulls in 20-something disco and house fans.

GLOBE-TROTTERS UNITE *Mirko Stanković*

I was working as a screen manager on movies and commercials before the NATO bombs fell in 1999. At this time, Serbia was isolated from the rest of the world. Things felt desolate, and the future was uncertain. I wanted to create a space where global free spirits could come together and exchange ideas and information. With some friends, I created that space in the basement of the building I was renting an apartment in. We called it the Federal Association of Globe-Trotters (see review, opposite). As a pledge of our commitment to defy borders in a city where the borders felt like they were clenching around us, we all contributed pieces of old furniture, pictures, and artefacts from all over the world. At a time when opportunities were limited, this was our way of living with no limits – of staying connected with each other and the world.

At first, it was mostly local people from Belgrade who came here, but as Serbia opened up, people started coming from everywhere. Diplomats, politicians, celebrities – even Oscar-winner Adrian Brody visited us. Now I own this place and plan to continually evolve it as Belgrade continues to evolve. I hope that more and more open-minded and open-hearted people from all over the world will come here to help in that process.

SERBIA

Akademija (Art Kafe 'Fleka'; Map p386; ☎ 627 846; www.akademija.net, in Serbian; Rajićeva 10; ☺ 10pm-4am Mon-Sat, noon-2am Sun) This dark, graffitied club is a Belgrade institution; alternative crowds and student activists have been rocking in this basement (to performers like Darkwood Dub) for the last two decades. Anything from funk and punk to reggae, electro or fetish happens in the bowels of Akademija. Despite recent refurbishments to bring this cult club into the 2000s, you can still feel its '80s soul.

Oh! Cinema! (Map p386; ☎ 328 4000; Kalemegdan Citadel; ☺ 11pm-4am) If only the former occupants of the citadel could see their descendants partying on its walls today. During the day, upbeat tunes at Oh! Cinema! coax you into early alcohol, and the view from the eastern bulwarks of the citadel keeps you drinking till dawn. This terrace bar is open only in summer.

Plastic (Map p386; ☎ 0646403956; www.club-plastic.com; cnr Dalmatinska & Takovska; ☺ 10pm-late Thu-Sat) A slick venue where DJs spin house, trance and techno, Plastic offers electric atmosphere with plenty of chill-out space to rest your dance-slammed bones. Be prepared to queue.

Bitef Art Cafe (Map p386; ☎ 063594294; www.bitefartcafe.co.yu; Skver Mire Trailović 1; ☺ 7pm-4am) Beloved particularly by funk, soul and jazz aficionados, Bitef Art Cafe is a converted church offering creative clubbing. It could be pop one night, a string quartet the next or even a straight-up sit-down performance.

DANUBE RIVER BARGES
Adjacent to Hotel Jugoslavija in Novi Belgrade is a kilometre-long strip of some 20 barges. Most are closed in winter. Get there with bus 15 or 84 from Zeleni Venac or bus 68, 603 or 701 from Trg Republike. Get out at Hotel Jugoslavija.

Blaywatch (Map p383; ☎ 064477771; www.blaywatch.net.yu; ☺ midnight-4am) The name says it all; equal-opportunists steer clear. This throbbing, fleshy place gets crowded, and dress codes may be enforced (sneakers bad on boys, skimpy good on girls).

Bibis (Map p383; ☎ 319 2150; www.bibis.co.yu; ☺ 10am-2am) With a subdued sports-bar vibe, Bibis is good for a chat and a drink before hitting larger and louder neighbouring barges. It's also popular in winter when other barges close.

Amsterdam (Map p383; ☎ 319 4971; ☺ 10am-4am) Floating cocktail bar and classy restaurant by day, sometimes with live bands at night.

Akapulco (Map p383; ☎ 778 4760; ☺ noon-3am) Where blinged-up boys come to flaunt their money and she-accessories. Stay away if you have a low turbofolk threshold.

Bahus (Map p383; ☎ 301 5802; www.bahus.rs; ☺ 10am-1pm) A chic multitiered A-list option with plush pastel lounge chairs geared for coffee or cocktails rather than clubbing.

SAVA RIVER BARGES
On the western bank of the Sava River is a 1.5km strip of floating bars, restaurants and discos known as 'splavs'. Most are only open in summer. Walk over Brankov Most, or take tram 7, 9 or 11.

Leading the pack at the time of research, enormous **Freestyler** (Map p386; ☎ 063300839; www.splavfree.rs; Brodaska bb; ☺ 1am-5am Thu-Sun) churns out house, techno and R&B to packed-in patrons. Nearby, **Exile** (Map p386; ☎ 0638190855; Savski kej bb; ☺ midnight-3am) pounds out techno and **Sound** (Map p386; Savski kej bb; ☺ midnight-3am) plays house and disco. Other floating favourites include **Babilon** (Map p386; Savski kej bb; ☎ 318 0232) and **Cruise** (Map p386; Savski kej bb; ☎ 215 7210).

Concerts & Theatre
Bilet Servis (Map p386; ☎ 303 3311; www.biletservis.co.yu; Trg Republike 5; ☺ 9am-11pm Mon-Sat, noon-10pm Sun) Concert and theatre ticketing agency.
Dom Omladine (Map p386; ☎ 324 8202; www.domomladine.org; Makedonska 22; ☺ ticket box 10am-10pm) Art and cultural events including music, film and multimedia.
Kolarčev University Concert Hall (Map p386; ☎ 630 550; Studentski Trg 5; ☺ box office 10am-noon & 6-8pm) Performances by Belgrade Philharmonia.
National Theatre (Map p386; ☎ 262 0946; www.narodnopozoriste.co.yu; Trg Republike; ☺ box office 10am-2pm Tue-Sun) Opera in winter.
Sava Centar (Map p383; ☎ 220 6060; www.savacentar.com; Milentija Popovića 9; ☺ ticket office 10am-8pm Mon-Fri, to 3pm Sat, 1hr before events) Major concerts and events.
Serbian Academy of Arts & Sciences (Map p386; ☎ 334 2400; www.saisu.ac.yu; Knez Mihailova 35; ☺ concerts 6pm Mon & Thu) Check windows for details on free concerts and exhibitions.

Cinemas
Cinemas showing the latest Hollywood blockbusters in English or with English subtitles:
Dom Sindikata (Map p386; ☎ 323 4849; www.dds.co.yu; Trg Nikole Pašića 5; tickets 200-250DIN)

Tuckwood Cineplex (Map p386; ☎ 323 6517; www
.tuck.co.yu; Kneza Miloša 7; tickets 150-280DIN)

SHOPPING

Belgrade's main street, Knez Mihailova, is
packed with global brands. If you seek souvenirs, consider jewellery, something lacy for
grandma's kitchen, or hand-knitted woollens
from vendors in Kalemegdan Park. Snoop
around **craft street market** (Map p386; cnr Kralja
Milana & Njegoševa; ⊗ 8am-5pm Mon-Sat) for handcrafted jewellery and original oil paintings.
Particularly nice Belgrade-themed stationery
can be found at IPS bookshop (see p382).

GETTING THERE & AWAY
Bus

Belgrade has two adjacent bus stations. **BAS**
(Map p386; ☎ 636 299; Železnička 4) serves the region,
Lasta (Map p386; ☎ 625 740; Železnička bb) deals with
destinations around Belgrade. If in doubt, it's
a fair guess to try BAS first.

Sample services are Subotica (440DIN, three
hours), Niš (460DIN, three hours), Podgorica
(940DIN, nine hours), Budva (1160DIN, 12
hours) and Novi Pazar (580DIN, three hours)
for Kosovo.

There are several daily services to Western
Europe; see the table, p422.

Train

The **central train station** (Map p386; ☎ 629 400; Savski
Trg 2) has a helpful **information office** (☎ 361 8497;
platform 1; ⊗ 7am-7pm). There's also a **tourist office**
(☎ 361 2732; ⊗ 9am-8pm Mon-Fri, 9am-5pm Sat, 10am-
4pm Sun) for basic city information, an **exchange
bureau** (⊗ 6am-10pm) and a **sales counter** (☎ /fax
265 8868; ⊗ 9am-4pm Mon-Sat) for Eurail passes at
the track end of the station.

You can also buy bus and train tickets in
town at Putnik Travel Agency (p390).

Overnight trains run from Belgrade to Bar
(1000DIN plus three-/six-berth couchette
1000/564DIN, 11½ hours). Frequent trains go
to Novi Sad (199DIN, 1½ hours) and Subotica
(420DIN, three hours).

For international trains, see p422.

GETTING AROUND
To/From the Airport

Nikola Tesla Airport is 18km from Belgrade.
The **JAT bus** (☎ 675 583) connects the airport
with the JAT bus terminal at Trg Slavija via the
train station (200DIN; 7am to 10pm hourly
from airport, 5am to 9pm hourly from town,

or coordinated with scheduled JAT flights).
Alternatively, bus 72 connects the airport
with Zeleni Venac (60DIN on bus, 46DIN
from newsstands; 5am to midnight from airport, 4.40am to 11.40pm from town, every
30 minutes).

Don't fall in the pit of taxi sharks outside
the airport (who will ask up to €30 for a 30-
minute ride that shouldn't cost more than
€15). Ask the tourist office in the arrivals
hall to call a taxi for you. Generally, a taxi
from the airport to Knez Mihailova should
be 1100DIN.

Car & Motorcycle

Parking in Belgrade isn't fun. It's regulated
by three parking zones (red, one hour; yellow, two hours; green, three hours) for which
tickets must be bought from kiosks or via SMS
(best avoided if you don't read Serbian).

Public Transport

Trams and trolleybuses serve limited routes,
but buses go all over downtown, and to Novi
Beograd and the suburbs.

Tickets cost 29DIN from a street kiosk
or 40DIN from the driver; punch tickets
on board.

Tram 2 is useful for connecting Kalemegdan
Citadel with Trg Slavija, bus stations and the
central train station.

Taxi

Whatever experience you have with taxi drivers at the airport and the train stations, don't
hold it against all of them – they're mostly a
good lot. Move away from transport hubs and
flag down a distinctly labelled cruising cab.

If the meter's not running, point this
out to the driver. Flag fall is 98DIN and the
rate per kilometre depends on the time of
day (and the company). A 5km trip costs
around 200DIN.

AROUND BELGRADE

ZEMUN ЗЕМУН

Some 8km northwest of central Belgrade on
the southern bank of the Danube, Zemun
was the most southerly point of the Austro-
Hungarian Empire when the Turks ruled
Belgrade. Considered part of Belgrade these
days, Zemun feels like a slow-paced 'town
within a city', lined with Austro-Hungarian

SERBIA

houses. It's hard to imagine that the notorious criminal 'Zemun clan' hailed from such a quaint place.

Above the market area and up the narrow cobbled street of Grobnjačka, remnants of the old village lead uphill towards the **Gardoš**, a fortress with origins going back to the 9th century. Fifteenth-century walls remain, as does the **Tower of Sibinjanin Janko**. Built in 1896 to celebrate the millennial anniversary of the Hungarian state and to keep an eye on the Turks, the tower guards the city like a misplaced lighthouse.

Down the stairs descending from the tower is **Nikolajevska church** (Njegoševa 43), dating to 1731. Gleaming out of the gloom is an astoundingly beautiful iconostasis carved in baroque style.

At the time of writing, **Zemun Museum** (☎ 316 5234; Glavna 9) was closed for extensive renovations that will hopefully be worth the wait.

Sleeping & Eating
Between Zemun and Belgrade, try fabulous floating Arka Barka (see p392).

Hotel Skala (☎ 307 5032; Bežanijska 3; s/d/apt 6300/8100/9000DIN; ✂ 🖳) At this top-notch choice the lobby wraps around a covered courtyard overlooking the basement restaurant, a charming place for meals under intimate arches. Rooms are homely, with warm wooden furniture and wi-fi.

Aleksandar (☎ 199 462; Kej Oslobođenja 49; meals 500DIN; ✆ 9am-midnight) A fun fish lunch can be found here, where the expansive menu's offerings are hauled from sea and river. Try fiery-red *riblja čorba* (peppery fish soup).

Venecija (☎ 307 7611; Kej Oslobođenja bb; meals from 600DIN; ✆ 9am-midnight) This is another good choice, with a white terrace overhanging the water and striped poles attempting to evoke Venetian vibes.

Reka (☎ 261 1625; www.reka.co.yu; Kej Oslobođenja 73b; fish mains 600-1000DIN) At this vibrant place offering live music most nights you can wash down grilled trout or smoked chicken (both 690DIN) with something from the wine list.

Bella Napoli (☎ 219 8162; www.bellanapoli.co.yu; Zmaj Jovina 35; meals 300-600DIN; ✆ noon-midnight Tue-Sun) An ambient Italian choice.

Getting There & Away
Zemun is a 45-minute walk from Belgrade. Cross Branko Bridge (Brankov Most) and follow bul Nikole Tesle through the green patch

until you can pick up the Kej Oslobođenja waterside walkway.

Alternatively, take bus 15 or 84 from Zeleni Venac market, or bus 83 outside the main train station. Tickets cost 40DIN on the bus, or 29DIN from a newsstand.

SMEDEREVO СМЕДЕРЕВО
☎ 026 / pop 77,800
Head to Smederevo if you like fortresses. This small town 46km southeast of Belgrade served as the capital in 1427, and hosted the seat of government again from 1805 to 1807. When Smederevo was liberated from Turkish rule it's said that Karađorđe was presented with the city keys under the old mulberry tree that still stands today.

Shockingly large, **Smederevo fortress** (admission 50DIN; ✆ 8am-8pm) is a triangular fort with 25 towers and a moat, built by Despot Đurađ Brankovic with the intention of holding off the Turks. The fortification was eventually captured in 1459, but given that it took more than 20 years to conquer, it is impressive that its labour force threw it up in only a couple of years. The main damage is the result of neglect, and the enormous explosion of an ammunition train in WWII.

Lovingly maintained **Smederevo Museum** (☎ 222 138; admission 70DIN; ✆ 10am-5pm Tue-Fri, to 3pm Sat & Sun) is a 'history of the town' museum with artefacts dating from Roman times. There's little in English, but walking around its exhibition spaces (probably by yourself) is pleasant.

The museum is a block left of the bus station. The fortress is just beyond, across the train tracks – if you can't see it there's no hope for you. The **tourist information center** (☎ 615 666; Kralja Petra I 8; ✆ 8am-8pm Mon-Fri, 9am-7pm Sat) can provide basic information.

Getting There & Away
There are regular buses to and from Smederevo (330DIN, 1½ hours, every 15 minutes) from Belgrade's Lasta station.

GOLUBAC FORTRESS ГОЛУБАЦ
The surreal experience of Golubac fortress takes a little effort but is well worth it for the imaginative high it'll give you.

The fortress was built by the Hungarians in the 13th century, later captured by the Turks, eventually becoming Serbian in the late 19th century. Nine stone towers remain in an evocative state of ruination. Elsewhere this would be chalked up as a highlight and a high admission fee charged, but here it sits as if no one noticed it grow supernaturally from Ðerdap Gorge. There are no hand railings or barriers; if you're not careful you could plunge to a gloomy end or get steamrolled by a vehicle hurtling through its tunnels.

Getting There & Away

A handful of buses head to Golubac (500DIN, two hours) from BAS bus station in Belgrade. Those continuing to Kladovo literally pass through the fortress; ask to be dropped off there.

Alternatively, the fortress is an hour's walk from Golubac bus station. Walk to the water's edge and you'll see the fortress on your right. Follow the path until you reach the stairs. Follow the road left; enjoy the view and watch for cars. And snakes.

VOJVODINA
ВОЈВОДИНА

Some of Serbia's highlights spring forth from the strikingly level plains of Vojvodina. The region is a rich mix of Hungarian and Balkans cultures and traditions. Its capital, Novi Sad, hosts Exit – one of the freshest festivals in the Balkans. Nearby are the rolling hills of Fruška Gora, pierced by monasteries and home to the enchanting town of Sremski Karlovci, once the base of the Serbian Orthodox patriarchate. Closer to Hungary in distance and identity is Subotica, an art deco dream.

Despite the laid-back pace prevailing in these parts, there's always a festival happening somewhere, in honour of anything from bee-keeping or beer to tobacco or tolerance.

NOVI SAD НОВИ САД

☎ 021 / pop 299,000

When it's not hosting Serbia's biggest music festival, Novi Sad is a happy town just for the hell of it. Cafes spill onto the main thoroughfare, which locals prowl for popcorn or ice cream, and atmospheric alleyways become energetic social centres after dark. All of this is presided over by Petrovaradin Citadel, atop a mighty volcanic rock.

Novi Sad is well organised, accessible and a great base for Fruška Gora.

Orientation

The train and intercity bus stations are next to each other at the northern end of bul Oslobođenja. A 2.5km walk straight down this and left on Pavla Papa leads to the centre. Alternatively, take bus 11Λ to the city bus station. One block south of here is Zmaj Jovina, the heart of Novi Sad, dominated by the Catholic cathedral with its chequered roof tiles. Leading off this are small streets of varying character; cobbled Dunavska is a hub of shops and cafes, while Laze Telečkog is the place to drink the night away.

Two road bridges lead over the Danube to the eastern bank and old town; Glavni Most delivers you to the foot of the citadel.

Information

For general info, consult the **Tourist Organisation of Vojvodina** (www.vojvodinaonline.com). There are two banks on central Trg Slobode: **Raiffeisen** (☎ 488 0200; ☽ 8am-7pm Mon-Fri, 9am-3pm Sat) and **UniCredit** (www.unicreditbank.co.yu; Trg Slobode 3; ☽ 9am-4.30pm Mon, Tue, Wed & Fri, to 6pm Thu).

Apoteka Pharmacy (☎ 402 820; www.apoteka novisad.co.rs; ☽ 7.30am-9pm Mon-Fri, 7am-9pm Sat) Gorgeous art deco pharmacy.

Autoturist (☎ 523 863; www.autoturist.co.yu; Mite Ruzica 2; ☽ 8am-8pm Mon to Fri, to 2pm Sat) Bus tickets and local tours.

Internet Club Net 21 (☎ 0642235010; Zmaj Jovina 14; per hr 50DIN; ☽ 24hr)

IPS Megastore (☎ 421 302; Zmaj Jovina 16; ☽ 9am-9pm Mon-Sat) CDs, DVDs, novels and travel guides.

JAT Airways (☎ 456 397; www.jat.com; Mihajla Pupina 18; ☽ 9am-5pm Mon-Fri)

KSR Beograd Tours (☎ 527 455; Svetozara Miletića 4; ☽ 7am-7pm Mon-Fri, to 1pm Sat) Train information and tickets at train-station prices.

Kym Internet Cafe (☎ 423 161; cnr Laze Telečkoq & Mite Tuzica; per hr 65DIN; ☽ 24hr) Minimum 30 minutes.

Main post office (☎ 614 708; Narodnih Heroja 2; ☽ 9am-9pm Mon-Sat, 10am-6pm Sun) Also telephone centre. Next to giant New Nork shopping centre.

Tourist information centre (☎ 421 811; www.novisadtourism.org.yu; Mihajla Pupina 9; ☽ 8.30am-8pm Mon-Thu, 7.30am-8pm Fri, 7.30am-2pm Sat) The place to start; professional people can direct you in and around Novi Sad.

Sights

PETROVARADIN CITADEL ПЕТРОВАРАДИН
Designed by French architect Vauban, the Petrovaradin Citadel is impressively perched overlooking the river. In the 88 years it took

to build the citadel (from 1692 to 1780) it's estimated that the daily death toll was 70 to 80 of the slaves, murderers and thieves who were 'earning their purgatory' by building it. Dubbed 'hell' by those unfortunate souls, it is now more affectionately referred to as the 'Gibraltar of the Danube'.

Petrovaradin was built to protect the town from Turkish invasions and was mainly populated by Austro-Hungarian army soldiers. Notable prisoners held within its dungeons include Karađorđe and a young Tito (albeit not at the same time). The town's 'ladies of the night' entertained the soldiers and the best Hungarian Roma came to play in the village below.

Within the citadel's walls the **museum** (433 613, 433 145; muzgns@eunet.yu; admission 100DIN; 9am-5pm Tue-Sun) is beautifully laid out but could use some English captions. There's striking artwork on the 1st floor.

The citadel's **clock tower** was erected by the Austrians, who introduced a 'clock tax' for each house that could see it – practically the entire town.

MUSEUM OF VOJVODINA

The **Museum of Vojvodina** (Muzej Vojvodine; 420 566; www.muzejvojvodine.org.yu; Dunavska 35-37; admission 100DIN; 9am-5pm Tue-Sun) houses historical, archaeological and ethnological exhibits. Building 35 covers Vojvodinian history from Palaeolithic times to the late 19th century; 37 takes the story to 1945 with harrowingly detailed emphasis on WWI and WWII. A committed visit will send you away with increased knowledge and appreciation of Serbia.

Festivals & Events

Some festivals are worth making the trip (and booking accommodation in advance) for. The biggest is July's **Exit festival** (see the boxed text, opposite), which secures a stellar line-up each year. The **Cinema City Festival** (www.cinemacity.org) in June may do for movies what Exit has done for music. September's **International Festival of Street Musicians** (www.cekans.org.yu) turns the town's streets into an open-air stage. **Novi Sad Jazz Festival** (www.kcns.org.yu) has been held each November since 1979 and gets better every year.

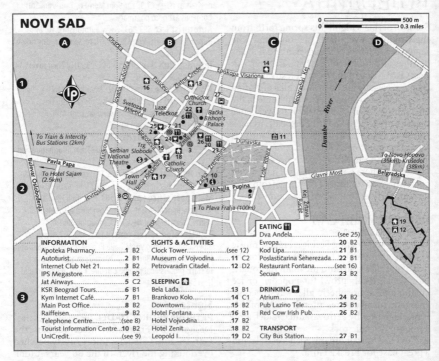

NOVI SAD

> ### ENTERING THE STATE OF EXIT
>
> Every July, people unite around Petrovaradin Citadel for the epic **Exit festival** (www.exitfest.org; 4 days approx €90, camping pass approx €18). The first, in 2000, lasted 100 days and is remembered for having energised a generation of young Serbs against Milošević. Since then it has grown to attract performers and audiences from around the region and beyond to positively promote cultural diversity while actively raising awareness on issues such as human trafficking, substance abuse and unemployment. At the 2006 Exit festival, revellers were issued with not tickets but passports to the State of Exit – the 'newest Balkan state' and a decidedly peaceful one. More than 190,000 visitors attended the star-studded 2007 Exit festival, 30% of whom were foreigners. Its line-up included the Beastie Boys, Groove Armada, Lauryn Hill, Robert Plant, Snoop Dogg and the Prodigy. The likes of Manu Chau, Primal Scream, the Sex Pistols and the Hives attended Exit in 2008...along with more than 100,000 people from the Balkans and beyond, collectively contributing to Petrovaradin Citadel's ongoing role as a bulwark of culture.

Sleeping

BUDGET

Downtown (☎ 64 192 0342; www.hotelsnovisad.com; Njegoševa 2; per person €10) Downtown can be booked online through hostelworld.com, but if you just rock up you'll be given coffee and conversation if not a bed. The hostel is in good order – bathrooms glisten and rooms can be arranged in a variety of configurations to suit different group sizes. There's one twin room.

Brankovo Kolo (☎ /fax 528 623; www.hostelns.com; Episkopa Visariona 3; d/tr/q per person €8/7/6; ☼ 1 Jul-25 Aug; **P** **Д**) A centrally located hostel with comfortable shared areas, Brankovo Kolo is a great option (only in summer). Book well ahead.

MIDRANGE

Hotel Zenit (☎ 621 444; www.hotelzenit.co.yu; Zmaj Jovina 8; s 4700-5700DIN; d 5700-6500DIN, tr 8200DIN; apt for 2/4/6 people 10,000/12,400/15,100DIN; **P** **✕** **Д**) A glass-fronted hotel with cosy rooms in a prime location, Zenit is popular with foreign visitors because it's efficiently run but comfortable and personal. There are two single rooms in the cheaper 4330DIN category that are significantly smaller than standards.

Hotel Fontana (☎ 621 779; www.fontana-ns.com; Pašićeva 27; s/d/tr 2800/3300/4000DIN; **P** **✕**) Casual, cosy Fontana has well-sized rooms with slanting wooden roofs overlooking the courtyard. Bathrooms are clean and serviceable (despite showers you have to share with a boiler and an overly affectionate shower curtain). The courtyard restaurant makes for a familial atmosphere.

Hotel Vojvodina (☎ 622 122; www.hotelvojvodina .co.yu; Trg Slobode 2; s/d from 3100/4400DIN) The last state-run hotel in town is often full because of its location overlooking the central square. Rooms are run-down compared to newer kids on the block, but atmosphere here dates to 1854.

Bela Lađa (☎ 06616594; Zlatne Grede 15; www.bela ladja.com; per person from €15; **P** **Д** **✕**) Bela Lada is something between a hostel and a hotel. Various room configurations can fit one to five people. Book ahead through www.hos telworld.com during festivals.

Hotel Sajam (☎ 420 766; www.hotelsajam.co.yu; Hajduk Veljkova 11; s/d/tr 3610/4480/5400DIN; **P** **✕** **Д**) Slightly out of town but reasonable value, Sajam has a bar and restaurant on premises and pleasantly lit rooms with writing desks. Breakfast coffee is undrinkable; buy a real one at the bar.

TOP END

Leopold I (☎ 488 7878; www.leopoldns.com; citadel; s 9900-10,725DIN, d 7425-14,025DIN, apt 15,676-29,700DIN) Standard rooms aren't the size you'd expect for the price you pay, but they're special. Renovated a year ago, Leopold I's infinite corridors evoke the luxurious era of the citadel in its heyday. Its 60 rooms are in Gothic, Renaissance or the more economical modern style. The cherry on the cake is the Leopold I apartment, truly fit for a kaiser – or a family of four.

Eating

Kod Lipa (☎ 615 259; Svetozara Miletića 7; meals from 250DIN; ☼ 8am-11pm) Atmosphere here transports you to traditional times of Vojvodinian cooking. Opened in the late 19th century, Kod Lipa has old photographs showing that little has changed since then. Descend into the converted cellars and smell mellow wine in the vast barrels; there's seating among them within secluded alcoves.

Dva Anđela (☎ 662 4989; Laze Telečkog 14; average main 500DIN; 🕑 9am-11pm Mon-Thu, 9am-1am Fri & Sat, 11am-11pm Sun) Dva Anđela is a slick new place with iPod-cool interiors located in the heart of the action along Laze Telečkog. The penne pasta with porcini (440DIN) is a treat, and salads are enormous. Nab a table out the front for prime people-watching position.

Sečuan (☎ 529 693; Dunavska 16; average main 550DIN; 🕑 10am-11pm) Opened in 1981 when Novi Sad hosted the table-tennis championships; locals still love it today.

Plava Frajla (☎ 613 675; www.plavafrajla.rs; Sutjeska 2; meals 300-400DIN; 🕑 9am-midnight) A popular choice for Novi Sadians, especially on raucous weekends when traditional music lifts spirits up to the chairs hanging from the roof. Find it at SPENS sport centre opposite the football stadium.

Restaurant Fontana (☎ 0643517914; www.restoran fontana.com; meals from 400DIN; 🕑 9am-late) This tucked-away oasis serves traditional food loved by locals. Eat in the ambient dining room or around the fountain in the courtyard. Staff can guide you to specialities like stuffed kebabs (550DIN).

Evropa (Dunavska 6; cakes 50-100DIN; 🕑 8am-midnight) Follow the crowds here for *žito*, the traditional dessert made of crushed wheat and walnuts.

Poslastičarnica Šeherezada (☎ 623 280; Zmaj Jovina 19; desserts 140DIN; 🕑 8am-1am) This ice creamery throws cold calorie bombs onto the main street.

Drinking

Laze Telečkog is lined with bars of different moods and characters.

Atrium (www.atriumclub.rs; Laze Telečkog 2; 🕑 9am-midnight) Wrapped around the promising corner of Laze Telečkog and Zmaj Jovina, Atrium offers seating in a faux library, upstairs on balconies, or on the main thoroughfare. Perfect for drinks or desserts.

Red Cow Irish Pub (cnr Dunavska & Zmaj Jovina; 🕑 8am-1am) A young crowd spends its evenings in this faux Irish pub. There's tonnes of seating in the bar area and the upstairs attic room. Go into the courtyard opposite the city library on Zmaj Jovina, and climb to the 1st floor.

Pub Lazino Tele (www.lazinotele.com; Laze Telečkog 16; 🕑 8am-1am) Part Irish pub and part London bar with red phone booths inside and tables

and drinks spilling outside. There's a bit of everything here: TV for sports fans, DJs and live musicians, a range of beers and a long list of cocktails…it's a good choice on a street of endless choices. Check the website for upcoming events.

Getting There & Away

There are frequent trains linking the **train station** (☎ 443 200; bul Jaše Tomića 4) with Belgrade (330DIN, 1½ hours) and Subotica (290DIN, 1½ hours).

The **bus station** (☎ 442 021; bul Jaše Tomića 6; 🕑 info counter 6am-11pm) is immediately next to the train station. There are frequent buses to Belgrade (590DIN, one hour, every 10 minutes) and Subotica (690DIN, two hours) but the latter are more expensive and slower than trains. Buses also go to Uzice (950DIN, five hours) and Zlatibor (1060DIN, six hours).

There are also bus links to Austria, the Czech Republic, France, Italy, Macedonia, Budapest, Germany and Sweden.

FRUŠKA GORA ФРУШКА ГОРА

Fruška Gora is an 80km stretch of rolling hills punctuated by 16 monasteries where life continues as it has for centuries. Thirty-five monasteries were built between the 15th and 18th centuries to preserve Serbian culture and religion from the Turks. The 16 that remain still play an important role in cultural life, with christenings and weddings on weekends.

There are around 800km of marked paths through the area, making time and good shoes the best approach to the park. For more, see www.npfruskagora.co.yu.

Krušedol and Novo Hopovo are perhaps the best-known and easily accessible monasteries.

Krušedol monastery, near Krušedol Selo, was built by Đorđe Branković between 1509 and 1516. The church – dedicated to the Annuciation – was burnt down by the Turks in 1716 and rebuilt later; the residencies date from 1753. The four central pillars are 16th-century originals. Vivid frescos leap from the walls as a biblical storyboard. Originally painted in 1545, they were repainted between 1745 and 1757.

Novo Hopovo, near Irig, is one of the oldest of the region's monasteries (1576), and in one of the loveliest settings for walks. It suffered severe damage during WWII. Restoration of the frescos revealed earlier work painted under the influence of Cretan masters who also worked at Mt Athos monastery in Greece. Many frescos are incomplete but present powerful images. Icons inside the monastery were painted in 1776 by Serbian baroque artist Teodor Kračun.

Grgeteg monastery was abandoned in 1690 but revived in the early 1700s. Its centrepiece is the icon of the Holy Mother Trojeručica (meaning 'of three hands'), a copy of the famous icon from Hilander monastery at Mt Athos, in front of which prayers are sung.

The 16th-century **Velika Remeta** was built entirely of bricks rather than stone. Its bell tower was erected in 1735; at almost 40m it's the highest in the region.

Other monasteries in the area include **Mala Remeta**, apparently first built with the support of King Dragutin Nemanjić, **Vrdnik** (or Ravanica), with a classicist church constructed in the early 1800s, and **Jazak**, built between 1736 and 1758 and reconstructed between 1926 and 1930.

It may be possible to stay at **Norcev** (☎ 480 0222; Partizanski put hh, Iriški Venac Elektrovojvodina; s from €32, d from €42, ste from €62) near Iriški Venac.

Getting There & Away

With your own wheels you can freely flit between monasteries. Otherwise, the easiest way to cover ground and gain insight is with a tour; ask at tourist offices in Novi Sad and Sremski Karlovci. Alternatively, take public transport to villages within the park and walk between sights; eg, take a bus from Novi Sad bound for Irig and ask to be let out at the Novo Hopovo monastery (150DIN, 30 minutes), an easy five-minute walk from the main road. From there, walk or catch local buses to other points such as Vrdnik. If you do this, bring a map like the Geokarta 1:60000 *Fruška Gora* (210DIN), available at bookshops in Novi Sad.

SREMSKI KARLOVCI
СРЕМСКИ КАРЛОВЦИ

The elegant buildings of Sremski Karlovci don't fit here at the edge of Fruška Gora. Located on the banks of the Danube as a gateway to Serbian Orthodox monasteries, the town is lathered in historical significance. The Romans brought grapevines from southern Italy, giving rise to the region's wine culture.

The **tourist organisation** (☎ 882 128, 883 855; www.karlovci.co.yu; Branka Radičevića 7; ☺ 9am-5pm Mon-Sat) on the main square offers maps and information and can arrange guided tours in and around Sremski Karlovci (including wine tasting) and Fruška Gora.

Sremski Karlovci was the centre of the Serbian Orthodox Church in the 19th century and has a magnificent baroque **Orthodox cathedral** (1758–62) with an impressive iconostasis and 18th-century icons. Also on the square are the neoclassical **town hall** (1806–11) and **grammar school building**, a cross between art nouveau and traditional Serbian style. The school began functioning in 1792 and now houses the School of Theology. The baroque **Four Lions fountain** was built in 1799 by Italian architect Giuseppe Aprilli; legend says that if you drink from it you will return to Sremski Karlovci and/or get married.

Off the square, down Mitropolita Stratimirovića, is the small white **Lower church** with a ghostly white plane tree.

The **Museum of Bee-Keeping and Wine Cellar** (☎ 881 071; muzpcela@eunet.yu; Mitropolita Stratimirovića 86) is run by Žarka Živanović, descendent of esteemed language professor and bee-keeper Jovan Živanović. The museum represents 40 generations of bee-keeping and six generations of winemaking, making it a good place to try the famous *bermet* wine.

The round **Chapel of Peace** sits on the southern side of town. It was here that the Peace Treaty between the Turks and Austrians was signed in 1699. The chapel (1817) was designed to resemble a Turkish military tent with four entrances enabling everyone to simultaneously enter as equal parties.

Sleeping & Eating

Hotel Dunav (☎ 883 735; www.hoteldunav.co.yu; Dunavska 5; s/d/tr 4180/5018/5818DIN) The only option in town is a good one, letting you eat and sleep by the Danube. The casino on the premises in no way detracts from the family-friendly feel.

Četri Lava (☎ 765 8160; Branka Radičevića 1; meals 200-400DIN) This cosy restaurant offers good-value meals in a cellar-style dining room. Try the trout (440DIN per 300g).

Getting There & Away

Buses 61 and 62 frequently travel to and from Novi Sad (100DIN, 30 minutes). If you catch a bus from a stop outside the main bus station you'll avoid the 35DIN platform charge. The last regular bus back from Sremski Karlovci leaves at 11.25pm; there's another a lot later at 2.30am.

SERBIA

SUBOTICA СУБОТИЦА

☎ 024 / pop 148,400

Hungarian cultural influences drift over the border into Subotica. Serbian and Hungarian languages mingle in the streets, the smell of goulash wafts through the air, and art nouveau buildings (1908–12) sparkle in this proud provincial town. It was in Subotica that Czinner – a central character in Graham Greene's *Stamboul Train* – was arrested en route to Constantinople. Subotica is a day trip from Belgrade or Novi Sad, or a stopover on the way to Hungary.

Orientation & Information

The art nouveau Modern Art Gallery is through the park opposite the train station on Đure Đakovića; it's one of the most beautiful buildings in the country. Facing the museum, walk left along Đure Đakovića. You will find the pedestrian street Korzo around 100m along on your right. The bus station is about 1km along.

Bookshop (☎ 551 845; ☺ 7.30am-7pm Mon-Fri, to 1pm Sat) Old-world bookshop through the park opposite the clock tower. Sells *Subotica Views* by Boška Krstić.

Exchange office (train station; ☺ 8am-6.30pm Mon-Sat, to 7pm Sun)

Left-luggage office (train station; per item 60DIN; ☺ 24hr)

Pireus Bank (☺ 9am-5pm Mon-Fri, to 1pm Sun) ATM and Western Union transfer.

Raiffeisen Bank (☺ 8am-7pm Mon-Fri, 9am-3pm Sat)

Tourist information office (☎ 670 350; ticsu@sub otica.net; town hall; ☺ 8am-8pm Mon-Sat, to noon Sun) Pamphlets and advice on the park side of the town hall.

Sights

Subotica's main attraction is art nouveau architecture. Most sights are along Korzo and on the main square, Trg Republike.

The **town hall** (Trg Republike), built in 1910, is a curious mix of art nouveau and something Gaudí may have had a playful dab at. It houses an engaging **historical museum** (admission 50DIN; ☺ 10am-2pm Tue-Fri, to 1pm Sat) displaying regional life and the skull of a mammoth. If the exquisitely decorated council chambers are open, don't miss them.

One of the most stunning buildings in Serbia is the graceful **Modern Art Gallery** (☎ 552 651; liksus@tippnet.co.yu; Trg Lenjina 5; admission 50DIN; ☺ 8am-6pm Mon-Fri, 9am-noon Sat), adorned with mosaics, floral patterns, ceramic tiles and stained-glass windows.

On the main square, the 1854 **National Theatre building** is a Romanesque terracotta structure resting on six heavy pillars; it houses Serbia's oldest theatre.

Along Korzo, the building shared by the **Continental** and **Piraeus** banks is another art nouveau gem. A little further away is the first art nouveau building to have sprung up in Subotica, the **synagogue**. The building is magnificent, making it all the more tragic that, apart from a commemorative stone placed in 1994 in memory of the 4000 Jewish citizens of Subotica killed during WWII, the building lies in inaccessible tatters. Hopefully, renovations will change this.

Sleeping

At the time of writing, fading Hotel Patria (a few hundred metres to the left as you leave the train station) was being extensively renovated. Hopefully, when it's up and running it will fill the midrange gap in accommodation.

Hostel Bosa Milećević (☎ 548 290; 7 Marije Vojnić Tošinice br 7; per person 930DIN) Hostel Bosa Milećević is a hidden budget gem, albeit too well hidden behind the Ekonomski Fakultet at Segedinksi put 11. Accommodation is in bright rooms with two beds, desks, lockable cupboards, fresh sheets and towels. Bathrooms and kitchenettes are communal, but you may have them to yourself.

Hotel Galleria (☎ 647 111; www.galleria-center .com; Matije Korvina 17; standard s/d 4800/6400DIN, apt s 8000-18,000DIN, d 9600-24,000DIN; Ⓟ ⓧ 🖳) The 'Atrium' plaza at the end of cafe-lined Matije Korvina houses the four-star Hotel Galleria, with fitness centre, rooftop restaurant and spacious rooms decked out in warm mahogany-look furniture. Bookshelves framing the bed are a nice touch. Two rooms are wheelchair equipped.

Hotel PBG (☎ 556 542; www.pbghotel.co.yu; Harambašićeva 21; s/d from 2320/4000DIN; Ⓟ ⓧ 🖳) This down-to-earth and more homely alternative to the Galleria is located slightly further from the centre.

Eating

Boss Caffe (☎ 551 111; www.bosscaffe.com; Matije Korvina 8; ☺ 7am-midnight Mon & Wed-Sat, to 1am Sun & Tue; Ⓥ) Truly the boss of Korvina, with pizzeria, cafe and bar, the best of Boss is immediately behind the Modern Art Gallery; enjoy art nouveau surrounds and eclectic food such as tacos (195DIN to 375DIN) or a generous vegetarian plate (385DIN). Many dishes are offered in starter and main sizes.

Baskuca (☎ 55 2292; www.baskuca.com; cnr JJ Zmaja & Cara Lazara; ⊙ 9am-2am Mon-Sat, 4pm-midnight Sun) This cool yellow-and-blue building is where hip Suboticans come for food and chat.

Ravel (☎ 554 670; Nušićeva 2; cakes 50-100DIN; ⊙ 9am-10pm Mon-Sat, 11am-10pm Sun) One of the loveliest cafes you're likely to set foot in. Ravel's art nouveau interior seems untouched for a century, with pastel-green walls and golden lamps. Choose a cake and soak up the sun by its large windows.

Getting There & Away
From the **train station** (☎ 555 606) there are two trains to Szeged, Hungary (240DIN, 1¾ hours). Trains to Belgrade (480DIN, 3½ hours) call at Novi Sad (400DIN, 1½ hours). It's possible to day trip to Subotica if you get an early train.

The **bus station** (☎ 555 566; Marksov Put) has hourly buses to Novi Sad (650DIN, two hours) and Belgrade (900DIN, 3½ hours).

PALIĆ ПАЛИЋ
Summer crowds from Serbia and Hungary flock to the resort of Palić. Its centrepiece is the 5-sq-km lake for boating, swimming and fishing, encircled by a 17km-long cycling and walking path. Bike- and boat-hire places are dotted around the lake, as are cafes and restaurants. Shops, supermarkets and restaurants can be found along Subotica road near the bus stop. In mid-July Palić hosts a **European film festival** (☎ 554 600; www.palicfilmfestival.com).

Accommodation is generally in villas with ornately carved wooden verandahs, many of which are modelled on Swiss summer houses. The **tourist information office** (☎ 753 111; www.palic .co.yu; Kanjiški put 17a; ⊙ 8am-6pm) can help filter through accommodation options.

From Subotica, take bus 6 diagonally opposite Hotel Patria (heading under the railway bridge) to Palić (40DIN, 20 minutes). Get out at the distinct gate with its Olympic-torch-shaped tower and walk down the lane. Alternatively, a taxi costs around 300DIN for the 8km drive.

VRŠAC ВРШАЦ
☎ 013 / pop 54,000
A nice town to wander through en route to Romania (10km away), freakily flat Vršac is full of reminders of Serbia's Austro-history.

Long, orderly streets are lined with well-preserved Austro-Hungarian buildings, with an occasional baroque gem. Nearby, the Vršac mountains add some altitude to the otherwise perfectly parallel Banat plain. Around 10% of Vršacians are Romanian.

Orientation & Information
From the centre, Miloša Obilića leads northwest towards the bus and train stations. At the forking intersection, the bus station is to the right and the train station straight on. They are flat 15- and 25-minute walks respectively.

The **Tourist Organization of Vršac** (☎ 831 056; www.to.vrsac.com; Trg Pobede 1; ⊙ 8am-7pm Mon-Sat) is on a distinctive corner behind the town hall. Next door is **Hemo.net** (per hr 100DIN; ⊙ 8am-11pm) internet cafe.

There are several banks, including **Hypo Group Bank** (Dvorska 1; ⊙ 8am-5pm Mon-Fri, to 1pm Sat).

Sights
The **Pharmacy on the Steps museum** (☎ 838 053; ⊙ 10am-1pm & 6-8pm Sun & sometimes Sat) is set in the oldest pharmacy in Vršac, dating to 1784. With rather inconvenient opening hours, it covers the history of pharmaceutical health-care in the area and pays tribute to the art of Paja Jovanović, whose brother worked here.

Banat Patriarchial Residence on Jaše Omića is a fine example of baroque architecture. Completed in 1763, the house contains a chapel dedicated to St Archangel Synod.

Across the road, the oldest **Orthodox church** in Vršac (1785) contains works of celebrated local artists, including Paja Jovanović.

The **Tower of Vršac** is believed to have been built in 1439 by Đurađ Brankovic. Little remains of the tower, but it offers wonderful views of the region. Walk 400m up the stairs (ask for directions at the distinct glass Millennium centre) or take a taxi for around 250DIN.

Vršac has been a wine-loving region since Roman times. Grozdjebal (Grape Ball) is held in the third weekend of September. Try to buy regional wines at **Vršački Vinogradi** (Svetosavski trg 1; ⊙ 8am-8pm Mon-Sat), diagonally opposite Hotel Srbija.

Sleeping & Eating
Hotel Srbija (☎ 835 545; hotelsrbija@hemo.net; Svetosavski Trg 12; s 2295-2580DIN; d 4020DIN; apt s/d/tr 3075/4780/6030DIN; ⊠) At this central hotel the

renovated 'lux' rooms offer minibars and newer bathrooms, but even standard rooms have TV and air-con.

Grand Caffe (☎ 0658900089; Trg Save Kovačevića 40; average meal 330DIN; ☽ 7am-midnight Mon-Fri, to 2am Sat & Sun) On the pedestrian area, this cafe offers pizza, pasta and pancakes.

Hermes Pekara (Trg Pobede 2; ☽ 6am-midnight Mon-Fri, 6am-1am Sat) A local favourite for freshly baked pasties, Hermes is opposite the tourist office.

Getting There & Away
More than 20 daily buses go to Vršacc (570DIN, 1½ to two hours) from Belgrade. Back to Belgrade, trains are less regular and much slower than buses (call ☎ 839 900).

SOUTHERN SERBIA

Some great adventures are to be found south of Belgrade. Zlatibor's rolling hills are a peaceful privilege to explore any time of year. Dramatic Kopoanik is a popular ski destination for Europeans in the know. Pressed against interesting Balkans neighbours is the melding cultural heritages of the Raška region (known interchangeably by the Turkish 'Sandžak'), the last to be liberated from Ottoman rule, in 1912. Following integration of the region into the Kingdom of Serbs, Croats and Slovenes, many Sandžak Muslims migrated to Turkey. It's estimated that there are more Muslims of Raška origin in Turkey than are left in the Raška region of southern Serbia, but even today many people in the region speak Turkish. Sadly, the quality of life in these parts lags behind that of the rest of Serbia, and it's not hard to detect resentment about this.

This all comes to a head in Novi Pazar, which feels more Turkish than some pockets of Istanbul. The skyline is shaped by minarets, and streets are distinctly Ottoman. Threaded through it all is a strong Serbian side, as in some of the country's most revered Orthodox monasteries.

TOPOLA ТОПОЛА
☎ 034 / 25,000
Topola is an easy and rewarding day trip 65km from Belgrade. This small town is where Karađorđe pitched the Serbian insurrection against the Turks in 1804 and where his grandson King Petar I built one of the most jaw-dropping churches in the country,

the Church of St George, which holds the mausoleum of the Karađorđević family.

Orientation & Information
The bus station is 10 minutes' walk north of the centre on the Belgrade road. It's a five-minute walk south from the Tourist Organisation to the museum and 15 minutes through the idyllic Oplenac area to the Church of St George and Petar House museum.

The **Tourist Organisation** (☎ 811 172; www.topolaoplenac.org.rs; Kneginje Zorke 13; ☽ 8am-5pm Mon-Fri, 10am-5pm Sat) can provide a town map.

Sights
One ticket (200DIN) grants you access to three impressive sights in Topola. Buy the ticket wherever you start.

Before it was a **museum** (Kralijice Marije; ☽ 9am-5pm), this was the place from which Karađorđe led his rebellion. In the entrance is Karađorđe's cannon – originally known as *aberdar* (herald), it could be heard all the way to Belgrade and would summon leaders to the very room now housing the bulk of the museum's collection. One of the handles of the cannon is missing; it was removed by Karađorđe's grandson King Petar I, who made it into a crown for his 1904 coronation.

Atop the centre of Oplenac hill's rich parkland is the **Church of St George** (Avenija Kralja Petra I; ☽ 8am-7pm). This white-marble, five-domed church was built by King Petar I between 1904 and 1912. The impressive 1500kg candelabrum hanging from the main cupola is a tribute to the 1389 Battle of Kosovo. More striking are the vibrant frescos magnificently rendered on every inch of the church, with over 40 million mosaic pieces in 15,000 stunning colours. Millions more mosaic pieces grace the mausoleum under the church, where Karađorđe, King Petar and 20 other members of the Karađorđević family have been laid to rest.

Opposite the church is **Petar House** (Avenija Kralja Petra I; ☽ 8am-7pm), used by workmen building the church and King Petar during his visits to inspect progress. It exhibits artefacts belonging to the royal family, including some extremely humanising portraits.

Your ticket also lets you visit the Wine Grower's House at the park entrance.

Sleeping & Eating
Hotel Oplenac (☎ 811 430; www.hoteloplenac.org; Avenija Kralja Petra I; s/d from 1830/2360DIN) At the foot of

SERBIA

> **REFLECTIONS ON HISTORY** *Dragan Reljić*
>
> We are surrounded by history in Serbia, but the world sees it more simply than it is. People were so happy about the fall of Milošević, but we have been left with a legacy of guilt. Since then, it's like we are blamed for all the problems of the region. Some of what the media says is true, but some of it is not. Yes, bad things have happened in our past, but we also have a proud history – one full of democratic revolution, triumph, love…
>
> Titoism wasn't communism in the way the world understood it. My parents had more opportunities when they were my age – under Tito, Yugoslavians could travel the world. But I am a historian who cannot travel to the countries I study. Under Tito, we lived with Albanians, Bosnians, Croatians…many people for so many years, but now we are divided. Kosovo? As a historian I am neutral, but as a Serbian I feel that the spirit of Serbia is in Kosovo.

the park west of the church, this hotel was built in 1934 by King Aleksandar. It has lost its sheen, but its happy situation in forested Oplenac offers pleasant immersion into local ambience and history.

Breza (☎ 812 463; Krajiskih Brigada 25; meals 300-400DIN; ☺ 8am 11pm) Five minutes' walk downhill from the town centre, this local favourite has an English menu of usual Serbian fare. Eating here is like eating on a friend's patio (which it probably will be by the time you finish your burger).

Getting There & Away
Frequent buses travel to and from Belgrade (500DIN, 1½ hours).

DESPOTOVAC ДЕСПОТОВАЦ
☎ 035 / 25,500
The reasons to come to this idyllic town in southern Serbia are the nearby Manasija monastery and Resava cave 20km away. Despotovac is on an eastern offshoot of the Belgrade–Niš corridor and epitomises a lazy rural town.

Sights
Manasija monastery, 2km north of Despotovac, stands out for the confronting fortress surrounding it. Fortified by 11 towers that loom over you when you approach, Manasija was a refuge for artists and writers fleeing the Turkish invasion of Kosovo in the first half of the 15th century. Resident monks undertook literary and copying work in the Resava school.

The monastery was burnt by the Turks in 1456, and an explosion of gunpowder stored on the premises by the Austrians caused further damage in 1718. The frescos that have survived date from the 1400s and are products of the Morava school of painting, heavily influenced by Greek masters. Many consider Manasija frescos to be the predecessors of the Serbian equivalent of Renaissance art.

A winding 20km beyond Despotovac, **Resava cave** (Resavska Pećina; ☎ 611 110; www.resavska-pecina.co.yu; adult/child 220/170DIN; ☺ 9am-5pm 1 Apr-1 Nov) was discovered in 1962. Some 4km have been explored, but only 80m are open to the public. The guided tour through several impressive halls takes around 40 minutes. Brace yourself for camera-snappy school groups and a temperature of 7°C; needless to say, bring a jacket.

Sleeping & Eating
A pleasant strip of restaurants and pizzerias leads to the bus station.

Kruna Motel (☎ 611 659; Rudnička bb; s/d 1500/2700DIN; P) On the main road, this motel is good value. Parquet floors, a balcony and slippers make you feel at home – so does the cooking. There's even a shower-head holder (a rarity in Serbia). Helpful hotel staff can organise transport to the cave and monastery for 1600DIN.

Grand Restaurant (☎ 611 552; meals 200-300DIN; ☺ 6am-midnight Mon-Sat, 3pm-midnight Sun) One of the nicest eating options, the Grand is just opposite the bus station and does frighteningly good grilled trout.

Getting There & Around
Sites aren't well served by public transport. A taxi will take you to both the cave and the monastery for around 1600DIN, including waiting time.

Belgrade buses leave four times a day to Despotovac (580DIN, 2½ hours). If you're day-tripping from Belgrade, check what time buses head back at Despotovac's **bus station** (☎ 063355641).

NIŠ НИШ
☎ 018 / pop 250,000

Niš is a lively city of curious contrasts: horse-drawn carriages trot alongside new cars, cocktails are sipped in cobblestone alleys, and traditional Serbian fare is served in an old Turkish hamam. Niš has had a grim history but makes the best of its old sites these days.

History
Niš was settled in pre-Roman times and flourished during the time of local-boy-made-good Emperor Constantine (280–337).

Turkish rule lasted from 1386 until 1877, despite several Serb revolts; the Ćele Kula, a Turkish tower of Serbian skulls, is a grim reminder of their failure. The massive Tvrđava Citadel is another remnant of Turkish dominion.

Niš had a tough time in the last century. The Nazis built one of the country's most notorious concentration camps here, ironically named 'the Red Cross'. More recently, Niš was an infamous gathering place for Serb nationalists during the '90s conflict.

Orientation
North of Nišava River, the Tvrđava Citadel shelters the adjacent market and bus station. The train station is west on Dimitrija Tucovića. The central business district is south of the river. The main pedestrian boulevard, Obrenovićeva, stretches before the citadel. The staircases dotted along it lead to an enormous underground shopping mall.

Crossing over Nikole Pašića is cobblestone Kopitareva ('Tinker's Alley'), once populated by merchants and now a trendy eating and drinking area.

The citadel hosts a **blues, rock and pop festival** in July and a **jazz festival** in October.

Information
Internet Caffe (☎ /fax 501 800; Trg Oslobođenja bb; per hr 30DIN; ☼ 7am-11pm) Four computers in the foyer of Hotel Ambassador.

KSR Beograd (☎ /fax 523 808; Trg Oslobođenja 9; ☼ 8am-4pm Mon-Fri, 9am-2pm Sat) Train tickets at station prices.

Post office (Voždova Karađorđa 13a; ☼ 8am-8pm) Internet access for 50DIN per hour.

Tourist Organisation of Niš (☎ 523 118; www.nistour ism.org.yu; Voždova Karađorđa 7; ☼ 7.30am-7pm Mon-Fri, 9am-1pm Sat) Niš maps and domestic bus bookings.

UnCredit Bank (Trg Obrenovićeva bb; ☼ 9am-7pm)

Sights
Built by the Turks in the 18th century, the **Tvrđava Citadel** (Jadranska; ☼ 24hr) is now a recreational area. Through the Stambol Gate immediately across the bridge is a courtyard full of restaurants, cafes and trinket shops. Miniature trains tour the citadel's park (40DIN).

Protected from the elements by a benign-looking chapel, the **Tower of Skulls** (Ćele Kula; ☎ 222 228; Braće Tankosić bb; adult/child 120/100DIN; ☼ 8am-8pm Tue-Sun Apr-Oct, 9am-4pm Tue-Sat, 10am-4pm Sun Nov-Mar) is an eerie sight. The story starts at the 1809 Battle of Čegar. With defeat inevitable, the Serbian duke of Resava kamikazed towards the Turkish defences, desperately firing at their gunpowder stores. In the process, he killed himself, 4000 of his own men and 10,000 Turks. The Turks still triumphed and, to deter future acts of rebellion, beheaded, scalped and embedded the skulls of the dead Serbs in this tower. Of the 952 skulls initially placed, only 58 remain – enough to give an impression of how ghoulish this sight would have been. Contrary to the original intention, the tower now serves as a proud monument of Serbian resistance.

Mediana (☎ 550 433; bul Cara Konstantina bb; museum adult/child 100/80DIN, site free; ☼ 8am-4pm Tue-Sat, 10am-6pm Sun, closed Nov-Apr), on the eastern outskirts of Niš, is what remains of Constantine's 4th-century Roman palace. Archaeological digging has so far revealed a palace, a forum and an expansive grain-storage area with some almost-intact pottery vessels. There is an archaeology collection at the small **museum** (☎ 511 531; Nikole Pašića 59; admission 100DIN; ☼ 10am-8pm Tue-Sun).

Sleeping
There aren't many choices in Niš, but they are good ones.

Hostel Niš (☎ 515 703; www.hostelnis.com; Dobrička 3a; dm/tw bed 1050/1550DIN; P ▢) All hostels should be like this one. Hostel Niš is central, clean, new, friendly, airy and easy to find, and has wireless internet and lockable drawers under the beds. It's a five-minute walk (towards the river and a block left) from the bus station.

Regent Club (☎ 524 924; www.regentclub.com; Obrenovićeva 10; s/d/tr 5450/7400/9450DIN, apt 11,280DIN; P ✖ ▢) The Regent Club is hidden in an arcade of travel agents. Rooms are enormous and well equipped, with complimentary coffee-making facilities, good-sized working desks, spa-showers and wi-fi. Prices plummet on weekends.

SERBIA

Hotel Niški Cvet (☎ 297 700; www.niskicvet.com; Kej 29 Decembra 2; s/d 5450/7800DIN, apt 10,300-13,850DIN; P ⊠ ◻) A modern hotel offering fantastic views over the citadel, Niški Cvet isn't as central as the Regent Club (and has cable rather than wi-fi) but offers fantastic views over the Nišava River and the citadel. Coordinated beds and curtains lend a touch of class, as do the slimline fittings in the restaurant.

Hotel Ambassador (☎ /fax 501 800; Trg Oslobođenja bb; s/d with air-con & TV 3110/4100DIN, without air-con & TV 2685/3680DIN; ⊠ ◻) Once the pride and joy of Niš and now a relic of another era, the Ambassador has stale rooms that are nonetheless satisfactory for a midrange hotel. Photos of Elizabeth Taylor greet you in the foyer (the poor thing was a guest in 1971), and there's a 500-billion-dinar note at reception. Internet in the foyer is free for guests.

Eating & Drinking

There's a wide range of fast-paced restaurants and cafes in the cobblestone Kopitareva area on the southern side of Nikole Pašića. A particularly good one is **Pleasure Caffe** (☎ 231 466; St Sava Park 31b; mains 200-500DIN; ⊙ 7.30am-11.30pm Mon-Fri, to 1am Sat & Sun) offering fresh food (like the 480DIN pepper steak) and nibbles while you work your way through the cocktail list; palindrome-geeks should order a Madam I'm Adam (190DIN).

Hamam (☎ 513 444; Tvrđava; meals 200-2000DIN; ⊙ 11am-midnight) The exterior is a crumbling Turkish bathhouse. The interior is an elegant restaurant serving tasty food in intimate alcoves under domed roofs. In addition to pizza, there's a wide range of national fare like dimljena vešalica (a roll of smoked pork stuffed with cream cheese and almonds). Start with a grilled pepper (15DIN).

Restoran Sindjelić (☎ 512 550; Nikole Pašića 36; meals from 400DIN; ⊙ 8am-1am Mon-Fri, to 2am Sat, to 1am Sun) This proud traditional Serbian restaurant serves hearty meals in elegant interiors or in the more casual outside area. A great choice for fine dining and leisurely drinking.

Tramvaj (Tramway; ☎ 257 909; Pobede 20; ⊙ 8am-midnight) Remember that 'j' is pronounced 'y', get on the tram, sit in a compartment and order an ice-cream concoction, like the Terrible Tram (190DIN).

Broz (Obrenovićeva bb; ⊙ 10am-late) A shiny bar dedicated to the late Broz (Tito) that would appeal to its namesake. A large photo-montage of Broz and Castro chuckling in the Havana

heat covers a wall, and a bust of the Marshal guards the ladies' toilets.

Getting There & Away

The **bus station** (☎ 355 177; Kneginje Ljubice) has frequent services to Belgrade (800DIN, three hours), and Brzeće (550DIN, 1½ hours) for Kopaonik, four daily to Novi Pazar (940DIN, four hours), and three to Užice (900DIN, five hours) for Zlatibor. There are regular buses to Pirot (320DIN, 1½ hours) and Vranje (550DIN, two hours), and three daily buses to Topola (630DIN, 2½ hours).

There are eight trains to Belgrade (800DIN, 4½ hours) and two to Bar (2400DIN, 11½ hours) from the **train station** (☎ 364 625).

AROUND NIŠ
Pirot Пирот
☎ 010 / pop 67,552

The highlight of Pirot is getting there from Niš. The 1½- to two-hour drive traces the Nišava River towards Bulgaria, slicing through jagged mountains on its windy way. Pirot is a compact town with an energetic market and a couple of charming sights, including a working ćilim factory.

The distinct Pirot ćilim carpets can be found all over Serbia. The technique arrived with the Turks and its Islamic design elements have become Christianised over time. The sheep-rearing villages around Pirot and cottage-industry carpet weaving have depended on each other for seven centuries but now suffer under slumping demand.

ORIENTATION & INFORMATION

From the bus station, walk south along the market. Further on across the bridge is Srpskih Vladara – the town's central square, containing landmark Hotel Pirot.

The frustratingly well-hidden **Turistička Organizacija Pirot** (☎ 320 838; www.topirot.com; Srpskih Vladara Br 77; ⊙ 7.30am-3pm Mon-Fri) is immediately opposite Hotel Pirot. Pick up a map here.

There are plenty of banks in the square, including **ProCredit** (Srpskih Vladara 48; ⊙ 9am-7pm Mon-Fri, to 1pm Sat) and **Raiffeisen Bank** (Srpskih Vladara; ⊙ 9am-7pm Mon-Fri, to 1pm Sat). The **post office** (Nikole Pašića) is near the bridge.

SIGHTS & ACTIVITIES

You can buy carpets and see them being painstakingly woven on vertical looms at the **Pirot Ćilim** (☎ 332 586; www.ponisavlje.co.yu; Dečanska 53;

SERBIA

☺ 7am-2pm). Little other than Serbian is spoken, but friendly staff are fluent in charades.

Nearby, the **Ponišavlje Museum** (☎ 313 850; muzej pirot@ptt.yu; Nikole Pašica 49; admission 100DIN; ☺ 8am-3pm Mon-Fri, 10am-2pm Sat & Sun) is housed in an authentic mid-19th-century *konak* (Turkish-style residence with distinctive wooden framing). It displays folk costumes, pottery and countless *ćilims*. At the western edge of town is the Kale fortress.

SLEEPING & EATING

Hotel Pirot (☎ 333 455; Maršala Tita 52; s/d/tr/apt 1650/2900/3750/3600DIN) Comfortable for a night or two, the state-run Pirot is in decent nick. Bright rooms have TVs and clean bathrooms, but there's little character beyond a temperamental elevator.

Golemi Most (☎ 312 800; Nikole Pašića St; ☺ 8am-10pm) Enjoy pizza or ice cream in this pink building at the main bridge.

GETTING THERE & AWAY

The small **bus station** (☎ 320 758; Trg Republike; ☺ 5am-9pm) is near the market. There are regular services to Belgrade (1100DIN, six hours) and Niš (270DIN, 1½ hours), and to Dimitrovgrad (120DIN, 45 minutes) on the Bulgaria border.

Vranje Врање

☎ 017 / pop 55,000

Some 35km from the Macedonia border, this large town laden with orange-tiled roofs holds little interest for travellers but is a pleasant enough place to stay en route. Streets are perpetually lined with coffee-sipping locals, and the large Roma community lends a cosmopolitan feel.

ORIENTATION & INFORMATION

From the bus station, head north up Kralja Stefana Prvovenčanog to reach the centre, the main **post office** (☺ 7am-8pm) and tonnes of banks, including **Raiffeisen** (☺ 9am-3pm Mon-Fri, to 1pm Sat).

The sparsely equipped **Tourist Organisation of Vranje** (☎ 417 545; 29 Novembra 2; ☺ 8am-7pm Mon-Fri) is hidden on the top floor of the building containing the library. Bookshops sell Vranje maps (110DIN).

SIGHTS & ACTIVITIES

From the centre of town, continue north up Kralja Stefana Prvovenčanog. On your right

is the distinctive **ethnographic museum** (☎ 424 018; Pionirska 1; adult/child 80/50DIN; ☺ 8am-3pm Mon-Fri, 10am-2pm Sat & Sun), in a *konak* that somehow survived the jumble of urbanisation around it.

Continue on the same road and peel off northeast on Petog Kongressa for the **hamam** (dating from the late 1600s) on your right just across the river. Restorations have dragged it almost completely away from recognisability.

Turning left at the intersection before the hamam takes you to **Beli Most**, the Turkish footbridge. The road narrows, and you lose sight of the trickle of water – keep it within earshot. The bridge is unspectacular in size and the river under it barely wet, but it comes with a love story: known as 'lovers' bridge', it was allegedly built by a remorseful Muslim father who accidentally shot his daughter instead of her Serbian Orthodox lover.

If you continue past the hamam you reach the interesting Roma area. Alternatively, cross the footbridge and loop down past the hamam back into town.

SLEEPING & EATING

Hotel Vranje (☎ 422 366; Trg Republike 4; s/d without air-con 2925/5050DIN, with air-con 5425/6675DIN) A central accommodation choice, the Vranje has friendly staff (in charge of an enormous retro switchboard!) and worn but comfortable rooms with TV. Higher prices equal more space.

There are numerous places to sit, drink and watch the world go by, and there's a bakery everywhere you look. For a quick coffee, cake or pastry, head to **Tada Duka** (☎ 425 245; cnr Kralja Stefana Prvovenčanog & Pionirska; pastries 70DIN), opposite the museum.

GETTING THERE & AWAY

The **bus station** (☎ 421 201) is at the southern end of town. There are regular buses from Niš (550DIN, two hours). From Vranje, there are regular services to Belgrade (1250DIN, five hours) via Niš, and frequent services to Skopje (450DIN, 1½ hours) in Macedonia.

There are train services south to Skopje and north to Belgrade, but these aren't frequent enough to be as useful as buses, and the **train station** (☎ 421 714) is a long, desolate walk west of the bus station or a 200DIN taxi ride.

NOVI PAZAR НОВИ ПАЗАР

☎ 020 / pop 54,000

Novi Pazar – the cultural heartland of the Sandžak region – is a gateway and warm-up to Kosovo. However, it's a mistake to compare the Islamic heritage of this region with that of its neighbour; southern Serbia's Muslims are Slavs who converted to Islam. Here the locals don't even try to pretend that the Turkish coffee is Serbian.

The fact that the Turks weren't ousted from here until 1912 has left an indelible mark on the town's character; even today Turkish is widely spoken. Many people are ethnically Bosnian, but the Serbian population increased as refugees came over from nearby Bosnia, Kosovo and Macedonia.

The nouveau-wacko Hotel Vrbak is a curious central landmark. It's attached to a bridge crossing the Raška River, which hurries through town. All around is a frantic jigsaw of architecture; apartment blocks that smack of socialism and the Ottoman bazaar punctuated by minarets remind you that you're standing at a crossroads of East and West.

Besides the tapestry of Turkishness, there are some idyllic Orthodox monasteries in the vicinity.

Orientation & Information

The Turkish quarter is on the southern side of the river. On the other side are numerous cafes, bars and restaurants on 28 Novembar street. Hotel Vrbak spans the river and defies description.

A taxi ride into town from the bus station costs around 90DIN. There are travel agencies and internet cafes around the bus station, and several banks including **ProCredit Bank** (28 Novembar 93; 8am-4pm). Information for travellers is thin on the ground; hopefully, the **Tourist Organization of Novi Pazar** (28 Novembar 27) will open its doors soon. Meanwhile, **Ecco Travel Agency** (23 832; www.ecco.co.yu; 28 Novembar 54; 9am-7pm Mon-Fri, to 2pm Sat) can help with local information.

Sights

Wandering around the Turkish area is a joy. Old cafes serve Turkish desserts, and small shops sell meat, nuts or copperware. Attempts to restore the ruined **hamam** (just off Maj) have failed dismally, leaving it at the mercy of coffee-drinking men. And who can blame them; the stunning atmosphere is worth checking out.

SOPOĆANI MONASTERY СОПОЋАНИ
Nestling in one of the most beautiful settings in Serbia, Sopoćani monastery is a Unesco-

protected treat. Built by King Uroš (who is buried here) in the mid-13th century, it was destroyed by the Turks at the end of the 17th century and only restored in the 1920s, the dome replaced in 1929. The church is Romanesque in external appearance, and frescos within are prime examples of European medieval art. They also miraculously (or perhaps divinely) survived more than two centuries exposed to the elements. The black on the walls is said to be glue that once held gold leaf.

Some of the monks speak English and will be glad to give you the historical lowdown. Ask to be pointed to the portrait of St Philippus, 'the Mona Lisa of Serbia' for his mysterious following eyes. The Assumption of the Mother of God fresco is one of the most renowned.

The monastery is well signed along the enchanting road leading to it. There's no public transport; a taxi from and to Novi Pazar costs around 800DIN, including waiting time.

If you want to linger longer in this lush area, stay at the monastery-style **Hotel Sopoćani** (313 663; Sopoćani bb; per person €15).

CHURCH OF ST PETER ПЕТРОВА ЦРКВА
Three kilometres from town on a bluff on the Kraljevo road, the small, stone Church of St Peter (Petrova Crkva) is the oldest in Serbia and the only pre-Nemanjić church; parts date to the 8th century. In the late 1950s the ancient cemetery around the church was discovered to hold the grave of a 5th-century Illyrian prince.

Inside the rough masonry, a step-down baptismal well and feet-polished flagstones provide a tangible sense of the ancient. The 13th-century frescos are incomplete due to damage. If the church is locked, ask at the nearby house to be let in.

ST GEORGE MONASTERY
ЂУРЂЕВИ СТУПОВИ
Perched on a hill visible from the Church of St Peter, and partly obscured by trees, the monastery of St George dates from 1170. The church is the result of Stefan Nemanja's promise to God that he would endow a monastery to St George if he was released from Turkish captivity. The monastery was damaged by Turks and by Germans in WWII. The small building currently serving as a trinket shop is one of the few to have survived the years; it was used as a prison in the Ottoman era. Many attempts have been made to restore the monastery, but none so energetically as those going on at the time of

writing. What was formerly little more than a ruin has recently emerged as a fully functioning monastery. Follow progress at www.podigni mostupove.com (mostly in Serbian).

A return taxi trip from Novi Pazar costs around 800DIN.

Sleeping

Hotel Tadž (☎ 311 904; www.hoteltadz.co.yu; Rifata Burdževića 79; **P** **⚇**) Despite its unspectacular entrance through the driveway and up some bland stairs, Hotel Tadž is the best hotel in town. Rooms have TV and wi-fi, and guests are free to use the computer in the foyer. The restaurant downstairs lacks the character of Novi Pazar, but this may be what you're looking for.

Hotel Atlas (☎ 316 352; Jošanički Kej bb; s/d/tr/apt 3000/5000/5800/6800DIN; **P** **⚇** **⚇**) Cosy beds and sparkling bathrooms give the feel of a modern hotel. There's internet available in the foyer, and the pleasant restaurant downstairs adds elegance. You could swing a small child in the apartment rooms, and have a spa bath afterwards. Find it on the main road behind the market area.

Hotel Vrbak (☎ 314 548, 314 844; Maršala Tita bb; s/d from 1200/2200DIN) Perhaps better reviewed as a sight rather than a sleeping option, Hotel Vrbak, teetering over the Raška River, suffers an architectural identity crisis. Window trimmings, Ottoman puffs, and the glass onion dome capping the foyer hint at the Orient, but the dilapidated state of things suggests that the Vrbak fell with Yugoslavia. This friendly, freaky place deserves patronage for its sheer quirkiness. Just check that everything in your room turns on, closes, flushes and smells as it should. Long live Vrbak.

Hotel Palma (☎ 335 400; Jošanički Kej bb; s/d 1000/2000DIN; **P**) Next door to Hotel Atlas, the Palma has no-frills rooms that are spacious, light, airy and a steal at this price. Friendly staff speak some German.

Hotel Kan (Cannes; ☎ /fax 315 300; Rifata Burdžovića 10; s 1914-2395DIN, d 2870DIN, tr 3830DIN) Opposite Vrbak, this small oriental-style hotel offers simple but clean rooms with cable TV and minibar. Walls feel makeshift and the windows could be bigger (though perhaps noise levels would be worse), but it's secure and central.

Eating

Ukus (1 Maj 59; meals 110-190DIN; ⏱ 8am-11pm) A down-to-earth hole-in-the-wall on the main street of the old town, Ukus turns out home-cooked food. Salads (30DIN to 50DIN) are fresh and zesty, and the paprika's possibly the best 30DIN you'll spend in Serbia. Things get eaten early – arrive in good time or be content with delicious *gulaš* (goulash; 190DIN). Unlike at many places in Novi Pazar, there's no macho vibe to deter female patrons.

Šadrvan (meals 100-250) This family-friendly place is at the Vrbak end of 28 Novembar. There are no surprises (*gulaš* is 250DIN, and *srpska* or *šopska* salads are 120DIN), but wrought-iron chairs out the front offer a comfortable place to discreetly watch passers-by.

Getting There & Away

From the **bus station** (☎ 318 354) frequent buses go to Belgrade (1000DIN, four hours), an overnight bus goes to Sarajevo (€15, seven hours), and four daily buses head to Pristina (€5, three hours) in Kosovo. There are also occasional services to destinations in Germany and Turkey. Zlatibor is reached via Raška.

There are regular buses to Novi Pazar from major hubs like Uzice (250DIN) and Kraljevo (450DIN).

AROUND NOVI PAZAR

Studenica Monastery Студеница

One of the most sacred and beautiful sites in Serbia, Studenica is nestled in mountainous forest alongside the Studenica River. The monastery was established in the 1190s by Stefan Nemanja and further developed by his sons Vukan and Stefan, who are entombed here. Active monastic life was cultivated by much-revered St Sava and continues today.

There are three churches within the impressive oval monastery walls. The central and most important is **Bogorodičina crkva** (Our Lady's church), containing the tomb of Stefan Nemanja, brought here by his brother Sava. Medieval architecture is acclaimed for its polished marble exterior and elaborately decorated windows and doorways. The frescos, dating back to the early 13th century, were repainted with wonderfully rich colours in 1569. Pilgrims gather at Bogorodičina crkva on 24 May to celebrate the feast day of Stefan Nemanja.

Next door is the comparatively small **Kraljeva crkva** (King's church), built in 1314 by King Milutin. It houses some of the best-preserved frescos in the country, including the *Birth of the Virgin*, which illustrates the evolving techniques of Serbian fresco artists.

SERBIA

The simplest of the three churches is **Crkva Svetog Nikole/Nikoljača** (St Nicholas' Church). Medieval tombs and frescos therein were buried for centuries until soil was removed to reveal them. Between St Nicholas' and King's church the foundations of the church dedicated to St John the Baptist can be seen.

GETTING THERE & AWAY

Getting to Studenica monastery isn't fun without your own transport. It's around 11km off the main road linking Novi Pazar and Kraljevo, and well signed all the way. Attempting the journey with public transport involves getting to the town of Ušće. From Novi Pazar there are regular buses bound for Ušće (every 15 to 30 minutes from 5am), from where it's remotely possible to get a local bus to the monastery; they don't always run as scheduled. Alternatively, negotiate a return journey with a taxi.

KOPAONIK КОПАОНИК
☎ 036

Serbia's prime ski resort is great for people who want a ski-holiday without glamour and prices to match. Kopaonik is situated around the Pančićev Peak (Pančićev Vrh, 2017m) overlooking Kosovo. It's a pleasant base for hiking and, with your own wheels, an adventurous base for monastery buffs.

Orientation & Information

The resort sits 1770m above sea level. The smaller subvillage of **Brzeće** (area code ☎ 037) is 14km below and linked to it with a ski lift.

In the centre of the resort are a couple of ATMs, a post office, mini-supermarkets, restaurants, clothing shops and a bookshop.

Many places open arbitrarily or close completely out of season, but prices plummet.

For more information, visit www.npkopaonik.com, www.kopaonik.net and Serbian-only www.raska-turizam.co.yu.

Activities
SKIING

The main appeal of Kopaonik is that snow is only a short walk away, sometimes just outside your hotel. Ski season generally runs from late November to late March or early April. There are 44km of ski slopes served by 23 lifts.

Ski Centre Kopaonik (☎ 471 203; www.skijalistasrbije .co.yu; 🕑 8am-3pm Mon-Thu, to 8pm Fri-Sun), at the base of the Hotel Grand, sells ski passes.

Balkan Holidays (www.balkanholidays.co.uk) and **Crystal** (www.crystalski.co.uk) are British outfits that book ski holidays in 'Kop'.

HIKING & BIKING

As a national park, Kopaonik offers interesting hiking and mountain biking. See p381.

Walks in the vicinity of the resort include that to Mt Kopaonik's highest point, where there's a monument to Serbian botanist Josef Pancic. A less demanding walk along the Samokovska River takes you to the granite boulders of Marko's Rock (Markova Stena). It's also possible to walk to Heaven's Chairs (Nebeske Stolice), the ruins of the highest Orthodox church in the Balkans. Between Brzeće and Kopaonik is Metodje, the site of holy water. Walking along the Brzeće River with its watermills is pleasant.

OTHER ACTIVITIES

If you have your own transport, Kopaonik can be used as a base for exploring monasteries. Studenica (opposite), St George (p411), Sopoćani (p411), Žiča, Crna Reka, Stara, Nova Pavlica and Gradac are all accessible with your own vehicle.

When numbers allow, monastery tours are possible. Interested persons are pooled by **Tourist Centar Kopaonik** (International CG; ☎ 471 977; www.kopaonik-genex.com/eng).

It may also be possible to arrange **rafting** on the Ibar River to the medieval town of Maglič. The rafting event **Veseli spust** (Merry Descent), ending in Kraljevo, is held each July. Enquire at your hotel or directly through Tourist Centar Kopaonik.

Sleeping

There are several large-scale hotels with restaurants, gym facilities, pizzerias, discos and shops. Expect to pay from 1500DIN to 3000DIN for a single and 1660DIN to 4000DIN for a double depending on the season and whether you take bed and breakfast or full board. Other options in addition to those below include two-star **Hotel Jugobank** (☎ 471 040; Kopaonik) and **Hotel Junior** (☎ 823 344; Brzeće; s/d from €40/50).

JAT Apartments (☎ 471 043; www.jatapartmani.com; Kopaonik; apt for 1/2/3/4/5 people plus tax from 1520/1680/ 2160/2960/3520DIN; 🖳) These airline-affiliated apartments are a good all-year option. Interiors are ageing, but all have kitchenettes, well-maintained bathrooms, good cupboard space for ski gear and plenty of linen.

SERBIA

SERBIA

TRUMPET TOWN

Every August the otherwise indistinct town of Guča blasts to life with the **Dragačevo Trumpet Festival** (Dragačevski sabor trubača). Since 1961, performers have descended on Guča with trumpets, trombones, tubas…anything with a brassy sheen that makes some noise. Organisers may have been seeing double when they counted almost half a million people here, but it's certain that more people attend each year, and from further afield than before.

'Raucous' doesn't come close to describing what the mostly Roma musicians manage to achieve at Guča. It's debaucherously hedonistic. Pigs and sheep spin on spits as visitors twirl with euphoric abandon and slap dinars on the sweaty foreheads of performers. It's been reported that around 3 tonnes of bread and an incomprehensible three million litres of beer are consumed over these four decadent days.

Bring a tent or book accommodation in advance – or don't bother; who can sleep with all that noise anyway? Packages including return transport from Belgrade and accommodation cost €205. For more information visit www.guca.co.yu.

Grand Hotel (☎ 471 037; www.kopaonik-genex.com; s €56-130, d €88-213; 🖳 🖭) Run by the pervasive Genex corporation, the Grand is the leader of the pack. It offers swimming pool, fitness centre, tennis courts, and ski slopes on your doorstep.

Eating

Several eateries are in the central courtyard of the resort. A good choice is modern **Gril Andreja** (☎ 471 977; meals 300-800; 🕑 8am-midnight), which serves simple salads and decadent meat platters; the Iznenađenje Andreja (2300DIN) is a masterpiece of almost everything on the menu, or there's simple fare such as spaghetti bolognese (650DIN) and house pizza (500DIN).

Etno Club Sunce (☎ 063771994; meals 200-700DIN; 🕑 8am-midnight) Away from manufactured resort-style dining, the Etno Club offers home cooking served in fireside alcoves. It's mostly meaty, other than the *vegetarianski tanjir* (300DIN). Find it down the unpaved road uphill from the centre.

Koala Restaurant (☎ 471 977; 🕑 8.30-midnight) This modern pizzeria is attached to Villa Bianca.

Boeing Restaurant (☎ 471 043; www.jatapartmani.com; Kopaonik; 🕑 8am-10pm) In the JAT Apartments complex, the Boeing serves bountiful buffets.

Getting There & Away

Getting to Kopaonik from anywhere other than Belgrade (1200DIN, six hours) or Niš (800DIN, four hours) isn't easy. During the summer and winter seasons there are three daily buses from Belgrade and one from Niš. Buses generally leave Kopaonik in the afternoon.

Getting to Kopaonik from local destinations is messy; there are connections from Kraljevo, Krušavec and Raška. Coming from Novi Pazar, pick up an infrequent connection in Raška (for Raška bus information call ☎ 737 555). Alternatively, a taxi from Raška costs around 1200DIN.

ZLATIBOR ЗЛАТИБОР
☎ 031 / pop 156,000

Zlatibor is a special region of rolling plains, ski fields, prophecies, traditions and hospitality. The area stretches from the Tara and Šargan mountains in the north to the Murtenica hills to the east, bordering BiH. The town center of Tržni at the heart of the region has everything you could need, but not far beyond it are quaint villages where locals are seemingly oblivious to the nearby ski slopes. The highest peak is Tornik (1496m). Geologically, the region is dominated by limestone.

Orientation & Information

Zlatibor is a patchwork of small settlements centred on the Tržni centar, a village of shops, eating and drinking places, a market and a bus stop.

Anitours (☎ /fax 841 855; www.anitours.co.yu; Tržni centar; 🕑 8am-7pm) Accommodation and tours for upwards of €10.

Igraonica Internet Caffe (Tržni centar; per hr 120DIN; 🕑 9am-midnight) Two internet cafes with the same name and price; both have fast connections.

Komercijalna Bank (☎ 845 182; Tržni centar; 🕑 8am-8pm Mon-Fri, 9am-3pm Sat Jan, Feb, Jul & Aug, 8am-4pm Mon-Fri, 9am-1pm Sat rest of yr) Western Union transfers, currency exchange and an ATM.

Post office (☎ 841 337; Tržni centar; ⊙ 7am-7pm) Also has phone centre and maps; at the town end of the lake.
Tomba (☎ 845 965; Tržni centar; ⊙ 8am-7pm) Apartments in large complex.
Zlateks (☎ 841 244; www.zlateks.co.yu; Tržni centar bus station; ⊙ 7am-8pm) Tourist agency at the bus station organising tickets, accommodation and tours.
Zlatibor Tourism Organization (☎ 841 646, 845 103; www.zlatibor.co.yu, in Serbian; ⊙ 8am-6pm Mar-Jun, to 10pm Jul-Feb) A useful website for Serbian speakers.

Sights & Activities

The Tržni centar is a well-facilitated base all year around. For suggested villages to visit from here, see the boxed text, p416.

Zlatibor's slopes are mostly mild, but a couple more difficult ones are planned. The two major skiing hills are Tornik and Obudovica. The **Nordic skiing trail** is located at the northern foothill of Šumatno Brdo and is 1042m at its highest point.

Rafting trips on the Drina can be arranged from Zlatibor through **Era Rafting Club** (☎ 0644131752; azara@ptt.yu).

Several walks of varying difficulty and duration originate, intersect or end in the Tržni centar. The red 66km **adventure trail**, for instance, takes eight to 12 hours and reaches an altitude of 1133m on its way to Mokra Gora. Within easy reach of the Tržni centar is the **monument** in memory of local victims of German aggression in 1941; head south along ulica Sportova, cross the footbridge and follow the footpath to the monument and its spectacular views.

If your dignity is expendable, take a **miniature train** from the car park behind the bus station for a return trip (per person 250DIN) into lush surrounds.

The wellness centre at Hotel Mona Zlatibor (below) can be used by nonguests. A one-hour relaxation massage costs 2500DIN and half an hour in the sauna 600DIN.

Sleeping

Private rooms and apartments offer more space, facilities and privacy for less money than resorts. There are two peak seasons: winter (January and February) and summer (June to August). Apartments in season typically cost €30 to €80 for two to six people and €10 to €30 less out of season. Find them through travel agents. The following hotels are open all year.

Hotel Mona Zlatibor (☎ 841 021; www.mona zlatibor.com; Naselje Jezero 26; s/d from 5980/8000DIN, apt from 7000DIN; P ⊠ 🖳 🕿) Rooms could

benefit from bigger windows, but this sleek new hotel and wellness centre opposite the bus station wants for little else. There's a modern restaurant with a grand piano and a sprawling buffet.

Club Satelit (☎ 841 188; www.satelit.co.yu; Obudojevica bb; s/d from €21/53; P 🕿) Closer to the base of the ski slopes than to the centre, this intimate place looks like a castle and feels like a mountain lodge. Rooms are comfortably furnished.

Olimp (☎ 842 555; www.hotelolimp.com; Naselje Sloboda bb; s/d/tr B&B from 2200/3600/4500DIN, s/d/tr half board 3000/4800/7500DIN; P 🕿) Though showing its age next to newer players, Olimp hangs on to comparative advantages such as an enormous swimming pool and a location just outside of the centre delivering spacious views and mountain breezes to your balcony.

Hotel Vis (☎ 841 467; snezana.teodosic@ozone-hotels .com; standard s/d 3200/5400DIN, s/d/tr apt 3700/6200/8400DIN) Vis has seen better days but offers charming Fawlty Towers character. Standard rooms are spacious and have balconies. Apartments are dark but pleasant for their multilevel design; check the view before you check in. The glass conservatory off the lobby is pleasant for coffee and cake. Prices drop for stays of a few days or longer.

Hotel Dunav (☎ 841 126; fax 848 411; Rujanska bb; s/d/tr 2500/4200/6300DIN) If you arrive lost and late, the overpriced but delightfully friendly Dunav, just past the bus stop, will welcome you with a comfy bed. Its crumbling facilities and cramped bathrooms are terrible value for money, but three meals are included.

Eating

Explore beyond the numerous cateries in the centre by dropping into local villages for wholesome food.

Grand Zlatibor (☎ 848 123; www.grand-zlatibor.co.yu; meals from 400DIN; ⊙ 11am-midnight) The Grand is a three-tiered affair that rises in class with each level; it's above an elegant attempt at an Irish pub, which is in turn above a not-so-elegant nightclub. The warm wooden atmosphere is just the place to try traditional Užice grilled dishes (420DIN to 720DIN) or horsemeat steak (950DIN).

Zlatiborska Koliba (☎ 841 638; meals 250-600DIN; ⊙ 8am-midnight) Wooden ceilings, a big brick-arched bar, an open fireplace and good Serbian food chased by slugs of *rakija* make this a suitable place to recover from skiing or hiking. In season there's live traditional music.

The house speciality is *teleća prsa* (veal, potatoes, *kajmak* and vegetables in an earthenware pot stewed over an open fire). It's at the foot of the ski slopes.

Restoran Jezero (☎ 841 100; average meal 650DIN; ⏱ 8am-midnight) Here the food's mostly Serbian with some Italian standards thrown in – and a pleasing choice of ice cream. Its prime location hanging over the lake is the drawcard.

Cafe Dukat (☎ 514 753; pastries 40-100DIN; ⏱ 7am-4pm) Where locals come for *burek* and yoghurt for breakfast or freshly baked muffins and croissants any time.

TP Palisad (⏱ 7am-8pm) For DIY general supplies, head to this supermarket at the town end of the lake.

Getting There & Around

Express buses leave the **bus stand** (☎ 841 244, 841 587) for Belgrade (700DIN, four hours) and Novi Sad (1005DIN, 6½ hours), and almost hourly buses depart for Užice (120DIN, 45 minutes, between 5.50am and 11.10pm), the nearest railhead. There are buses to Kraljevo (440DIN), from where there's onward transport to southern locations such as Novi Pazar. Contact Zlateks (p415) for more information.

Without your own wheels the easiest way to explore the region is to join locally organised tours (see p414).

Minibuses ply villages in season, but at other times public transport is inconvenient; pick up village connections from the hub of Užice. The other option is to negotiate a taxi; getting to a village at the edge of the region and back to the Tržni centar will cost around 2000DIN return.

AROUND ZLATIBOR

Zlatibor is one of the most special regions in Serbia. In addition to the key suggestions below, see the boxed text, right) for more exploratory ideas.

Sirogojno Сирогојно
☎ 064

The **Open-Air Museum** (☎ 802 291; www.sirogojno.org .yu; adult/child 120/70DIN; ⏱ 9am-4pm Oct-Apr, to 7pm rest of yr) is in the village of Sirogojno, 26km from Zlatibor. If it weren't for the ticket counter and school groups, you'd swear you'd stepped back in time to a 19th-century Serbian village. High-roofed, fully furnished wooden houses are spread across a pleasant mountainside and are open for your exploration. Forget it

---

WORTH THE TRIP: VILLAGES AROUND ZLATIBOR

Those with the time and inclination should consider visiting the following villages in the region:

- **Gostilje** for homestays with cattle breeders and fruit growers, and walks to the local watermill and waterfall.

- **Kremna** for easy access into Tara National Park and 19th-century Tarabić family prophecies accurately predicting the assassination of the king and queen of Serbia and – hopefully inaccurately – WWIII.

- **Rožanstvo** for the 2km-long Stopića cave, in which water cascades down tiers of stone baths.

- **Stublo** for a 12th-century Uvac monastery.

- **Dobroselica and Jablanica** for wooden churches.

---

if you're not a fan of cultural history, but it's truly transporting for enthusiasts and their children. Purchase an English-language guide (80DIN) on your way in.

There are regular bus connections to Sirogojno from Užice. Alternatively, Zlateks (p415) organises a tour of Sirogojno (700DIN) that takes you to the Open-Air Museum. A return taxi trip from the Tržni centar costs around 2000DIN return, including waiting time.

Mokra Gora Мокра Гора
☎ 31

Flanked by the mountains of Zlatibor, Šargan and Tara, Mokra Gora is a key village for several reasons beyond its picturesque setting, the healing waters of 'Bela Voda' (good for your eyes and goddamn awful for your palate) and its vantage point to Tara National Park and BiH's Višegrad.

One of those reasons is the village of **Drvengrad** (Küstendorf; ☎ 800 686; www.mecavnik.info; Mećavnik hill; adult/child 180/100DIN; ⏱ 9am-9pm), built by enigmatic filmmaker Emir Kusturica in 2002 for his film *Life Is a Miracle*. The first **Küstendorf Film Festival** (http://kustendorf-filmand musicfestival.org/) was held here in January 2008 to showcase the work of film students around the world.

Just as Kusturica intended, Drvengrad is an enchanting place celebrating local culture. The village is built in the 19th-century style typical of the region, but quirky and colourful flourishes give the village a fantastical feel. The Stanley Kubrick cinema shows extracts of Kusturica's films. Take Bruce Lee Street down past the church for some prime panoramas. The central **restaurant** (☎ 800 688) serves sensational food; enjoy bacon and eggs for breakfast (150DIN) with Che Guevara Biorevolution juice (130DIN), and lunch on veal in *kaymak* (500DIN) with homemade bread balls (150DIN). If you can't get enough of this merry town, there's a **hotel** (☎ 0648830213; s/d €30/50, apt €120-150; 🖳 🐾) in the same style and spirit but with modern comforts such as indoor swimming pool, gym and wi-fi.

The other key reason to venture to Mokra Gora is the **Šargan 8 railway** (☎ 031-800 505, bookings 510 288; www.zeleznicesrbije.com; 2½hr trip 500DIN; ☼ Apr-Sep), a tourist train of key importance to Serbs. At the end of the 19th century several things were predicted in the village of Kremna by the prophet Mitar Tarabić. Among them, the assassination of the Serbian king and queen, WWIII and the construction of a recreational railway.

The Šargan 8 was once part of a narrow-gauge railway linking Belgrade with Sarajevo and Dubrovnik. Construction started in 1921 and finished at 15,440m four years and 200 lives later. The railway was closed in 1974, but 3.5km reopened 25 years later after teams of volunteers cleared the track with the help of the Serbian army, and train stations were resurrected from the 1920s. The project was completed during the NATO bombings of 1999 and Šargan 8 was triumphantly opened to tourists. The joy of the journey is its disorienting twists and turns. Each time you pop out of one of the 22 tunnels en route, the view seems to have inverted; the village of Drvengrad is intermittently visible out the left and the right windows.

The train leaves daily at 10.30am and 1.25pm and at 8am and 4.10pm if there are enough people to warrant it.

By far the easiest way to get to Mokra Gora is with your own wheels. Otherwise, take a bus from Užice or negotiate a taxi. The better option is a tour from the Tržni centar. Travel agencies pool clients through Zlateks (p415) into groups of 20, charging 700DIN for a trip covering the railway and Drvengrad.

SERBIA DIRECTORY

ACCOMMODATION

More hostel options have opened in recent years, though they can be a pain to find. Contact the Youth Hostel Organisation (p391) for deals. A key website for hostel bookings in Belgrade is www.hostelworld.com.

The cheapest option is private rooms and apartments, which can be organised through travel agencies. 'Wild' camping is possible outside national parks.

Unless otherwise stated, prices include breakfast and private bathroom. If you depend on internet access, check that the wi-fi offered actually works.

ACTIVITIES
Birdwatching

Serbia's birdwatching scene is underrated; several spots have rich bird life, including areas around Belgrade (p390). Keen birdwatchers should contact the **League for Ornithological Action of Serbia** (www.ptica.org). See also p380.

Skiing

Main ski resorts are Zlatibor (p414) and Kopaonik (p413), both of which are also popular for summer hiking. The ski season is from December to March.

Trekking & Climbing

National parks (p381) offer quiet respite for walkers; Tara National Park has almost 20 marked paths ranging from about 2km to 18km. Zlatibor offers accessible walks (p415) covering a range of cultural sites. Climbers will enjoy the canyons of the Drina River.

Kayaking & Rafting

It's possible to kayak and raft at Tara National Park along the Drina River; contact the **'Drina-Tara' Rafting Club** (www.raftingtara.com, in Serbian) or **Era Rafting Club** (☎ 0644131752; azara@ptt.yu). BAS-affiliated rafting club **'Bodo'** (www.tarabodo.com) also organises rafting on the Tara.

There's a quirky rafting event on the Ibar River every July; see p413.

BOOKS

Tim Judah looks at Serbian history from the landmark Battle of Kosovo in *The Serbs: History, Myth and the Destruction of Yugoslavia*. Sabrina Ramet's *Balkan Babel* is an engaging look at Yugoslavia from Tito to Milošević. Åsne Seierstad's *With their Backs to the World* (2005) offers insightful portraits of local Serbs after 1999. Vesna Goldsworthy's memoir *Chernobyl Strawberries* provides a portrait of a young Serb in Yugoslavia and the UK.

Momo Kapor's *A Guide to the Serbian Mentality* is a tongue-in-cheek but insightful look at the Serbian psyche from a Serbian perspective.

Matthew Collin's *Guerilla Radio: Rock 'N' Roll Radio and Serbia's Underground Resistance* is a fast-paced and edgy tale about B92 radio station, which stood up to Milošević and became a force of resistance in Serbia.

White Eagles over Serbia is a romping fusion of Yugoslavian commentary and good old-fashioned 1950s espionage by literary heavyweight Lawrence Durrell. For more, see p22.

BUSINESS HOURS

Banks are open from around 8am to 5am Monday to Friday and 8am to 2pm Saturday. On weekdays many shops open 8am to 6pm, and some open until early afternoon on Saturday. Restaurants are generally open 8am to 11pm or midnight, and bars are open 9pm until around 3am. Take all of this with a grain of salt (see the boxed text, p434).

COURSES

The **Serbian Language and Culture Course** (www.srpsk ijezik.edu.yu; Oslobodioci Valjeva 31, Valjevo; min 20 classes over 2 weeks €310) affiliated with Belgrade University can arrange accommodation and board.

Courses in Roma culture are offered at **Amala Summer School** (www.galbeno.co.yu) in Valjevo, 100km southwest of Belgrade,

focusing on Roma culture, music and dance, and Romany and Serbian language.

CUSTOMS

If you're bringing in more than €5000 (or €5000 worth of equipment) you must complete a currency declaration form on arrival and show it on departure. It's unlikely, but customs officials could confiscate your cash if you don't declare it.

DANGERS & ANNOYANCES

Travelling around Serbia is generally as safe as elsewhere for the traveller who exercises the usual caution. The only exceptions to this can occur around border areas, particularly the southeast border with Kosovo, where Serb-Albanian tensions remain. Check the situation before attempting to cross overland into Kosovo, and think twice about driving there with a Serbian-plated car.

A particularly hard-to-avoid annoyance is smoking, which happens even in nonsmoking zones.

DISCOUNT CARDS

The EURO<26 discount card (www.euro26 .org.yu) gives cardholders discounts on rail travel, air travel with JAT, and some hotels.

EMBASSIES & CONSULATES

A complete list of embassies and consulates in Serbia and Serbian embassies around the world is available at www.mfa.gov.yu /worldframe.htm. Countries represented in Belgrade (area code ☎ 011):

Albania (Map p383; ☎ 306 6642; embassy.belgrade@ mfa.gov.al; bul Mira 25a)
Australia (Map p386; ☎ 330 3400; belgrade .embassy@dfat.gov.au; Čika Ljubina 13)
BiH (Map p383; ☎ 329 1995; ambasadabih@sbb.co.yu; Milana Tankosića 8)
Bulgaria (Map p386; ☎ 361 3980; bulgamb@eunet.yu; Birčaninova 26)
Canada (Map p386; ☎ 306 3000; bgrad@interna tional.gc.ca; Kneza Miloša 75)
Croatia (Map p386; ☎ 367 9150; crobg@mvpei.hr; Kneza Miloša 62)
France (Map p386; ☎ 302 3500; ambafr_1@eunet .yu; Pariska 11)
Germany (Map p386; ☎ 306 4300; germany@sbb .co.yu; Kneza Miloša 74-76)
Hungary (Map p386; ☎ 244 0472; mission.blg@kum .hu; Krunska 72)

Netherlands (Map p386; ☎ 202 3900; bel@minbuza.nl; Simina 29)
UK (Map p386; ☎ 264 5055; ukembbg@eunet.yu; Resavska 46)
USA (Map p386; ☎ 361 9344; http://belgrade
.usembassy.gov; Kneza Miloša 50)

FESTIVALS & EVENTS

Pop, rock, techno and electronic aficionados from all over Europe flock to Novi Sad's Exit festival (see the boxed text, p401) in July and maybe on to Belgrade's Beer Festival in August.

On a different note, there's the boisterous Dragačevo Trumpet Festival (see the boxed text, p414).

Vojvodina and Belgrade are particularly known for putting on good parties; see p400 and p390.

GAY & LESBIAN TRAVELLERS

Once upon a time, the Serbian Criminal Code made sex between consenting (male) adults illegal. This was repealed in 1994, but homophobia hasn't been done away with. The gay and lesbian scene remains underground; for more information, see www.gay-serbia.com and p432.

HOLIDAYS

Public holidays in Serbia:
New Year 1 January
Orthodox Christmas 7 January
St Sava's Day 27 January
Nation Day 15 February
Orthodox Good Friday April (see p433 for dates)
Orthodox Easter Monday April (see p433 for dates)
International Labour Days 1 and 2 May
Victory Day 9 May
Republic Day 29 November
St Vitus's Day 28 June

St Sava's Day, Victory Day and St Vitus's Day are working days but are as revered as public holidays.

Orthodox churches celebrate Easter between one and five weeks later than other churches.

INTERNET RESOURCES

B92 Network (www.b92.net/eng) Daily English-language news.
National Tourist Organisation (www.serbia-tourism.org)

Serbian Government (www.serbia.sr.gov.yu)
Serbian Ministry of Foreign Affairs (www.mfa.gov.yu)
Serbian Orthodox Church (www.spc.yu/eng) Official site.

LANGUAGE

Serbian is the common language. Many people speak English and German from years working abroad.

Hungarians in Vojvodina use the Latin alphabet, Serbs use both Latin and Cyrillic. See the Language chapter (p454) for useful phrases and the Cyrillic alphabet.

MAPS

Freytag & Berndt offers the useful 1:385,000 *Serbia and Montenegro*. Cartographia produces the 1:800,000 *Serbia, Montenegro, Bosnia & Herzegovina and Macedonia*.

Autoatlas-Srbija i Crna Gora/Beograd by M@gic M@p is a useful reference.

Plan Grada Beograd is a detailed Belgrade city map. Maps are also available from tourist offices and bookshops throughout the region. A creative one is the colourful *Belgrade Witty Map* (270DIN).

MONEY

Serbia retains the dinar, although some hotels may want payment in euros. One dinar amounts to 100 para, but you'd need a trainload to buy anything

Western Union (www.westernunion.com) transfers can be made at most banks and major post offices. ATMs are plentiful in major towns. Cards are widely accepted by businesses. Exchange offices readily change hard currencies into dinars and back again; look for the large, yellow, diamond-shaped 'Menjačica' signs. Exchange machines generally accept euros, US dollars and UK pounds and can change up to €200 at a time. Most banks charge a commission to change travellers cheques.

POST

Parcels should be taken unsealed to the main post office for inspection.

You can receive mail, addressed poste restante, in all towns for a small charge.

TELEPHONE & FAX

Press the 'i' button on public phones for dialling commands in English. Calls to

SERBIA

EMERGENCY NUMBERS

- Ambulance ☎ 94
- Fire service ☎ 93
- Motoring assistance in Belgrade ☎ 987
- Motoring assistance outside Belgrade ☎ 011 9800
- Police ☎ 92

Europe/Australia/North America cost around 50/100/80DIN a minute.

Long-distance calls can also be made from booths in post offices.

Fax

Faxes can be sent from large hotels or post offices (take photocopies, as originals may be kept). Faxing costs 170/253/253DIN per page to Europe/Australia/North America.

Phonecards

Phonecards can be bought in post offices and tobacco kiosks for 300DIN (for local-call cards) and 600DIN (for international-call cards). Halo Plus cards allow longer calls locally, in the FYR region or internationally, depending on which category you buy. Calls to Europe/Australia/North America cost 13/40/40DIN per minute.

There are three mobile operators in Serbia. **MT:S** (www.mts.telekom.yu) numbers begin with 064 and 065, **Telenor** (www.telenor.co.yu) numbers begin with 062 and 063, and **VIP mobile** (www.vipmobile.co.yu) numbers begin with 060 and 061. Phone numbers can be purchased at branches around town for around 200DIN and recharge cards at supermarkets and kiosks.

TOURIST INFORMATION

Top marks to Novi Sad and Belgrade; both have plenty of English material and friendly fountains of knowledge behind the desk. Tourist-office addresses throughout the country can be found at www.serbia.travel/cms/item/info/en/TouristOrg.html.

The usefulness of tourist offices outside Serbia (affiliated with JAT Airways) depends entirely on the person sitting at the desk.

In addition to the **National Tourist Office of Serbia** (www.serbia.travel), the **Tourist Organization of Belgrade** (www.tob.co.yu) is a useful starting point.

TOURS

Look for a tour company that suits through the **National Association of Travel Agencies** (YUTA; Map p386; ☎ 011-322 8686; www.yuta.co.yu; Kondina 14, Belgrade). Tourist offices can usually connect you to local and regional tour agents.

Ace Cycling & Mountaineering Center (☎ /fax 018-247 287; www.ace-adventurecentre.com; B Krsmanovica 51/8, Niš) organises guided cycling and walking tours in Serbia.

TRAVELLERS WITH DISABILITIES

Some top-end hotels cater for travellers with disabilities, but uneven pavements, stairs, slopes and limited lift access make getting around town difficult. Many places of interest are in the older towns, but the older the town the harder the access.

VISAS

Tourist visas for fewer than 90 days aren't required by citizens of most European countries, Australia, New Zealand, Canada and the USA. The **Ministry of Foreign Affairs** (www.mfa.gov.yu/visas/visasr.htm) has full details.

If you're not staying at a hotel or private home you must register with the police within 24 hours of arrival and subsequently on changing address.

WOMEN TRAVELLERS

Other than cursory interest shown by men towards solo women travellers, travelling is hassle-free and easy. In Muslim areas some women wear a headscarf but most adopt Western fashions.

TRANSPORT IN SERBIA

This section deals with travel to, from and throughout Serbia. For travel within the Western Balkans, see p439.

GETTING THERE & AWAY
Air

Serbia is well served by regional airlines from intercontinental hubs. Travellers from Australasia can fly to Dubai and pick up a JAT flight to Belgrade, or with Lufthansa via Frankfurt, or Austrian Airlines via Vienna. Travellers from North America pick up connecting flights in London or Frankfurt. Other than Germanwings, none of the European discount airlines flies to Belgrade.

DEPARTURE TAX

Departure tax for domestic/international flights is €8.50/16.50, which may be covered in the price of your ticket. Children under two incur no such tax.

Belgrade's **Nikola Tesla Beograd Airport** (☎ 011-209 444, 0648485402, 063255066; www.airport-belgrade .co.yu) handles most international flights. Office telephone numbers below are for Belgrade (area code ☎ 011):

Aeroflot (airline code SU; ☎ 328 6071; www.aeroflot .com) Hub Moscow Sheremetyevo.

Aerosvit (airline code VV; ☎ 328 3430; www.aerosvit .ua/eng) Hub Kyiv.

Air France (airline code AF; ☎ 638 378; www.airfrance .com) Hub Paris Charles de Gaulle.

Alitalia (airline code AZ; ☎ 676 692; www.alitalia.com) Hub Rome.

Austrian Airlines (airline code OS; ☎ 324 8077; www .aua.com) Hub Vienna.

British Airways (airline code BA; ☎ 328 1303; www .britishairways.com) Hub London Heathrow.

ČSA (Czech Airlines; airline code OK; ☎ 361 4592; www .csa.cz) Hub Prague.

Germanwings (airline code 4U; ☎ 526 7005; www .germanwings.com) Hub Cologne.

JAT (airline code JU; ☎ 311 4222; www.jat.com) Hub Belgrade.

Kuban Airlines (airline code KIL; ☎ 303 7106; www .alk.ru) Hub Krasnodar.

Lufthansa (airline code LH; ☐ 303 4944; www .lufthansa.com) Hub Frankfurt.

Montavia (airline code GZP; ☎ 362 0690; www.mont avia.com) Hub Moscow.

Montenegro Airlines (airline code YM; ☎ 262 1122; www.montenegro-airlines.cg.yu) Hub Podgorica.

Norwegian Air Shuttle (airline code DY; www.norwe gian.no) Hub Fornebu.

Olympic Airways (airline code OA; ☎ 303 6850; www .olympic-alrlways.gr) Hub Athens.

Swiss International Air Lines (airline code LX; ☎ 303 0140; www.swiss.com) Hub Zurich.

Tunisair (airline code TU; ☎ 323 3174; www.tunisair .com) Hub Tunis.

Turkish Airlines (airline code TK; ☎ 303 6195; www .turkishairlines.com) Hub Istanbul.

Land

Serbia is easily entered from any of its neighbours, though Kosovo poses complications. Make sure you are registered with the police (it's the duty of your hotel/host to do this) and have registration paper(s) with you when leaving.

Decent maps of the region such as the Freytag & Berndt map (see p419) and the National Tourist Office of Serbia brochure *In Serbia by Car* show borders.

BICYCLE

There are no problems bringing bicycles into the country. Outside Vojvodina, some areas can be hilly. There are not many cyclists here, so drivers are not cycle-savvy.

BORDER CROSSINGS
BiH

Border crossings are at Sremska Rača, Badovinci, Trbušnica, Zvornik and Kotroman.

Croatia

Crossing points are at Bijeljina, Batrovci, Šid, Bačka Palanka, Bogojevo, Apatin and Bezdan.

Kosovo

At the time of research the main crossings between Kosovo and Serbia were at Jarinje (gate 1) and Banja (gate 31). Additionally, there were gate 3 in Medare, gate 4 in Mutivoda and gate 5 in the Presevo valley. Note that, because Serbia does not acknowledge crossing points into Kosovo as international border crossings, it may not be possible to enter Serbia from Kosovo unless you first entered Kosovo from Serbia (or Albania, Macedonia or Montenegro).

Gates 1 and 31 were temporarily closed after damage was caused by angry mobs on 19 February 2008 after Kosovo's declaration of independence two days before. Before attempting to cross here, check the situation with your embassy.

Also see the travel advisory boxed text, p270.

Macedonia

There are crossings at Preševo and Đeneral Janković. (Note that the latter is controversial because Serbia considers it part of the Serbia border with Macedonia, but it is physically in Kosovo.)

BUS

There's well-developed bus service to Western Europe and Turkey. Contact Bas Turist (p383) or Lasta (p383) for further information. For sample routes, see the table, p422.

SERBIA

INTERNATIONAL BUS SERVICES FROM BELGRADE

Destination	Price (DIN)	Duration (hr)	Departures
Amsterdam	9840	9	Wed & Sat
Banja Luka	1665	7½	daily
Bratislava	2600	12	Wed & Sun
Ljubljana	3000	7½	daily
Malmö	10,890	12	Fri & Sun
Milan	4920	17½	Wed, Sat
Paris	7600	28	Mon, Tue, Wed, Fri & Sat
Sarajevo	1640	8	daily
Split	3800	12½	daily except Sun
Vienna	2560	9½	Mon, Tue, Wed & Thu
Zurich	5700	23	Tue & Sat

CAR & MOTORCYCLE

Drivers need an international driving permit (available from your home motoring association), and vehicles need green card insurance or insurance (from €80 a month) purchased at the border. See p447.

Driving Serbian-plated cars into Kosovo is not advised, and often not permitted by rental agencies or insurers.

TRAIN

International rail connections out of Serbia originate in Belgrade. Heading north and west, most call at Novi Sad and Subotica and go east via Niš. For sample daily services from Belgrade, see the table, right.

Several trips from Serbia offer a nice slice of the Balkans; the scenic route to Bar on the Montenegrin coast is one. For more, visit www.serbianrailways.com.

GETTING AROUND
Bicycle

Cyclists are rarer than they should be; in larger cities such as Belgrade and Novi Sad bicycle paths are improving, as is pedestrian respect for them. Vojvodina is relatively flat, but the main roads make for dull days. Mountainous regions such as Zlatibor offer some good mountain biking in summer months. More interesting winding roads come with the downside of narrow shoulders.

For info on cycling tours, see p420.

Bus

Bus services are generally reliable and extensive, but outside major hubs, sporadic connections may leave you in the lurch for a few hours. This is particularly true in southern Serbia; don't count on being able to get from anywhere to everywhere, at any time. You may have to double back to transport hubs.

Buses are rarely full and there's usually a row available for everyone; reservations are only worthwhile for international buses, during holidays and where long-distance journeys are infrequent. Receipts are given for luggage carried below (20DIN to 50DIN per piece).

Prices quoted in this book won't always be spot on; fares vary depending on which company is running the route.

Car & Motorcycle

Independent travel by car or motorcycle is an ideal way to discover Serbia. Outside main cities parking is generally no problem; most hotels offer guests free parking. Carefully scrutinise parking signs in Belgrade and other

TRAIN SERVICES FROM BELGRADE

Destination	Price (DIN)	Duration (hr)
Bucharest	4200	14
Budapest	2780	7
Istanbul	5190	26
Ljubljana	4150	10
Moscow	10,000	50
Munich	9000	17
Sofia	2600	11
Thessaloniki	4200	16
Vienna	6950	11
Zagreb	3100	7

Prices include sleeper.

large towns. You may have to purchase tickets from machines or kiosks or via SMS.

Traffic police are everywhere and accidents happen all the time. Drive on the right, buckle up, don't drink (the blood-alcohol limit is 0.05%) and stick to speed limits (120km/h on motorways, 100km/h on dual carriageways, 80km/h on main roads and 60km/h in urban areas).

AUTOMOBILE ASSOCIATIONS
The **Automobile and Motorcycle Association of Serbia** (Auto-Moto Savez Srbije; Map p386; ☎ 011-333 1200; www .amss.org.yu; Kneginje Zorke 58, Belgrade), temporarily at Ruzveltova 18, Belgrade (Map p383), provides extensive information on its website, and roadside assistance (call ☎ 987).

FUEL & SPARE PARTS
Filling up is no problem in medium-sized towns, but don't squeeze it to the last drop; there are few late-night petrol stations. Spare parts for major brands (check with your dealer before you travel) are readily available.

HIRE
Several companies have offices at Belgrade airport, including **AVIS** (☎ 011-209 7062; www.avis-ser bia.co.yu; ☉ 8am-8pm), **Budget** (☎ 011-228 6361; www .budget.co.yu; ☉ 8am-8pm Mon-Fri, to 6pm Sat, to 5pm Sun), **Europcar** (☎ 011-228 9028; www.europcar.co.uk; ☉ 8am-9pm Mon-Fri, noon-9pm Sat & Sun) and **Hertz** (☎ 011-228 6017; www.hertz.co.yu; ☉ 8am-8pm).

The typical cost of a small hire car in Serbia is €50 per day. Check where you are *not* able to take the car.

Train
Serbian Railways (☎ 011-361 4811; www.serbianrailways .com; Nemanjina 6, Belgrade) serves Novi Sad, Subotica and Niš from Belgrade. Train enthusiasts will enjoy the Šargan 8 railway in Mokra Gora (p417). There's also an attempt to sell day trips on the *Romantika* tourist train (see p390).

Generally, trains aren't as regular and reliable as buses, with fewer services and more breakdowns. Tickets can be booked direct through Serbian Railways or through travel agents.

Western Balkans Directory

CONTENTS

The regional directory provides a general overview of information applying to the whole of the Western Balkans. It's a diverse region of millions of people, so we've had to generalise a bit. For more specific information, refer to the relevant country directories.

ACCOMMODATION

For each accommodation listing in this book, we've generally used the currency in which the hostel, hotel or guesthouse quotes their prices; some in local currency and others in euros

---

BOOK YOUR STAY ONLINE

For more accommodation reviews and recommendations by Lonely Planet authors, check out lonelyplanet.com/hotels where you'll find the insider low-down on the best places to stay. Reviews are thorough and independent. Best of all, you can book online.

PRACTICALITIES

- Standard European electricity is used (220V to 240V/50Hz to 60Hz); as throughout Europe, the region uses standard electricity plugs with two round prongs.

- The metric system is used for weights and measures.

- Every country in the region is in the Central European time zone (GMT+1).

- For useful websites covering the region, see p24.

---

or US dollars. Some establishments quote in one currency but expect or accept payment in another.

Accommodation suggestions and reviews in this book are listed in three broad categories: budget, midrange and top end. Because these vary across the region (Croatia is in a different economic class from Albania, for instance), they are categorised according to local price ranges, not by some regional standard. Within each category, we've ordered reviews according to our personal opinion. This is of course a subjective way to do things; just because Goran's place is listed before Mira's doesn't necessarily mean that there's an enormous difference, but perhaps Goran's is closer to the centre or has a bigger bathroom.

The cheapest places to shack up are camping grounds, followed by hostels and student accommodation. Guesthouses, *pensions* and private rooms offer good value and some hotels offer comparably low prices. In some regions, self-catering flats offer fantastic value. Those in cities may need to be arranged well in advance during season and may demand a minimum stay. Countryside cottages may suit people travelling in groups.

Peak holiday periods and major festivals can make accommodation scarce; book ahead. Sometimes even camping grounds fill up, particularly near large towns and cities. Popular destinations such as Dubrovnik and

Hvar can fill up quickly at any time. Make reservations as many weeks ahead as possible, at least for the first night or two. A two-minute international call (or Skype call) seems a more sensible use of time and money than spending a day of your holiday looking for accommodation.

Accommodation-booking desks at airports rarely cover the lower hotel strata; tourist offices generally have more extensive accommodation lists, and the helpful ones will go out of their way to find you a place to hang your hat.

Camping

There are many camping grounds throughout the region. Even those intended for motorists are often easily accessible with public transport and almost always have space for backpackers with tents. Many camping grounds rent small on-site cabins, bungalows or caravans for double or triple the regular camping fee. Some camping grounds are usefully affiliated with outdoor-activity companies.

The standard of camping grounds varies a lot. Some have pristine facilities, others offer basic squat toilets and sporadic water supply. Croatia's coast has nudist camping grounds galore (signposted 'FKK', the German acronym for 'naturist') in secluded locations for those who don't mind letting it all hang out.

Depending on facilities, location and demand, camping grounds may only be open from April to October, May to September, or perhaps only June to August. A few private camping grounds are open year-round. In popular resorts, bungalows will probably be full in July and August.

You're sometimes allowed to build a campfire – ask first. Camping in the wild is usually illegal; ask locals about the situation before you pitch your tent on a beach or in an open field.

Guesthouses & Pensions

Small private *pensions* (or *pansions*) are common in the Western Balkans. Priced between hotels and private rooms, *pensions* typically have fewer than a dozen rooms and sometimes a small restaurant or bar on the premises. You'll get more familial service at a *pension* than you would at a hotel, which may come at the expense of a teensy bit of privacy,

though many are run with the unobtrusive efficiency of hotels.

Homestays & Private Rooms

Homestays are often the most authentic way to experience daily life in the region. Bring small gifts for your hosts – it's a deeply ingrained cultural tradition.

In most countries, travel agencies can arrange accommodation in local homes or you will be approached at train or bus stations by people with rooms to let. This can be good or bad – it's impossible to generalise. Just make sure you check the room and clearly negotiate the price before you commit, and don't leave valuables behind when you go out. When in doubt, arrange rooms through tourist offices, which have lists of places registered for room rental.

The other option is to find a place yourself; look for pleasant buildings marked with signs reading *Zimmer frei* (German), *sobi* (Macedonian) or *room* (English!).

Hostels

There isn't a hostel scene throughout the whole region as yet; it's in its foetal stages in Albania, Kosovo, Macedonia and Montenegro. Where there are hostels, they are generally cheap, secure and available to everyone – not just card-carrying youths. Many hostels are part of the national Youth Hostel Association (YHA), which is affiliated with Hostelling International (HI). Hostel cards are seldom required but may net small discounts. Cards can be purchased at some hostels, through national hostelling offices or through HI (www.iyhf.org); also see p432.

In our experience, most hostels provide clean linen, towels, soap and toilet paper. In extremely rare situations you may be required to bring or hire a sleeping sheet. Hostels generally provide a bed, communal bathrooms

---

WHERE BB IS KING

Throughout the region when a building has no official number its address is usually written with the street name followed by 'bb'. This stands for *bez broja* – 'without a number'. Be aware that rural 'bb's might give a village name rather than a street.

and shared kitchens. Some extend to a couple of twin rooms and fancier facilities such as internet access.

The downside of hostels (aside from their absence in some places) is that they can be a bugger to find in unsigned buildings hidden down obscure laneways; at least touts at bus/train stations can show you the way! Some savvier hostels will meet you somewhere or pick you up.

More private hostels have opened in recent years, which often are more akin to small hotels. Some are terrific, but others you need to be wary of; we've had reports of some places operating as 'hostels' when they're only registered for private room rental.

Some hostels (in bigger cities such as Belgrade) have 24-hour receptions; others require you to arrange an arrival time in advance. Generally, people prearrange such accommodation online through websites like www.iyhf.org, www.hostelworld.com or www.hostelbookers.com, but out of season you can just rock up. A reliable site for bookings and frank traveller reviews is www.hostels.com/en/easterneurope.html.

UNIVERSITY ACCOMMODATION

Some universities rent out space in student halls, particularly during July and August. This is quite popular in Croatia and is taking off in Serbia. Accommodation is sometimes in single rooms, but mostly in doubles or triples (which you may have all to yourself). Cooking facilities may be available. Enquire at the college or university, at student information services or local tourist offices.

Hotels

Hotels can be decadent five-stair affairs or low-key establishments as cheap as private rooms. We've tried to cover the spectrum of budgets in each country, unless the choice is between the overpriced Stalin-style Jugo-petro-no-go and a cheap and cheerful guesthouse. Generally prices include breakfast.

Some bigger cities have sparkling international chain hotels which offer the same high standard you would expect anywhere in the world.

There are still some communist-era hotels across the region. Many have moved into private hands, but that doesn't necessarily mean they've had so much as a change of sheets since Tito went to meet Marx.

But, call us nostalgic travel writers, so long as you don't mind sleeping in mattresses moulded into the shape of previous guests and eating the occasional stale breakfast while pigeons pick the crumbs from last night's folk-fest off the floor, some of these crumbling oldies offer precisely the kind of character you may want to experience while you're in the Balkans. As for the others – nothing a quick whack with a wrecking ball wouldn't fix.

Motels

On the outskirts of many towns (generally a few kilometres out, towards major transport arteries) you often find a couple of motels. These can be comfortable affairs with some business facilities, sometimes of a higher, newer standard than crustier hotels in town. The downside to these is that they're generally oriented towards motorists so may be hard to reach without your own wheels. On the other hand, there may also be some 'motels' in the centre, which don't necessarily provide parking, or much else.

Throughout this book we've generally not added motels on the outskirts. We just thought you should know they're there.

ACTIVITIES

Activity options in the region are endless; you can mountaineer and paraglide or have rural adventures on a mountain bike or a donkey. See country chapters for more.

Canoeing & Kayaking

Some great kayaking and canoeing outfits operate out of Croatia's Elafiti and Kornati Islands (see p253) as well as Montenegro's Herceg Novi (p341). In BiH, areas around Banja Luka and the Una River around Bihać offer some pleasant paddling, often with little advance preparation (see p163). Also consider paddling on Macedonia's Lake Ohrid (p308).

Cycling

The hills and mountains of the Western Balkans can be heavy going, but this is offset by the abundance of things to see. Physical fitness is not a major prerequisite for cycling the flat expanses of northern Serbia. There are some interesting mountain-bike trails around Krupa in the Vrbas canyons of BiH (p160), and northern Albania is attracting more mountain bikers these days. Cycling is increasingly popular in Croatia's Istria (p199) and Kvarner (p210), where tourist offices can provide maps with marked routes, as well as on the Macedonian coast (p308).

See p445 for more information on bicycle touring, and the individual destination sections for rental outfits.

Diving

The sparkling waters and varied marine life of the Adriatic support a thriving diving industry, particularly in Croatia, where cave diving is a speciality (see p253), and increasingly in Montenegro (see p368) and in Macedonia's Lake Ohrid (p307).

Hiking

There's some excellent hiking along trails in forests, mountains and national parks throughout the Western Balkans. Public transport often gets you to trailheads, and chalets or mountain huts offer dormitory accommodation and basic meals. Generally, ski areas become hiking hubs in summer months.

Some specifically great hiking areas include the Paklenica and Risnjak National Parks in Croatia (p253), the national parks of Macedonia (p327) and its spectacular gorges at Lake Matka (p297) near Skopje.

Zlatibor (p414) in southern Serbia offers some relatively mild but scenically rewarding hiking. There are excellent routes throughout Montenegro (p368).

Mt Tomorri National Park in Albania (p79) is a true hiking frontier, as is the Balkans Peace Park (see the boxed text, p61).

The best months for hiking are from June to September, especially late August and early September, when the summer crowds will have disappeared.

Landmines in BiH and Kosovo (and parts of Slavonia in Croatia) mean that hiking should *not* be undertaken without first seeking information from national parks, tourist offices or qualified guides.

Skiing

Ski resorts around the Western Balkans offer lower prices and smaller crowds than elsewhere in Europe. The season generally lasts from early December to late March, though at higher altitudes may extend an extra month either way. Snow conditions vary from year to year and region to region, but January and February tend to be the best (and busiest) months.

Host of the 1984 Winter Olympics, BiH offers inexpensive skiing at the resorts of Jahorina, Bjelašnica and Vlašić (p163). Macedonia's Mavrovo ski resort (p298) is establishing a name for itself, as are Serbian resorts at Kopaonik (p413) and tamer Zlatibor (p414). The next Montenegrin skiing discovery will be Durmitor (p365). Hopefully, Kosovo's Brezovica (p278) will be back in business soon.

White-Water Rafting

Rafting is possible from March to October on a growing number of scenic rivers, including the Una near Bihać in BiH (p163) and the Tara in Montenegro's World Heritage–listed Durmitor National Park (p365). It's also possible to raft on the Drina (from BiH or Serbia) and the Ibar (p417). Rafting in Albania is also on the rise (p64).

Yachting

The most famous yachting area is the passage between the long, rugged islands off Croatia's Dalmatian coast (p253). Yacht tours and rentals are also available (for those who aren't on a budget) in Montenegro; see p368.

SAFETY GUIDELINES FOR WALKING

Before setting off, consider the following:

- Pay any fees and acquire necessary permits.
- Be sure you are healthy and comfortable walking for a sustained period.
- Only embark on tracks within your realm of experience.
- Obtain reliable information about physical and environmental conditions along your intended route (eg from park authorities), including track-specific weather conditions.
- In BiH and Kosovo seek out authoritative information about landmines from park authorities (or NATO in Kosovo).
- Be aware of local laws, regulations and etiquette about wildlife and the environment.

428 WESTERN BALKANS DIRECTORY •• Business Hours

RESPONSIBLE HIKING & CAMPING

To help preserve the ecology and beauty of the Balkans, consider the following tips (and those on p21).

Rubbish

■ Carry out *all* your rubbish including easily forgotten items like silver paper, orange peel, cigarette butts and plastic wrappers. Make an effort to carry out rubbish left by others.

■ Never bury rubbish: it takes years to decompose and may be dug up by animals, which could be injured or poisoned by it. Digging also disturbs soil and ground cover and encourages erosion.

■ Minimise waste by taking minimal packaging and no more food than you need. Take reusable containers or stuff sacks.

■ Sanitary napkins, tampons, condoms and toilet paper should be carried out; they decompose poorly.

Human Waste Disposal

■ When camping in the wild (after checking to see that it's allowed), bury your business in a hole at least 15cm deep and at least 100m from any nearby water. Same goes with portable toilet tents.

Washing

■ Don't use detergents, toothpaste etc in or near watercourses, even if they are biodegradable.

■ For personal washing, use biodegradable soap and a water container (or a lightweight, portable basin) at least 50m away from the watercourse. Disperse waste water widely to allow the soil to filter it fully.

■ Wash cooking utensils 50m from watercourses using a scourer, sand or snow instead of detergent.

Erosion

■ Hillsides and mountain slopes, especially at high altitudes, are prone to erosion. Stick to existing tracks and avoid short cuts.

BUSINESS HOURS

Saturday and Sunday are usually days off, though many shops, restaurants and cafes are open every day, and banks and post offices sometimes open for half of Saturday. Even in predominately Muslim areas, Sunday rather than Friday (the Muslim day of prayer) is taken off. Beyond this, all we can say is good luck: premises sometimes close for long lunches or just for the hell of it. Often someone can be telephoned or tracked down to reopen things, but often not. For specific details, see country directories.

CHILDREN

The family-oriented folk in these parts are all the more friendly when children are involved. Travelling with kids adds a whole new dimension to your trip and provides you with many opportunities to interact with people (and your kids many opportunities to have their cheeks pinched). Having a break from sightseeing at the local playground or swimming pool can be a nice respite for you and your kids, and may even introduce you to people that childless travellers would never have the opportunity to meet.

Child-friendly local culture pervades; often kids will stay out with their parents to the early hours. More activities are now geared towards children, and more facilities are factoring them in; car-rental firms often hire children's safety seats for a price. Some restaurants and hotels even offer high chairs; fewer will have cots (cribs). The choice of baby food, infant formulas, soy and cow's milk, disposable nappies (diapers) and the like can be as great in supermarkets as it is back home – even in Kosovo and Albania – though prices for imported items can be disproportionately high.

- If a well-used track passes through a mud patch, walk through the mud so as not to increase the size of the patch.
- Avoid removing the plant life that keeps topsoils in place.

Fires & Low-Impact Cooking

- Don't depend on open fires for cooking; chopping wood in trekking areas can cause rapid deforestation. Cook on a lightweight kerosene, alcohol or Shellite (white gas) stove and avoid those powered by disposable butane gas canisters.
- Encourage your trekking mates to be outfitted with enough clothing so that fires are not a necessity for warmth.
- If you use local accommodation, select places that don't use wood fires to heat water or cook food.
- If you light a fire (in areas that get few visitors), use only dead or fallen wood in an existing fireplace. Remember the adage 'the bigger the fool, the bigger the fire'; use only what you need.
- Ensure that you fully extinguish fires by spreading embers and flooding them with water.

Wildlife Conservation

- Don't buy items made from endangered species.
- Discourage the presence of wildlife by not leaving food scraps behind. Place gear out of reach and tie packs to rafters or trees.
- Don't feed the wildlife, as this can lead to animals becoming dependent on hand-outs, to unbalanced populations and to diseases.

Private Property

- Wild camping is not always allowed; sometimes permits are required. Check at local tourist offices or seek permission to camp on or cross private land from landowners.

Environmental Organisations

- The WWF (www.panda.org) has various Balkans-based conservation projects.
- CEEweb for Biodiversity (www.ceeweb.org) is a network of conservation organisations throughout the region and beyond. One issue it addresses is sustainable development of tourism.

One irritation can be protecting your child from inhaling the cigarette fumes of nearby smokers (some of whom are virtually children themselves). A polite request and a friendly chat will quickly get over this.

In Albania, praise won't be lavished on your child – and nor should you lavish praise on Albanian kids – there are concerns about the all-observant 'evil eye'.

Sidewalks in some areas make prams inconvenient; better to go with a sling or pouch.

For more advice, grab a copy of *Travel with Children* by Cathy Lanigan.

CLIMATE CHARTS

The Western Balkans can be boiling hot and freezing cold, but neither extreme will prevent travel. In fact, this is a fascinating place to visit at any time of year – even winter. July and August can be uncomfortably hot, particularly in the cities, but this is the time when mountains and beaches are at their best. From a climatic point of view, May, June and September are the best months in which to visit the region, with nowhere too warm or too cool. See p430 for climate charts.

CUSTOMS

The usual allowances for tobacco (200 to 250 cigarettes), alcohol (2L of wine, 1L of spirits) and perfume (50g) apply to duty-free goods purchased at airports or on ferries. The tobacco quota can sometimes be exceeded – locals understand how expensive cigarettes are in the wider world (and sympathise with the addiction!). Customs checks are pretty cursory and you probably won't have to open your bags, but don't be lulled into a false sense of security. There may also be restrictions on the import/export of local currency, although

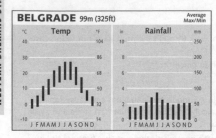

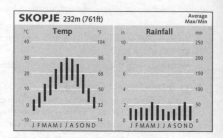

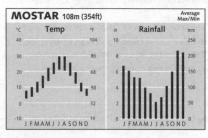

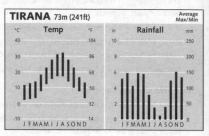

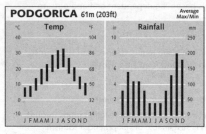

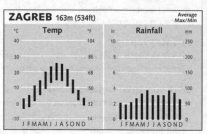

the amounts allowed these days are actually quite large.

While there's no problem bringing in and taking out personal effects, be aware that antiques, books printed before 1945, crystal, gemstones and precious metals (gold, silver, platinum), securities and valuable works of art may still have to be declared in writing or even accompanied by a 'museum certificate' (available from the place of purchase) in many countries.

DANGERS & ANNOYANCES

Brace yourself for the shocking first sentence of the crucial Dangers & Annoyances section: the Western Balkans is slightly *safer* than the developed-world average.

Without wanting to gloss over things (and with another reminder to consult individual chapters), the fact is that the horrors of recent wars have severely skewed perceptions about

the region. The leftover dangers are primarily landmines (in Kosovo, BiH, and Slavonia in Croatia) and ethnic tensions in very select areas (at the time of writing limited to border regions of Serbia and Kosovo, which were prone to flare up around key political events). The policies that your country supports or has supported with respect to this region will not be held against you.

Tell your concerned parents (or kids) that a traveller's personal safety in the Western Balkans is generally more assured than in the big cities of Western Europe, North America or Australia, albeit with a much higher threat of passive smoking. Street smarts that you apply in those places will see you through this region. As with anywhere in the world, you're going to be less of a target if you don't flash expensive gear around and you don't stagger home through dark streets. Predominantly Muslim regions (Kosovo, Albania, parts of

BiH, Serbia and Macedonia) have less alcohol-induced crime; something like 50% of street crime and violence is alcohol related.

There is a significant organised-crime underworld in the Western Balkans, but if you don't bother it, it won't bother you. Concerned locals may shock you with tales of muggings and thefts, but bear in mind that they may be comparing the situation to things under communism, when the crime rate seemed lower because it was rarely reported in the media.

Cavalier driving habits, badly maintained roads (particularly in Albania) and vehicles, and road hazards (like livestock) increase the risk of traffic accidents. See p446 for more information, and country chapters for local peculiarities.

Corruption

We do still get occasional reports of encounters with corrupt low-level individuals, but systemically this is on its way out. Unless your physical safety is threatened, do *not* pay bribes. Stay level-headed and remind your wannabe extortionist that you will take the matter up with your embassy. If they 'threaten' to take you down to the station, thank them for the opportunity to speak to their superiors, who will likely let you go and reprimand the officer in question. All of this applies, of course, when you haven't committed a real crime.

Drugs

Always treat drugs with a great deal of caution. There are drugs available in the region, but none of them are legal. The local penalties are severe and prison conditions aren't good.

Scams

We've had reports about shopkeepers (and even hotels, though rarely) making charge-slip imprints with credit cards on the sly, then copying signatures from the authorised slip. There have also been reports of unscrupulous people making quick and high-tech duplicates of cards. Keep your card in sight, let it go only for as long as it absolutely needs to be gone and consider cancelling it if you think something is amiss.

Now that local currencies have settled, there is essentially no black market, so if you come across one, walk the other way.

The time-old taxi scam (overcharging) is rife, but generally only around transport hubs. Move away from train and bus stations and hail down a friendly cruising cab.

Theft

Theft can happen; the threat comes from local thieves and, sadly, fellow travellers. The most important things to guard are your passport, other documents, tickets and money – in that order. It's best to carry these next to your skin and not in bumbags, which scream 'tourist' and look stupid. If you're new in town, it may be safer and more efficient to leave your luggage (but not your valuables) at train-station lockers or luggage-storage counters while you get your bearings and find a place to stay.

Carry your own padlocks for hostel lockers and for your backpack to deter people from rifling through your stuff. A chain or long-latch lock can be handy for fastening your stuff on trains, or onto hostel furniture when there aren't lockers.

Snatch thieves are most active in dense crowds, especially in bus and train stations and on public transport. Cameras and shoulder bags are a joy for these guys; put them over your head rather than just on your shoulder, or better yet use a day-pack. At restaurants and cafes, keep your bag on your lap or put your chair leg through its strap. Wearing your backpack on front makes pick-pocketing harder, but we don't approve of it because, again, it looks stupid. It also highlights the fact that you're a tourist, potentially with valuables so valuable that you're prepared to look ridiculous to protect them. Worse, it implies that you think there are lots of thieves out there. Rather than wander around looking pregnant with paranoia, we say just keep your valuables in money belts or inside pockets, and only put things you're prepared to lose in accessible pockets and bags. Also get into the habit of being more alert when you're engulfed in a crowd.

Also guard against modern theft – if you're online banking in internet cafes, it goes without saying you should diligently protect your details.

Don't leave valuables lying around your hotel room or in parked cars. Cars with foreign and/or rental-agency plates attract attention – watch out for snatch thieves when you pull up at traffic lights. Report incidents to police and ask for a written statement for the purpose of claiming insurance. Also remember that some items aren't covered by insurance if you leave them unattended. More on this at p433.

Violence

As elsewhere in Europe, there are very small groups of skinheads and neo-Nazis in the region that have targeted Roma. It is highly unlikely that travellers – of whatever colour – will encounter any violence.

DISCOUNT CARDS

Bear in mind that discount cards may only work in theory.

Camping Card International

The Camping Card International (CCI) is a camping-ground ID valid for a year that includes third-party insurance. The CCI can serve as a guarantee, whereby you hand over your CCI and keep your passport with you. Many camping grounds offer a small discount (usually 5% to 10%) to card holders.

CCIs are issued by automobile associations, camping federations and sometimes camping grounds. See www.campingcardinternational.org for a list of national bodies that issue cards.

Hostel Cards

A hostelling card can be useful, though not mandatory, for staying at hostels. Most hostels don't require you to be a hostelling association member, but sometimes charge less if you have a card. Some hostels will issue one on the spot or after a few days' stay, though this might cost more than getting one at home. For more on this, see p425.

International Student, Youth & Teacher Cards

An International Student Identity Card (ISIC), a plastic ID-style card with your photograph, provides discounts on many forms of transport (including airlines and local transport), cheap or free admission to museums and sights, and inexpensive meals in some student cafeterias and restaurants. If you're under 26 but not a student, you are eligible to apply for an International Youth Travel Card (IYTC), issued by the Federation of International Youth Travel Organisations, or the Euro<26 card (which is currently not recognised in Albania, BiH and Macedonia). Both go under different names in different countries and give much the same discounts and benefits as an ISIC. An International Teacher Identity Card (ITIC) identifies the holder as an instructor and offers similar deals. All these cards are issued by student unions, hostelling organisations and youth-oriented travel agencies.

For more information, visit www.isic.org and check destination chapters for applicability in specific countries.

Senior Cards

Make sure you bring proof of age; many attractions offer reduced-price admission for people over 60 or 65, or sometimes as low as 55 for women (we know that 55 is not senior, but take the discounts where you can!). For around €20, European residents aged 60 and over can get a Railplus Card as an add-on to their national rail senior pass, entitling the holder to train-fare reductions of 25%.

Start asking about benefits at your local senior citizens' advice bureau; discounts may already apply to travel packages and travel agents at home.

EMBASSIES & CONSULATES

Be aware of what your embassy can and can't do for you; generally speaking, it won't be much help in emergencies if the trouble you're in is remotely your own fault. You are bound by the laws of the country you are visiting.

In genuine emergencies you might get some assistance, but only if other channels have been exhausted. Free tickets home are exceedingly unlikely – embassies expect you to have insurance. If you have all your money and documents stolen, it might assist with getting a new passport, but a loan for onward travel is almost always out of the question.

See individual country chapters for addresses of embassies and consulates in the Western Balkans.

GAY & LESBIAN TRAVELLERS

While no longer illegal anywhere in the Western Balkans, homosexuality is still not completely socially acceptable. The majority of local gay men and women are reluctant to admit their sexual orientation, outside the small but thriving bar and club scene in Zagreb (Croatia) and Belgrade (Serbia), where the most progressive attitudes can be found. The gay scene in Albania is alive, albeit not yet organised. In Skopje (Macedonia) and Sarajevo (Bosnia) it's deep underground, and outside of large population centres, gay and lesbian life is almost nonexistent, taking place largely online (through sites such as www.gayromeo.com). Perhaps times are slowly a-changin', though;

the first ever **Mr Gay Balkans** (http://mistergaybalkans
.com) was held in 2006, with the winner representing the region at the annual **Mr Gay Europe** (www.mrgayeurope.com) competition.

The short of it is that, even where tolerance is on the up, it pays to be careful about how openly GLB or T you are. Same-sex pairs travelling together and sharing rooms will generally be assumed to be in platonic relationships. International websites such as www.gaydar
.com and www.gay.com may be useful.

Refer to individual country directories for more.

HOLIDAYS

Schools get the summer months off (usually July and August) as well as breaks for Easter and Christmas. These dates are generally followed even in countries with a large Muslim population, such as BiH and Albania. What newly self-declared independent Kosovo's public holidays will be isn't clear yet. See country directories for details of local holidays and festivals.

Orthodox churches celebrate Easter between one and five weeks later than other churches. See the boxed text, below, for Easter dates over the next few years.

Muslim regions of the Western Balkans celebrate two major festivals or *bajrams*: the end of Ramadan and the Feast of the Sacrifice. Muslim religious holidays follow the lunar calendar, which is 11 or 12 days shorter than the Gregorian calendar, so the dates of the *bajrams* fall 11 or 12 days earlier each (Gregorian) year. To make it even more interesting, the exact dates depend on the sighting of the new moon. In some cases, an imam from one town will spot a sliver of the moon a day earlier or later than his colleagues, so the local faithful will celebrate on a different day, which means the dates below are only approximate. See the boxed text, right, for Muslim festival dates over the next few years.

MUSLIM FESTIVAL DATES		
Year	End of Ramadan	Feast of the Sacrifice
2009	19 September	27 November
2010	9 September	16 November
2011	30 August	6 November
2012	18 August	26 October

INSURANCE

Murphy's law dictates that if you don't get insurance, you'll need it. Our mantra is this: if you can't afford travel insurance, you can't afford to travel. Policies offered by **STA Travel** (www.statravel.com) and other student-travel organisations are usually good value, as is the quick and easy online system offered by **World Nomads** (www.worldnomads.com).

Always check the fine print. Medical is obviously the most important part of the policy you get; you may prefer a policy that pays doctors or hospitals directly so you don't have to claim money back later. Generally, medical costs in the region aren't exorbitant, but check that policies cover ambulance and emergency flights home for serious injuries. Some policies let you choose your own doctor.

Some policies specifically exclude 'dangerous activities', which can include scuba diving, motorcycling, horse riding, skiing and even short treks. Some even exclude entire countries (such as BiH and Kosovo) or regions within countries.

For more on health insurance, see p451. For details on car insurance, see p447.

INTERNET ACCESS

Practically every decent-sized town has internet access for reasonable hourly rates. Some internet cafes are well-run, laid-back places where it's easy to socialise. Others are unmarked smoky dens full of teenagers playing Doom or surfing anatomically oriented websites.

More and more hotels in every price category are offering free internet access, whether dial-up, cable or wireless. In many towns you'll see signs for free wi-fi in restaurants, cafes and hotels. These signs are often metaphysical conjectures rather than statements of fact; sometimes it works like a dream, sometimes not at all. If internet is important to you, check whether it works before you commit to a room or restaurant. If you're travelling with a laptop

ORTHODOX & STANDARD EASTER DATES		
Year	Standard Easter	Orthodox Easter
2009	12 April	19 April
2010	4 April	4 April
2011	24 April	24 April
2012	8 April	15 April

or hand-held computer, be aware that your modem may not work once you leave your home country. To get around this you can buy a global modem or a local PC-card modem.

In this book, where the internet icon is used in reference to accommodation, it means that the hotel has internet-enabled computer facilities, or wi-fi for BYO laptop users.

MONEY

The main problem you'll face as you travel around the region is constant currency changes as you flit between the denar, dinar, lekë, convertible mark, kuna and euro. Most local currencies are impossible to officially change once you're outside the particular country, so spend them or change them into euros before you move on – or trade small amounts with passengers or bus drivers coming from your next destination. There's no longer any particular desire for 'hard' currency (long gone are the days when hoteliers would slash rates if you paid in US dollars) and the convertibility of all currencies makes them stable and reliable ways to carry cash.

ATMs & Credit Cards

There are plenty of ATMs in cities, major regional centres and tourist spots throughout the Western Balkans. These days you can also use credit cards (particularly Visa, MasterCard and Amex) at upmarket restaurants, shops, hotels, car-hire firms, travel agencies and many petrol stations, though cash is still preferred. Always have backup cash; many big hotels in Albania, for instance, are prepared to accept credit cards, but the system isn't always working.

Cash or debit cards that you use at home to withdraw money directly from your bank or savings account can be used throughout the region at ATMs linked to international networks such as Cirrus and Maestro. The major advantage of using ATMs is that you don't pay commission charges to exchange money and the exchange rate is usually at a better interbank rate than that offered for travellers cheques or cash exchanges.

Charge cards such as Amex and, to a lesser extent, Diners Club have offices in most countries and can generally replace a lost card within 24 hours, but they aren't widely accepted off the beaten track. Charge cards may also be hooked up to some ATM networks. Credit and credit/debit cards such

> ### DON'T BELIEVE US
>
> Throughout this book we state opening hours as they're publicly stated. These are a useful guide, but they're frequently ignored. When there are no customers left a cafe will close early. When staff at a museum or tourist office get tired, they may nip out for a nap. Internet cafes will offer a 'back in five' post-it note and come back in 50. On the other hand, during high season things may stay open later than usual. Learn from our frustrations; if you're making a long journey to a particular place, consider calling ahead to check that the doors will be open when you get there.

as Visa and MasterCard are more widely accepted because they tend to charge merchants lower commissions.

If you rely on plastic, always have a backup (like a spare €100 or even a spare credit card).

Cash

This is, of course, the easiest way to carry money, but obviously if you lose it, it's gone. The most favoured currency throughout the Western Balkans is the euro. In Montenegro and Kosovo the euro is to all intents the official currency. The US dollar and the UK pound may also be accepted, though pounds can sometimes only be exchanged in major cities.

It's possible to exchange virtually any other major world currency in big cities, but you are inevitably at the mercy of the exchange office and its rates. Exchange machines accepting euros, US dollars and UK pounds are becoming more prolific in major cities, usually at transport hubs. It's best to change your money into euros before you leave home.

Moneychangers

Before handing over cash always check the commission and rate. Shop around, never stop at the first place you see, and if you happen to be in a tourist area you can rest assured you'll be offered lower rates everywhere else. Some airports, such as Nënë Tereza Airport in Albania, also offer rather unfavourable rates.

Tipping

Throughout the Western Balkans you tip by rounding up restaurant bills and taxi fares to the next whole figure. In some countries restaurants will already have added a service charge to your bill, so you don't have to round it up much (if at all). A tip of 10% is quite sufficient if you feel you have been well looked after. Waiters in any place catering mostly to foreign tourists will usually expect such a tip. If 'rounding up' means you're only giving honest waiters a couple of cents, add some more coins.

Travellers Cheques

If you still use travellers cheques you mustn't have heard through your pith helmet that even the Western Balkans has moved on. You may have to do some exploring to find banks that are familiar with them and you'll probably have to pay a commission when you do (unless you take Amex and Thomas Cook cheques to Amex and Thomas Cook offices). In some places you may also need to show your original receipt to cash travellers cheques.

Western Union

If it all goes horribly wrong don't despair. While it's a horrid (and highly unusual) situation, as long as you know the phone number of a friend or relative back home, they can wire money to you anywhere in the region via Western Union. We don't bother listing WU representatives in this guide, as there are literally thousands of them catering to locals working overseas and sending money home. Just look for the distinctive yellow-and-black sign, either standing alone or at banks and post offices. The sender will be given a code that they then communicate to you and that you take to the nearest office, along with your passport.

PHOTOGRAPHY & VIDEO

Film and camera equipment is available everywhere, with bigger cities obviously offering a wider choice.

Use your common sense; it's never a good idea to photograph military sites or personnel. Also be sensitive about taking photographs of poverty, urban decay and war damage, which might offend people.

Always ask permission before photographing people and the interiors of churches and mosques. Museums will often demand that you buy permission to photograph or film.

Increasing numbers of processing labs are now equipped to burn digital images onto CDs. If you want to do this yourself at an internet cafe, you may need to bring a USB cable or card reader. Some provide both, but others won't let you plug anything in.

POST

Details of post offices are provided in the information sections of each city or town in individual country chapters, and postage costs are given in the country directory. Both efficiency and cost vary enormously both within the region and within individual countries; what should take five to 14 days can take a few weeks or a month. If you're posting important items, it pays to certify post or use a global service like DHL.

Poste restante (having letters sent to you care of local post offices) is often only possible in central offices in major towns. It is also unreliable, and (with apologies to the 17 people in the world's travel community who don't use email), archaic. If you desperately need something posted to you, it's probably best to find a friendly hotel or a friend of a friend who can receive mail at their address.

To send a parcel from the Western Balkans you usually have to take it unwrapped to a main post office. Parcels weighing over 2kg often must be taken to a special customs post office. Staff will usually wrap the parcels for you. They may ask to see your passport and note the number on the form. If you don't have a return address within the country, put your name care of any large tourist hotel to satisfy them.

SOLO TRAVELLERS

Going it alone in the Western Balkans can be enormously rewarding: there's the perfect mix of lesser-known sights that you can soak up in atmospheric isolation, and a developing tourism scene that can see you cross paths with some interesting people. In lonelier areas where this isn't the case (solo travellers are thin on the ground in Albania and Kosovo), there's generally an expat community (or at least an Irish pub) that may let you into the fold, albeit reluctantly.

The great privilege of travelling alone (other than the freedom to do what you want, see what you want and travel at your own pace) is that you're more likely to meet and socialise with locals whom you'd otherwise never speak to. If you do get lonely, head to the nearest hostel; it's amazing how easy it is to find a travel companion for a day, a week or however long you're on the same trail.

One downside to factor in during peak seasons in high tourist areas is that singles may be expected to fork out room rates for a double.

TELEPHONE

Cities throughout the region have a huge number of private call centres and state-run centres inside post-office buildings, increasingly the domain of entrepreneurs who offer discounted rates. Many internet cafes are also now offering cheap international phone calls. Check country chapters for more specific details.

Mobile Phones

Mobile phones can come in handy when you need to call hotels ahead, or come across a closed museum saying 'call this number', or when your hotel reception is closed. All the mobile-phone networks in the region use the GSM standard. If you plan to stay for a while, consider buying a SIM card to slip into your phone (check with your provider at home before you leave that your handset has not been blocked). SIM cards can cost as little as €5 and can be topped up with widely available cards. Alternatively, if you have roaming, your phone will usually switch automatically over to a local network. This can be expensive if you use the phone a lot but can be very useful for ad hoc calls on the road.

Phone Codes

Every country's international dialling code and international access code is given in the Fast Facts section at the beginning of the corresponding chapter. To call abroad simply dial the international access code for the country you're calling from.

Every town has its local code within the country listed directly underneath its chapter heading. To make a domestic call to another city in the same country in the Western Balkans, dial the area code with the initial zero and the number.

Phonecards

Local telephone cards, available from post offices, telephone centres, newsstands and retail outlets, are prolific.

There's a wide range of local and international phonecards; check call costs for specific destinations to find the most appropriate one.

TIME

The Western Balkans lies within the Central European time zone (GMT+1). This means it's in the same time zone as Italy, Austria and Hungary, but if you're entering the region from Greece, Bulgaria or Romania you'll need to put your clock back one hour (don't forget this after the 45-minute boat ride from Corfu!). Greenwich Mean Time (GMT) is five hours ahead of New York, eight hours ahead of Los Angeles and 10 hours behind Sydney. All countries employ daylight-saving time. Clocks are put forward an hour usually on the last Sunday in March and set back one hour on the last Sunday in September.

TOURIST INFORMATION

The quality and presence of tourist information across the Western Balkans varies enormously. Every country in the region offers some sort of tourist-information service. Serbian and Croatian tourist-information centres are a cut above the rest, but as with anything else it all depends on how enthused the person sitting behind the desk is.

TRAVELLERS WITH DISABILITIES

Probably the biggest challenge travellers with limited mobility will face in the region is unkempt footpaths. Steep hills, uneven stairs and cobblestones can pose challenges even for able-bodied travellers. Generally, the older and prettier a town is, the more difficult it can be to get around, particularly in a wheelchair.

Many museums and sites don't offer disabled access. Other than top-notch establishments, many hotels have either no lift or the old-fashioned type, which is near-impossible to get a wheelchair into. In Croatia, many public-toilet and transport facilities are wheelchair accessible, but rickety public transport throughout the region shows that making things disabled-friendly has not been a high priority.

On the upside, people are extremely friendly and help is never far away.

If you have a physical disability, get in touch with your national support organisation and ask about the countries you plan to visit.

The **Royal Association for Disability & Rehabilitation** (RADAR; ☎ in UK 020-7250 3222; www.radar.org.uk; 12 City Forum, 250 City Rd, London EC1V 8AF) is a helpful place to start.

VISAS & DOCUMENTS
Passport

Your most important travel document is your passport, which should remain valid until well after you plan to return home. If it's just about to expire, renew it before you travel; some countries insist that passports remain valid for a specified period (usually three to six months) beyond the expected date of your departure from that country, though in practice this is rarely checked.

Once you start travelling, carry your passport (or a copy of it) at all times and guard it carefully. Some countries have laws requiring you to always carry official documentation. The hassle of losing your passport is reduced considerably if you have recorded its number and issue date, or have photocopies of data pages. Spend a few minutes being smart before you head off by emailing scanned copies of important documents to yourself.

Many hotels hold onto your passport for the duration of your stay. A Camping Card International (CCI) or driving licence can get around this, but leaving your passport at the front desk can also be a good way to make sure it's safe. We've not come across any problem doing this; as one local hotelier put it, 'Can you imagine what would happen if I lost your passport!? I would be thrown into jail and you would be moved to a nicer hotel!'

Visas

A visa is a stamp in your passport or a separate piece of paper permitting you to enter the country in question and stay for a specified period of time. Often you can get the visa at the border or at the airport on arrival, but not always, especially if you're travelling by train or bus and the procedure is likely to hold up others. Check first with embassies or consulates of countries you plan to visit; otherwise, you could find yourself stranded at the border. With a valid passport and visa (if required) you'll be able to visit all Western Balkans countries for up to three months. You're also required to have some sort of onward or return ticket and/or 'sufficient means of support', which in practice is rarely checked unless you turn up at a border or airport immigration control looking as though you've been sleeping in a dumpster for a week. Appearances do make a difference, even if it's the least dirty T-shirt you can find.

For those who do require visas, it's important to remember that these will have a 'use-by' date, and you'll be refused entry after that period has elapsed.

Consulates sometimes issue visas on the spot, although some levy a 50% to 100% surcharge for 'express service'. If there's a choice between getting a visa in advance and getting one at the border, go for the former option if you have the time. They're sometimes cheaper in your home country and can spare you bureaucratic procedures.

Decide in advance if you want a tourist or transit visa. Transit visas, usually valid for just 48 or 72 hours, are often cheaper and issued faster, but it's usually not possible to extend a transit visa or change it to a tourist visa.

The visa form may instruct you to report to police within 48 hours of arrival. If you're staying at a hotel or other official accommodation (camping ground, hostel, private room arranged by a travel agency etc), this will be taken care of for you. If you're staying with friends or relatives, or in a private room arranged on the street or at the train station, you're supposed to register with the police yourself. During the communist days these regulations were strictly enforced, but things have relaxed nowadays. Consult visa sections in relevant country directories for full information.

VOLUNTEERING

If you're interested in staying put and being useful for a while, consider volunteering. Many organisations that could use your help are listed at www.idealist.org.

One organisation worth considering is **Balkan Sunflowers** (www.balkansunflowers.org), a

---

THE VISA GAME

Citizens of the EU, US, Canada, Australia and New Zealand, and many others, won't need visas in advance for any country in the Western Balkans. People arriving in Albania are required to pay €10 if arriving by air and €1 if arriving by sea or land. However, visa regulations do change; check with individual embassies before travelling.

not-for-profit organisation initially established for the benefit of Kosovar refugees that continues to work for social reconstruction, primarily with young people. Another is the **Western Balkans Programme to Fight HIV and AIDS** (www.balkans-fight-hiv.org), which uses volunteers in each country of operation. For more interesting organisations, also see p21.

WOMEN TRAVELLERS

Though there's a certain amount of variation throughout the region, travel for women in the Western Balkans is only marginally more challenging than it is in Western Europe but much easier than it is in, say, Turkey. In big cities such as Belgrade, women wandering around at night are just as safe – if not more so – than they are elsewhere in Europe.

Despite feminism's advances in many countries in the region, women remain underrepresented in positions of power, in both governmental and corporate spheres. At the risk of generalising, women in the Western Balkans still wield influence rather than the levers of power themselves. The amazing women that you will come across in the region hint at a more affirmative future.

In the most culturally conservative areas, there are noticeably fewer women out and about. In some areas, women are simply less active in social and cultural life than their male counterparts; this is true of parts of Kosovo, Muslim areas of Macedonia and Serbia, and Albania and BiH. But even in these places the dress code is very relaxed, with the headscarf the choice of a minority. Modest attire is appropriate in places of worship of all denominations.

There's often a stark difference between urban and rural attitudes, the former more progressive than the more conservative latter. Needless to say, a woman wandering into an all-male bar in the arse-end of Albania may raise some eyebrows. In areas where you can feel a macho vibe, you're wise to follow local customs, such as sitting closer to the front than the back on public transport, and next to other women.

As elsewhere in the world, women travellers should keep their street smarts about them, remember that flirting may in some contexts be construed as angling for sex, and hang on to their sense of humour.

For some inspiration, consider reading *Black Lambs & Grey Falcons: Women Travelling in the Balkans* – extraordinary tales of extraordinary women, compiled in homage to the Western Balkans' perennial woman traveller Rebecca West.

Transport in Western Balkans

CONTENTS

GETTING THERE & AWAY

This section covers getting to and from countries of the Western Balkans from outside the region. Consult the transport sections in country chapters for information on getting to and from specific countries within the region.

The number of inexpensive carriers serving the region is climbing, but for the moment it's more economical – and exciting – to travel overland with extensive bus and train services.

There's a vast network of flights servicing the rest of Europe, but coming from or going further afield you may have to travel via hubs outside the region. Those coming from outside Europe generally travel via gateway cities in Western Europe to take advantage of cheaper fares and frequent connections.

THINGS CHANGE

The information in this chapter is particularly vulnerable to change. Check directly with the airline or a travel agent to make sure you understand how a fare (and ticket) works and be aware of the security requirements for international travel. Shop carefully. The details given in this chapter should be regarded as pointers and are not a substitute for your own careful, up-to-date research.

The more romantic and economical way to arrive in the region is by train from neighbouring countries. There are also lots of bus connections from neighbouring countries and beyond to Austria, Switzerland and Germany, and all the way north to Scandinavia and east to Turkey.

There are many ferry services linking Croatia, Montenegro and Albania with Italy, plus a couple of short rides connecting Greece and Albania.

ENTRY REQUIREMENTS

You won't be surprised to learn that all countries require visitors to have passports with at least six months' validity. Visitors from most countries can visit most of the countries and territories in the region for up to 90 days without needing to get a visa in advance, and entry is usually free. The small exception to this is Albania, where land and sea entry costs €1 and air arrival €10. For more, see p437 and directory sections in country chapters.

AIR

All of the capitals and quite a few regional cities are served by a range of European airlines. Broadly speaking, the less touristy the destination, the more expensive the flight, so flying into Pristina (Kosovo) and Tirana (Albania) is poor value compared to landing in Zagreb (Croatia) or Belgrade (Serbia). For departure taxes out of particular countries, check the transport section of the country chapter. Travellers from anywhere outside Europe should look at getting a flight on a busy route to Western Europe and then a connecting flight into the region. Airlines such as Austrian Airlines, Swiss International Air Lines and Lufthansa may have deals where you fly from North America or Australia and get a flight to the Western Balkans for free. These airlines may also offer open-jaw tickets, where you can fly into one city and out of another, which can save a bit of backtracking.

Airports & Airlines

The Western Balkans has six major airports and a host of smaller ones. The biggest are in Belgrade and Zagreb. See the country chapters

---

TRAVELLING TO THE WESTERN BALKANS ON THE CHEAP

If saving money is more important than saving time, consider a cheap flight to Western Europe followed by a low-cost carrier to the edge of the region, then overland travel by bus, train or boat. It can work out very reasonably if you fly from London, Amsterdam or Paris to Austria, Hungary, Slovenia, Italy's Adriatic coast (eg Bari, Brindisi or Ancona) or to Thessaloniki or Corfu in Greece. Lots of Italian Adriatic ports have ferries to Croatia, Montenegro and Albania, and there are ferries from Corfu to Albania as well. There are buses and trains from all over the continent into the region.

    Germanwings (www.germanwings.com) now offers cheap flights to various Balkans locations. Croatia and countries on the edge of the region are extremely well served by **Ryanair** (www .ryanair.com), **easyJet** (www.easyjet.com), **Air Berlin** (www.airberlin.com), **Wizz Air** (www.wizzair.com) and **SkyEurope Airlines** (www.skyeurope.com). **Germania Express** (www.gexx.de) flies to Pristina. **Bmi baby** (www.bmibaby.com) will also get to you close to the region.

---

for more information. Airlines flying to and from the Western Balkans:

Ada Air (airline code ZY; www.adaair.com) Hub Tirana.

Adria Airways (airline code JP; www.adria-airways.com) Hub Ljubljana.

Aer Lingus (airline code EI; www.aerlingus.com) Hub Dublin.

Aeroflot (airline code SU; www.aeroflot.com) Hub Moscow Sheremetyevo.

Aerosvit (airline code VV; www.aerosvit.ua/eng) Hub Kyiv.

Air Baltic (airline code BT; www.airbaltic.com) Hub Riga.

Air France (airline code AF; www.airfrance.com) Hub Paris Charles de Gaulle.

Air India (airline code AI; www.airindia.com) Hub New Delhi/Mumbai.

Albanian Airlines (airline code LV; www.albanianair lines.com.al) Hub Tirana.

Albatros Airways (airline code 4H; www.albatrosair ways.net) Hub Tirana.

Alitalia (airline code AZ; www.alitalia.it) Hub Rome.

Austrian Airlines (airline code OS; www.aua.com) Hub Vienna.

BH Airlines (airline code JA; www.bhairlines.ba) Hub Sarajevo.

British Airways (airline code BA; www.britishairways .com) Hub London Heathrow.

Croatia Airlines (airline code OU; www.croatiaairlines .hr) Hub Zagreb.

ČSA (Czech Airlines; airline code OK; www.csa.cz) Hub Prague.

EasyJet (airline code EZY; www.easyjet.com) Hub London Luton.

Emirates (airline code EK; www.ekgroup.com) Hub Dubai.

Germania Airlines (airline code ST; www.gexx.de) Hub Berlin.

Germanwings (airline code 4U; www.germanwings .com) Hub Cologne.

Hemus Air (airline code DU; www.hemusair.bg) Hub Sofia.

JAT (airline code JU; www.jat.com) Hub Belgrade.

KLM (airline code KL; www.klm.com) Hub Amsterdam.

Kosova Airlines (airline code KOS; www.flyska.com, in Albanian) Hub Pristina.

Kuban Airlines (airline code KIL; www.alk.ru) Hub Krasnodar.

LOT Polish Airlines (airline code LOT; www.lot.com) Hub Warsaw.

Lufthansa (airline code LH; www.lufthansa.com) Hub Frankfurt.

Macedonian Airlines (MAT; airline code IN; www.mat .com.mk) Hub Skopje.

Malév Hungarian Airlines (airline code MA; www .malev.hu) Hub Budapest.

Meridiana (airline code IG; www.meridiana.it) Hub Olbia.

Montavia (airline code GZP; www.montavia.com) Hub Moscow.

Montenegro Airlines (airline code YM; www.montene groairlines.com) Hub Podgorica.

Norwegian Air Shuttle (airline code DY; www.norwe gian.no) Hub Fornebu.

Olympic Airways (airline code OA; www.olympicairlines .com) Hub Athens.

Royal Jordanian (airline code RJ; www.rja.com.jo) Hub Amman.

Ryanair (airline code FR; www.ryanair.com) Hub London Stansted.

SAS Scandinavian Airlines (airline code SK; www .scandinavian.net) Hub Copenhagen.

Scandjet (airline code FLY; www.scandjet.se) Hub Gothenburg.

SkyEurope Airlines (airline code NE; www.skyeurope .com) Hub Warsaw/Bratislava/Budapest.

SN Brussels Airlines (airline code SN; www.flysn.com) Hub Brussels.

Swiss International Air Lines (airline code LX; www .swiss.com) Hub Zurich.

Tunisair (airline code TU; www.tunisair.com) Hub Tunis.

Turkish Airlines (airline code TK; www.turkishairlines .com) Hub Istanbul.

Tickets

Buying flight tickets directly from airlines can yield some decent prices, but it's often easiest and cheapest to book airline tickets online through a host of websites; see the boxed text, right. Shop around, but always make sure that the price you're quoted includes the relevant taxes; these can make the difference between a good price and a great price. For recommended travel agencies in the Western Balkans, see the Information sections for each capital city.

Albania

Tirana's Nënë Tereza Airport is served by several airlines, including national carrier Albanian Airlines, which flies to Athens, Bologna, Frankfurt, Istanbul, London, Pristina, Rimini, Rome and Turin.

Adria Airways flies to Tirana from Copenhagen, London, Amsterdam, Brussels, Frankfurt, Paris, Munich, Zurich, Vienna, Ljubljana and Barcelona. Aegean Airlines flies to Athens and Alitalia to Rome. Major airlines flying in and out of Tirana include Austrian Airlines (to and from Vienna) and British Airways (to and from London); the latter runs flights into Albania from Gatwick for as low as £85.

Surrounding countries are well served by national carriers to and from Albania, including Bulgarian Airways for Sofia, JAT Airways to Belgrade, Lufthansa to Munich and Malev Hungarian Airlines to Budapest. Greek destinations (Athens and Thessaloniki) are served by Olympic Airlines. Belleair is a new budget airline that runs from Tirana to several destinations throughout Italy as well as a couple in Germany and Switzerland and one to Belgium. This may be a good option to get you to Italy's Adriatic coast, from where you can ferry to the Albanian ports of Vlora and Durrës.

Turkish Airlines connects Tirana with London but also serves several more remote destinations in Africa, the Middle East, the Indian subcontinent and central Asia.

Generally an effective way of flying into Albania is with a cheap ticket to Italy and onwards to Tirana.

Bosnia & Hercegovina

The main airport in Bosnia and Hercegovina (BiH) is Međunarodni Aerodrom in Sarajevo, which is served by a handful of major airlines including Austrian Airlines, British Airways,

Lufthansa and Adria Airways. The national carrier, BH Airlines, flies relatively inexpensively to Belgrade, Frankfurt, Cologne/Bonn, Istanbul, Skopje, Stuttgart, Zagreb and Zurich. It's also possible to fly to Istanbul from Mostar and from Banja Luka to Zurich or Belgrade. An economical way of moving to/from BiH may involve getting to Dubrovnik, Split or Zagreb and picking up onward connections from there either overland or with Croatia Airlines.

Croatia

There are a handful of airports in Croatia, which are all well connected to each other and to European capitals. Zagreb has links to Munich, Prague, Paris, Frankfurt, Vienna, Amsterdam, Zurich, London, Cologne, Berlin, Sarajevo, Rome and Copenhagen amongst other destinations. Zadar airport is now well-served by budget airlines, including Ryanair to London and Dublin, SkyEurope to Prague and Vienna, and Germanwings to Cologne, Stuttgart and Dortmund. Split has flights to Copenhagen, Bratislava, Paris, Prague, Vienna, Rome, Brussels, Oslo, Amsterdam, Gatwick and several major cities in Germany. Rijeka also serves Germany particularly well, as well as London and Oslo. Pula airport connects to several towns in the UK, as well as Edinburgh, Amsterdam, Paris, Belgrade and Moscow. Lots of tourist traffic flies in and out of Dubrovnik airport, particularly in summer. Flights include those bound for Tallinn (Estonia), Oslo, Brussels, Vienna, Bratislava, Amsterdam, Dublin, Edinburgh, Rome, Paris and Tel Aviv, as well as several major cities in Poland, Germany, Spain and the UK.

ONLINE TICKETS

Some recommended websites to book air tickets include those listed below. They usually levy a booking fee on any flights bought, but even if you don't buy through them, their software can be very useful for checking that the flight prices offered to you by other travel agents are the best ones available.

- www.ebookers.com
- www.flybudget.com
- www.itasoftware.com
- www.opodo.com
- www.statravel.com

CLIMATE CHANGE & TRAVEL

Climate change is a serious threat to the ecosystems that humans rely upon, and air travel is the fastest-growing contributor to the problem. Lonely Planet regards travel, overall, as a global benefit, but believes we all have a responsibility to limit our personal impact on global warming.

Flying & Climate Change

Pretty much every form of motorised travel generates CO_2 (the main cause of human-induced climate change) but planes are far and away the worst offenders, not just because of the sheer distances they allow us to travel, but because they release greenhouse gases high into the atmosphere. The statistics are frightening: two people taking a return flight between Europe and the US will contribute as much to climate change as an average household's gas and electricity consumption over a whole year.

Carbon Offset Schemes

Climatecare.org and other websites use 'carbon calculators' that allow travellers to offset the level of greenhouse gases they are responsible for with financial contributions to sustainable travel schemes that reduce global warming – including projects in India, Honduras, Kazakhstan and Uganda.

Lonely Planet, together with Rough Guides and other concerned partners in the travel industry, supports the carbon offset scheme run by climatecare.org. Lonely Planet offsets all of its staff and author travel.

For more information check out our website: www.lonelyplanet.com.

Kosovo

Pristina International Airport is well served from Ljubljana, Tirana, Vienna, London, Berlin, Stuttgart, Hamburg and Cologne, Budapest, Copenhagen and Istanbul. Other than those offered by Germanwings, flights are not particularly good value for money.

Macedonia

Skopje's international airport serves several destinations with Macedonian Airlines, including Vienna, Amsterdam, Rome and Zurich. Other airlines pitch in to connect Skopje with Budapest, Berlin, Tirana, Istanbul, Prague, Ljubljana, Milan, Belgrade, Split, Zagreb, Paris, Amsterdam and Sofia.

Smaller Ohrid international airport serves Belgrade, Llubljana, Vienna, Zurich, Dusseldorf, Amsterdam and Tel Aviv.

Montenegro

Montenegro's Podgorica airport serves Belgrade, Budapest, Zagreb, Vienna, Frankfurt, London, Paris, Zurich, Ljubljana, Rome, Skopje, Moscow and St Petersburg.

Serbia

Belgrade is a well-connected hub, with flights to major cities in Europe. JAT Airways is the national carrier; its regular services include Amsterdam, Vienna, Paris, Prague, Tivat, London, Frankfurt, Moscow, Stockholm, Trieste, Copenhagen, Istanbul, Zurich, Skopje, Moscow and Sarajevo.

LAND

For details of overland transport in and out of individual countries, refer to the Transport sections in the country chapters.

With the advent of the EU, border crossing in the region has never been simpler. The region can be entered from all sides with no problems, bar Kosovo, which at the time of writing was complicated by its declaration of independence from Serbia. Some of the major routes are Croatia from Slovenia or Italy, Serbia from Hungary, and Macedonia from Greece.

Austria

Austria has been a popular destination for guest workers from the Western Balkans for decades, and there are lots of bus and train services heading south into the region. **Eurolines** (www.eurolines.at) runs buses from Vienna to major cities in Croatia, as well as Bosnia and Serbia. Interestingly, ticketing is more efficiently organised from the Western Balkans than from Vienna. There are also daily trains from Vienna to Belgrade (€85, 11 hours) via Budapest, and a couple to Zagreb (€50, 6½ hours) via Slovenia.

TRANSPORT IN
WESTERN BALKANS

Bulgaria

There's a daily train from Sofia to Belgrade (€25, 11 hours) via Niš. There are four buses a day between Sofia and Skopje (€15, five hours) in Macedonia. Find more information through Sofia's central bus station (go to www.centralnaavtogara.bg).

Germany

Deutsche Touring (a division of Eurolines) handles bus connections between German and Croatian cities. As there are too many to list here, it's best to consult www.deutsche-touring.de. As a general idea, bus fares into Croatia cost €50 to €60, depending on which town you're headed to.

There are also several train connections that can get you into the region; a common one is a daily train from Munich to Zagreb (€90, 9½ hours).

Greece

From Albania there are border crossings into Greece at Kakavijë, Kapshtica, Qafë Bot and Dogana Tre Urat. Long queues in summer months can make for long delays. Generally, there are regular bus services to Greece from ethnic Greek areas of southern Albania. To Albania there are several daily buses from Thessaloniki (€35, 10 hours) and Athens (€50, 24 hours) to Tirana. There are also buses from Ioannina to Saranda (€8, 1½ hours) and Gjirokastra (€6, 1½ hours), and to Korça from Kastoria and Thessaloniki (€20, five hours). Buses to Athens leave Saranda at 8pm, arriving in Athens at 6am (€26).

A new international bus route recently commenced between Skopje and Thessaloniki, leaving Monday, Wednesday and Friday at 6am, returning 5pm (1280MKD one way, four hours). Taxis and minibuses also ply the route between Skopje and Thessaloniki (€15 to €25) – a minimum of four people is required to justify the journey. Some travel agencies arrange 'shopping trips' with minivans. There's also a daily train (€12, five to six hours), which doesn't always run on time.

There's a daily train from Belgrade to Thessaloniki (€52, 16 hours)

Hungary

By train there's a daily service from Budapest to Belgrade (€35, seven hours), as well as two daily trains from Szeged in southern Hungary to Subotica (€3, 1¾ hours) in Serbia's northern Vojvodina region.

Croatia is well served from Hungary; regular daily trains go from Budapest to Zagreb (€30, 6½ hours) or Split (€66, 16 hours).

There are big discounts on return train fares from Hungary to the Western Balkans – up to 65% to Croatia and 40% to Serbia and Montenegro.

There are daily buses from Budapest to Serbia, either to Subotica (€16, four hours) or Belgrade (€46, 10½ hours). There are also regular buses to Split (€50, 13 hours) and weekly buses to Zadar (€46, 10 hours) in Croatia.

Italy

Trieste is well connected with the Croatian coast, particularly Kvarner and Istria. There are six daily buses from Rijeka (60KN, 2½ hours) as well as regular services to and from Pula, Split and Dubrovnik. But the far more popular and efficient way to travel between Italy and Croatia is by boat; see p444.

Romania

By train there's a daily service between Belgrade and Bucharest (€35 to €57 with sleeper, 14 hours). Unfortunately, there doesn't seem to be any regular bus service between Serbia and Romania.

Turkey

There are several bus services from countries of the Western Balkans to Istanbul and other destinations in Turkey. Istanbul is an 11-hour bus ride from Skopje and can also be reached with an overnight train from Belgrade (26 hours) or by bus from other Serbian destinations. From Prizren in Kosovo, Istanbul is a 10-hour bus ride.

RIVER

There are no regular passenger ferries along the stretches of the Danube within the region. There are international tourist cruises on the Danube, but they're generally designed for pleasure-seekers rather than travellers trying to get anywhere, and are usually run from Germany or Austria. The **Danube Tourist Commission** (www.danube-river.org) oversees friendly use of the waterway, and lists river-cruise operators.

SEA

There's a dazzling array of ferries between Italy and Croatia, and Montenegro and

Albania, as well as a charming little jaunt between Corfu in Greece and southern Albania. Schedules change almost as frequently as the weather, but broadly speaking there are more boats crossing the Adriatic between May and September, and fewer from October until the end of April.

Italy

This is one of the most popular ways to get to the Balkans. Catching cheap flights to Ancona, Venice, Brindisi or Bari and then taking the ferry can often work out cheaper than a direct flight to Tirana or Split. Regular boats from several companies connect Italy with Albania, Croatia and Montenegro.

ALBANIA

Prices between Albania and Italy range from €30 to €90 in high season.

Agemar (www.agemar.it) runs a car ferry three times a week to Durrës from Trieste (deck passage/car €80/115, 22 hours) and five times a week to Durrës from Bari (deck passage/car €42/€90, three hours). **Tirrenia Navigazione** (www.tirrenia.it) also runs ferries from Bari to Durrës (seat €50, seven to nine hours) as does **Azzurraline** (www.azzurraline.com) – chair/car €45/80, eight to nine hours – and **Venezia Lines** (www.venezialines.com) – €80, 3½ hours – which claims to do it faster.

Skenderbeg Lines (www.skenderbeglines.com) runs daily except Sunday between Brindisi and Vlora (€40, 4½ hours).

CROATIA

Speedy catamarans running from Venice and Trieste to coastal resorts in Istria include the following. From May to early October, **Venezia Lines** (www.venezialines.com) operates to various ports in Istria, such as Poreč (2½ hours), Rovinj (3½ hours), Rabac (four hours) and Pula (three hours) as well as the island of Mali Lošinj (five hours) in the Kvarner Gulf. Peak-season summer fares are between €53 and €63 one way (€89 and €117 for a roundtrip). **Commodore Travel** (www.commodore-travel.hr) in Pula has a weekly boat service to Venice between June and September (370KN, 3½ hours). **Ustica Lines** (www.usticalines.it) has fast boats to Poreč and Rovinj (one way/return 150/280KN, around two hours) between May and September.

Further south on Croatia's coast, **Jadrolinija** (☎ Ancona 071-20 71 465, Bari 080-52 75 439, Rijeka 051-211 444; www.jadrolinija.hr) runs car ferries from Ancona

to Split (346KN to 477KN, 10 hours, three to seven weekly) and Zadar (325KN to 448KN, seven hours, three to four weekly), a line from Bari to Dubrovnik (346KN to 477KN, eight hours, one to four weekly), a year-round ferry from Pescara to Split (346KN to 477KN, 10 hours, twice weekly) and a summer ferry from Pescara to Hvar (346KN to 477KN, nine hours, once weekly). Prices are for a deck seat; couchettes and cabins cost more, and bringing a car costs an extra 50% of the price.

Split Tours (☎ Ancona 071-20 40 90, Split 021-352 553; www.splittours.hr) runs the Blue Line car ferries connecting Ancona with Zadar and Split, and continuing on to Stari Grad (Hvar) for the same prices as Jadrolinija. It also connects Ancona with Vis in the summer.

SNAV (☎ Ancona 071-20 76 116, Naples 081-76 12 348, Split 021-322 252; www.snav.com) has a fast car ferry linking Split with Pescara (€36 to €90, 4¾ hours, daily) and Ancona (€36 to €90, 4½ hours, three to seven weekly) and Pescara with Hvar (€36 to €90, 3¼ hours, daily). **Sanmar** (www.sanmar.it) handles the same route for a similar price.

Venezia Lines (☎ 041-52 22 568; www.venezialines.com; Santa Croce 518/A, Venice 30135) runs passenger boats from Venice to the following destinations once, twice or three times weekly, depending on the destination and the month: Pula (low/high season €50/55, three hours), Rovinj (low/high season €48/53, 3¾ hours) and Poreč (low/high season €48/53, 2½ hours). The company also covers other Istrian destinations and runs some routes from Rimini and Ravenna.

Emilia Romagna Lines (www.emiliaromagnalines.it) also runs summer passenger boats (14 April to 30 September) from Italy to Croatia. Routes run from Cesenatico, stopping at Rimini and Pesaro, to Rovinj (low/high season €57/62, 3¼ hours), Lošinj (Lussino; low/high season €62/72, four hours), Zadar (low/high season €72/82, 4½ hours) and Hvar (low/high season €71/82, 5½ hours).

In Croatia, contact **Jadroagent** (Map p205; ☎ 052-210 431; www.jadroagent.hr; Riva 14) in Pula and **Istra-Line** (☎ 052-451 067; www.istraline.hr; Šetalište 2) in Poreč for information and tickets on boats between Italy and Croatia.

MONTENEGRO

Ferry services connect Montenegro (Bar and Kotor) with Italy (Bari and Ancona).

Montenegro Lines (☎ 030-303 469; www.montenegrolines.net; ferry terminal, Bar) has boats from Bar to

Bari (€60, 10 hours, three weekly, nearly daily from July to September) and Ancona (€72, 16 hours, twice weekly from July to early September). Cars cost €68 to €90 and cabins are an additional €12 to €68 depending on the type and season.

Azzurra Line (☎ +39-80-592 8400; www.azzurraline .com) has weekly ferries between Bar and Bari (deck passage €48, seat €55, cabin €67 to €91, car €78, 10 hours) and between Kotor and Bari (deck passage €55, seat €65, cabin €75 to €189, car €72, nine hours) but only from June or July to September.

If you're transporting a car into Montenegro there's an additional €6.50 fee.

Greece
Privately operated boats run between Corfu and Saranda in southern Albania in season. There are two morning ferries (9am) from Corfu to Saranda. **Ionion Cruises** (www.ionian cruises.com) runs the 'flying dolphin', a high-speed trip (€17.50, 45 minutes) with return service at 11am and 4pm. The ferry is slower but cheaper (€15, 1½ hours).

GETTING AROUND

This section covers getting between the different countries of the Western Balkans. For information on getting around within countries, refer to country chapters.

AIR
Major regional air hubs in the region are Zagreb and Belgrade. All major cities in the Western Balkans are well connected, with several regular flights, but these generally don't offer good value for money. For instance, it costs around €190 to fly from Zagreb to Skopje. Flights to smaller cities such as Pristina and Ohrid tend to be far more expensive (and less interesting) than overland travel. Flying within a particular country isn't common, given the small size of countries – factoring in trips to and from airports, you generally don't save much time against a bus or train ride. The only route commonly used by visitors is from Zagreb to Dubrovnik in Croatia. Airlines based in the region tend to be fairly small and receive moderately good ratings for their punctuality and service. See country chapters for more details.

Airlines in the Western Balkans:
Albanian Airlines (airline code LV; ☎ 355 4-230 857; www.albanianairlines.com.al) Hub Tirana. Flies to Pristina.
BH Airlines (airline code JA; ☎ 387 33-218 605; www .bhairlines.ba) Hub Sarajevo. Flies to Belgrade, Skopje and Zagreb.
Croatia Airlines (airline code OU; ☎ 385 1-487 2727; www.croatiaairlines.hr) Hub Zagreb. Flies to Dubrovnik, Podgorica, Pristina, Sarajevo, Skopje, Split and Zadar.
JAT (airline code JU; ☎ 381 11-311 2123; www.jat.com) Hub Belgrade. Flies to Banja Luka, Niš, Ohrid, Podgorica, Pula, Sarajevo, Skopje, Tirana and Tivat (Montenegro).
Kosova Airlines (airline code KOS; ☎ 381 38-249 185; www.flyska.com, in Albanian) Hub Pristina.
Macedonian Airlines (MAT; airline code IN; ☎ 389 2-3218 077; www.mat.com.mk) Hub Skopje.
Montenegro Airlines (airline code YM; ☎ 382 81-405 501; www.montenegroairlines.com) Hub Podgorica. Flies to Belgrade, Niš, Skopje and Tivat.

Another useful airline just outside the region is **Adria Airways** (airline code JP; ☎ 386 1-369 1010; www .adria-airways.com), hub Ljubljana, which flies to Podgorica, Sarajevo, Pristina, Tirana, Ohrid and Skopje.

BICYCLE
The experience of cycling around the region varies quite a bit from country to country. While major cities in Serbia have dedicated bike paths to which car drivers are becoming increasingly sensitive, Albania, on the other hand, has average road conditions with a populace of inexperienced drivers. The other countries and regions fall roughly between these two extremes. See Transport sections of the country chapters for more information on local cycling conditions.

The key to a successful bike trip is to travel light, and don't overdo it on the first few days. Even for the shortest and most basic trip it's worth carrying the tools necessary for repairing a puncture. You might want to consider packing spare brake and gear cables, spanners, Allen keys, spare spokes and strong adhesive tape. At the risk of stating the bleeding obvious, none of the above are much use unless you know what to do with them. Maintenance is also important: check your bike thoroughly each morning and again at night when the day's touring is over. Take a good lock and always use it when you leave your bike unattended.

The wearing of helmets is not compulsory but is certainly advised.

A seasoned cyclist can average about 80km a day but this depends on the terrain and how much weight is being carried. Again, don't overdo it – there's no point burning yourself out during the initial stages.

If you want to bring your own bike, most airlines allow you to put a bicycle in the hold for a surprisingly small fee. You can either take it apart and pack all the pieces in a bike bag or box, or simply wheel it to the check-in desk, where it should be treated as a piece of check-in luggage. You may have to remove the pedals and turn the handlebars sideways so that it takes up less space in the aircraft's hold; check all this with the airline before you pay for your ticket. If your bicycle and other luggage exceed your weight allowance, ask about alternatives or you may find yourself being charged a ransom for excess baggage.

Within Europe, bikes can usually be transported as luggage subject to a fairly small supplementary fee.

BUS

Buses are a widely used means of transport throughout the Western Balkans; they're inexpensive, usually efficient, mostly comfortable and get to places trains can't go. (In Albania this may include off-road places – sometimes literally off the road: buses have driven into abysses between Tirana and Elbasan, and the daily *furgon* to Theth also reminds you of your mortality.)

Often major bus stations are positioned near major railway stations so you can use a combination of bus and train depending on what's leaving when. Getting between major destinations is a breeze, but closer distances between smaller towns can be trickier. Minibuses (kombis) may be useful here. The ticketing system varies in each country, but advance reservations are rarely necessary. Buses can be bought at bus stations or on board buses. Often there's a small platform fee at larger stations and there's generally a small charge for stowing luggage.

See individual country chapters for more details about long-distance buses.

CAR & MOTORCYCLE

Travelling by car or motorcycle gives you an immense amount of freedom and is generally worry-free in most of the Western Balkans, though travelling by car can be tricky between EU and non-EU countries. Cities can also raise stress levels as you try to negotiate convoluted one-way systems or find somewhere to park. Tito got to work building a decent highway network in Yugoslavia, so driving in FYR countries is relatively straightforward. Albania falls somewhat behind on this front; while roads are steadily improving (Tirana to Dhërmi is great, as is Tirana to Pogradec, minus some fate-tempting sharp edges, and Tirana to Shkodra), we don't pretend that road trips here will necessarily be fun, safe or easy. Another special consideration relates to Kosovo; at the time of writing this was certainly off many insurers' radars, and driving Serbian-plated cars was ill-advised.

Parking

Local parking habits are quite carefree in the southern part of the Western Balkans in particular, so it's possible you can be blocked in by someone double-parking next to you. Where parking is more organised be aware of where and how to purchase parking tickets. Sometimes parking that looks illegal (on sidewalks) is actually permitted and maybe even metered. Theft from vehicles can be a problem throughout the region, so check what sort of parking your hotel offers.

Automobile Associations

Every country except Albania has a national automobile association that can help with on-road mishaps, maps and more.

UK motoring organisations such as the **RAC** (www.rac.co.uk) and the **Automobile Association** (www.theaa.com) have excellent information on their websites, including driving tips and conditions for all the countries of the Western Balkans.

Driving Licence

Proof of ownership of a private vehicle (a vehicle-registration document for British-registered cars) should always be carried when touring Europe. An EU driving licence is acceptable for driving throughout most of the Western Balkans, as are North American and Australian licences. But to be on the safe side – or if you have any other type of licence – you should obtain an international driving permit (IDP) from your national motoring organisation.

Fuel & Spare Parts

Finding the right type of fuel is no longer a problem in the Western Balkans. Fuel prices vary from country to country and may bear little relation to the general cost of living. As in the rest of the world, the price of fuel has risen in recent years.

Unleaded petrol of 95 or 98 octane is widely available throughout the region. As usual, unleaded fuel is slightly cheaper than super (premium grade), and diesel is about 40% cheaper than unleaded. In some countries, glitzy petrol stations are popping up like mushrooms along highways, in other countries they're placed erratically; there may be many within a few kilometres of each other and none for an incredibly long stretch. Don't dawdle in filling up your tank – especially if you're travelling off the main highways.

Hire

Hiring a car is quite straightforward. The big international firms will give you reliable service and a good standard of vehicle, and many have representatives at airports. Prebooked rates are generally lower than walk-in rates at rental offices, but either way you'll pay about 20% to 40% more than in Western Europe. However, renting from small local companies is nearly always cheaper.

You should be able to make reservations online; websites:

Avis (www.avis.com)
Budget (www.budget.com)
Europcar (www.europcar.com)
Hertz (www.hertz.com)

If you're coming from North America, Australia or New Zealand, ask your airline if it has any special deals for rental cars in Europe. You can often find very competitive rates.

Although local companies not connected with any chain will usually offer lower prices than the multinationals, when comparing rates beware printed tariffs intended only for local residents, which may be lower than the prices foreigners are charged. If in doubt, ask. The big chain companies sometimes offer the flexibility of allowing you to pick up the vehicle from one place and drop it off at another at no additional charge.

Minimum age requirements vary from country to country and from one company to another. Generally, the rule is that you need to have held a full licence for a minimum of one year. You also generally need a major credit card, though a large wad of cash as a deposit can also be persuasive.

Insurance

Third-party motor insurance is compulsory throughout Europe. For non-EU countries make sure you check the requirements with your insurer. For further advice and more information contact the **Association of British Insurers** (www.abi.org.uk).

In general you should get your insurer to issue a green card (which may cost extra), an internationally recognised proof of insurance, and check that it lists all the countries you intend to visit. You'll need this in the event of an accident outside the country where the vehicle is insured. The European accident statement (known as the *constat amiable* in France) is available from your insurance company and is copied so that each party at an accident can record information for insurance purposes. The Association of British Insurers has more details. Never sign accident statements you cannot understand or read – insist on a translation and sign that only if it's acceptable.

If the green card doesn't list one of the countries you're visiting and your insurer cannot (or will not) add it, you will have to take out separate third-party cover at the border of the country in question. Generally, this is only a problem if you plan to drive across to Bulgaria or into Albania.

Taking out European breakdown cover with the **RAC** (☎ in UK 0800 550 055; www.rac.co.uk) covers you in all the countries in this book in its zone 2 option. That offered by the **AA** (☎ in UK 0870 085 2721; www.theaa.com) may also be a smart investment, though it doesn't cover Serbia, Montenegro, Albania, Macedonia or Kosovo. Non-Europeans might find it cheaper to arrange for international coverage with their own national motoring organisation before leaving home. Ask your motoring organisation for details about free and reciprocal services offered by affiliated organisations around Europe.

Some insurance packages (especially those covering rental cars) do not include all European countries; for example, hiring a car in Italy and driving it to Croatia will cause problems unless you have the correct insurance stamp (ask the agency to insure you for wherever you plan to travel). When you're organising insurance, check where you're able to travel with your vehicle.

Road Rules & Safety

Motoring organisations are able to supply members with country-by-country information on motoring regulations, or they may produce motoring guidebooks for general sale.

Every vehicle travelling across an international border should display a sticker that shows the country of registration. It's compulsory to carry a reflective safety vest and warning triangle almost everywhere in Europe, for use in the event of a breakdown. Many other countries require that a first-aid kit and a spare-bulb kit be carried in the vehicle at all times. Also bear in mind that in most countries, dipped headlights must be used at all times – even during the day – and that snow chains are required in certain areas between November and April. The **AA** (www.theaa.com) offers detailed country-specific information.

Driving at night can be particularly hazardous in rural areas as roads are often narrow and winding, and you may encounter horse-drawn vehicles, cyclists, pedestrians and domestic animals. In the event of an accident you're supposed to notify the police and file an insurance claim. If your car has significant body damage from a previous accident, point this out to customs upon arrival and have it noted somewhere, as damaged vehicles may only be allowed to leave the country with police permission.

Standard international road signs are used throughout all of the Western Balkans, though they may appear sporadically in Albania. You drive on the right-hand side of the road throughout the region and overtake on the left. Keep right except when overtaking, and use your indicators for any change of lane and when pulling away from the kerb. You're not allowed to overtake more than one car at a time, whether it's moving or stationary (eg pulled up at a traffic light).

Speed limits are posted, and are generally 110km/h or 120km/h on motorways (freeways), 100km/h on highways, 80km/h on secondary and tertiary roads, and 50km/h or 60km/h in built-up areas. Motorcycles are usually limited to 90km/h on motorways. In towns you may only sound the horn to avoid an accident.

Everywhere in the Western Balkans the use of seat belts is mandatory, and motorcyclists and their passengers must wear a helmet. In some countries, children under 12 and intoxicated passengers are not allowed in the front seat. Driving after drinking *any* alcohol is a serious offence – most Western Balkans countries have a 0% blood-alcohol concentration (BAC) limit.

HITCHING

Hitching is never entirely safe, and we wouldn't recommend it. In parts of the region hitching is a common way for locals to get around; in Albania it's an alternative to buses, which in some areas wind down in the early afternoon, leaving people stranded. On the other hand, hitching is on the decline in Macedonia. Wherever you are, there's always a risk when you catch a ride with strangers. It's safer to travel in pairs and to let someone know where you're planning to go. Once you've flagged down a vehicle, it's safer if you sit next to a door you can open. Ask the driver where they're going before you say where you're going. Trust your instincts if you feel uncomfortable about getting in, and get out at the first sign of trouble. You can find more pointers at www.bugeurope.com/transport /hitch.html, and information on ride sharing at http://europe.bugride.com/, www.hitchhikers .org and www.bugeurope.com.

LOCAL TRANSPORT
Boat

On Croatia's coast the national Jadrolinija car ferries operate year-round on the Bari–Rijeka–Dubrovnik coastal route, stopping at Zadar, Split and several islands. The ferries are more comfortable than buses on the same route but also more expensive. Local ferries connect the bigger offshore islands with the mainland and with each other. Some of the ferries only operate a few times a day, and once they're full the remaining motorists must sit and wait for the next service. There are no regional services to and from Montenegro, which is more commonly accessed from Italy. Albania's ferry services generally go between Himara and Saranda on the Ionian coast during season. The ferry trip on Lake Koman is a joy.

Minibus

The shared minibus or *furgon* is a quick but slightly cramped form of both intercity and city transport, particularly in Albania. They leave when full, and you pay when you're on board. They will stop frequently to let passengers on and off. *Furgons* often have very limited space for luggage, which is when you'll thank yourself for packing light.

TRAIN

Trains are the most atmospheric, comfortable and fun way to make long overland journeys in the Western Balkans. All major cities besides Tirana are on the rail network (and Pristina was struggling at the time of writing). The train trip from Belgrade to Bar via Podgorica is particularly spectacular.

When you travel overnight you'll get a bed reservation included in the price of your ticket, although you may have to pay a few euros extra for the bedding once on board. Each wagon is administered by a steward or stewardess, who will look after your ticket and make sure that you get off at the correct stop – crucial if you arrive during the small hours. Each wagon has a toilet and washbasin at either end, although their state of cleanliness can vary massively. Be aware that toilets may be closed while the train is at a station.

If you plan to travel extensively by train, it's worth getting hold of the *Thomas Cook European Rail Timetable,* updated monthly, which gives a complete listing of train schedules, has reservation information and indicates where supplements apply. This trainophile's bible is available from Thomas Cook outlets and can be ordered online at www.thomascookpublishing.com.

If you intend to stick to one or a handful of countries it might be worth getting hold of the national timetable(s) published by the state railway(s). A particularly useful online resource for timetables in the Western Balkans is the DeutscheBahn website at www.bahn.de, which lets you easily look up the most popular routes in Europe. Another good source of information is www.raileurope.com.

Classes

Throughout the Western Balkans there exists a similar system of train classes to that in Western Europe. Short trips, or longer ones that don't involve sleeping on the train, are usually seated like a normal train: benches (on suburban trains) or aeroplane-style seats (on smarter intercity services).

There are generally three classes of sleeping accommodation; some countries have a different name for them, but for the sake of simplicity we'll call them 3rd, 2nd and 1st class.

Third-class accommodation is not available everywhere, but it's the cheapest way to sleep, although you may feel your privacy has been slightly invaded. The accommodation consists of six berths in each compartment.

Second class has four berths in a closed compartment. If there are two of you, you

will share your accommodation with two strangers. However, if there are three of you, you'll often not be joined by anyone.

In 1st class you pay for space rather than any sort of Orient Express–style opulence. There won't be a white-linen restaurant car or a piano bar, but your two-berth apartment may be adorned with plastic flowers to make you feel as though you got some value for money.

Costs

While it's reasonable, train travel is pricier than bus travel in some countries. First-class tickets are double the price of 2nd-class tickets, which are in turn approximately twice the price of 3rd-class tickets.

Reservations

It is always advisable to buy a ticket in advance. Seat reservations are also advisable but only necessary if the timetable specifies they're required. Out of season, reservations can be made pretty much up to an hour before departure, but never count on this. On busy routes and during summer, try to reserve a seat several days in advance. Booking tickets via travel agencies before you leave home is more expensive than booking on arrival in the Western Balkans but may offer some peace of mind.

Train Passes

For general information about train passes, go to www.raileurope.com.

INTERRAIL

InterRail passes can only be used by European residents of more than six months' standing. The pass allows free train travel in a certain country (with a One Country pass) or several countries (with a Global pass) during a certain period of time. Some are valid over a continuous period of time, while others are flexibly valid. An InterRail Global pass is valid in 30 countries, including BiH, Croatia, Macedonia, Montenegro and Serbia. Prices depend on age and class; youth passes for people younger than 25 are cheaper than adult passes, and child passes are 50% cheaper than adult passes.

For some examples of prices; a three-day One Country pass for Serbia or Macedonia for an adult/youth travelling 2nd class is €49/32. A Global Pass valid for five days in a 10-day period costs €249/159, or €599/399 for one continuous month. Terms, conditions and occasional surcharges may apply on certain trains. For more information, visit www.interrailnet.com.

BALKAN FLEXIPASS

The Balkan Flexipass offered by **Rail Europe** (www.raileurope.com) covers rail travel in Macedonia, Serbia and Montenegro, as well as Bulgaria, Greece, Romania and Turkey. It covers travel in 1st class only, and costs from US$283 for five days' travel in one month to US$591 for 15 days' travel in one month. Discounted passes are available for both youths (under 26) and seniors (over 60); five days' travel costs US$166/226 youth/senior and 15 days' travel costs US$356/475.

Health

CONTENTS

Travel health depends on your predeparture preparations, your health care while travelling and how you handle any medical problem that does develop. The Western Balkans is generally an exceptionally safe place in terms of staying healthy, with no tropical diseases and an extensive, if sometimes basic, health-care system.

Prevention is the key to staying healthy while abroad. A little planning, particularly for pre-existing illnesses, will save trouble later: see your dentist before a long trip, carry spare contact lenses or glasses, and take your optical prescription with you.

BEFORE YOU GO

Bring medications in their original, clearly labelled containers, along with a signed and dated letter from your physician describing your medical conditions and medications, including generic names. If carrying syringes, be sure to have a physician's letter documenting their medical necessity.

INSURANCE

If you're an EU citizen, an E111 form, available from health centres, covers you for most medical care. The E111 will not cover you for nonemergencies or emergency repatriation home. If you do need health insurance, strongly consider a policy that covers you for the worst possible scenario, such as an accident requiring an emergency flight home.

> **TRAVEL-HEALTH WEBSITES**
>
> It's usually a good idea to consult your government's travel-health website before departure, if one is available.
> **Australia** www.dfat.gov.au/travel/
> **Canada** www.travelhealth.gc.ca
> **UK** www.doh.gov.uk/traveladvice/
> **USA** www.cdc.gov/travel/

Find out if your insurance plan will make payments directly to providers or reimburse you later for overseas health expenditures. The former option is preferable.

RECOMMENDED VACCINATIONS

The World Health Organization (WHO) recommends that all travellers be covered for diphtheria, tetanus, measles, mumps, rubella and polio, regardless of their destination. Since most vaccines don't produce immunity until at least two weeks after they're given, visit a physician at least six weeks before departure.

INTERNET RESOURCES

The WHO's useful publication *International Travel and Health* is revised annually and is available online at www.who.int/ith/. Some other useful websites include www.mdtravelhealth.com (travel-health recommendations for every country, updated daily), www.fitfortravel.scot.nhs.uk (general travel advice for the layperson), www.ageconcern.org.uk (advice on travel for the elderly) and www.mariestopes.org.uk (information on women's health and contraception).

IN THE WESTERN BALKANS

AVAILABILITY & COST OF HEALTH CARE

Good basic health care is readily available, and for minor illnesses pharmacists can give advice and sell over-the-counter medication. They can also advise when more specialised help is required and point you in the right

HEALTH

direction. The standard of dental care is usually good.

Medical care is not always readily available outside major cities, but embassies, consulates and five-star hotels can usually recommend doctors or clinics.

INFECTIOUS DISEASES
Poliomyelitis
Poliomyelitis is spread through contaminated food and water. Its vaccine is one of those given in childhood and should be boosted every 10 years, either orally (a drop on the tongue) or as an injection.

Rabies
Spread through bites or licks on broken skin from an infected animal, rabies is always fatal unless treated promptly. Animal handlers should be vaccinated, as should those travelling to remote areas where a reliable source of postbite vaccine is not available within 24 hours. Three injections are needed over a month. If you have not been vaccinated, you will need a course of five injections starting 24 hours or as soon as possible after the injury. If you have been vaccinated, you will need fewer injections and have more time to seek medical help.

Tickborne Encephalitis
Spread by tick bites, tickborne encephalitis is a risk in Croatia in the summer months. It is a serious infection of the brain and vaccination is advised for those in risk areas who are unable to avoid tick bites (such as campers, forestry workers and walkers). Two doses of vaccine will give a year's protection, three doses up to three years'.

Typhoid & Hepatitis A
Both of these diseases are spread through contaminated food (particularly shellfish) and water. Typhoid can cause septicaemia; hepatitis A causes liver inflammation and jaundice. Neither is usually fatal. Typhoid vaccine (Typhim Vi, Typherix) will give protection for three years. In some countries, the oral vaccine Vivotif is also available. Hepatitis A vaccine (Avaxim, VAQTA, Havrix) is given as an injection; a single dose gives protection for up to a year, and a booster gives 10 years' protection. Hepatitis A and typhoid vaccines can also be given as a single-dose vaccine (Hepatyrix or ViATIM).

TRAVELLER'S DIARRHOEA
To prevent diarrhoea, avoid tap water unless it has been boiled, filtered or chemically disinfected (with iodine tablets), and steer clear of ice. Only eat fresh fruit or vegetables if cooked or peeled; be wary of dairy products that might contain unpasteurised milk. Eat food that is heated through and avoid buffet-style meals. If a restaurant is full of locals the food is probably safe.

If you develop diarrhoea, be sure to drink plenty of fluids, preferably an oral rehydration solution (eg Dioralyte). If you start having more than four or five stools a day, you should take an antibiotic (usually a quinolone drug) and an antidiarrhoeal agent (such as loperamide). If diarrhoea is bloody, persists for more than 72 hours, or is accompanied by fever, shaking, chills or severe abdominal pain you should seek medical attention.

ENVIRONMENTAL HAZARDS
Heat Exhaustion
Heat exhaustion occurs following excessive fluid loss with inadequate replacement of fluids and salt. Symptoms include headache, dizziness and tiredness. Dehydration is already happening by the time you feel thirsty – drink sufficient water to produce pale, diluted urine. To treat heat exhaustion, replace lost fluids by drinking water and/or fruit juice, and cool the body with cold water and fans. Treat salt loss with salty fluids such as soup or Bovril, or add a little more table salt to foods than usual.

Insect Bites & Stings
Mosquitoes are found in most parts of Europe. They may not carry malaria but can cause irritation and infected bites. Use a DEET-based insect repellent.

Bees and wasps only cause real problems to those with a severe allergy (anaphylaxis). If you have a severe allergy to bee or wasp stings carry an EpiPen or similar adrenalin injection.

Water
Tap water is generally safe to drink in the main cities and resorts. Do not drink water from rivers or lakes, as it may contain bacteria or viruses that can cause diarrhoea or vomiting.

TRAVELLING WITH CHILDREN
All travellers with children should know how to treat minor ailments and when to seek

medical treatment. Make sure the children are up to date with routine vaccinations, and discuss possible travel vaccines well before departure as some are not suitable for children less than one year old.

WOMEN'S HEALTH

Travelling during pregnancy is possible, but there are important things to consider. Always have a medical check up before planning your trip. The most risky times for travel are during the first 12 weeks of pregnancy and after 30 weeks. Antenatal facilities vary greatly between countries and you should think carefully before travelling to a country with poor medical facilities or where there are major cultural and language differences from home.

SEXUAL HEALTH

Emergency contraception is most effective if taken within 24 hours of unprotected sex. Condoms are available throughout the region.

Language

CONTENTS

This language guide offers basic vocabulary to help you get around the Western Balkans. For more extensive coverage of the languages included in this guide, pick up a copy of Lonely Planet's *Eastern Europe Phrasebook*.

ALBANIAN

PRONUNCIATION

Written Albanian is phonetically consistent and pronunciation shouldn't pose too many problems for English speakers. Each vowel in a diphthong is pronounced and the **rr** is trilled. However, Albanian has certain letters that exist in English but are rendered differently.

ë	often silent; at the beginning of a word it's like the 'a' in 'ago'
c	as the 'ts' in 'bits'
ç	as the 'ch' in 'church'
dh	as the 'th' in 'this'
gj	as the 'j' in 'joke'
j	as the 'y' in 'yellow'
q	as the 'ch' in 'cheat'
x	as the 'ds' in 'adds'
xh	as the 'j' in 'jewel'
y	'ee' pronounced with rounded lips, as the 'ew' in 'new'

ACCOMMODATION

Where's a ...?	Ku ka një ...?
camping ground	vend kampimi
guesthouse	bujtinë
hotel	hotel
youth hostel	fjetore për të rinj

Do you have any rooms available?	A keni ndonjë dhomë të lirë?
a single room	një dhomë më një krevat
a double room	një dhomë më dy krevat

How much is it per night/person?	Sa kushton për një natë/njeri?
Does it include breakfast?	A e përfshin edhe mëngjesin?

CONVERSATION & ESSENTIALS

Hello.	Tungjatjeta.
Goodbye.	Mirupafshim.
Yes.	Po.
No.	Jo.
Please.	Ju lutem.
Thank you.	Faleminderit.
That's fine.	Eshtë e mirë.
You're welcome.	S'ka përse.
Excuse me.	Me falni.
I'm sorry.	Më vjen keq.
Do you speak English?	A flisni anglisht?
What's your name?	Si quheni?
My name is ...	Unë quhem ...

SHOPPING & SERVICES

bank	bankë
chemist/pharmacy	farmaci
the ... embassy	... ambasadë
market	treg
newsagency	agjencia e lajmeve
post office	postë
telephone centre	centralin telefonik
tourist office	zyrë turistike

I'm looking for ...	Po kërkoj për ...
How much is it?	Sa kushton?
What time does it open/close?	Në ç'ore hapet/mbyllet?

TIME, DAYS & NUMBERS

What time is it?	Sa është ora?
today	sot
tomorrow	nesër
yesterday	dje
in the morning	në mëngjes
in the afternoon	mbasdite

Monday	e hënë
Tuesday	e martë
Wednesday	e mërkurë
Thursday	e enjte
Friday	e premte
Saturday	e shtunë
Sunday	e diel

1	një
2	dy
3	tre
4	katër
5	pesë
6	gjashtë
7	shtatë
8	tetë
9	nëntë
10	dhjetë
100	njëqind
1000	një mijë

SIGNS – ALBANIAN

Hyrje	Entrance
Dalje	Exit
Informacion	Information
Hapur	Open
Mbyllur	Closed
E Ndaluar	Prohibited
Polici	Police
Rajoni I Policisë	Police Station
Banjat	Toilets
Burra	Men
Gra	Women

TRANSPORT

What time does the ... leave/arrive?	Në ç'orë niset/arrin ...?
boat	anija
bus	autobusi
tram	tramvaji
train	treni

I'd like ...	Dëshiroj ...
a one-way ticket	një biletë për vajtje
a return ticket	një biletë kthimi

(1st/2nd) class	klas (i parë/i dytë)
bus stop	stacion autobusi
Can you show me (on the map)?	A mund të ma tregoni (në hartë)?

Directions

Where is ...?	Ku është ...?
Go straight ahead.	Shko drejt.

Turn left.	Kthehuni majtas.
Turn right.	Kthehuni djathtas.
near/far	afër/larg

BOSNIAN/CROATIAN/ MONTENEGRIN/SERBIAN

WHO SPEAKS WHAT WHERE?

From a linguistic perspective, the differences between Bosnian, Croatian, Montenegrin and Serbian are slight (they are all classed as South Slavic languages), and the four are mutually intelligible. From a cultural perspective, the story is significantly different, with distinctions based on religion, ethnicity and geography all contributing to create a heady mix of official and preferred languages and writing systems. In effect, the resolution of the Balkans conflict meant that each nation had a strong desire to reflect its independence through the recognition of its own official languages.

Croatia is perhaps the simplest to classify. the official language is Croatian and the official writing system is the Roman alphabet. Serbia is also fairly straightforward, with Serbian the official language and the Cyrillic alphabet the official writing system (although in reality both Cyrillic and Roman alphabets have equal status and are in common use in government, schools and the media). Things become somewhat complicated in Bosnia and Hercegovina, however, where three languages share official status. Bosnian itself is almost identical to Croatian (with a few lexical variations). It's spoken by the Muslim community (Bosniaks) and is written in the Roman alphabet. Croatian is spoken by the Bosnian Croats; it too is written in the Roman alphabet. Serbian is spoken by the Bosnian Serbs and is written in the Cyrillic alphabet. Finally, Montenegro's official language is Montenegrin, but Bosnian, Croatian, Serbian (plus Albanian!) are also in official use, and both Roman and Cyrillic alphabets have official status. To make everything even more interesting, both the Serbian variety spoken in Bosnia and Montenegro are more similar to Croatian in pronunciation but almost identical to Serbian spoken in Serbia proper when it comes to variations in vocabulary. Simple, isn't it?

LANGUAGE

PRONUNCIATION

The writing systems of these languages are phonetically consistent: every letter within a word is pronounced and its sound will not vary from word to word. With regard to the position of stress, only general rules can be given: the last syllable of a word is never stressed, and in most cases the accent falls on the first syllable in the word.

It's worth familiarising yourself with the Serbian/Montenegrin Cyrillic alphabet (see the boxed text, p458). Bosnian and Croatian use a Roman alphabet and many letters are pronounced as in English – the following are some of the departures from the English alphabet and its pronunciation.

c	as the 'ts' in 'cats'
ć	as the 'tch' sound in 'future'
č	as the 'ch' in 'chop'
đ	as the 'dy' sound in 'verdure'
dž	as the 'j' in 'just'
j	as the 'y' in 'young'
lj	as the 'lli' in 'million'
nj	as the 'ny' in 'canyon'
š	as the 'sh' in 'hush'
ž	as the 's' in 'pleasure'

The most noticeable difference between Serbian on one side and Bosnian, Croatian and Montenegrin on the other lies in the pronunciation of the vowel 'e' in certain words. A long **e** in Serbian becomes 'ije' in the other varieties, eg *reka/rijeka* (river), and a short **e** in Serbian becomes 'je', eg *pesma, pjesma* (song). Sometimes, however, the vowel **e** is the same in all languages, as in *selo* (village). To simplify matters, this chapter gives the Serbian pronunciation only in the Cyrillic translations. Several notable variations in vocabulary between the four language varieties are indicated in the following phrases by 'B/C/M/S' for Bosnian/Croatian/Montenegrin/Serbian.

ACCOMMODATION

hotel
  hotel   хотел
guesthouse
  privatno prenoćište   приватно преноћиште
youth hostel
  omladinsko prenoćište   омладинско преноћиште
camping ground
  kamping   кампинг

Do you have any rooms available?
  Imate li slobodne sobe?
  Имате ли слободне собе?
How much is it per night/per person?
  Koliko košta za noć/po osobi?
  Колико кошта за ноћ/по особи?
Does it include breakfast?
  Da li je u cijenu uključen i doručak?
  Да ли је у цену укључен и доручак?

I'd like ...
  Želim ...   Желим ...
  a single room
  sobu sa jednim krevetom   собу са једним креветом
  a double room
  sobu sa duplim krevetom   собу са дуплим креветом

EMERGENCIES – BOSNIAN/CROATIAN/ MONTENEGRIN/SERBIAN

Help!
  Upomoć!
  Упомоћ!
Call a doctor!
  Pozovite liječnika (B/C)/lekara (M/S)!
  Позовите лекара (M/S)!
Call the police!
  Pozovite policiju!
  Позовите полицију!
Go away!
  Idite!
  Идите!
I'm lost.
  Izgubljen/Izgubljena sam. (m/f)
  Изгубљен/Изгубљена сам. (m/f)

CONVERSATION & ESSENTIALS

Hello.
  Bog. (C)/Zdravo. (B/M/S)   Здраво.
Goodbye.
  Zbogom.   Збогом.
Yes.
  Da.   Да.
No.
  Ne.   Не.
Please.
  Molim.   Молим.
Thank you.
  Hvala.   Хвала.
That's fine.
  U redu je.   У реду је.
You're welcome.
  Nema na čemu.   Нема на чему.
Excuse me.
  Oprostite.   Опростите.

I'm sorry.
Žao mi je.   Жао ми је.
Do you speak English?
Govorite li engleski?   Говорите ли енглески?
What's your name?
Kako se zovete?   Како се зовете?
My name is ...
Zovem se ...   Зовем се ...

SHOPPING & SERVICES
I'm looking for ...
Tražim ...
Тражим ...
  a bank
  banku   банку
  the ... embassy
  ... ambasadu   ... амбасаду
  the market
  tržnicu (C)
  pijacu (B/M/S)   пијацу
  the post office
  poštu   пошту
  the telephone centre
  telefonsku centralu   телефонску централу
  the tourist office
  turistički biro   туристички биро

How much is it ...?
Koliko košta ...?   Колико кошта ...?
What time does it open/close?
U koliko sati se otvara/   У колико сати се отвара/
zatvara?   затвара?

TIME, DAYS & NUMBERS

What time is it?	*Koliko je sati?*	Колико је сати?
today	*danas*	данас
tomorrow	*sutra*	сутра
yesterday	*jučer*	јуче
in the morning	*ujutro*	ујутро
in the afternoon	*popodne*	поподне
Monday	*ponedjeljak*	понедељак
Tuesday	*utorak*	уторак
Wednesday	*srijeda*	среда
Thursday	*četvrtak*	четвртак
Friday	*petak*	петак
Saturday	*subota*	субота
Sunday	*nedjelja*	недеља
1	*jedan*	један
2	*dva*	два
3	*tri*	три
4	*četiri*	четири
5	*pet*	пет
6	*šest*	шест

7	*sedam*	седам
8	*osam*	осам
9	*devet*	девет
10	*deset*	десет
100	*sto*	сто
1000	*hiljadu* (B/M/S)/	хиљаду
	tisuću (C)	

SIGNS – BOSNIAN/CROATIAN/MONTENEGRIN/SERBIAN

Ulaz/Izlaz	Entrance/Exit
Улаз/Излаз	
Otvoreno/Zatvoreno	Open/Closed
Отворено/Затворено	
Informacije	Information
Информације	
Policija	Police
Полиција	
Stanica Policije	Police Station
Станица Полиције	
Zabranjeno	Prohibited
Забрањено	
Toaleti/WC	Toilets
Тоалети/WC	

TRANSPORT
What time does the ... leave/arrive?
Kada ... polazi/dolazi?
Када ... полази/долази?
  boat
  brod   брод
  bus
  autobus   аутобус
  train
  vlak (C)/*voz* (B/M/S)   воз
  tram
  tramvaj   трамвај

  one-way ticket
  kartu u jednom pravcu   карту у једном правцу
  return ticket
  povratnu kartu   повратну карту
  1st class
  prvu klasu   прву класу
  2nd class
  drugu klasu   другу класу

Where is the bus/tram stop?
Gdje je autobuska/tramvajska stanica?
Где је аутобуска/трамвајска станица?
Can you show me (on the map)?
Možete li mi pokazati (na karti)?
Можете ли ми показати (на карти)?

LANGUAGE

WAXING CYRILLICAL

The following list shows the letters of the Macedonian and Serbian/Montenegrin Cyrillic alphabets. The letters are common to all languages unless otherwise specified.

CYRILLIC	SOUND	PRONUNCIATION
А а	a	short as the 'u' in 'cut'
		long as in 'father'
Б б	b	as in 'but'
В в	v	as in 'van'
Г г	g	as in 'go'
Д д	d	as the 'd' in 'dog'
Ѓ ѓ	j	as in 'judge'
		(Macedonian only)
Ђ ђ	j	as in 'judge'
		(Serbian/Montenegrin only)
Е е	e	short as in 'bet'
		long as in 'there'
Ж ж	zh	as the 's' in 'measure'
З з	z	as in 'zoo'
Ѕ ѕ	dz	as the 'ds' in 'suds'
		(Macedonian only)
И и	i	short as in 'bit'
		long as in 'marine'
Ј ј	y	as in 'young'
К к	k	as in 'kind'
Л л	l	as in 'lamp'

CYRILLIC	SOUND	PRONUNCIATION
Љ љ	ly	as the 'lli' in 'million'
М м	m	as in 'mat'
Н н	n	as in 'not'
Њ њ	ny	as the 'ny' in 'canyon'
О о	o	short as in 'hot'
		long as in 'for'
П п	p	as in 'pick'
Р р	r	as in 'rub' (but rolled)
С с	s	as in 'sing'
Т т	t	as in 'ten'
Ќ ќ	ch	as in 'check'
		(Macedonian only)
Ћ ћ	ch	as in 'check'
		(Serbian/Montenegrin only)
У у	u	as in 'rule'
Ф ф	f	as in 'fan'
Х х	h	as in 'hot'
Ц ц	ts	as in 'tsar'
Ч ч	ch	as in 'check'
Џ џ	j	as the 'j' in 'judge'
Ш ш	sh	as in 'shop'

Directions
Go straight ahead.
Idite pravo naprijed.   Идите право напред.
Turn left.
Skrenite lijevo.   Скрените лево.
Turn right.
Skrenite desno.   Скрените десно.
near/far
blizu/daleko   близу/далеко

MACEDONIAN

It's worth familiarising yourself with the Macedonian Cyrillic alphabet (above). In the pronunciation guides for the following phrases, stress in words is marked as italic.

ACCOMMODATION
hotel
хотел   *ho*·tel
guesthouse
приватно сместување   *pri*·vat·no smes·*tu*·van·ye
youth hostel
младинско   *mla*·din·sko
пренокиште   pre·*no*·chish·te
camping ground
камп   kamp

Do you have any rooms available?
Да ли имате слободни соби?
da li *i*·ma·te *slo*·bod·ni *so*·bi
How much is it per night/person?
Која е цената по ноќ/особа?
ko·ya e *tse*·na·ta po noch/*o*·so·ba
Does it include breakfast?
Да ли е вклучен појадок?
da li e *vklyu*·chen *po*·ya·dok
a single room
еднокреветна соба
ed·no·*kre*·vet·na *so*·ba
a double room
соба со брачен кревет
so·ba so *bra*·chen *kre*·vet
a twin room
двокреветна соба
dvo·*kre*·vet·na *so*·ba

CONVERSATION & ESSENTIALS
Hello.
Здраво.   *zdra*·vo
Goodbye.
До гледање.   do *gle*·da·nye
Yes.
Да.   da
No.
Не.   ne

Please.
Молам.   *mo*-lam
Thank you.
Благодарам.   bla-*go*-da-ram
That's fine.
Мило ми е.   *mi*-lo mi e
You're welcome.
Нема зошто.   ne-ma *zosh*-to
Excuse me.
Извинете.   iz-*vi*-ne-te
I'm sorry.
Простете.   *pro*-ste-te
Do you speak English?
Зборувате ли   zbo-*ru*-va-te li
англиски?   *ang*-li-ski
What's your name?
Како се викате?   *ka*-ko se *vi*-ka-te
My name is ...
Jac се викам ...   yas se *vi*-kam ...

EMERGENCIES – MACEDONIAN

Help!
Помош!   *po*-mosh
Call a doctor!
Викнете лекар!   *vik*-ne-te *le*-kar
Call the police!
Викнете полиција!   *vik*-ne-te po-*li*-tsi-ya
Go away!
Одете си!   *o*-de-te si
I'm lost.
Се загубив.   se *za*-gu-biv

SHOPPING & SERVICES
bank
банка   *ban*-ka
chemist/pharmacy
аптека   *ap*-te-ka
embassy
амбасада   am-ba-*sa*-da
my hotel
мојот хотел   *mo*-yot *ho*-tel
market
пазар   *pa*-zar
newsagency
киоск за весници   *ki*-osk za *ves*-ni-tsi
post office
пошта   *posh*-ta
stationers
книжарница   kni-*zhar*-ni-tsa
telephone centre
телефонска   te-le-*fon*-ska
централа   *tsen*-tra-la
tourist office
туристичко биро   tu-ris-*tich*-ko *bi*-ro

I'm looking for ...
Барам ...   *ba*-ram ...
How much is it?
Колку чини тоа?   *kol*-ku *chi*-ni *to*-a
What time does it open/close?
Кога се отвора/затвора?   *ko*-ga se *ot*-vo-ra/*zat*-vo-ra

TIME, DAYS & NUMBERS
What time is it?   Колку е часот?   *kol*-ku e *cha*-sot
today   денес   *de*-nes
tomorrow   утре   *u*-tre
yesterday   вчера   *vche*-ra
morning   утро   *u*-tro
afternoon   попладне   po-*plad*-ne

Monday   понеделник   po-*ne*-del-nik
Tuesday   вторник   *vtor*-nik
Wednesday   среда   *sre*-da
Thursday   четврток   *chet*-vrtok
Friday   петок   *pe*-tok
Saturday   сабота   *sa*-bo-ta
Sunday   недела   *ne*-de-la

1   еден   *e*-den
2   два   dva
3   три   tri
4   четири   *che*-ti-ri
5   пет   pet
6   шест   shest
7   седум   *se*-dum
8   осум   *o*-sum
9   девет   *de*-vet
10   десет   *de*-set
100   сто   sto
1000   илјада   *il*-ya-da

TRANSPORT
What time does the next ... leave/arrive?
Кога поаѓа/пристигнува идниот ...?
ko-ga po-*a*-ja/pris-*tig*-nu-va *id*-ni-ot ...
boat
брод   brod
bus
автобус   *av*-to-bus
train
воз   voz
tram
трамвај   *tram*-vay

timetable
возен ред   *vo*-zen red
bus stop
автобуска станица   av-*to*-bus-ka *sta*-ni-tsa

I'd like ...
Сакам ...
sa-kam ...

a one-way ticket
билет во еден правец   bi-let vo e-den pra-vets
a return ticket
повратен билет   pov-ra-ten bi-let
1st class
прва класа   pr-va kla-sa
2nd class
втора класа   vto-ra kla-sa

Can you show me (on the map)?
Можете ли да ми   mo-zhe-te li da mi
покажете   po-ka-zhe-te
(на картава)?   (na kar-ta-va)

Directions

Where is ...?
Каде е ...?   ka-de e ...

Go straight ahead.
Одете право напред.   o-de-te pra-vo na-pred
Turn left/right.
Свртете лево/десно.   svr-te-te le-vo/des-no
near/far
блиску/далеку   blis-ku/da-le-ku

Also available from Lonely Planet:
Eastern Europe Phrasebook

Glossary

You may encounter some of the following words during your time in Albania (Alb), Bosnia and Hercegovina (BiH), Croatia (Cro), Kosovo (Kos), Macedonia (Mac), Montenegro (Mon) and Serbia (Serb). Some words used in several countries are marked as (Sla).

acropolis – Classical Greek term for the upper town, often with a castle and temples
amam (Mac) – derived from the Turkish word *hamam*, meaning public baths
an (Mac) – derived from the Turkish word *han*, meaning inn

bairam or **bajram** – a Turkish word meaning festival; also used for the major Muslim religious festivals in the Western Balkans
ban (Cro) – term for a duke or viceroy
bb (Sla) – *bez broja* – literally, 'without a number' – used in street addresses
Bektashi – a Muslim sect or dervish order who revere the Prophet Mohammed's son-in-law, Ali
besa (Alb) – sacred oath, often in relation to a blood feud
bey – Turkish term for a governor or lord
bez broja (Sla) – see *bb*
bezistan, bezisten – Turkish term for a covered market, often connected financially and/or physically to a mosque
BiH – Bosnia and Hercegovina
Bogumils – a heretical sect of the medieval Christian church in BiH
bura – cold northeasterly coastal wind in winter
buregdz/vinica (BiH) – a bakery selling *burek*
burek, byrek – a filo-pastry pie with various fillings
burekdžinica (Mac) – a bakery selling *burek*

campanile – bell tower
čaršija (Sla) – from the Turkish term for a market; usually means 'downtown' or 'old town'
ćevabdžinica (Sla) – a shop selling *ćevapčići*
ćevapi, ćevapčići (Sla) – grilled minced lamb or beef
convertible mark (BiH) – KM; the currency of BiH
Crna Gora – Montenegrin name for Montenegro

Dalmatia – the half of Croatia bordering the Adriatic Sea
denar – MKD; the currency of Macedonia
dinar – DIN; the currency of Serbia
djamija (Mac) – see *džamija*
dnevna karta (Cro) – 'day ticket' for public transport
dolazak (Cro) – arrival, as in train arrival time
domaća rakija (Sla) – homemade spirits

džamija (BiH, Mon, Serb) – a main mosque, from the Arabic word *jami* meaning mosque; a mosque where Friday sermons are heard

fis (Alb) – clan
FKK – 'Freie Körper Kultur', a German phrase meaning 'free body culture', or wear as little as you want. This acronym denotes nudist beaches in Croatia.
furqon (Alb) – a minivan that takes paying passengers on a fixed route
FYROM – Former Yugoslav Republic of Macedonia, a name used by the UN for Macedonia because of Greek protests, much resented in Macedonia

garderoba (Sla) – left-luggage office
Gheg (Alb) – dialect of northern Albania and Kosovo
gostionica (Sla) – guesthouse, inn

hamam – Turkish word for public baths
han – Turkish word for inn
HDZ (Cro) – Hrvatska Demokratska Zajednica or Croatian Democratic Union, a Croatian political party
Helveti – a Muslim sect or brotherhood of dervishes
Hrvatska (Cro) – the Croatian name for Croatia

iconostasis – in Orthodox churches, a wall highly decorated with icons separating the congregation from the inner sanctum
Illyrians – early, pre-Slavic inhabitants of the Western Balkans

Jadrolinija (Cro) – Croatia's national coastal ferry company

kabas (Alb) – instrumental Albanian polyphonic music
kafana (Mon, Serb) – cafe
kajmak (Sla) – devastatingly rich cream dish
kale – Turkish word for fortress
kanun (Alb) – canon of traditional Albanian law and customs
Karađorđević – 19th- and 20th-century Serbian royal family
karst – limestone
kavana (Cro) – cafe
kebapčići (Sla) – kebabs (grilled Turkish-style meat dishes)
kebapdžinica (Sla) – a shop selling *kebapčići*
KFOR – Kosovo Force, the NATO-led international peacekeeping force in Kosovo
klapa (Cro) – Croatian a cappella music
konoba (Cro, Mon) – small family-run bistro
kuna (Cro) – KN; the currency of Croatia

lekë (Alb) – the currency of Albania

maestral – warm wind that blows over the Mediterranean from the Sahara
mafil (Alb) – an indoor balcony where women can watch guests in the guest room
manastir (Mon, Serb) – Orthodox monastery or convent
minaret – the tower on a mosque from which the call to prayer *(azan)* is broadcast
musaka (Sla) – same as Greek moussaka, a baked dish made of layers of meat, potato and eggplant

NDH (Cro) – Nezavisna Država Hrvastka, Independent State of Croatia, the Fascist puppet state that nominally ruled half of the Western Balkans during WWII
ne vozi nedjeljom ni praznikom (Sla) – term in ferry schedules meaning no services on holidays or Sundays
Nevruz – ancient spring festival of Persian origin, celebrated as a holiday by Bektashi followers

odlazak (Sla) – departure, as in departure time of a train

pasha – Turkish term for military governor
pivo (Sla) – beer
plaža (Sla) – beach
polazak (Sla) – arrival, as in arrival time of a train
polje (Sla) – field or plain
poslovni (Sla) – express, as in express train

qilim (Alb) – a woven rug or kilim

raki (Alb) – distilled spirits
rakija (Sla) – distilled spirits
ražnjići (Sla) – shish kebab
restauracija (Sla) – restaurant
ris (Sla) – lynx
Roma – name for the Romany-speaking communities of the Western Balkans, sometimes called Gypsies
rruga (Alb) – street
RS – Republika Srpska (Serb Republic), Serbian entity in BiH

salata (Sla) – salad
samostan (Cro) – Catholic monastery
šar planinec (Mac) – famously protective Macedonian sheepdog
sevdah (BiH) – from the Turkish word *sevda*, meaning love, traditional Bosnian folk music, sometimes dubbed the 'Bosnian blues'
SFOR – Stabilisation Force, the NATO-led international peacekeeping effort in BiH
sheshi (Alb) – square or plaza
Shqipëria (Alb) – the Albanian name for Albania
Sigurimi (Alb) – Albanian communist-era secret police
skara (Mac) – barbecued meat, ubiquitous menu item in Macedonia

Slavonia – the inland half of Croatia, between Hungary and BiH
šljivovica (Sla) – a potent spirit made from plums
soba (s), **sobe** (pl), **sobi** (pl; Sla) – rooms, meaning rooms for rent
sofra – a large metal plate for serving food, from the Turkish word for dinner table
stanica (Sla) – a bus station or train station
stećci (BiH) – medieval tombstones
stelae – Roman funerary stones, a kind of gravestone
sveta/sveti (Sla) – saint and/or holy, eg Sveti Jovan (St John) or Sveta Bogorodica (Holy Mother of God)

tartufe (Sla) – truffle, underground fungus adored by gourmets
tekija (Sla) – shrine and/or place of worship for Muslim sects such as the Bektashi
tekke – see *tekija*
teqe (Alb) – see *tekija*
Tosk (Alb) – offical dialect of Albania
trg (Sla) – square or plaza
Trgovski Centar (Mac) – shopping centre
turbe – Muslim gravestones and/or tombs
turbofolk – an unholy mix of folk tunes 'updated' with Europop music

UÇK (Alb) – Ushtria Çlirimtare Kombetare, National Liberation Army, an ethnic Albanian rebel group active in Kosovo and Macedonia in the late 1990s
ulica (Sla) – street, abbreviated to 'ul'
UNMIK – UN Mission in Kosovo, the interim government of Kosovo
Unprofor – UN Protective Force, peacekeeping force, first in Croatia, later in BiH, during the 1990s conflict
Ustaša (s), **Ustaše** (pl) – brutal Croatian fascist party installed in power by the Nazis during WWII
UXO – unexploded ordnance

Vlach – a rural community, traditionally shepherds, who speak a Latin-derived language called Aromanian
vladika (Mon) – title of a Montenegrin prince-bishop
VMRO (Mac) – Vnatresno-Makedonska Revolucionerna Organizacija, Internal Macedonian Revolutionary Organisation, early Macedonian liberation movement
Vojvodina – Serbian province north of the Danube River
vozi svaki dan (Cro) – means 'service every day' in ferry schedules

wi-fi – wireless internet technology

xhamia (Alb) – mosque
xhiro (Alb) – Albania's highly social evening stroll

Zimmer frei – German for 'room free'

The Authors

MARIKA McADAM — Coordinating Author, Kosovo, Serbia

Marika is an Australian writer and lawyer currently based on the precipice – and antithesis – of the Balkans, in Vienna. Having backpacked through Croatia, Serbia and Bosnia and Hercegovina (BiH) in 2004 and road-tripped down the Dalmatian coast in following years, she jumped at the opportunity to travel the region again. Her earlier memories of Serbia as grim and grumpy were completely eclipsed in these recent travels by experiences with fun and friendly Serbs whom she laughed with about nothing and everything. And whatever its status, the experience of resolutely persistent and unfailingly hospitable Kosovo was a privilege that marked her forever (literally – she burnt her arse in a jacuzzi). Marika also wrote the Destination Western Balkans, Getting Started, Itineraries, Snapshots, Western Balkans Directory and Transport in Western Balkans chapters.

JAYNE D'ARCY — Albania

After watching Celtic Tigers eat up and commercialise Irish culture in the mid-'90s, Jayne's been attracted to countries with more character and lower GDPs. Albania hit her radar in 2006, when she joined her first ever package tour, and while complaining about the hard mentality of her fellow tourists, she was pretty stoked to get a new passport stamp and see some amazing ruins in relative peace. The changes in Albania since then are astonishing, and the similarities to the 'old Ireland' are huge (homemade spirits, dodgy roads), but the Albanian Tiger is yet to emerge. Apart from travel writing, Jayne writes features on children, people and the environment.

CHRIS DELISO — Macedonia

Chris Deliso's long experience of seductive Macedonia began a decade ago and has, since 2002, evolved to full fledged residential status. As a travel writer and journalist, he has covered most everything there is to cover here, but delights in uncovering the country's many hidden places for visitors – from mountain wilds and ancient ruins shrouded by vineyards to rustic village eateries and secret lakeshore beaches. For Chris, researching the present guide involved off-roading in remote locales, swimming in four lakes and rivers, handling real ancient Macedonian gold, eating plenty of grilled meats and sampling one superb wine after another in the Tikveš wine region. He has also co-written Lonely Planet's *Greece*, *Greek Islands* and *Bulgaria* guides.

LONELY PLANET AUTHORS

Why is our travel information the best in the world? It's simple: our authors are passionate, dedicated travellers. They don't take freebies in exchange for positive coverage so you can be sure the advice you're given is impartial. They travel widely to all the popular spots, and off the beaten track. They don't research using just the internet or phone. They discover new places not included in any other guidebook. They personally visit thousands of hotels, restaurants, palaces, trails, galleries, temples and more. They speak with dozens of locals every day to make sure you get the kind of insider knowledge only a local could tell you. They take pride in getting all the details right, and in telling it how it is. Think you can do it? Find out how at **lonelyplanet.com**.

THE AUTHORS

PETER DRAGIČEVIĆ   Montenegro

After a dozen years working for newspapers and magazines in both his native New Zealand and Australia, Peter finally gave in to Kiwi wanderlust, giving up staff jobs to chase his typically (for an antipodean) diverse roots around much of Europe. While it was family ties that first drew him to the Balkans, it's the history, the natural beauty, the convoluted politics, the cheap *rakija* and, most importantly, the intriguing people that keep bringing him back. This is the 10th Lonely Planet title he's contributed to, including writing the Macedonia and Albania chapters for the previous edition of the *Eastern Europe* guide.

MARK ELLIOTT   Bosnia & Hercegovina

British-born travel writer Mark Elliott was only 11 when his family first dragged him to Sarajevo and stood him in the now-defunct concrete footsteps of Gavrilo Princip. Fortunately, no Austro-Hungarian emperors were passing at the time. He has since visited virtually every corner of BiH supping fine Hercegovinian wines with master vintners, talking philosophy with Serb monks and Sufi mystics, and drinking more Bosnian coffee than any healthy stomach should be subjected to. When not travel writing he lives a blissfully quiet life in suburban Belgium with the lovely Danielle, whom he met while jamming blues harmonica in a Turkmenistan club.

VESNA MARIĆ   Croatia (Zagreb, Dalmatia)

Vesna was born in BiH while it was still a part of Yugoslavia, and she has never been able to see Croatia as a foreign country. A lifetime lover of Dalmatia's beaches, pine trees, and food and wine, she expanded her knowledge by exploring Zadar and Zagreb, two cities she discovered anew. Researching this book was a true delight. Vesna also wrote the chapter's introductory material, the Croatia Directory and the Transport in Croatia section.

ANJA MUTIĆ   Croatia (Hrvatsko Zagorje, Slavonia, Istria, Kvarner Region)

It's been more than 16 years since Anja left her native Croatia. The journey took her to several countries and continents before she made New York her base 10 years ago. But the roots are a-calling. She's been returning to Croatia frequently for work and play, intent on discovering a new place on every visit, be it a nature park, an offbeat town or an island. She's happy that Croatia's many beauties are appreciated worldwide but secretly pines for the time when you could have a leisurely seafront coffee in Hvar without waiting for a table.

Behind the Scenes

THIS BOOK

This 2nd edition was written by Marika McAdam, Jayne D'Arcy, Chris Deliso, Peter Dragičević, Mark Elliott, Vesna Marić and Anja Mutić. The 1st edition was written by Richard Plunkett, Vesna Marić and Jeanne Oliver. This guidebook was commissioned in Lonely Planet's London office, and produced by the following:

Commissioning Editors Will Gourlay, Fiona Buchan, Sally Schafer
Coordinating Editors Sarah Bailey, Carolyn Bain
Coordinating Cartographer Jacqueline Nguyen
Coordinating Layout Designer Carol Jackson
Senior Editors Helen Christinis, Katie Lynch
Managing Cartographer Mark Griffiths
Managing Layout Designer Sally Darmody
Assisting Editor Diana Saad
Assisting Cartographers Alex Leung, Khanh Luu, Brendan Streager
Assisting Layout Designer Indra Kilfoyle
Cover Designer Michael Ruff
Project Manager Rachel Imeson
Language Content Coordinator Quentin Frayne

Thanks to Sasha Baskett, Nicholas Colicchia, Eoin Dunlevy, Mark Germanchis, Chris Girdler, Ali Lemer,

Rosie Nicholson, Trent Paton, Jo Potts, Branislava Vladisavljević, Glenn van der Knijff

THANKS
MARIKA McADAM

As always, the folk I met on the road are what make this job the best one in the world. Thank you for agreeing with me that different language, culture, history and religion don't have to get in the way of a shared sense of humour.

A first-time coordinating author couldn't have had a better team to learn from than Jayne D'Arcy, Chris Deliso, Peter Dragičević, Mark Elliott, Vesna Marić and Anja Mutić. Travelling with books written by these fine folk has been a joy, writing one with them a thrill. People like commissioning editor Will Gourlay are the reason I've loved Lonely Planet since I was 10 years old.

Thanks also to my big sister Lorina, who was unquestioningly up for anything in Serbia. I'll never forget her trusting expression when she turned around after two hours in a bus bumping through the arse-end of southern Serbia to innocently ask where we were going. And to Jo, who came along to Kosovo, put up with months of stress throughout writing about it afterwards, and during the

THE LONELY PLANET STORY

Fresh from an epic journey across Europe, Asia and Australia in 1972, Tony and Maureen Wheeler sat at their kitchen table stapling together notes. The first Lonely Planet guidebook, *Across Asia on the Cheap*, was born.

Travellers snapped up the guides. Inspired by their success, the Wheelers began publishing books to Southeast Asia, India and beyond. Demand was prodigious, and the Wheelers expanded the business rapidly to keep up. Over the years, Lonely Planet extended its coverage to every country and into the virtual world via lonelyplanet.com and the Thorn Tree message board.

As Lonely Planet became a globally loved brand, Tony and Maureen received several offers for the company. But it wasn't until 2007 that they found a partner whom they trusted to remain true to the company's principles of travelling widely, treading lightly and giving sustainably. In October of that year, BBC Worldwide acquired a 75% share in the company, pledging to uphold Lonely Planet's commitment to independent travel, trustworthy advice and editorial independence.

Today, Lonely Planet has offices in Melbourne, London and Oakland, with over 500 staff members and 300 authors. Tony and Maureen are still actively involved with Lonely Planet. They're travelling more often than ever, and they're devoting their spare time to charitable projects. And the company is still driven by the philosophy of *Across Asia on the Cheap*: 'All you've got to do is decide to go and the hardest part is over. So go!'

course of this project proposed a lifetime of his love and support; yes, please!

JAYNE D'ARCY

Thanks to Sharik Billington for taking on Albania with me and my three-year-old, to Miles, for coping with all the cheek-pinching, to Will Gourlay for sending me up the Accursed Mountains in the first place, and to Orieta Gliozheni in Korça, Stavri Cifligu in Tirana, Marius Qytyku in Berat, Yolanda Kebo in Saranda and Edward Shehi and his Italian tourists in Voskopoja. Thanks Dr Shannon Woodcock at La Trobe University, Australia, Mada at Sunrock, Corfu, and everyone else along the way who had the keys and let us in.

CHRIS DELISO

It would be impossible to thank everyone who deserves recognition here, since my gratitude is great and goes back 10 years. For this specific book, then, I would like to mention the following: Jason Miko, Aleksandar Konevski, Aleksandar Danilovski, Ivo Marussi (Skopje); Nikola Kiselinov, Danijel Medaroski, Vilijam Hristovski, Risto and Anita Stojoski, Dimitri, Cobi and Darko (Ohrid and around); Kiril Jonovski (Prespa); Patrice Koerper, Elena Petkovska, Gorki Baloyannis, Nesad Azenovski and Petar Cvetkovski (Bitola and around); Saško Atanasov, Aleksandar Panov, Divna Jordanovska, Violeta Jankova, Efrem Ristov, Konstantin and Stevo (Tikveš wine region); Stevče Donevski (Kratovo); Anne Withers, Saško Dončovski, Ace Stojanov, and especially Dragi Pop-Stojanov and family (Strumica). My biggest gratitude goes to Buba and Marco. Extra thanks go to Lonely Planet's Will Gourlay for his enthusiasm and expertise in making this book happen, to coordinating author Marika McAdam for holding it all together, and to the editorial production and map-making teams for their hard work in finishing it off.

PETER DRAGIČEVIĆ

A huge thanks to all the wonderful people who helped me along the way, especially my beloved Dragičević cousins, Goran and Jadranka Marković, Dragana Ostojić, Slavko Marjanović, Jack Delf, Hayley Wright and Danica Ćeranić. Extra special thanks to Milomir Jukanović. Cheers to all the other LPers on this title – it's been a blast!

MARK ELLIOTT

A particularly fine team at LP made writing this chapter an especially enjoyable task. Mark Griffiths very helpfully expedited a vastly improved Sarajevo map, Will Gourlay infected everyone with inspiring Balkans enthusiasm and the delightful Marika graciously coped with my annoyingly endless barrage of suggestions. In Bosnia many thanks are due to Edis Hodžić, Guillaume Martin, Olivier Janoschka, Snezhan in Trebinje, Vlaren at Tvrdoš Monastery, Semir in Blagaj, Narmina in Mostar, Branislav Andrić in Višegrad and so many more, including the mysterious 'angel' who provided me with such insights to the Belašnica highland villages, then disappeared without my ever knowing his name. As ever, my greatest thanks go to my endlessly inspiring wife, Dani Systermans, and to my unbeatable parents who, three decades ago, had the crazy idea of driving me to Bosnia in the first place.

VESNA MARIĆ

Hvala to Maja Gilja, my mother, Toni and Marina Ćavar, Ružica, Stipe, Ante, Dana and Loreta Barać. Also *hvala* to Kristina Hajduka, and Janica and Matej. Thanks to Gabriel and all the travellers I chatted to along the way. Thanks also to Anja Mutić and Will Gourlay.

ANJA MUTIĆ

Hvala mojim prekrasnim roditeljima – Mom for her cooking and laughter and Dad for the drives and encouragement. *Gracias* to the Barcelona family, especially my nephew Biel for his hilarious Croatian pronunciation. *Obrigada*, Hoji, for being there before, during and after. A huge *hvala* to my friends in Croatia who gave me endless contacts and recommendations and whose names would easily fill several pages – this book wouldn't be the same without you. A big thank you goes to commissioning editor Will Gourlay for his support and enthusiasm. Finally, to the inspiring memory of my grandmother Mira, who still guides my travels.

OUR READERS
Many thanks to the travellers who used the last edition and wrote to us with helpful hints, useful advice and interesting anecdotes:

Minoru Arisawa, Mike Beer, Luis Blanco, Geoff Brown, Gareth Collman, Gemma Ding, Steve Draper, Robert Durenkamp, Milena Dzordeski, Aled Edwards, Fred Fisher, Helen Forster, Erik Futtrup, Lee Garratt, Eva Gies, Cecilia Harlitz, Tony Hartley, William Hind, Esther Hobson, Dag Hongve, Javi Jimenez Romo, Jerome Kenyon, Giel Klanker, Ewald Koch, Matthias Kopp, Shawna Kristin, Nick Kukic, Eva Lasky, Nadia Lipsey, Jorn Lund, Stephen Madge, Kay McKenzie, Diljana Mihajlovic, Hugo Miranda, Despina Monokrousou, Mads Nielsen, Klaus Paben, Salvatore Palumbo, Stephen Passant, Patrick Picard, Leo Planken, Joseph Quaye, Frank Röhl, Jay Ruchamkin, Sasha Savic, Marie Schnoz, W Sirk, Stefan Sjöblom, M Smith, Karsten Staehr, Sandie Stringfellow, Peter Tang, Claude Tomisich, Jaume Tort, Anastasios Tsagklas, Zoran Tuntev, Menno Verschuren, Vanessa Voss, James Watson, Tameeka Wells, Philipp Wendtland, Frank Wilson, Kyle Wood, Zachary Wynne, Jeffrey Ziemba, Daniël Zoetelief

ACKNOWLEDGMENTS
Many thanks to the following for the use of their content:
Globe on title page ©Mountain High Maps 1993 Digital Wisdom, Inc.

Internal Photographs by Anja Mutić p4; Chris Deliso p4, p263 (#7); Jayne D'Arcy p4, p264 (#6); Marika McAdam p4; Mark Elliott p4, p266 (#4); Peter Dragičević p4; Vesna Marić p4; Koca Sulejmanovic/ AFP/Getty Images p265 (#7). All other photographs by Lonely Planet Images, and by Andrew Burke p267 (#6); Greg Elms p262 (#3); Patrick Horton p264 (#4), p266 (#1), p267 (#3); Tim Hughes p268; Doug McKinlay p263 (#5); Martin Moos p263 (#6); Witold Skrypczak p261.

All images are the copyright of the photographers unless otherwise indicated. Many of the images in this guide are available for licensing from Lonely Planet Images: www.lonelyplanet images.com.

BEHIND THE SCENES

Index

INDEX

INDEX

Lokrum Island (Cro) 250
Lopar (Cro) 219-20
Lošinj Islands (Cro) 219
Lovćen National Park (Mon) 6, 357-8, 6
Lukomir (BiH) 130

M

Macedonia 281-332, **283**
  accommodation 327
  activities 327-8
  architecture 286
  arts 286-7
  books 328
  border crossings 330
  business hours 328
  cinema 286-7
  climate 282
  costs 282
  culture 286
  customs regulations 328
  dance 287
  disabilities, travellers wih 330
  economy 286
  embassies 328-9
  emergencies 329
  environmental issues 289
  EU membership 285-6
  exchange rates, see inside front cover
  fax services 329-30
  festivals 267, 329
  food 287-8
  geography 288
  history 282-6
  holidays 329
  internet resources 329
  itineraries 282
  language 329, 458-60
  magazines 328
  mobile phones 330
  money 329
  music 287
  national parks 289
  newspapers 328
  planning 282
  population 286
  postal services 329
  radio 328
  religion 286
  safety 328
  telephone services 329-30

tourist information 330
travel to/from 330-1
travel within 331-2
TV 328
visas 330
Magarevo (Mac) 315-16
magazines 23-4
  Albania 93
  Macedonia 328
  Montenegro 368
Makarska (Cro) 235-6
Mali Lošinj (Cro) 219
Malovište (Mac) 315
maps
  BiH 165
  Kosovo 279
  Montenegro 370
  Serbia 419
Mariovo (Mac) 9, 314, 9
Mavrovo National Park (Mac) 265, 298-9
measures 424
medical services 451-2, see also individual locations
Međugorje (BiH) 139-41
metric conversions, see inside front cover
migration 36
Milošević, Slobodan 34, 35, 105
Mladić, Ratko 106
Mljet Island (Cro) 242-4
mobile phones 436
  Albania 97
  BiH 166
  Croatia 256
  Macedonia 330
  Montenegro 370
  Serbia 420
Mokra Gora (Ser) 416-17
monasteries
  Cetinje monastery (Mon) 360
  Dečani monastery (Kos) 277
  Dobrilovina Monastery (Mon) 366
  Dobrun Monastery (BiH) 148
  Gomionica Monastery (BiH) 160
  Gračanica Monastery (Kos) 276
  Grgeteg monastery (Ser) 403
  Guča Gora (BiH) 154
  Jazak (Ser) 403
  Krušedol monastery (Ser) 402
  Mala Remeta (Ser) 403
  Manasija monastery (Ser) 407
  Monastery of St Mary (Alb) 83
  Monastery of St Nicholas (Alb) 88
  Monastery of Sveta Bogorodica-Eleusa (Mac) 326

Monastery of Sveta Petka (Mac) 310-11
Monastery of Sveti Arhangel Mihail (Mac) 324
Monastery of Sveti Gavril Lesnovski (Mac) 324
Monastery of Sveti Gjorgji (Mac) 321
Monastery of Sveti Joakim Osogovski (Mac) 323
Monastery of Sveti Leontij-Vodoča (Mac) 326
Monastery of Sveti Nikola (Mac) 320
Norcev (Ser) 403
Novo Hopovo (Ser) 402-3
Ostrog Monastery (Mon) 364, 261
Pološki Monastery (Mac) 320
Sopoćani Monastery (Ser) 411
St George Monastery (Ser) 411-12
Studenica Monastery (Ser) 412-13
Sveti Jovan Bigorski monastery 298-9
Sveti Naum (Mac) 307-8
Sveti Pantelejmon monastery (Mac) 293
Treskavec Monastery (Mac) 318
Tvrdoš monastery (BiH) 145
Velika Remeta (Ser) 403
Vrdnik (Ser) 403
money 19-20, 432, 434-5, see also inside front cover
  Albania 96
  BiH 165
  Croatia 255-6
  Kosovo 279
  Macedonia 329
  Montenegro 370
  Serbia 376, 419
moneychangers 434
  Albania 96
  Croatia 255
Montenegro 333-72, **335**
  accommodation 367-8
  activities 368
  architecture 339
  arts 338-9
  books 368-9
  border crossings 371
  business hours 369
  cinema 338-9
  climate 334
  costs 334
  culture 338
  customs, local 340
  customs regulations 369

000 Map pages
000 Photograph pages

INDEX

000 Map pages
000 Photograph pages

484

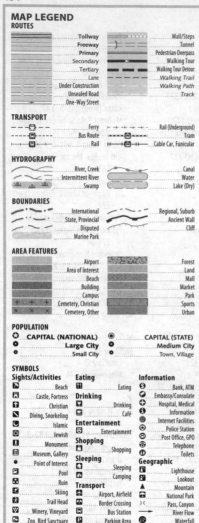

MAP LEGEND

ROUTES

Tollway	Mall/Steps
Freeway	Tunnel
Primary	Pedestrian Overpass
Secondary	Walking Tour
Tertiary	Walking Tour Detour
Lane	Walking Trail
Under Construction	Walking Path
Unsealed Road	Track
One-Way Street	

TRANSPORT

Ferry	Rail (Underground)
Bus Route	Tram
Rail	Cable Car, Funicular

HYDROGRAPHY

River, Creek	Canal
Intermittent River	Water
Swamp	Lake (Dry)

BOUNDARIES

International	Regional, Suburb
State, Provincial	Ancient Wall
Disputed	Cliff
Marine Park	

AREA FEATURES

Airport	Forest
Area of Interest	Land
Beach	Mall
Building	Market
Campus	Park
Cemetery, Christian	Sports
Cemetery, Other	Urban

POPULATION

CAPITAL (NATIONAL)	CAPITAL (STATE)
Large City	Medium City
Small City	Town, Village

SYMBOLS

Sights/Activities
Beach, Castle, Fortress, Christian, Diving, Snorkeling, Islamic, Jewish, Monument, Museum, Gallery, Point of Interest, Pool, Ruin, Skiing, Trail Head, Winery, Vineyard, Zoo, Bird Sanctuary

Eating
Eating

Drinking
Drinking, Café

Entertainment
Entertainment

Shopping
Shopping

Sleeping
Sleeping, Camping

Transport
Airport, Airfield, Border Crossing, Bus Station, Parking Area

Information
Bank, ATM, Embassy/Consulate, Hospital, Medical, Information, Internet Facilities, Police Station, Post Office, GPO, Telephone, Toilets

Geographic
Lighthouse, Lookout, Mountain, National Park, Pass, Canyon, River Flow, Waterfall

LONELY PLANET OFFICES

Australia
Head Office
Locked Bag 1, Footscray, Victoria 3011
☎ 03 8379 8000, fax 03 8379 8111
talk2us@lonelyplanet.com.au

USA
150 Linden St, Oakland, CA 94607
☎ 510 250 6400, toll free 800 275 8555
fax 510 893 8572
info@lonelyplanet.com

UK
2nd fl, 186 City Rd,
London EC1V 2NT
☎ 020 7106 2100, fax 020 7106 2101
go@lonelyplanet.co.uk

Published by Lonely Planet Publications Pty Ltd
ABN 36 005 607 983

© Lonely Planet Publications Pty Ltd 2009

© photographers as indicated 2009

Cover photograph: Beach at the Dominican monastery, Brač Island, Croatia, Johanna Huber/SIME.

Many of the images in this guide are available for licensing from Lonely Planet Images: www.lonelyplanetimages.com.

MIX
Paper from responsible sources
FSC™ C021741
www.fsc.org